DEFECTIVE COPY
FOR REVIEW PURPOSES ONLY
NOT FOR RESALE

C0-ALL-286

The Most Valuable Players
in Baseball, 1931–2001

The Most Valuable Players in Baseball, 1931–2001

by TIMM BOYLE

McFarland & Company, Inc., Publishers
Jefferson, North Carolina, and London

Library of Congress Cataloguing-in-Publication Data

Boyle, Timm.
The most valuable players in baseball, 1931–2001
by Timm Boyle
p.   cm.
Includes index.

ISBN 0-7864-1029-9 (illustrated case binding : 50# alkaline paper)

1. Most Valuable Player Award (Baseball)— History — Chronology.
2. Baseball players— United States— Statistics.   I. Title
GV877.B65   2003   796.357'64 — dc21   2002011774

British Library cataloguing data are available

©2003 Timm Boyle. All rights reserved

*No part of this book may be reproduced or transmitted in any form
or by any means, electronic or mechanical, including photocopying
or recording, or by any information storage and retrieval system,
without permission in writing from the publisher.*

Cover photograph: 1994 National League MVP Jeff Bagwell *(Courtesy of the Houston Astros)*

Manufactured in the United States of America

*McFarland & Company, Inc., Publishers
Box 611, Jefferson, North Carolina 28640
www.mcfarlandpub.com*

To the best family a man could ever have.

To my wife, Deanna,
whose wonderful qualities of patience and acceptance help keep me on track.

And to Jon, Tyler and Kaitlyn,
whose lives have filled my heart to overflowing with love.

Also, to my mother, Jeanne,
and Carol, Bill and Dave.

Acknowledgments

If it weren't for a couple of guys named Dave, this book would not exist, and I want to express my heartfelt gratitude for everything they did to make it possible. The writing and research that Dave Masterson and Dave Laude put into this project was indispensable.

I also want to thank Dan Schlossberg and Marty Appel, who always took time out of their busy writing schedules to answer my questions and steer me in the right direction.

Contents

The M·V·Ps 5

Preface

I'm obviously biased, but I believe that Major League Baseball's Most Valuable Player award is the most fascinating honor in all of sports.

Why? For one, its history dwarfs that of awards in other sports. More importantly, it's the one award that defies all description, rhyme or reason. The Rookie of the Year honor always goes to a first-year player, while the Cy Young accolade is always presented to a pitcher. But the Most Valuable Player award can be garnered by any player at any position for almost any reason.

Often the MVP is the best overall player in the league, but not always. Frequently the MVP guides his team to a post-season berth, but not necessarily. Every time we think that only a player on a pennant contender can be named MVP, an Ernie Banks or an Andre Dawson is selected. Every time we assume that only an everyday player can capture the honor, a Roger Clemens, Dennis Eckersley or Willie Hernandez is chosen. Every time we figure that only a slugger will catch the voters' fancy, an Ichiro Suzuki is picked.

The only consistent factor regarding baseball's Most Valuable Player award is that it's inconsistent. And it's almost always surrounded by controversy.

The Baseball Writers Association of America (BBWAA) took over responsibility for naming official winners in 1931, and annual heated debates concerning the worthiness of the victors are due as much to the variety of skills possessed by MVPs as to the lack of strict guidelines used in their selection.

Although hard and fast standards are absent, certain qualities connected with MVP winners have become apparent in the 70-plus years of the award. In examining the candidates, voters have favored some attributes more highly than others, and while a clear-cut pattern has never really evolved, the selection of more than 140 MVPs and the study of those winners provide insight into recurrent MVP characteristics.

Two basic trends stand out almost every year: MVP winners enjoy banner statistical campaigns and, in more cases than not, are members of pennant- or division-winning ballclubs. At the very least, MVP picks nearly always play for clubs which have finished among the upper half of their competition in the standings. Rare is the MVP who labors for a non-contender.

Home run hitters and big RBI men often catch the attention of the voters, with a less significant qualification being a high batting average. Overall ability — hitting, running, throwing and fielding — is important, but the greatest emphasis usually is placed on the player's might in wielding the bat.

Certain positions seem to merit special consideration among MVP voters during specific time periods. Leadership was a quality that voters regarded highly in the first few decades of the award, which helps explain why catchers and player-managers won a significant number of MVP awards early on. Pitchers took home the hardware more frequently prior to the 1956 creation of the Cy Young Award, which has lessened the likelihood of a hurler capturing the MVP. Outfielders have always been represented well, but have come to even more prominence in recent years.

Unfair as it may seem, the city in which a player performs apparently does occasionally have a bearing on the selection of the recipient. Joe Gordon and Spud Chandler, both New York Yankees, are prime examples. In each case, personal statistics were excellent, yet hardly dominant. But the team for which they played and the media coverage received by the club were unmatched in baseball. And although Dale Murphy probably didn't need Ted Turner's help in garnering two consecutive awards, the advent of cable superstations such as TBS in Atlanta certainly helped Murphy gain the same type of exposure that Sammy Sosa of Chicago has through WGN-TV.

A player's past performance also comes into the voting picture at times. Players who have established a reputation through previous standout efforts can tip the scales ever so slightly in their favor, especially in close MVP races. On the other hand, winning the MVP award too many times might prove to be an obstacle in gaining further honors. Three-time winners Jimmie Foxx and Mickey Mantle, for example, found garnering a fourth MVP impossible, despite admirable efforts that seemed more than worthy of consideration.

And while repeat winners are alternately aided and hampered by their previous wins to varying degrees, other steadily outstanding players such as Mel Ott, Johnny Mize, Ralph Kiner, Eddie Murray, Greg Maddux, and Manny Ramirez never quite crossed the initial threshold. This might be due to the fact that they failed to produce any single-season, record-breaking performance to capture the public's fancy, such as Joe DiMaggio's 56-game hitting streak, Roger Maris' 61 homers, Maury Wills' 104 stolen bases or Barry Bonds' 73 round-trippers. Those rare times when a player conquers history are almost always honored with an MVP, but even this particular qualification does not assure a lock on the award, as base thief Lou Brock and slugger Mark McGwire might point out.

Flashy fielders rarely win unless they augment their glovework with an exceptional season at the plate. An obvious exception — there's always an exception when it comes to the MVP award — was the brilliant shortstop Marty Marion, whose fielding wizardry was spotlighted in 1944 because he played for the World Champion Cardinals. At the same time, others equally extraordinary at the same position and more productive at the plate and on the bases, such as Pee Wee Reese, Luis Aparicio and Ozzie Smith, were bypassed.

If the MVP has a black eye, it's because of the inexcusable behavior of a small minority of voters who allow their personal feelings to influence their votes. The classic example occurred in 1947 when Boston writer Mel Webb left Ted Williams completely off his ballot, despite the fact that the Splendid Splinter had won the Triple Crown. Even a 10th place vote from Webb for Williams would have been enough to give him the award that season over Joe DiMaggio. This was hardly the first time Williams had been snubbed by the writers, whose clashes with Teddy Ballgame were legendary. In 1942, Williams earned the Triple Crown and also paced the American League in slugging, total bases, runs and walks, but placed second to Gordon, who led the league in strikeouts, grounding into double plays and most errors at his position.

In summary, an MVP can display any number of varying talents, but those abilities are often assessed differently from season to season by the voters, without any apparent logic. Also, a ballplayer who earns the honor one year may be a vastly different type of athlete from the winner of the previous campaign.

And that's exactly what makes baseball's Most Valuable Player award so intriguing and appealing. Jack Lang, longtime head of the BBWAA, has brilliantly refused to narrow the criteria for selecting MVPs. Each year his instruction to the voters is that every player is eligible. Who will win is usually a mystery ... just the way it should be.

Introduction

Baseball's Most Valuable Player award ranks as the most prestigious individual honor in the game. But its establishment and current status did not come overnight. More than three decades of professional baseball had already been played before an official MVP honor was first bestowed.

The MVP concept is said to have originated from the 1875 awarding of a silver tray, water pitcher and loving cup to James "Deacon" White of the Boston Red Stockings in the National Association. Thirty-five years later, Hugh Chalmers, president and general manager of the Chalmers automobile company, announced that he would present a car to the player who produced the highest batting average in 1910. This turned into a fiasco because several players conspired to help Napoleon Lajoie edge Ty Cobb in this race, and Chalmers wound up giving cars to both players to avoid further controversy.

Chalmers altered his award the next year to make it less specific, designating it for the player who proved to be the "most important" and "most useful" to his team and the league. Realizing the value of linking his product with the fast-growing national sport, and understanding the importance of adding legitimacy to the selections, Chalmers officials convinced the game's sportswriters to help choose the worthy performers.

In 1911, a committee consisting of one writer from each of the 16 major league cities selected Frank Schulte of the Chicago Cubs and Ty Cobb of the Detroit Tigers as the first MVPs in the National and American leagues, respectively. The Chalmers award continued through the 1914 season, but World War I and an overall lack of interest brought about the discontinuation of the Chalmers honor.

Major league officials decided to institute an MVP award eight years later, and again sportswriters were recruited to determine the winners. The American League began this practice in 1922, with George Sisler of the St. Louis Browns copping the first League Award. Unfortunately, there were several flies in the ointment regarding this new award. Rules stating that a writer could select only one player per team on his ballot kept several qualified players out of the running, as did the stipulations that player-managers and previous winners were ineligible. The National League amended two of those rules when it began its League Award in 1924, and Dazzy Vance of Brooklyn captured the senior circuit's first such honor.

The League Awards ran into even rougher waters in the late 1920s when winners began using their newly exalted status as bargaining tools for upgrading salaries. Club owners responded by howling at their respective league offices until, finally, the issue drew to a head in 1928. Mickey Cochrane, AL winner that year, engaged in a spirited salary squabble with Philadelphia Athletics owner Connie Mack, with the feisty catcher claiming that an MVP deserved a much larger pay hike than the one he was offered. Following that dispute, American League officials discontinued their League Award, while the National League continued for one more year before dropping its accolade.

The Sporting News picked up the MVP ball and ran with it beginning in 1929. Because the American League did not select a winner that season, the national sports weekly took matters into its own hands and named Al Simmons the winner. With the National League dropping its League Award in 1930, the popular baseball publication selected Bill Terry, that league's last .400 hitter, as the MVP for the season. Other unofficial MVP awards were presented by the Baseball Writers Association of America (BBWAA) and the Associated Press in 1929 and '30.

The birth of the modern MVP award occurred at a December 11, 1930, meeting in which BBWAA officials voted to establish a permanent award in both leagues. This award is still recognized as baseball's officially sanctioned laurel, and a player from each league has been chosen by the BBWAA every year since 1931. *The Sporting News* continued to select winners off and on, and since 1948 has named a Player of the Year and Pitcher of the Year in each league.

Two baseball writers in each major league city are in charge of the BBWAA balloting, with a total of 28 ballots cast. Each eligible writer selects 10 MVP candidates, ranking them in order of preference. The top man on each list is awarded 14 points, with the second player receiving nine, the third eight, and so on.

Only 14 players have received all of the first-place votes since 1931. These unanimous selections are Hank Greenberg in 1935, Carl Hubbell in '36, Al Rosen in '53, Mickey Mantle in '56, Frank Robinson in '66, Orlando Cepeda in '67, Denny McLain in '68, Reggie Jackson in '73, Mike Schmidt in '80, Jose Canseco in '88, Frank Thomas in '93, Jeff Bagwell in '94, Ken Caminiti in '96 and Ken Griffey Jr. in '97.

Barry Bonds is the only player in the history of the MVP award to win it four times. Three-time recipients are Jimmie Foxx, Joe DiMaggio, Stan Musial, Roy Campanella, Yogi Berra, Mantle and Schmidt. Two-time MVPs are Hubbell, Greenberg, Hal Newhouser, Ted Williams, Willie Mays, Ernie Banks, Roger Maris, Robinson, Johnny Bench, Joe Morgan, Robin Yount, Dale Murphy, Cal Ripken Jr., Thomas and Juan Gonzalez.

More popular and prestigious than ever, the Most Valuable Player award remains atop the list of cherished prizes awarded annually to baseball's outstanding performers.

Here then are the yearly selections of the Most Valuable Player award as chosen by the BBWAA. You may not agree with every selection, but considering the variables in the word *valuable*, there can be no disputing that each of the honorees fits the unwritten guidelines in one way or another.

The M·V·Ps

1931 NATIONAL LEAGUE—FRANKIE FRISCH

Frank Francis Frisch
B. September 9, 1898, Bronx, New York
D. March 12, 1973, Wilmington, Delaware

Year	Team	Games	AB	Hits	Avg.	HR	RBI	Runs	SB
1931	SL NL	131	518	161	.311	4	82	96	28

The Season

Crowded breadlines were a more familiar sight during the 1931 season than were packed ballyards. It was, after all, the Depression era. Interest in the National Pastime was still high, but the economy was such that the majority of unemployed fans satisfied their baseball appetites on the street corner, watching electronic scoreboards register inning-by-inning tallies of their favorite teams' games.

For St. Louis Cardinals fans, the sweet consistency of home team victories in 1931 provided a welcome distraction from the economic gloom. The Redbirds easily defended their 1930 National League pennant with a 101–53 year, fielding a club that MVP Frankie Frisch later referred to as the greatest on which he ever played. The St. Louis nine were never really challenged, finishing 13 games ahead of the second-place New York Giants.

Although the pennant race may have been lacking in drama, the batting title competition was among the fiercest and closest in the game's history. It ended with Cardinal Chick Hafey (.3489) barely edging out Bill Terry (.3486) of the Giants and another Redbird, Jim Bottomley (.3482).

The Cardinals then snapped the Philadelphia Athletics' two-year hold on the World Championship with a seven-game victory over the A's in a rematch of the 1930 fall classic, thanks to a .500 average by Pepper Martin and a pair of wins each by Bill Hallahan and Burleigh Grimes.

Back on July 12, the largest crowd in the history of St. Louis' Sportsman's Park (45,715 in a 35,000-seat ballpark) doubled its pleasure during a doubleheader. Due to the throng spilling over onto the field, a number of normally routine fly balls went for ground-rule doubles, and the contest established records for most two-baggers in a single game (11) and in a twin bill (21).

The Brash Flash

Baseball records show that wherever Frankie Frisch played, team success followed like a faithful puppy. In the 13 seasons prior to his 1931 MVP year, the dynamic "Fordham Flash" established a winner's reputation, dominating play and filling a leadership role on two teams that captured a total of six National League pennants and two World Championships. Since becoming a bona-fide regular in 1921, the future Hall of Famer had never dipped below the magic .300 mark, and was recognized at that time as the greatest switch-hitter the game had ever known.

As a vital cog in the legendary John McGraw's magnificent New York Giant machine, Frisch participated in four straight World Series from 1921 to 1924. Historians will note that this dynasty began when the flashy collegiate from Fordham University took a permanent hold on the third slot in the Giant batting order.

Frisch, whose .348 average in 1923 is tied for the best ever by a switch-hitter (Pete Rose hit .348 in 1969), paced the NL in hits (223) and fielding (.973) in '23, runs (121) in '24, and fielding again in both 1927 (.979) and '28 (.976).

Only player-manager Rogers Hornsby of the St. Louis Cardinals, still commonly acknowledged as the most talented right-handed hitter in the game's history, kept Frisch from being referred to as the top second baseman of his day. In one of the most talked-about trades of all time, Frisch and pitcher Jimmy Ring were swapped to St. Louis for Hornsby, who had just led his club to the 1926 World Championship and had won six batting titles in the past seven years.

St. Louis fans felt betrayed, bitterly protesting the departure of the popular "Rajah." But Frisch was determined to dispel those sentiments, and did so quickly. He played like a man possessed in his initial Cardinal campaign, hitting .337, leading the league in stolen bases and establishing a record for chances accepted by a second baseman. That season he came within a single vote of being named league MVP.

The Fordham Flash's animated presence on the right side of the St. Louis keystone came to exemplify all that was aggressive about the new-breed Cardinals. It was soon apparent that the heads-up dynamo was the spiritual flag-bearer for one of the National League's most successful franchises. His scrambling style of play again paid dividends with pennants in 1928 and 1930.

The all-out energies expended by the switch-hitter in 1931 were, as always, contagious among his teammates, the result being yet another Redbird pennant fluttering in the Sportsman's Park breeze.

Baseball writers recognize a catalyst when they see one, and as usual, Frisch's style of play defined that term in 1931, earning him the first senior circuit Baseball Writers Association of America MVP. From a statistical standpoint, it was a puzzling selection because at least four National Leaguers put up numbers that far outweighed those compiled by the Dutchman. Only one year earlier, Frisch had enjoyed one of his finest campaigns, ripping league pitching for a .346 average. But the .311 mark in 1931, although respectable, eventually turned out to be five points lower than Frisch's lifetime average. The 33-year-old did lead the league in stolen bases that season with 28, his third and final thievery crown.

Yet the voters clearly saw beyond mere boxscore dimensions in the MVP balloting. In Frisch they saw a bona-fide pacesetter whose ability to inspire championship performances from his teammates was plainly evident again in 1931.

Frankie's image as an incendiary leader was fortified in that year's World Series. With typical abandon, Frisch shrugged off a bad case of lumbago that nearly had him bedridden. Bandaged like a mummy, he rapped out seven hits and fielded 35 chances flawlessly to help win a seven-game Series against Connie Mack's powerful Philadelphia Athletics.

But in an already satisfying career, the best was yet to come. The Cards slipped in 1932 and '33, and Frisch was handed the managerial reins in mid-season of the latter year. A full-fledged character himself, Frisch presided over the most raucous assemblage of baseball zanies ever to congregate in the same clubhouse—the Gashouse Gang. Still batting third and playing second base—and now calling all the important moves—the veteran secured a niche for himself in baseball annals as he guided the colorful Cardinals to another World Championship in 1934.

Frisch, who struck out more than 18 times only twice during a 17-year career, did it all without possessing the power of many stars of his day. In fact, the spray hitter held the record for

most World Series games played without a home run (50 games, 197 at-bats). Ironically, Frisch hit the first-ever NL homer in an All-Star Game (1933), and the following year became the first player to lead off an All-Star Game with a four-bagger.

Retiring as a player in 1937, Frisch went on to accumulate a total of 16 managerial years for the Cards, Pirates and Cubs. Known for his umpire baiting, he would argue especially vigorously when his teams played in New York, and some of the men in blue suspected it was so that Frisch could get a jump-start on visiting his New Rochelle home after being ejected.

The "Old Flash," as he later referred to himself, was given his greatest baseball thrill with enshrinement in the Hall of Fame in 1947. A painting of the aggressive competitor adorns the hallowed halls of that museum. Its title typifies the sweeping bravado he brought to 2,311 games as a player: "Keep hustling."

Top 5 MVP Vote-Getters

1. Frankie Frisch, St. Louis—65
2. Chuck Klein, Philadelphia—55
3. Bill Terry, New York—53
4. Woody English, Chicago—30
5. Chick Hafey, St. Louis—29

1931 AMERICAN LEAGUE—LEFTY GROVE

Robert Moses Grove
B. March 6, 1900, Lonaconing, Maryland
D. May 22, 1975, Norwalk, Ohio

Year	Team	Games	W	L	ERA	IP	SO	BB	ShO
1931	Phil AL	41	31	4	2.06	288.2	175	62	4

The Season

Perhaps the 1927 New York Yankees were the greatest baseball team of

all time. Maybe. Then again, the 1929–31 Philadelphia Athletics might possess equal claim to that accolade.

In 1931, the A's captured their

third consecutive American League crown, finishing 13½ games ahead of the Yanks. Three of four future Hall of Famers on the A's squad—Jimmie Foxx,

Al Simmons and Mickey Cochrane — were known for their powerful bats, but it was the pitching that sowed the pennant seeds.

The Athletics were runners-up to the hard-hitting Yankees in several offensive categories, but A's pitchers led the league in ERA (3.47), threw twice as many shutouts (12) as any AL club and allowed the fewest runs per game (4.1).

The "Big Three" of Most Valuable Player Lefty Grove, George Earnshaw and Rube Walberg accounted for 72 of Philadelphia's 107 wins, while Simmons led the league in hitting (.390) for the second straight year.

After winning two World Series in a row (1929-30), the heavily favored A's fell victim to Pepper Martin and the St. Louis Cardinals in 1931, bowing out in seven games.

Boston's Earl Webb, who had never hit more than 30 doubles in a season, clubbed 67 two-baggers, still the highest total ever, while Lou Gehrig of New York drove in 184 runs, still the AL standard. Babe Ruth belted the 600th home run of his career August 21, and Wes Ferrell of Cleveland pitched a no-hitter and drove in four runs with a homer and double April 29 against St. Louis.

Late February of 1931 was not a good time to be a current or former American League president. On February 27, E.S. Barnard passed away at age 57 after having succeeded AL founder Ban Johnson in 1927. The following day, Johnson died after a long illness. On May 27, AL Secretary Will Harridge was elected to succeed Barnard.

Lefty Lightning

To opposing batters, Lefty Grove was a dark, intimidating enemy who, like a deadly serpent, could uncoil and strike at a moment's notice. To teammates, he was a moody, tempestuous companion, but also a savage competitor and winner. And to manager Connie Mack and Philadelphia Athletics fans, he was "Mr. Reliable."

Considered the greatest left-handed pitcher in American League history, Grove blew away one hitter after another during a dazzling, 17-year, 300-win career. Lefty fashioned an enviable 3.06 lifetime earned run average and struck out well over 2,000 batters.

The 6-foot-3, 190-pounder used only an occasional curve or forkball; nine times out of 10 he threw pure heat. That speed enabled Grove to lead the AL in wins four times, winning percentage on five occasions (no other pitcher did it more than three times), and shutouts and complete games three times each. He held the highest winning percentage (.680) of any 300-game winner.

A whistling fastball was virtually all the cocky southpaw needed as he sailed through his first seven seasons in the majors (1925–31), leading the American League in strikeouts every time. And despite sensational seasons of 24–8, 20–6, 28–5, 25–10 and 24–8 in his first nine campaigns, it was the Hall of Famer's wondrous 1931 record of 31–4 that solidified the lasting recognition he so richly deserved. The stunning mark — no pitcher won 30 games in a season for the next 37 years — alongside his minuscule, league-leading 2.06 ERA, allowed the speed-ball artist to outpoll such sluggers as Lou Gehrig and Al Simmons in the 1931 MVP voting.

Lefty also topped AL hurlers in strikeouts with 175 and shutouts with four in 1931, and 16 of his 31 triumphs were in succession. Two other junior circuit moundsmen, Smokey Joe Wood and Walter Johnson, also had run off streaks of 16 straight wins in previous years, and the fiery left-hander let it be known he was not pleased when his string ended one shy of the outright record. After a 1–0 defeat by the St. Louis Browns — the lone run the result of an error by substitute outfielder Jim Moore — Grove tore apart the clubhouse, denting lockers and shredding uniforms. He then won his next five starts for what would have been a major league record of 22 consecutive victories were it not for the loss to the Browns.

But the man with the sizzling fastball and cantankerous attitude had little else to be upset about in 1931. While American League hitters were chewing up pitchers to the tune of a .278 composite batting average, Grove was mowing down everyone in sight, limiting opposing batsmen to a .229 mark.

Along with 20-game winners George Earnshaw and Rube Walberg, as well as heavy hitters Jimmie Foxx, Mickey Cochrane and Simmons, Grove pushed the A's into a second consecutive World Series against the St. Louis Cardinals, and the third in a row overall. He contributed by winning the first and third games of the '31 Series, but the A's faltered in the seventh meeting, and Mack's dynasty began its swift disintegration.

The lightning-quick lefty's success in 1931 came as no surprise to those who had seen him perform in post-season competition the two previous years. Grove won two of three World Series decisions with a 1.42 ERA as the A's knocked off the Cardinals four games to two in the 1930 World Series. Even in his one loss, the fireballer tossed a five-hitter.

And in 1929, although a sore pitching hand is said to have kept him from starting a World Series game, Lefty produced two impressive relief jobs against the powerful Chicago Cubs. One of those was a two-inning stint in Game 4, during which he struck out four of the six men he faced. The A's scored 10 runs in the seventh inning in that contest to overcome an 8–0 deficit and win 10–8 for the most remarkable comeback in Series history. The setback took the heart out of the Cubs, who bowed out in the next game.

Born Robert Moses Grove, Lefty quit school early, working as a day laborer in the western Maryland coal mines and for the railroads. Grove broke into big league baseball at the relatively late age of 25, preferring to stay with Jack Dunn's Baltimore Orioles of the International League in the early 1920s. The budding star won 27 games twice and 25 once for the O's. Philadelphia A's owner Mack bought Grove for $100,600 in 1925, the $600 tacked on to make it the highest total ever paid for a minor leaguer.

In his rookie year with the A's, Grove was only 10–12, but it would be the last season that Lefty would fall below the .500 mark. The gifted southpaw hit his stride in 1927 when he began a series of seven consecutive 20-win seasons. Over a four-year span beginning in 1928, he compiled a mighty 103–23 record for an incredible .817 winning percentage.

After nine splendid years with the powerhouse A's, during which he won 195 games and struck out 1,523 batters, Lefty was sold to the Boston Red Sox as part of Mack's massive housecleaning project.

Grove's fastball had lost a little of its velocity, and his stamina was not what it once was, but he gave the Red Sox a shot in the arm, winning 20 games and leading the league in ERA at 2.70 in 1935. He paced the circuit in

earned run average three more times (2.81 in 1936, 3.08 in 1938 and 2.54 in 1939) for a total of nine career ERA titles. No other pitcher has led his league in ERA more than five times. Grove finally won his 300th and last game at the age of 41.

Following his retirement, Grove returned to the town of his birth, Lonaconing, Maryland, and opened a bowling alley that became the social center of the area.

How fast was Lefty Grove during his prime? New York's Bill Dickey said he was the fastest he ever saw, and Joe Sewell of the Indians described Lefty's heater as "a flash of white sewing thread coming at you."

That's how fast Lefty Grove was,

and not only for the first five or six innings. When asked how he handled hitters in the last couple of frames, the seemingly tireless Grove responded, "In the eighth inning I bear down; in the ninth I just blow it by them."

And, like a chain of dominoes, batters would topple one by one, victims of the king of the hill.

Top 5 MVP Vote-Getters

1. Lefty Grove, Philadelphia — 78
2. Lou Gehrig, New York — 59
3. Al Simmons, Philadelphia — 51
4. Earl Averill, Cleveland — 43
5. Babe Ruth, New York — 40

1932 NATIONAL LEAGUE — CHUCK KLEIN

Charles Herbert Klein
B. October 7, 1904, Indianapolis, Indiana
D. March 28, 1958, Indianapolis, Indiana

Year	Team	Games	AB	Hits	Avg.	HR	RBI	Runs	SB
1932	Phil NL	154	650	226	.348	38	137	152	20

The Season

The brilliant four-man pitching rotation of the Chicago Cubs — Lon Warneke, Guy Bush, Pat Malone and Charlie Root — led that club to the pennant with a 90–64 record in 1932. Even the mid-season firing of uncompromising manager Rogers Hornsby couldn't upset the Chicago express that edged the Pittsburgh Pirates by four games before running into trouble against Babe Ruth's Yankees in the World Series.

Meanwhile, the Philadelphia Phillies were battering National League pitchers at an alarming rate, scoring an average of 5½ runs per game. The top three RBI spots in the league belonged to Philadelphia hitters Don Hurst (143), Chuck Klein (137) and Pinky Whitney (124), but Philly hurlers were

the worst in the league with a composite 4.47 ERA.

That sorry staff could have used the elastic right arm of brash Cardinal rookie Dizzy Dean, who burst onto the scene with 18 wins and a league-high 191 strikeouts. Johnny Frederick of the Brooklyn Dodgers was the definitive pinch-hitter in 1932, blasting six home runs in his specialist role. His fourth pinch-hit round-tripper was recorded on the same day (August 14) that 49-year-old teammate John Quinn became the oldest pitcher to win a major league game.

Cubs shortstop Billy Jurges, on the other hand, was lucky his 24th birthday in May wasn't his last. On July 6, Jurges was shot in the shoulder and hand in his Chicago hotel room by spurned girlfriend Violet Popovich Valli, a local nightclub and theater singer.

Pittsburgh catcher Earl Grace saw his consecutive errorless streak of 110 games end September 7 with a throwing miscue. He set an NL record by committing only one error this season.

Ferocious Phillie

Had the timing been right and his team more successful, Chuck Klein of the Philadelphia Phillies could conceivably have captured five consecutive Most Valuable Player awards. From 1929 through 1933, the muscular left-handed hitter terrorized National League pitchers with a five-year batting average of .359, 180 home runs and 693 RBIs.

It's nearly impossible to grasp the magnitude of the impressive numbers Klein piled up in his first five years as a fulltimer. During that span (1929–33), he led the NL in major offensive categories 19 times. Only once in that period did he fail to top the league in homers.

In his prime, the right fielder was an imposing figure. His 185 pounds, carried on a 6-foot frame, were mainly distributed in a huge upper torso. Klein's enormous arm strength was renowned throughout the league, as was his reputation as an impassioned competitor.

The Philadelphia strongboy's powerful uppercut stroke was perfectly suited for the park in which he played 13 of his 17 seasons. The Baker Bowl, home of the Phillies, was distinguished by a towering metal fence in right field that was a mere 280 feet, six inches from home plate, and Klein took full advantage of its proximity.

Nostalgic recollections of Klein's exploits filled Philadelphia newspapers when he died in 1958, and long-forgotten attempts by the local media to gain Hall of Fame residence for the old favorite were renewed, but to no avail. Fortunately, that honor finally came by vote of the veteran's committee in 1980.

The reasons behind this lengthy wait are somewhat obscure. Some believe a lack of fielding skills kept Klein from entering sooner, while others downplayed the amazing 1929 through 1933 effort by labeling the remainder of his career mediocre by comparison.

Yet, even while the burly Klein was lofting baseballs over and against the metal Baker Bowl fence with great regularity, his dominance was largely overlooked due to Philadelphia finishes that were nearly always near the bottom of the heap. That changed briefly in 1932 when the club had its best year in 14 seasons, placing fourth at 78–76.

The 1932 team's modest accomplishment gained Klein the degree of notoriety needed to capture the Most Valuable Player award. It was another exceptional campaign for the pride of Philadelphia, who topped the National League in hits (226), home runs (38), runs (152), stolen bases (20) and slugging (.646), while hitting .348 and pacing a ferocious Phils attack that was far and away the best in the senior circuit. No player has led his league in both homers and stolen bases since Klein did it in 1932.

The MVP award as it now exists had not yet been established when Klein was having two of his most productive seasons. In his first full year, 1929, the 24-year-old blasted an NL-record 43 home runs, while batting .356 and driving in 145 runs. In 1930, he managed to improve that performance, posting league bests in batting (.386), runs (158) and doubles (59), while smashing 40 homers and racking up 170 RBIs. Klein's RBI total is surpassed in NL annals only by Hack Wilson's 190 of the same year, but even Hack couldn't top the Philly hero's 288 runs produced (RBIs plus runs, minus home runs), still the highest NL total ever. In addition, Klein set a modern-day record for assists by an outfielder with an amazing total of 44.

The golf-stroke swing of the relentless left-hander produced a .337 average in 1931, as he again led the league in home runs, RBIs, slugging and runs. The inaugural MVP that went to Frankie Frisch of the pennant-winning Cardinals should arguably have gone to Klein, who finished second in the voting.

He was runner-up again in 1933, despite winning the Triple Crown with league highs of .368, 28 home runs and 120 RBIs, as well as NL bests in hits (223), doubles (44), slugging (.602) and on-base percentage (.422). Klein's Triple Crown achievement was only the third of four post–1900 National League efforts.

Convinced that the league's top hitter would assure them the pennant, the Chicago Cubs acquired Klein in 1934, and although flashes of past greatness surfaced occasionally, his league-leading days were over. Baseball experts used many combinations of the following theories to explain the precipitous decline: he could no longer hit lefties, didn't have the Baker Bowl ballfield as his ally anymore, couldn't cope with the pressure of playing with a contender and was seeing better pitching while playing for a front-runner.

Years later, Cub teammate Billy Herman related what he believed to be the real reason for the sudden loss of lightning in Klein's bat. Shortly after joining the Chicago team, Klein pulled a hamstring muscle that eventually turned black and blue, swelling to gargantuan proportions. He continued to play, keeping the injury a secret, but was never the consummate batsman he had been.

Still, he did average close to .300 in his two-year Chicago tenure, contributing substantially to the Cubs' 1935 pennant and hitting .333 in his only World Series appearance.

In 1936, Klein was dealt back to Philadelphia, where he celebrated by clobbering four home runs in one game at Pittsburgh's Forbes Field July 10, with two of those mammoth shots reaching the right center field roof.

His last .300 year was 1937. By 1939, he was swapped to Pittsburgh, then back to the Phillies for a final time in 1940. From 1942 to 1944, Klein was a player-coach for Philadelphia, rarely taking the field.

His final years bore no resemblance to the dominance that comprised the first third of his career, but this son of an Indianapolis steelworker had few regrets. Klein had started with a simple dream: to escape a lifestyle that offered little more than molten metal and blowtorches. In his quest, he emblazoned the Klein name in NL record books and forged a bronze plaque for himself in the Hall of Fame.

Top 5 MVP Vote-Getters

1. Chuck Klein, Philadelphia — 78
2. Lon Warneke, Chicago — 68
3. Lefty O'Doul, Brooklyn — 58
4. Paul Waner, Pittsburgh — 37
5. Riggs Stephenson, Chicago — 32

1932 AMERICAN LEAGUE — JIMMIE FOXX

James Emory Foxx
B. October 22, 1907, Sudlersville, Maryland
D. July 21, 1967, Miami, Florida

Year	Team	Games	AB	Hits	Avg.	HR	RBI	Runs	SB
1932	Phil AL	154	585	213	.364	58	169	151	3

The Season

Revenge is sweet. New York manager Joe McCarthy attained a taste of that pleasing nectar in 1932 when his team swept the Chicago Cubs in the World Series. Cub owner William Wrigley had released McCarthy as manager late in the 1930 season, saying he wanted a mentor who could deliver a World Championship. The Yankees made McCarthy their skipper in 1931, and the following campaign he gained retribution.

The Yankee pennant snapped a string of three straight AL flags for Philadelphia, although the A's were still a powerful bunch. The runner-up Athletics led the league in hitting (.290) and blasted 173 homers, the most ever at that time. But the Yanks, who had the only staff ERA under 4.00 in the hard-hitting American League, breezed to first place by 13 games.

Babe Ruth's most famous homer came in the fifth inning of Game 3 of the World Series against Charlie Root, and speculation has never ended as to whether the Bambino was actually "calling his shot" when he pointed in the general direction of the Wrigley Field bleacher seats prior to his blast.

Ruth teammate Lou Gehrig, who had just concluded another high-grade season, hit .529 with three homers and eight RBIs in the four-game Series, connecting for nine hits and scoring the same number of runs.

Back on June 3, Gehrig hit four consecutive home runs and narrowly missed a fifth in a victory over Philadelphia, while on August 21, Cleveland's Wes Ferrell became the first pitcher of the century to win at least 20 games in each of his first four seasons.

And in a wild 18-inning game July 10, Cleveland's Johnny Burnett set a major league record with nine hits in an 18–17 loss to Philadelphia.

The Right-Handed Ruth

The stories surrounding the mammoth home runs off the bat of Jimmie Foxx are nearly as legendary as the man himself. It was not uncommon for a rookie to marvel at a long-distance shot off the bat of another slugger, only to be told, "You think that one was hit far? You should have seen the one Foxx hit here!"

And so it went at every American League park until the rookie, with a vision of majestic brute strength in his mind, finally arrived at Shibe Park for the first time and watched in awe as the "right-handed Babe Ruth" peppered the upper deck with baseballs. And as the rookie matured to manhood, so grew his appreciation of perhaps the strongest man ever to play the game.

A Jimmie Foxx home run did not lope lazily out of an outfielder's reach, sinking softly into the first few rows of bleachers; it rocketed off his bat and soared to uncharted heights as flabbergasted fans and ballplayers alike tried in vain to follow its space-bound flight. After a 1931 World Series homer by "Double X," St. Louis bullpen pitcher Jim Lindsey quipped, "We were watching that ball for two innings."

But for the Philadelphia Athletics and Boston Red Sox first baseman, it wasn't feast or famine, home run or strikeout. Foxx hit well over 500 career round-trippers, and also posted a .325 lifetime batting average and led the AL in on-base percentage three times.

His first of three Most Valuable Player awards came, ironically, in 1932, the year the A's failed to win the pennant for the first time since 1928. Foxx outpolled a couple of members of the World Champion Yankees named Lou Gehrig and Babe Ruth, and a look at Jimmie's '32 season reveals the logic behind the baseball writers' decision.

Big Jim was No. 1 in the American League in five vital offensive areas—home runs (58), RBIs (169), total bases (438), slugging (.749) and runs (151)—while placing second in batting at .364 and walks with 116. He also was third in the league in hits with 213, and his 58 blasts were the most ever by a right-handed hitter and second only to Babe Ruth's 60 at that time.

James Emory Foxx was only 16 years old when he signed his first professional baseball contract with the local team in Easton, Maryland, but was already full grown. And a physically mature Jimmie Foxx meant nightmares for pitchers, and extra insurance policies for third basemen.

Ted Williams, who played with the right-handed terror on the Red Sox for more than three years, said he never saw anyone hit a ball harder than Foxx. The "Maryland Mauler" developed bulging biceps and strapping shoulders from heavy work at the Eastern shore farm on which he grew up, and at six feet and 190 pounds was an awesome sight at the plate, both as a batter and a catcher.

Managing the Easton squad in 1925 was ex–Philadelphia Athletics third baseman Frank "Home Run" Baker, and when both the Yankees and A's displayed interest in the power-packed receiver, Baker showed loyalty to his old boss by steering Foxx toward A's owner and manager Connie Mack.

Jimmie Foxx. (National Baseball Hall of Fame Library, Cooperstown, N.Y.)

From the beginning, there was no question that the muscular newcomer could hit major league pitching. In a 10-game, "let's see what you can do" stint in 1925, Foxx hit at a .667 clip for the A's. But finding a position for him was a problem that wasn't fully resolved until 1929 when Foxx settled in at first base. Prior to that decision, young Jimmie was sent to Providence of the International League, where he hit .327 and played behind the plate.

Foxx appeared in enough games for the Athletics in 1928 to accumulate 400 at-bats, but more important, hit .328 with 13 homers and 79 RBIs, clearly demonstrating that a place had to be found for him in the starting lineup. Mack decided to install the 21-year-old prodigy at first base in 1929, and it's no coincidence the move directly preceded three consecutive Philadelphia pennants.

The slugging first sacker ripped American League pitching for a .354 average, belting 33 homers and driving in 117 runs. He was third in slugging at .625 and fifth in total bases with 323, helping lead the A's to a stunning 18-game margin of victory over the defending World Champion New York Yankees in the pennant race. Foxx then hit .350 with a pair of valuable home runs in the four games-to-one World Series win against the Chicago Cubs in 1929.

The 1930 season was even more productive for Double X, who raised his totals in RBIs to 156, home runs to 37, slugging to .637 and total bases to 358. Foxx hit .335 and was beginning to be seen as the successor to Babe Ruth.

Foxx had another fine fall classic in 1930, hitting .333 with a homer, two doubles and three RBIs as the A's made it two World Championships in a row with a six-game victory over the St. Louis Cardinals. His two-run wallop yielded a 2–0 A's win in the pivotal fifth game.

Slipping somewhat in 1931, Jimmie hit .291, the only time he was under .300 in his 11-year tenure with Philadelphia. Although the sturdy batsman was fourth in the AL in homers with 30 and fifth in slugging at .567, it was definitely a sub-par season for Foxx. Jimmie picked up in the '31 World Series, stroking eight hits (including a home run) and batting .348 against St. Louis, which took the Series in seven games.

Despite the disappointing loss to the Cardinals, Foxx was headed for MVP awards the following two seasons and another in 1938 in what was blossoming into a supremely successful career.

Top 5 MVP Vote-Getters

1. Jimmie Foxx, Philadelphia — 75
2. Lou Gehrig, New York — 55
3. Heinie Manush, Washington — 41
4. Earl Averill, Cleveland — 37
5. Lefty Gomez, New York — 27

1933 National League — Carl Hubbell

Carl Owen Hubbell
B. June 22, 1903, Carthage, Missouri
D. November 21, 1988, Scottsdale, Arizona

Year	Team	Games	W	L	ERA	IP	SO	BB	ShO
1933	NY NL	45	23	12	1.66	308.2	156	47	10

The Season

As if in anticipation of better days ahead, prohibition was relaxed slightly in 1933 with beer becoming a legal drink just prior to the start of the baseball season. Prohibition would be lifted completely in December.

Rejoicing with their suds, fans were treated to the July 6 spectacle of the first All-Star Game, as nearly 50,000 shook off the Depression's throes to watch the American League best the National 4–2 at Comiskey Park in Chicago. Fittingly, 1931 MVP Frankie Frisch of St. Louis smashed the NL's initial four-bagger. (Frisch would hit another the next year, accounting for the first two NL All-Star home runs.)

It was a wonderful campaign for Bill Terry's New York Giants, who won their first World Championship in 11 seasons. Picked to finish fourth, Terry's charges surprised by staying near the top, then moving into first place in early June and staying there, winning by five games over Pittsburgh.

The Giants staff was the best in baseball in 1933, with Carl Hubbell, Hal Schumacher, "Fat Freddie" Fitzsimmons and Roy Parmelee as the starting rotation, but the team's inspiration was provided by rookie shortstop Blondy Ryan. With Ryan injured and remaining in New York, the Giants suffered a disastrous mid–July road trip, losing seven straight. Their lead had shrunk to 2½ games when Ryan wired the following message to Terry: "They cannot beat us. En route. J.C. Ryan." He rejoined the club and played hurt, and "They Cannot Beat Us" was adopted as the war cry of the Giants, who recovered and pulled away for the pennant.

The Scroojie King

The pitch is common to the repertoires of a number of hurlers today, but nobody ever used the screwball with such exclusivity and effectiveness as the masterful Carl Hubbell. The elusive sphere mystified hitters in three different ways—dipping, dancing and disappearing—delivered with robotic nonchalance and pinpoint control from the benign lefty with the low-slung pants.

When Hubbell pitched, his opponents were regularly perched at dugout railings, closely observing the craftsman at work. They caught an eyeful in the 1934 All-Star Game. All but lost in baggy flannels, the "Meal Ticket," not known for strikeouts, fanned five future Hall of Famers (Babe Ruth, Lou Gehrig, Jimmie Foxx, Al Simmons and Joe Cronin) in a row, a feat retold religiously by baseball scribes prior to nearly every All-Star affair. Hubbell, who often stated he would rather get a man out with one pitch than three, confessed years later that he had altered that strategy and went for the whiff against the next batter, Bill Dickey, who broke the string with a single.

Carl Owen Hubbell was born in 1903 in Carthage, Missouri, and grew up on his family's pecan farm in Oklahoma. His love was baseball, which he played for an oil company team following high school graduation. Originally signed by the Detroit Tigers, he was discouraged from experimenting with the screwball by Tiger manager Ty Cobb, who warned against potential arm troubles. Consequently, Hubbell kicked around in the minor leagues from 1923 to '28, posting journeyman

records before turning in earnest to the magic pitch at mid-season of the latter year. An 11-inning shutout, witnessed by a Giant scout, led to a $30,000 bid and a trip to New York for the future "Scroojie King."

Five years later, the lanky lefty was pitching the New York Giants to the 1933 World Championship. It was his first year as a full-fledged star, with the fadeaway breaking ball accounting for a league-low 1.66 ERA. Hubbell, roommate Mel Ott and player-manager Bill Terry carried a no-name supporting cast to a 91–61 mark and the pennant.

It was the first of five straight 20-plus win seasons for Hubbell, whose 23–12 mark notched the first of two MVP awards, the second coming in 1936. He easily outshone every hurler in the game in '33, leading the NL in wins, ERA, shutouts (10) and innings pitched (308.2), and was the recognized stopper for the best mound corps in baseball. Had the writers leaned toward a hitter for the MVP award, it would have gone to 1932 winner and this year's runner-up, Chuck Klein. The Phillies slugger won the Triple Crown with a .368 average, 28 home runs and 120 RBIs.

During one stretch of the 1933 regular season, Hubbell set an NL record by holding the opposition scoreless for 45⅓ straight innings, 18 of those coming in a Herculean, six-hit shutout against the Cardinals, which he considered his greatest pitching feat. Ten of his 33 starts were shutouts, and his 309 innings pitched were tops in the National League. To cap it off, the gaunt-faced lefty and his wicked butterfly pitch registered two complete-game World Series wins versus

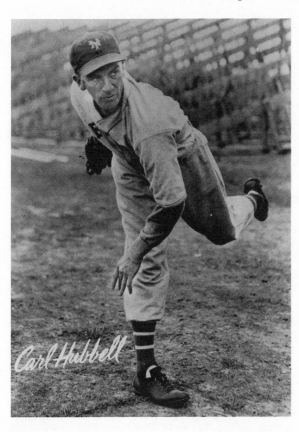

Washington as the Giants won in five. Hubbell allowed no earned runs in 20 innings during that 1933 fall classic.

The modest man who wore the moniker "King Carl" came of age in 1933. In the five previous years, he had averaged slightly more than 15 wins per season and fired a no-hitter against the Pirates in 1929, the first by a lefty in 11 seasons. But those were basically transition years:

time to refine the devastating screwball, marry the high school sweetheart and get comfortable in the 60-foot-6-inch surroundings he would soon dominate. The best was yet to come, including two more World Series and another MVP season.

Top 5 MVP Vote-Getters

1. Carl Hubbell, New York — 77
2. Chuck Klein, Philadelphia — 48
3. Wally Berger, Boston — 44
4. Bill Terry, New York — 35
5. Pepper Martin, St. Louis — 31

Carl Hubbell. (Courtesy San Francisco Giants.)

1933 AMERICAN LEAGUE—JIMMIE FOXX

James Emory Foxx
B. October 22, 1907, Sudlersville, Maryland
D. July 21, 1967, Miami, Florida

Year	Team	Games	AB	Hits	Avg.	HR	RBI	Runs	SB
1933	Phil AL	149	573	204	.356	48	163	125	2

The Season

Perhaps remembering the success he'd enjoyed when 27-year-old player-manager Bucky Harris led his team to a World Championship in 1924, Washington Senators owner Clark Griffith went the youth leadership route again in 1933, and the move paid off.

Shortstop Joe Cronin, 26, was handed the managerial reins at the beginning of the 1933 campaign, and responded with an American League pennant as the Senators outlasted the defending World Champion Yankees

by seven games. Griffith's son-in-law contributed on the field as well, hitting .309 and banging in a team-high 118 runs. But Washington fell victim to the New York Giants in a five-game World Series.

Babe Ruth's two-run homer helped the AL win the first-ever All-Star Game, 4–2 July 6 at Comiskey Park, and two months later, the West won the first Negro League East-West All-Star Game, 11–7, at the same venue.

On September 19, two brothers on opposing teams hit a home run in the same game for the first time. Cleveland

pitcher Wes Ferrell allowed a round-tripper by brother Rick Ferrell, a Boston catcher, and went deep himself against Hank Johnson. Philadelphia's Al Simmons became the last American League player to collect 200 hits five years in a row when he stroked exactly 200 safeties in his first year with the White Sox.

Always ahead of his time, Chicago Cubs President William Veeck recommended a series of interleague games to unconvinced baseball officials. Veeck's idea would eventually come to fruition — 64 years later.

Double for Double X

How to improve on the previous season, in which he captured the Most Valuable Player award and narrowly missed winning the Triple Crown, was answered by Jimmie Foxx in 1933 the only way he could have: by earning his second consecutive MVP honor and securing the first American League Triple Crown since 1909.

With totals of 48 homers, 163 RBIs and a .356 batting average, Foxx's closest competitors (Babe Ruth with 34 homers, Lou Gehrig with 139 RBIs and Heinie Manush with a .336 average) lagged light-years behind. Foxx also was tops in the AL in slugging at .703 and total bases with 403, while scoring 125 runs and collecting 204 hits. Over a two-game period in June 1933, the future Hall of Famer connected for four straight home runs to tie a record. Two months later, he hit for the cycle and set an AL record with nine RBIs in a win over Cleveland.

Never considered a slick fielder, the first baseman was proficient enough to lead the league in assists with 93. But for all his colossal efforts, Jimmie took a pay cut from $16,333 to $16,000 the next year as owner and manager Connie Mack tried unsuccessfully to combat the results of the Depression.

By 1934, Foxx was the lone survivor of the glory-year stars who had made the Philadelphia Athletics one of the best teams in the history of the game. Sold to help keep Mack monetarily afloat were Lefty Grove, Rube Walberg and Max Bishop to the Boston Red Sox; Al Simmons, George Earnshaw, Jimmy Dykes and Mule Haas to the Chicago White Sox; and Mickey Cochrane to the Detroit Tigers.

Despite the fact that the team, which fell to fifth place in 1934, was depreciating around him, "Double X" maintained his high standards. The cheerful, easygoing powerhouse was runner-up in home runs with 44 and slugging at .653, and fourth in RBIs with 130 and total bases with 352. Pitchers had learned to fear him, as evidenced by his league-leading 111 walks.

In his final campaign with the once-great A's in '35, Foxx paced the American League in slugging (.636) and tied for the home run title with Detroit's Hank Greenberg (36). "The Beast" went animal with 340 total bases (second in the AL), 115 RBIs (third), a .346 average (third) and 114 walks (third). But Philadelphia plummeted all the way to the cellar in 1935.

Foxx's prowess notwithstanding, Mack could no longer resist the big bucks being offered for his long ball hitter. Jimmie's move to the Boston Red Sox and their intimately close left field wall certainly didn't damage his home run production, nor did the new surroundings hurt his wallet. Millionaire owner Tom Yawkey handed his new star a contract for $32,000, nearly double his highest salary in Philadelphia.

Yawkey's $150,000 purchase earned his pay in 1936 by placing third in the AL in homers with 41, RBIs with 143 and slugging at .631. He also racked up 369 total bases, but the Red Sox slipped from fourth place to sixth. Boston moved up a notch to fifth in 1937, thanks to Foxx, their leading home run hitter (36) and RBI man (127).

The powerfully built first baseman, who also made spot starts at third base, catcher and in the outfield during his 20-year career, had outstanding seasons with both the A's and Red Sox, putting together several impressive streaks.

Spanning parts of three decades, Jimmie drove in 105 runs or more every season for 13 years in a row (1929–41), and batted .300 or better in 10 of 12 consecutive full seasons (1928–39). From 1929 to 1940, Foxx's slugging average was in the .600s six times and the .700s on three occasions. The first sacker also led the AL in fielding percentage three times.

Double X played in seven All-Star Games; hit 30 or more homers for a dozen straight years beginning in 1929; and, starting in his first MVP year (1932), hit at least 35 homers in nine consecutive seasons. Many of those round-trippers were mammoth shots, but unfortunately, exact distances are unknown because homers were seldom measured in those days.

When asked once how far a Jimmie Foxx home run had traveled off him, New York pitcher Lefty Gomez pointed to the upper reaches of Yankee Stadium and said, "I don't know how far it went, but it takes 45 minutes to walk up there."

And, as Foxx approached his third career MVP season in 1938, there was still plenty of pop left in his bat.

Top 5 MVP Vote-Getters

1. Jimmie Foxx, Philadelphia — 74
2. Joe Cronin, Washington — 62
3. Heinie Manush, Washington — 54
4. Lou Gehrig, New York — 39
5. Lefty Grove, Philadelphia — 35

1934 National League — Dizzy Dean

Jay Hanna Dean
B. January 16, 1910, Lucas, Arkansas
D. July 17, 1974, Reno, Nevada

Year	Team	Games	W	L	ERA	IP	SO	BB	ShO
1934	SL NL	50	30	7	2.66	311.2	195	75	7

The Season

The year 1934 will forever be linked with the derring-do antics of the St. Louis Cardinals, better known as the Gashouse Gang.

Down eight games to the New York Giants in early September, the St. Louis club mounted a magnificent stretch run that resulted in both teams sporting 93–58 records with only two games remaining.

At that point, a seemingly innocuous pre-season comment by Giant player-manager Bill Terry came back to haunt him. "Brooklyn?" he had flippantly asked when questioned about the Dodgers' 1934 chances, "Are they still in the league?"

Using that quote as a rallying point, the incensed Dodgers demonstrated to Terry just how dangerous a running mouth can be, knocking off the Giants in the last two games of the regular season and shattering New York's pennant hopes.

That set the stage for a seven-game set between the Gashouse Gang and the Detroit Tigers in the World Series, a closely fought affair until the Cardinals routed the American Leaguers 11–0 in the final contest. In that deciding seventh game, frustrated Tiger fans pelted St. Louis left fielder Joe "Ducky" Medwick with so much debris that Commissioner Kenesaw Mountain Landis demanded Medwick's removal.

The peerless screwball of New York Giant hurler Carl Hubbell gained undying status in the 1934 All-Star Game as five future Hall of Famers — Babe Ruth, Lou Gehrig, Jimmie Foxx, Al Simmons and Joe Cronin — fell victim to its elusiveness, all striking out in succession.

The early stages of baseball's fading innocence were typified in three 1934 events: the Pittsburgh Pirates became the last team to begin playing home games on Sunday, starting April 29 after Pennsylvania's Blue Law was repealed; Landis sold the broadcast rights to the World Series for $100,000 to the Ford Motor Company; and night baseball in the NL was authorized by a vote of league owners.

Following the season, eventual commissioner Ford Frick was promoted from publicity director to National League president.

The Legend Is a Card

In his day he was as much a part of American folklore as a Western gunslinger or a World War I flying ace. The stories surrounding his brief but legendary career were always outrageous and, in most instances, true.

Jay Hanna "Dizzy" Dean was a symbol of his era: boisterous, bold, charismatic and a little bit larger than life. For five years he was among the best moundsmen in the game — bragging and challenging before, during and after each contest, then backing up his words with deeds that fired the imagination.

Dean could turn his vast talents on and off like a faucet. He would clown and toy with opposing batters until the moment of truth arrived; then the playful attitude was replaced with a crackling fastball or sweeping curve.

No game or situation, regardless of its supposed sanctity, was off-limits for Dizzy's constant barrage of boast-filled predictions. Before the 1934 season began, the Cardinal ace bragged loudly that "me and (younger brother) Paul," another Redbird hurler, would win 45 games between them and lead the Cardinals to the pennant. The Deans won 49. Prior to the World Series, the elder Dean predicted to all within earshot that he and Paul would each win two games. They did precisely that.

Dizzy was forever carrying on a steady banter with opponents from the mound. In the 1934 World Series, he openly taunted Detroit Tiger star Hank Greenberg late in Game 7. The Cards were coasting to an 11–0 win, and Dean, who had fanned Greenberg twice, was feeling especially frisky. "What's wrong, Mickey?" he shouted to Tiger player-manager and that year's American League MVP Mickey Cochrane. "No pinch-hitters?" He then whiffed the dangerous Greenberg for a third time.

Dean's MVP campaign fulfilled promises of dominating brilliance. As a rookie in 1932, the 21-year-old won 18 games with league highs in innings pitched (286) and shutouts (four). That inaugural mark was followed by a 20-win season in 1933, with the swaggering upstart topping the National League in strikeouts both years. In 1933, he set an NL record by fanning 17 Chicago Cubs in one afternoon.

He was 28–12 in 1935 and 24–13 in 1936. Dean's durability evidenced itself in NL highs in complete games and innings pitched both years. It was more of the same excellence through the first half of 1937 until a wicked line drive off the bat of Earl Averill in the All-Star Game broke a toe on Dean's right foot. His unyielding insistence on an early comeback drastically altered a once fluid pitching motion and placed an unnatural strain on his prized right arm. Bursitis developed quickly, and by season's end the smoke on Dean's fastball had vanished.

He was traded to the Chicago Cubs in 1938, and as a mere wisp of his once invincible self, still managed to beguile the enemy with slow curves and changeups to register a 7–1 mark and help his new mates to a pennant. However, it was painfully apparent that at age 27, Dean's comet-like talent had burned out.

Yet from 1932 to 1936, it would have been difficult to refute the brash hurler's oft-stated claim that he was the best pitcher in baseball. During those five years, the controversial Cardinal won 120 games and notched four strikeout titles. His watermark year of 1934 was the first time a National League pitcher had scaled the hallowed 30-win plateau since Grover Cleveland Alexander did it in 1917. No NL moundsman has duplicated the effort since.

During that memorable MVP campaign, the 23-year-old third-year man took the mound in nearly one-third of his club's 154 regular-season games. On September 21, Dizzy and brother Paul set a major league record that stood for 58 years by allowing a total of only three hits in a double-header sweep of Brooklyn. Dizzy's three clutch victories in the final week of the season put the Gashouse Gang over the hump and into the World Series. Dean appeared in three of the seven World Series games and won two, including the title clincher, a shutout on only one day of rest. Besides leading the league in victories, he was tops in winning percentage (.811), shutouts (seven) and strikeouts (195).

It was heady stuff for the son of a poor itinerant farm worker. Dean was born in 1910 in Lucas, Arkansas. His mother died when he was 3, and he and his brothers spent their youth working the cotton fields of the Southwest. Formal schooling for young Jay Hanna ended in grade four. Following an armed forces hitch, Jay pitched for a semipro team where he was spotted and signed by Cardinal scout Don Curtis in 1930.

Before another decade had elapsed, the good-natured field hand had achieved the pinnacle of baseball success and plunged into the depths of near oblivion. His final three years with the Cubs saw the once magnificent performer win but nine games, and at age 30, Dean retired.

Months after his retirement, Dean's golly-gee innocence was booming over the local airwaves in his job of radio broadcaster for Cardinals and St. Louis Browns games. His vast popularity continued unabated in the new profession, and in 1950, Dean signed on with national television to work baseball's *Game of the Week*. Some school teachers deplored his misuse of the English language, which included constant malapropisms and impromptu phraseology ("he slud into third"), but the objectors were in the minority.

Dean's amiable presence was a welcome companion for baseball until he left broadcasting in the late 1960s. He died of a heart attack in 1974 at age 63. In 1953, 16 years after his dominant pitching days had passed, Dean was elected to the Hall of Fame.

For four generations, baseball aficionados were treated to a rare combination of athletic superiority and good-humored eccentricity from Dean. He was a country rogue in St. Louis flannels — sometimes a hellcat, sometimes a charmer, always a hurler supreme.

Dizzy Dean … an American folk hero.

Top 5 MVP Vote-Getters

1. Dizzy Dean, St. Louis — 78
2. Paul Waner, Pittsburgh — 50
3. Jo Jo Moore, New York — 42
4. Travis Jackson, New York — 39
5. Mel Ott, New York — 37

1934 AMERICAN LEAGUE — MICKEY COCHRANE

Gordon Stanley Cochrane
B. April 6, 1903, Bridgewater, Massachusetts
D. June 28, 1962, Lake Forest, Illinois

Year	Team	Games	AB	Hits	Avg.	HR	RBI	Runs	SB
1934	Det AL	129	437	140	.320	2	76	74	8

The Season

Sporting a team batting average of exactly .300, the Detroit Tigers won 101 games to capture the American League pennant over the 94–60 New York Yankees. The Tigers went from fifth place in 1933 to the top of the heap, winning 26 more games and copping their first crown since the Ty Cobb–led 1909 squad.

The Motor City team was the best run-producing club in the majors, but ran into the whirlwind National League entry, the St. Louis Cardinals, in the World Series. The Gashouse Gang bested the Tigers in a thrilling seven-game affair.

Nineteen-thirty-four was Babe Ruth's final year as a Yankee. The Bambino, 39, slowing down at bat and in the field, hit only .288 with 22 home runs. One of those round-trippers came July 13 and was the 700th of his career.

Other individual highlights this season included Detroit rookie Schoolboy Rowe tying a junior circuit record with 16 straight wins; St. Louis Browns hurler Bobo Newsom pitching nine innings of no-hit ball against the Red Sox September 18, only to lose in the 10th after giving up his first hit; and Washington catcher Moe Berg setting an AL mark with his 117th consecutive errorless game April 21.

The women's liberation movement took a step forward March 20 when Mildred "Babe" Didrickson pitched one inning of an exhibition game for the Philadelphia Athletics, holding the Brooklyn Dodgers scoreless and hitless.

Motor City Messiah

Gordon Stanley "Mickey" Cochrane was an intense student of baseball — a hard worker who spent many hours perfecting his numerous natural talents. His left-handed line drive swing was acquired through arduous hours in the batting cage, the result being a lifetime .320 average that is unsurpassed by any retired catcher in the game's history.

On the bench, Mickey would survey the action with a cool demeanor, but inside he was a calculating machine, constantly on the lookout for the edge that could give his team a win. As a handler of pitchers he was unparalleled, mollifying the outbursts of a Lefty Grove or spurring on the more gentle souls such as George Earnshaw to the peak of their ability.

Cochrane was everything a catcher should be and more, the extra ingredient being basepath speed and savvy that made the feisty Irishman as good a base runner as anyone on the Athletics, his first club.

The Detroit Tigers were most interested in his ability to rile a ballclub when they purchased him from the Philadelphia A's prior to the 1934 sea-

son. Taking on the role of player-manager for the first time, the fiery catcher hit .320 and led the Tigers to the promised land, fulfilling his assignment as Detroit's messiah. "Black Mike" was the undisputed commander on and off the field for the American League champions. Recognizing his importance in the Tigers' success story, the baseball writers voted him the MVP.

Were the award based purely on statistics, a couple of New York Yankees would have finished well above the MVP recipient. First baseman Lou Gehrig won the Triple Crown with a .363 average, 49 home runs and 165 RBIs, and also posted league highs in slugging and total bases. Pitcher Lefty Gomez paced the junior circuit in wins (26), ERA (2.33), strikeouts (158), shutouts and complete games.

Nineteen-thirty-four may have been the crowning glory in Cochrane's career, but it was hardly a solitary season of excellence. His stylish ability and consistently outstanding record always get him strong backing when the stove league question, "Who was the greatest catcher of all time?" pops up. In 13 seasons, Cochrane hit over .300 nine times. He was one of the most enduring catchers ever, with 11 consecutive seasons of 100 or more games caught, and in five of those years he went over the 130-game mark. The aggressive backstop played on five pennant winners and three World Championship teams.

He dreamed as a youth of not only playing major league baseball, but managing a team as well. From early on, Cochrane exhibited a sharp mind, and was an excellent pupil both on the baseball sandlots and in the classroom, eventually graduating from Boston University. His heads-up style of play caught the eye of a representative from the Dover club of the Eastern Shore League, and Mickey signed his first professional contract.

He was an infielder at the time, but when the team needed a catcher, Mickey volunteered. Within a year he was demonstrating major league ability, and Connie Mack, owner and manager of the Philadelphia Athletics, went to great lengths to procure the youngster. Mack bought controlling

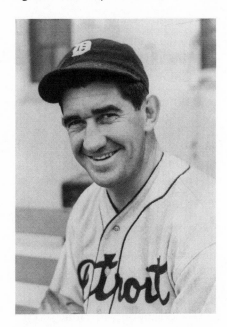

Mickey Cochrane. (Courtesy Detroit Tigers.)

interest in the Portland minor league team, purchased Cochrane from Dover, groomed his skills at Portland and then bought his contract. The entire transaction cost Mack nearly $200,000 and much paperwork, but he later claimed it was one of the best maneuvers and investments he ever made.

In his first year at Philadelphia (1925), Cochrane stepped immediately into the starting catcher slot, hit .331 and displayed the natural leadership qualities that would soon be his trademark. In 1928, he earned the League Award, the predecessor to the MVP.

By 1929, Mack had pieced together his Athletics dynasty, and Philadelphia won the first of three consecutive pennants, with World Championships coming in 1929 and '30. Cochrane was exceptional in all three pennant drives, hitting .331, .357 and .349, respectively. He led AL catchers in fielding with a .993 mark in both 1930 and '32, and paced the league in on-base percentage (.459) in 1933.

Although Mack recognized his receiver to be the heart of the ballclub, Mickey was not spared when Philadelphia backed up the truck in the years immediately following the 1931 World Series. Cochrane put in two more good seasons for Philadelphia, but prior to 1934, Mack sold him to Detroit for $100,000.

There Mickey directed his new club to the pennant, and Detroit fans turned the city into a madhouse. The bushy-eyed Cochrane was the center of local attention, and civic groups awarded him numerous gifts, including a new car. Unfortunately, Detroit fell to St. Louis and player-manager Frankie Frisch in the 1934 World Series. It marked the final fall classic in which each team was led by a player-manager.

But Cochrane's bunch bounced back, repeating as pennant winners in 1935, this time defeating the Chicago Cubs in a six-game World Series for the Tigers' first World Championship. Cochrane scored the winning run in the deciding game, after the 32-year-old had caught 110 games while hitting .319 in the regular season.

In 1936, Mickey slipped to .270 in 44 games. While the Tigers dropped from contention, the high-key Cochrane agonized and suffered a nervous breakdown that put him in the hospital.

Disaster struck early in 1937. After hitting a home run off Bump Hadley of the New York Yankees in his previous at-bat, Mickey took a Hadley fastball to the right temple and went down in a heap at home plate. He was unconscious for 10 days, hovering between life and death before finally pulling through. But at age 34, his playing days were over.

The zestful Cochrane personality was unsuited for bench managing, or so said Detroit owner Spike Briggs when Mickey was replaced during the 1938 season.

He eventually returned to the game as a scout, coach, Philadelphia Athletics general manager and vice president for the Tigers, but those closest to him said he was an unhappy man, lacking the once familiar spirit after his son was killed in World War II. Cochrane died in 1962.

Twenty-three years after his 1947 induction into the Hall of Fame, baseball's writers voted Mickey Cochrane the best catcher in the game's first 100 years. And although that ranking may be honorary and still open to dispute, there can be no argument that in numbers of ways to best an opponent, he was the most diverse receiver of them all.

Top 5 MVP Vote-Getters

1. Mickey Cochrane, Detroit — 67
2. Charlie Gehringer, Detroit — 65
3. Lefty Gomez, New York — 60
4. Schoolboy Rowe, Detroit — 59
5. Lou Gehrig, New York — 54

1935 NATIONAL LEAGUE — GABBY HARTNETT

Charles Leo Hartnett
B. December 20, 1900, Woonsocket, Rhode Island
D. December 20, 1972, Park Ridge, Illinois

Year	Team	Games	AB	Hits	Avg.	HR	RBI	Runs	SB
1935	Chi NL	116	413	142	.344	13	91	67	1

The Season

Like a crafty jockey, Chicago manager Charlie Grimm paced his charges for most of the 1935 season, allowing the New York Giants and St. Louis Cardinals to battle for the lead along the rail in the National League pennant race.

But Grimm finally applied the whip in September, and the Cubs sped forward with 21 consecutive wins, passing the Cards in the stretch drive and winning by four lengths. Chicago then suffered a six-game World Series defeat to Detroit.

The Cubbies not only put runs on the board in 1935, leading the NL with 847, they also were adept at keeping the opposition off of it. Chicago pitchers were the best in baseball with a 3.26 ERA, aided by a league-high 163 double plays.

Cubs hitters paced the senior circuit with a .288 mark, while a pair of 20-game winners — Bill Lee and Lon Warneke — helped Chicago pitch a league-best 81 complete games and place second in strikeouts with 589.

The first night game in major league baseball history was played May 24 in Cincinnati, with the Reds downing Philadelphia 2–1. By 1948, every big league park had lights, with the exception of Chicago's Wrigley Field, which featured day games exclusively until 1988.

In Babe Ruth's NL debut April 16, the largest opening day crowd (25,000) in Boston Braves history showed up to see him belt a 430-foot homer off Carl Hubbell. On May 25, Ruth slugged three home runs, including his 714th and final one (a 600-foot shot), for the Braves at Pittsburgh. Eight days later, Ruth announced his retirement.

Hartnett's Heroics

Without a doubt, the most widely remembered moment in the career of Chicago Cubs catcher Gabby Hartnett is his famous 1938 home run, delivered in the twilight during a tight pennant race: the "homer in the gloamin'." And equally without question, the rugged backstop's finest season came in 1930 when he accumulated lifetime highs of 37 home runs, 122 RBIs and a .630

slugging average, in addition to hitting .339.

But in 1930, the Most Valuable Player award was still a year away from official recognition, and in '38, another catcher, Cincinnati's Ernie Lombardi, was the choice. So what exactly did Charles Leo Hartnett accomplish in 1935 to convince baseball writers to select him as the National League MVP?

On paper, Hartnett was not nearly as productive as St. Louis' Joe Medwick or Wally Berger of Boston. But fortunately, MVP awards are not granted solely on the basis of eye-catching statistics.

Not that the big, tomato-faced catcher was lacking in impressive stats. Hartnett hit a hefty .344 in 1935 to place third in the National League, and slugged at a .545 clip, good for fifth. He also tagged 13 homers and drove in 91 runs. But perhaps even more important in the eyes of the scribes were the subtle intangibles Gabby contributed on a daily basis. Hartnett helped mold the majors' best pitching staff, which included four hurlers with at least 15 wins apiece. His arm, probably the strongest in baseball at the time, kept enemy base runners cautious.

The 1935 World Series, in which Hartnett produced a pair of two-hit games and collected at least one safety in five of the contests, was the second of four Series appearances for the 6-foot-1, 195-pounder from Rhode Island. After going 0-for-3 in a pinch-hitting role in the 1929 fall classic, he hit .313 with a home run and two doubles in the Yankees' sweep of the Cubs in 1932, then legged out a triple in another New York whitewash in 1938.

What had led up to the 1938 pennant was far more thrilling for Cubs fans and their catcher than what took place during the World Series. With the season more than half completed and the Cubs perched in third place, 6½ games behind Pittsburgh, Charlie Grimm was dismissed as manager and future Hall of Famer Hartnett was picked to take over as player-manager. Going into the final week of the season, the Cubs were 1½ games behind the Pirates.

In the first of a three-game series at Wrigley Field, the Cubs cut the Pirates' lead to one-half game. With the clubs deadlocked at 5–5 in the second contest and darkness settling in, the right-handed clutch hitter came to the plate with two outs and nobody on base in the bottom of the ninth inning. The umpires had decided to suspend the game if it was still tied after nine frames. Pittsburgh reliever Mace Brown tried to slip an 0-2 pitch past Gabby, but he lashed a line drive into the left field bleachers, a "homer in the gloamin'," to put the Cubbies into first place to stay.

The 1938 season was Hartnett's last hurrah. The Cubs finished fourth in 1939, then slid to fifth in '40. Gabby was released at the end of the 1940 season, signing on as a player-coach with the New York Giants.

The easy-going man nicknamed "Gabby" by a Chicago sportswriter served as manager in three minor league cities before retiring. Returning to baseball in 1965, Hartnett joined the Kansas City Athletics as a baseline coach. On his 72nd birthday, Gabby passed away at his home in Park Ridge, Illinois.

Charles Leo Hartnett, born in 1900 in Rhode Island, grew up in Millville, Massachusetts. The first of 14 children of a local streetcar conductor and bus driver, he joined the Eastern League and became a starting catcher immediately. The Cubs purchased him in 1922, and two years later, he took over on the big league level. From 1924 to 1928, Hartnett hit no worse than .275, batting .302 in '28 and clubbing 24 home runs in '25. He drove in 80 runs in 1927 while catching 125 games.

But just as he appeared to be coming into his own, Gabby suffered a scary arm injury in spring training of 1929, limiting him to 25 games that season. Several theories regarding the mysterious ailment made the rounds, including one from Gabby's mother claiming that the catcher's injury was psychosomatic, probably related to his wife's pregnancy. Later, teammate Woody English said the sore arm was caused by the recoil of a gun that Hartnett used to shoot clay pigeons in Chicago's Lincoln Park.

Cubs fans feared their catcher's career might be cut short, but after a winter's rest, the right arm returned to form. So did Gabby, who enjoyed his best season in 1930, beginning a stretch of 100 or more games caught eight years in a row.

The durable receiver set a record for consecutive chances by a catcher without an error (452) in 1933 and '34, and led the National League in fielding and assists six times each. Hartnett hit a career-high .354 in 1937, missing Chief Meyers' NL mark for catchers by only four points. He also was named to six straight All-Star Teams (1933–38).

Despite a workman-like attitude, Hartnett had a colorful, boisterous side to him as well. When he believed that his pitcher was focusing too much attention on a base runner at first, he would sometimes step toward the mound between pitches and say loudly, "Don't throw over there. Let him run. I'll throw him out by eight or 10 feet." And on pop fouls near the stands, Hartnett would occasionally entertain the fans by yelling, "I never dropped a pop fly in my life," before hauling it in.

Gabby always seemed to be in the right place at the right time. He was Carl Hubbell's catcher when the left-handed screwball artist whiffed five eventual Hall of Famers in succession during the 1934 All-Star Game; he was behind the plate for Babe Ruth's "called shot" in the 1932 World Series; and in his first major league outing in 1922, Hartnett caught none other than Grover Cleveland Alexander, who requested Gabby as his personal catcher the rest of the season.

And to this day, many old-timers who recall his Wrigley Field heroics remember Gabby Hartnett as their personal favorite as well.

Top 5 MVP Vote-Getters

1. Gabby Hartnett, Chicago — 75
2. Dizzy Dean, St. Louis — 66
3. Arky Vaughn, Pittsburgh — 45
4. Billy Herman, Chicago — 38
5. Joe Medwick, St. Louis — 37

1935 AMERICAN LEAGUE — HANK GREENBERG

Henry Benjamin Greenberg
B. January 1, 1911, New York, New York
D. September 4, 1986, Beverly Hills, California

Year	Team	Games	AB	Hits	Avg.	HR	RBI	Runs	SB
1935	Det AL	152	619	203	.328	36	170	121	4

The Season

The Detroit Tigers repeated as pennant winners in 1935, this time taking a close-to-the-vest World Series from the Chicago Cubs, four games to two.

After getting blanked in Game 1, Detroit rallied to win the next three, one in extra innings. The Tigers finally brought home the city's first World Championship in Game 6 when in the bottom of the ninth inning, Leon "Goose" Goslin singled home jubilant player-manager Mickey Cochrane with the winning run.

As in the previous year, the Tigers displayed the most potent attack in baseball. Their infield accounted for an average of 105 RBIs per man. The Detroit team was hardly one-dimensional, however, with the best fielding in the league and second-best pitching to the runner-up New York Yankees, who finished three games back.

Connie Mack's Philadelphia Athletics, mired in the cellar all season, were an enigma in 1935. With hitters such as Jimmie Foxx, "Indian" Bob Johnson and Pinky Higgins providing the long ball, the Mackmen led the league in round-trippers, but still managed to finish last in the AL in runs scored.

In a couple of "firsts," Philadelphia's Roger "Doc" Cramer became the first AL player to produce six consecutive hits in a nine-inning game twice (he had also accomplished the task in 1932), while Vern Kennedy of Chicago tossed the first no-hitter ever at Comiskey Park — and the first in the junior circuit in four years — blanking Cleveland 5–0 and contributing a bases-loaded triple.

Surely the most bizarre play of the season occurred September 7 when Boston's Joe Cronin ended a 5–3 loss to Cleveland by hitting a line drive off the head of third baseman Odell Hale and into the hands of shortstop Bill Knickerbocker, who started a triple play.

A Tiger Earns His Stripes

In the days when the Detroit Tigers were the main challengers to a rarely interrupted string of Yankee pennants, Hank Greenberg was one of the league's biggest guns. As respected throughout the league for his talent and class as Bob Feller and Joe DiMaggio, big Hank lacked the latter star's fielding grace and New York media coverage, but carried the same DiMaggio mystique, dignity and good looks. And like the Yankee Clipper, Greenberg could hit like a demon.

Despite a nagging self-doubt concerning his status as Detroit's top run producer, the 24-year-old placed the weight of the Tigers' clean-up position squarely on his broad shoulders during his 1935 MVP year. Early in the season, the defending American League champions were struggling to put runs on the board, and in only his third year in the bigs, Greenberg summoned up the fortitude to request that manager Mickey Cochrane insert him in the fourth spot of the Tiger attack. Cochrane grinned knowingly at this coming-of-age attitude, and acquiesced. From that point on, the Detroit team began scoring runs in bunches, 170 of which were driven in by the booming bat of the 6-foot-3½-inch, 210-pound right-handed slugger.

Hank's long, poetic swing accounted for 36 home runs that year,

tying Jimmie Foxx for the league lead. His RBI total was an astounding 51 better than his closest competitor, Lou Gehrig. And as was the norm throughout his career, the Detroit powerhouse registered a top-notch batting mark, hitting .328 while guiding the Tigers to the pennant.

Hank suffered a major setback in the 1935 World Series when, after hitting a first-inning home run, broke his wrist while trying to score from first base on a single during the second game of the confrontation with the Chicago Cubs. His mates went on to win without the big guy's services, however, and this softened Henry's disappointment.

Nineteen-thirty-five was the first of six campaigns in a war- and injury-shortened career that would implant the Greenberg persona directly in the midst of baseball's luminaries. But where Hank was concerned, the time to enjoy victories was always short. Weeks after the World Series but before baseball's writers had officially named him the league's MVP, he was back in training, with rehabilitation heavy on his mind.

The feeling that he always had to prove himself came as much from his heritage as his strong work ethic. The first Jewish superstar ballplayer battled anti-Semitism from owners, coaches, players and fans for much of his career, but always overcame. "I found (taunting) was a spur to make me do better," Greenberg said. "Because … if you struck out, you weren't just a bum, but a Jewish bum."

The New York native was rarely satisfied, even after achieving his goals. As a youngster growing up in the Bronx, the tall, gangly Greenberg was

Hank Greenberg. (Courtesy Detroit Tigers.)

ferred the veteran Harry Davis, a sharp glove man with a weak stick. Davis was at first base on opening day, but that slight only made Greenberg strive harder to break into the lineup. Approximately one-third of the way through the campaign, Greenberg received his opportunity, and once seized, never let go. He started 116 games for the Tigers that initial season, hit .301, parked 12 home runs and drove in 87 teammates. It was an impressive debut for the soft-spoken young man, and the first of eight straight years in which he would be above the .300 mark in batting.

In 1934, Detroit hired new manager Mickey Cochrane, who helped instill confidence in the blossoming first sacker by naming him sole possessor of that position. Hank lived up to Cochrane's expectations, hitting a resounding .339 and leading the Tigers in homers (26) and RBIs (139). His 63 doubles paced the circuit, and still stood as the fourth highest single-season total ever. Although he was not religious, Hank felt a strong affinity toward fellow Jews, and brought attention to the Jewish faith with a highly publicized decision to sit out a game on Yom Kippur during the '34 pennant race. Detroit snatched the AL flag, and despite a loss to the Cardinals in the World Series, Hank hit .321 with seven RBIs in his first post-season affair.

Then came the MVP year of 1935, and with it the World Championship. In only three years, the explosive Greenberg stroke had helped resurrect baseball fever in the Motor City while setting the stage for two more Tiger pennants, another World Championship and one more MVP season.

Top 5 MVP Vote-Getters

1. Hank Greenberg, Detroit — 80
2. Wes Ferrell, Boston — 62
3. Joe Vosmik, Cleveland — 39
4. Buddy Myer, Washington — 36
5. Lou Gehrig, New York — 29

far from a natural athlete. He would compensate for his ungainliness by arriving earlier, working harder and staying longer on the practice field than any of his chums. That resolute attitude would remain throughout his life.

Shortly after his graduation from high school, Greenberg was pursued by the Yankees, Tigers, Senators and Pirates. Scouts from all four teams were in attendance one July day when the 18-year-old polled a monumental home run while playing for a woolen mill company team. A quartet of contract offers was made, and Hank, with advice from his father, signed with the

Tigers because they agreed to wait until he had completed college, and to pay for his tuition.

He lasted only one semester at New York University, as the need to prove himself a major leaguer became too overwhelming to ignore. The Tigers shipped him to Hartford of the Eastern League, and later to Raleigh where he began distinguishing himself as a batsman of some repute, albeit an awkward first baseman.

The Tigers brought the 22-year-old up to the big club in 1933, where the rookie met immediate resistance from manager Bucky Harris, who pre-

1936 National League — Carl Hubbell

Carl Owen Hubbell
B. June 22, 1903, Carthage, Missouri
D. November 21, 1988, Scottsdale, Arizona

Year	Team	Games	W	L	ERA	IP	SO	BB	ShO
1936	NY NL	42	26	6	2.31	304	123	57	3

The Season

Five of baseball's mythical pantheons gained eternal prestige in 1936, with charter membership in baseball's version of Mount Olympus, the Hall of Fame. The quintessential quintet, in order of voting preference, were Ty Cobb, Babe Ruth, Christy Mathewson, Honus Wagner and Walter Johnson. The Cooperstown, New York, facility would admit other tenants in yearly groups, but the supremacy of this inaugural five would remain unmatched.

Future Hall of Famers did battle in the 1936 All-Star Game, the first victory by a National League team since the game's inception. The closely fought affair featured shutout stints by Carl Hubbell and Dizzy Dean, with Joe "Ducky" Medwick driving in the winning run.

Giants owner Horace Stoneham had all but thrown in the towel for 1936, as on July 1 his club rested, seemingly immobile, in fifth place. But just as Stoneham started toying with the idea of rebuilding for 1937, the New Yorkers took off. Two months later, thanks to a 35–5 spurt, the Giants were on top of the standings, having passed St. Louis and Chicago.

The Giants went on to capture the pennant with a 92–62 record, finishing five games ahead of the Cubs and Cards, but were overrun four games to two by the cross-town Yankees in the first World Series meeting between these teams in 13 years.

Prior to the season, the new owners of the Boston Braves asked local media to select a different nickname for the team. "The Bees" was the choice, but it never really caught on, and was discontinued after five years.

On April 14, St. Louis rookie Eddie Morgan became the first player to hit a pinch-hit home run in his first major league at-bat. It turned out to be the only homer of Morgan's brief career.

Royal Replay

Sportswriters of the day referred to him as "King Carl" in their daily accounts, but the common complaint in the press box was that he was "exceptional but boring." It had been easy writing about the previous New York Giant pitching legend, Christy Mathewson, the scribes said, for "Matty" exuded charm both on the field and off. But Carl Hubbell was so mild-mannered, so somber in his work, that he defied adjectival praise.

Yet in 1936, the machine-like Hubbell accomplished a feat unmatched by any National League pitcher when he won his second Most Valuable Player award. No other NL hurler — Hall of Famer or otherwise — has ever captured more than one, and with the advent of the Cy Young Award in 1956, the odds are against anyone ever tying, let along surpassing, Hubbell's achievement.

Matty may have been more fanciful in his years as the Giants' top hurler, but Hubbell guided that same club through a long period of prosperity, providing equal dependability, if not with the same style.

Although the writers found it difficult to extract colorful copy from Hubbell's business-like pitching and low-key lifestyle, the fans recognized athletic genius when they saw it, with attendance always increasing whenever

the "Meal Ticket" took the mound. This was especially true from mid-1936 through early 1937, when the invincible workhorse spun 24 consecutive wins, still the NL record. Hubbell's incredible streak began May 17, 1936, with a 6–0 shutout of Pittsburgh, and his 24th victory was notched May 27, 1937. In those 24 wins, he fashioned a 1.95 ERA. The streak ended May 31 when Brooklyn pounded him for five runs on seven hits in fewer than three innings.

Hubbell was rivaled in mound supremacy during that period by his exact opposite, the braggadocio Cardinal, Dizzy Dean. In head-to-head match-ups, the quiet lefty won 8-of-11 games from his vocal opponent.

Hubbell's 253 career wins are the most ever by a Giant southpaw, and are topped only by Mathewson in the team's annals. His lifetime victory total was not bettered by a National League left-hander until Warren Spahn turned the trick in 1959.

But Hubbell and his mystifying screwball were without equal in 1936. The hollow-faced southpaw, at the peak of his popularity, began the season slowly, and fans wondered aloud if the unconventional delivery that his "out" pitch demanded had taken its toll. Then he caught fire, registering 16 straight triumphs from mid-season to the end of the year, leading the Giants from fifth place past the Cubs and Cardinals into the World Series. His final 26–6 record represents the zenith victory mark of his career, and Hubbell also topped the circuit that season in ERA (2.31) and winning percentage (.813).

In the 1936 World Series, he won one of the two games the Giants

Carl Hubbell. (Courtesy San Francisco Giants.)

managed to take from the powerful New York Yankees, capturing Game 1 in distinguished fashion, 6–1.

The Giants, again bolstered by the high-kicking Hubbell, returned to the World Series in 1937, with the southpaw again pacing the league in wins and winning percentage (.733). But after going 22–8 in the regular season, he could only generate another split in two decisions as the Giants fell to the Yankees once more.

Though he would play six more campaigns, 1937 was the last time Hubbell would appear in a World Series. His 4–2 post-season record was admirable, despite the Giants winning only one World Championship in three tries, and his 1.79 ERA is clear evidence that the best teams in the junior circuit were also awed by his ability.

Following the 1937 season, warnings issued a dozen years earlier by Ty Cobb concerning the dangers of throwing the screwball came to fruition. Chipped pieces of bone were removed from Hubbell's pitching limb prior to 1938, and from then on his left elbow was a continual source of trouble. In 1938, he started only 22 games, his lowest number in 10 years, and dropped to an equally disappointing 13–10 record. He remained effective as a spot starter, and his ERA never wandered above 4.00, but the end was near.

By the time he retired in 1943, delivering the screwball had altered the bone structure in his left arm to such an extent that his palm nearly faced forward where the back of his hand should have been. But as wearing as the "scroojie" might have been on Carl, records indicate that hitters facing him suffered the majority of the anguish. In 535 mound appearances, he racked up a 253–154 overall mark for a .622 winning percentage. His lifetime ERA is a stingy 2.98, and in 3,590 innings, he allowed only 725 walks, fewer than two a game. In 16 big league seasons, Hubbell had 14 winning years.

The Giants, for whom he had played his entire career, rewarded Carl for his reliable service with the team's farm director's post immediately upon his retirement. Hubbell passed away at the age of 85.

Perhaps the ultimate tribute to the man can be found in the following: the same sportswriters who complained about his lack of charisma voted Hubbell two MVP awards and induction into the Hall of Fame in 1947. The "Scroojie King" is proof positive that calm majesty still carries more weight than colorful mediocrity.

Top 5 MVP Vote-Getters

1. Carl Hubbell, New York — 60
2. Dizzy Dean, St. Louis — 53
3. Billy Herman, Chicago — 37
4. Joe Medwick, St. Louis — 30
5. Paul Waner, Pittsburgh — 29

1936 AMERICAN LEAGUE — LOU GEHRIG

Henry Louis Gehrig
B. June 19, 1903, New York, New York
D. June 2, 1941, New York, New York

Year	Team	Games	AB	Hits	Avg.	HR	RBI	Runs	SB
1936	NY AL	155	579	205	.354	49	152	167	3

The Season

The New York Yankees made a shambles of the American League pennant race in 1936, racking up 102 victories to win by 19½ games.

Nineteen-thirty-six National League MVP Carl Hubbell pitched the New York Giants to a 6–1 win over the Yanks in Game 1 of a six-game World Series, breaking their 12-game Series winning streak. But the Bronx Bombers rallied to capture the first of four consecutive World Championships, including a Series-record 18-run outburst in Game 2.

The Yankees' forte during the regular season was brute strength. They bashed 182 home runs, the most until that time and the highest total before the Giants connected for 221 in 1947. Three of those homers came May 24 off the bat of Yankee second baseman Tony Lazzeri, who set a single-game

Lou Gehrig. (Courtesy New York Yankees.)

Only Henry Aaron and Ruth possess more lifetime RBIs, while only Ruth and Ted Williams own higher career slugging averages.

The "Iron Horse" was the first player in the 20th century to hit four homers in one game, and he belted a major league record-23 grand slams. Gehrig appeared in every game from June 1, 1925, when he replaced Wally Pipp, to April 30, 1939. Along the way, Lou collected the League Award (predecessor to the MVP) in 1927, the Triple Crown in 1934 and the Baseball Writers Association of America's Most Valuable Player honor in 1936.

But for the first dozen years of his career, Gehrig played second fiddle to his teammate, the one and only Babe Ruth. When the Babe left New York in 1935, Gehrig had the spotlight to himself for a season; but the next year, up came a regal rookie named Joe DiMaggio, who quickly became the darling of Yankees fans. Meanwhile, Gehrig continued in his quiet, efficient manner until he was struck down by amyotrophic lateral sclerosis, a muscle and spinal disease better known today as Lou Gehrig's disease.

The illness forced his departure from the Yankee lineup early in the 1939 season and soon led to his death in 1941, only 17 days short of his 38th birthday.

Lou's 1936 MVP award was earned on the basis of a .354 average, 49 home runs and 152 RBIs, as well as another Yankees pennant and World Series crown. The six-time All-Star led the American League in homers, slugging (.696), runs (167) and walks (130); was second in RBIs and total bases (403); and fourth in batting. In the Yankees' four games-to-two triumph over the cross-town Giants in the Series, Lou hit .292 with two homers and seven RBIs.

By all rights, the proud Yankee should have walked off with an MVP trophy in 1934. Gehrig not only won the Triple Crown, leading the league in hitting (.363), home runs (49) and RBIs (165), but also paced the AL in total bases with 409 and slugging at .706. But Detroit catcher Mickey Cochrane snared the honor in a close vote.

That was merely one of the many

AL record with 11 RBIs against Philadelphia, including two grand slams, another round-tripper and a triple.

Two future superstars, New York's Joe DiMaggio and Bob Feller of Cleveland, broke into baseball in 1936. DiMaggio tied a major league record June 24 with two homers in one inning, while Feller set an AL mark and tied a major league standard with 17 strikeouts September 13. Feller had fanned 15 in his first big league start August 23.

Dignified Hero

Today he is generally acknowledged as the greatest first baseman ever, and his record of 2,130 consecutive games played stood for 56 years. Yet until his premature, tragic death, Lou Gehrig was not fully appreciated, having spent virtually his entire career in the shadows of either Babe Ruth or Joe DiMaggio.

In a 17-year career, all with the Yankees, Gehrig hit .340 with 493 home runs and 1,990 runs batted in.

exceptional campaigns the Yankees' handsome slugger enjoyed. Gehrig hit at least 27 home runs in each of a dozen straight years (1927–38), and had more than 40 round-trippers five times, including 49 twice. He batted .300 or better 12 times in a row (1926–37) with a high of .379 in 1930, and the first sacker's slugging average was in the .700s on three occasions.

But Gehrig's most significant contribution was runs batted in. He sent at least 107 runners scampering across the plate in 13 consecutive seasons (1926–38), leading the league five times. His 184 RBIs in 1931 are still an American League record. Gehrig was the only player in major league history to drive in 150 or more runs five times. He was also the only one to collect at least 165 RBIs four times and 170-plus RBIs on three occasions.

In seven World Series, Larrupin' Lou never batted below .286, and was particularly effective in 1928 and 1932 when the Yanks swept the Cardinals and Cubs, respectively. Lou teed off on Card pitching with four home runs, nine RBIs and a .545 average. The Hall of Famer was equally merciless against Cub hurlers, batting .529, stroking three homers, driving in eight runs, scoring nine times and collecting nine hits.

The only one of four children to survive infancy, Henry Louis Gehrig quickly learned the Protestant work ethic while growing up in Manhattan. He was a model son to his immigrant parents, to the point of embarrassment at being labeled a "mama's boy" by friends. Considered the best high school baseball player in the country,

the 17-year-old blasted a grand slam into the right field bleachers at Chicago's Wrigley Field to break a tie and give the High School of Commerce a victory over Lane Tech in the New York intercity championship game.

Originally signed by John McGraw's Giants, Gehrig protected his amateur status at Columbia University — competing in both football and baseball — by playing for the Eastern League under the name "Henry Lewis." But his contract was voided and he returned to college. As a Yankees rookie in 1925, Gehrig slammed 20 homers and drove in 68 runs while batting .295 in what was to be his least productive year in 14 full seasons.

The 6-foot, 200-pound left-hander combined with Babe Ruth to form the most awesome one-two punch in baseball history, and despite the fact that the introverted Gehrig was the opposite of the Babe in many ways, they were good friends until Ruth criticized Lou's mother in 1933. A rift developed and the two barely spoke to one another for several years.

While the Bambino received the vast majority of accolades handed out by local media, Gehrig better represented the Yankee image of dignified superiority. The polite, serious-minded gentleman was totally loyal to teammates and devoted to his job.

But the debilitating effects of the illness that would soon take his life began to show themselves in 1938 when he hit .295, 45 points below his lifetime average. By 1939, Gehrig could no longer pull the ball, and routine plays at first base were a struggle; he collected only four singles in eight games.

After a teammate sincerely congratulated him for a simple play in the field, Lou knew it was time to call it quits.

He took himself out of the lineup following 2,130 consecutive games, and although remaining in uniform the rest of the season and being named an honorary captain, the "Iron Horse" never played another game. "Lou Gehrig Day" was held July 4, 1939, at Yankee Stadium, and the quiet hero brought tears to the eyes of fans, teammates and opponents as he said goodbye. Less than two years later, Lou Gehrig was dead. His uniform No. 4 was retired, the first Yankee so honored, and a monument was dedicated to him at Yankee Stadium. A year later, Gary Cooper portrayed him in the movie *Pride of the Yankees*.

When the bright light of day shone down on Gehrig as he gave his famous farewell speech, it was obvious he had finally emerged from the shadows of Ruth and DiMaggio. Lou told the 61,808 admirers in attendance that he considered himself the luckiest man on the face of the earth. But in this one respect he was wrong — the luckiest men on earth were those who'd known him as a teammate and friend.

Top 5 MVP Vote-Getters

1. Lou Gehrig, New York — 73
2. Luke Appling, Chicago — 65
3. Earl Averill, Cleveland — 48
4. Charlie Gehringer, Detroit — 39
5. Bill Dickey, New York — 29

1937 National League—Joe Medwick

Joseph Michael Medwick
B. November 24, 1911, Carteret, New Jersey
D. March 21, 1975, St. Petersburg, Florida

Year	Team	Games	AB	Hits	Avg.	HR	RBI	Runs	SB
1937	SL NL	156	633	237	.374	31	154	111	4

The Season

The New York Giants pocketed their second consecutive pennant in 1937, coming from behind to beat out the Cubs by three games. Mel Ott tied Triple Crown and MVP winner Joe Medwick in home runs with 31 to contribute to the Giants' league-leading 111 round-trippers. But the New Yorkers were overwhelmed four games to one by the cross-town Yankees in the World Series.

For the first time in 34 years, two rookie pitchers on the same club won 20 games. The Boston Bees finished 16 games out of the running in fifth place, but certainly couldn't blame freshmen right-handers Jim Turner (20–11, 2.38 ERA) and Lou Fette (20–10, 2.88). Between them, the pair led the National League in ERA, shutouts and complete games.

A line drive off the bat of Earl Averill in the 1937 All-Star Game broke 1934 MVP Dizzy Dean's toe and aided the demise of the zany St. Louis hurler's career. Another former MVP moundsman, Carl Hubbell, extended his unbeaten streak to 24 over two seasons, while Pittsburgh outfielder Paul Waner broke Rogers Hornsby's modern-day National League record by collecting 200 hits for the eighth time.

The longest NL consecutive games played streak ended at 822 when Pittsburgh first baseman Gus Suhr missed a game June 5 while attending his mother's funeral. On August 6, the first two batters in a game hit home runs for the first time in the century when Roy Johnson and Rabbit Warstler of Boston teed off against Chicago's Tex Carleton.

Two-Fisted Slugger

When Joe Medwick came on the National League scene for his first full season in 1933, it was with the same blatant audacity of a gunslinger bursting through the swinging doors of a Western saloon, pounding his fist on the bar to order a shot of whiskey and turning a challenging scowl toward the nearest patron.

The St. Louis Cardinals left fielder, nicknamed "Ducky" for his peculiar waddle, typified the aggressive, enraged style the Gashouse Gang displayed in the 1930s. Medwick hammered pitches, many well out of the strike zone, to all parts of the ballpark, then ran the bases like a bull on the loose, ready to use his spikes and fists at whatever base he ended up.

But the hot-tempered Hungarian didn't limit his fisticuff activities to the enemy. Teammates Rip Collins, Tex Carleton and Ed Heusser all faced the wrath of an angered "Muscles" Medwick at one time or another, and all three were cold-cocked by one punch. Joe even joined teammates Dizzy and Paul Dean in a scuffle with *New York News* reporter Jack Miley and *Chicago Tribune* writer Irv Kupcinet in a Tampa hotel just prior to the 1937 season.

But what Medwick's passion for the game cost him in friends, it earned him in respect from opposing pitchers, particularly in 1937 when he led the league in virtually every offensive statistic.

The last NL player to win the Triple Crown hit .374 with 31 home runs and 154 RBIs, and also was the league's top producer of runs (111), hits (237), doubles (56) and total bases (406). He had the best slugging per-centage in the league at .641, appeared in the most games and accumulated the highest number of at-bats. As if that wasn't enough to set him apart from other National Leaguers, Medwick led all outfielders in fielding with a .988 mark.

The Cardinals finished 15 games behind the New York Giants in fourth place, which normally might have cost him the MVP award; but Medwick so outshone his contemporaries in 1937 that he garnered the award over second-place Chicago's Gabby Hartnett in a close vote. The 5-foot-10, 187-pound bundle of energy was especially adept at plating fellow Redbird base runners. Joe sandwiched a pair of runner-up titles in the RBI race around three straight runs-batted-in crowns in the years 1935 to 1939.

Ducky's hard, hacking swing and adequate speed made him a natural for "in the gap" extra base hits. He led the NL in doubles three years in a row (1936–38) and was second four times. He had 40 or more two-baggers on seven occasions, with a high of 64 in 1936, still a league record. His 18 triples were tops in the senior circuit in 1934, as were his 223 hits in '36.

A colorful character, Medwick's quick temper often resulted in trouble. Following a hard slide into Detroit third baseman Marv Owen and a scuffle in the sixth inning of the final 1934 World Series game, Tigers fans pelted Ducky with fruits, vegetables, bottles and just about everything else they could get their hands on when he took his left field position. Commissioner Kenesaw Mountain Landis demanded Medwick's removal from the contest, and the Cards went on to clinch the Series 11–0.

Two more full seasons in St. Louis—in which he hit .322 and .332, belted 35 homers and accumulated 239 RBIs—preceded his trade to Brooklyn in 1940. Six days later, while facing his old teammates, Medwick took a fastball to the temple from Bob Bowman which knocked him unconscious and precipitated a brawl. Medwick and Bowman had quarreled prior to the game, and Dodgers President Larry MacPhail accused the pitcher of purposely hitting his outfielder. To save his hurler from retribution by the Dodgers and their fans, St. Louis manager Billy Southworth had Bowman escorted from the field by police.

Medwick continued to hit around .300 for the next seven years with NL clubs Brooklyn, New York, Boston and St. Louis.

Ducky was a manager in the bushes from 1949 to 1951, and 15 years later returned to St. Louis as a minor league hitting instructor. Medwick and others believed his unpopularity with the writers delayed his admittance to the Hall of Fame, but he was finally inducted in 1968, 20 years after his retirement. While assisting the Cards in spring training of 1975, Joe died of a heart attack at age 63.

Joseph Michael Medwick was born to Hungarian parents November 24, 1911, in New Jersey. A gifted athlete, Joe's first love was football, and his dream was to don the blue and gold of Notre Dame. Even after signing a minor league contract with the Cardinals, Joe was hoping to display his gridiron skills in South Bend, Indiana, and so used the name "Mickey King" to protect his amateur status. But after hitting .419 with 22 home runs and 100 RBIs for Scottsdale, he put football permanently on the back burner.

In the early '30s, Medwick was one of the first and best of the Cardinals' new farm system. He moved up to the Houston squad for the 1931 season and promptly paced the Texas League in several offensive categories. It was there that a young girl in the stands, observing a waddle in Joe's walk, gave him the lasting nickname "Ducky."

Medwick was promoted to St. Louis at the tail end of 1932, and immediately took over left field. Joe's motto when he swaggered into St. Louis was "base hits and buckerinos," and his hunger for money nearly matched his appetite for excellence throughout a 17-year career.

The kid wasted no time establishing himself as a major leaguer. After a solid rookie campaign (.306, 18 HRs, 98 RBIs), the dangerous bad-ball hitter raised his average to .319 and his RBIs to 106 as the Cards rolled to the 1934 World Championship. Ducky collected 11 hits for a .379 average and five RBIs in the seven-game Series.

The 10-time All-Star followed up with splendid seasons the next two years, batting in the .350s and averaging 20 homers and 132 RBIs. In 1936, he tied an NL record by stroking 10 consecutive hits over three games. But he didn't appear in another World Series until 1941 when his Brooklyn Dodgers were defeated by the Yankees.

Joe Medwick played the game to win, whether that meant plowing into a shortstop to break up a double play or streaking around second to claim an extra base on a drive into the gap. And when it was high noon on the baseball diamond, gunslinging Joe was a good hombre to have on your side.

Top 5 MVP Vote-Getters

1. Joe Medwick, St. Louis—70
2. Gabby Hartnett, Chicago—68
3. Carl Hubbell, New York—52
4. Jim Turner, Boston—30
5. Lou Fette, Boston—29

1937 National League—Charlie Gehringer

Charles Leonard Gehringer
B. May 11, 1903, Fowlerville, Michigan
D. January 21, 1993, Bloomfield Hills, Michigan

Year	Team	Games	AB	Hits	Avg.	HR	RBI	Runs	SB
1937	Det AL	144	564	209	.371	14	96	133	11

The Season

The New York Yankees grabbed the brass ring again in 1937, breezing to the pennant by 13 games over Detroit and whipping the cross-town Giants in the World Series for the second year running, this time four games to one.

Easily the most powerful club in the big leagues, the Yanks swatted 174 home runs and balanced that explosive attack with the best pitching in the American League. Yankee moundsmen twirled 15 shutouts, tying the White Sox staff for the league lead, with the New Yorkers boasting the only 20-game winners in Lefty Gomez and Red Ruffing.

Hank Greenberg and Charlie Gehringer led the Detroit charge. Greenberg tallied 183 RBIs, only one short of Lou Gehrig's 1931 league record and still the third highest total in baseball history, while Gehringer won the batting crown.

Rookie teammate Rudy York established a major league record for home runs in a month (18 in August), eclipsing the 17 Babe Ruth tagged in September 1927. York's record stood for 61 years until Sammy Sosa of the Cubs blasted 20 in June during his 1998 MVP year. But the Yankees countered with the two, three and four RBI men in Joe DiMaggio (167), Gehrig (159) and Bill Dickey (133).

The Bronx Bombers continued slamming the horsehide in the World Series, scoring 28 runs in five games. The AL team set the pace from the start, winning the first two contests by identical 8–1 scores.

It was a bad year for 1934 MVPs. Mickey Cochrane of the Tigers had his career ended by a Bump Hadley fastball that struck him in the head and left him unconscious for 10 days, while Dizzy Dean of the St. Louis Cardinals suffered a fractured toe from an Earl Averill line drive in the All-Star Game. It was a better year for Chicago catcher Luke Sewell, who was behind the plate for his third no-hitter since 1931 when Bill Dietrich dominated St. Louis June 1.

From the Shadows

An actor who performs with restrained understatement often sacrifices glowing reviews for an effective interpretation of his role. Such was the craft and essence of Charlie Gehringer, who was so subtly superb in his 19-year characterization as the Detroit Tigers second baseman that his excellent work often went unnoticed.

But in 1937, Gehringer's methodical brilliance took center stage, as the 34-year-old's .371 batting average paced the American League. The bulwark of the Tiger infield edged New York's Joe DiMaggio for MVP honors — no small task considering DiMaggio's league-leading totals in home runs, slugging and total bases for the World Champion Yankees. But the overall performance of Gehringer's effortless glove work, combined with his best year at the plate, earned the second sacker the prestigious award.

It was the first time in four AL campaigns that a player from a pennant-winning team had not copped MVP honors, and it gave second-place Detroit its third such award in four years. In those four seasons, the graceful Gehringer registered averages of .356, .330, .354 and finally his MVP year mark, which topped his closest competitor by 20 points.

As usual, Charlie led all second basemen in fielding percentage in 1937, the fifth of seven such titles. The left-handed, line drive hitter was equally smooth with a hickory stick in his hands. At 5-foot-11 and 180 pounds, Gehringer owned a level stroke that had an affinity for finding the outfield alleys, and packed enough power to rank fourth in career home runs by AL second basemen. It is somewhat unconventional for a second baseman to bat third in a lineup, but 11 years of 80 or more RBIs, including seven of 100-plus, more than justified Gehringer's presence in that spot.

Born in 1903 in Fowlerville, Michigan, Charlie grew up on his father's chicken farm, where he and his brother whiled away the hours on a homemade baseball diamond. Gehringer excelled in athletics early, earning a baseball scholarship to the University of Michigan. Ex-Tiger star Bobby Veach, on a tip from a hunting buddy of Gehringer's, scouted Charlie at Michigan. Veach liked what he saw and arranged a tryout for Gehringer in front of Detroit manager Ty Cobb. The youngster was lured off campus to sign a major league contract for little more than traveling money.

The unassuming, sticky-fingered infielder was schooled in the art of second base, and within two years was starting for the parent club. Gehringer hit .277 during his 1926 rookie season, then improved to .317 and .320 the next two campaigns. In 1929, he added power to his arsenal, hitting 13 home runs to go with a .339 mark and pacing the junior circuit in runs (131), hits (215), doubles (45), triples (19) and stolen bases (27).

By 1930, fellow competitors considered him a star, but most fans took his low-key performances for granted. Gehringer's practice was to stay in the background; so much so, the story

Charlie Gehringer. (Courtesy Detroit Tigers.)

goes, that he would say "hello" at the start of spring training, hit over .300 for the season and mutter "goodbye" as he packed his gear for the winter. Yankees shortstop Broadway Lyn Lary hung the nickname "The Mechanical Man" on the quiet Tigers star.

The Tigers vacillated in the standings during Charlie's first eight campaigns, but the near flawless fielder continued to contribute .300 averages and steadily increasing power while missing very few starts. In the 1934 pennant year, Gehringer hit .356, drove in 127 runs and topped the circuit in hits (214) and runs scored (134). At age 32, when the Tigers took the 1935 World Championship, "The Great Robot" hit .330 with 201 hits, 19 homers and 108 RBIs. The Tigers slipped to second the following year, but Gehringer scarcely missed a beat, hitting .354 with 116 RBIs and an AL-best 60 doubles, still the sixth highest total in baseball history.

Following the 1937 MVP season, he put in three more stellar years, all above the .300 mark in hitting. The Tigers slid to fourth in 1938, but Gehringer and teammates Hank Greenberg and Rudy York combined for 111 home runs, one of the best AL marks ever for a trio. Also in '38, Gehringer played in his sixth and final All-Star Game, establishing a still-standing record for highest batting average (.500) for players with 20 or more at-bats in All-Star play. A .325 average in 1939 was followed by .313 in 1940, and a final pennant for Gehringer and his Tigers. Charlie's uncanny consistency throughout his career is reflected in the .321 mark he registered for three World Series, one point higher than his lifetime average.

Finally, in 1941, the years of hard labor took their toll. The dour-faced Gehringer played that campaign with an agonizingly bad back, and his average nose-dived to .220. He had wanted to leave the game after 1940, but Tigers management, pointing to a war-depleted roster, urged him to stay. Gehringer retired after a 1942 season that saw him used primarily as a pinch-hitter. Saying little, giving all,

the sad-eyed Gehringer had been a blessing for five Detroit managers.

Gehringer applied those same positive traits to the auto accessory industry following his retirement, then returned to baseball for a short stint as the Tigers general manager. Recognizing that his personality lacked the outgoing quality necessary for the post, Charlie appointed his own successor in 1951 and remained as club vice president until 1959.

Elected to the Hall of Fame in 1949, Gehringer served on the Hall's veteran's committee, which considers for entrance players who have used up their first eligibility period. Charlie passed away in 1993, only four months shy of his 90th birthday.

It's safe to say that few names crossing that committee's desk represent players who equaled the consistently exceptional standards set by the career of Charlie Gehringer. For if that were a prerequisite, the Hall would be a lonely place, indeed.

Top 5 MVP Vote-Getters

1. Charlie Gehringer, Detroit — 78
2. Joe DiMaggio, New York — 74
3. Hank Greenberg, Detroit — 48
4. Lou Gehrig, New York — 42
5. Bill Dickey, New York — 22
5. Luke Sewell, Chicago — 22

1938 NATIONAL LEAGUE — ERNIE LOMBARDI

Ernesto Natali Lombardi
B. April 6, 1908, Oakland, California
D. September 26, 1977, Santa Cruz, California

Year	Team	Games	AB	Hits	Avg.	HR	RBI	Runs	SB
1938	Cin NL	129	489	167	.342	19	95	60	0

The Season

Four teams battled early for the National League crown in 1938 — the Cubs, Pirates, Giants and Reds — but in the end, Chicago's strong pitching prevailed.

Gabby Hartnett, the 1935 NL MVP who took over Chicago's managerial reins at mid-season, put his team over the hump September 28 with his famous "homer in the gloamin'." At that point in the season, the race was down to the Cubs and Pittsburgh, who were locked in a 5–5 game in the bottom of the ninth inning at Chicago's Wrigley Field. With darkness descending and two men out, Hartnett clobbered a game-winning round-tripper to launch the Cubs into first, a

blow from which the Bucs could not recover.

Exciting as it was, the 1938 pennant race paled in comparison to the individual pitching feat of Cincinnati's Johnny Vander Meer. The lefty caught lightning in a bottle with two consecutive no-hit games, including a 6–0 decision against Brooklyn June 15 in the first-ever night game at Ebbets Field. Less than a month later, Vander Meer was the winning pitcher in the All-Star Game.

The Cubs went down to ignominious defeat in the World Series, losing four straight to the Yankee express. The only contest that warmed the hearts of Chicago fans was Dizzy Dean's Game 2 effort in which, without benefit of his once blazing fastball, the

proud Diz used his head and heart to hold the powerful Yankees to two runs in seven innings before finally succumbing 6–3.

Few players have hit home runs in their first big league at-bat, and it's even more rare when two do it in the same game, let alone the identical inning. But in the first frame of an April 19 contest at Philadelphia, both Brooklyn's Ernie Koy and the Phillies' Heinie Mueller homered in their first major league at-bats.

Proboscis Power

Ernie Lombardi didn't just hit a baseball, he fairly crushed it. Sizzling line drives and ground balls were the rule rather than the exception when Ernie connected, and opposing infielders who regularly played 10 to 20 feet back on the outfield grass still found themselves handcuffed by the sheer force of Big Lom's drives.

Had Lombardi's swing been more prone to an upward stroke, there is little doubt he would have significantly increased his lifetime total of 190 home runs. No one in the game slammed the sphere harder than the 6-foot-3-inch, 230-pound catcher. Those who saw him will also concur that nobody ever traveled 90 feet at a slower clip than the hulking backstop, whose painfully sluggish stride allowed fielders the luxury of recovering his ground ball shots and throwing him out time and again. Yet, despite his plodding pace on the basepaths, Lombardi had an underground reputation as a savvy base runner.

The easy going receiver might have been one of baseball's greatest hitters for average had he possessed even moderate running ability, yet even his snail-like gait could not completely diminish the purity of his batting eye. Only three times in baseball history have catchers managed to win batting titles. "The Schnozz," whose giant nose dominated a massive presence, registered two of those hitting crowns. Additionally, Lombardi was forced to combat infield shifts used regularly against him. But the infielders — all but the first baseman playing to the third base side of second and back on the outfield grass — failed to stop him from attaining a lifetime .306 mark.

From 1932 to 1942, Lombardi ranked alongside Chicago's Gabby Hartnett as the best catcher in the NL. That reputation was tarnished somewhat during the 1939 World Series in an incident referred to as "Lombardi's snooze." During Game 4 of the Yankees' sweep of Cincinnati, with the score tied 4–4 in the top of the 10th inning and runners on first and third, Joe DiMaggio singled. When Reds outfielder Ival Goodman bobbled the ball, Charlie Keller dashed from first to home, where Lombardi awaited a relay throw. The ball and Keller arrived simultaneously, and Ernie was kneed in the groin during a tremendous collision.

Stumbling, then falling from the impact, Lombardi was subsequently blamed for not retrieving the dropped baseball that lay just a few feet from the pay station as DiMaggio made a full circle of the bases. Bucky Walters, who was pitching at the time, decried the unjust criticism his catcher received, pointing out that as the hurler it was his responsibility to back up home plate, which he failed to do.

Ernie overcame the media lambasting and helped lead the 1940 Reds to another pennant and a World Championship over the Detroit Tigers. He hit .319 during the regular schedule, but was able to start only one post-season game due to a disabling ankle injury.

Two seasons later, he was traded to the Boston Braves, where he hit .330 to lead the league, the last time a catcher earned the hitting crown. Before 1943, he again changed teams, this time going to the Giants, where he finished his career with five campaigns in which he averaged .288.

It had been a 17-year haul for the Oakland, California, native, who began his professional career in the Pacific Coast League. Minor league averages of .398, .377, .366 and .370 landed him a spot in the big time with the Brooklyn Dodgers in 1931, where at age 23 he hit a respectable .297; but he was unable to dislodge Al Lopez from the signal-calling position. Shipped to Cincinnati the following year, he became a starter, hitting .303 with 11 homers. By 1935, Ernie was slashing baseballs with brutal effectiveness, racking up a

Ernie Lombardi. (Courtesy Cincinnati Reds.)

career-high .343 average and tying a major league record with a double in each of four consecutive innings during a May 8 game against Philadelphia.

Ernie's hitting prowess was matched by his ability on defense. Although he had no running speed to speak of, he was agile in his catching gear, aided by gigantic hands that would often snatch errant pitches barehanded out of thin air. He handled an improving Cincinnati pitching staff with ease and dexterity, and gave all of his hurlers a big target behind the plate. Apparently Lombardi was quite comfortable with his value to the Reds, because year after year he would risk being traded by holding out during spring training in hopes of garnering a bigger contract. He was less at ease, however, with his reputation as a lady's man. Throngs of women would wait for him to leave the park in his street clothes following a game, and he would often hang out in the clubhouse long after the final pitch to avoid the admirers.

The Reds were looked upon as a bona-fide pennant threat in 1938, but after an early season rush, faded to fourth, finishing 82–68. But "Bocci," as teammates referred to him, shone as never before, slamming his way to a league-leading .342 average that was to be 36 points above his lifetime mark. Lombardi's .524 slugging percentage was fifth in the league, and he reached career highs in the following categories: at-bats (489), games caught (123), hits (167), doubles (30), runs (60) and RBIs (95).

For his prodigious efforts, the writers named Lombardi the National League MVP, the first Cincinnati Red to earn that distinction. It was a memorable campaign for the 30-year-old, eighth-year man, who was behind the plate for both of Johnny Vander Meer's no-hit performances.

Two pennants, a World Championship and a second batting crown followed that MVP season, as the giant pull-hitter continued to rack up impressive numbers. After being released by the Giants following the 1947 slate, he returned full circle in his baseball odyssey, playing one last season in the Pacific Coast League at age 40.

Lombardi lived the rest of his life in quiet retirement on the West Coast, awaiting a Hall of Fame call that never came. The Schnozz died in 1977, his place as the greatest catcher in Cincy history already taken by a more handsomely virile Johnny Bench. But the veteran's committee added Lombardi to the Hall in 1986.

There are those who will tell you

that had Ernie Lombardi ever hit ground balls on modern-day artificial turf, there would be infielders walking around today with dents in their chests.

Top 5 MVP Vote-Getters

1. Ernie Lombardi, Cincinnati — 229
2. Bill Lee, Chicago — 166
3. Arky Vaughn, Pittsburgh — 163
4. Mel Ott, New York — 132
5. Frank McCormick, Cincinnati — 130

1938 AMERICAN LEAGUE — JIMMIE FOXX

James Emory Foxx
B. October 22, 1907, Sudlersville, Maryland
D. July 21, 1967, Miami, Florida

Year	Team	Games	AB	Hits	Avg.	HR	RBI	Runs	SB
1938	Bos AL	149	565	197	.349	50	175	139	5

The Season

After loafing through September and dropping 11 of their final 15 games, the New York Yankees entered their third consecutive World Series and 10th in the past 18 years as only slight favorites.

But, as in the last time the two clubs met in post-season play (1932), New York rocked the Chicago Cubs four straight, becoming the first team to win three World Series in a row. The sweep meant eight straight victories for Yankees manager Joe McCarthy over his former Cubs team.

Despite the late-season swoon, the Yankees were in a class by themselves in 1938. They headed the American League in runs scored, home runs and slugging, but it wasn't all an offen-

sive show. New York pitchers were foremost in ERA, complete games and shutouts.

Detroit's Hank Greenberg made a run at Babe Ruth's single-season home run record, but fell two shy, ending up with 58 circuit clouts to tie Jimmie Foxx for most homers by a right-handed batter.

Nineteen-year-old pitcher Bob Feller, in his first full season in the Cleveland Indians' rotation, set a modern-day record by striking out 18 Tigers in one game October 2. Another hurler, Lefty Grove, led the AL in ERA (3.08) for the eighth of nine times. Two years after his MVP season, Lou Gehrig hit his 23rd and final grand slam, a major league record that is still intact.

Finally, the inventor of the box-

score and the first baseball writer, Henry Chadwick, was inducted into the Hall of Fame by a special committee that also enshrined Alexander Cartwright for originating baseball's basic concepts.

Renewed Magnificence

When Jimmie Foxx donned his Boston Red Sox uniform on the first day of spring training in 1938, there were those who wondered whether he had another exceptional season in him.

His batting average had slipped 53 points from 1936 to '37, with five fewer home runs and 16 fewer RBIs. Some believed his recently acquired nightlife antics were taking their toll on a once iron-hard body, and he was beginning to suffer severe sinus trouble. But if the

30-year-old Foxx's career was headed downhill, he for one certainly wasn't aware of it.

He had already accomplished several magnificent feats, having won two Most Valuable Player awards (1932 and '33), earned the Triple Crown (1933) and played on three pennant and two World Champion squads. Now it was time to help the improving Red Sox become a contender under manager Joe Cronin.

Foxx did just that, dominating the league with a renewed vigor, winning a record-third MVP trophy and narrowly missing out on another Triple Crown, as Boston jumped from fifth place to second. The Red Sox hit a major league-leading .299 in 1938, but the big story was "Double X."

Pacing the league in five offensive departments, Foxx was denied his second Triple Crown by Hank Greenberg, who belted 58 homers to Jimmie's 50. Incredibly, the pair together outhomered more than half of the American League teams in 1938. "The Beast," who broke a major league record by collecting two or more home runs in nine games, led in hitting at .349, RBIs with a career-high 175, slugging at .704 and total bases with 398. He also tied for the lead in walks (119), was second in home runs and runs (139), and placed third in hits (197). And speaking of walks, Foxx set an AL record and tied a major league mark with six walks in one game, June 16 against St. Louis.

Fenway Park, with its short left field porch, was a godsend for the free-swinging right-hander, who clubbed 35 of his 50 round-trippers in Boston. In fact, though he played only six full years at Fenway, 220 of his 534 career homers were tagged as a member of the Red Sox.

The man many considered the only home run hitter in Babe Ruth's class in the 1930s captured his fourth and final homer title in 1939 when he smacked 35. Four home run crowns

may not seem like a substantial number for a bomber such as Foxx, until one remembers that he played in the same time period and league as such clouters as Ruth, Lou Gehrig, Joe DiMaggio and Greenberg.

Foxx also led in slugging with a .694 mark in 1939 (his fifth slugging title), and was runner-up to DiMaggio in hitting (.360) and to teammate Ted Williams in total bases (324). Jimmie was on base enough times to score 130 runs, third in the AL, and he even saw action as a pitcher. But the Red Sox finished a distant second to the perennially favored Yankees.

Dipping below .300 in 1940 for only the third time in his career, Foxx still could thrash the baseball. He rapped 36 home runs to give him exactly 500 for his career. Jimmie was fourth in RBIs with 119 and fifth in slugging at .581, while hitting .297. Boston sank to fourth that year, then bounced back to second in Foxx's last full season in Beantown.

Nineteen-forty-one saw Double X reach the .300 mark for the 11th time in 14 full campaigns, but his home run total dwindled to 19. By 1942, too much liquor and too little sleep had sapped the 34-year-old's talents; with a .270 average, Jimmie was released on waivers and picked up by the mediocre Chicago Cubs, who were three years away from a wartime pennant.

Platooned at first base with Phil Cavarretta, The Beast was now a harmless kitten, hitting .205. He decided to hang up the bat and glove after the 1942 campaign, but a year later the Cubs convinced him to give it one more try. While many players were serving in the war, Foxx played sparingly for Chicago in 1944, then went to the Philadelphia Phillies for the 1945 season. He hit his final seven home runs in Philly, appearing in 89 games, including nine as a pitcher. His career mark as a moundsman was 1–0 with a 1.52 ERA.

Jimmie retired again, this time for

good; but he stayed in baseball, managing the St. Petersburg Instructional League team in 1947 and '48, and the Bridgeport club of the Colonial League for part of '49. Foxx was voted into the Hall of Fame in 1951 and made his final professional baseball appearance in 1958 as a coach for Minneapolis of the American Association.

Jimmie Foxx had been one of the most powerful, skilled hitters of all time, and also one of the most well-liked men to play the game. Unfortunately, his extreme generosity mixed with a naiveté born of innocence. Several imprudent investments set him back, as did an over-anxiousness to pick up checks, many of which were bar tabs. Never one to turn down a drink, Foxx became a heavy imbiber, and his drinking, as well as ill health and money problems, were splashed across the newspapers during his last few years.

Jimmie suffered a heart attack in 1963, but recovered and was only a few months shy of his 60th birthday when he choked to death on a piece of meat while visiting a brother in Miami, Florida.

James Emory Foxx was a man who possessed that rare combination of raw strength and a friendly, easy going manner. He'll always be remembered by those who saw him play for his frequent, towering home runs, but also for a quick smile. And he'll be recalled for his most complimentary nickname: "The Right-Handed Babe Ruth."

Top 5 MVP Vote-Getters

1. Jimmie Foxx, Philadelphia — 305
2. Bill Dickey, New York — 196
3. Hank Greenberg, Detroit — 162
4. Red Ruffing, New York — 146
5. Bobo Newsom, St. Louis — 111

1939 NATIONAL LEAGUE—BUCKY WALTERS

William Henry Walters
B. April 19, 1909, Philadelphia, Pennsylvania
D. April 20, 1991, Abington, Pennsylvania

Year	Team	Games	W	L	ERA	IP	SO	BB	ShO
1939	Cin NL	39	27	11	2.29	319	137	109	2

The Season

Utilizing a tough pitching staff, stingy defense and plenty of speed, the Cincinnati Reds staved off a late St. Louis threat in 1939 to win their first pennant in two decades. The Reds' 4½-game cushion over the Cardinals was made possible by a pitching staff that led the National League in ERA (3.27), complete games (86) and strikeouts (637).

The Reds had finished dead last in 1937, but jumped to fourth the following year. They continued their upward climb in '39 behind the slugging of Frank McCormick (128 RBIs, 312 total bases) and Ernie Lombardi (20 home runs), and the pitching of Bucky Walters and Paul Derringer, who won 52 games between them in '39.

But even the Reds were no match for the tyrannizing New York Yankees, who made Cincinnati their fourth straight World Series victim with a sweep.

A major league baseball first occurred August 26 when W2XBS televised a double-header between Cincinnati and the Brooklyn Dodgers at Ebbets Field. Announcer Red Barber's call was heard by the approximately 500 television set owners in the New York area. Among the advertisers were Ivory Soap, Mobil Oil and Wheaties. Walters holds the distinction of being the first winning pitcher on television.

Roberto Alomar wasn't the first player to spit at an umpire. On September 15, Billy Jurges of the New York Giants and ump George Magerkurth exchanged saliva while debating a fair-foul call on a drive down the left field line at the Polo Grounds. Both were suspended for 10 days and fined $150.

Born-Again Bucky

Had it been entirely up to him, William Henry Walters never would have thrown a pitch in the major leagues. Bucky was a strong-armed but light-hitting third baseman who by his own admission would have been happy to remain at his position for the next 10 years and, if necessary, eventually eke out a living as a utility infielder, just to stay in baseball.

When approached prior to the 1935 season by Philadelphia Phillies manager Jimmie Wilson, who thought Walters might make a pretty fair pitcher, the four-year infielder resisted. He was fully aware that a strong stick was not part of his arsenal, but he had an intense love for the game and pictured himself as an everyday player. With the exception of a handful of minor league pitching outings and a pair of starts late the previous year, third base was as close to the mound as Bucky cared to be.

Fortunately for Walters, he saw the handwriting on the wall. The solid spring training performance of recently acquired Johnny Vergez was threatening to push Bucky out of his third base slot. So, with the assurance that he'd get a chance to win back the hot corner position if he failed as a hurler, Walters met the challenge.

He didn't exactly burn up the National League in his first few seasons on the hill, but once traded to Cincinnati, the side-armed flamethrower turned into the league's best pitcher in the late 1930s and early '40s.

Bucky's MVP trophy in 1939 made him the second of three consecutive MVPs from the Reds. Walters was nothing less than sensational that year, leading the league with 27 wins

and a 2.29 ERA. The 6-foot-1, 180-pound right-hander also paced the circuit in strikeouts (137), complete games (31) and innings pitched (319), while guiding the Reds to the pennant in his first full year with the team.

Bucky's sinking fastball hardly mystified the New York Yankees in the 1939 World Series, however. He was racked for six earned runs on 13 hits, and tagged with two losses.

Walters again led the NL in ERA (2.48), wins (22), complete games (29) and innings pitched (305) in 1940, as Cincinnati made it two consecutive pennants. This time Bucky was a significant factor in the World Series. He helped even the Series against Detroit at one game apiece with a 5–3, three-hit victory, the first post-season win for an NL pitcher since 1937. Then, with his team down three games to two and facing elimination, the Reds ace shut out the Tigers on five hits with a 4–0 win, belting a home run to boot. Cincinnati went on to capture the finale 2–1 for its first World Championship in 21 years.

William Henry had played sandlot ball in Philadelphia in the late '20s, getting his first break when a scout sent him to Montgomery, Alabama. With financial assistance from a grandmother, Bucky arrived at Montgomery, but failed to make the club.

The 22-year-old broke into the majors with the Boston Braves in 1931 as an infielder, but played only nine games and was sent back to the bushes. After two years of limited action, Walters was purchased by the Red Sox in 1934 and sold to the seventh-place Phillies, where he played in 83 games, including two as a pitcher.

The right-hander's first full year as a moundsman was 1935 when he

Bucky Walters. (Courtesy Cincinnati Reds.)

was 9–9 for Philadelphia. Walters then had the dubious distinction of losing more games (21) than any pitcher in 1936, although he led the league with four shutouts.

Following another bland year (14–15) with the Phillies and dropping eight of his first dozen decisions in 1938, the hard-throwing but wild hurler was obtained by his first big league manager, Bill McKechnie. Exchanged for catcher Virgil Davis, pitcher Albert Hollingsworth and $55,000, Walters joined the Reds between Johnny Vander Meer's two consecutive no-hitters. Apparently some of the excitement rubbed off because Walters won 11-of-17 decisions for the fourth-place club the rest of the year, and ended up at 15–14, his first winning season.

Bucky used 1938 as a launching pad, and didn't suffer another losing year until 1948 when, at age 39, he was 0–3. During his six most successful campaigns (1939–44), Walters was 121–73 with an ERA of 2.70. In 1941, he paced the senior circuit in complete games (27) and innings pitched (302).

Walters, who relied almost exclusively on the fastball, seemed to be headed toward mediocrity following records of 15–14 in 1942 and 15–15 in '43. But, approaching the twilight of his career, the square-jawed competitor exhibited flashbacks of 1939 and 1940 when he won an NL-best 23-of-31 decisions with an ERA of 2.40 in 1944, while also playing his position flawlessly.

The glory days, however, were over for Walters. He took over as Cincy's manager late in 1948 and was at the helm for all but the final three games in '49, compiling an overall mark of 81–123 as a big league skipper.

Walters ended up with a career batting average of .243, stroking 23 home runs and 99 doubles, driving in 234 runs and pitching in four All-Star Games. He earned only $22,000 in 1940 after winning the MVP award, but said that because of his love for the game and a childlike fantasy that he'd be around forever, he would have played for half as much, as long as it meant remaining in baseball. Bucky passed away in 1991, the day after his 82nd birthday.

Bucky Walters' love affair with baseball existed long before his conversion to pitcher. But it was the predestined switch that revitalized his career and gave the born-again ballplayer new life.

Top 5 MVP Vote-Getters

1. Bucky Walters, Cincinnati — 303
2. Johnny Mize, St. Louis — 178
3. Paul Derringer, Cincinnati — 174
4. Frank McCormick, Cincinnati — 159
5. Curt Davis, St. Louis — 106

1939 AMERICAN LEAGUE — JOE DIMAGGIO

Joseph Paul DiMaggio
B. November 25, 1914, Martinez, California
D. March 8, 1999, Hollywood, Florida

Year	Team	Games	AB	Hits	Avg.	HR	RBI	Runs	SB
1939	NY AL	120	462	176	.381	30	126	108	3

The Season

Another season, another Yankee World Championship; the Bombers were doing it with ridiculous ease these days. This time they moved so far out in front early in the season that second place became the competitive focal point for league fans midway through the year.

The New Yorkers eventually went on to capture 106 wins, finishing 17 games ahead of the Boston Red Sox. It was the Yanks' fourth straight pennant and fifth in eight years. Even a splendid rookie, Ted Williams, could not keep the Bosox close to the relentless Yankees, who clubbed a league-high 166 home runs, including a major league record-13 during a doubleheader sweep of Philadelphia June 28.

Nineteen-thirty-nine marked the end of an era, as Lou Gehrig finally gave in to a killing disease and ended his incredible consecutive games played streak at 2,130. A packed Yankee Stadium crowd paid tribute to "The Iron Horse" on a memorable day held in his honor July 4, and Gehrig became the first major leaguer to have his uniform number (4) retired. In December, he was elected to the Hall of Fame.

Replacing Gehrig, in a sense, was the latest Yankee sensation, Charlie "King Kong" Keller, who hit .334 during the regular season and led a four-game World Series sweep of the Cincinnati Reds with a .438 average, three home runs and six RBIs.

On May 16, fans at the first American League night game saw Cleveland defeat the A's 8–3 in 10 innings at Shibe Park in Philadelphia.

Perfection in Pinstripes

Thanks to the medium of television, his face is probably more well known today than when he was the most highly publicized player in the game of baseball. All the way up until his death in 1999, he radiated quiet class and distinguished earnestness. Some may remember him as "Mr. Coffee," but those who seek and appreciate baseball lore knew him for what he really was: Joe DiMaggio, a hero to an entire generation.

In 1939, there was seemingly nothing 24-year-old "Joltin' Joe" could not do on a baseball diamond. It was the year he won the first of three Most Valuable Player awards, notching his initial batting title with a stupendous .381 average that even he would never match again.

To say that Joe missed hitting .400 by an eyelash that year is not stretching the point. He was blasting away at a .412 pace with three weeks left in the season when a nervous eye twitch inexplicably took hold, dragging him from his lofty heights the remainder of the campaign.

DiMaggio was the eighth of nine children, the son of a crab fisherman in the San Francisco Bay Area. Joe's papa disapproved of his sons playing baseball, but when 18-year-old Joe became the prime target of $75,000 contract offers from major league teams, the immigrant father was overwhelmed. Three DiMaggios eventually made the big time, brothers Dom and Vince attaining success that was all but overshadowed by the sibling who would so elegantly wear Yankee pinstripes.

The most famous DiMaggio burst into prominence with the power of unexpected lightning, hitting safely in 61 straight games in his first professional season with the San Francisco Seals. Only 18, he shattered the previous Pacific Coast League record of 49 in a row, hitting .340 in the process. High-rolling offers came from virtually every big league club.

But the Seals, smelling even bigger bucks, decided to hold onto the youngster for one more year, a costly move that eventually delayed his major league debut by two seasons. In 1934, DiMaggio tore tendons in his knee and missed 88 Seals games. Despite a .341 average, every club except the Yankees backed away, with the Yanks dropping their purchase price from $75,000 to $25,000. The Seals accepted, on the stipulation that DiMag be allowed one more year on their club. In that 1935 season, DiMaggio batted .398, slugged 34 home runs and drove in 154, while winning the league MVP. Fifteen general managers screamed in unison at their respective scouts, and awaited with trepidation the force coming their way.

Despite a major buildup, the statuesque outfielder actually exceeded early expectations. In terms of pure run production, his first three seasons—1936, 1937 and 1938—were possibly his best campaigns, and in each case the Yankees won a World Championship.

The most herald rookie since Ty Cobb, DiMaggio hit .323, slugged 29 four-baggers, smacked a league-high 15 triples and drove in 125 runs. On June 24 of that 1936 season, he tied three major league records during a 10-run fifth inning by hitting two homers. He also equaled the modern-day mark of four extra base hits in a game with a pair of doubles. His sophomore effort

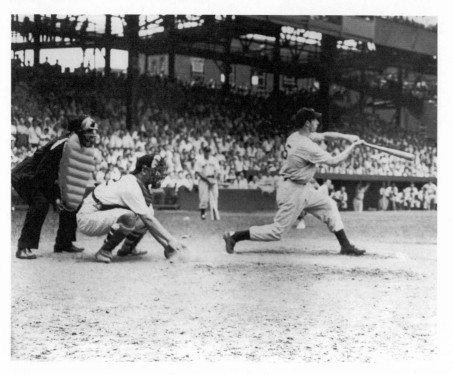

Joe DiMaggio. (Courtesy New York Yankees.)

may have been his best overall, as he parked 46 home runs to lead the league, reached a career high in RBIs with 167, paced the circuit in both runs (151) and slugging (.673), and hit .346. Nineteen-thirty-eight was almost as impressive: 32 HRs, 140 RBIs and a .324 average at age 23.

The pristine clarity of a DiMaggio swing was one of the most wondrous sights to behold in baseball. He would settle comfortably into a wide right-handed batting stance, shoes always exactly 3½ feet apart. At the last possible fraction of a second, he'd stride shortly, seemingly snatch the speeding baseball from the catcher's mitt and reverse its flight with added impetus into the far reaches of the park.

Early in his career, Joe was a shy, discreet figure. Initially confused by the fuss made over his abilities, DiMaggio would gradually grow into his role as the club's unquestioned deity, handling the adulation as he would a long run on a fly ball — with casual grace and style.

There was an air of spiritual attraction about the classy leader. He was a soft-spoken pillar of stateliness, an earnest authority figure who relished privacy but drew crowds like a magnet. Fellow ballplayers treasured his presence, both on and off the field, reverently referring to him as "Number 5" or "The Big Guy."

In full Yankee regalia, DiMaggio radiated an aura of tranquil self-con-

fidence. He luxuriated in pressure situations, leading his mates to 10 World Series in 13 seasons. There the spotlight shone brightly on the Yankee Clipper, and he responded with eight Series home runs and 30 runs batted in, numerous fielding gems, and nine World Championships.

His 1939 MVP year corresponded with the fourth of those titles, the campaign beginning with a minor triumph. After three seasons of nagging injuries and a holdout, Joe finally suited up and played in his first year-opening contest. But the good fortune didn't last long. In game 10, he tore a muscle in his right leg while attempting an impossible catch, and subsequently missed 34 games. DiMaggio recovered to scorch AL pitching and lead the New Yorkers to their fourth straight World Championship, becoming the first and only player in the history of baseball to begin his career with four consecutive World titles.

Despite the fact that he started 117 games, DiMaggio captured his first MVP. Lou Gehrig, suffering from an incurable disease, had retired early that season, and the writers were now paying homage to the new Yankee kingpin. It was the advent of an admiration society that continues to this day.

Top 5 MVP Vote-Getters

1. Joe DiMaggio, New York — 280
2. Jimmie Foxx, Boston — 170
3. Bob Feller, Cleveland — 155
4. Ted Williams, Boston — 126
5. Red Ruffing, New York — 116

1940 National League — Frank McCormick

Frank Andrew McCormick
B. June 9, 1911, New York, New York
D. November 21, 1982, Manhasset, New York

Year	Team	Games	AB	Hits	Avg.	HR	RBI	Runs	SB
1940	Cin NL	155	618	191	.309	19	127	93	2

The Season

After catching the bouquet the previous year, Cincinnati became the bride in 1940, seizing its second straight National League pennant and being crowned the World Champion for the first time since the infamous Black Sox scandal in 1919.

Again, the Reds did it with pitching and defense, leading the majors in ERA (3.05) and fielding average (.981). Most Valuable Player Frank McCormick and 1938 MVP Ernie Lombardi were Cincy's only productive hitters, but for the second year in a row, both 1939 MVP Bucky Walters and Paul Derringer were 20-game winners.

Having cruised to the NL flag by a dozen games over Brooklyn, the Reds needed the full seven to defeat Detroit in the 1940 World Series. It was the first National League World Championship since 1934.

The Series was highlighted by the gutsy performance of 40-year-old Cincinnati coach Jimmie Wilson, who was activated the day before the first game after Lombardi suffered an injury. Wilson, who had not caught a complete game in three years, shocked the baseball world by hitting .353 and forbidding the Tigers to steal a base over seven games. In fact, Jimmie pilfered the only base of the Series.

Only two months prior to the Series, Cincinnati backup catcher Willard Hershberger, who had been filling in for the injured Lombardi, committed suicide in Boston's Copley Plaza Hotel. Hershberger, whose father had killed himself 12 years earlier, was reportedly distraught over his pitch calling efforts during a close loss to New York three days previously.

Umpire George Magerkurth, who had been fined and suspended in 1939 for engaging in a spitting battle with Billy Jurges of the Giants, was attacked by a Brooklyn fan during an on-field argument at Ebbets Field. Dodgers manager Leo Durocher was later suspended and fined for "inciting a riot."

Pennant Propeller

Frank McCormick was about as excited as a 19-year-old young man could be. He'd just had a tryout with the New York Giants in the Polo Grounds and thought he'd done rather well. Maybe he hadn't knocked every pitch out of sight, and he knew there were faster young men in the state of New York, but he had hit the ball with authority and made the routine plays in the outfield.

And now a Giant coach was approaching Frank to give him the news, hopefully to tell him that they liked what they'd seen and wanted him to put on a major league uniform. Who needed that lousy job at the art gallery, anyway? Sure, he'd broken $450 worth of Early American glass a couple of weeks earlier, but it was an accident, and certainly didn't justify his subsequent firing. But before long it wouldn't matter; soon he'd be signing a professional baseball contract.

The Giant coach couldn't have selected a more ironic method of telling Frank McCormick that he just wasn't good enough. "Son," the coach said, "if you have a good job, I'd advise keeping it." Frank's hopes had been dashed, but not his spirit. He passed up a chance to go into police work, continuing to struggle at his first love, baseball; two

years later, he made the Cincinnati Redlegs ballclub. McCormick appeared in only a dozen games for the Reds in 1934, and after a couple of years in the minors, was brought up again at the tail end of the 1937 season and became a regular the following year.

The husky, likeable first baseman, who on the advice of a sandlot coach had switched from the outfield, came on the scene with a bang. McCormick led the National League in hits in each of his first three full seasons, culminating in 1940 when he batted .309, tagged 19 home runs and drove in 127 to earn the Most Valuable Player award and guide the Reds to their second consecutive pennant and a World Series triumph over Detroit.

The 1940 campaign saw big Frank pace the NL in doubles with a career-high 44, and in hits with 191, while placing runner-up in RBIs with 127 and total bases at 298. The MVP trophy was the third straight to be awarded to a Cincinnati ballplayer. The pride-oriented Redleg had a tough World Series, batting only .214, but doubled and scored the tying run in the 2–1 victory in the decisive seventh game.

McCormick had played a significant role in Cincinnati's pennant-winning effort the previous year, leading the league in RBIs (a career-best 128) and hits (209), and running second in batting (.332) and total bases (312). Frank's .495 slugging average was his highest ever, and the 6-foot-4, 205-pounder's 18 homers marked the first of seven times that McCormick was in double figures in that category. And even though the Yankees swept Cincinnati in the 1939 World Series, McCormick was a terror at the plate, collecting two hits each in three of the contests and batting .400.

Following the 1940 MVP year, McCormick slipped to his lowest average in a full season, .269, but belted 17 home runs and set a record by striking out only 13 times in 603 at-bats. Frank narrowly missed driving in 100 or more runs for the fourth year in a row, settling for 97. He did drive in 102 runs in 1944, the fourth time he reached the 100 plateau in his career, and his 20 round-trippers that season were a career high.

Nineteen-forty-five was McCormick's last year with the Reds; in 1946, he went to the Philadelphia Phillies, where he spent his final full season as a regular, batting .284 with 11 home runs and 66 RBIs. McCormick played with both the Phils and Boston Braves in 1947, then ended his career in '48 with the Braves, picking up a hit in the World Series loss to Cleveland.

When Frank retired, he held several NL defensive records for a first baseman, including highest single-season fielding average (.999 in 1946). He rejoined the Reds as a scout, coach and broadcaster from 1955 to '68 before dying of cancer in 1982.

Frank Andrew McCormick was born June 9, 1911, in New York City, and by the age of 17 knew he wanted to be a major league baseball player. Sandlot coach George Halpern arranged a tryout for him with the Philadelphia Athletics in Yankee Stadium, but Frank was unimpressive at the plate, and was not seriously considered.

Halpern secured another look-see for his hard-hitting outfielder in 1934, this time with the Reds in Beckley, West Virginia. McCormick came through, made the team and hit .350 before being called up to the Reds.

The .299 lifetime hitter batted .300 or better his first five years in the majors, and five of his first seven full campaigns. A proficient extra base hitter, McCormick pounded out 40 or more doubles three years in a row (1938–40) and stroked at least 20 two-baggers in 10 straight seasons (1938–47). Frank was the unanimous choice as the National League's All-Star first baseman in 1938, the first of

Frank McCormick. (Courtesy Cincinnati Reds.)

nine consecutive All-Star selections for the big guy. In that same year, he gave teammate Johnny Vander Meer a psychological boost during the right-hander's second consecutive no-hitter by tagging a three-run homer in the third inning.

Frank McCormick claimed that winning the 1940 World Championship was his greatest thrill in baseball. It wasn't the money, Frank insisted, but rather the intense joy and boundless satisfaction he derived from being called a champion.

Top 5 MVP Vote-Getters

1. Frank McCormick, Cincinnati — 274
2. Johnny Mize, St. Louis — 209
3. Bucky Walters, Cincinnati — 146
4. Paul Derringer, Cincinnati — 121
5. Freddie Fitzsimmons, Brooklyn — 84

1940 AMERICAN LEAGUE — HANK GREENBERG

Henry Benjamin Greenberg
B. January 1, 1911, New York, New York
D. September 4, 1986, Beverly Hills, California

Year	Team	Games	AB	Hits	Avg.	HR	RBI	Runs	SB
1940	Det AL	148	573	195	.340	41	150	129	6

The Season

The 1940 season began in classic style, with Cleveland Indians fireballer Bob Feller no-hitting the Chicago White Sox on opening day, the first pitcher to accomplish that feat since Leon "Red" Ames in 1909.

The American League then settled into a torrid pennant race, with the Detroit Tigers finally edging the Indians by one game, while the New York Yankees finished two back. The Detroit flag was its third in seven years and broke the Yankee string of four straight AL titles.

The hard-hitting gang from Detroit led the majors in runs scored (888) and in team batting (.286). They then ran into a resilient Cincinnati Reds team in the World Series. With the championship one victory away, the Tigers dropped the final two contests to lose in seven.

Three-time MVP Jimmie Foxx hit his 500th career home run against Philadelphia pitcher George Caster September 24 during the same inning that three of Foxx's Boston teammates — Ted Williams, Joe Cronin and Jim Tabor — also went deep.

The name "DiMaggio" had taken on a special luster in American League cities by 1940, and "Joltin' Joe" added to that sheen by pacing league hitters with a .352 average for the New York Yankees.

Encore from the Outfield

By the time the 1940 season had begun, Hank Greenberg's prowess with the bat had been well defined throughout the majors. Only 29 years old and entering what is usually a ballplayer's prime, the Tigers' biggest weapon was more than merely an expert at turning fastballs into bleacher souvenirs; he was a celebrity throughout the land.

The good-looking bachelor was an excellent story for baseball writers throughout the junior circuit. He was amiable, articulate and interesting beyond the realm of locker room conversation, but getting him to bare his soul was a real challenge. The moment talk shifted to his own vast accomplishments, Greenberg turned strangely pessimistic. He seemed to reflect a brooding insecurity, as if his achievements were a freakish mistake and his talent might vanish the next day. The long practice hours he put in during his career were Hank's defense against what might be considered an inordinate fear of failure. Long after everyone else had accepted him as a baseball superstar, Hank Greenberg was still seeking that goal.

And many years later, people are still acknowledging Greenberg's voluminous resume, thanks in part to a 2000 documentary titled *The Life and Times of Hank Greenberg*. Aviva Kempner directed the 95-minute film, a work she began shortly after his 1986 death from cancer.

This self-driven attitude reflected his lifestyle long after he had retired from baseball. He was part of the Cleveland Indian success story in 1954, as the team's minor league director when it won an AL record-111 games. Later he joined the Chicago White Sox in an executive capacity, and that team won the 1959 pennant. During that time he became a millionaire, investing his baseball earnings wisely.

Money consciousness was always evident in Hank's nature, even as a player. Following a spectacular 1937 season in which he hit .337, blasted 40 home runs and drove in a league-leading 183 runs, Greenberg's production dropped to .312, 33 HRs and 112 RBIs two years later. Although the Tigers wanted him to take a $10,000 salary cut for 1940, Hank, a shrewd negotiator throughout his career, turned the tables on management and received a $10,000 increase. The Tigers had requested that Hank make a move from first base to the outfield, despite the fact that he'd led AL first basemen in fielding in 1939 (.993). He reasoned that the added work necessary to make him into a decent fly-shagger required compensation. Thus the raise — and the pennant — because Hank's move to left field allowed Detroit to squeeze the big bat of first baseman Rudy York into its already fearsome lineup.

With Greenberg and York powdering opposing pitchers, the Tigers went from fifth place in 1939 to champions in 1940. Detroit's new left fielder responded to his position with 41 home runs, 150 RBIs, 50 doubles and a .670 slugging mark, all of which led the league, while batting .340. The enigmatic slugger topped off that effort with his best World Series, hitting .357 with a round-tripper and six RBIs. He was named the American League MVP for the second time, the first to cop the honor at two different positions.

Hank's baseball prime was interrupted by World War II, when at age 30 he was the first star in his sport to enlist in the Armed Forces; he spent 4½ years serving his country. "Hammerin' Hank" was no desk jockey, flying many a dangerous bombing mission, including the initial air strike of Japan. He came out of the service in 1945 at mid-season, then hit a pennant-clinching, ninth-inning grand slam for the Tigers in the final game of the regular season. In his first full year after the war, the 35-year-old blasted 44 home runs and drove in 127 runs, both league highs.

Despite that excellent comeback, Detroit waived him out of the American League prior to the 1947 season after Greenberg had applied for the vacant job of Tigers general manager and was turned down by owner Walter Briggs. The Pittsburgh Pirates picked him up, and Greenberg, after threatening to retire, negotiated what writers of the day reported as the first NL $100,000 salary.

He played for one year as a Pirate, and despite hitting 25 home runs, leading the league in walks (104) and tutoring star-in-the-making Ralph Kiner, was totally dissatisfied with a .249 batting average. At age 36, Greenberg retired.

In nine big league seasons, and three others shortened by injury and war, Hank tallied a .313 lifetime average, 1,276 RBIs and 331 home runs. Greenberg stands in the top 20 all time in the home run percentage category, and was inducted into baseball's Hall

of Fame in 1956. A dreamer's speculation of what might have been, based on average full-year performances prior to the military, projects the following: 549 career home runs and 2,094 RBIs, both of which would have outclassed all but Babe Ruth at that time.

Still, the sensitive slugger left behind a record that requires nothing in the way of apologies. And his flair for responding to dramatic situations gives Hank a permanent place in baseball's hero department. For example:

- In his last 1941 game prior to induction in the Army, Hank left Tiger fans cheering with two circuit clouts.
- In 1945, Hank's bases-loaded home run on the last day of the campaign clinched the pennant.
- Amid much public attention and a hot 1934 pennant race, Greenberg declared he would not play on Rosh Hashana, the Jewish New Year. At the last second, he reversed that stance and smashed two home runs. He then sat out on Yom Kippur.
- In a spectacular 1937 bid to best Lou

Gehrig's still-standing AL record of 184 RBIs in one season, Greenberg fell only one shy.

- In another attempt to outdo a seemingly unbeatable mark, Hank assaulted Ruth's hallowed total of 60 home runs in one season. During that 1938 run at the Babe, Greenberg set a major league mark by hitting two or more home runs in 11 games, but came up a pair short. His 58 homers, 119 RBIs and 144 runs all led the league.

All "might-have-beens" aside, Hank Greenberg was a ballplayer for the ages.

Top 5 MVP Vote-Getters

1. Hank Greenberg, Detroit — 292
2. Bob Feller, Cleveland — 222
3. Joe DiMaggio, New York — 151
4. Bobo Newsom, Detroit — 120
5. Lou Boudreau, Cleveland — 119

1941 National League — Dolph Camilli

Adolph Louis Camilli
B. April 23, 1907, San Francisco, California
D. October 21, 1997, San Mateo, California

Year	Team	Games	AB	Hits	Avg.	HR	RBI	Runs	SB
1941	Bkn NL	149	529	151	.285	34	120	92	3

The Season

As flamboyant as Bill Veeck and domineering as George Steinbrenner, Brooklyn Dodgers General Manager Larry MacPhail was perhaps the most interesting personality in baseball in 1941 when he put together "the best team money could buy."

No Brooklyn regular that year came from the Dodger farm system,

but the renegades blended their talents beautifully. Following a 20-year dry spell, the Dodgers won the National League pennant with 100 victories under the leadership of manager Leo Durocher.

Twenty-two-year-old Brooklyn center fielder Pete Reiser became the NL's youngest batting champion ever when he hit .343, while teammates Kirby Higbe and Whit Wyatt were the

league's only 20-game winners. "Da Bums" led the way in batting (.272), homers (101) and pitching (3.14 ERA).

Dodger fans' wild post-season celebrations were squelched by the cross-town Yankees, who took the first of seven World Series confrontations in 16 seasons between the two clubs in a five-game set.

Mel Ott, the youngest player in major league history to reach 100 home

Dolph Camilli. (Courtesy Los Angeles Dodgers.)

level across home plate, the image was one of a tentative rookie merely hoping to get some wood on the ball.

But it didn't take long for pitchers to learn better. What Camilli lacked in an intimidating presence at the plate, he more than made up for with a vicious, level swing, sending outfielders scampering to all parts of the park in pursuit of screaming line drives.

The southpaw first baseman never came close to winning a batting title, nor did he conduct a serious assault on Babe Ruth's home run record; but he was a consistent slugger who gave the Brooklyn Dodgers exactly what they needed in the late 1930s and early '40s: power. Speed, defense and pitching were already present, but with the exception of the muscular Camilli, purchased from the Phillies prior to the 1938 season, no Dodger had hit more than 14 home runs in any year since 1932. Dolph rectified that situation immediately, blasting 24, 26 and 23 homers in his first three Dodger campaigns. But that was just a warm-up for the 1941 season when the San Francisco native hit .285, cracked 34 home runs and drove in 120. His efforts helped Brooklyn win the pennant for the first time since 1920, and convinced writers to name him the National League's MVP.

His home run and RBI totals were career highs, and both paced the NL in 1941. Dolph was also runner-up in slugging (.556), total bases (294) and walks (104).

Camilli was a viable threat at the plate throughout the 1941 season, but down the stretch when the Dodgers were battling to stay a step ahead of the pesky Cardinals, he waxed brilliant in the clutch. Some of his late-season heroics included:

- A three-run homer September 11 to help nudge St. Louis 6–4 in 11 innings, giving the Dodgers a two-game lead;

- A key base hit during a five-run 11th inning September 15 in a 5–1 triumph over the Reds;

- An RBI triple against the Pirates September 17 that led to a 6–4 win; and

- A homer, his 34th of the season,

runs (22 years, 132 days), achieved two career milestones in the same game, recording his 400th home run and 1,500th RBI in a win over Cincinnati June 1. Following the season, Ott was named player-manager for the New York Giants.

Pittsburgh Pirates manager Frankie Frisch inspired one of Norman Rockwell's best known oil paintings when the 1931 NL MVP carried an open umbrella onto the field during a rainy game in Brooklyn August 19. The sarcastic gesture produced some hearty laughs, as well as an ejection by umpire Jocko Conlan.

On June 6, Pittsburgh's Rip Sewell was nearly as busy catching the baseball as he was throwing it, establishing a single-game NL record for assists by a pitcher with 11 in a 4–3 win over New York.

Although the league's fans grew in numbers, they were seeing a slightly inferior brand of baseball, as more than half of the major leaguers from 1940 were active in the Armed Forces by '41. One of those wearing baseball flannels was eventual three-time MVP Stan Musial, who stroked two hits in his major league debut for the Cardinals September 17.

Dodger Power Source

When 5-foot-10, 185-pound Dolph Camilli would crouch slightly in the left-handed batter's box, allowing his bat to dangle at a nearly horizontal

another safety and three RBIs in an 8–3 conquest of his old team, Philadelphia, September 21.

Not that Dolph was a one-man show by any means. Dodger GM Larry MacPhail had fleeced several clubs of some of their best players to assemble his 1941 cadre of talent. This wild bunch that engaged in beanball wars, brawls and lengthy arguments with umpires was easily the most despised team in baseball, its temperament personified in manager Leo Durocher. Strangely enough, as strong as Camilli was, he never was involved in on-field fisticuffs. When asked once how well Dolph could handle himself in a fight, Durocher said that nobody knew because nobody wanted to find out.

Camilli was the first of MacPhail's acquisitions. After borrowing $200,000 from the Brooklyn Trust Company, most of which was used to refurbish the Ebbets Field stands, first-year GM MacPhail talked bank president George V. McLaughlin into loaning the club an additional $50,000 to obtain Camilli. MacPhail's line of reasoning was that the Dodgers were lacking only power in their pennant quest, and that Camilli, who was dissatisfied with his salary in Philly, could provide the needed punch.

A model of consistency — both at first base, where he played 1,476 games in a 12-year career, and at bat — Dolph led National League first basemen in fielding percentage at .994 in 1937 and never dipped below .989 in his six years with the Dodgers. He also put together eight seasons in a row with at least 23 home runs.

A lifetime .277 hitter, Camilli rose to a career-high .339 with a league-best .446 on-base percentage in 1937, his last year with the Phillies. Senior circuit pitchers, well aware of his mean stroke, learned to pitch around the fearsome swinger, who twice paced the league in walks and was second three other times.

The flashy fielder entered the big time at age 26. After failing to show much at the plate in a short stint with the Cubs, he was sent to Philadelphia in 1934. In three full seasons with the Phils, Camilli averaged 27 homers and 88 RBIs, while hitting over .300 twice. But Philly management wouldn't budge from its $12,500 salary offer, and the disgruntled first baseman headed to Brooklyn in 1938.

His average slipped 88 points to .251 in his initial year as a Dodger, but everyone knew he wasn't there to win a batting crown. His 24 homers and 100 RBIs in '38 seemed like Ruthian numbers to the power-starved Brooklyn fans. Camilli peaked in 1941, then followed that MVP season with another fine campaign in '42, pounding 26 home runs and driving in 109.

That was to be his final productive effort. Dolph lost his home run stroke, tallying only six in 1943 at the age of 36, and rather than report to the Giants, to whom he'd been traded, returned to his ranch.

After serving as player-manager for Oakland of the Pacific Coast League in 1944, Camilli came back for an abbreviated season with the Boston Red Sox in '45. He managed and coached several minor league teams in the next decade, and basked in fatherly pride in 1960 when 23-year-old son Doug joined the Dodgers. Dolph scouted for both the New York Yankees (1960–67) and California Angels (1969–71) before retiring from baseball. He passed away in 1997 at the age of 90.

Camilli did not shatter records, nor did he warrant Hall of Fame residence. But the dependable, solid contact hitter filled a power role in Brooklyn that no other player could, and helped bring Flatbush fans a season they'd never forget.

Top 5 MVP Vote-Getters

1. Dolph Camilli, Brooklyn — 300
2. Pete Reiser, Brooklyn — 183
3. Whit Wyatt, Brooklyn — 151
4. Jimmy Brown, St. Louis — 107
5. Elmer Riddle, Cincinnati — 98

1941 AMERICAN LEAGUE — JOE DiMAGGIO

Joseph Paul DiMaggio
B. November 25, 1914, Martinez, California
D. March 8, 1999, Hollywood, Florida

Year	Team	Games	AB	Hits	Avg.	HR	RBI	Runs	SB
1941	NY AL	139	541	193	.357	30	125	122	4

The Season

What a season for baseball. Two of the game's greatest stars produced hitting achievements in 1941 that have not been matched since.

Joe DiMaggio of the New York Yankees set a record by hitting safely in 56 consecutive games, while Boston's Ted Williams batted .406, becoming the first man since Bill Terry (.401 in 1930 for the New York Giants) to reach that magic mark, and the last to do so.

The Yanks broke out of the gate slowly, but when DiMaggio started hitting, the New Yorkers began ringing up one win after another until they were far in front of the league. The Bronx Bombers finished 17 games ahead of the Red Sox, breaking a record by clinching the pennant September 4.

The AL champs then went on to best the cross-town Brooklyn Dodgers four games to one in the World Series. The turning point came in Game 4 when the Dodgers seemingly had it won 4–3. A third strike to New York's Tommy Henrich on what would have been the final out slipped away from Brooklyn catcher Mickey Owen, and Henrich reached first. The floodgates had been opened and the Yanks swirled in, scoring four times to win 7–4.

On June 2, baseball and the nation mourned the loss of Lou Gehrig, who died of amyotrophic lateral sclerosis at age 37. Following the season, Lou Boudreau became the youngest (24 years, four months, eight days) big league manager of the century when Cleveland named him player-manager.

The Streak

It felt like a good year right from the start. He had hit the ball well in spring training, and midway though the first month of the 1941 regular season, Joe DiMaggio was clipping away at a .528 pace. Including exhibition games, he had slapped at least one hit in each of his last 27 contests. Then came the slump — a prolonged period in which the Yankee center fielder's average plummeted 222 points.

Joe was at his wit's end, wondering if the hits would ever start to fall, when almost innocuously the streak began. A scrub infield hit against the White Sox in a 13–1 New York loss May 15 started things rolling. The Yanks were in fourth place at the time, 6½ games behind Cleveland. Fifty-five games and 90 DiMaggio hits later, the Yankees were in first place, six games up on the Indians. In a hitting display that grows more amazing with each passing season, "Joltin' Joe" delivered at least one hit in every one of those contests.

The first record to fall was the

Joe DiMaggio. (Courtesy New York Yankees.)

Yankee mark of 29 consecutive games, jointly held by Roger Peckinpaugh and DiMaggio's predecessor in center field, Earle Combs. On July 1, Joe tied, then broke, George Sisler's 1922 AL record of 41 during a double-header. With Sisler's record overtaken, the Yankee Clipper discovered that the press boys had unearthed yet another milestone at which he could shoot: Willie Keeler's 44 in a row.

Four nerve-wracking games later, Joe conquered Keeler's 1897 mark in style with a round-tripper. Still the streak continued, until finally, before a packed house in Cleveland's Municipal Stadium, two fielding gems by Indians third baseman Ken Keltner and a final double play grounder to shortstop Lou Boudreau halted the big guy at 56 consecutive games. All three DiMaggio outs had been well-pounded, and had one gone through, the streak could eventually have reached the stratospheric 73 mark because the very next game, DiMag began again, hitting safely in his next 16 contests.

During the 56-game streak, he hit .408 with 15 homers, 55 RBIs and symbolic totals of 56 runs scored and 56 singles. Game by game the DiMaggio name had become the most familiar in the land. Les Brown and His Band of Renown recorded a hit song called

Joltin' Joe. Many of DiMaggio's teammates, steeped in superstition, wore the same underwear throughout the record-setting period, prompting one ex-Yankee to recall that after a while the team clubhouse was an odorous place to be.

But this golden season would have been incomplete without the annual DiMaggio injury. On August 19, he sprained an ankle rounding first base and was forced to miss almost a month. Playing only 139 games, he still managed to lead the league in RBIs with 125, sport a .357 batting average and swat 30 home runs.

The inevitable honors followed the 1941 season: MVP and the Associated Press' Outstanding Male Athlete of the Year award. The streak was definitely a major factor in DiMaggio's MVP award, because runner-up Ted Williams led the league in batting (.406), homers (37), runs (135), slugging (.735) and walks (145). To top off a perfect campaign, Joe's wife, Dorothy, gave birth to his first child, Joe Jr. Twenty-eight years later, the amazing hitting spree was still fresh in the minds of baseball zealots. A poll of diverse experts of the game voted the 56-game hitting streak the greatest achievement in baseball history.

The MVP campaign had certainly

compensated for what DiMaggio considered his biggest disappointment up to that time: the Yankees' failure to win the 1940 pennant.

Joe had again missed the season opener that year, thanks to a strained knee tendon. When he returned May 8, his club was in a three-way struggle with Detroit and Cleveland that went down to the final day. Pacing the Yankees in every significant offensive category, Joe captured his second consecutive batting title (.352), hit 31 home runs and batted in 133. But the Yanks finished third, two games out, as Detroit won the flag.

Nineteen-forty-one's successes resurrected national consciousness in the Yankee dynasty and its regal star. At 26 years of age, his already impressive reputation had been greatly enhanced. When DiMaggio stepped into the batting cage or walked down the street, activity stopped as those on hand drank in his courtly presence. He was the epitome of Yankee class, a living advertisement of the ingrained confidence that seemed to surround the greatest baseball team around.

The winter of 1941-42 briefly changed the public's positive perception of the man. Yankee management, pointing to expected hard times ahead during World War II, asked DiMaggio to take a $5,000 cut in salary for 1942. He flatly refused, and the team's salary negotiators put their top player in a bad light by stating in the press that DiMaggio was unwilling to make a patriotic sacrifice by taking less money. He finally settled for a $5,000 raise, but was booed by AL fans in every city.

DiMaggio hit .305 with 21 homers and 114 RBIs as the Yankees won the pennant, and for the first time, he played in every game. His .333 World Series mark was not enough, however, to stave off a band of young upstarts from St. Louis, who downed New York four games to one.

But baseball took a back seat to the war, and after much thought, DiMaggio gave up his exempt classification and enlisted in the United States Army.

He was 28, in his baseball prime, and would lose three potentially productive years of his career, along with a $43,500 annual salary that was bound to increase. But DiMaggio would be back.

Top 5 MVP Vote-Getters

1. Joe DiMaggio, New York — 291
2. Ted Williams, Boston — 254
3. Bob Feller, Cleveland — 174
4. Thornton Lee, Chicago — 144
5. Charlie Keller, New York — 126

1942 NATIONAL LEAGUE — MORT COOPER

Morton Cecil Cooper
B. March 2, 1913, Atherton, Missouri
D. November 17, 1958, Little Rock, Arkansas

Year	Team	Games	W	L	ERA	IP	SO	BB	ShO
1942	SL NL	37	22	7	1.78	278.2	152	68	10

The Season

President Franklin Delano Roosevelt gave baseball the official go-ahead prior to the spring of 1942, erasing all doubts concerning the game's future during the war years. Due to the draft and enlistments, many of the major league franchises were forced to bring up unproven youngsters from their farm systems and call back retired veterans to fill rosters.

The level of play throughout the big leagues degenerated accordingly, but the St. Louis Cardinals, nurtured by the strongest minor league system in baseball, fielded an enviable group of talented men, including outstanding rookie Stan Musial. This Cardinal bunch, managed by Billy Southworth, mounted one of the most exciting pennant drives in baseball history, rallying from 10½ games behind in August to overtake the Brooklyn Dodgers. The Cards' 106 wins and Brooklyn's 104 were the most by an NL pennant winner and runner-up since 1909.

After dropping the first World Series game, the Cardinals stunned the New York Yankees by coming back with four straight wins for the World Championship.

On September 13, the same day that Chicago shortstop Lennie Merullo tied a major league record with four errors in one inning, his son was born. Merullo named him "Boots."

Prior to the season, the Cubs dropped their contractual plans to install lights at Wrigley Field due to the military's materials shortage. The war ended three years later, but Wrigley Field would not host a night game for 46 seasons.

Home Front Hero

Mort Cooper's seasons in the sun were short ones. Only three extraordinary campaigns highlighted the big right-hander's 11-year career, but those were enough to keep memory's flames burning for a lifetime.

Cooper was a wartime phenomenon — a hard thrower who peaked in his mound efforts during the 1942 through 1944 schedules when a majority of regular major leaguers were fighting World War II. He was outstanding in those campaigns, possibly the best pitcher in the National League. Unfortunately, a sore arm coincided with the return of the war veterans, leaving an eternal doubt as to whether Cooper would have performed quite as brilliantly against top-notch competition.

Having joined the Cards at the tail end of 1938, Mort became a member of the starting rotation the following year, averaging 12 wins for the next three seasons. The imposing battery combination of the Cooper brothers came into being in 1940 when Mort's brother, Walker, joined the club as a catcher. Both were big men weighing 210 pounds, with Mort standing 6-foot-2 and the younger sibling an inch taller. Mort's best years took place when Walker was calling for the assortment of forkballs and overhand fastballs that baffled hitters.

In all, Cooper racked up a lifetime record of 128 wins against 75 defeats (a marvelous .631 winning percentage), and a career ERA of 2.97. His three World Series appearances yielded a "tough-luck" 2-3 mark with a 3.00 ERA. Twice he led the league in wins and shutouts, his top campaign being 1942 when he paced the circuit in victories, shutouts and ERA, and claimed the MVP.

Cooper was the league's best pitcher again in 1943, the Cards repeating as pennant winners. He was 21-8 for an NL-best .724 winning percentage, and posted a 2.30 ERA. One of those victories was a one-hitter against the Dodgers, marred only by Billy Herman's "dying quail" single late in the game. Even more memorable was a 4–3 World Series victory against the Yankees that year, which he and Walker dedicated to their father, who had died that morning.

Mort's last big year was 1944, when he fashioned a 22–7 record and a 12-strikeout blanking of the St. Louis Browns in Game 5 of the World Series. Salary squabbles prior to 1943 and 1945 infuriated Cardinal owner Sam Breadon, who traded Cooper to the Boston Braves early in '45.

Arm troubles began cropping up immediately after the swap, limiting Cooper to 13 decisions (9–4). A measure of past effectiveness returned in 1946, as Mort went 13–11. But after starting the next season 2–5, the forkballer was traded to the New York Giants, where he compiled the worst mark of his career, finishing 3–10.

At age 34, the tall hurler decided to call it quits. He stayed away in 1948, although he was restless and unhappy. He mounted one more grueling comeback try, training diligently in the winter of '48, and earned a spot with the Chicago Cubs in 1949. But his comeback was a disaster. He made one mound appearance, retired no one and gave up two hits and a walk. This time, he hung up his glove for good.

As a youth, Mort threw so hard that only Walker was able to catch him. After wowing the locals, Mort signed his first professional contract at age 20 when he joined the Western League. Shortly thereafter, the Cardinals claimed the Missouri youth and advanced him through their farm system.

The key to Cooper's success came in 1941 when Jim Weaver, an ex-Pittsburgh Pirate pitcher, taught him how to throw a forkball. The 28-year-old's natural affinity for the off-speed delivery led to a quick mastery of the pitch. Shortly thereafter, he orchestrated back-to-back one-hitters. Nineteen-forty-two was a glorious year for the elder Cooper, who led the Cardinals in an inspiring pennant drive that culminated in a double-header sweep of the Dodgers. The young Cardinals had trailed Brooklyn by 10½ games in early August, but after winning 27-of-30, pulled to within one game of first place. In the opening contest, Cooper pulled his mates even with the Dodgers by firing one of his league-leading 10

shutouts. The Cards then won the second affair.

An old knee injury kept Mort out of the military during World War II, and he took advantage of his exempt status to become the league's top moundsman in 1942. He was the starting pitcher for the NL in the All-Star Game, and went on to post league bests in wins (22), ERA (1.78) and shutouts, while finishing second in strikeouts (152) and innings pitched (279). Cooper also started the 1943 All-Star Game, and he owned the dubious distinction of being the only player in All-Star history to be declared the losing pitcher in consecutive games.

Superstition played a sidebar role during Cooper's MVP campaign. The big righty had scoffed at bad luck implications that went with the No. 13 on the back of his jersey. But in 1942, he changed his stance. Noting that he stopped winning after registering his 13th victory the previous year, he changed to No. 14 after gaining his 13th win of 1942. The switch was followed by another triumph, so Cooper went up to the next uniform number, and was once more successful in securing a win.

After returning to No. 13, he promptly lost the opening game of the World Series 7–4 to the Yankees. Although the Cards would go on to take the next four contests, Cooper did not win a game, posting a 5.54 ERA over 13 innings.

But the poor World Series performance did not dim the excellence of his regular-season campaign, and post-season honors included the league MVP and a spot as the NL pitcher on *The Sporting News'* all-star team.

Top 5 MVP Vote-Getters

1. Mort Cooper, St. Louis — 263
2. Enos Slaughter, St. Louis — 200
3. Mel Ott, New York — 190
4. Mickey Owen, Brooklyn — 103
5. Johnny Mize, New York — 97

1942 AMERICAN LEAGUE — JOE GORDON

Joseph Lowell Gordon
B. February 18, 1915, Los Angeles, California
D. April 14, 1978, Sacramento, California

Year	Team	Games	AB	Hits	Avg.	HR	RBI	Runs	SB
1942	NY AL	147	538	173	.322	18	103	88	12

The Season

The United States was becoming increasingly involved in World War II by the spring of 1942, and baseball, anxious to contribute to the cause, donated well over $1 million to wartime charities that year.

Players, umpires and officials agreed to take 10 percent of their pay in war bonds, and the St. Louis Browns gave free passes to 39,000 servicemen. Fans also participated, returning souvenir baseballs which were then offered to the military for recreational purposes. All 16 big league clubs hosted charity games, raising $506,000 for the war effort. The Yankees supplied $80,000 of that bulk from an August 23 pre-game exhibition that saw 47-year-old Babe Ruth hit a pitch off Walter Johnson, 54, into the right field stands.

On July 7, a group of American League all-stars defeated a military all-star team featuring Bob Feller, Sam Chapman and Cecil Travis 6–0 in front of 60,000 fans in Cleveland. Gate receipts provided $160,000 to a military relief fund.

New York made it six American League pennants in seven years in 1942, all with Joe McCarthy at the helm. The Yanks posted 103 victories to win the flag by nine games over the Red Sox, whose Ted Williams earned the first Triple Crown since Lou Gehrig in 1934, and his second consecutive batting title.

The Bronx Bombers then out-hit, out-homered, out-fielded and out-stole the St. Louis Cardinals in the World Series, but became the first team since 1915 to win a Series opener before dropping four straight. New York's 1942 post-season losses matched its total number of defeats in its last eight Series appearances from 1927 through '41.

By finishing in third place, the St. Louis Browns squeezed into the upper half of AL teams for the first time since 1929, when they took fourth.

Acrobatic Kid

Joe Gordon entered major league baseball as an already hardened 23-year-old man, but left the game as a 54-year-old kid. In between, the acrobatic second baseman blasted home runs for the New York Yankees and Cleveland Indians, contributing to six pennant winners and five World Series victors, as well as serving as a manager for half a decade.

Although his best season was 1948 when he belted 32 homers and drove in 124 runs for the World Champion Indians, Gordon was awarded the MVP trophy as a Yankee in '42. "Flash" hit .322 for his best average ever, tagged 18 home runs and collected 103 RBIs, guiding New York to another American League flag.

Due to his family's bleak economic condition, little Joe was forced to face the hard realities of life and grow up quickly. But once he established himself as a big league ballplayer, the kid in him suddenly burst forth.

When the quick, wiry infielder wasn't spearing ground balls headed for the outfield, "Trigger Joe" was off on hunting and fishing trips or raising dogs. The right-handed slugger, who pounded an AL-record 253 lifetime homers for a second baseman, spent hours practicing his broadcasting skills at home with a tape recorder.

Jumping from hobby to hobby during an 11-year playing career, he was finally able to enjoy the varieties of life. In high school he had been interested in only one thing: baseball. Joe began playing as a catcher, but preferred the challenge of Legion ball, joining an East Side Commercial American team that was searching for an infielder. He played well at shortstop and helped his team win the 1931 state championship.

Gordon acquired an athletic scholarship from the University of Oregon, and within a year the big league scouts were on his trail. The Yankees quickly shoved a contract toward him, but Joe declined, deciding to finish college. Gordon hit .418 his sophomore year and was named the league's most outstanding player.

After college, Flash made the Yanks' Class AA team in Oakland in 1936, taking over at shortstop a couple of weeks into the season and hitting .300 in 143 games. Joe spent the next year at the Triple A level in Newark, where the Bears won their league by 25½ games. The 5-foot-10, 175-pounder performed so well that the Yankees never hesitated in giving regular second baseman Tony Lazzeri his unconditional release, figuring Gordon was fully prepared for the big time.

Joe clubbed 25 homers in his freshman campaign in 1938 as a Yankee regular, playing in a home park that measured more than 400 feet to left-center field. He also drove in 97 runs while appearing in 127 games. The next three seasons, the acrobatic infielder averaged 27 home runs and 100 RBIs, twice tagging 32 doubles.

The flashy glove man outpolled Triple Crown winner Ted Williams for the MVP crown in 1942, thanks to a solid offensive season and the writers' growing disaffection with the Red Sox left fielder. While it could be argued that the MVP nod in a close competition should go to a player on a pennant winner, the vote against Williams was a sham. Teddy Ballgame paced the majors in batting (.356), home runs (36), RBIs (137), slugging (.648), total bases (338), runs (141) and walks (145), yet finished 21 points behind Gordon, who led the league in strikeouts (95), grounding into double plays (22) and most errors at his position (28).

The agile Gordon, who robbed many a hitter with sprawling stops and off-balance throws, had a career-high batting average in 1942, augmented by 29 doubles and a .491 slugging percentage. Fortunately for the second sacker, the MVP balloting occurred before the Yanks' World Series loss to St. Louis. Joe hit only .095 in the five-game set and was picked off second base by Cardinals catcher Walker Cooper in the ninth inning of the last game.

Following his MVP season, Gordon slumped significantly, ending with 17 home runs, 69 RBIs and a .249 average in 1943. Uncle Sam then came calling, and "GI-Joe" spent the next two years in the Army.

He came back to the majors in 1946, but had lost a considerable amount of sharpness, batting .210 with only 11 round-trippers and 47 RBIs. The Yanks then sent Gordon to Cleveland in exchange for pitcher Allie Reynolds. The still powerful second baseman, who now had a realistic target to shoot for in left-center field, cracked 29 homers during his first campaign in Cleveland, the most he'd had since 1940.

Gordon enjoyed his top season ever in 1948, helping garner a pennant for the Indians, who beat out the Red Sox in a one-game playoff. He then contributed a home run and a pair of RBIs to Cleveland's six-game World Series triumph over the Braves.

Flash's final two years as a ballplayer were mediocre ones, and at age 35 he decided to hang it up. Eight years later, Gordon was back in a Cleveland uniform as the Indians' manager,

Joe Gordon. (Courtesy New York Yankees.)

where he complied a 184–151 record from 1958 to mid–1960. In the first-ever manager-for-manager trade, Indian front office boss Frank Lane swapped Gordon for Tiger skipper Jimmie Dykes in 1960. Joe finished the year with the Tigers, then piloted the Kansas City Athletics in 1961 and the K.C. Royals in '69. He died at age 63.

In six World Series, Gordon hit four home runs, netted 16 RBIs and scored a dozen runs. His best effort was 1941 when he paced a four games-to-one victory over Brooklyn by hitting .500 with a homer in the opener and a contest-winning RBI single in the fifth game.

Joe Gordon not only made acrobatic fielding plays from his second base position and smacked home runs into the left field seats, he brought a contagious, youthful exuberance to the game unmatched by any player in his era.

Top 5 MVP Vote-Getters

1. Joe Gordon, New York—270
2. Ted Williams, Boston—249
3. Johnny Pesky, Boston—143
4. Vern Stephens, St. Louis—140
5. Tiny Bonham, New York—102

1943 National League—Stan Musial

Stanley Frank Musial
B. November 21, 1920, Donora, Pennsylvania

Year	Team	Games	AB	Hits	Avg.	HR	RBI	Runs	SB
1943	SL NL	157	617	220	.357	13	81	108	9

The Season

The beginning of the 1943 season was a pitcher's dream and a hitter's nightmare. Due to wartime restrictions, the "balata" ball, made from reprocessed rubber, was used on an experimental basis. In four opening day games, only 11 runs were scored, and it was 11 games into the season before a home run was hit. It took Chicago 1,120 at-bats over 32 games before its first round-tripper, provided by Bill Nicholson. On May 9, the old ball made a comeback.

Both hitters and pitchers had a tough time warming up prior to the regular season, suffering through the northern climes during spring training. Following a suggestion by Office of Defense transportation head Joseph B. Eastman, Commissioner Judge Kenesaw Mountain Landis urged all big league clubs to train north of the Ohio and Potomac rivers and east of the Mississippi, with the exception of the Cardinals and Browns, who could train anywhere in Missouri.

If the Cards minded the cold, they certainly didn't show it once the season began. St. Louis made a shambles of the pennant race, outdistancing Cincinnati by 18 games. Cardinal pitchers Howie Pollet, Max Lanier and defending MVP Mort Cooper finished 1-2-3 in the ERA standings, and Cooper threw back-to-back one-hitters versus Brooklyn and Philadelphia.

In a World Series rematch, however, the Cardinals were punished in five games by the Yankees, who hosted the first three contests because of travel restrictions.

Fans got plenty of amusement out of the dew-drop ball — later called a blooper or eephus ball — delivered by Pittsburgh moundsman Rip Sewell this season. The pitch looped 18 to 20 feet high on its way to batters, who must have felt as if they were playing in a slow-pitch softball league. Hitters were not laughing, however, as Sewell finished among the top five pitchers in wins (21), ERA (2.54), innings pitched, complete games and winning percentage.

The Donora Greyhound

Baseball has had its superstars; they've come and gone, and they won't be forgotten. The sport has also enjoyed its share of colorful characters and men of great integrity. They too will be remembered. But among the thousands of athletes who have worn major league uniforms, one stands out for his unique talents and personality. He is Stan Musial.

Called "baseball's happy warrior, baseball's perfect knight" by then-Commissioner Ford Frick, Stan is nationally esteemed both for his gargantuan on-field performances and flawless off-field demeanor. Low-key yet delightful, self-confident yet unassuming, Stan makes life pleasant for all those with whom he comes in contact.

A better than average fielder and savvy base runner, Musial is regarded as one of the greatest ballplayers of all time. His incredibly consistent hitting and durability allowed him to break more than 50 major league and National League records over a 22-year career.

Musial demolished the sophomore jinx myth in 1943, and at the same time clearly demonstrated he was a hitter to be feared. Coiled up in his corkscrew, peekaboo batting stance, Musial would suddenly lash out with a fury, attacking pitches regardless of their nature or location. By season's end, the left-hander had pitchers on the ropes in every ballpark, battering away with a combination of hits to all fields and an occasional knockout punch over the wall.

"The Man," so named by Brooklyn fans for his never-ending success in Ebbets Field, led the NL in seven offensive categories during his first MVP season in 1943. He was tops in hitting at .357, slugging at .562, total bases with 347, hits with 220, doubles at 48, triples with 20 and on-base percentage at .425. In most of those departments, the league's runner-up was nowhere in sight. Musial also was second in runs scored with 108 and tied for fifth in RBIs with 81.

As a result of his punishing attack on league hurlers and more-than-adequate defensive work in right field, Stan was voted the Most Valuable Player for the first of three times. Musial collected five hits for a .278 average in the World Series that season, but the Yankees were just too much for St. Louis to handle.

Born and raised in the steel mining area of Donora, Pennsylvania, the fifth of six children was christened Stanislaus, but was known as Stanley when he began school. Basketball was the natural athlete's best high school sport, and his father tried to persuade him to accept a University of Pittsburgh roundball scholarship, but to no avail. Stan had decided the first time he picked up a bat that he wanted to be a major league baseball player.

Musial started out as a pitcher. He received a chance to show his wares at age 17, trying out with a Cardinal farm team in nearby Monessen; and the following year, the left-hander inked his first professional contract to play with Williamson of the Mountain State

Stan Musial. (National Baseball Hall of Fame Library, Cooperstown, N.Y.)

League. The southpaw was mediocre in his first season (6–6, 4.66 ERA), but came back to post a 9–2 record in 1939 while batting .352. Stan also enjoyed success off the diamond, marrying Lillian Labash, his boyhood sweetheart, on his 19th birthday.

Nineteen-forty was a turning point for Stan, and an example of how seeming tragedy can lead to ultimate good. Though wild, Musial recorded an 18–5 mark for Daytona Beach of the Florida State League, playing in the outfield when not pitching. But while diving for a ball late that season, Musial fell on his throwing arm. The wing was still virtually lame by the time he reported to Columbus, Georgia, in the spring of 1941.

At this point, Cardinal manage-ment, which had never held a great deal of hope for Stan's success as a pitcher, moved the 6-foot, 175-pounder to the outfield, hoping his arm would recover sufficiently to allow him to make the necessary throws. Musial, who later said he'd always had considerably more confidence in his hitting than his pitching, eagerly took on the new challenge.

Assigned to Class AA Springfield at the beginning of the '41 campaign, he had no idea he'd end up with the big club before the season ended. Musial exploded at Springfield, batting .379 with 26 home runs in only 87 games. Having outgrown that competition, he was promoted to Rochester of the Triple A International League where he hit .326 in 54 games prior to being called up to the Cardinals in September as a replacement for the injured Enos Slaughter. The youngster did his share to help in the pennant drive, batting .426 in a dozen contests, but St. Louis fell short by 2½ games to Brooklyn.

The quiet rookie's first full big league season started slowly, and St. Louis manager Billy Southworth began using his future superstar only against right-handed pitchers. But soon Musial broke out of his doldrums and began bashing the ball to all parts of the field.

"The Donora Greyhound" ended up hitting .315 in 1942, only three points behind teammate Slaughter, and good for third in the league. The Cardinal rookie was also third in the NL in triples with 10 and fourth in slugging at .490. The '42 edition was one of the best Redbird teams ever, as illustrated by its 4–1 World Series win over the fearsome Yankees. Musial later called it the greatest Series in which he ever played. The young outfielder drove in the winning run in Game 2, and was instrumental defensively in the Series, robbing Joe Gordon of a home run in the seventh inning of the third game, which St. Louis won 2–0.

At 21 years of age, Musial's brilliant career was off to an impressive start. He would accomplish even more in the ensuing seasons, including winning his second and third MVP awards before the decade was complete.

Top 5 MVP Vote-Getters

1. Stan Musial, St. Louis — 267
2. Walker Cooper, St. Louis — 192
3. Bill Nicholson, Chicago — 181
4. Billy Herman, Brooklyn — 140
5. Mort Cooper, St. Louis — 130

1943 AMERICAN LEAGUE — SPUD CHANDLER

Spurgeon Ferdinand Chandler
B. September 12, 1907, Commerce, Georgia
D. January 9, 1990, South Pasadena, Florida

Year	Team	Games	W	L	ERA	IP	SO	BB	ShO
1943	NY AL	30	20	4	1.64	253	134	54	5

The Season

Despite losing stalwarts Joe DiMaggio, Phil Rizzuto and Tommy Heinrich to the military, the Yankees won their third consecutive pennant, this time going 98–56 to beat out a surprising Washington Senator squad by 13½ games. It was the irrepressible Joe McCarthy's eighth and final title as New York's skipper.

Bill Dickey, the Bronx Bombers' elder statesman at age 36, filled an important part-time role for his team, hitting .351 and helping guide Yankee pitchers to the American League ERA team title.

Revenge was sweet for the Yankees in the World Series, as they vanquished the St. Louis Cardinals four games to one, reversing the outcome of the previous fall classic. Dickey was the Series batting star, leading both clubs in RBIs and striking the deciding blow in the clincher, a two-run homer.

Some of the best moves made by Boston player-manager Joe Cronin this season were inserting himself into the lineup as a pinch-hitter. In a three-day period, Cronin slammed three three-run pinch-hit home runs, including two during a June 17 double-header. He wound up setting an AL record with five pinch-hit homers for the year.

In the first-ever night All-Star Game, the AL was a 5–3 winner at Philadelphia's Shibe Park July 13, thanks to a three-run homer by Boston's Bobby Doerr. The fans at Shibe had little else to cheer about this season, as their A's tied a junior circuit record for futility with 20 consecutive losses.

Persistence Pays Off

It was a long, hard climb to the top for the resolute Spud Chandler, but once he reached his destination, the Yankee ace became one of the toughest pitchers to beat in the history of baseball.

Chandler's sights were firmly set on being a Yankee from the time he was a youngster. He spent an unusually long apprenticeship in that club's farm system before finally reaching the majors, but it was well worth the wait.

Everything came together for the enduring right-hander in 1943. At age 36, when most ballplayers are winding down their careers, Chandler blossomed into the league MVP. He was the Yanks' most dependable hurler that year (20–4), tossing a yeoman-like 253 innings for the World Champions and never allowing more than four runs in a game. There had never been a Yankee pitcher named MVP before Chandler, and there has not been one since.

One of the oldest American League players to claim the MVP, he racked up league bests in wins, ERA (1.64), winning percentage (.833), complete games (20) and shutouts (five). Chandler was the first AL pitcher since Lefty Grove to nab the MVP. His dual win of the ERA and winning percentage titles made him only the fourth moundsman to top both categories in one season.

After toiling 5½ years in the minors, Spud joined the team of his dreams in 1937 as a 29-year-old rookie. In his first start, he fired a four-hitter at the White Sox, but was blanked 1–0. Chandler saw limited action that campaign, as the pitching-strong Yankees romped to the pennant and World Series

crowns. His first good year came in 1938 when he went 14–5, and the Yanks cruised to another World Championship.

Strictly a spot starter the next two seasons, Spud compiled a combined 11–7 record with few opportunities for greatness. Time seemed to be passing the veteran by, and at age 33 he wondered apprehensively whether he would ever get a true shot at the starting rotation.

The answer came the following year. Chandler had worked earnestly all spring on a new pitch, a slider that he perfected in a remarkably short time. Spud started 20 games in 1941, compiling a 10–4 record and a 3.19 ERA, plus four saves. The Yankees won 101 games and the pennant, and after having watched the team's four previous World Series from the bench, Chandler made his first post-season appearance. Unfortunately, an unearned run off Chandler in Game 2 led to a 3–2 loss, the only Yankee defeat in the Series win over Brooklyn.

New York won the AL flag again in 1942, the veteran Chandler reaching the 200 mark in innings pitched for the first time and posting a sparkling 16–5 record. He was among the league leaders in win percentage (.762), ERA (2.38) and wins that season, but as luck would have it, was out-dueled in his only World Series start, despite giving up only three hits and one run.

Chandler's rise to the majors was a long time coming following his days at the University of Georgia, from which he graduated with a bachelor of science degree. Set on wearing the Yankee emblem, he turned down offers from the Cardinals and Cubs, finally signing for less money when the Yankees came

Spud Chandler. (Courtesy New York Yankees.)

calling. Although his minor league record was excellent, Chandler had to toil longer than usual before being promoted to the parent club, due to the Yankees' pitching depth.

The 6-foot, 181-pound hurler finally made the big time in 1937. While hardly overwhelming with his fastball, he displayed superb control and an enviable propensity for keeping the ball low. Known for his vehement intensity, Chandler was an alarming presence in the locker room prior to a start. He would mentally work himself into a lather, then carry that calculated ire to the mound. Spud referred to his wrathful pitching persona as "outward determination."

After his magnificent MVP year in 1943, Chandler was drafted into the military. But at age 39, he triumphantly returned to regain his position as the Yankees' "Angry Ace," posting a 20–8 record in 1946. The following year, the Yankees were turning to youth, and the 40-year-old saw action only in spot assignments. In only 17 appearances, he registered a 9–5 record, and surprised the Yankee brass by leading the circuit in ERA with a 2.46 mark. He was relegated to the bullpen in the seven-game World Series victory over Brooklyn, and limited to a couple of ineffective innings in Game 3.

It was time to call it a career, and he did so as a champion. Despite reaching the majors at an advanced age and losing two years to the war, Chan-

dler had tallied 1,485 innings in 11 seasons, fashioning a 109–43 record and an excellent 2.84 ERA. He never had a losing season while posting a .717 lifetime winning percentage.

Chandler's stamina, the hallmark of his career, was on display for all to see in his final start of the 1943 regular season, when he worked 14 innings to best the Washington Senators 2–1 for his 20th win. The grim righty frequently helped his own cause, producing his highest batting average during his MVP year by hitting .258. His 1943 heroics continued in the World Series, where he notched the only two Series wins of his career, both complete-game gems, and held the Cardinals to one earned run in 18 frames.

Spud became a Yankee scout upon his retirement, but lost patience with the organization and quit when his pleas to sign Herb Score and Frank Lary — who together won 41 games in 1956 — went unheeded.

Chandler's is an amazing story among MVPs. His was a lengthy, arduous haul to the summit, and a steady pursuit of greatness that continued long after less-motivated men would have given up. But as his brilliant winning percentage indicates, Spud Chandler just would not be beaten.

Top 5 MVP Vote-Getters

1. Spud Chandler, New York — 246
2. Luke Appling, Chicago — 215
3. Rudy York, Detroit — 152
4. Billy Johnson, New York — 135
5. Bob Johnson, Washington — 116

1944 NATIONAL LEAGUE — MARTY MARION

Martin Whiteford Marion
B. December 1, 1917, Richburg, South Carolina

Year	Team	Games	AB	Hits	Avg.	HR	RBI	Runs	SB
1944	SL NL	144	506	135	.267	6	63	50	1

The Season

By 1944, the St. Louis Cardinals were the only major league team still exhibiting pre-war talent. Manager Billy Southworth effortlessly steered his gifted club to a 105-win season and its third straight pennant. While other teams were being ravaged by the military draft, the Redbirds could still dip into their vast farm system and pluck out a Ted Wilks, who in 1944 went 17–4.

The New York Giants also feted an exciting rookie pitcher in "Big Bill" Voiselle, who notched a 21–16 mark. Meanwhile, the Cincinnati Reds trotted out Joe Nuxhall, who in his brief stay became the youngest player (15 years, 10 months) ever to appear in the majors.

Under new ownership, the Phillies changed their nickname to Blue Jays following a fan contest. But the club couldn't chirp its way out of last place in 1944 or '45, and went back to Phillies for the 1946 season.

St. Louis fans had a glorious time in 1944. Not only did the Cardinals romp to another pennant, but in the American League, the usually punchless St. Louis Browns captured their only flag to assure a hometown World Series. Sportsman's Park was the site of all the Series games, and the event took on added dimensions when it was discovered that rival managers Southworth and Luke Sewell shared the same St. Louis apartment.

The Browns, a scrappy group of veterans, shocked the baseball world by winning two of the first three World Series games. But the favored Cardinals regained their composure to triumph in six.

In a 19-day span, Boston knuckleball pitcher Jim Tobin was involved in two no-hitters, but if anyone tells you he witnessed either of them, ask for a ticket stub. Tobin homered and no-hit Brooklyn April 27 in front of fewer than 2,000 fans at Braves Field, then was beaten 1–0 May 15 by Cincinnati's Clyde Shoun, who tossed a no-hitter before just over 1,000 spectators.

Not to be outdone, Tobin teammate Red Barrett set a major league record August 10 when he needed only 58 pitches to win a nine-inning game against Cincinnati. The 2–0 Braves win was the shortest night game ever at one hour, 15 minutes.

Mr. Shortstop

Luis Aparicio, Rabbit Maranville, Roy McMillan, Phil Rizzuto, Pee Wee Reese, Mark Belanger, Ozzie Smith, Omar Vizquel and various others were magicians at the shortstop position. But one, and only one, bore the distinctive title "Mr. Shortstop." His name was Marty Marion, a defensive wizard who anchored the infields of some of the most celebrated St. Louis Cardinal teams in history.

Marion was the first player selected MVP by baseball's writers solely on the strength of his fielding ability. Marion was the initial shortstop to be earmarked "most valuable," and his intangible contributions to the 1944 World Championship transcended the usual set of hitting statistics tallied by many other winners of the award.

The fifth-year man was the spectacular constant of the Redbird infield that season and many others, playing 144 games steadily, often brilliantly. He became the sixth St. Louis Cardinal to earn the MVP in 14 years of the award, edging Bill Nicholson of Chicago by one point in the voting despite "Swish's"

National League bests in home runs (33), RBIs (122) and total bases (317).

The Cardinals finished 105–49 in 1944, 14½ games in front of their closest adversaries. A major portion of St. Louis' success story belongs to Marion, who was not only extraordinary afield, but was also the most productive shortstop in the National League with the bat, driving in 63 runs. Besides wowing the St. Louis faithful with his fielding, he hit .267, four points higher than his lifetime mark.

Although the 26-year-old managed only a .227 World Series average following his MVP campaign, his prowess with the glove was painfully apparent to the St. Louis Browns. In Game 4, his tentacles snared a ground ball over second base, turning a sure-fire base hit into a fancy double play that took the heart out of a promising Browns rally. The Cards won that game 5–1 to even the Series at two games apiece.

"Slats" was hardly a total washout with the bat, exceeding the old axiom that an excellent fielding middleman need only hit .250 to justify his presence in a lineup. Marion carried a career .263 average, and six times went over the .270 mark, twice driving in 70 or more runs.

In his rookie year of 1940, the 22-year-old became a starter and hit .278. Over the next three seasons, Marion batted .252, .276 and .280, with the team winning two pennants and a World Championship. Marty's exploits captured the hearts of fans, as he led the league in assists in 1941, topped the circuit in doubles (38) in 1942 and won a starting spot on the All-Star Team in 1943.

It was his infield play that most electrified onlookers. "The Octopus" could routinely go deep in the hole between short and third to shoot down opposing hitters on their way to first. Extremely agile for a 6-foot-2 man, Marion was the antithesis of the small-but-quick shortstop, using his gangly build to utmost advantage.

Three times he topped the senior circuit in fielding percentage, and twice led in assists, putouts and double plays. His most impressive years with the glove came in 1946 and '47 when he bested all shortstops in putouts and double plays, and made the All-Star squad both times. In the latter season, he registered his finest marks, driving in 74 runs with a .272 average.

The Cardinals won another World Championship in 1946, and in '47 Marty helped put together major league baseball's first pension package for players, proposing the original plan and serving as NL representative.

He again headed all shortstops in fielding in 1948, hit .252 and scored a career-high 70 runs. Mr. Shortstop was selected to the All-Star Team once more, but begged off due to a recurring back problem that plagued him throughout the season.

The same childhood knee injury that had kept him out of World War II was beginning to take its toll on Mar-ion, and would shorten his career. In 1949, he was limited to 134 games, and by 1950, he appeared in only 106 contests. The latter year saw Marion play in his final All-Star Game. Except for a few outings as a player when he managed the Browns in 1952 and '53, Marion was through as a regular.

The knee injury can be traced to age 9 when Marty fell and shattered his right leg and thigh. Subsequent operations left his right leg one inch shorter than his left, and although those who saw him skim across the dirt to snatch a ground ball might not believe it, the out-of-kilter alignment wreaked havoc on his back muscles and made it difficult for him to bend as the years wore on.

Considering those medical circumstances, it's a wonder Marion made it to the big leagues at all. His first opportunity came with Chattanooga, an affiliate of the Washington Senators. His brother, Red, who later played briefly in the majors, gained a tryout for Marty, and the Senators immediately signed him. But owner Calvin Griffith unwisely vetoed the pact, and the younger Marion soon landed in the Cardinals' system, his career a jewel in St. Louis baseball history.

Marion last wore a major league uniform in 1956 when he managed the Chicago White Sox to a second consecutive third-place finish, following two campaigns at the helm of the Browns and one guiding the Cardinals. Marion never tasted a piece of the first-place pie as a skipper, but his magnificent solidity as a player and the three World Championship teams he played on assure him a place of esteem.

Like many invaluable glovemen who have secured the game's toughest infield position, Marion has been denied Hall of Fame entrance because of a less than scintillating bat. But with Luis Aparicio, Peewee Reese and Phil Rizzuto breaking the shortstop logjam into the Hall, can Marty Marion be far behind?

Top 5 MVP Vote-Getters

1. Marty Marion, St. Louis — 190
2. Bill Nicholson, Chicago — 189
3. Dixie Walker, Brooklyn — 145
4. Stan Musial, St. Louis — 136
5. Bill Voiselle, New York — 107
5. Bucky Walters, Cincinnati — 107

1944 AMERICAN LEAGUE — HAL NEWHOUSER

Harold Newhouser
B. May 20, 1921, Detroit, Michigan
D. November 10, 1998, Detroit, Michigan

Year	Team	Games	W	L	ERA	IP	SO	BB	ShO
1944	Det AL	47	29	9	2.22	312.1	187	102	6

The Season

President Franklin Delano Roosevelt campaigning for a fourth term in 1944 was not surprising, but the St. Louis Browns winning the pennant was a shock. The Browns, who edged Detroit by one game, swept their final four-game series with the Yankees, taking the clincher 5–2 on a pair of two-run homers by Chet Laabs in front of their first sellout crowd since 1925.

Although St. Louis' George McQuinn was the top World Series hitter with a .438 mark, and Browns pitchers had a composite ERA of 1.49, the Cardinals took advantage of 10 Browns errors to win the "streetcar series" in six games. It was the Browns' one-and-only World Series appearance, and the first-ever fall classic in which all games were played west of the Mississippi River.

The flamboyant Dizzy Dean was scheduled to announce the Series on

Hal Newhouser. (Courtesy Detroit Tigers.)

plishments of players whose greatest successes were achieved in the early to mid–1940s when many of the game's stars were serving their country in World War II. The theory is a logical one, and probably applies to a vast majority of the flash-in-the-pan celebrities.

But Hal Newhouser, whose three choicest years were 1944–46, was not an overnight sensation, nor a mouse who played only while the cats were away. Unfortunately, he is often incorrectly included in those ranks. Immaturity and attitude problems kept Newhouser from reaching his glowing potential prior to the war, while severe bursitis in his left shoulder prevented him from continuing his brilliance past his late 20s. The fact of the matter is, Hal displayed a legitimate claim to upper-class status in 1946, when the best players were back from the war, by again dominating American League pitchers and recording his third consecutive 25-plus-win season.

After four big league campaigns ranging from mediocre to poor, Newhouser came into his own in 1944 on the way to becoming the league's finest war-years pitcher. "Prince Hal," who was classified 4-F because of a heart ailment, amazingly won 29 games that season, while losing only nine and posting a 2.22 ERA. His win and strikeout (187) totals topped the circuit, and if it weren't for teammate Dizzy Trout, Newhouser would have also been the leader in ERA, shutouts (six), complete games (25) and innings pitched (312). His splendid performance resulted in the first of two con-

secutive Most Valuable Player awards, edging Trout by four points.

Trout and Newhouser were a deadly force in '44, combining for 56 victories, the most by a pair of teammates since 1908. Despite their prowess, the Tigers were edged by one game in the pennant race by the surprising St. Louis Browns.

Twenty-three years earlier, Harold Newhouser had been born into a poor Detroit family, but by age 16 had made a name for himself, bedeviling American Legion hitters with a fine assortment of blazing fastballs and wicked curves. Hal tossed two no-hitters while winning 15 straight games in 1937, then added three more no-hit gems while recording 19 victories in a row the following season.

A rule prohibiting professional contact with Legion players kept big league scouts at bay. But following the '38 campaign, Detroit Tigers scout Aloysius J. "Wish" Egan visited the Newhouser home, laying several $100 bills in front of Hal and his father before driving away with a signed contract.

The Newhousers' elation lasted only a couple of hours, however. Shortly after Egan's departure, Cleveland General Manager Cy Slapnicka, accompanied by star pitcher Bob Feller, arrived at the Newhouser residence, offering Hal $15,000 in cash and a $4,000 car to ink an Indians pact. Despite the disparity in offers, the left-handed hurler said later he felt he'd done the right thing by signing with his hometown team.

Newhouser was a brooder and sulker during his first five years of professional baseball, earning a loner's reputation. Although Hal turned himself around both professionally and personally in 1944, he continued to carry an image of gruffness, reinforced by icy glares toward hitters with the audacity to rip his pitches.

The Tigers sent Newhouser to Alexandria of the Evangeline League in 1939, but he outgrew it quickly, advancing to Beaumont of the Texas League. The wild southpaw had a shabby 5–14 record there, but many of his losses were by one or two runs, earning him the nickname "Hard-luck

nationwide radio, but Judge Kenesaw Mountain Landis nixed the idea, based on Dean's "unprofessional" on-air demeanor and creative use of grammar. Landis, who had been baseball's czar since 1920, passed away in November due to coronary thrombosis at age 78.

The war was taking its toll, as evidenced by only 40 percent of those players who'd started the 1941 campaign still being active in '44. On June 6, all games were cancelled as the nation held its breath while allied forces invaded occupied France. Later that month, the Yankees, Dodgers and Giants gathered at the Polo Grounds to play a six-inning exhibition in front of 50,000 people, raising money for war bonds.

The Browns' Nelson Potter, who would win 19 games this season, became the first pitcher suspended for throwing a spitball.

Newhouser's New Image

A natural tendency among baseball historians is to belittle the accom-

Hal." Detroit called him up at the tail end of the season, and he wore a Tiger uniform for the next 14 years.

From 1940 to 1943, Newhouser not only lost 17 more games than he won, with an earned run average in the 3.75 range, but also had as difficult a time controlling his temper as he did his curve ball. Fielding miscues by teammates sent his temperature soaring, as did a lack of supportive hitting. That, combined with frustration from issuing nearly six walks every nine innings, made Newhouser irritable and unpleasant. When he requested a trade following the '43 season, teammates and Detroit fans were hoping he'd be accommodated.

Sensing a diamond in the rough,

Tiger General Manager Jack Zeller held onto Newhouser, while recently acquired catcher Paul Richards and manager Steve O'Neill began the often tedious but eventually rewarding task of honing the rough-edged hurler. During the winter of 1943 and spring of '44, the goodwill ambassadors convinced Hal that an attitude adjustment might bring about a change of fortunes.

Determined to shed his crusty outer skin, Newhouser went into the 1944 season a changed man. And while the competition was admittedly weakened by the draft, the resultant effects of his new image were crystal clear on paper and in the eyes of teammates who played with a renewed gusto behind him.

With a 29–9 season under his belt in 1944, and sporting a fresh disposition that would carry over into the following year, the suddenly effective lefty anticipated continued success in '45, when he would gain his second consecutive MVP honor.

Top 5 MVP Vote-Getters

1. Hal Newhouser, Detroit — 236
2. Dizzy Trout, Detroit — 232
3. Vern Stephens, St. Louis — 193
4. Snuffy Stirnweiss, New York — 129
5. Dick Wakefield, Detroit — 128

1945 National League — Phil Cavarretta

Philip Joseph Cavarretta
B. July 19, 1916, Chicago, Illinois

Year	Team	Games	AB	Hits	Avg.	HR	RBI	Runs	SB
1945	Chi NL	132	498	177	.355	6	97	94	5

The Season

Little did Chicago Cubs fans who celebrated a 1945 National League pennant realize what significance the first-place finish held. The Cubbies would not win another title of any kind until 1984, and 57 years later they still had not returned to the World Series.

Chicago's pitching staff was the finest in the senior circuit, featuring solid starters in Hank Wyse, Claude Passeau, Paul Derringer and Ray Prim. Additionally, the Cubs gained the services of ex-Yankee ace Hank Borowy for $100,000 for the final two months of the season when the righty miraculously cleared waivers in the American League. Borowy went on to post an 11–2 Cub record in the pennant stretch, the team winning the NL title by three games.

The World Series, captured by the

Detroit Tigers in seven games, was preceded by a war-year's assessment of the talent of the two pennant winners by Chicago sportswriter Warren Brown. "I don't think either of them can win," he wryly observed. He was almost right.

Other noteworthy events this season included a modern-day, NL-record 37-game hitting streak by Boston Brave Tommy Holmes, who is the only major leaguer ever to lead his league in both fewest strikeouts (nine) and most home runs (28) in the same season. Brooklyn shortstop Tommy Brown became the youngest major league player to hit a home run when the 17-year-old teed off on Pittsburgh's Preacher Roe August 20. Earlier in the month, New York's Mel Ott clobbered the 500th home run of his career.

On August 28, Brooklyn Dodgers General Manager Branch Rickey held a private meeting with Jackie Robinson,

the results of which would soon shake the very foundation of the game. Following the season, Rickey announced the controversial signing of the African-American ballplayer.

Favorite Son

The last MVP link Chicago Cubs fans have had with a pennant winner was longtime local favorite Phil Cavarretta, who hit the mother lode in 1945 and experienced a year that far surpassed any other in his distinctive 22-season career. A dependable .293 lifetime hitter, Cavarretta soared to .355 for the flag-winning Cubs.

Nineteen-forty-five was Phil's 11th full season in the majors, and besides leading the National League with a towering average and an impressive on-base percentage (.449), the slick-swinging left-hander established single-year bests in RBIs (97) and slugging percentage (.500, good for third in the league), while providing excellent glovework at first base and in the outfield. The Chicago team was built around the grim-faced hustler, and Cavarretta delivered consistently in the Cubs' last pennant campaign. The MVP voting saw him garner 15 of a possible 24 first-place votes, making the Cubs captain an easy victor over Boston Brave Tommy Holmes, despite the latter's NL highs in five offensive categories.

Phil's popularity with Windy City fans belied a gruff personality that was forthright but oftentimes undiplomatic. Workmanlike performances over an elongated stretch were what endeared him to Chicagoans. He was a tough competitor who, except for his incredible MVP campaign, usually averaged from .270 to .290.

Originally attempting to make the big time as a southpaw pitcher, he was converted to an everyday player by Cubs manager Charlie Grimm, who brought him up for seven games in 1934. The 18-year-old hit .381 in that short stay, and Grimm promptly replaced himself at first base with Cavarretta to start the 1935 season. "Jolly Charlie" christened him "Philibuck" because it sounded like a tough name for the hard-nosed youngster, and Cavarretta answered with an excellent rookie campaign, hitting .275 with 82 RBIs in a pennant year.

But Phil would not be as productive again until 1943. In the interval, he hit between .270 and .286 (except for an uncharacteristic .239 in 1938), and moved in and out of the Cubs lineup, switching between first base and the outfield.

Finally, at age 27, Cavarretta found a home at first base, playing in 143 games and batting .291. He followed that performance with a .321 mark in 1944, topping the league with 197 hits and gradually building for his full MVP assault in 1945.

At 5-foot-11½ and 175 pounds, Cavarretta rarely hit for power, yet drove in 920 runners while flirting with a lifetime .300 average. He holds the unusual distinction of spoiling three late-game no-hitters, and on six occasions stroked five or more hits in a single contest. In three World Series (1935, 1938 and 1945), he compiled a .317 batting average. A four-time All-Star selection, he holds the All-Star Game record for consecutive times reaching base in one game at five (triple, single, three walks), in the 1944 summer classic.

Cavarretta's incredible longevity makes him the answer to an interesting trivia question: Who is the only player to be on a major league roster at the same time as the two greatest home run hitters of all time — Babe Ruth and Hank Aaron?

Phil served a 2½-year hitch as player-manager of the Cubs beginning in mid–1951. With the team floundering, owner P.K. Wrigley hoped Cavvy's desire would prove infectious to the players, but the club still finished last. Cavarretta provided one of the few Cub highlights, inserting himself as a pinch-hitter in a 4–4 contest and blasting a game-winning grand slam against Phillies ace Robin Roberts.

The Cubs rose to fifth place under Phil's leadership in 1952, but plummeted to seventh in 1953. Immediately prior to the 1954 season, Cavarretta prophesied to Wrigley that new directions had to be taken or the team would be a long time reaching respectability. The remarks cost Phil his job. Undaunted, he changed Chicago uniforms and hit .316 in a part-time role with the White Sox, then retired early in 1955.

Born in 1916 in Chicago, the first-generation Italian was a baseball fanatic from the time he could lift a bat. Cavarretta was a Cub worshipper who starred as a pitcher at Lane Tech High School. In a Cub tryout, he hit the first pitch thrown to him out of the park. Signed out of high school by his favorite team, he made the majors within three months, slamming a game-winning four-bagger in his initial contest.

Eleven years later, at age 29, Cavarretta was not only the Cubs' best performer, but the most valuable in the NL as well. Phil's hot bat paced the Cubs through a tough 1945 pennant race and helped break a three-year, first-place stranglehold by St. Louis. The Cubs lost the World Series in seven games to the Tigers, but Cavarretta led all hitters with a .423 average while contributing 11 hits, seven runs and five RBIs.

With dreams of returning to the fall classic as a manager, Phil labored as a minor league skipper for 11 years following his playing days, but never received another major league shot as head man. He did come back as a coach for four campaigns, served one season as a scout and finally became a batting instructor for the New York Mets during their 1973 pennant year.

Cavarretta's proletarian execution as a ballplayer was highly esteemed over the long haul by Chicago fans, and for one fleeting season the entire National League saw firsthand why Cub backers held this blue collar worker in such high regard.

Top 5 MVP Vote-Getters

1. Phil Cavarretta, Chicago — 279
2. Tommy Holmes, Boston — 175
3. Red Barrett, Boston/St. Louis — 151
4. Andy Pafko, Chicago — 131
5. Whitey Kurowski, St. Louis — 90

1945 American League — Hal Newhouser

Harold Newhouser
B. May 20, 1921, Detroit, Michigan
D. November 10, 1998, Detroit, Michigan

Year	Team	Games	W	L	ERA	IP	SO	BB	ShO
1945	Det AL	40	25	9	1.81	313.1	212	110	8

The Season

At no time was the depletion of baseball talent more obvious than in the war year of 1945 when the American League employed a one-armed outfielder and a one-legged pitcher.

Having lost his right arm at age 6, Pete Gray put his handicap behind him, rose through the minor league ranks and made the St. Louis Browns squad, though he hit only .218 in his only big league season. An Air Force serviceman who'd lost his right leg in a plane crash, Bert Shepard pitched one game for the Senators with the aid of an artificial limb.

Also indicative of the lack of stars, Snuffy Stirnweiss' .309 batting average was the lowest by a league leader since 1905, and his circuit-pacing .476 slugging mark was the weakest since 1919. Boston's David "Boo" Ferriss took advantage of the lack of hitting, setting an AL record by pitching 22 scoreless innings to start the season.

Fans who went to Washington's Griffith Stadium to see the long ball were disappointed. Of the Senators' 27 home runs this season, only one — an inside-the-park homer by Joe Kuhel — came in front of the hometown crowd.

The war also caused the cancellation of the All-Star Game for the first and only time since the summer classic's inception in 1933.

Returning to the United States from his Air Force duties at mid-season, Tigers powerhouse Hank Greenberg belted a grand slam to defeat the Browns on the final day of the season and give Detroit the pennant by 1½ games over Washington. Greenberg then contributed five extra base hits, including a couple of home runs, and seven RBIs in the Tigers' four games-to-three World Series victory over the Cubs.

Prior to the '45 campaign, Kentucky Senator Albert Benjamin "Happy" Chandler was named Commissioner following the death of Judge Kenesaw Mountain Landis the preceding fall.

Hungry Hal Repeats

Once Hal Newhouser had experienced the sweet taste of success in 1944, he ravenously went after more of the same. In 1945, when more than half of the major leaguers from '43 were in the military, Newhouser became the first player to win back-to-back Most Valuable Player awards since Jimmie Foxx (1932–33). Hal is still the only American League pitcher to capture the coveted prize more than once.

Newhouser won 207 games with a lifetime ERA of 3.06 in a 17-year career, recording 33 shutouts. When he was on the hill, the bullpen usually took the day off. Twice the durable southpaw led the AL in complete games, and four times he was runner-up.

The thin, sandy-haired moundsman, whose duels with Bob Feller are legendary, neither smoked nor drank, but was known to consume large quantities of food in a sitting. Teammate Dizzy Trout claimed that Hal devoured a five-pound roast one evening. But his appetite for food was overshadowed by his hunger for mound supremacy.

The 1944 MVP competition had been fierce, with Detroit teammates Newhouser and Trout compiling virtually identical statistics. But in 1945, it was all Newhouser. The left-handed pitcher, who combined power with finesse, was overwhelming in the last year of the war, discarding batters like gum wrappers with an easy, fluid motion and varying speeds.

Newhouser was clearly baseball's most proficient hurler in '45, leading the American League in nearly every department. He was the junior circuit's best in wins (25), ERA (1.81), strikeouts (212), shutouts (eight), innings pitched (313.1), complete games (29) and winning percentage (.735). His 36 starts also topped the league.

Although his stunning numbers in 1944 failed to generate a Detroit post-season berth, Newhouser's 1945 performance helped the Tigers win the pennant for the first time in five years. As in the '35 World Series, the Tigers bested the Cubs, with Hal collecting both of his lifetime Series triumphs, including the finale. Despite a 6.10 ERA, he whiffed a record-22 batters in the fall classic, walking only four.

After putting together 54 victories over two seasons, Newhouser still had something to prove in 1946 when many of baseball's greats returned from the war. There was already talk that Hal would dip to his pre-war valley of mediocrity and soon fade from the scene. But "The Prince" would hear none of it. By mid-August, he was 20-4, and ended up pacing the league again in wins with 26 and ERA at an incredible 1.94, while finishing runner-up in win percentage (.743), strikeouts (275), complete games (29) and innings pitched (292).

The sturdy left-hander leveled out at 17-17 with a 2.87 ERA in 1947 when he was named the AL's starting pitcher in the All-Star Game, but came on strong again in '48, pacing the league in wins with 21 and posting a 3.01 earned run average. His 21st triumph came against Bob Feller and Cleveland on the final day of the regular season, forcing the Indians into a one-game playoff against Boston for the league title. Unfortunately, that was also the year Hal's bursitis began to give him trouble; although he won 18 and 15 games the next two years, his ERA jumped to 3.36, then 4.34.

Newhouser, who won exactly 200 games for Detroit, saw his pitching opportunities dwindle in the next few years as the bursitis worsened, with only 22 innings of work in 1953, his last year as a Tiger. But the Indians, who had tried to sign him at age 17, decided he could assist as a reliever, acquiring the 33-year-old for the 1954 season. They were right, as Hal went 7–2 with a 2.51 ERA in fewer than 47

innings, helping the Indians win their first pennant since 1948. Cleveland was heavily favored in the World Series, but the New York Giants surprised with a four-game sweep.

Following retirement, Newhouser took on a vice president's job at a Pontiac, Michigan, bank, but kept his hand in baseball as a scout for the Baltimore Orioles (1956–61) and Cleveland (1961–64). Hal knew how to spot pitchers, as he proved by signing Dean Chance. The Orioles let Chance slip through the expansion draft, however, and the tall right-hander went on to lead the AL in wins with 20 and ERA at 1.65 for the Los Angeles Angels in 1964.

Newhouser became the only Tiger pitcher to enter the Hall of Fame when

the veteran's committee selected him in 1992. Hal passed away in 1998 at the age of 77.

Because Hal Newhouser's most sensational seasons came during the war years, there will always be some who minimize his accomplishments. But those who saw him pitch in his prime are convinced he could have won in any era.

Top 5 MVP Vote-Getters

1. Hal Newhouser, Detroit — 236
2. Eddie Mayo, Detroit — 164
3. Snuffy Stirnweiss, New York — 161
4. Boo Ferriss, Boston — 148
5. George Myatt, Washington — 98

1946 National League — Stan Musial

Stanley Frank Musial
B. November 21, 1920, Donora, Pennsylvania

Year	Team	Games	AB	Hits	Avg.	HR	RBI	Runs	SB
1946	SL NL	156	624	228	.365	16	103	124	7

The Season

From 1942 to 1945, baseball was seriously imperiled by the enemy overseas, as World War II put a dent in the available talent. But by 1946, many players were exchanging their military outfits for baseball uniforms.

Suddenly another foe, this one from the south, threatened to deplete major league resources. Millionaire Jorge Pasquel, in an attempt to create a Mexican baseball league, began enticing the game's stars with large sums of money. Brooklyn Dodgers outfielder and holdout Luis Olmo was the first noteworthy player to be persuaded, signing for $40,000 for three years.

Back in the United States, the Cardinals and rookie manager Eddie Dyer captured their fourth flag in five years, though they needed a two

games-to-nothing victory over Brooklyn in the first-ever major league playoff to determine a pennant winner.

In a fitting climax to the initial post-war season, St. Louis nudged the Boston Red Sox in a seven-game World Series, taking the clincher 4–3 when Enos Slaughter made his famous gallop home from first base on a two-out double by Harry "The Hat" Walker. Cards pitcher Harry Brecheen won three games with a 0.45 ERA.

On April 18, Jackie Robinson became the first black player in organized baseball in the 20th century when he suited up for the Montreal Royals of the International League. Providing a taste of what was to come, Robinson stroked four hits, including a home run, in his debut, and wound up as the league's batting champion (.349).

Cubs pitcher Claude Passeau's

major league-record errorless streak of 273 consecutive chances, dating back to September 21, 1941, came to an end May 20.

More Magic from "The Man"

A stylish, classy leader, Stan Musial provided an unparalleled example of hitting wizardry and baseball smarts during an illustrious 22-year big league career. And while statistics alone do not tell the whole story, they are essential in any attempt to grasp the magnitude of the congenial star's accomplishments.

The lifetime .331 hitter earned seven batting titles and six slugging crowns. He led the National League in doubles eight times; total bases, hits and on-base percentage six times each;

and runs scored and triples on five occasions each. The sturdy outfielder and first baseman played in at least 140 games 14 times, and was the only man to appear in 1,000 games at both positions. He also led the league in fielding three times.

Musial hit .310 or better a sensational 17 times, drove in 100 or more runs in 10 seasons, slapped at least 30 doubles on 16 occasions (with a high of 53 in 1953) and collected 200 or more hits a half-dozen times. He slugged over .500 16 times, reaching .702 in 1948, and scored more than 100 runs in 11 different campaigns. Amazingly, he never struck out more than 46 times in one season.

His record-breaking efforts included most seasons of 100 or more games played, most extra base hits and total bases, and even most homers in a double-header (five). At his retirement in 1963, Musial's NL career marks encompassed most at-bats, runs, hits, doubles and RBIs, and the only player with a more impressive set of lifetime credentials was Ty Cobb.

After spending 1945 in the Navy, Musial wasted little time in 1946 re-establishing himself as the best hitter in the National League, earning his second of three Most Valuable Player trophies and becoming the first NL player to do it at two different positions.

The easy going gentleman was the NL leader in batting (.365), runs (124), total bases (366), slugging (.587), hits (228), doubles (50) and triples (20). He was also third in RBIs with 103 and tied for fifth in homers at 16. "The Man," who had already proven his individual talents, exhibited an unselfish, team-oriented spirit when he willingly agreed to switch from the outfield to first base, where he played 114 games in '46. From then on, Musial split his time between the two positions. Returning to his roots, Stan appeared in one game as a pitcher in 1952.

Prior to the '46 season, Musial, whose salary was a paltry $13,500, was seduced by a $65,000 cash advance and a total of $130,000 for five years by Jorge Pasquel to play in a Mexican baseball league. Floored by the offer, Stan bit his upper lip and turned down the enticement, determined to force the Cards into upping his pay the following season.

Musial's Cardinals finally shook off the resilient Dodgers in '46, defeating them in a playoff for the pennant, then went on to nip the Red Sox in the World Series. Stan hit only .222 in the seven-game set, but topped Series participants with four doubles, and added the same number of RBIs. Appreciating his loyalty and continued fine play, the Cards rewarded Musial with a $31,000 salary for the 1947 season, representing $5,000 more per annum than he would have made in Mexico.

Following his initial MVP effort in 1943, Musial, a pre-war father with a draft deferment, stayed in baseball in 1944 while many of his compatriots were drafted or enlisted. Stanley had a virtually identical season to the one he'd enjoyed the previous year, batting .347 — the third of 16 straight .300 seasons — with 12 homers and 94 RBIs, plus league bests in hits (197), doubles (51), slugging (.549) and on-base percentage (.440).

It was Musial's third full campaign, and for the third straight year the Cardinals made it to the World Series, this time bumping the underdog Browns four games to two. Stan's seven hits tied him for the Series leadership, and he also had a home run and two RBIs, hitting .304 and slugging .522.

With Musial serving his country in World War II as a ship repairman in 1945, the Cards failed to win the pennant, finishing three games behind the Cubs. Stan played some ball in the Navy, both at home and in the South Pacific, and it was during this time that he developed his peekaboo batting stance. His feet close together, the left-hander would curl his body to the point where he'd have to peek over his right shoulder at the pitcher. With the seemingly awkward stance, it was said that Stan resembled a kid peering around a corner to see if the cops were coming.

Although Stan Musial played in World Series in each of his first four full seasons, he would never appear in another. Ironically, the next time the Cardinals returned to the fall classic was in 1964, the year after he retired. But the amiable, egoless star would continue to rewrite the record book in his remaining 17 seasons, with another MVP year still ahead of him.

Top 5 MVP Vote-Getters

1. Stan Musial, St. Louis — 319
2. Dixie Walker, Brooklyn — 159
3. Enos Slaughter, St. Louis — 144
4. Howie Pollet, St. Louis — 116
5. Johnny Sain, Boston — 95

1946 AMERICAN LEAGUE — TED WILLIAMS

Theodore Samuel Williams
B. August 30, 1918, San Diego, California
D. July 5, 2002, Inverness, Florida

Year	Team	Games	AB	Hits	Avg.	HR	RBI	Runs	SB
1946	Bos AL	150	514	176	.342	38	123	142	0

The Season

The return of war-year heroes to American League clubs helped boost attendance to an all-time high, as the junior circuit turnstyles clicked to the tune of 9,621,182 fans in 1946.

Easy victors in the AL were the Boston Red Sox, with a 104–50 record and 12-game margin over the runner-up Detroit Tigers. Although Boston made the flag fight less than exciting, the thrill of the long ball returned to the American League as home runs zoomed from 430 to 653, thanks largely to the returning legion of power hitters.

The Red Sox possessed a pleasing blend of hitting (league-leading .271 average) and run scoring (792, the best in baseball), in addition to the top fielding average in the AL. Despite being heavy World Series favorites, Boston lost a seven-game thriller to the St. Louis Cardinals.

Other American League highlights included a surprising batting title by Washington's Mickey Vernon (.353) and a not-so-unexpected no-hitter by Bob Feller, his second. Feller struck out 348 batters this season to apparently break the major league record set in 1904 by Philadelphia A's pitcher Rube Waddell, but baseball historians eventually raised Waddell's total from 346 to 349.

Only two years prior to his MVP season, Cleveland's Lou Boudreau established a big league record with five extra base hits in a game July 14 versus Boston, a mark that would not be matched for 24 years.

Finally — The Thumper

He was the most prolific hitter of his era. Ted Williams, a picture of perfection at the plate, powered baseballs for average as well as home runs, leading the league in both categories a combined 10 times. He drove scathing line drives over and through absurd-looking defensive shifts designed solely to stop him, but the pull-hitter was rarely halted. When all else failed, the opposition merely walked him, giving Teddy the highest on-base percentage in the game's history. In sheer popularity, he bowed to the other titanic American League figure of the time, Joe DiMaggio; but for pure ability to swat the white sphere, Williams was second to no man.

Nineteen-forty-six was not the best season Williams had experienced in his career, but the circumstances were finally ripe for his first MVP award. Williams had astonished all with a .406 average in 1941, and followed with a Triple Crown campaign the next season. But the MVPs went to pennant-winning Yankees DiMaggio and Joe Gordon.

It was the 28-year-old's first campaign since the war, his initial appearance in three years, and Williams started 1946 with a crack of thunder, smashing a 400-foot homer on opening day. By season's end, he had racked up league-leading totals in slugging (.667), walks (156), total bases (343), runs (142) and on-base percentage (.497). His .342 average was second in the league, as were his 38 homers and 123 RBIs. In the All-Star Game that year, he had the single-best mid-season affair ever with two homers and a pair of singles, one round-tripper coming off Rip Sewell's celebrated blooper pitch.

This was the season Ted first confronted the "Williams Shift," devised by Cleveland Indians player-manager and future MVP Lou Boudreau. After Williams had annihilated the Indians with three home runs and a single in the first game of a July twin bill, Boudreau placed all but his third baseman and left fielder on the right side of the diamond. One week later, Williams went 3-for-4 in the first game of a double-header against St. Louis, then hit for the cycle in the nightcap to reach seven consecutive safeties in one day.

The strategy, soon adopted by every AL club, seemed to finally catch up to Ted in the last month of 1946. With Boston already assured of a pennant, "The Lord of Fenway" hit only .250 in September and lost his leads in all three Triple Crown categories. Still, he managed some degree of satisfaction by clinching the pennant with an inside-the-park home run to the vacated left field area. When asked later if it was the easiest home run he'd ever hit, Williams responded, "Hell, no. It was the hardest I ever had to run."

"The Kid" entered his first and only World Series with a badly bruised right elbow, courtesy of an exhibition game errant pitch. He failed miserably in a seven-game loss to the St. Louis Cardinals, hitting only .200 with no extra base hits and one RBI, and the Beantown writers burned him for his ineffectiveness.

Williams' harsh treatment by Boston's scribes was as frequent as his lusty line drives, and can be traced to the slugger's antagonistic personality. Opinionated, explosive in temperament and wrathful to all who would upset his single-minded purposefulness on the diamond, the 6-foot-4, 198-pounder lashed back repeatedly at his press box foes. Occasionally, he'd get into it with the fans as well. In fact, he was fined $5,000 by the Red Sox for spitting at Boston fans who booed him August 7, 1956, after he misplayed a

Ted Williams. (National Baseball Hall of Fame Library, Cooperstown, N.Y.)

windblown fly ball off the bat of Mickey Mantle.

Ted's first unsavory taste of adversity came in 1938 when he joined Boston in spring training. Despite demonstrating that he was capable of handling big league pitching, a cocky demeanor earned him a ticket to the Red Sox farm team in Minneapolis. The 20-year-old had no control over his famous temper and showed little interest in base running or fielding. During a game he would be seen absentmindedly practicing his swing with an imaginary bat in the outfield. But by 1939, those mythical strokes were stinging American League pitching in earnest for a sensational .327 rookie average, with 31 homers and a league-leading 145 RBIs.

The league's freshman phenomenon continued his barrage the next campaign with a .344 effort and a league-best 134 runs, and by 1941 he set upon junior circuit hurlers for his legendary .406 season. Hitting .39955 going into the last day of the year, the 23-year-old refused manager Joe Cronin's offer to sit on the bench and thus have the average rounded into the magical .400 by statisticians. "The Splendid Splinter" proceeded to go 6-for-8 in the double-header. Yet, there was no MVP for the curly-haired slugger in '41, despite additional AL highs in homers (37), slugging (.735), runs (135) and walks (145). This was the year of DiMaggio's 56-game hitting streak, and the Yankee Clipper was voted the award.

In 1942, Ted "slipped" to a league-leading .356 average with other top league marks in home runs (36), RBIs (137), slugging (.648), runs (141) and walks (145). But in an obvious vote against Williams, New York second baseman Joe Gordon outpolled the player who was clearly head and shoulders above his competition. In 1943, Williams was drafted into the Marines for a World War II hitch. He lost three prime years to the war effort, then two more during the Korean conflict when Uncle Sam called again.

This second stint was the unkindest cut of all. Ted was 34 when drafted in 1952, and he justly bemoaned his age, the fact that he had already served his country and his status as the sole provider for his family. Purportedly an excellent pilot, Williams flew 39 missions over Korea, nearly perishing during a crash landing, and suffering a permanent hearing impairment.

His lofty goal as a Southern California youth was to be the greatest hitter who ever lived, and these five years in the military all but ended that dream. It has been said that Williams existed for his next turn in the batter's box. As a child, he was passionately in love with baseball, and most especially with the science of hitting. Ted took advantage of the sunny California skies, spending every spare moment hefting a bat.

Following a stellar high school career, he joined the San Diego Padres in the Pacific Coast League at age 17, and hit .271, then .290 with 23 home runs the next season. The Red Sox signed him to a major league contract in 1937, and in his last minor league effort, Williams copped the Triple Crown.

With visions of an unlimited future, Williams advanced to the majors. In five prodigious campaigns, "The Thumper" established himself as baseball's offensive sovereign, and by 1946 was on the verge of entering a three-year period he would later deem "hellaciously exciting," but the most disappointing of his majestic career.

Top 5 MVP Vote-Getters

1. Ted Williams, Boston — 224
2. Hal Newhouser, Detroit — 197
3. Bobby Doerr, Boston — 158
4. Johnny Pesky, Boston — 141
5. Mickey Vernon, Washington — 134

1947 NATIONAL LEAGUE—BOB ELLIOTT

Robert Irving Elliott
B. November 26, 1916, San Francisco, California
D. May 4, 1966, San Diego, California

Year	Team	Games	AB	Hits	Avg.	HR	RBI	Runs	SB
1947	Bos NL	150	555	176	.317	22	113	93	3

The Season

Possibly the most controversial season in history, 1947 featured the suspension of a manager, a bitter World Series rivalry and the advent of the black player in major league baseball. Brooklyn Dodgers owner Branch Rickey forever changed the course of baseball when he brought Jack Roosevelt Robinson to the majors.

Several St. Louis Cardinal players tried to organize a league-wide strike early in the campaign to protest Robinson's presence in the previously all-white major leagues. But National League President Ford Frick laid down the law, threatening suspensions for any players participating in such a walkout. Robinson wound up leading the NL in stolen bases and placing second in runs on his way to earning baseball's recently established Rookie of the Year award.

Immediately prior to the '47 campaign, Brooklyn manager Leo Durocher was ousted for one year by Commissioner "Happy" Chandler for "conduct detrimental to baseball." The removal of "The Lip," accused of associations with gamblers, followed a hostile feud between the Dodgers skipper and Larry MacPhail, one of the Yankees owners, who had hired coach Chuck Dressen away from Durocher. The hassles were renewed when the two clubs met in the first-ever televised World Series, which the Yankees won in seven games.

Nineteen-forty-seven's Hall of Fame inductees — Mickey Cochrane, Frankie Frisch, Lefty Grove and Carl Hubbell — all had been league MVPs. Also that season, the New York Giants powered a mind-boggling 221 home runs, the most ever at that time.

A tremendous home run race between New York's Johnny Mize and Pittsburgh's Ralph Kiner ended in a dead heat with both players belting 51. It marked the first time in 17 years that any National Leaguer had reached the 50-homer plateau.

Boston Anchor

Prior to the 1947 season, Boston Braves manager Billy Southworth took newcomer Bob Elliott aside and told him that with hustle and desire, he could be the National League's Most Valuable Player. Southworth might not have fully believed his own words, but he turned out to be a prophet.

Few others believed it, including Elliott, even after the voting. When *The New York Times* rushed a photographer to his San Diego home, Bob was leisurely painting the house, unaware he'd been chosen for the prestigious award.

The 30-year-old Boston third baseman, who'd spent seven full seasons with Pittsburgh, failed to crack the top five in home runs, slugging or total bases in 1947, and perhaps equally important, his team finished eight games out in third place. The tough, reliable hitter had enjoyed a fine season, to be sure, placing second in batting at .317 and doubles with 35, as well as driving in 113 runs; however, five NL pitchers had won at least 21 games, and two sluggers had slammed more than 50 homers.

But Elliott, whose 15-year career was marked by steady if not spectacular play, was finally appreciated by baseball's writers, who made him the first Brave MVP ever. After seven years

in which his home run production had never exceeded 10, the right-hander clobbered 22 in 1947. His average, RBIs and .517 slugging percentage all were career highs. Another marked area of improvement for Elliott was his fielding. He had played exclusively in the outfield until age 25, but was placed at third base in 1942, and it took five years to get a handle on the position. In fact, he committed more errors than any NL third sacker three years running (1942–44). But by '47, Elliott led league hot corner men in fielding average (.956).

Born Robert Irving Elliott November 26, 1916, in San Francisco, he began his professional baseball career in 1936. His 43 hits for Pittsburgh in '39, 16 of which were of the extra base variety, convinced Pirates management that the 22-year-old right fielder was ready for fulltime duty. Incoming skipper Frankie Frisch was happy to pencil Elliott's name in the starting lineup 147 times his rookie year of 1940, and the Bucs won 10 more games than in '39, moving into the first division. Elliott was a factor in his team's climb, batting .292 with 50 extra base hits.

The right fielder suffered moderately from the sophomore jinx, slipping to only three homers and a .273 average, despite a dozen more ribbies than he had as a rookie. But in 1942, a move to third base corresponded with a dramatically improved hitting stroke.

In the next four seasons, three of which were played almost entirely at third base, the 6-foot, 185-pounder never hit below .290, reaching .315 in '43 and averaging 30 doubles and more than 100 RBIs per year. The lifetime .289 batter was a particular menace to

NL hurlers in 1943 when he was second in RBIs (101), third in total bases (258) and triples (12), and fourth in hitting and slugging (.444).

Bob split his time between the hot corner and the outfield in 1945 and '46, and as the Pirates faded, so did Elliott's stick production. Bob's average dipped to .263 the latter year, and he drove in 40 fewer runs. Frisch was fired as manager at the tail end of the season, and the Pirates brass decided it might be worth losing an everyday player to acquire the right mentor.

Boston utility infielder Billy Herman, who'd shown his baseball smarts in a 14-year playing career with the Cubs and Dodgers, was targeted. The Braves were more than willing to swap Herman for Elliott, who would become their first consistent third baseman since Pinky Whitney in the mid–1930s.

The new surroundings suited Bob just fine, as he demonstrated with his MVP effort. Meanwhile, Herman failed to finish the season with the last-place Pirates, prompting St. Louis Cardinals manager Eddie Dyer to credit Boston with "the greatest trade ever made."

Elliott was nearly as proficient in 1948 when he led the NL in walks (131) and helped the Braves to their first pennant in 34 years. Although Cleveland took the World Series in six games, Boston's third baseman provided some dramatic moments, crushing two consecutive home runs off Indians fireballer Bob Feller in Game 5. Elliott topped all Series participants in slugging (.619) and homers (two), as well as tying for the lead in hits (seven), RBIs (five), runs (four) and assists (14), while batting .333.

Three more solid seasons with Boston followed for the hard-nosed competitor, who drove in more runs (903) than any player during the 1940s. But by age 35, Bob was slowing down, and the Braves sent him to the Giants for the 1952 season, where he hit only .228. The seven-time All-Star selection wound up his playing career in the American League in '53 with the St. Louis Browns and Chicago White Sox.

Elliott tried his hand as a Pacific Coast League skipper for San Diego and Sacramento from 1954–59, and in 1960 was hired to pilot the Kansas City Athletics, who finished last. Six years later, Bob passed away.

Bob Elliott was unspectacular, but steady; hardly charismatic, but reliable. His selection as the 1947 MVP came as a surprise to most baseball fans and players, but it was a refreshing change of pace, and proof that clutch performances on the diamond can outweigh gaudy statistics.

Top 5 MVP Vote-Getters

1. Bob Elliott, Boston — 205
2. Ewell Blackwell, Cincinnati — 175
3. Johnny Mize, New York — 144
4. Bruce Edwards, Brooklyn — 140
5. Jackie Robinson, Brooklyn — 106

1947 AMERICAN LEAGUE — JOE DIMAGGIO

Joseph Paul DiMaggio
B. November 25, 1914, Martinez, California
D. March 8, 1999, Hollywood, Florida

Year	Team	Games	AB	Hits	Avg.	HR	RBI	Runs	SB
1947	NY AL	141	534	168	.315	20	97	97	3

The Season

After a three-year dry spell, the Yankees regained the World Championship, going 97–57 and besting runner-up Detroit by 12 games. Bucky Harris, in his first year at the New York helm, guided another power-laden club that topped the league in runs, home runs, batting average and slugging percentage.

For the first time in 16 years, two junior circuit no-hitters were tossed in the same season, with Don Black of Cleveland turning the trick against the Philadelphia Athletics, and A's pitcher Bill McCahan shutting down the Washington Senators. Both were 3–0 games.

The 1947 World Series was a bonafide thriller, going the full seven games before the Yankees finally downed the Brooklyn Dodgers. Yankees right-hander Bill Bevens narrowly missed baseball immortality in Game 4 when he came within one out of throwing the first no-hitter in Series history. The villain who broke up the masterful performance was Cookie Lavagetto, who not only ruined the no-hitter, but drove in the tying and winning runs with a double. New York's Johnny Lindell led all hitters in the fall classic, batting .500 and driving in seven runs.

On July 5, Cleveland's Larry Doby became the American League's first black player. Earlier in the year, Negro League superstar Josh Gibson died of a brain tumor at age 35.

Censor's Choice

Although most baseball historians are hesitant about directly besmirching the DiMaggio persona, they

Joe DiMaggio. (Courtesy New York Yankees.)

can League in eight significant offensive categories. Not that DiMaggio's final MVP effort was worthless; nor was his post-military career disappointing. Far from it. Despite losing three prime years to the Army, the graceful fly-chaser came back to regain his place as one of the AL's most feared hitters and revered personalities.

The military brought about tough times for Joe, who suffered from painful ulcers and a sense of helplessness as his marriage disintegrated while he was stationed far from his wife and son. He rose to the rank of staff sergeant, served 31 months in a physical training program for Air Force cadets, played on Army baseball teams and entertained troops in the United States and abroad.

DiMag found it hard to get back in stride when he finally returned to baseball in 1946. In 132 games, he hit only .290, the first time he had ever dipped below .300 in any organized league. The fans who initially cheered his return were booing by year's end. A bone spur in the heel of his left foot didn't help.

Nineteen-forty-seven began with an operation on that heel, and DiMaggio missed the first few weeks of play. But in his first at-bat of the year, he blasted a home run. He went on to finish second in the league behind Williams in total bases (279) and slugging (.522), and third in RBIs (97), and he topped the Yankee club in average (.315) and home runs (20). For the first time in his career, Joe led AL outfielders in fielding percentage (.997).

It was his ninth year in the big show, and probably his eighth-best campaign. But the Yankees had regained the pennant, their first since 1943, and there was no mistaking that DiMaggio had keyed the charge.

In the seven-game World Series against Brooklyn, DiMaggio helped his mates to another World Championship with two home runs, his Game 5 shot providing the deciding edge in New York's 2–1 win. He almost had a third homer in Game 6, but Al Gionfriddo made a running catch of his 415-foot blast, robbing him of a game-tying four-bagger.

The big numbers surfaced for the

agree "Joltin' Joe" never quite regained the awesome dominance he had demonstrated prior to joining the military. There were some remarkable campaigns, to be sure, and when he approached the point of being completely healthy, the post-war "Yankee Clipper" would lash out with his old form. But, except for 1948, every time DiMaggio began putting it all together again, another injury would drag him down, and each time it would be more difficult for the aging star to recuperate.

His third MVP award in 1947 was more or less a gift from baseball writers. Ted Williams won the Triple Crown that season, but made countless enemies in the press corps for his refusal to cooperate. One such foe was Boston writer Mel Webb, who left Williams off his ballot entirely. Even a 10th-place vote from Webb would have been enough to give the award to Williams, who lost by one point. In typical fashion, the "Splendid Splinter" shrugged off the MVP snub by saying, "I lost to the Big Guy, didn't I?"

So even though 1947 wasn't close to being one of DiMaggio's better campaigns, he was voted top honors in what amounted to a revenge vote against Williams, who led the Ameri-

last time in 1948 when DiMaggio led the AL in home runs with 39 and RBIs with 155. He was again hitting the ball in a deadly style, but the Yankees finished third, 2½ games out.

Two operations on his right heel caused him to miss the first 76 games of 1949. His first appearance of the season, against Boston, was the stuff of which melodramas are created. In a three-game set, DiMaggio blasted four home runs and drove in nine as the Yankees swept in Fenway Park. Joe went on to hit .346, and New York won the pennant and World Series.

In 1950, at age 35, he helped New York to yet another World Championship with a .301 average, 32 circuit clouts, 122 RBIs and a league-best .585 slugging percentage. Injuries again limited him to 139 games, and DiMaggio considered retirement. Only a scorching .370 stretch in the final six weeks convinced him to try it one more time.

But 1951 was the worst year of all. DiMaggio suffered from neck spasms,

played in only 116 games and managed a .263 batting average with 12 home runs and 71 RBIs. At age 37, following the 1951 World Series triumph, he announced that he was through.

In 13 seasons, the Clipper had registered a .325 lifetime average, smashed 361 homers, driven in 1,537 runs and scored 1,390 times. The numbers, impressive as they are, fail to tell the whole story.

Yankee management retired uniform No. 5 upon DiMaggio's retirement. After a short stint hosting postgame radio and television shows, he virtually vanished from the public eye. His 274-day marriage to Marilyn Monroe, their divorce and her subsequent death left him sullen and somewhat of a recluse.

Thirteen years after his 1955 induction into the Hall of Fame, he reemerged as a batting instructor for the Oakland A's and Yankees. In 1979, he was appointed to the Baltimore Orioles' board of directors.

The great DiMaggio seemed more

at home during his final years whenever the spotlight turned his way, still moving with the same effortless grace and affluence he displayed in the wide-open expanses of center field, and the masses still gravitated to his regal presence as they did in his heyday. Joe passed away in 1999 at the age of 84.

A 1969 baseball commissioner's poll named DiMaggio the game's greatest living ballplayer, and an Associated Press vote dubbed him the fifth greatest ballplayer of all time.

Whatever he did, the sentiment from the 1941 song still rang true: "We want you on our side, Joe DiMaggio."

Top 5 MVP Vote-Getters

1. Joe DiMaggio, New York — 202
2. Ted Williams, Boston — 201
3. Lou Boudreau, Cleveland — 168
4. Joe Page, New York — 167
5. George Kell, Detroit — 132

1948 NATIONAL LEAGUE — STAN MUSIAL

Stanley Frank Musial
B. November 21, 1920, Donora, Pennsylvania

Year	Team	Games	AB	Hits	Avg.	HR	RBI	Runs	SB
1948	SL NL	155	611	230	.376	39	131	135	7

The Season

Although the National League's pennant race paled in comparison to the one American League fans enjoyed in 1948, the Boston Braves were happy with the results. And why not? They beat out St. Louis by 6½ games for their first flag since 1914, despite winning only 91 times, the NL's lowest total for a pennant winner in a decade.

Under manager Billy Southworth, the only non-Hall of Fame skipper to win more than three pennants, Boston had a pleasing blend of league-leading hitting (.275) and pitching (3.38 ERA).

The Braves' title hopes dimmed midway through the season when spark plug second baseman Eddie Stanky broke an ankle, but Boston kept winning. The dream season ended, however, when the Braves were downed four games to two in the World Series by the Cleveland Indians and AL Most Valuable Player Lou Boudreau. Nineteen-forty-seven MVP, third baseman Bob Elliottt, paced Boston in the Series with a .333 average, two homers and five RBIs. A record crowd of 86,288 attended the fifth game in Cleveland.

July 16 was an interesting day for

managers. Leo Durocher shocked the baseball world by leaving Brooklyn and replacing Mel Ott with the Giants, Burt Shotton returned as the Dodgers' skipper, and Eddie Sawyer relieved Ben Chapman in Philadelphia.

Stan Turns Slugger

Upon attending his first major league baseball game at Forbes Field, 17-year-old Stan Musial closely scrutinized the action from his grandstand seat for several innings before turning to the sports editor of his hometown newspaper and boldly declaring he could hit big league pitching.

The scribe may have given his companion a knowing smile and thought young Stanley rather brash, but 10 years later, Musial would not only handle major league pitching, he'd annihilate it on the way to his third Most Valuable Player award in six years.

Stan had so many exceptional seasons for the St. Louis Cardinals, with whom he played his entire career, it's difficult to keep track of them. But 1948 stands out as not only his best campaign, but perhaps the finest overall post-war year for any ballplayer. Musial played in all 155 of his team's games, collecting five hits in four different contests and ripping National League pitching apart with a .376 average, clubbing 39 home runs and cracking 46 doubles and 18 triples among his 230 hits. He slugged at a phenomenal .702 clip, the highest NL percentage since 1930 and a mark that would not be topped by a senior circuit player in 46 years. Scoring 135 runs and driving in 131, Musial contributed to 225 of his squad's 742 tallies that season.

The sweet-swinging left-hander's batting and slugging averages were career highs, as were his homers, RBIs, hits and runs. Musial's 429 total bases were the sixth highest single-season total ever. During a three-game series at Ebbets Field in 1948, Stan hit safely 11 times in 15 at-bats, prompting Dodgers fans to label him "The Man," a term of pure respect which stuck throughout his career.

It was during the '48 season that Musial, who led the NL in eight offensive categories, observed that home run hitters such as Ralph Kiner were commanding high salaries, and began aiming more often for the fences. His previous high had been 19 homers in '47, but he more than doubled that mark in 1948, and in so doing boosted his RBI total by 36.

One round-tripper not included in his stats that season was a two-run shot at Sportsman's Park in St. Louis during the All-Star Game. Homers in All-Star competition were hardly new for Musial, who appeared in 24 mid-season classics, belting six home runs and hitting .317. His most notable All-Star performance came in 1955 when he tagged a solo homer in the bottom of the 12th inning at Milwaukee's County Stadium to give the National League a 6–5 victory. The blast was especially sweet for Musial because that game marked the first time since 1947 that "The Man" had not been voted to the starting team. Other All-Star four-baggers included a two-run job at Ebbets Field in 1949, a clutch blow at Washington's Griffith Stadium to help the NL win 7–3 in 1956 and a mammoth drive into the third deck at Yankee Stadium in 1960.

A year prior to his third MVP effort, Musial had a scare when he suffered from appendicitis and infected tonsils, missing five games. Weakened by the illnesses, Stan was hitting only .200 by mid–June, but recovered to bat .312 for the season. The iron man missed only 24 games between 1943 and 1956, and played in 895 consecutive contests from April 15, 1952, to August 22, 1957, the seventh longest streak in baseball history.

Musial failed to garner a record-fourth Most Valuable Player award in his remaining 15 seasons, but won three straight batting titles in 1950–52. His seventh and final hitting crown came in 1957 when the 36-year-old batted .351.

Musial also led the National League in total bases and runs scored three more times, and was the top RBI man in 1956 with 109. In virtually every year from 1949 to 1958, the portside swinger was in the top four in nearly all offensive departments. With five more years left in his magnificent career, Musial recorded his 3,000th hit in 1958. That year Musial was rewarded

with a $100,000 salary, making him only the third player in baseball history to reach that mark.

As Musial aged, his average dipped, and by 1959 he was down to .255. But the 41-year-old grandfather came back in 1962 to hit .330 with 19 homers and 82 RBIs. After one more season, Stan called it a career.

A look at Musial's standing among baseball's career leaders gives a glimpse of his magnificence. He was among the top 10 in eight categories, and the top 20 in three others. His 6,134 total bases were second all-time, while his 725 doubles were third and both his 3,630 hits and 1,951 RBIs fourth. Stan was also seventh in runs, 10th in walks, 17th in slugging, tied for 19th in home runs and 28th in batting. He was the Cardinals' all-time leader in virtually every offensive department.

Following his retirement, Musial was appointed a Cardinals vice president, then was named general manager in 1967 when St. Louis won the pennant. He left the position the next year to become senior vice president. Stan, who was selected as a chairman for President Lyndon Johnson's physical fitness program in the 1960s, was elected to the Hall of Fame in 1969, his first year of eligibility.

One of the most popular players of all time, Stan Musial became the first Cardinals player to be honored by the retiring of his uniform — No. 6. A statue of "The Man" stands proudly outside Busch Stadium in St. Louis, a tribute to one of the few athletes whose impeccable character mirrored his incredible abilities.

Top 5 MVP Vote-Getters

1. Stan Musial, St. Louis — 303
2. Johnny Sain, Boston — 223
3. Al Dark, Boston — 174
4. Sid Gordon, New York — 72
5. Harry Brecheen, St. Louis — 61

1948 AMERICAN LEAGUE—LOU BOUDREAU

Louis Boudreau
B. July 17, 1917, Harvey, Illinois
D. August 10, 2001, Olympia Fields, Illinois

Year	Team	Games	AB	Hits	Avg.	HR	RBI	Runs	SB
1948	Cle AL	152	560	199	.355	18	106	116	3

The Season

The 1948 season can be described as both unique and dramatic, but also tragic. Unique, because for the first time in the history of the American League, two teams tied for first place, forcing a one-game playoff. Dramatic, because by Labor Day only 1½ games separated Boston, Cleveland and New York. A couple of weeks later, the veritable knot at the top was pulled even tighter, with the Indians and Red Sox tied for first and the Yankees closing to one game back.

The Indians, who held opponents scoreless for 47 consecutive innings during August and who set attendance records both for a single game (82,781) and the season (2.6 million), had a chance to clinch on the final day of the regular campaign, but were shelled 7–1 by Detroit, while the Red Sox were bombing New York 10–5 to move into a first-place tie with the Indians.

Taking center stage in this drama was Cleveland player-manager Lou Boudreau, who collected four hits, including two homers, to lead the Indians to an 8–3 playoff victory over Boston. The Tribe then scalped another Beantown team, the Braves, in a six-game World Series featuring the pitching of Bob Lemon (2–0, 1.65 ERA) and the hitting of Larry Doby (.318).

And 1948 was a tragic year for baseball fans because the great Babe Ruth died of throat cancer at New York Memorial Hospital August 16 at the age of 53. Two months earlier, Ruth's uniform No. 3 was retired during a ceremony in his final Yankee Stadium appearance.

On July 7, Cleveland owner Bill Veeck signed 42-year-old Negro League pitcher Satchel Paige, a move that was criticized as merely a publicity stunt. But Paige won six of seven decisions to help the Indians capture the pennant.

Precocious Pilot

When a couple of headstrong personalities clash in baseball, the result is usually the removal from the scene of one of those persons. Fortunately for Cleveland Indians fans in 1948, the exception, rather than the rule, occurred.

The precocious Lou Boudreau had been chosen player-manager of the Indians six years earlier. While most 24-year-old major league players were still adjusting to life away from Mom and Dad, Boudreau was giving orders to men who'd played their first sandlot games before he was born.

But by 1948, eccentric Indians owner Bill Veeck was tiring of the fiery Boudreau's mediocre record (450–464), and tried to deal him to the St. Louis Browns. Cleveland fans may not have been overly pleased with the tangible results of the scrappy skipper's tenure either, but they recognized a keen baseball mind, not to mention a good ballplayer, when they saw one.

Their intense protests, including a newspaper-sponsored vote that resulted in 90 percent of respondents in favor of retaining him, helped keep Boudreau in Cleveland and resulted in a 1948 World Championship. It was the first World Series victory for the Tribe since 1920, leading to Veeck's now-famous comment: "Sometimes the best trades are the ones you never make." Veeck later wrote, "Lou was deter-mined to prove I was a jerk. And he did."

Few players did more for their team than Lou Boudreau in 1948. "Good Kid" not only hit a sparkling .355 with 18 home runs and 106 RBIs, but also played brilliantly at shortstop, using his vast knowledge of the hitters and flawless instinct to make up for an average arm and a lack of speed.

During the 1948 regular season, Boudreau was second in the league in hitting, third in hits (199), fourth in slugging average (.534) and fifth in total bases (299). His homer total was a career high, as were his runs batted in, 116 runs scored and 98 walks.

The cagey Boudreau's Indians finished in a tie for first place with the Ted Williams-led Boston Red Sox, and in a one-game playoff October 4, Boudreau took matters into his own hands, swatting a pair of homers in the Indians' triumph, which featured Gene Bearden's 20th win. Then, in the World Series, the squatty shortstop hit .273 with four doubles to pace the Indians to a four games-to-two victory over the Boston Braves. Following the season, Lou was named the American League's Most Valuable Player by a wide margin over Joe DiMaggio.

Two more years as player-manager of Cleveland were followed by a couple of seasons with the Red Sox, giving him a 15-year playing career. Three brief, inauspicious managing stints followed: the Red Sox from 1952 to '54 (229–232), the Kansas City Athletics from 1955 to '57 (151–260) and the Chicago Cubs in 1960 (54–83).

Although his baseball abilities and smarts are well-chronicled, the Harvey, Illinois-born Boudreau wasn't a one-dimensional athlete in his younger years. The three-time all-state basketball star helped Thornton High School win the Illinois state championship in 1933. He was also a catalyst for the University of Illinois hoops squad that won a Big Ten crown in 1937.

But baseball was his first love. After two years in the minors, he came up to the Tribe in 1938, quickly making a name for himself. Lou led the league in hitting in 1944 with a .327 mark, the first of four times he batted over .300 in a five-year span.

Boudreau is widely known for his 1946 implementation of the Ted Williams shift, in which he placed all of his infielders except the third baseman on the right side of second base. In the first game of a double-header July 14, Boudreau tied a record with five extra base hits (four doubles and a home run). But Williams managed to overshadow Boudreau in that 11–10 Red Sox win at Fenway Park with three home runs, including a grand slam, a single, eight RBIs and four runs. Following a double by "The Thumper" in game two, Boudreau unveiled the new defense against Williams, who grounded out and walked twice in three plate appearances. The St. Louis Cardinals copied the shift in the 1946 World Series, holding the frustrated Williams to a .200 batting average.

The youngest man to serve as a player-manager for a full season also was the last one to win a World Championship. No other shortstop would crack the .350 mark in batting for 48 years. Many of those hits were well-placed in outfield alleys, as the six-time All-Star smacked a career-high 46 doubles in 1940 and swatted exactly 45 two-baggers to lead the league in 1941, '44 and '47.

In the field, Boudreau was equally impressive. Some other shortstops possessed greater range or stronger arms, but once Lou reached a grounder, the batter was as good as out. The vacuum cleaner led AL shortstops in fielding a record-tying eight times, including marks of .978 in 1944, .982 in '47 and .975 in '48. Boudreau paced junior circuit shortstops in double plays five times (his 134 double plays in 1943 were a record) and in putouts on four occasions.

The former father-in-law of 1968 AL MVP Denny McLain was a Chicago Cubs radio broadcaster for many years. His uniform No. 5 was retired by the Indians, who renamed the street bordering Municipal Stadium "Boudreau Boulevard." A fan of the bowling alley and racetrack, Boudreau was elected to baseball's Hall of Fame in 1970. He passed away as a result of heart failure from complications of diabetes in 2001 at the age of 84.

Loved by fellow players and fans alike, Lou Boudreau was a true competitor who respected the game. He played it, managed it and announced it in the same fashion — with expertise and professionalism.

Top 5 MVP Vote-Getters

1. Lou Boudreau, Cleveland — 324
2. Joe DiMaggio, New York — 213
3. Ted Williams, Boston — 171
4. Vern Stephens, Boston — 121
5. Bob Lemon, Cleveland — 101

1949 NATIONAL LEAGUE — JACKIE ROBINSON

Jack Roosevelt Robinson
B. January 31, 1919, Cairo, Georgia
D. October 24, 1972, Stamford, Connecticut

Year	Team	Games	AB	Hits	Avg.	HR	RBI	Runs	SB
1949	Bkn NL	156	593	203	.342	16	124	122	37

The Season

Although Jackie Robinson had broken the color barrier two years previously, it wasn't until 1949 that African-Americans appeared in the All-Star Game. The 16th edition of the midsummer classic featured Robinson, Roy Campanella and Don Newcombe on the National League team, while Larry Doby suited up for the American League. The AL took advantage of five NL errors to win 11–7 at Ebbets Field in Brooklyn.

The Dodgers captured their second pennant in three years, but needed a late surge and a St. Louis downfall. Trailing the Cardinals by 1½ games as late as September 21, Brooklyn took two of three from the Redbirds, then nudged the Phillies 9–7 in 10 innings on the final day to win by one game. But the Dodgers suffered their fifth straight World Series setback when the Yankees won in five games.

The most bizarre event of the '49 season occurred in June when a schizophrenic woman shot Philadelphia first baseman Eddie Waitkus with a .22 caliber rifle in Chicago's Edgewater Beach Hotel. Waitkus, who had never met the woman, was out for the rest of the year, but came back in 1950 to resume his career.

Pittsburgh pitcher Ernie "Tiny" Bonham, who had helped the New York Yankees win three pennants and two World Series, was not as fortunate. Less than three weeks after earning his 103rd career win — an 8–2 decision

Jackie Robinson. (Courtesy Los Angeles Dodgers.)

Had Robinson been a mellow, subdued sort to whom grace under pressure came naturally, his willingness to turn the other cheek would have been less remarkable. But he was far from meek, far from mild-mannered. Robinson was a battler, a combative militant. His deftness at squelching those innate instincts during his rookie year of 1947 was even more amazing than his accomplishments on the diamond.

In addition to the tremendous pressures Robinson faced that first season, he was required to switch to the unfamiliar position of first base with the Dodgers, who already had Eddie Stanky at Jackie's originally spot, second base. With spikings, beanballs and vicious racial insults constantly directed toward him, Robinson had to be on his toes at all times. But he soon had the opposition on the alert as well, establishing himself as the most electrifying player in baseball.

Robinson produced a sparkling initial campaign, hitting .297 with 12 homers and 48 RBIs, leading the National League in stolen bases with 29 and placing second in runs scored at 125. For his efforts, the 28-year-old was dubbed the major league's first Rookie of the Year. But his crowning moment of glory came in 1949 when he became the first black man to earn the MVP award.

Having proven himself a legitimate big leaguer, Robinson could now shed his cloak of compliance and exhibit his true self, which was revealed in an aggressive, dish-it-out style of play. When verbally or physically attacked, he fought back. More comfortable in this role, the fierce competitor who would do anything to win was the league's most significant player in 1949. The right-handed hitter was the NL's best in batting (.342) and stolen bases (37), runner-up in RBIs (124) and hits (203), and third in slugging (.528), runs (122), doubles (38) and triples (12). He single-handedly kept Brooklyn in contention much of the season, and despite straining ligaments in his right leg in August, continued to play every day as the Dodgers edged St. Louis for the pennant.

Red Schoendienst, the Cardinals

over Philadelphia — Bonham died September 15 following an appendectomy and stomach surgery.

Man of Destiny

Like the early settlers who ventured into unknown territories, charting new courses, Jackie Robinson was a pioneer, blazing a trail across rivers of hatred, valleys of ignorance and hills of prejudice. While those around him scoffed, ridiculed, berated and threatened, he agonized through the intense humiliation with a closed mouth, holding back the anger and frustration, and resolving in his heart to become a man of destiny.

As the 20th century's first African-American major leaguer, Robinson needed more than his diverse physical skills, which were plentiful; he was also required to display a strength of character rarely seen. It was Jackie's inner fortitude, as much as his on-field contributions, which qualified him for Branch Rickey's "great experiment."

Rickey could have selected any of a number of outstanding black ballplayers, including Josh Gibson, Satchel Paige, Buck Leonard or Monte Irvin. As gifted an athlete as Robinson was, there were better players available. But Rickey was looking for more than physical prowess; he sought a man who possessed a determined spirit, one who had the strength to meet the inevitable taunts with a quiet presence of mind … at least for one season.

second baseman in 1949, once said of Robinson, "If it weren't for him, the Dodgers would be in the second division."

Participating in a World Series was never a realistic consideration for Robinson as a youth. Jackie was born in a small shack in the middle of a Georgia cotton field, but the family soon moved to Pasadena, California. Brother Mack became a track star, finishing second to Jesse Owens in the 200-meter run at the 1936 Olympics. Jack gradually discovered he too owned athletic skills, earning a partial scholarship to UCLA and starring in four sports, including football (12 yards per carry, tops in the nation) and basketball (Pacific Coast Conference scoring leader two straight years).

Robinson quit school to help support his mother, then enlisted in the Army, serving as a second lieutenant during World War II before receiving his discharge in 1944. He proved, both literally and figuratively, that he would take a back seat to no one, and was acquitted in an Army court martial after refusing to sit in the back of a bus. Robinson joined the Kansas City Monarchs of the Negro League at age 26, was scouted by the Dodgers and signed with the Triple A Montreal Royals in 1946, where he led the International League in hitting (.345) and topped second basemen in fielding.

Following his MVP season in 1949, Robinson continued to rattle the opposition with basepath antics, and hit well above .300. He stole 197 bases in a 10-year career — the Dodgers winning six pennants during that span — but his true base running value to his team was centered in an ability to upset the pitcher. Nineteen of Robinson's 197 career stolen bases were thefts of home, including five in one season.

Blessed with a fielding whiz partner in shortstop Pee Wee Reese, Jackie led NL second basemen in double plays four consecutive years (1949–52). Most fans remember the 1951 Dodgers-Giants playoff for Bobby Thomson's home run, but not many recall that Robinson put Brooklyn into that series on the final day of the regular season with a brilliant defensive play and a 14th-inning homer. When Junior Gilliam came up in 1953, the versatile Robinson, who had led league second sackers in fielding three times including a phenomenal .992 mark in 1951, moved to the outfield where he spent most of his time from 1953–56.

At the conclusion of the 1956 season, the Dodgers tried to trade Robinson to the New York Giants for Dick Littlefield and $35,000, but the 37-year-old instead chose retirement. He worked for a restaurant chain, did public relations jobs for New York Governor Nelson Rockefeller and loudly criticized baseball for the lack of blacks in management posts.

Jackie's later years were marred by sadness and illness. Jackie Jr. came home from Vietnam a heroin addict. After his arrest for possession of drugs and a firearm, he kicked the habit, but was killed in an automobile accident in 1971. Meanwhile, Robinson's health was waning, as his diabetes worsened and eyesight began to fail. The Hall of Famer died on October 24, 1972, at age 53.

Baseball has honored this courageous pioneer on several occasions, including 1994 when the Rookie of the Year award was re-designated the Jackie Robinson Award, and again in 1997 with a celebration of the 50th anniversary of his major league debut, which included every team retiring uniform No. 42.

A lifetime .311 hitter who excelled in clutch situations, Jackie Robinson will be remembered as an exceptional ballplayer and a winner. But more important, he'll always have a special place in the hearts of men and women who value freedom and dignity. As the words on his Hall of Fame plaque read: "Jackie Robinson led the way."

Top 5 MVP Vote-Getters

1. Jackie Robinson, Brooklyn — 264
2. Stan Musial, St. Louis — 226
3. Enos Slaughter, St. Louis — 181
4. Ralph Kiner, Pittsburgh — 133
5. Pee Wee Reese, Brooklyn — 118

1949 AMERICAN LEAGUE — TED WILLIAMS

Theodore Samuel Williams
B. August 30, 1918, San Diego, California
D. July 5, 2002, Inverness, Florida

Year	Team	Games	AB	Hits	Avg.	HR	RBI	Runs	SB
1949	Bos AL	155	566	194	.343	43	159	150	1

The Season

Despite a key injury to spiritual leader Joe DiMaggio, the New York Yankees stormed to a dramatic pennant in 1949, sweeping Boston in a season-ending two-game series to slip past the Red Sox by one game.

Slick second baseman Jerry Coleman was added to the Yankees roster in '49, as was hard-swinging left fielder Gene Woodling. But the most important Bomber addition was the impish little manager with the funny way of talking, Casey Stengel. In his first year at the helm, Stengel guided a club that was without a .300-hitting regular, brilliantly platooning his lineup and utilizing the league-leading relief pitching skills of Joe Page (27 saves) to their utmost.

In contrast, the runner-up Red Sox packed a powerful wallop, with four regulars hitting over .300. As a team, they topped the circuit in runs, home runs and batting average.

Future Hall of Famers George Kell of Detroit and league MVP Ted Williams battled to the last game of the season for the hitting crown, each finishing at .343. Kell won by two percentage points on the fourth decimal.

In the World Series, the Yanks met and defeated their archrivals from Brooklyn for the third time in less than a decade, this time in five games. Future physician and AL president Bobby Brown provided New York's big stick, hitting .500 and leading both clubs in RBIs (five).

The best individual pitching performance of the season came from eventual MVP Bobby Shantz. The Philadelphia A's rookie threw nine consecutive innings of hitless relief May 6 in a 13-inning, 5–4 victory over Detroit.

Finally, 1937 MVP Charlie Gehringer was elected to the Hall of Fame.

The Joy of Hitting

"Hitting a baseball," Ted Williams once said, "is at the center of my heart."

An average fielder who eventually mastered the tricky left field wall in Fenway Park, Williams concentrated a vast majority of his baseball energies on hitting. The intimate joy of bringing his swing to a state of near sublimity has probably never been surpassed in terms of study, practice and focus. The record shows as much.

Number 9's lifetime slugging percentage of .634 ranked second in baseball annals only to Babe Ruth. Six times the left-hander topped the AL in hitting, missing a seventh by two-tenths of a percentage point and an eighth because his plethora of walks left him short of the required number of official at-bats. In fact, Williams'

2,019 walks — third on the all-time list — kept him from attaining even greater hitting heights in a variety of categories.

At age 23, he batted .406, the last to reach the .400 barrier. Sixteen years later, he fell short of the mark by five hits, ending at .388. A .344 career average — ninth all time — is embellished by 521 lifetime homers, third on the list when he retired, and no one can argue that the "Splendid Splinter" would not have made a serious assault on Ruth's total of 714 round-trippers had not five years in the military so rudely interrupted. In the Red Sox record book, he was among the top two all time in eight offensive departments.

In four separate decades, he was one of the AL's brightest stars, who fittingly put on superb exhibitions in many of the 18 All-Star Games in which he performed. Ted's .304 All-Star average was highlighted by a game-winning home run in the 1941 contest, a 4-for-4 outing in '46 (including two home runs) and a career-altering 1950 accident in which he broke an elbow while barreling into the left field wall, then remained in the game to drive in the lead run for the American League.

Immediately following his 1946 MVP came some of Ted's most productive, yet frustrating, years. In '47, "Teddy Ballgame" won the Triple Crown in a prodigious one-man barrage, yet lost the MVP to Joe DiMaggio. Williams captured his fourth batting crown in 1948, but the Red Sox came up shy, losing the pennant race in a sudden-death playoff game to the Cleveland Indians.

The 1949 MVP season was bittersweet, with emphasis on the *bitter*. Playing every game, the left fielder hit .343 and topped the league in home runs (43), RBIs (159), runs (150), doubles (39), walks (162) and on-base percentage (.490), but his club was again edged out for the pennant on the last day of the season.

Bad luck and the Yankees were mainly responsible for keeping Williams out of the fall classic, but politics played a major role in limiting Ted to two MVP awards. He could have rightfully claimed the award in 1941, 1942, 1947 and 1957, especially in '47 when

Boston sportswriter Mel Webb left him completely off the ballot, despite Williams' Triple Crown credentials. Had the slugging outfielder been listed even 10th on that scribe's tally, the 1947 award would have been his. In contrast to the MVP voting, *The Sporting News* named Williams baseball's Player of the Year five times.

The last decade of Williams' career was marvelous, despite a shattered elbow and the Korean war, which robbed him of his power, youth and dream of becoming the greatest hitter in the game. Williams revised his goal and set his sights on being acknowledged as the best *old* hitter, and achieved just that.

With advancing years and nagging injuries bearing down hard, "The Thumper" registered batting marks from 1954 to '58 that read .345, .356, .345, .388 and .328, the last two seasons resulting in batting titles at ages 39 and 40. During that time, he averaged 29 homers per campaign.

A painful neck injury dropped him to .254 in 1959; but at 42 years of age, Ted came back to close out his 19-year career with a .316 effort and 29 four-baggers, going out in a blaze of glory with a home run in his final at-bat.

Williams was voted into the Hall of Fame in 1966, his initial year of eligibility. He spent the next 30 years or so dividing his time between his other passion, fishing, and promoting the Jimmy Fund, a cancer charity for children.

Each spring he would return, larger than life, as a special hitting instructor for Red Sox minor leaguers, passing on his vast knowledge of hitting mechanics freely, even detailing minute idiosyncrasies of the batter's box in his well-read book, *The Science of Hitting*.

Ted's impact as a hitting guru was never more evident than in the early stages of his four-year stint as manager of the Washington Senators and Texas Rangers. Under the influence of their hitting-conscious skipper, Washington rose from 10th place to fourth in the Eastern Division in Williams' first season, with every one of the Senator starters showing rises in batting average. Williams earned Manager of the

Year honors in 1969, but one year after the franchise shifted to Texas, he returned to the fishing boats. In 1999, he was honored by baseball at the All-Star Game.

Serious health problems, resulting in the use of a pacemaker, were followed by open-heart surgery in early 2001, prompting Ted to keep a lower profile. He died of cardiac arrest in 2002 at the age of 83. But during his later years, he had learned to show the same patience with a rod and reel that he did with a bat in his hands, calmly applying fundamental skills and precise execution to make the big connection … just waiting for those strikes.

Top 5 MVP Vote-Getters

1. Ted Williams, Boston — 272
2. Phil Rizzuto, New York — 175
3. Joe Page, New York — 166
4. Mel Parnell, Boston — 151
5. Ellis Kinder, Boston — 122

1950 NATIONAL LEAGUE — JIM KONSTANTY

Casimir James Konstanty
B. March 2, 1917, Strykersville, New York
D. June 11, 1976, Oneonta, New York

Year	Team	Games	W	L	ERA	IP	SO	BB	Saves
1950	Phil NL	74	16	7	2.66	152	56	50	22

The Season

Entering the 1950 season, the Philadelphia Phillies had finished in last place a record-17 times, their only pennant coming in 1915. The Whiz Kids reversed that trend, capturing the National League flag in theatrical fashion on the final day of the season when Dick Sisler's 10th-inning home run beat second-place Brooklyn.

Sisler's shot saved the Phillies from blowing an almost sure championship, as the club had squandered a seven-game lead with one week to go.

The Phils had the best team ERA in the league, and their biggest gun was Del Ennis, a slow-moving outfielder who hit .311 with 31 round-trippers and a league-best 126 RBIs. Although Philadelphia pitching held up against the New York Yankees in the World Series, three consecutive one-run defeats preceded a fourth-game wipeout.

The low-scoring Series was hardly indicative of a season that saw baseballs regularly leaving NL confines. The senior circuit's 1,100 homers in 1950 were the most in one season by either league at that time. Four of those blasts were recorded in one contest by Brooklyn's Gil Hodges, the husky Dodger becoming the first 20th century National Leaguer to accomplish the feat in a nine-inning game.

A thrilling All-Star Game July 11 featured Ted Williams fracturing an elbow slamming into the wall to catch Ralph Kiner's drive, then driving in a run with a single; Kiner belting a game-tying home run in the ninth inning; and Red Schoendienst giving the NL its first All-Star Game win as a visiting team, 4–3, with a 14th-inning homer.

One-Man Cavalry

In 1950, his palmball was nearly unhittable. Batters lunged at the off-speed delivery, sliders cut the corners of the plate repeatedly and an occasional fastball kept everyone honest. Rallies consistently brought his team from behind, and once leads were procured, the reliable bullpen ace safeguarded them like precious gold bars. The season belonged to Jim Konstanty.

The first pitcher in baseball annals to crack the 70-appearance mark in one year, Konstanty's watermark MVP effort gave new respect to the role of relievers in the baseball scheme. The big Philadelphia right-hander was practically the whole senior circuit show in 1950 when it came time for dousing fires. The closest reliever was 14 saves behind Jim's total, and in appearances, Konstanty (74) was 23 ahead of his nearest rival.

During that memorable campaign, the 33-year-old was indispensable to the Phillies, winning a major league record-16 games in relief and saving an NL record-22, accounting for 42 percent of Philadelphia's pennant-winning total of 91 wins.

The brawny hurler's standing as the game's top reliever made his starting assignment in Game 1 of the World Series all the more astounding. Strapped for a live arm, manager Eddie Sawyer turned once more to Konstanty, who responded with a four-hit, one-run performance against the Yankees in his only start of the year. It wasn't good enough, however, as Philadelphia lost 1–0.

Konstanty made two more fruitless appearances in relief in the four-game Yankees sweep, and while the Phillies' poor showing was disheartening, the pain was eased somewhat when the award givers honored Jim with the MVP.

The resolve and courage he displayed throughout a bitter pennant fight was reminiscent of his early life, when from age 16 he fended entirely for himself. Living with a younger brother in a cheap flat, Jim won a half-scholarship to Syracuse University, where he lettered in basketball, soccer, boxing and baseball.

Transformed from an outfielder to a pitcher early in his minor league career, Konstanty labored from 1940 to 1944 without much success in the Cincinnati system. He made it to the majors with the Reds for the 1944 season, but a one-year stint in the Navy in 1945 and a trade to the Boston Braves the following year found him back in the bushes once again.

Konstanty, who looked more like a professor than a ballplayer, might have passed through the majors without fanfare had it not been for his hometown undertaker. Andrew Skinner coached Konstanty in the winter of 1946, and that collaboration marked the turning point in Jim's career. With no baseball background, Skinner used a pitching instruction manual to help his buddy develop an effective slider and perfect a palmball.

When Sawyer became Jim's manager and turned him into a relief pitcher in 1947, the die was cast for fu-ture brilliance. Late in 1948, Sawyer moved into the skipper's post for the Philadelphia Phillies, bringing Konstanty along, despite the latter's sorry bush league marks. There was something about the way the 6-foot-1½, 202-pound pitcher responded to pressure, Sawyer explained, and Konstanty proved his mentor right in 1950.

Unfortunately, that stunning 1950 success turned out to be a one-season brush with greatness. By 1951, hitters were learning to lay off Konstanty's palmball, which usually dropped out of the strike zone prior to reaching home plate. From 1951 until his retirement after the 1956 season, Casimir James was, for the most part, a run-of-the-mill hurler.

Traded to the Yankees near the tail end of the 1954 season, Konstanty was temporarily revitalized, helping New York to the 1955 pennant with a 7–2 record. But the next year, manager Casey Stengel opted for youth out of the bullpen, and at age 39, Jim was swapped to the Cardinals. He retired following the season and returned to the sporting goods store he had owned and operated since 1947 in Oneonta, New York. Konstanty, the only NL relief pitcher to earn the MVP award, died 20 years later of liver cancer.

If lifetime statistics were the sole basis on which to judge a career, those compiled by James Konstanty during an 11-year stint would hardly merit a second glance. The bespectacled reliever's 66–48 record with 74 saves and 3.46 ERA is respectable, but hardly indicative of the influence he had on the game. Only 11 percent of NL games were "saved" in 1950, but by 1962 that number had nearly doubled. The fireman is now an integral part of every pennant contender.

The palmball artist's major league career, on the whole, was a rough and struggling existence. But his single Herculean effort of 1950 will always be remembered as a major contribution toward liberating baseball's bullpen aces from relative obscurity to an era of indispensability.

Top 5 MVP Vote-Getters

1. Jim Konstanty, Philadelphia — 286
2. Stan Musial, St. Louis — 158
3. Eddie Stanky, New York — 144
4. Del Ennis, Philadelphia — 104
5. Ralph Kiner, Pittsburgh — 91

1950 AMERICAN LEAGUE — PHIL RIZZUTO

Philip Francis Rizzuto
B. September 25, 1917, Brooklyn, New York

Year	Team	Games	AB	Hits	Avg.	HR	RBI	Runs	SB
1950	NY AL	155	617	200	.324	7	66	125	12

The Season

Two managers who won nearly 6,000 games between them were at the helms of their teams for the final time in 1950. Cornelius McGillicuddy, better known as Connie Mack, suffered through a 52–102 season with the Philadelphia Athletics, and the 88-year-old mentor finally decided to call it quits, ending an amazing 53-year career that saw him win nine pennants. Joe McCarthy, who had won an incredible eight flags and seven World Championships in a dozen years with the Yankees, left his post as the Red Sox skipper midway through the year due to illness.

The Yankees, under Casey Stengel, outlasted Detroit by three games for another in a seemingly endless array of pennants, then held the Phillies to five runs in their sixth World Series sweep and 13th World Championship overall.

Some of the season's more interesting events included St. Louis

Phil Rizzuto. (Courtesy New York Yankees.)

Browns pitcher Harry Dorish stealing home June 2 (no other AL pitcher has done it since); Boston producing the most lopsided score in 50 years — 29–4 over St. Louis at Fenway Park June 8, thanks in part to a combined seven home runs by Bobby Doerr, Walt Dropo and Ted Williams; and New York's Johnny Mize hitting three home runs in a game for a record-sixth time in a loss at Detroit September 15.

It was a relatively easy year for the arms of junior circuit catchers. Dom DiMaggio of Boston was the league leader in stolen bases with 15, the lowest total ever for the AL's top man in thefts.

The Little Guy

It didn't take long for Phil Rizzuto to determine what his three most hated words were. He heard them over and over again as he tried to compete with boys his own age, but hardly his size. "You're too small." The words were es-

pecially exasperating for Phil in high school, when at 4-foot-11 he was a full foot shorter than most of his teammates. The frustration continued at a 1936 tryout, when Dodgers manager Casey Stengel told him to get a shoeshine box because he'd never be a big leaguer.

But Rizzuto refused to be intimidated. Though he only reached the height of 5-6, the 150-pound spark plug became the all-time greatest Yankee shortstop, appearing in nine World Series during a 13-year career and winning the Most Valuable Player award in 1950. "Scooter" hit a glittering .324 in his MVP campaign, placing second in the American League in runs scored (125), hits (200) and stolen bases (12), and third in doubles (36). He even smacked a career-high seven homers and led AL shortstops in putouts and fielding average.

Phil carried the aging Yankees for much of the year, raising his average to .441 two months into the season. He was the AL's starting shortstop in the

All-Star Game, playing all 14 innings, and helped New York win another pennant. Rizzuto had a poor World Series, hitting only .143, but his glove aided the Yankees in their sweep of the Whiz Kids from Philadelphia.

The Yankee veterans had not exactly rolled out the red carpet for Rizzuto when the tiny Italian came up to the parent club in 1941. Rizzuto and second baseman Jerry Priddy were ostracized by the established players, who didn't want to see Joe Gordon or Frank Crosetti lose their jobs to these upstarts. As it turned out, Priddy failed in his attempt to wrest the second base job from Gordon, but Rizzuto quickly secured his position as *the* Yankees shortstop, working his way into teammates' hearts with an aggressive, heads-up style of play. Before long, the same players who had given him the cold shoulder were enviously protecting their scrappy little infielder from those who tried to take advantage of his size.

Phil had a distinctive rookie season, hitting .307 and pacing AL shortstops in double plays. The agile, slick-fielding Rizzuto was the American League's top man at his position for most of his career, leading the way in double plays three times, fielding average and putouts twice each, and assists once.

Shortly after enlisting in the Navy in 1943, Rizzuto married Cora Esselborn. He had health problems during his three-year stint, contracting malaria. It was a weak and rusty Rizzuto who returned to the Yankees in 1946. Two more mediocre seasons followed, with minor injuries and dizzy spells making the 1948 campaign a particularly bleak one for the 30-year-old infielder.

But, suddenly revitalized, Rizzuto came on strong in 1949, finishing second in MVP voting after batting .275, stealing 18 bases (runner-up in the AL) and fielding at a league-best .971 clip. He led his team in games played, hits, runs, doubles, triples, stolen bases, total bases and at-bats, as the Yanks won another World Championship. The classy shortstop followed that solid year with an MVP season in 1950, his last extraordinary effort. In the ensuing six years, Phil would hit no higher than .274, falling all the way to .195 in 1954, although he continued to amaze onlookers with his deft fielding abilities.

Rizzuto had been a loyal employee, but he was released in August 1956 to make room for recently acquired Enos Slaughter. Phil was incensed at the maneuver, but soon joined Mel Allen in the booth as a broadcaster, making famous his resounding "Holy cow" and "Did you see that?" blurtings as a Yankees announcer through 1996.

As a teenager in New York, Rizzuto must have figured that the broadcast booth would probably be the closest he'd ever come to landing a job in baseball. His size was a constant deterrent in his efforts to impress scouts, most of whom overlooked the flashy fielding skills and surprising snap in his swing. But the Yanks saw beyond Rizzuto's physical limitations and signed the speedster for $75 a month in 1936, when he played for the Bassett, Virginia, Class D team. He moved up to Norfolk of the Piedmont League the next year, and spent 1939 and 1940 with the Triple A squad in Kansas City, being named Minor League Player of the Year in '40.

Soon after Phil came up to the big

show, teammates learned of his various phobias, including a fear of flying and a revulsion toward anything that crawled, such as snakes, spiders and mice. Practical jokes abounded with Rizzuto as the unwitting target. Outfielder John Lindell was the major prankster, often scaring him into thinking their plane's engines were on fire, and filling the shortstop's glove with any bugs he could locate.

Although a virtual hypochondriac off the field, Rizzuto was nothing short of courageous on it, chasing pop flies at full speed, diving to block ground balls and standing his ground at second base when enemy runners attempted to break up double plays. Yankees hurler Vic Raschi, when asked about his best pitch, said it was anything hit in the direction of Rizzuto. A lifetime .273 hitter, Phil's market value was greatly enhanced by the intangibles. He was always a threat to steal a base, and his intelligent positioning and wide range made him one of the Yankee fans' favorites.

Rizzuto was also an excellent bunter, a craft that was all but ignored during this homer-happy era. Detroit third baseman George Kell was particularly impressed with Scooter's ability to keep an opposing third sacker hon-

est. "You can't rest in the field when Rizzuto's up," Kell said. "He's a wonderful bunter and a strong enough hitter so that you can't play him too shallow."

Rizzuto had to wait nearly 40 years following his playing days to enter the Hall of Fame. Yankees owner George Steinbrenner frequently criticized the veteran's committee for its unwillingness to vote Rizzuto in, and it wasn't until former ballplayers and Rizzuto supporters such as Yogi Berra, Pee Wee Reese and Bill White joined the committee that Phil finally made it into the Hall in 1994.

By outward appearances, diminutive Phil Rizzuto was not an impressive sight, but his triumph in overcoming a short stature to star in the major leagues made him a giant in the eyes of the fans.

Top 5 MVP Vote-Getters

1. Phil Rizzuto, New York — 284
2. Billy Goodman, Boston — 180
3. Yogi Berra, New York — 146
4. George Kell, Detroit — 127
5. Bob Lemon, Cleveland — 102

1951 NATIONAL LEAGUE — ROY CAMPANELLA

Roy Campanella
B. November 19, 1921, Philadelphia, Pennsylvania
D. June 26, 1993, Woodland Hills, California

Year	Team	Games	AB	Hits	Avg.	HR	RBI	Runs	SB
1951	Bkn NL	143	505	164	.325	33	108	90	1

The Season

On October 3, 1951, what is acknowledged by many as the single most exciting moment in sports history occurred. The New York Giants, who had rallied from 13½ games behind the Brooklyn Dodgers to tie for the National League pennant, now

needed to pull another rabbit out of their hats.

Brooklyn held a 4–1 advantage going into the bottom of the ninth inning in the third and final playoff game, but the Giants pushed one run across and had a pair of runners on base with one out. Dodgers manager Chuck Dressen summoned Ralph

Branca to face Bobby Thomson, who came through with "the shot heard 'round the world," a three-run homer, giving the Giants the flag. Fittingly, it was the first game to be telecast coast to coast.

New York, which won 37 of its last 44 regular-season contests, employed two 23-game winners in Larry

Roy Campanella. (Courtesy Los Angeles Dodgers.)

Jansen and Sal Maglie, but neither could post a victory in the Giants' four games-to-two World Series loss to the cross-town Yankees.

Two rookie outfielders who played in that '51 Series, Willie Mays and Mickey Mantle, went on to capture five MVP trophies between them. Mays was the NL's Rookie of the Year that campaign. Veteran outfielder Ralph Kiner of Pittsburgh hit an All-Star Game home run for the third consecutive year.

On September 13, St. Louis became the first senior circuit team to play two different opponents on the same day since the early 1900s. The Cardinals knocked off New York 6–4 in the afternoon, then fell 2–0 to Boston in the nightcap of an unusual double-header.

NL President Ford Frick became baseball's third commissioner when he was given a seven-year contract at $65,000 per annum by club owners September 20.

Campy Came to Play

In days past, Roy Campanella would take vicious cuts at the plate, his right knee nearly scraping the ground from the force of his swing. He would spring from his crouch behind home plate like a cat, whistling a rocket past his pitcher's ear and into the waiting glove of an infielder. But during the 35 years following his stunning baseball career, he sat in a wheelchair, paralyzed from the waist down and barely able to use his arms, the result of a sickening car crash on an icy road near Long Island in 1958. The accident forever changed the course of his life, forcing Roy out of the game he treasured with all of his heart. Despite the physical agony of the injuries and the emotional trauma that followed, one thing remained constant: his ardent passion for life.

It is highly ironic that Campanella, once a powerfully physical man, was forced to spend so much time virtually motionless. From 1948, when he became the major league's first African-American catcher, to 1957, when he involuntarily concluded a spectacular career, the stocky, muscular man behind the mask was the National League's best at his position, with only the Yankees' Yogi Berra in his class.

Here was a man who came to play every day, despite bruised and battered hands, knotted thigh muscles and fatigue bordering on exhaustion. His day-in, day-out efforts and five World Series appearances were appreciated by the writers, who honored him with three Most Valuable Player awards in only five seasons.

Nineteen-fifty-one began on a scary note for Campanella, who narrowly escaped serious injury when a gas heater blew up in his face. More physical woes were to come for the 29-year-old once the season got underway, such as bone chips in an elbow following a collision at home plate with Whitey Lockman, a concussion after being knocked unconscious by a pitch and a leg injury suffered on the final day of the regular season. But overall, 1951 was a joyous, rewarding campaign for the Brooklyn Dodgers catcher.

Exhibiting a quiet demeanor off the field, but a fiery, competitive spirit on it, Campanella became the National League's best backstop that season. Campy hit a career-high .325, fourth best in the league, powered 33 home runs (third) and drove in 108 (fourth).

He was third in the NL in slugging at .590 and doubles with 33, and fourth in total bases with 298. While runners were stealing bases at a 60 percent success rate across the majors, Campy was gunning down two-thirds of those bold enough to test the rifle-like arm that helped him lead all catchers in assists (72) and double plays (12) in 1951.

Roy was born in Philadelphia to an Italian father and an African-American mother, and at an early age was expected to help out by mowing lawns, selling newspapers and delivering milk. He took on the challenge of catching when he learned it was the only open spot on the high school team. In 1936, he was offered a chance to join the Bacharach Giants, a black semipro team that regularly toured four East Coast states.

At 15, Roy preferred baseball to homework, and when the Baltimore Elite Giants of the Negro National League suggested a tryout, the bulky backstop leaped at the opportunity, signing a contract for $60 a month. Campanella made the team, quit school and for the next nine years played ball year 'round, spending his winters on the diamonds of such countries as Venezuela and Puerto Rico, and playing in three Negro League All-Star Games. Campanella credited Homestead Grays standout catcher Josh Gibson with helping him develop and improve his skills behind the plate.

Following the 1945 season, the portly catcher was involved in a series of exhibition games against major leaguers, where he learned that Brooklyn Dodgers owner Branch Rickey had shown interest in him. Impressed by reports about the solid receiver's lively bat and strong arm, Rickey offered Campanella a minor league contract.

Saying he'd think it over, the slugging backstop traveled to Venezuela for the winter season, but received word again from Rickey and decided to return to the States and sign with Nashua, a Class B Dodger farm team, for the 1946 season. Campanella hit .290 with 13 homers and 96 RBIs for Nashua, and was named the league's MVP. When skipper Walt Alston was ejected from a game that season, he turned the reins over to Campy, who became the first black man to manage in organized baseball. Nashua won that contest 7–5.

Along with roommate Don Newcombe, Campanella was promoted to Montreal in 1947. Roy obviously was ready for the Dodgers the following season, but Rickey felt his future star was the right person to break the color line in the American Association, and sent him to St. Paul, Minnesota. With Campanella tearing up that league and the Dodgers struggling, skipper Leo Durocher convinced Rickey to bring Campanella up midway through the campaign.

Campy played in 83 games—collecting three hits in his first start—smacked nine homers and batted .258, but the Dodgers finished third, 7½ games out. His first full season, 1949, in which he made the All-Star squad for the first of eight straight years, began a string of nine consecutive campaigns in which Campanella caught 100 or more games. A .287 average, 22 home runs and 82 RBIs helped the Dodgers edge the Cardinals for the pennant. The 27-year-old catcher homered in the World Series, but the Yankees cruised to a five-game triumph. In 1950, when the Dodgers fell two games short of Philadelphia's Whiz Kids, Roy raised his home run total to a resounding 31.

Campanella had proven his capabilities as a steady, reliable receiver, an intelligent handler of pitchers and a consistent hitter. Three MVP awards in five years would follow for the likeable, roly-poly man who was as quick with a smile as with his bat.

Top 5 MVP Vote-Getters

1. Roy Campanella, Brooklyn — 243
2. Stan Musial, St. Louis — 191
3. Monte Irvin, New York — 166
4. Sal Maglie, New York — 153
5. Preacher Roe, Brooklyn — 138

1951 AMERICAN LEAGUE—YOGI BERRA

Lawrence Peter Berra
B. May 12, 1925, St. Louis, Missouri

Year	Team	Games	AB	Hits	Avg.	HR	RBI	Runs	SB
1951	NY AL	141	547	161	.294	27	88	92	5

The Season

While the National League feted a sizzling pennant race between the Giants and Dodgers, the Yankees stayed comfortably ahead of the Cleveland Indians to win the American League flag by five games.

Always the showman, first-year St. Louis Browns owner Bill Veeck outdid even himself when he sent 43-inch-tall Eddie Gaedel to bat against the Detroit Tigers August 18. Gaedel, wearing uniform No. ⅛, walked on four pitches, Veeck was chastised by league officials and the Browns received a ton of publicity.

Individuals who earned plenty of ink included the trio of 20-game winners on the Cleveland pitching staff—Bob Feller, Mike Garcia and Early Wynn—who were joined by three other junior circuit hurlers in the "20" circle. One of Feller's victories was his third and final no-hitter, but "Rapid Robert" was upstaged by Yankee Allie Reynolds, who fired two no-hit games, including one to clinch a tie for the pennant.

After losing Games 1 and 3 against the Cinderella New York Giants, the Yankees took the final three World Series contests to rack up their third straight championship. Except for Monte Irvin (.458) and Al Dark (.417), Yankee hurlers and their composite 1.87 Series ERA kept their New York counterparts in check.

Inducted into the baseball Hall of Fame in 1951 was three-time Most Valuable Player Jimmie Foxx, who played a vast majority of his career with the Philadelphia Athletics and Boston Red Sox.

The Clown Prince

If Joe DiMaggio was the most elegantly prestigious ballplayer in New York Yankee history, his alter ego was fellow pinstriper Yogi Berra. Homely beyond reproach, the stocky little catcher compares favorably in two departments with his Bronx Bomber teammate: both were well-loved by the fans and could knock the stuffings out of a baseball.

The youngest of four boys growing up in an Italian family in the St. Louis section known as "The Hill," Lawrence Berra owes much to his older brothers. All three had been forced to give up baseball opportunities to help support the impoverished Berra clan, but successfully coaxed their parents into allowing Yogi to have a chance at the game. Berra tried out for the St. Louis Cardinals with childhood buddy Joe Garagiola in 1942, but turned down a $500 offer, which was half of what his pal received. Soon thereafter, the Yankees swept in and signed the young catcher.

Yogi Berra. (Courtesy New York Yankees.)

From the first day he donned a New York uniform, fans, writers and fellow players realized there was something peculiarly special about the happy-go-lucky little package of talent. He immediately became one of the most likeable men in the sport — simple in his tastes, unintentionally hilarious in conversation and as colorful as the characters in the comic books he read so religiously. Despite superficial appearances, Yogi has shown himself to be one of the more astute baseball minds of his time, able to grasp the ethereal particulars of the game quickly as player, coach or manager.

Berra's acumen was clearly apparent in 1951, when at age 26 he led the Yankees in home runs (27) and RBIs (88), while pacing league backstops in putouts, assists and double plays to earn his first of three MVP awards.

Overcoming a shaky 4-for-19 start and a prolonged season-ending slump, Berra finished with a .294 average and became the eighth Yankee to cop the coveted Most Valuable Player honor, as well as the first AL catcher since Mickey Cochrane in 1934.

Because of the enduring dry spell he suffered through toward the conclusion of 1951, Berra had counted himself out of the MVP competition. But Yogi's chances were boosted by the Yankees pennant, and there was no mistaking his major contributions to that team and the 13 other pennant winners on which he played. Winning was what Berra was all about. Nobody in baseball history has played on more

World Championship teams (10) than the waddle-in-his-walk receiver.

Despite the daily grind that went with his position, Berra finished fourth in the league in homers during his initial MVP year, and this combination of power and behind-the-plate dominance helped the sixth-year pro edge out pitchers Ned Garver (20 wins) of the Browns and Allie Reynolds (two no-hitters) of the Yanks, who followed Yogi in the balloting.

Berra's obvious ability to call pitches and handle Yankee hurlers was evident throughout his career, but it was especially noteworthy in 1951 when Vic Raschi and Ed Lopat won 21 games each, and Reynolds posted 17 triumphs. Reynolds' second no-hitter was in jeopardy after Berra dropped a pop foul off the bat of Boston's Ted Williams with two outs in the ninth inning. But on the next pitch, Williams popped it up again, and this time Berra squeezed it for the final out, as well as a Yankee clinching of a tie for the AL pennant. Following the game, Yankee executive Del Webb said to Berra, "When I die, I hope they give me a second chance the way they did you."

Nineteen-fifty-one was the first payoff in a career that had promised big Yankee dividends as early as 1946 when Yogi homered in his first major league game. Immediately befriended by New York stars DiMaggio and Phil Rizzuto, Berra soon learned to shrug off the initially painful taunts concerning his physical appearance, and started stinging the horsehide mercilessly. He hit .305 in 1948, and was the starting All-Star Game receiver in '49. This was the year that new manager Casey Stengel made Berra a fulltime catcher, and not so coincidentally, the Yanks rattled off five consecutive World Championships. The next season, Berra was acknowledged by *The Sporting News* as the top backstop in either league, and placed third in the MVP voting.

In what many view as the best campaign of his career, the compact left-handed hitter pounded out 28 homers, drove in 124 runs, hit .322 and led AL catchers in putouts and double plays in 1950. The MVP, however, went to teammate and good buddy, Rizzuto.

Experts and fans puzzled at the sight of so unathletic a figure producing such extraordinary results. Berra's mug (and if ever there was a face to fit that word, this was it), replete with oversized ears, crooked teeth and five o'clock shadow, was never in danger of adorning a picture frame in a bobby-soxer's bedroom. But, as Garagiola astutely observed some years later, Berra's face turned out to be his fortune, distinctively setting him apart from the throngs: a built-in recognition factor that served him well throughout his career.

Yet as Berra himself said, "You don't hit with your face," and his ability to deliver with men in scoring position soon gained notoriety equal to his features and irregular pundits. Despite being a notorious bad-ball hitter, Yogi never struck out more than 38 times in a season. Berra spurned the free pass and scorched shoe-top sliders and nose-jamming fastballs with the same relish. The free-swinger perplexed AL hurlers throughout his career, finishing with 1,430 RBIs, a .285 lifetime average and 358 home runs, including 306 as a catcher. He was among the top five Yankees all time in six offensive departments, and among the top 10 in nine.

"When you get to the seventh inning," rival manager Paul Richards observed of Berra, "he's the most dangerous hitter in baseball."

Sportswriters were equally amused and confused by Berra's brand of patchwork quotations, expressed with an elocutionary style that would have brought Henry Higgins to his knees:

- On Yogi Berra Day, Sportsman's Park, St. Louis: "I want to thank you all for making this day necessary."
- Analyzing Yankee pennant chances in 1982: "We have deep depth."
- After watching an old Steve McQueen movie: "He must have made that before he died."
- Following Johnny Bench's breaking of Yogi's record for career homers by a catcher: "I always knew the record would stand until it was broken."

This amalgamation of looks, mangled quotes and teeming baseball talent was only beginning to gain momentum in 1951. Along with Mickey Mantle, Lawrence Peter Berra would continue to secure a monotonous string of Yankee pennants and World Championships well into the 1960s, picking up two more MVPs and a Hall of Fame berth on his carnival romp through the American League.

Top 5 MVP Vote-Getters

1. Yogi Berra, New York — 184
2. Ned Garver, St. Louis — 157
3. Allie Reynolds, New York — 125
4. Minnie Minoso, Cleveland/ Chicago — 120
5. Bob Feller, Cleveland — 118

1952 National League—Hank Sauer

Henry John Sauer
B. March 17, 1917, Pittsburgh, Pennsylvania
D. August 24, 2001, Burlingame, California

Year	Team	Games	AB	Hits	Avg.	HR	RBI	Runs	SB
1952	Chi NL	151	567	153	.270	37	121	89	1

The Season

Following an agonizing conclusion to their 1951 season, the Brooklyn Dodgers mended their fans' broken hearts by winning the pennant by 4½ games for first-year owner Walter O'Malley.

Carl Erskine's June 19 no-hitter against the Cubs provided Brooklyn with its best individual performance of the year, but it was the season-long work of Rookie of the Year Joe Black (15–4) out of the bullpen that pushed the Dodgers into the World Series.

The Ebbets Field crew featured a fearsome lineup, compiling league highs in runs, home runs and stolen bases. But following a familiar script, the Dodgers lost in seven games to the Yankees in the World Series.

Unusual achievements during the season included Warren Spahn's record-tying 18-strikeout performance in a 15-inning loss to Chicago June 14; a May 21 outburst in which the Dodgers suffocated the Reds with 15 first-inning runs, setting an NL record by having 19 consecutive batters reach base; and a home run April 23 by New York Giants relief pitcher Hoyt Wilhelm in his first major league at-bat. Wilhelm, who earned his initial career win that day—and his first of 15 relief victories this season—would not hit another homer in a 21-year, Hall of Fame career.

Despite such entertaining spectacles, National League attendance reached a post–World War II low of 6 million, a depth which would not be touched again. The largest non-contributors to the turnstile tally were the seventh-place Braves, who drew fewer than 300,000 customers in their last year in Boston.

Right-hander Robin Roberts posted 28 victories for Philadelphia this season, the highest total since 1934 NL MVP Dizzy Dean recorded the same amount in 1935. Pittsburgh slugger Ralph Kiner tied for the top senior circuit spot in home runs with 37, marking the seventh straight year in which he either led or tied for the league lead in that department.

Sauer Grapes MVP

Rangy, long ball-hitting Hank Sauer was "The Mayor of Wrigley Field" for only six seasons, but during that time he was as popular a Bruin as any personality in the history of the Chicago Cubs.

The faithful had previously loved Gabby Hartnett and Phil Cavarretta, the team's two MVP predecessors who helped bring pennant flags to the franchise. But Sauer, surrounded by ineptitude, seemed to inspire even more fan adulation. Like Ernie Banks who followed, Sauer's credible performances were often the only semblance of professionalism on a squad that consistently finished in the second division. And while Banks earned the "Mr. Cub" sobriquet for his efforts, it was "Big Henry" who was regularly showered with packets of chewing tobacco by adoring bleacher fans when he took his left field position.

One of the most soft-spoken men in baseball, Sauer was thrust into the eye of a controversial storm in 1952 when he was named the National League's MVP. Scathing newspaper attacks from various big league cities decried the selection of the slow-moving outfielder, pointing contemptuously to an unspectacular .270 batting average, his team's fifth-place finish, a lack of skills in the outfield and other deserving candidates, such as Robin Roberts (28 wins) and Joe Black (15–4 for pennant-winning Brooklyn). Absent from most of the criticism were Sauer's estimable RBI (121) and home run (37) totals, both of which topped the league.

So what should have been a sensational triumph for the Pittsburgh native turned out to be a dubious victory in the eyes of dissenting critics. Hank, born into a large, lower-class family, had worked diligently to achieve this moment of glory. Sauer and his brothers would play baseball incessantly, using homemade equipment, including a redesigned boxing glove that was converted into Hank's first mitt.

Older brother Ed was the first Sauer to make it to the big leagues, playing sparingly for the Cubs, Cardinals and Braves for four seasons beginning in 1943. He managed only five home runs in his career, but that total, combined with Hank's 288 round-trippers, put the Sauer boys eighth on the all-time brothers list for homers at that time.

The Yankees signed Hank to his first contract in 1937, and he played distinctively for three minor league campaigns before being claimed by Cincinnati in 1941.

After seeing limited action in the 1941 and '42 seasons, he was drafted into the Coast Guard, where he spent the next two years. He hit .293 in 31 games for Cincinnati in 1945, but once again returned to the bushes, earning a Minor League Player of the Year award before reaching the big leagues in 1948 as a 31-year-old rookie.

The turning point in Sauer's career came in 1947 when minor league manager Jewel Ens persuaded him to switch from a 35-ounce bat to a 40-ouncer. Sauer obliged, and the result was a 50-homer season for Syracuse and a minor league player of the year award.

The nine-year minor league struggle made it all the more difficult for Sauer to absorb the 1952 MVP criticism, and the same writers who had led the attack were quick to gleefully emphasize his 1953 failings when Hank slumped to 19 home runs and 60 RBIs.

But Sauer rebounded for 41 round-trippers and 103 RBIs for the Cubs in 1954 before faltering to a .211 average in '55. Chicago traded Sauer in 1956 to the Cardinals, who then swapped the veteran to the Giants. The power stroke returned one more time in 1957, as the 38-year-old socked 26 home runs in the Polo Grounds before traveling with the Giants to the West Coast for two more campaigns.

The "Big Dutchman's" 15 major league seasons were that of a model ballplayer. He preferred in most instances to let his potent bat do the talking. A lifetime home run ratio of one every 16.6 at-bats placed the 6-foot-4, 199-pound righty among the top 30 all time in that category.

From 1948 through 1952, he never hit fewer than 30 circuit clouts, averaging 102 RBIs per year during that span. After belting 35 homers in his first full season in 1948, Sauer and Cincinnati teammate Frankie Baumholtz were traded to the Cubs for Peanuts Lowrey and Harry Walker in what turned out to be the steal of the decade for Chicago.

In 1950, he was the unwitting source of an All-Star Game controversy when Brooklyn Dodgers manager Burt Shotton attempted to usurp the rules and bench Sauer, the fans' choice in the balloting, for Duke Snider. Lacking a true center fielder among his three elected outfielders, Shotton publicly stated that Sauer was the worst fielder of the three and would sit down in favor of Snider. A public outcry followed, and Shotton relented, with Sauer starting in right field.

The placid yet authoritative figure overcame this and the MVP ridicule to carve out an exemplary National League career. Following his retirement, the Giants latched onto Hank and made him a part of their organization as a scout for 35 years. His son, Hank Jr., played minor league baseball. Hank Sr. passed away in 2001 at the age of 84 while playing golf near his Millbrae, California, home.

But the most indelible portrait of Sauer can be found in his 1952 MVP season when the outfielder's league-leading marks in home runs and RBIs almost single-handedly lifted a weak Chicago Cubs team to a .500 effort. Besides pacing the league in two of three Triple Crown categories, he was runner-up in slugging percentage at .531 and total bases with 301.

Sauer tore up the league in the first half of that season, crashing 23 homers (including three in one game) and driving in 69 runs by the All-Star break. During the mid-season classic, Hank hit the game-winning round-tripper off Bob Lemon in a National League victory, a moment he later called his biggest thrill in baseball. After winding down to a near crawl at the end of the year, Sauer still managed to edge Robin Roberts in the MVP balloting, 226 points to 211, despite his team's fifth-place finish. One hour after the call came informing Sauer of his MVP award, his son was born.

There were surely more multifaceted individuals who graced major league arenas in the early 1950s, but for expertise in giving baseballs four-bagger relocations, The Mayor's record meets the standards set by more-heralded heroes of his era, such as Ralph Kiner and Gil Hodges, among the NL power elite. In deportment, however, Hank Sauer was second to none.

Top 5 MVP Vote-Getters

1. Hank Sauer, Chicago — 226
2. Robin Roberts, Philadelphia — 211
3. Joe Black, Brooklyn — 208
4. Hoyt Wilhelm, New York — 133
5. Stan Musial, St. Louis — 127

1952 AMERICAN LEAGUE — BOBBY SHANTZ

Robert Clayton Shantz
B. September 26, 1925, Pottstown, Pennsylvania

Year	Team	Games	W	L	ERA	IP	SO	BB	ShO
1952	Phil AL	33	24	7	2.48	279.2	152	63	5

The Season

As the 1952 season progressed, it appeared that perhaps the New York Yankees' World Championship streak would come to an abrupt halt. The Bronx Bombers, who had won three consecutive crowns, were trying to cope without the retired Joe DiMaggio and the injured Ed Lopat.

A powerful Cleveland squad seemed the likely candidate to derail the New York express. The Indians led the American League late in August, and ended up pacing the circuit in runs and homers, as well as boasting three 20-game winners. But under the near-genius guidance of manager Casey Stengel, the Yankees nudged the Tribe by two games, then defeated the Brooklyn Dodgers in a seven-game World Series.

The post-season highlight was second baseman Billy Martin's seventh-game sprint and knee-high catch of a Jackie Robinson pop-up with two outs and the bases loaded. That seventh-inning heroic helped give New York a 4–2 victory and its fourth World Championship in a row.

Detroit pitcher Virgil Trucks matched Allie Reynolds' feat of the previous year by twirling a pair of no-hitters in 1952. The status of the second gem August 25 against New York was in doubt until Tigers shortstop Johnny Pesky convinced official scorer John Drebinger to change a third-inning infield hit by Phil Rizzuto to an error. Actually, Drebinger had originally ruled the play an error on Pesky, but had been talked into changing it to a hit by New York World Telegram reporter Dan Daniel.

And speaking of a lack of hitting, St. Louis and Cleveland tied a major league record for fewest hits in a game April 23 when they combined for only two during a 1–0 Browns victory. A pair of Bobs—Cain of St. Louis and Feller of the Indians—both tossed a one-hitter.

Miniature with Moxie

When baseball scouts seek pitching prospects on high school and college diamonds these days, they're looking primarily for one thing: heat. They want a boy who can pump the ball at 90-plus miles per hour. Curves, control, knowing how to set up a hitter … all these can be taught; but raw speed is a God-given gift.

One hurler without that seemingly vital pitch in his arsenal was Bobby Shantz. The 5-foot-6, 139-pounder rarely blew pitches by hitters in the genre of other left-handed MVPs, such as Sandy Koufax and Lefty Grove. Instead, the crafty southpaw used sharp-breaking curve balls and an occasional knuckler, pinpoint control and natural savvy to thwart the opposition. In addition to his quietly effective pitching, Shantz was an excellent fielder, earning eight Gold Glove awards.

Shantz began coming into his own in 1951, his third year with the Philadelphia Athletics, when he started out at 7–6 and finished 18–10 for a sixth-place ballclub. But that stretch run effort was only a prelude for one of the most outstanding seasons ever put together by a pitcher.

Bobby started changing speeds on his fastball in 1952, and results were immediate. The diminutive left-hander jumped to a 14–2 record, pitched 14 consecutive complete games (winning 11 of them) and captured his 20th victory against three defeats with nearly two months remaining in the season. His 24–7 mark gave him the American League crown in triumphs and winning percentage (.774), and he also led the way in opponents' on-base percentage (.272). The writers ignored the A's fourth-place finish, presenting Shantz with the MVP award.

Bobby's 2.48 ERA was third in the league, as were his five shutouts and 152 strikeouts, and the lefty's 27 complete games were good for the runner-up spot. In his one inning of work in the 1952 All-Star Game, the pint-sized competitor whiffed three slugging National Leaguers—Whitey Lockman, Jackie Robinson and Stan Musial—in succession.

Unfortunately for Shantz and the Athletics, he failed to heed a bit of advice he'd received that year. Not a prolific hitter, Bobby loved stepping into the batter's box as much as toeing the rubber. Despite repeated warnings from manager Jimmy Dykes, Shantz continued to swing from the right-hand side where he had more power, rather than bat lefty to help protect his valuable left arm. Bobby paid the price when he was struck on the left wrist by a wicked fastball, breaking it in two places. Seeking his 25th win that day, with one scheduled start remaining, the injury put him out for the year.

In his first 1953 start, Shantz tore muscles in his left shoulder, apparently the result of favoring the wrist, and won only five games that season. His 1954 effort was even more short-lived. On opening day, Bobby re-injured the shoulder, and although he picked up the win, appeared in only one other contest that year. The financially troubled Athletics fell to seventh place in 1953 and the cellar in '54 before moving to Kansas City for the 1955 campaign. The A's first MVP since Jimmie Foxx (1933) saw his woes continue in K.C., where he won only seven games in two years. But then his big break arrived.

The Yankees, looking for help on the mound and in the infield, sent six marginal players to the Athletics for right-hander Art Ditmar and bright young prospect Clete Boyer. The 31-year-old Shantz was merely a throw-in, but ended up being the Bronx Bombers' salvation in 1957, leading the league in ERA at 2.45, winning 11 games and saving five others.

The lithe lefty, referred to by Casey Stengel as "Little Feller," helped the Yanks win pennants in 1957, '58 and '60. Shantz pitched five scoreless innings in the seventh game of the 1960 World Series against the Pirates.

Shantz, who compiled a 2.73 ERA in four years as a Yankee, was not protected in the 1961 expansion draft and, ironically, landed with Pittsburgh. He was 6–3 for the Pirates in 1961, then went to the expansion Houston Colt .45s the next season. He finished the year with the Cardinals, and in his final campaign, was sent to the Cubs in the lopsided 1964 deal that brought Lou Brock to St. Louis. Bobby went to his eighth ballclub, the Phillies, late in '64 before retiring.

When Shantz was offered his first shot at professional baseball, he almost turned it down out of a fear of failure. After playing sandlot ball in Philadelphia, scouts told him he had a very good arm, but that his size was inadequate. Finally, in 1947, A's scout Harry O'Donnell arranged a tryout for the 21-year-old at Class A Lincoln, Nebraska; but Bobby hesitated, convinced he was too small to make it. His father talked him into giving it a try, and the little southpaw won 18 games in 1948, making the parent club the subsequent year. In his second big league game in 1949, Shantz used a dazzling assortment of off-speed curves and knucklers to hurl nine consecutive no-hit innings in relief against Detroit, getting credit for the win and securing a spot in the starting rotation.

Throughout his career, Shantz

displayed a big league mind in a Little League body. And while he never instilled trepidation in hitters with a blazing fastball, he kept them off-balance and outsmarted them long enough to be considered one of the best little left-handers in the game.

Top 5 MVP Vote-Getters

1 Bobby Shantz, Philadelphia—280
2. Allie Reynolds, New York—183
3. Mickey Mantle, New York—143
4. Yogi Berra, New York—104
5. Early Wynn, Cleveland—99

1953 NATIONAL LEAGUE—ROY CAMPANELLA

Roy Campanella
B. November 19, 1921, Philadelphia, Pennsylvania
D. June 26, 1993, Woodland Hills, California

Year	Team	Games	AB	Hits	Avg.	HR	RBI	Runs	SB
1953	Bkn NL	144	519	162	.312	41	142	103	4

The Season

The 1953 edition of the Brooklyn Dodgers was an awesome one, as demonstrated by its 105 victories, the most in baseball since World War II, and league-leading totals in runs, homers, hitting, slugging and stolen bases. Five of the eight Brooklyn regulars hit over .300, including batting crown recipient Carl Furillo (.344), who injured his hand September 6 in a brawl with the hated Giants and was out for the rest of the season.

Brooklyn was especially tough at Ebbets Field this season, tying the St. Louis Cardinals' 1942 record for most wins in a home ballpark with 60.

Despite having garnered their second pennant in a row and fourth in seven campaigns, the Dodgers' postseason difficulties continued with another World Series loss to the New York Yankees. Brooklyn had a composite batting average of .300 in the six-game set, but committed seven errors, dropping its seventh consecutive fall classic. One bright moment for the Dodgers occurred in the third game when Carl Erskine struck out 14 batters for a Series record.

The Braves, who had resided in Boston since the National League was formed in 1876, found a new home in Milwaukee. It was the first franchise shift in the majors in a half-century, and the initial major league action for Milwaukee fans since 1901 when the Milwaukee Brewers were American League charter members. Apparently pleased with the new surroundings, the Braves jumped from seventh place the previous year all the way to second in manager Charlie Grimm's first full season.

Dizzy Dean, the 1934 NL MVP, was elected to baseball's Hall of Fame in 1953.

The Receiver Repeats

While Jackie Robinson was the best-known black major leaguer in the late 1940s and early '50s, teammate Roy Campanella was the most popular of the Dodgers' various African-American players. But linking Robinson and Campanella is like comparing apples to oranges. They both played the game with heart and soul, and there the similarity ended.

Roy Campanella. (Courtesy Los Angeles Dodgers.)

To Robinson, baseball was a cause first, then a game. Following two years of squelching his emotions at the insistence of Branch Rickey, Jackie let loose in 1949 and never quit reminding baseball that despite its token attempts at integration, it was still a white man's game and needed to change. To Campanella, baseball was merely a way to have fun and earn money simultaneously. The hefty catcher once said that in order to play ball for a living, one had to be a man, but also had to have a lot of little boy within him. For his attitude, Roy was dubbed an "Uncle Tom" by Robinson, but Campanella brushed the demeaning remark aside.

The 5-foot-9, 190-pound bundle of optimism enjoyed a tragically brief but enviable 10-year career in the National League, breaking most offensive records for catchers. His 242 lifetime home runs were an NL high for a catcher until Johnny Bench came along, and they represented the top total for receivers in Dodgers history. He was the first catcher to hit 20 or more round-trippers three years in a row, and he reached that pinnacle seven times. For nine consecutive years, the Brooklyn backstop caught at least 100 games, with a high of 140 in both 1951 and '53. Campanella accumulated 100 or more RBIs and hit .300 in three different seasons, and slugged at a .500 clip or better on four occasions. He is one of only a handful of National Leaguers to be named the Most Valuable Player three times.

The second of those awards came in 1953, two years after the first. A hand injury had slowed Roy down considerably in 1952 — his average slipping to .269 — although he still managed 22 homers and 97 RBIs while leading league catchers in fielding with a .994 mark. The Dodgers won the '52 pennant, but fell in a seven-game World Series to the Yankees. Campy roared back in '53, putting together career-high numbers in home runs (41, third in the NL), RBIs (142, first), slugging (.611, third), runs scored (103), putouts (802) and games played (144). His homer and RBI totals were the most ever by a catcher at that time.

Nineteen-fifty-three was an outstanding year for several other Dodger sluggers as well. Owner Rickey, taking advantage of Ebbets Field's 365-foot power alley in left-center, stocked his lineup with the right-handed strength of Gil Hodges, Carl Furillo, Robinson and Campanella. The staff ERA in 1953 was an unimpressive 4.10, but the team's 208 homers offset that inadequacy, and the Brooks won the pennant by 13 games. Roy's robust stroke figured prominently in the cakewalk, and he was a solid contributor in the World Series. A Campanella homer in the eighth inning provided the winning run in a 3–2 Game 3 triumph, and his six runs scored tied for the top mark among Series participants. But once again the Dodgers fell to the Yankees, this time in six games.

Like many MVP winners, Campanella's World Series totals did not mirror his regular-season efficiency. The deceptively quick and agile backstop hit .237 in five post-season experiences, all against the Yankees, collecting four homers and 12 RBIs. In 32 games, he stroked 27 hits, including five doubles, and scored 14 runs. As a team, the Dodgers were even less effective in Series play during Roy's tenure, winning only once (1955) in five attempts.

In addition to the on-field contributions, Campanella displayed another, less tangible quality through his leadership capabilities. When the Dodgers were slumping, he would keep his teammates loose with jokes and stories about the old days in the Negro Leagues, when he would play ball by sunlight (sometimes up to three dou-ble-headers in a day) and travel by moonlight. While the nine years spent in the Negro and Mexican leagues were draining ones, Roy's memories were much brighter than those associated with his 1954 season.

If 1952 had been a bleak year for the Brooklyn catcher, '54 was even more dismal. True to his character, Campanella tried to play with a broken bone in his left wrist, and it took a benching by manager Walter Alston to convince the rugged competitor he needed surgery. He totaled only 111 games, batting a career-low .207 with 82 hits. Nineteen of those safeties were homers, however, and he managed to drive in 51 runs. It was the only campaign in which Campanella failed to lead league receivers in any defensive category. With the Dodgers finishing five games behind the pennant-winning Giants, the injury-riddled 32-year-old had little about which to feel satisfied.

The following season would bring back the good times for Roy, who would help lead the Dodgers to that elusive World Series championship. But it would be Campanella's final successful season before a tragic accident ended his career, and nearly his life.

Top 5 MVP Vote-Getters

1. Roy Campanella, Brooklyn — 297
2. Eddie Mathews, Milwaukee — 216
3. Duke Snider, Brooklyn — 157
4. Red Schoendienst, St. Louis — 155
5. Warren Spahn, Milwaukee — 120

1953 American League — Al Rosen

Albert Leonard Rosen
B. February 29, 1924, Spartanburg, South Carolina

Year	Team	Games	AB	Hits	Avg.	HR	RBI	Runs	SB
1953	Cle AL	155	599	201	.336	43	145	115	8

The Season

The Yankee machine churned out a record-fifth consecutive World Championship in 1953, breezing to the pennant by 8½ games, then besting the Brooklyn Dodgers in a six-game World Series. Casey Stengel's bunch out-hammered a powerful Dodger club in the fall classic, with Yankee second sacker Billy Martin taking on the hero role, collecting a dozen safeties for a .500 average.

During the regular season, the New York team led the American League in runs, average, slugging, ERA and least runs allowed. This prodigious output was directly contrasted with that of the miserable last-place Browns, who finished their final season in St. Louis with exactly 100 defeats.

Typifying the futility of that franchise was rookie Bobo Holloman, who fired a no-hitter in the first start of his career, only to wind up back in the farm system within three months and out of the majors for good.

Gene Stephens and Sammy White of the Red Sox made the record book June 18, the former pounding out three hits in one inning and the latter scoring three times in that same frame. Boston's 17-run seventh inning included 14 hits and six walks.

On June 15, an 18-game Yankees winning streak and a 14-game St. Louis losing skid both came to an end. The 3–1 Browns victory included Johnny Mize's 2,000th career hit.

Despite a .325 lifetime batting average, 361 homers, more than 1,500 RBIs and a record 56-game hitting streak, Joe DiMaggio did not receive enough votes for Hall of Fame enshrinement in his first year of eligibility.

Unanimous Pick

The single-minded determination personified by Al Rosen throughout his life could be used as a prime example for motivational seminars and positive thinking manuals. The unwavering hustler was and is a winner, and his entire attitude toward life exudes that philosophy.

Goal setting has always been a part of Rosen's existence, and with an eye staunchly fixed on a major league career, Al signed a Class D Cleveland Indians contract in 1942. But it was eight long years before he attained his objective, struggling incessantly to correct his biggest deficiency: fielding ground balls. Attention to that cause brought slow but steady improvement, and after averaging 37 errors per year, Rosen cut that total in half in 1949, assuring himself of a clear shot with the Indians.

Rosen exploded onto the major league scene to stay in 1950, leading the American League with 37 home runs—an AL rookie record that stood for 37 years—and driving in 116 in his first full season. A more telling triumph was the 26-year-old's satisfying league leadership in assists. He topped the 100 mark in RBIs again during an impressive sophomore effort, hitting a record-tying four grand slams. Rosen then led the junior circuit with 105 RBIs in 1952 while crashing 28 round-trippers and lifting his average over .300 for the first time. The Indians finished second to the Yankees in both 1951 and '52.

Then came the incredible 1953 MVP endeavor, when only one point in his .336 batting average separated the prematurely gray-haired slugger from a Triple Crown. Mickey Vernon's Washington teammates helped deny Rosen that particular plum, purposely running amuck on the basepaths in the last inning on the final day of the season to assure that Vernon would not have to bat again and jeopardize his .337 average.

But no one could take away the blockbusting Rosen's single brightest day in the sun the following year. Playing with a broken index finger, the Indian mainstay demonstrated to his hometown fans why he was the leading All-Star vote-getter by powering two distant homers and registering five RBIs, both record-tying efforts for an All-Star Game.

"The Hebrew Hammer" was the unquestioned darling of Municipal Stadium at that point in his career, but by 1955 he was the object of the most consistently vicious fan derision in Cleveland history. As Rosen fought unsuccessfully to overcome the hindrance of a permanently impaired finger, his batting marks gradually declined, and the booing became relentless. The situation reached an intolerable level for Cleveland manager Al Lopez, who privately told friends that the continual disrespect heaped upon Rosen was one of the factors in his decision to take over the Chicago White Sox managerial reins following the 1956 season.

Nineteen-fifty-five and '56 were an especially painful period for the 5-foot-10, 180-pound Rosen. Despite the injury and a new position, first base, "Flip" had managed to hit an even .300 with 102 RBIs in the pennant-winning year of 1954; however, he slipped to .250 in the four-game World Series upset loss to the New York Giants. In the face of a hostile home crowd, he led the second-place Tribe with 81 RBIs in 1955, but stumbled to an all-time low .244 average. Still hampered by the bad finger, he tallied only 61 RBIs, 15 round-trippers and a .267 average the following campaign, after which the 32-year-old retired.

Despite his vast big league accomplishments, the fabulous 1953 campaign stands out as the right-handed hitter's claim to fame, and for good reason. Following that year, Rosen's name headed the MVP ballot of every one of the 24 baseball writers eligible to vote for the award. His .336 average for 1953 was 51 points above his lifetime mark, with career highs in hits, home runs, runs, RBIs, slugging percentage and stolen bases.

Playing every game at third base for the Tribe, Rosen's 43-homer output established an AL record for hot corner players. In compiling 201 hits, he became the first American Leaguer in 16 years to go over 200 safeties and 40 circuit clouts in the same season.

A pair of grand slams and a 20-game hitting streak highlighted the impressive assault, which included league-leading statistics in five offensive categories: homers, RBIs (145), total bases (367), slugging (.613) and runs (115).

Born in 1924 in South Carolina, Rosen soon moved with his family to Miami, Florida, where he spent the majority of his youth. By age 13, he was playing professional softball with the older men of the community.

Eternally aggressive and possessing an extremely sharp and retentive mind, he eventually graduated with a degree in business administration and worked for an investment firm during his baseball career. Rosen put his education to use in the baseball world following his retirement as a player, presiding over the New York Yankees' return to prominence in 1978 as the club's president. A clash with owner George Steinbrenner culminated in Al leaving to become vice president and general manager of the Houston Astros, where he presided over a West Division title in 1980. Rosen also served as a GM for the San Francisco Giants,

who won the West Division in 1987 and the NL pennant in '89.

There remains, however, a question mark in the baseball fraternity concerning what Rosen might have accomplished had he not retired at such a young age. But Al's pride would not let him continue to perform at anything less than 100 percent efficiency, and the injured finger had negated that possibility.

Yet well after retirement, he looked fit to powder a fastball to the far reaches of Municipal Stadium.

Top 5 MVP Vote-Getters

1. Al Rosen, Cleveland — 336
2. Yogi Berra, New York — 167
3. Mickey Vernon, Washington — 162
4. Minnie Minoso, Chicago — 100
5. Virgil Trucks, St. Louis/Chicago — 81

1954 NATIONAL LEAGUE — WILLIE MAYS

Willie Howard Mays
B. May 6, 1931, Westfield, Alabama

Year	Team	Games	AB	Hits	Avg.	HR	RBI	Runs	SB
1954	NY NL	151	565	195	.345	41	110	119	8

The Season

The New York Giants combined power and pitching to rise from fifth place the previous year to the pennant. Lodged in first place the final four months of the season, the Giants beat out defending champion Brooklyn by five games. New York was only fifth in the league in hitting (.264), but had the best ERA (3.09) and tied the Dodgers for most homers (186).

Pinch-hitter supreme Dusty Rhodes, who was strategically used during the regular season by manager

Leo Durocher, homered in the first two games of the World Series, and came through with timely pinch-hit singles in the second and third contests as the upset-minded Giants swept the Indians, snapping a string of seven consecutive NL Series defeats.

Impressive individual major league achievements in 1954 included 24 saves by Brooklyn's Jim Hughes, the most ever in the National League at that time, and Wally Moon of the Cardinals homering in his first and last at-bats of the campaign on the way to earning Rookie of the Year honors. In

the minors, Roswell's Joe Bauman blasted 72 home runs to establish an all-time record in organized baseball.

Home runs played a big part in significant events this season. During a double-header split against New York May 2, Stan Musial of St. Louis became the first player to hit five home runs in the same day; Joe Adcock's four homers and a double July 31 gave the Milwaukee slugger a record-18 total bases for one game; and Hank Aaron belted his first of 755 career round-trippers April 23.

Willie Mays. (Courtesy San Francisco Giants.)

Crowd Pleaser

Whether racing from underneath his cap to flag down a seemingly uncatchable fly ball, exploding at the turn to advance from first to third on a sharp single or swinging from his heels and smacking one of his many home runs, Willie Mays was quite possibly the most exciting player to grace the major leagues.

The crowd-pleasing performer was special for more than his 660 career homers, 1,903 RBIs and .302 batting average; his natural charisma and boundless enthusiasm for the game of baseball also set him apart from his contemporaries. One of the few athletes who combined tremendous power with considerable speed, Mays possessed the unique ability to beat an opponent in a myriad of ways. His bat, glove, arm, legs, mind … all were lethal weapons.

Never was a player more suited to patrol the vast expanses of the Polo Grounds in New York than Mays, whose instant acceleration and sure-handedness enabled him to snare soft liners and Texas Leaguers behind second base, cut off line drives in the alleys, and haul in deep blasts that approached the 482-foot wall in dead center field. And after five full seasons in New York, where he earned the first of two MVP awards, Willie was no less spectacular in blustery Candlestick Park in San Francisco. The "Say Hey Kid" sparkled on the West Coast for 14 seasons, setting countless records at the plate and in center field before returning to New York, where he finished his career as a Met in 1973.

Born in the Birmingham, Alabama, suburb of Westfield, Willie Howard's parents divorced before he started his elementary schooling. By the time he was a teenager, Mays was competing with and against men twice his age on his father's steel mill team. The boy's talents were not limited to baseball, however. He led the country in scoring on the high school basketball court, and shone at a variety of positions on the gridiron.

At 15 years of age, when blacks were just beginning to break into the majors, Mays quit school to join the Birmingham Barons of the Negro League. Four years later, New York Giants scout Eddie Montague stumbled upon the flashy center fielder while arranging to purchase first baseman Alonzo Perry. The Barons received $10,000 for Willie, who was given a $5,000 signing bonus and assigned to Trenton, New Jersey, of the Interstate League midway through the 1950 season.

Mays quickly advanced to Minneapolis of the American Association, where he was hitting .477 after a month and a half with the Millers, and being tutored in the finer points of the game and off-field deportment by roommate and former Negro League star Ray Dandridge. Mays was then called up to the Giants, appearing in 121 games in 1951, batting .274 and clubbing 20 homers. The right-handed slugger, who won Rookie of the Year honors that season, took part in the first of five World Series following New York's remarkable comeback and defeat of the Dodgers in a three-game playoff. But he batted only .182 in the six-game World Series setback at the hands of the Yankees.

The shy, reserved Mays had lacked confidence, especially at the plate, when first brought up to the Giants, staggering to a 1-for-25 start. His self-esteem dwindling rapidly, Willie broke down and cried in the Giants clubhouse one afternoon until comforted by manager Leo Durocher, who assured the 20-year-old rookie that the center field job was his even if he failed to get another hit all year.

With a restored self-image, Mays relaxed, but the opposition never could again. Though he missed most of 1952 and all of '53 after being drafted into the Army, No. 24 returned to enjoy one of the most brilliant careers on record. The dominance began in 1954. Mays hit a National League-best .345 for the flag-winning Giants — going 3-for-4 on the final day of the season to edge out teammate Don Mueller (.342) and

Duke Snider (.341) for the batting title — and also led the league in slugging at .667 and triples with 13. He was runner-up in total bases with 377, and his 41 round-trippers, 119 runs scored and 195 hits all were third in the NL. The 5-foot-10½, 170-pounder rapped 33 doubles and collected 110 runs batted in. Defensively, the center fielder participated in a circuit-leading nine double plays.

He was the catalyst in the New York pennant drive, then hit .286 with three RBIs in the surprising four-game sweep of Cleveland in the World Series. In the first Series contest, Willie made one of the most memorable catches of all time when he robbed Vic Wertz of extra bases with an over-the-shoulder grab of the left-handed slugger's 462-foot wallop. Mays won the NL MVP award by a comfortable margin, and immediately became a nationwide favorite. It didn't hurt his image any when he was photographed playing stickball with kids on the streets of Harlem. All of which

prompted Durocher to quip, "If he could cook, I'd marry him."

But 1954 was only the first in a lengthy string of banner years for the Alabama native during a 22-year career. Showing that rare combination of power and speed, Mays put together six straight campaigns of belting at least 20 homers and stealing 20 or more bases. Mays' career rankings have held up well since his retirement nearly 30 years ago. He was third all time in home runs (660) and total bases (6,066), sixth in runs (2,062), seventh in games (2,992), eighth in RBIs (1,903), 10th in at-bats (10,881) and hits (3,283), 17th in walks (1,464), 18th in slugging (.557), and 29th in doubles (523). His 13 consecutive seasons of 300-plus total bases were surpassed only by Hank Aaron, and his 22 extra-inning homers were tops all time. "The Wonder" had more outfield putouts (7,095) and total chances than any player in history, and was tied for 16th in outfield double plays (60).

It used to be said that the All-Star

Game was made for Willie Mays, and for good reason. He tied Stan Musial and Hank Aaron in appearances with 24, and twice (1963 and 1968) was named the contest's MVP. Mays set a record by collecting a total of six hits in the two 1960 games, including a Yankee Stadium home run.

With an MVP award under his belt in 1954, Mays was just coming into his own. The following decade would see him emerge as the league's most dynamic player, and in 1965 Willie would earn his second MVP trophy.

Top 5 MVP Vote-Getters

1. Willie Mays, New York — 283
2. Ted Kluszewski, Cincinnati — 217
3. Johnny Antonelli, New York — 154
4. Duke Snider, Brooklyn — 135
5. Al Dark, New York — 110

1954 AMERICAN LEAGUE — YOGI BERRA

Lawrence Peter Berra
B. May 12, 1925, St. Louis, Missouri

Year	Team	Games	AB	Hits	Avg.	HR	RBI	Runs	SB
1954	NY AL	151	584	179	.307	22	125	88	0

The Season

It took an extraordinary season to break the string of five straight New York Yankee pennants, and that's just what Al Lopez's Cleveland Indians produced in 1954, winning an American League-record 111 games. That total bested the 1927 Yankee mark of 110, and gave the Tribe an eight-game winning margin over runner-up New York, as well as only its third pennant in team history.

Again leading the Indian charge in 1954 was their unmatched assem-

blage of starting pitchers — Bob Lemon, Early Wynn and Mike Garcia — the first two notching 23 victories each and Garcia compiling 19. Cleveland featured only five returnees from its 1948 World Championship team, but newcomers such as mid-season acquisition Vic Wertz kept the Indian wrecking crew rolling along. Center fielder Larry Doby was the biggest gun, topping the AL in both home runs (32) and RBIs (126).

The Yankees hardly faded in 1954, racking up 103 wins, the most in Casey Stengel's reign as manager. Meanwhile,

Paul Richards' "Go-Go" White Sox rounded out the trio of teams that managed to go over the .500 mark, finishing third with 94 conquests.

At the other end of the spectrum, the Browns left St. Louis and took up residence in Baltimore. Now known as the Orioles, they limped home in seventh place with 100 losses, but sent more fans through the turnstiles than during any of the 52 seasons that the team played in St. Louis.

Heavy favorites going into the World Series, the record-setting Indians met up with the pinch-hitting mastery of Dusty Rhodes and the fielding wizardry of Willie Mays, and were blown away in four straight, despite a .500 average from Wertz.

A trade to end all trades, begun November 18 and concluded December 1, involved 18 players moving between the New York Yankees and Baltimore Orioles. Among those switching teams were pitchers Bob Turley and Don Larsen, and outfielder Gene Woodling. Only two years later, Larsen would make World Series history.

Surprise Win

Winning the 1954 MVP award surprised Yogi Berra as much as it pleased him. Despite producing another superb effort, the Yankees backstop had once again counted himself out of the running before the campaign was completed. After all, he reasoned, the Indians registered an American League-record number of wins, so surely the writers would honor someone from that exemplary pennant squad. But for the second year running, the baseball scribes shunned a member of the flag-winning team, denying Cleveland a second consecutive MVP and picking Berra instead.

Considering the tendency toward bestowing the accolade on members of front-runners, Yogi had seemingly stood a better opportunity for the laurel in the two previous campaigns. Both 1952 and '53 had been Yankee pennant years, with Berra excelling in each, hitting .273 and .296 with homer totals of 30 and 27, while catching 273 games. Both times there had been World Championships, and in addition to his potent stick, Berra gave innumerable demonstrations of behind-the-plate acrobatics that sent enemies reeling.

During this Yankee reign, head man Casey Stengel called Berra "my assistant manager," a prophetic reference. Following his playing days, Yogi guided both New York clubs — the Yankees (1964) and Mets (1973) — to pennants, signing on once more with the AL entry as skipper for the '84 season, but being bounced after a 6–10 start in 1985.

Yogi Berra. (Courtesy New York Yankees.)

That quick hook by Yankees owner George Steinbrenner so infuriated Berra that he vowed never again to set foot in Yankee Stadium until King George was no longer in power. Fourteen years later, Berra buried the hatchet and appeared at opening day ceremonies honoring the 1998 World Champions. Yogi, who served as a Houston Astros coach from 1986–89, compiled a .522 winning percentage as a big league skipper. Through the 2001 season, he was a special advisor to the Yankees organization. His managerial head had also been on the chopping block in '84, when the Yanks sputtered early on. But the club rallied heavily in the second half, saving Yogi from being dismissed.

In 1954, Berra led by example, catching a personal-high 149 games and finishing third in the AL in total bases with 285. The left-handed spray hitter was even more prominent in the RBI department, producing a career-best total and missing that title by one (126–125) to Larry Doby of the Indians. Berra also batted .307, finishing fifth in the league.

By this time, Berra was the unquestioned deity among junior circuit signal callers, rivaled only by Roy Campanella in the National League for ultimate supremacy behind the mask. The 1954 MVP effort served to further strengthen his standing at the top of the heap. He led the league in putouts and double plays, whacked 22 home runs and was far ahead of his AL catching opponents in nearly every offensive statistic.

Still short of his 30s, the amiable Berra represented money in the bank for the Yankees, who recognized what solidity behind the plate means to pennant contenders. Bill Dickey, the nonpareil of his day, had prodded the preceding Bomber dynasty through its years of dominance, and Elston Howard waited just ahead to assume a similar role in the '60s. But the Eisenhower era was Yogi Berra territory in every sense.

Projecting a squat, unsophisticated persona, Berra hardly radiated an image of success and prosperity, but in reality he was already in the champagne-and-caviar tax bracket. Yogi and Phil Rizzuto wisely invested in a bowling alley during the 1950s boom period, and the Yankee catcher also made big money by sinking cash into and endorsing the chocolate soft drink Yoo-Hoo, which turned into another lucrative financial source. Additionally, he was the highest-paid catcher in the game, a content husband and father, and owner of two MVP awards.

And there was much more to come. Or, to put it in Yogi's own words, "It ain't over 'til it's over."

Top 5 MVP Vote-Getters

1. Yogi Berra, New York — 230
2. Larry Doby, Cleveland — 210
3. Bobby Avila, Cleveland — 203
4. Minnie Minoso, Chicago — 186
5. Bob Lemon, Cleveland — 179

1955 NATIONAL LEAGUE — ROY CAMPANELLA

Roy Campanella
B. November 19, 1921, Philadelphia, Pennsylvania
D. June 26, 1993, Woodland Hills, California

Year	Team	Games	AB	Hits	Avg.	HR	RBI	Runs	SB
1955	Bkn NL	123	446	142	.318	32	107	81	2

The Season

The Brooklyn Dodgers returned to the top of the National League under sophomore manager Walter Alston in 1955, winning their first 10 games for a major league record and beating out second-place Milwaukee by a comfortable 13½-game margin. It was the Dodgers' fifth pennant in nine years, and third in the past four campaigns. Brooklyn was the class of the NL, leading the way in batting, slugging, runs, homers, stolen bases and ERA.

When the Yankees captured the first two World Series games, it appeared that Brooklyn was headed for its eighth consecutive post-season setback. But with Duke Snider crashing four homers, driving in seven runs and hitting .320, the Dodgers became the first team to rally from a 2–0 Series deficit, winning in seven.

Brooklyn's Sandy Amoros, inserted into left field for defensive pur-

poses in the seventh game, started a key sixth-inning double play with a one-handed running catch near the foul line, robbing Yogi Berra of extra bases. Johnny Podres went on to blank the Yankees 2–0 in the decisive contest. The two powerful squads combined for a World Series-record 17 homers in the first six games.

Two prominent NL pitchers wielded heavy lumber this season. Brooklyn's Don Newcombe set a league record for hurlers with his seventh home run September 5 in the same game that he earned his 20th win, while a homer by Milwaukee's Warren Spahn August 15 at Sportsman's Park in St. Louis gave him at least one round-tripper in every National League ballpark during his career.

Ernie Banks of Chicago, who would win two MVP awards before the end of the decade, established a major league record with five grand slams, while Bill Bruton of Milwaukee won his third stolen base crown in a row.

Tragedy Strikes

Roy Campanella wasn't alone in thinking that 1958 would be his comeback year. Coaches and teammates felt the same way about the Brooklyn catcher, who had faded in the past two years. Following a third Most Valuable Player award in 1955, Campanella's home run and RBI production had fallen off, and his batting average had dipped drastically. But he had experienced off-years immediately after winning the coveted MVP before, and at 36 years of age still had some pop left in his bat, plus a strong, accurate arm. Many, including Campy, believed the new, warmer surroundings of Los Angeles — where the Dodgers were moving for the 1958 season — and the short left field fence at the Coliseum would suit the husky backstop just fine.

But those dreams turned into an ugly nightmare the evening of January 28, 1958. Roy was returning home to Long Island from his liquor store when the car he was driving hit a patch of ice, skidded down a hill and crashed full force into a telephone pole. The auto flipped over, crushing Campanella against the steering wheel. Unable to move, he was forced to wait a half-hour until he could be pulled out and rushed to Glen Cove Community Hospital, where a doctor attempted in vain to alleviate the damage. X-rays revealed that both the fifth and sixth cervical vertebrae were broken. Roy was permanently paralyzed from the waist down, and could barely move his arms.

As if his physical problems weren't enough, emotional tribulations soon cropped up as well, as his wife, Ruthe, was unwilling to cope with a paralyzed husband. Campanella eventually brought a suit against her for legal separation, and the two were in and out of the courts in a messy ordeal. Then, nearly five years to the day after Roy's accident, Ruthe suffered a heart attack while speaking to her husband on the phone, and died at age 40.

After years of being a physically dominant man, Campanella was devastated by his sudden inability to function in a normal manner. But he never gave up. Walter O'Malley, who had purchased the club following the 1950 season, was gracious to Campanella, paying him a $50,000 salary for 1958, then donating the same amount from the gate receipts of a Dodgers-Yankees exhibition game in 1959 to help with the beloved catcher's hospital expenses. More than 93,000 people honored the brave backstop that evening. In his first public appearance since the tragic mishap, Roy received a deafening ovation when he was wheeled into Yankee Stadium immediately prior to the third 1958 World Series game against Milwaukee. In 1969, he was elected to the Hall of Fame, and three years later, the Dodgers retired his uniform No. 39.

While Campanella could not help but wish that fate had been kinder, he continued to exhibit a zest for life. His autobiography, *It's Good to Be Alive*, has been an inspiration to its many readers. Mrs. Roxie Doles, a next-door neighbor, became Roy's third wife, and the couple lived in Hartsdale, New York. Campy passed away in 1993 at the age of 71.

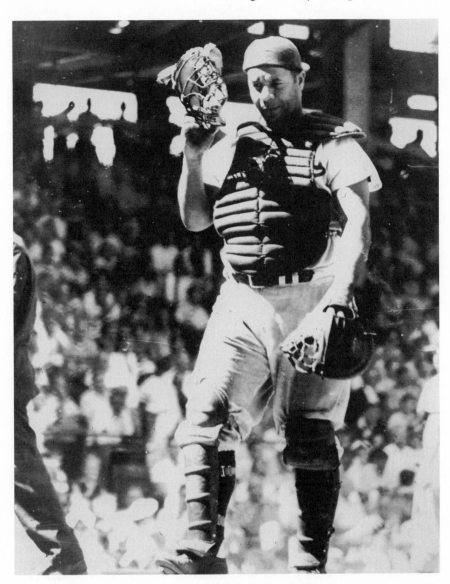

Roy Campanella. (Courtesy Los Angeles Dodgers.)

Among the trophies that adorned his home is the one earned in 1955 as the National League's Most Valuable Player. Although his personal stats did not match the 1953 effort, the '55 campaign was perhaps his sweetest. The Dodgers, after three consecutive World Series losses to the menacing Yankees, finally turned the tables on New York, capturing the World Championship in a seven-game set. Campanella, who stumbled to an uncharacteristic .207 average in 1954, came back with a vengeance the next season, hitting .318, fourth best in the NL. Roy socked 32 home runs and drove in 107, while slugging at a .583 clip. He also paced league catchers in putouts for the fifth of six times. Campy had a solid Series, rapping out seven hits, including three doubles and two homers, and collecting four RBIs.

Campanella's third MVP award was won by a mere five points over teammate and center fielder Duke Snider. The "Duke of Flatbush" ripped NL pitching in 1955 to the tune of 42 home runs, 34 doubles and a league-high 136 RBIs. The .309 hitter also paced senior circuit players in runs (126), while racking up a .628 slugging percentage, 338 total bases and 104 walks.

Although his offensive production wavered during his final two years, Campanella continued to be a stalwart defensive receiver, leading league backstops in putouts in '56 and in fielding average in '57. The Dodgers finished third in their concluding season in Brooklyn, and when Campy removed his uniform on that last day of the year, little did he know he'd never wear it again.

His tenure in the big leagues was brief, but Campanella took advantage of every moment, never letting up for a second. The three MVP awards he earned in such a short stay were unprecedented. The natural tendency is to pity Roy Campanella for the cruel fate he suffered. But admiration and respect are more appropriate responses, for he was a man with a deep richness of baseball experiences and a unique appreciation for the essence of life.

Top 5 MVP Vote-Getters

1. Roy Campanella, Brooklyn — 226
2. Duke Snider, Brooklyn — 221
3. Ernie Banks, Chicago — 195
4. Willie Mays, New York — 165
5. Robin Roberts, Philadelphia — 159

1955 American League — Yogi Berra

Lawrence Peter Berra
B. May 12, 1925, St. Louis, Missouri

Year	Team	Games	AB	Hits	Avg.	HR	RBI	Runs	SB
1955	NY AL	147	541	147	.272	27	108	84	1

The Season

The Chicago White Sox had the highest team batting average in the American League, allowed the fewest runs and, as usual, stole the most bases. Nellie Fox and George Kell hit over .300 for Chicago, with Jim Rivera and Minnie Minoso finishing 1–2 in the stolen base race. Billy Pierce added a circuit-leading 1.97 ERA, but manager Marty Marion's exciting team still fell short of the mark, ending in third place.

Detroit, featuring the slugging of Al Kaline and Ray Boone, outpaced all clubs in run production, but could only rise as high as fifth place. Kaline became the youngest batting champion ever by hitting .340 at the age of 20.

As usual, the Yankees landed on top of the standings, beating out the defending champion Indians by three games and the White Sox by five. New York pitching was the basis for its 1955 success, as the club's hurlers recorded a league-low 3.23 ERA.

After winning the first two games of the World Series, the Bronx Bombers were eventually bested in seven by the Brooklyn Dodgers.

A couple of young fireballers raised some eyebrows around the league.

Herb Score of Cleveland fanned 245 to lead the AL and break Grover Cleveland Alexander's rookie record of 235, while Bob Turley of the Yankees also topped the 200 mark (210). Sure-handed outfielder Larry Doby of Cleveland set a junior circuit record with 166 consecutive games without an error.

An added footnote for 1955 was the successful move by the Athletics from Philadelphia to Kansas City, where the team escaped the cellar, moving up to sixth place.

Finally, three-time MVP award winner Joe DiMaggio was inducted into the Hall of Fame in his third year of eligibility.

Back to Back

The incalculable worth of fireplug Yogi Berra to the 1955 New York Yankees goes far beyond the second consecutive MVP honor granted him at season's end. Manager Casey Stengel came closest to summarizing Berra's value to the World Champions that year when he succinctly stated: "Take him out and we fall apart."

After catching 149 games the previous season, Berra overcame an assortment of aches, pains and fatigue to squat behind the pay station in 145 more contests in 1955. With the Yankees entrenched in a titanic pennant struggle with the Indians and White Sox, Yogi was not about to take many pit stops. While handling the New York pitching corps and acting as field general for the pinstripe troops, the weary receiver managed to hoist his bat and lash out for 27 home runs, 108 RBIs and a .272 average, guiding his mates to the pennant. And at age 30, Berra earned his third MVP.

With more than 1,000 regular season games already accumulated behind the plate, the plodding obligations of the position had begun to take their toll on Berra. Following his final Most Valuable Player year, there would be no more 140-plus catching campaigns for Berra, who nonetheless remained a vital part of the Yankee dynasty through 1961.

In 1956, he matched his season-high mark with 30 round-trippers, scaling the century mark in RBIs for the last time with 105 and calling Don Larsen's perfect game in the World Series as an added exclamation point. Five more years of distinguished service followed. By 1961, however, the clutch hitter's big bat (22 homers, .271) was that of an outfielder and infrequent receiver. Following the 1963 campaign when the 38-year-old hit .293 as a part-timer, Berra hung up his gear and took over as Yankees manager.

The living comic book caricature was through as a player, winding down to mortal proportions as all athletes eventually must. But in 1955, the Berra who donned catching gear for the proud Bombers seemed physically imbued with steel components. To many baseball fans, Mickey Mantle represented Yankee dominance during this period, but those in the know pointed to Berra's team-high 108 RBIs and recognized him as the club's lifeblood.

In his third MVP season, Berra went over the 140-mark in games caught for the fifth time in six years, and it was this constant presence combined with the marvelous hitting statistics that gave Yogi the edge in the Most Valuable Player voting over runner-up Al Kaline of the Tigers, 218 to 201.

In copping the honor, Berra became the third three-time MVP winner in the AL, following in the footsteps of Jimmie Foxx and Joe DiMaggio. Yogi then went out and substantiated his place among this brilliant company by hitting .417 in the pressure cooker of a seven-game World Series loss to the Brooklyn Dodgers.

Berra had come to the Yankees an uncut diamond, already having confirmed his mettle under fire in more intimidating circumstances as a Coast Guard rocket gunner who landed on Normandy during the D-Day invasion. Prior to the military stint, Berra put himself in the spotlight by knocking in 23 runs in the space of two days for Norfolk in 1943.

It was that particular memory that persuaded Yankee brass to refuse a $50,000 New York Giants offer for Berra's services when he was still wearing Coast Guard togs. A less-discerning management might have jumped at the cash, for the stumpy little catcher hit only .253 in his final minor league season before joining the military, and was hardly a defensive specialist at the time. But there was no escaping the fact that nearly every time a teammate was perched in scoring position, the urchin responded with a hit.

Yogi Berra. (Courtesy New York Yankees.)

By 1949, the confidence that New York's front office displayed in Berra's potential was paying dividends, as Yogi was unchallenged in the AL for overall catching excellence. Berra's hitting was an almost immediate sensation when he joined the bigs in 1946, but his receiving style was far short of spectacular until 1949. During that campaign, ex-Yankee great and Hall of Famer Bill Dickey personally took Berra under his wing and drilled him in the finer points of the important position.

"Bill Dickey," Berra would later say, "taught me all his experience." The 12 cumulative titles in putouts, assists and fielding percentage indicate the pupil caught on very well, indeed. Berra held the record for consecutive chances accepted (950) without an error, a 148-game string that began in July 1957, continued through a perfect 1.000 fielding campaign in '58 and finally ended in May 1959.

His World Series records, many of which may never be broken, included most games (75) and hits (71). He trailed only Mickey Mantle and Babe Ruth in most Series home runs, and was second in RBIs and runs. Berra, a 15-time All-Star, was elected to the Hall of Fame in 1972.

Yet for all his achievements, Berra remained an atypical athletic hero, continuing to spew entangled quotes to a highly responsive media, and appearing strangely out of place in a world where he was surrounded by smug athletes who glibly articulated the intricacies of everything from the gross national product to the 19th special clause in their baseball contracts.

But while these more worldly types came and went, the simple seren-

ity of Yogi Berra remained a welcome constant.

Top 5 MVP Vote-Getters

1. Yogi Berra, New York — 218
2. Al Kaline, Detroit — 201
3. Al Smith, Cleveland — 200
4. Ted Williams, Boston — 143
5. Mickey Mantle, New York — 113

1956 National League — Don Newcombe

Donald Newcombe
B. June 14, 1926, Madison, New Jersey

Year	Team	Games	W	L	ERA	IP	SO	BB	Sho
1956	Bkn NL	38	27	7	3.06	268	139	46	5

The Season

There were several superb individual performances this season, complementing a hard-fought, three-way pennant race that went down to the wire.

Brooklyn's Sal "The Barber" Maglie did himself proud with a no-hitter September 25, which was also a major boost for his pennant-bound Dodgers. Pittsburgh first baseman Dale Long homered in eight consecutive games to set a record, while future two-time MVP and 1956 Rookie of the Year Frank Robinson of Cincinnati broke into the league with 38 round-trippers, tying Wally Berger's rookie mark set in 1930.

Five past and future MVP award winners distinguished themselves in All-Star play, with Willie Mays, Stan Musial, Ted Williams and Mickey Mantle all crashing home runs. But the standout in the NL's 7–3 win was Cardinals third sacker Ken Boyer, who sparkled afield and rapped out three hits. Mays, between MVP seasons, led the circuit with 40 stolen bases, the highest NL total since 1929.

The defending World Champion Dodgers won the pennant by one game over the Milwaukee Braves. The Dodgers' victory was made possible by a late-season surge, and for the sixth time in 10 years, Brooklyn squared off

against the Yankees in the World Series. Once more the Series went the full route, with New York coming out on top.

The Cy Young Award was established in 1956, with only one winner in the major leagues per year prior to 1967, when both leagues began naming their own recipients. National League MVP Don Newcombe of Brooklyn was the first Cy Young winner.

The power-laden Reds, who moved into third place, only two games off the pace, tied a major league record with 221 home runs.

On May 7, future NL President Bill White of the New York Giants hit a home run in his first major league at-bat.

Mound Monster

A hulking giant of a man, Don Newcombe was a combative, flame-throwing hurler whose mere presence on the hill was enough to send shivers up the spine of any enemy standing 60 feet, six inches away. Along with Jackie Robinson and Roy Campanella, the towering Madison, New Jersey, native helped break the color line in the National League and became the major league's first outstanding starting pitcher of his race.

Always big for his age, "Newk"

was throwing batting practice to neighborhood semipro teams by the time he was 9 years old, and he excelled in football and baseball in high school. After a stint in the Army — lying about his age to get in — he tried out for and made the all-black Newark Eagles in 1943, and a pitcher was born.

At age 17, he went 7–5 for Newark, and within two years had caught the eye of Brooklyn Dodgers general manager Branch Rickey, who signed him to a contract five months after snagging Robinson. In 1946, Don posted a 14–4 record for Nashau, the Brooklyn entry in the New England League, then followed with a 19–6 mark.

Following a 14–4 record for Montreal, the hawk-nosed fastball artist joined Brooklyn in 1949 in time for a Dodger pennant and Rookie of the Year award (17–8 and a league-leading five shutouts). Don handcuffed National League batters for 32 consecutive scoreless innings during one outstanding streak that season, and was runner-up to Warren Spahn in the strikeout race. On July 8, he became a part of history when Hank Thompson of the New York Giants stepped into the box, marking the first time a black pitcher and hitter had faced off against each other in a major league game.

Newcombe followed his successful debut with an even better 19-win effort as a 24-year-old in 1950, a season

Don Newcombe. (Courtesy Los Angeles Dodgers.)

Years later, the once superlative speedball flinger admitted his drinking problem, fought back and rehabilitated himself. He took a job as director of community relations with the Los Angeles Dodgers, making the major league rounds in spring training to warn of the pitfalls of drink, and offering help to potential baseball-playing alcoholics.

In his appeals, Newcombe offered his personal story as the perfect example of a ruined career. In 1956, when all was well, he was the overwhelming choice for the National League's Most Valuable Player award, having posted a superlative 27–7 record and snared the inaugural Cy Young honor.

After a slow start, the 30-year-old won six in a row in July, seven of eight the next month and five out of six in September. At one point in that stretch, he was virtually untouchable, winging his way to 39⅔ scoreless frames in a row. His 27th triumph of the season clinched the pennant for the Dodgers.

Newk garnered 223 of a possible 336 points in the MVP balloting, with eight of 24 first-place votes, earning a spot on every writer's card. Teammate Sal Maglie was a distant second with 183 points. The Cy Young and MVP, added to his Rookie of the Year award from 1949, made Newcombe the only pitcher in history to capture all three accolades.

In addition to outdistancing the next closest pitcher by seven victories, the hard-working Newcombe topped the NL in win percentage (.794) and opponents' on-base percentage (.257), was second in both fewest hits (7.3) and walks (1.5) per nine innings (1.5), and third in shutouts (five).

Tired and overworked, he could not overcome a World Series jinx that haunted him through three fall classics. In two 1956 starts, he was hammered mercilessly and yanked prior to the fourth inning. The brutal finish (21.21 ERA) to an otherwise excellent campaign left Don with a lifetime Series record of 0–4.

In fact, despite a lifetime winning percentage (.623) that ranked among the top 40 pitching marks of all time, Newcombe couldn't shake a reputation

that ended with a heartbreaking loss on the final day of the year to Robin Roberts and the Whiz Kids of Philadelphia, who edged the Dodgers by two games for the flag.

After notching his first 20-win campaign and leading the league in strikeouts with 164 in '51, Newk served another two years in the Army before returning in 1954 to post a sore-armed 9–8 record. Nineteen-fifty-five was smoke city for the lumbering 6-foot-4, 220-pounder, who was 15–1 by mid–July with a .406 batting average and six home runs to boot. The overpowering Dodger ended with a 20–5 record and an NL-best .800 winning percentage.

In his prime, Newcombe was a ferocious competitor whose concentration and stamina on the hill made him the ace of the Dodgers mound corps

and the bane of NL batsmen. Possessing an easy-flowing style, the long-armed righty threw effective, jug-handled curves and jumping fastballs that fairly exploded into the glove of roommate and best friend Roy Campanella.

The monstrous talent was laid to waste, however, following a striking 1956 MVP year. Gripped by alcoholism, Don withered away to an 11–12 slate in 1957, then started the 1958 season 0–6 before Brooklyn sent him packing to Cincinnati.

He rallied for one more winning season in '59 (13–8), but talent alone could no longer sustain the 33-year-old; after going 6–9 for the Reds and Cleveland Indians in 1960, Newcombe retired. Gravitating in the direction of his decline, Newcombe ran a liquor store in Newark.

for not coming up large in big games. In addition to his World Series misfortunes — including yielding a ninth-inning home run to New York's Tommy Henrich in a 1–0 loss to begin the 1949 fall classic that spoiled an otherwise brilliant performance — Newcombe gave up Dick Sisler's 10th-inning dinger that gave Philadelphia the 1950 pennant by two games over the Dodgers. A tiring Newcombe also failed to shut down the Giants in the third game of the 1951 NL playoffs, giving way to Ralph Branca and Bobby Thomson's subsequent pennant-clinching homer.

Don Newcombe paid his dues for the brief period of success he enjoyed in the major league spotlight, absorbing the racial slings and arrows as a pioneer for black ballplayers, and eventually crumbling under the weight of a misunderstood ailment all too common in the profession. In between, however, he was among the most intimidating figures ever to grace NL pitching mounds. And, like a true champion, he has battled adversity and returned to form, and is once more at the top of his game.

Top 5 MVP Vote-Getters

1. Don Newcombe, Brooklyn — 223
2. Sal Maglie, Brooklyn — 183
3. Hank Aaron, Milwaukee — 146
4. Warren Spahn, Milwaukee — 126
5. Junior Gilliam, Brooklyn — 103

1956 AMERICAN LEAGUE — MICKEY MANTLE

Mickey Charles Mantle
B. October 20, 1931, Spavinaw, Oklahoma
D. August 13, 1995, Dallas, Texas

Year	Team	Games	AB	Hits	Avg.	HR	RBI	Runs	SB
1956	NY AL	150	533	188	.353	52	130	132	10

The Season

New York's powerful Yankees again breezed to the pennant in 1956, winning their seventh flag in eight years. In a World Series rematch with the Brooklyn Dodgers, the Yanks came out on top in another seven-game affair.

The Dodgers won the first two Series contests, but the Bombers came back with a pair of victories, setting the stage for Don Larsen's perfect game. Larsen needed only 97 pitches in the 2–0 gem in Game 5. A Dodger victory in Game 6 merely delayed the final outcome, as Casey Stengel's sluggers decisively routed Brooklyn 9–0 in the finale.

The regular season was preceded by the election of two-time MVP Hank Greenberg to the Hall of Fame, as well as the death of baseball patriarch Connie Mack at age 93. Mack, who began his career as a Washington catcher in 1886, helped establish the American League in 1901 and served as the Athletics manager for 50 years, winning nine pennants and five World Series.

Nine years after baseball's color line was finally broken, an exhibition game between the A's and the Pirates had to be cancelled in Birmingham, Alabama, due to a local ordinance barring blacks and whites from competing against each other.

Although there was plenty of hitting to entertain American League fans, this was an especially good year for pitchers, with six league hurlers going over the 20-win mark. Jim Derrington of Chicago became the youngest pitcher (16 years, 10 months) to start a game in more than 50 years, losing 7–6 to Kansas City, while Boston's Mel Parnell no-hit the White Sox.

The Mick Lets Loose

It was, arguably, the best single season of his fabulous career. The devil curveball, which to this point had shackled the immense natural talents of Mickey Mantle, was no longer an annoyance. Outside benders were flicked easily to the opposite field in 1956, and now totally unfettered, the broad-shouldered 24-year-old did a number on American League hurlers.

The son of a poor miner, Mickey Charles Mantle was weaned on baseball from the time his small hands could grip a diminutive bat. Named after 1934 AL MVP Mickey Cochrane — the personal hero of Mantle's father, Mutt — the newborn's journey toward the major leagues was plotted for him from the beginning. Mickey was groomed by dad to be a switch-hitter from the time he was 5.

So, when the Yankees came calling in 1949, there was little hesitation in signing a Class D pact calling for a mere $140 a month and a paltry $1,150 bonus. Two years later, writers covering the Yankees' spring training camp couldn't believe their eyes as the 19-year-old shortstop pounded one long drive after another ... and from either side of the plate.

When Mantle joined the Yankees in the spring of 1951, the dynasty appeared ready to crumble. Joe DiMaggio, the banner carrier for the once overpowering New Yorkers, was plagued by numerous ailments and on the verge of beginning his final season. But so impressive was Mickey in his first turn with the big boys that even the hallowed DiMag was moved to remark that the newcomer was the greatest prospect he had ever seen.

Mantle made that Yankee ballclub ahead of schedule following a switch to the outfield — he'd committed more than 100 errors at shortstop over two minor league campaigns — and after a half-season of long four-baggers and frequent strikeouts, was sent back to the minors to hone the rough edges off his promising swing. He returned from the farm to the big club near season's end to compile a .267 average with 13 homers in 96 games, and was in the opening lineup for the World Series, playing right field beside DiMaggio. A knee-popping injury which was to bother him throughout his career limited Mickey to a brief, inconsequential appearance in that 1951 affair.

"The Commerce Comet" hit .311 in 1952 and returned to the World Series, where he battered Brooklyn pitching for a .345 average and two home runs, earning his second championship ring in two seasons. It was becoming apparent that the new middleman in the Yankees outfield was the next link in the Ruth-Gehrig-DiMaggio chain of New York superstars.

Nineteen-fifty-three started like gangbusters for the 21-year-old, who was tearing up the league at a .353 pace before going into a horrendous slump, due to a pulled thigh muscle. Returning too early from the injury, Mickey limped home with a .295 average, 21 homers and 92 RBIs. One of those home runs was a 565-foot blast at Washington's Griffith Stadium, leading Yankee pitcher Bob Kuzava to quip, "I never saw a ball hit so far. You could have cut it up into 15 singles." Mantle hit only .208 in the World Series against Brooklyn, but two of his five Series safeties were game winners, and New York had another World Championship.

Mickey Mantle. (Courtesy New York Yankees.)

Mantle hit an even .300 in 1954 with the first of six runs scored titles (129), and followed with marks of .306, a league-high 37 homers and 99 RBIs the next year as the Yanks repeated as flag winners. Also in 1955, Mantle paced the junior circuit in slugging (.611), triples (11), walks (113) and on-base percentage (.433).

It seemed that only a steady stream of vexing injuries could effectively halt No. 7 at this juncture in his career. Sad to say, the numerous hurts took a nasty toll beginning in 1947 when he contracted osteomyelitis in his left ankle.

But during spring training of his 1956 MVP campaign, the Mick appeared almost injury-free, and optimism bubbled over from every corner of the Yankee camp. He did not disappoint. A pair of opening day mammoth blows over the distant center field wall in Washington — witnessed by President Dwight Eisenhower — were merely a taste of what was to come. On May 30, he reached 20 home runs faster than any player ever, and did it in dramatic fashion. His rocket off the right field upper deck façade missed exiting Yankee Stadium by 18 inches, and would have traveled approximately 600 feet if given the opportunity. By July, he was ahead of Babe Ruth's 60-homer pace of 1927.

At this point, Mickey was the premiere gate attraction throughout the

American League, but a mid-season strain in his right knee finally slowed him down. He returned to the lineup to swat a home run in the All-Star Game; then, in an important four-game set with the contending White Sox late in the season, Mantle hit a pair of homers, two triples, two doubles and a couple of singles, personally accounting for 11 RBIs as the New Yorkers swept the series.

A combination of Mantle pressing too hard and a pulled groin muscle ended his race against Ruth, but his 50th homer, September 18 versus Chicago, clinched the pennant. When the season had finished, Mantle was the proud possessor of the Triple Crown, with 52 homers, 130 RBIs and a crackling .353 average. He was also tops in slugging (career-high .705), runs scored and total bases, and for an encore, pounded out three round-trippers off the Dodgers in the World Series. During Don Larsen's perfect game, Mickey not only homered, but also saved the day by chasing down a Gil Hodges blast and retiring the Dodger slugger with a slick, backhanded grab.

To no one's surprise, Mantle was the unanimous choice for 1956 MVP. He also received *The Sporting News'* Player of the Year award.

Following his retirement, thanks to his affiliation with a Las Vegas gambling casino, Mantle was barred from participation in major league baseball, but was re-instated in 1985. Living off his famous moniker, Mickey's job consisted of playing an occasional round of golf with the hotel's best clients. He reportedly took the job because one of his sons had contracted Hodgkins disease, and he needed the cash to pay medical bills.

Age was almost an embarrassment to Mantle as he restlessly searched for fulfillment beyond the baseball diamond, still longing for the competition. He unashamedly admitted to dwelling on the records he might have established but missed due to injury, including falling short of 3,000 hits and a .300 lifetime average.

Mantle's on-field regrets faded in comparison to the remorse he felt for far too many years of heavy drinking, once he realized his liver was shutting down. A 1993 stay in the Betty Ford Clinic and television appearances warning kids about drug and alcohol

abuse were followed by a liver transplant in 1994 at Baylor University Hospital, where an inoperable cancer lesion was discovered. He died at age 63 in 1995.

Eulogizing the Mick at his funeral, sportscaster Bob Costas said, "I just hope God has a place for him where he can run again, where he can play practical jokes on his teammates and smile the boyish smile, because God knows no one's perfect. And God knows there's something special about heroes."

But Mantle's regrets were far in the future following his exceptional 1956 MVP season. "When I was young and healthy," he once said, "I believe I was the best." The man can hardly be refuted.

Top 5 MVP Vote-Getters

1. Mickey Mantle, New York — 336
2. Yogi Berra, New York — 186
3. Al Kaline, Detroit — 142
4. Harvey Kuenn, Detroit — 80
5. Billy Pierce, Chicago — 75

1957 National League — Hank Aaron

Henry Louis Aaron
B. February 5, 1934, Mobile, Alabama

Year	Team	Games	AB	Hits	Avg.	HR	RBI	Runs	SB
1957	Mil NL	151	615	198	.322	44	132	118	1

The Season

After blowing a one-game lead with three to go and being nudged out for the National League pennant by the Brooklyn Dodgers in 1956, the Milwaukee Braves were determined not to let it happen again this season.

They didn't. The Braves won nine of their first 10 and cruised to the NL flag by eight games over St. Louis.

Most Valuable Player Henry Aaron clinched the pennant for Milwaukee September 23 when he belted a two-run, 11th-inning homer to beat the Cardinals 4–2.

In Fred Haney's first full season as the Braves skipper, his was the best team in baseball. Powerful Milwaukee led the majors in runs scored and home runs.

The Braves' feverish, seven-game

World Series victory over the New York Yankees featured the masterful pitching of Lew Burdette, who became the first hurler in more than a decade to win three games in one World Series. The right-hander tossed 24 consecutive scoreless innings in the Series and won the seventh game 5–0 on only two days of rest. It was the franchise's first World Championship in 43 years.

On June 12, three-time MVP Stan

Musial broke Gus Suhr's NL record for consecutive games played with his 823rd. Less than a month later, Musial, Aaron and Willie Mays were named by Commissioner Ford Frick to replace Cincinnati's Gus Bell, George Crowe and Wally Post in the NL's starting lineup for the All-Star Game after Reds fans stuffed the ballot box and elected eight Cincy starters.

Duke Snider's 40 home runs in 1957 allowed the Dodgers basher to tie Ralph Kiner's NL record with five consecutive seasons of 40-plus dingers.

In perhaps the most bizarre incident of the season, Philadelphia outfielder Richie Ashburn broke the nose of fan Alice Roth with a foul ball, then hit her with another foul ball moments later as she was being escorted from the park on a stretcher. Roth was the wife of *Philadelphia Bulletin* sports editor Earl Roth.

The Hammer

Never in the history of baseball have two men with such divergent personalities been compared as closely as Henry Aaron and Babe Ruth. The two greatest home run hitters of all time both played right field, but the similarity ends there.

Everything the bulky Babe did was with a swaggering bravado, from whipping three bats around his head in the on-deck circle to blasting baseballs out of sight and hurling abuse toward opposing dugouts as he trotted around the bases.

Aaron, on the other hand, with his tired eyes, nonchalant movements and unassuming manner, displayed a quiet, almost subdued consistency throughout his amazing career. As he serenely stepped up to the plate, Aaron would humbly walk behind the umpire and slip silently into the batter's box; only then would he reverently place his helmet upon his head.

Yet the inevitable comparisons between the two increased in direct proportion to Hammerin' Hank's home run total. By the middle of the 1973 season, Aaron was closing in on the Babe's 714 mark, and only a man of Henry's caliber and even temperament

Hank Aaron. (National Baseball Hall of Fame Library, Cooperstown, N.Y.)

could have stood up to the constant pressure bearing down on him.

In addition to the assault from the media, Aaron was forced to cope with vicious hate mail from racists who dreaded a black man breaking the immortal Ruth's record. For his patience and unswerving dedication, Aaron was rewarded. On April 8, 1974, the all-time home run king deposited an Al Downing pitch over the left field fence at Atlanta Stadium for his historic 715th career home run.

Aaron's magnificent home run record began to take shape in his MVP year, 1957, his fourth season in big league baseball. Hank matched his uniform number by slugging 44 round-trippers to lead the National League. He also paced the senior circuit in RBIs with 132, total bases with 369 and runs scored with 118. He was second in hits with 198 and third in both slugging percentage (.600) and batting (.322).

More important to the 23-year-old Aaron was the fact that he steered the Braves to the NL flag, coming through with the key blow—a two-run, 11th-inning homer—in the pennant-clinching contest. Aaron then led all hitters with a .393 average, three homers and seven RBIs in a World Series triumph over the Yankees. He followed up his 1957 effort with a .326 average, 30 home runs and 95 RBIs in

1958 as the Braves made it two pennants in a row.

Henry Louis Aaron did not appear destined for superstardom in 1952 when he left Mobile, Alabama, with two dollars, two pairs of pants and two sandwiches on his way to join a black barnstorming team named the Indianapolis Clowns. But a year and a half later, after Hank won Rookie of the Year honors in the Northern League (1952) and an MVP award in the Sally League (1953) in the Braves organization, he was clearly on his way.

Aaron's chance to make it with the parent club came in 1954 when recently acquired Bobby Thomson broke a leg during an exhibition game. Hank responded by batting .280 with 13 homers and 69 RBIs.

Aaron reached the .300 mark (.314) in his sophomore season for what was to be the first of 14 times, then preceded his MVP year by leading the league in batting (.328), hits (200), doubles (34) and total basses (340) in 1956. Following another solid season in 1958, the steel-wristed slugger paced the circuit with a career-high .355 average in 1959, and added 39 homers, 123 RBIs and league highs of 400 total bases and a .636 slugging percentage. But the Braves dropped two successive playoff games to Los Angeles after tying for first place.

Although Aaron had stolen a total of only 20 bases in his first six seasons, he stepped up the pace in 1960 and averaged nearly 22 thefts per year for the next nine campaigns, with a high of 31 in 1963. He also topped the NL in homers (44), RBIs (130), runs (121) and slugging (.586). Henry is remembered mostly for his 755 career home runs and .305 lifetime batting average, but he was a heady base runner and a steady, sure-armed outfielder as well.

Of course, what he knew best was how to hit the long ball. While Ruth's towering home runs came in clusters—54 in 1920, 59 in 1921, 60 in 1927 and 54 in 1928—Aaron's line drive shots were accumulated in consistent batches. Henry's home run totals ranged from a low of 24 to a high of 47 for an unmatched 19 consecutive years (1955–73).

Taking his home run swing to Atlanta when the club moved south in 1966, Aaron tagged 44 homers, drove in 97 runs and hit .300 in 1969 to help guide his team to first place in the Western Division during the first year of divisional play.

Aaron picked up his 3,000th hit in 1970, and bashed a career-high 47 round-trippers in '71, gaining his fourth slugging crown (.669). Hank slumped to his Braves' career-low average of .265 with 34 home runs in 1972, but then made a strong bid for Ruth's all-time record in '73 with 40 homers, ending the campaign with 713.

The Hammer pounded the record-tying blow on opening day of 1974 in Cincinnati against Jack Billingham, but then was considerate enough to wait until returning to the home folks before shattering what had seemed for many years to be an unbreakable record: the Babe's 714 home runs.

During an amazing 23-year career, Aaron declared several times that he wanted to be a Brave forever. But following the 1974 season, the 40-year-old long ball artist was dealt back to his old home town to join the Milwaukee Brewers, where he hit 22 more homers as a designated hitter to add to his astonishing total.

In addition to the homers, Aaron also ranked No. 1 all time in RBIs (2,297) and total bases (6,856), second in at-bats (12,364), tied for third in runs (2,174), third in hits (3,771) and games (3,298), ninth in doubles (624), 20th in slugging (.555), and 22nd in walks (1,402). He ranked first all-time in Braves franchise history in nine key offensive categories.

Aaron was a fairly quiet hero as a player, but he's used his position as an American icon since his retirement to criticize baseball on a number of occasions—including as recently as during the 2000 All-Star Game break—for its poor record on minority hiring. Baseball officials usually respond with promises of improvement following Aaron's comments, but very little has been accomplished. When the Chicago White Sox named Jerry Manuel as manager in 1997, he was the only black skipper hired since 1992, covering 36 managerial openings.

Baseball's record is even bleaker when it comes to hiring minorities for front office positions, which is where Aaron has served the Braves. He was vice president and director of player development from 1976–89, and is currently the senior vice president and assistant to the president. In 1999, baseball honored Aaron for his lifetime achievements on his 65th birthday, and introduced the Hank Aaron award, which is now presented annually to recognize the best overall hitters in both leagues. Elected to the Hall of Fame in 1982, Aaron is a member of the Hall's veteran's committee.

Comparisons between Aaron and Ruth will continue for as long as baseball is played. But Aaron will never be known as "another Babe Ruth." He will simply be known as the most proficient home run hitter ever.

Top 5 MVP Vote-Getters

1. Hank Aaron, Milwaukee — 239
2. Stan Musial, St. Louis — 230
3. Red Schoendienst, New York/Milwaukee — 221
4. Willie Mays, New York — 174
5. Warren Spahn, Milwaukee — 131

1957 AMERICAN LEAGUE — MICKEY MANTLE

Mickey Charles Mantle
B. October 20, 1931, Spavinaw, Oklahoma
D. August 13, 1995, Dallas, Texas

Year	Team	Games	AB	Hits	Avg.	HR	RBI	Runs	SB
1957	NY AL	144	474	173	.365	34	94	121	16

The Season

Dominating almost every offensive and defensive category, the New York Yankees won their third consecutive pennant, finishing eight games ahead of the White Sox. But in the World Series, the Yankees lost in seven games to a solid bunch from Milwaukee.

Chicago's runner-up status was somewhat of a moral victory because the club had finished in third place in each of the previous five seasons. Led by the league's top three base stealers — Luis Aparicio, Jim Rivera and Minnie Minoso — the White Sox became the first junior circuit club in 12 years to go over the 100 mark in thefts. Al Lopez's team also led the league in fielding.

Cleveland, feeling the career-altering loss of Herb Score via a line drive to his cheekbone May 7 off the bat of New York's Gil McDougald, tumbled all the way to sixth place from second the previous year. Less than two months earlier, the Indians had turned down an unprecedented $1 million offer for Score by the Red Sox.

Last-place Washington's spirits were buoyed somewhat by the 21-strike-out effort of Tom Cheney in a 16-inning game, and the first home run crown captured by a Senator. Roy Sievers' 42 round-trippers led the way, and the big right-hander also paced the league in RBIs with 114.

The Baltimore Orioles gave their franchise its first .500 season in 12 years, thanks in part to an AL record-setting four consecutive June shutouts by its pitching staff.

A Leader Emerges

Taking on the leadership role of the most successful franchise in sport was a tall order for the naturally shy Mickey Mantle, but by 1957, the once demure youth had confidently assumed the position. His teammates looked to the 25-year-old to provide a winning example, and he responded in brilliant fashion, nabbing a second consecutive MVP award and steering the Yankees to another World Series.

Retaining his boyish country charm, the small-town native developed into a clubhouse cut-up specializing in practical jokes. Easy going among friends and fellow Yankees, Mantle remained withdrawn around strangers.

Jim Bouton, Mickey's teammate in the early 1960s, pointed out in his book, *Ball Four*, that the sacrosanct hero was a dichotomy of characters, both admirable and detestable at various times. Bouton stated that Mantle would frequently push aside kids seeking autographs and make reporters grovel for stories if he was perturbed about something they had written. But at other times, he could be gregarious, going out of his way to sign hundreds of baseballs and spending long hours in the locker room with local scribes recounting the day's events.

Over the years, Mantle developed into a bona-fide hell-raiser and late-night carouser. He was one of several Yankees who were fined $1,000 for their part in the Copacabana Club incident May 16, 1957, when a patron accused Hank Bauer of assault. Billy Martin, with whom Mickey was tight, also was involved in the melee, and was traded to Kansas City a month later amid speculation that management felt he was a bad influence on Mantle. But Mickey always delivered on the ballyard. Intent on living his life to the fullest, he squeezed every ounce of ability from his pain-wracked body.

The ailments won out in the end, denying the switch-hitting center fielder No. 1 career totals in any major offensive category. He did, however, establish a number of World Series marks. His name topped the lifetime fall classic tallies for home runs (18), runs (42), RBIs (40), total bases (123) and walks (43).

Without the thickset slugger, even the Yankees would not have been part of so many post-season affairs. Once again in 1957, Mantle was the difference in New York's success. In some ways, Mickey's effort that year was even more impressive than the previous campaign, despite a generally lower statistical yield. He played a majority of the season on a pair of bad legs, but those bric-a-brac wheels were still strong enough to outdistance all American League players in number of times crossing the plate (121). Mantle's 146 bases on balls were also the top total in the junior circuit, and his .365 average was a high that exceeded his league-leading 1956 figure (.353).

His 34 home runs were third in the AL, and despite sitting out 15 games with a variety of hurts, the dynamo still led the Yankees in every significant hitting department. A troublesome right shoulder — the result of a collision with Red Schoendienst — and the usual knee ailments limited the star to 19 at-bats in a seven-game World Series, and the Yankees dropped the 1957 classic to the Milwaukee Braves.

Back-to-back Most Valuable Player awards are a measure of individual ascendancy, and the greatest switch-hitter the game has ever seen

Mickey Mantle. (Courtesy New York Yankees.)

went on to prove that he was certainly no two-year fluke. Before concluding an 18-year career in 1968, Mantle had polled 163 right-handed homers and 373 round-trippers from the port side for a lifetime tally of 536, 10th all time. His importance to the Yankee tradition is reflected in the fact that two-thirds of the seasons in which he played resulted in World Series appearances. He was named to 17 consecutive All-Star Teams as a further testament to his popularity and staying power, and he is one of only four AL ballplayers to win three MVPs.

Mantle was really feeling his oats after the 1957 season, staging his first, brief holdout prior to 1958. But he couldn't stand being out of uniform, even though by this point it meant wrapping his entire right leg in elastic bandages prior to every contest. Before much longer, the left leg required the same treatment. The Yanks won the pennant again in '58, aided by Mantle's third home run crown (42) and league-leading marks in runs (127) and walks (129), plus a solid .304 average. Miraculously, the wounded gazelle also swiped 18 bases.

After an "off" 1959 campaign in which he posted a sparkling .995 fielding average, Mantle began a stint in which he managed to play 153 games for two years running, the only time in his career he would accomplish that feat. The results were predictable. In 1960, he led the league with 40 homers and 119 runs while driving in 94, and the Yanks captured the AL pennant. Despite Mick's 10-for-25 (.400) World Series performance, which included three home runs and 11 RBIs, the Pirates bested the Bombers.

The following year was one in which the masses took Mantle's side in the race against Babe Ruth, cheering on the switch-hitter over teammate Roger Maris as both traded four-baggers at a mind-blowing pace. Between them, the M&M boys clouted a two-man record-115 home runs. The experts expected Mickey to top the Babe, but injuries stopped him short at 54, while Maris eventually triumphed with 61. Mantle might have come closer to Maris had he not heeded the advice of Yankees announcer Mel Allen and visited a particular doctor for a lingering cold. An injection led to a high fever, and Mickey missed several games after having the infected area cut open and lanced.

Still, it was a glory-filled year for the 29-year-old Mantle, who led the league in runs (132 for the sixth time), slugging (.687) and walks (126), while hitting .317 and driving home 128.

In the midst of his prime baseball years, the Yankee destroyer and his fans looked forward to seven or eight more seasons of superb productivity. Instead, they would get one more Mantle MVP and a quick decline in the fortunes of baseball's proudest franchise and most fragile superstar.

Top 5 MVP Vote-Getters

1. Mickey Mantle, New York — 233
2. Ted Williams, Boston — 209
3. Roy Sievers, Washington — 205
4. Nellie Fox, Chicago — 193
5. Gil McDougald, New York — 165

1958 NATIONAL LEAGUE—ERNIE BANKS

Ernest Banks
B. January 31, 1931, Dallas, Texas

Year	Team	Games	AB	Hits	Avg.	HR	RBI	Runs	SB
1958	Chi NL	154	617	193	.313	47	129	119	4

The Season

After more than 60 years in Brooklyn and New York, the Dodgers and Giants moved to Los Angeles and San Francisco, respectively, for the 1958 season. The Giants, who played in tiny Seals Stadium, rose from sixth place the previous year to third, while the Dodgers, in the colossal Coliseum, dropped from third to seventh.

Lodged in Milwaukee for their sixth season, the Braves earned a second consecutive National League pennant, outdistancing second-place Pittsburgh by eight games. The Braves paced the circuit in both batting (.266) and earned run average (3.21), and took a 3–1 World Series lead over the Yankees. But the Bronx Bombers, behind the four homers and eight RBIs of Hank Bauer, rallied to win the Series.

Tragedy and elation were in store this year for two players who won three MVP awards each. Dodger catcher Roy Campanella saw his career end January 29 in a horrible automobile accident that left him paralyzed below the waist, while Cardinal outfielder Stan Musial became the eighth player in major league history to reach the 3,000-hit plateau, with a double May 13.

Individual achievements included future MVP Orlando Cepeda grabbing Rookie of the Year honors, 1954 Most Valuable Player Willie Mays capturing his third stolen base title in a row and St. Louis' Sam Jones striking out 225 batters, the most in the league in 22 years.

Beacon in the Darkness

For Chicago Cubs fans, the 21 seasons that followed the 1945 pennant were bleak ones, indeed. The Cubs flailed helplessly in a sea of ineptitude, finishing last or next to last a dozen times during those years. For two consecutive decades, Chicago was a second division ballclub, a patsy for the rest of the National League.

Fortunately for their die-hard supporters, the extremely gifted, eternally optimistic Ernie Banks came along, making many of those gloomy seasons bearable. The tall, 22-year-old Texas native came directly to the majors via the Kansas City Monarchs of the Negro League in 1953. Before he left, Banks had established himself as one of the all-time greats, collecting more than 500 home runs over a 19-year career and hitting a respectable .274.

In addition to his offensive prowess, Banks was a good glove man. Although his range was never spectacular, the slick shortstop led the league in fielding three times during his first eight full seasons; and when he switched to first base in 1962, Ernie made the move gracefully, pacing NL first sackers in putouts five times and fielding once.

Beyond his on-field skills, Banks gave the impression of being one of the most genuinely happy people on earth, and his ardent zeal for the game and cheerful attitude were strikingly contagious. Often arriving early at the park to sign autographs and talk with the fans, he became a beloved ambassador of goodwill, both in the "friendly confines" of Wrigley Field and on the road. Repeatedly chanting "Let's play two today" and "It's a beautiful day for a ballgame," "Mr. Sunshine" was greatly admired by those who watched him perform on the ballfield, and cherished by those fortunate enough to come into contact with him.

Ernest's start in life was not particularly auspicious, and hardly indicative of the success that would follow. One of a dozen children in a poor Dallas family, the skinny youngster helped out by shining shoes and picking cotton. Banks joined a fast-pitch softball loop following his freshman year in high school, copying the batting stance of league opponent Hank Thompson, who later played for the New York Giants.

Banks impressed the locals with his strong hitting and good glove work, and at age 17 was granted a tryout with a black semipro hardball team known as the Detroit Colts, based in Amarillo. Ernie quickly became the team's shortstop, playing two summers before graduating from high school. Then in 1950, the Monarchs signed Banks for $300 a month.

This first professional experience was interrupted the next year when he was drafted into the Army, but after a two-year stint overseas, the quick-wristed slugger was back in Kansas City. The Cleveland Indians and Brooklyn Dodgers had shown interest in Banks while he was in the service, but neither team followed up when the 22-year-old returned to the States in March 1953. The Cubs, however, scouted the smooth athlete and purchased him for $10,000 late in the '53 campaign, immediately bringing Ernie to Chicago.

"Bingo" was an instant hit with the Cubs. He played in his team's final 10 games—ripping four extra base hits, including two home runs, and batting .314. Cub fans took to the dedicated, likeable young man right from the start, and he responded by hitting .275 and tagging 19 round-trippers in his rookie year of 1954. Ernie ran off a streak of 424 consecutive contests

Ernie Banks. (National Baseball Hall of Fame Library, Cooperstown, N.Y.)

two consecutive MVP seasons in 1958 and '59. Clearly the National League's dominant force in '58, Banks smashed his own record for homers by a short-stop with a league-high 47 among the Cubs' franchise-record 182 dingers. The 27-year-old also led the senior circuit in RBIs with 129, a .614 slugging average and 379 total bases. Ernie was runner-up in runs scored with 119 and triples with 11. Despite Banks' success, the mediocre Cubs moved up only two notches in the standings.

Unfortunately, this would typify Ernie's career. The sweet-dispositioned ballplayer failed to realize one career-long goal: to play in a World Series. In fact, he held the all-time record for most games played (2,528) without appearing in a fall classic.

Fortunately for Ernie, he didn't need to constantly be in the limelight to appreciate life. Rather than lament the fact that with more talented team-mates he could benefit from increased national media exposure, Banks often praised those around him, including owner Phil Wrigley, who many thought was less than diligent in his efforts to bring a winner to Chicago.

Eventually, the Cubs would emerge as a legitimate pennant threat prior to No. 14's retirement. But on the more immediate horizon was 1959, when Banks would become the first National Leaguer to cop the MVP award in two straight years.

Top 5 MVP Vote-Getters

1. Ernie Banks, Chicago— 283
2. Willie Mays, San Francisco—185
3. Hank Aaron, Milwaukee—166
4. Frank Thomas, Pittsburgh—143
5. Warren Spahn, Milwaukee—108

played before being sidelined in 1956 by an infection in his right hand. Banks returned to appear in 717 games in a row prior to taking a breather in 1961.

The season which best forecast the young shortstop's future excellence was 1955 when he broke a record for his position by belting 44 homers, third in the league. Five of those blasts came with the bases full to set another major league mark. Ernie was also third in the NL with 355 total bases, and fourth in both RBIs (117) and slugging percentage (.596). In addition, the classy pivot man was best in fielding at .972. The Cubs' sixth-place finish was actually an improvement over 1954, but when Banks "slipped" to 28 circuit clouts and 85 RBIs in 1956, Chicago once again became the league's doormat.

"Mr. Cub" snapped back the following campaign, setting the table for

1958 American League—Jackie Jensen

Jack Eugene Jensen
B. March 9, 1927, San Francisco, California
D. July 14, 1982, Charlottesville, Virginia

Year	Team	Games	AB	Hits	Avg.	HR	RBI	Runs	SB
1958	Bos AL	154	548	157	.286	35	122	83	9

The Season

For the first time in the history of the franchise, the New York Yankees had sole proprietorship of The Big Apple in 1958. Both the Dodgers and Giants had opted for the greener pastures of the West Coast, and the Yanks celebrated the departures with yet another World Championship.

The Bronx Bombers left the gate quickly and made a shambles of the pennant race, winning by 10 games over the Chicago White Sox, the latter club playing bridesmaid for the second straight year.

The resilient New Yorkers then enjoyed some measure of revenge in the World Series against the team that had bested them the previous year, the defending champion Milwaukee Braves. Down three games to one, the Yankees proceeded to match a World Series feat last accomplished in 1925 by the Pittsburgh Pirates, winning the last three contests for the championship.

Besides the usual Yankee heroics, the 1958 season also saw the final batting title won by the remarkable Ted Williams. The two-time MVP hit .328 at age 40.

Lonely Mercenary

The love of baseball is, for many, a thirst never really quenched. Starry-eyed fans who have never lived a major league existence yearn for a chance at the glittering diamond life far beyond the time when such desires are still plausible.

The rare dream was a reality for Jackie Eugene Jensen throughout the 1950s, and it was an auspicious one in 1960 when he willingly chose to walk away from the game. It was widely assumed at the time that his well-publicized fear of flying was the kinky-haired slugger's only reason for the premature defection. True, Jensen freely acknowledged that he was "terrified" of flight, but that particular reality was only a small part of the right fielder's impetus for leaving baseball.

Few knew what it felt like for a dedicated family man to be caught up in a solitary and nomadic lifestyle.

"It just looks like I'm not built for this type of life like some ballplayers," he lamented during his 1958 MVP year. "You're always away from home and you're lonesome. As soon as I can, I intend to get out."

"Unfathomable blasphemy" was the reaction of baseball zealots who could not or would not identify with the feelings of a man who they pictured as an ingrate about to step off the gravy train. After all, it had taken eight years for Jensen to gain some semblance of baseball notoriety prior to winning the ultimate tribute in 1958. And with the spotlight finally turned his way, he responded in 1959 with 28 home runs and a league-high 112 runs batted in.

The hardworking Jensen had not exactly been dormant prior to his prodigious 1958 campaign. Since coming to the Red Sox from Washington in 1954, he had put together four consistently productive seasons. From 1954 through 1957, the clean-up hitter's RBI totals were 117, an AL-best 116, 97 and 103.

But at age 31, in his ninth major league season, the 1958 edition of the low-profile Jensen was no longer possible to ignore. By mid-year, *Sports Illustrated* was calling him "the best right fielder in baseball," and the heady claim was justified by his final statistics. His 122 RBIs led the league and were a personal best, as were his 35 home runs (fifth in the league), 99 walks (second) and .535 slugging percentage.

The Red Sox finished third that year, but Jackie was honored with the MVP. His future looked bright in Beantown, but within three seasons, the heir apparent to Ted Williams would be a mellifluous Fenway Park memory.

Jensen left behind a brief but enviable 11-year record. A .279 lifetime average included five years with 100 or more RBIs and eight seasons of 80 or more runs driven across. He was quick enough to lead the league in stolen bases with 22 in 1954, and powerful enough to reach the stands for 199 career home runs. His glove work was steady and sure, much like the man.

Jensen's undistinguished big league start belied the stalwart force he was later to become. Originally dubbed "the Golden Boy," he arrived in the big show with the New York Yankees in 1950, his Hollywood image a direct contrast to a personality that naturally shunned center stage. He was a well-publicized bonus baby, California handsome, driving a flashy yellow convertible and sporting a gorgeous wife, Zoe Ann Olsen of Olympic diving fame. The dominant Yankees were anticipating that Jensen would replace his childhood idol, the aging Joe DiMaggio.

But after two inglorious years, the glut of Yankee farm talent and, more specifically, the 1951 arrival of Mickey Mantle, made Jensen expendable. In early 1952, he was traded from the perennial champs to the yearly downtrods, the Washington Senators. Jensen played regularly for two years in the Capitol City before being swapped again in 1954 to the Red Sox.

There the close left field wall, the Green Monster, and the bullnecked pull-hitter became line-drive acquaintances. From 1954 to 1959, no one in all of baseball — not Mantle, not Williams and not the more highly touted Detroit star, Al Kaline — drove in more runs than Jensen. Some of those runners crossed the plate on Jensen's AL-high 11 triples in 1956.

National attention had finally turned the way of "the Golden Boy," but by this time, his baseball mission was strictly mercenary. "It's the money and nothing but money that keeps me in baseball today," he openly stated in 1959.

If one looks beyond Jensen the ballplayer, his motivation was not all that difficult to understand. He'd already had his share of publicity, even before coming to the majors. He was All-San Francisco two years running in three high school sports, and at the University of California, he'd rushed for 1,010 yards as an All-America fullback his senior year on an undefeated team (including a 67-yard touchdown run in the Rose Bowl). And the previous spring, he had pitched Cal to an NCAA baseball championship.

The predilection to be near his wife and children was equally understandable when his earlier life is examined. The product of a broken home, Jensen rarely saw his hardworking mother, and from the time he was 5 to the age of 17, his family was uprooted 16 times, always one step ahead of a bill collector.

"I guess I just appreciate my current family more than most people," he stated on numerous occasions. "But for seven months of the year, I spend less than half the time with the people I love most."

He attempted to sever his ties with the sport three different times: after the 1953 season, following the 1959 campaign and early in the 1961 year. Except for the 1960 season, which he sat out in its entirety, all were aborted attempts to leave.

Finally, Jensen retired for good at age 34 after the 1961 schedule was completed. His ultimate baseball ambition had been realized: to quit. Twenty-one years later, he was dead.

In the end, some will say that the muscular blond's 11 years in the big time were unnecessarily cursory, that he could have had four to five more years of productivity. But considering his relatively brief stay on this earth and what he really wanted most from life, those 11 short seasons in the sun were very long ones indeed.

Top 5 MVP Vote-Getters

1. Jackie Jensen, Boston — 233
2. Bob Turley, New York — 191
3. Rocky Colavito, Cleveland — 181
4. Bob Cerv, Kansas City — 164
5. Mickey Mantle, New York — 127

1959 NATIONAL LEAGUE — ERNIE BANKS

Ernest Banks
B. January 31, 1931, Dallas, Texas

Year	Team	Games	AB	Hits	Avg.	HR	RBI	Runs	SB
1959	Chi NL	155	589	179	.304	45	143	97	2

The Season

Going for a third consecutive National League pennant, Milwaukee came up with a pair of 21-game winners, plus individual leaders in batting, home runs, slugging and total bases — but no flag. The Los Angeles Dodgers, on the other hand, were only sixth in the league in hitting, and lacked a hurler with more than 17 wins. But it was L.A. that captured the NL title and brought the West Coast its first World Championship by defeating the Braves two games to none in a playoff, then downing the "Go-Go" White Sox in a six-game World Series.

Twenty-four-year-old Dodger righty Larry Sherry had a part in all four of his team's Series victories, gaining two saves and a pair of wins.

The single most exciting event of the 1959 season was Harvey Haddix's 12 perfect innings against Milwaukee May 26. Unfortunately for Haddix and Pittsburgh, Lew Burdette was nearly as effective for the Braves, who won 1–0 in 13 frames. Another Pirate pitcher who made a name for himself was reliever Elroy Face, compiling an incredible 18–1 record with 10 saves.

Past and future MVPs excelled in 1959. Henry Aaron's 400 total bases were the most in baseball in more than a decade, Sandy Koufax set an NL mark and tied a major league record by striking out 18 San Francisco batters in one game, and Willie Mays made it four consecutive stolen base titles.

Baseball began a four-year experiment in 1959, staging two All-Star Games per season.

All in the Wrists

Fingers dancing near the handle of his bat, right elbow pointed directly behind him, the smooth, repetitious underswing while waiting for the pitcher to start his windup ... No. 14 was a picture of serenity at the plate. That image shattered abruptly, however, when the tall, wiry slugger snapped his iron-like wrists, the ball jumping off his bat and sailing onto Waveland Avenue behind the left field bleachers at Wrigley Field.

Ernie Banks entered 1959 as one of the National League's top stars. He had proven himself a full-fledged menace to NL pitchers, averaging 45 homers, 115 RBIs and a .300 average the past two seasons, and earning an MVP award in 1958. Ernie would end up a career .274 batter, and his 512 lifetime homers were good for a 14th-place tie with Eddie Mathews.

But "Mr. Cub" was more than just a skilled ballplayer to Cub fans — he was practically worshipped. Just the mention of the name *Ernie Banks* brought to the minds of Chicago's sports-conscious populace joy, optimism and class. His incessant smile and eternal enthusiasm were key ingredients in Cub fans' abilities to withstand the barren years of mediocre-to-wretched baseball on the North Side, and in their hopeful outlook and "wait until next year" attitude.

Prior to his retirement following the 1971 season, Banks was voted the Greatest Cub Player of All Time by the fans, was named Chicagoan of the Year in 1969 by the Chicago Press Club and became the first African-American to be enshrined in the Texas Sports Hall of Fame. Ernie stayed with the Cubs as a first base coach after 1971, then became a roving instructor in the minors before taking over as director of marketing, handling group sales. Banks was the eighth player to be elected to the Hall of Fame on the first ballot, in 1977, and later that year was selected to the club's Board of Directors. The *Chicago Tribune* purchased the Cubs from the Wrigley family in 1982, and shortly thereafter Ernie was dismissed, reportedly because of frequent absences from scheduled appearances.

Back in 1959, being a standout athlete was enough for Ernie. Setting out to become the first senior circuit player to win back-to-back MVPs, Banks succeeded magnificently. Ernie

drove in a career-high 143 runs in '59, the most in the league since 1937, and an amazing 91 more than his nearest teammate. His effortless style at the plate also accounted for 45 home runs and a .596 slugging average, both runner-up totals in the NL. Had not Mathews belted his 46th round-tripper in a post-season playoff game, Banks could have claimed his third consecutive home run crown. He was solid at shortstop too, leading the league in assists and setting major league records for fielding average (.985) and for committing only a dozen errors in 155 games.

Banks continued to pound opposing moundsmen into submission the following season, cracking a league-leading 41 homers for an amazing four-year total of 176, far more than any other player in that time span. His 331 total bases in 1960 were second in the circuit, 117 RBIs third and .554 slugging percentage fifth. He also snared his third and final fielding crown at shortstop (.977).

Figuring Jerry Kindall had more range at shortstop, the Cubs moved 30-year-old Banks to left field for 23 games in '61. But eyesight problems and a lack of feel for the position made it a short-lived experiment. He closed the season at first base, which became his permanent spot. Following his marriage to receptionist Eloyce Johnson, a nagging knee injury reasserted itself, and in 1963 Ernie suffered through his worst campaign, managing only 18 home runs and 64 RBIs, while batting an anemic .227. But Banks rebounded in 1964 and '65, averaging 25 homers and 100 RBIs.

The affable first sacker had never met a man he didn't like — until manager Leo Durocher took over the club in '66. Loudly claiming prior to the campaign that the Cubs were not an eighth-place team, Leo proved to be a prophet as his squad plunged to 10th. The fiery Durocher lashed out verbally at Ernie, letting him know in no uncertain terms that everyone was expendable, including the humble veteran.

Typical of his determined character, the 6-foot-1, 180-pounder quietly demonstrated he was still one of the

league's premier power hitters. His 23 circuit clouts and 95 RBIs in 1967, plus Leo's emphasis on fundamentals, helped the Cubs leap to third place, their best finish in 21 years. They held onto third the following year, as Ernie ripped 32 homers, third in the NL.

An air of eager anticipation filled the Cubs spring training camp in 1969, as for the first time in Banks' career, Cubs fans were realistically thinking pennant. In the first year of division play, Chicago led the East for 156 straight days and was up by eight games in mid–August. Then disaster struck. Not even the 38-year-old's 23 home runs, 106 RBIs nor his league-high .997 fielding average could keep the Miracle Mets from overwhelming the tired Cubs down the stretch in Banks' final full season. He played a total of 111 games his last two years, and though the Cubs challenged both times, Ernie again fell short of his dream — to play in a World Series.

In 1984, "Mr. Cub" received one of his greatest thrills when he was made an honorary coach of the division-winning Cubs during the playoffs, throwing out the ceremonial first ball in the opener. More than 30 years following his retirement, Banks' career rankings are noteworthy. In addition to his standing in home runs, he was among the top 25 in RBIs (1,636), extra base hits (1,009) and total bases (4,706), and among the top 40 in at-bats (9,421) and games (2,528).

Ernie Banks, who spent his entire 19-year career with the Cubs, will forever be linked with the North Side club in the minds of baseball fans everywhere. His unwavering loyalty, perpetual optimism and astonishing skills will never be forgotten. As columnist Dick Young once wrote, "Ernie Banks is a beautiful man."

Top 5 MVP Vote-Getters

1. Ernie Banks, Chicago — 232½
2. Eddie Mathews, Milwaukee — 189½
3. Hank Aaron, Milwaukee — 174
4. Wally Moon, Los Angeles — 161
5. Sam Jones, San Francisco — 130

1959 American League—Nellie Fox

Jacob Nelson Fox
B. December 25, 1927, St. Thomas, Pennsylvania
D. December 1, 1975, Baltimore, Maryland

Year	Team	Games	AB	Hits	Avg.	HR	RBI	Runs	SB
1959	Chi AL	156	624	191	.306	2	70	84	5

The Season

It had been four full decades since the "Black Sox" had shamed Chicago's American League fans with their despicable 1919 World Series antics, and as if cursed, the team suffered through the longest pennant dry spell in the circuit. But manager Al Lopez and his band of swifties changed all that in 1959 by scrapping their way to the top of the heap with panache, pitching and an airtight defense.

The mighty Yankees fell to third place, and the main challenge to the White Sox came from Cleveland, which topped the league in runs, home runs, batting average and slugging. But in the end, pitching-rich Chicago won handily by five games.

An April 22 win against Kansas City best exemplified Chicago's excuse for an offense. In the seventh inning, the Chisox scored 11 runs on only one hit, upsetting their opponents with 10 walks, a hit batsman and three men reaching on errors.

Despite an opening game 11–0 win, the White Sox speed merchants were bested in six games in the World Series by the Los Angeles Dodgers.

In other 1959 AL action, Rocky Colavito of Cleveland became the third major league player to lash four consecutive round-trippers in a game.

Twelve years after Jackie Robinson broke major league baseball's color line, the Boston Red Sox became the last team to field a black player when they used Pumpsie Green as a pinch-runner in a July 21 game.

Heart of a Giant

It was only fitting that Chicago White Sox "Mighty Mite," Nelson Fox, wear the Most Valuable Player crown following the 1959 success of the team that carried his personal stamp of aggressive, overachieving hustle. The handwriting was on the wall on opening day when the port-side swinging second baseman poked his first home run in two years to win a 14-inning squeaker over Detroit.

The South Side pepper pot was rolling along at a .332 clip in late July, and Chicago fans, desperate for a pennant, held their collective breath as Fox and company inched away from the pack. When it was over, the White Sox found themselves in the World Series for the first time since 1919, but this time even "Little Nellie's" .375 performance and flawless fielding could not turn the tide.

Jacob Nelson Fox had been bucking the odds in baseball since first deciding to pursue a professional career. The youngest child of a carpenter and ex-semipro second baseman, Nellie attempted the nigh-impossible and succeeded as a scrawny 16-year-old in convincing Philadelphia Athletic patriarch Connie Mack to sign him to a minor league pact.

Starting in Class B as an outfielder-first baseman in 1943, Fox was soon switched to second base and demoted to Class D. He performed respectably enough to move slowly up the A's minor league ladder until a one-year hitch in the Korean conflict momentarily halted his progress.

While others wrote him off as a short-term utility man, Fox practically willed himself into becoming the most reliable keystone man in the AL throughout the 1950s. By the end of the decade, only Ted Williams among all active American Leaguers had accumulated more hits.

When he finally hung up his glove, Fox did so with a splendid lifetime fielding mark of .984. From 1952 through 1960, he topped league second sackers in two-to-four fielding categories per year. Over his career, he turned in a total of 33 titles in putouts, assists, double plays, total chances per game and fielding average.

Such acumen with the glove did not come easily. Following his first full year with the Athletics, Nellie was traded to the White Sox for reserve catcher Joe Tipton. In 1950, he became a starter, and the next year, Sox manager Paul Richards declared Fox his personal project. The 23-year-old responded to the countless hours of infield and hitting practice, and by 1951, had raised his batting average 66 points to .313. From then until 1958, Fox and his pesky bat averaged .305.

As a seasoned veteran, it was his hustle and baseball savvy that was most in evidence. He executed the important aspects of the game on a regular basis—bunting, handling routine chances nearly perfectly and taking the extra base whenever the opportunity was presented. He was a regular fixture in the Sox lineup, playing in a then league-record 798 consecutive contests at second base. Immediately prior to that streak, he played in all but one of 275 games at second. There was seldom even a mid-season break for Fox, who was named to 12 AL All-Star Teams, slapping a two-run single in the 1954 classic to help his team win 11–9.

A relentless student of the game, Fox was handpicked by another of baseball's great minds, serving as manager Ted Williams' coach and right-hand man for the Washington Senators. The battling spirit of the little guy finally gave way to cancer in 1975.

Those who knew him or saw him play recall the unlikely portrait of the athlete he presented. Left cheek bulging with a gigantic wad of chewing tobacco, there was little in the 5-foot-10-inch, 160-pound frame that seemed to warrant special precaution from the opposition. He even appeared somewhat humorous when he ran — a kind of waddling, unnatural gait.

Little Nel rarely unleashed the long ball, but his Punch-and-Judy batting style would regularly base-hit the enemy to death. Choking up significantly on a fat-handled bat, Fox would guide the sphere to the opposite field with a short swing that concluded with his body lurching toward first base. That style resulted in the pugnacious second sacker leading the AL in singles seven consecutive seasons (1954–60) and pacing the league in hits four times. So rarely did he strike out that Nellie ranked as the third most difficult batter to whiff in baseball annals, and he never fanned more than 18 times in a season. In fact, he established a record for consecutive games without striking out (98) in 1958.

The beloved working stiff was honored in '59 with a Nellie Fox Night in Chicago, and repaid the faithful tenfold by aiding the Sox in their successful pennant run. The No. 2 man in the Chicago batting order finished with a .306 average (fourth in the league), 191 hits (second) and league-leading defensive marks for his position in putouts, assists and fielding average, again playing every game for his club. For his efforts, he became the first White Sox winner of the MVP award, and the first AL second baseman to get the nod since Joe Gordon 17 years earlier.

Fox drew 295 points and 14 first-place votes to teammate Luis Aparicio's 255 figure, the victory owed to Nellie's more consistent hitting. With teammate Early Wynn finishing third in the

Nellie Fox. (Courtesy Chicago White Sox.)

MVP voting, the White Sox became the first AL team to produce the top three MVP vote-getters in a season.

Nellie retired after 1965 with a lifetime .288 batting average built on 2,663 hits in 2,367 games. The sure-handed infielder ranked second all time in double plays for a second baseman (1,619), third in putouts (6,090), fourth in games (2,295) and seventh in assists (6,373). His 1956 putout total of 478 was fourth all time for a single season, and his 141 double plays in 1957 tied for fourth.

Even those figures, however, do not adequately reflect the vivacious enthusiasm the hard-nosed flyweight exhibited through 19 major league seasons. While more talented visages lit up the baseball horizon for fleeting periods, Nellie Fox demonstrated that through

hard work and steady hammering, someone of lesser physical skills could still have a telling effect in the long run.

Fox narrowly missed being enshrined in the Hall of Fame by baseball writers, falling two votes shy in his final year of eligibility (1985). But the veteran's committee selected the White Sox sparkplug for Hall induction in 1997.

Top 5 MVP Vote-Getters

1. Nellie Fox, Chicago — 295
2. Luis Aparicio, Chicago — 255
3. Early Wynn, Chicago — 123
4. Rocky Colavito, Cleveland — 117
5. Tito Francona, Cleveland — 102

1960 NATIONAL LEAGUE — DICK GROAT

Richard Morrow Groat
B. November 4, 1930, Wilkinsburg, Pennsylvania

Year	Team	Games	AB	Hits	Avg.	HR	RBI	Runs	SB
1960	Pit NL	138	573	186	.325	2	50	85	0

The Season

The steady bats of Dick Groat, Roberto Clemente and Dick Stuart, punctuated by the reliable arms of Vernon Law, Bob Friend and Elroy Face, spearheaded the Pirates to their first pennant since 1927. This time, however, the Bucs would not be bullied by the Yankees in the World Series. Pittsburgh captured four squeakers and the World Championship when Bill Mazeroski unloaded a Series-winning home run in the bottom of the ninth in game seven, marking the first time in major league history that a season had ended with a four-bagger. The defeat was especially bitter for New York, which had hammered Pirate pitching by scores of 16–3, 10–0 and 12–0.

Although no National League regular-season deeds could quite match the dramatic flair of Mr. Mazeroski's timely swat, there were numerous individual achievements worth noting, including three no-hit outings. Warren Spahn, at age 39, fired the first no-hitter of his already illustrious career, and claimed his 20th victory of the season at the same time. Immediately after being traded in mid-season to the Chicago Cubs, Don Cardwell tossed a no-hitter at the St. Louis Cardinals. Lew Burdette's gem against Cardwell's old squad, the Phillies, marked the first time since 1906 that three NL teams had been dealt the ultimate in single-game frustration in one season.

And speaking of pitching performances, San Francisco's high-kicking rookie, Juan Marichal, became the first NL hurler since 1900 to throw a one-hitter in his debut, striking out 12 in a 2–0 win over Philadelphia.

In an unusual "trade," Chicago manager Charlie Grimm and announcer Lou Boudreau swapped jobs after a 6–11 start. The Cubs were 54–83 in Boudreau's brief tenure.

On September 15, past and future MVP Willie Mays tied a modern day record with three triples in a game as San Francisco edged the Phillies 8–6 in 11 innings.

Court General

When the Pittsburgh Pirates copped the 1960 World Championship, the usually invisible contributions of the Bucs' main man in the middle, Dick Groat, were finally endorsed in a manner that hearkened back to his college days eight years earlier.

The Pennsylvania native had led the nation's college basketball players in points with a record-831 in 1951, then topped the country in assists in 1952, retiring as the No. 1 scorer in college history. "Dick the Great" was a legend at Duke University for his crafty ability on the hardcourt, where he snared two All-America awards in basketball and baseball.

Impressed with Dick's shortstopping abilities, Branch Rickey signed him to the Pirates for a $25,000 bonus immediately upon graduation. The cool steadiness of the 21-year-old was instantly apparent when Groat went straight from the college campus to the Pittsburgh shortstop post in mid–1952, and rang up a .284 average in 95 games. Right from the start, he was all business, rarely smiling, almost never laughing — burning with a furious passion to succeed that was reflected in an extremely intense visage.

The devotion he brought to his job paid dividends in 1960, the 29-year-old's seventh year in the bigs. Groat roared out of the gate and was hitting .350 well into the season, pro-

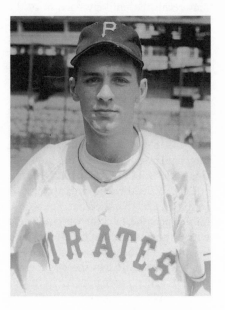

Dick Groat. (Courtesy Pittsburgh Pirates.)

viding game-winning performances at the bat and in the field on a regular basis for the high-flying Pirates. A 6-for-6 day, including three doubles, helped Pittsburgh defeat Milwaukee 8–2 May 13, and on September 17 versus Cincinnati, the infielder collected his 1,000th career hit. Dick finished at .325, the highest figure in the majors. In the heat of a tough pennant race, the Pirate captain went 16-for-23 and 27-for-56 before a Lew Burdette pitch fractured his wrist, causing him to miss 16 late-season contests. Groat rebounded to collect six hits, including a pair of two-baggers, and two RBIs in the team's 4–3 World Series triumph over the Yankees.

Groat's MVP award came much easier than his slender six-point margin in the batting race. Dick was a landslide winner in the balloting, compiling 276 points and far outdistancing teammate and runner-up Don Hoak, who received 162. Groat became the first Pirate to earn the MVP and the third straight shortstop to capture the honor. He joined Ernie Banks, winner of the two previous awards, as the only Most Valuable Players never to play a day of minor league ball. In addition to the MVP, Groat was chosen as the recipient of the annual Lou Gehrig Memorial Award, given to the player who best exemplifies the spirit of the former Yankee first baseman.

Nineteen-sixty's team and individual triumphs vindicated Groat, who had given up a career in pro basketball in 1956 at the request of the Pirates. Dick had played a single season with the Fort Wayne Pistons in 1952 in the then-fledgling National Basketball Association before a two-year hitch in the Army disturbed his two-sport career. But based on the shaky foundation of the NBA and the longevity potential the diamond game offered, Groat decided to give baseball his full-time attention. Since rejoining the Pirates in 1955, he had turned in a six-year .286 batting average that included season highs of .315 in 1957 and .300 in '58. Despite personal success, the shortstop was beginning to feel somewhat frustrated due to his team's inability to capture a pennant and the realization that he could seldom determine the outcome of a baseball game with the same dazzling effectiveness he had displayed on the college hardcourt.

As the Pirates gradually rose to power in the late 1950s, the contributions of Pittsburgh's take-charge guy began having a subtle but telling effect. Unlike the more publicized power boys, the right-handed poke hitter came through with timely singles, steady fielding and a prevailing attitude toward victory which vociferously spurred his mates to the limits of their abilities.

"He's the guy the Pirates can least afford to lose," observed Milwaukee hurler Warren Spahn, and that sentiment was echoed by many opponents throughout Dick's nine-year stay in the Steel City.

The obvious respect Groat commanded was hardly imparted in No. 24's lifetime statistics, which are substantial but not indicative of the significant part he played on two pennant winners. The .286 career batting average compiled over 14 years needs no defense, however, since a majority of Dick's shortstop contemporaries were far less effective at the plate.

Groat bested the opposition in quietly deceptive ways: getting on base, rapping a single to keep a critical rally alive, making a difficult pivot at second base or positioning himself perfectly in the field. Far from the premiere hitter in the NL, Dick made every at-bat count, rarely striking out, and gaining a reputation as a reliable hit-and-run man and clutch RBI provider. Like fellow shortstop MVP Lou Boudreau of the 1948 Indians, Groat was average in terms of size and below par in the speed department. But the prematurely bald Pirate ranked near the head of the class in gaming instinct and never-let-up passion.

Those particular ingredients were just what the St. Louis Cardinals needed in 1963 when general manager Bing Devine swung a deal that brought the 32-year-old to the Redbirds. Groat came through with a .319 season and a league-high 43 doubles, then contributed a .292 average in 161 games in the pennant-winning 1964 campaign. The gritty shortstop held down a starting St. Louis spot for another year, was traded to Philadelphia in 1966 and then shipped to San Francisco, where he played sparingly in 1967.

Groat may always wonder whether he might have achieved even more acclaim in professional basketball than he did as a baseball player, but members of his 1960 and 1964 championship teams certainly benefited from the infectious aura of confident determination radiating from the key position in their infield. Dick Groat was more than an efficient shortstop — he was an inspiring court general.

Top 5 MVP Vote-Getters

1. Dick Groat, Pittsburgh — 276
2. Don Hoak, Pittsburgh — 162
3. Willie Mays, San Francisco — 155
4. Ernie Banks, Chicago — 100
5. Lindy McDaniel, St. Louis — 95

1960 American League — Roger Maris

Roger Eugene Maris
B. September 10, 1934, Hibbing, Minnesota
D. December 14, 1985, Houston, Texas

Year	Team	Games	AB	Hits	Avg.	HR	RBI	Runs	SB
1960	NY AL	136	499	141	.283	39	112	98	2

The Season

The New York Yankees won their fifth pennant in six years in 1960, outdistancing the surprising runner-up Baltimore Orioles by eight games.

The powerful New Yorkers, who broke an AL record by bashing 193 homers during the regular season, continued a vicious assault on opposing pitchers in post-season play—setting World Series milestones for batting (.338), runs (55), hits (91) and extra base hits (27). Normally a light hitter, second baseman Bobby Richardson led the charge by clubbing a grand slam, driving in six runs in one game and establishing a Series mark with 12 RBIs. Despite the awesome offensive display, the Yankees fell in seven games to the Pirates.

Following the Series, Yankee skipper Casey Stengel was dismissed because of age, ending a sensational 25-year managerial career. The 70-year-old "Professor" retired having won more World Series games (37) than any manager in history, and his extremely successful teams captured seven of 10 fall classics.

Also retiring after the 1960 campaign was the incomparable Ted Williams, who early in the year became the fourth player in major league history to go over the 500 mark in homers. One of those dingers came September 2 against Washington's Don Lee, 20 years after Williams had homered off Lee's father, Thornton, of the Chicago White Sox. Another round-tripper came September 26 in the two-time MVP's final career at-bat.

In an unusual move, Cleveland and Detroit traded managers, with Joe Gordon going to the Motor City and Jimmy Dykes heading to the Indians.

New York-Bound

To the small-town man from North Dakota, Kansas City was a fine place to be late in 1959. The city was large enough to give him the recreational pursuits he desired, but small enough to provide the privacy he and his family cherished. Roger Maris had just finished a decent campaign in which the left-handed batter had hit .273 with 16 homers and 72 RBIs. With the Athletics building through youth, Roger's place on the club seemed secure, and the 25-year-old was satisfied, settled and at peace with the world.

But a surprising December announcement changed all that, uprooting a disillusioned Maris and his family, and sending him on a bittersweet nine-year adventure which would include tremendous personal triumphs and intense pain and suffering. Within two years, the shy, reserved right fielder would accomplish what many thought to be nearly impossible, yet would be forced to venture through an emotional hell he never dreamed existed.

Once the Yankees' farm club, and now facetiously referred to as such because of the constant shuffle of ballplayers between the two towns, Kansas City pulled off yet another headline-making swap with the New Yorkers. This time the Athletics exchanged promising prospect Maris for elder statesmen Don Larsen, Hank Bauer and Norm Siebern, as well as young Marv Throneberry. Roger and wife Pat were deeply disappointed by the trade, which would place Roger in a limelight he'd never known nor fancied. Maris would now be under the watchful eyes of the nation's media capital, where the fans didn't merely

hope for production from their ballplayers—they ruthlessly demanded it. Had the saddened "Rajah" realized the tumultuous odyssey that was in store for him in the ensuing years, he might have retired on the spot.

In 1960, Maris' performance for his new team elevated him to star status for the first time. In his Yankee debut April 19 at Boston, Maris provided a sign of things to come by connecting for four hits, including two homers, and driving in four runs. The modest man with the flattop haircut took advantage of Yankee Stadium's short right field porch, utilizing his smooth stroke to power 39 home runs and lead the American League in RBIs with 112 and slugging percentage at .581. Maris was also runner-up in total bases with 290 and runs scored at 98. Although Roger posted a career-high .283 batting average, many thought Mickey Mantle would corral his third MVP trophy in five years. But Maris surprised, edging the popular center fielder in the voting by three points, 225 to 222. Maris played in all seven games of the 1960 World Series loss to Pittsburgh, hitting .267 with two homers and a pair of RBIs.

Thanks to a splendid performance in his initial year in New York and the city's thorough media coverage, Maris was becoming a household word. It would, however, take the bizarre events of the following season to cast the unsuspecting ballplayer permanently into the annals of baseball lore.

He had already come a long way from American Legion ball in Fargo, North Dakota, where he attracted attention with his mammoth home runs. The Cleveland Indians were the first to sit up and take notice, but Roger was

Roger Maris. (Courtesy New York Yankees.)

year, but was sidelined when he broke a few ribs in a head-first slide. He finished with only 14 homers in 116 games, doubling that amount the next campaign, during which he was traded to Kansas City for Vic Power and Woodie Held. In '59, his circuit clout total dipped to 16, but Rog drove in 72 runs and hit a very respectable .273. He was off to another quick start that year before an appendix operation rudely intervened. The port-side swinger was hitting at a torrid pace following his return, but after the surgery, his average plummeted 80 points.

Following the 1960 MVP season, Maris would play eight more years for two teams, repeating as the AL's Most Valuable Player in '61 and achieving worldwide notoriety for breaking Babe Ruth's long-standing, single-season home run record. Roger wound up with 275 career homers and a .260 batting average in nearly 1,500 games. Though he never hit .300, Maris smashed 20 or more home runs six times, including five years in a row (1960–64), and on three occasions went over the 100 mark in RBIs. Revealing his status as a team player, the Yankees won five AL pennants during Maris' first five years in New York, and the Cardinals earned two NL flags during his only two seasons in St. Louis (1967–68).

But career accomplishments are not what come to mind when the name *Roger Maris* is bandied about. Rather, it is the incredible 1961 season — with its fantastic achievements, harrowing circumstances and unusual outcome — that will forever be linked with the slugging right fielder.

Top 5 MVP Vote-Getters

1. Roger Maris, New York — 225
2. Mickey Mantle, New York — 222
3. Brooks Robinson, Baltimore — 211
4. Minnie Minoso, Chicago — 141
5. Ron Hansen, Baltimore — 110

less than impressive in his debut pro tryout. Also showing interest were the Cubs, but they too passed him up.

At this point, the rugged, 18-year-old, all-around athlete seriously considered a career in pro football. He changed his mind, however, when the Indians asked for a second look, and this time Roger succeeded in making the club. In 1953, his home run production was minimal for the Indians farm club in Fargo, until manager JoJo White took the youngster aside and told him to forget about hitting the ball

where it was pitched and start swinging for the fences. Maris began concentrating on pulling the ball with an uppercut swing, and in 1954 bashed 32 round-trippers for the Fargo/Moorhead Twins. Hardly a one-dimensional player, the strong-armed, aggressive right fielder made all of the routine plays and most of the difficult ones.

After two more seasons in the minors, Roger was brought up to the Indians in 1957, and immediately made his presence felt. He was leading the AL in home runs and RBIs early in the

1961 National League — Frank Robinson

Frank Robinson
B. August 31, 1935, Beaumont, Texas

Year	Team	Games	AB	Hits	Avg.	HR	RBI	Runs	SB
1961	Cin NL	153	545	176	.323	37	124	117	22

The Season

Confounding pre-season predictions, Cincinnati held off the Dodgers to win its first flag since 1940.

Los Angeles hurler Sandy Koufax certainly did his part in bringing the Dodgers within four games of the top, fanning 269 hitters to break Christy Mathewson's modern-day National League record of 267 set in 1903.

The Reds countered with Joey Jay's 21 wins, plus 16 saves each from relievers Bill Henry and Jim Brosnan, to outlast L.A. Cincy ran into one of the best Yankee squads of all time in the World Series, however, and could win only one game.

Milwaukee left-hander Warren Spahn, 40, seemed to defy nature, getting even better at a time in his career when most hurlers had long since retired. The crafty, 17-year veteran became the second oldest major league pitcher (behind Cy Young) to throw a no-hitter when he blanked San Francisco 1–0 April 28. In his next start, Spahn two-hit the Dodgers in a 4–1 win May 3.

Chicago Cub owner Phil Wrigley instituted his infamous rotating manager system, wherein members of the team's coaching staff each took a short term at the helm. The procedure netted seventh-place results. The Cubs did manage to finish ahead of the last-place Phillies, who set a 20th century record by losing 23 games in a row. The New York Mets, who were awarded a National League charter in 1961 and started play the following year, would transcend the futility of these franchises.

Crosley Field King

The strapping figure of Frank Robinson has been an imposing force on the baseball scene since 1956, as a hard-driving player, as one of the most publicized big league managers, and finally as the no-nonsense major league vice president of on-field operations and again as a manager.

Robinson's career is dotted with "firsts." He is the only ballplayer to win Most Valuable Player awards in both leagues, and was the first black manager hired by a major league club. He was also the first African-American skipper to be fired, then hired again.

The slugger's place in baseball lore would have been secure even had he never gone on to fame in a managerial capacity. Besides compiling impressive lifetime statistics, the tremendously versatile performer was quick on the basepaths with excellent running instincts. Barreling into opposing infielders typified his aggressive style. A vast majority of his career was spent in the outfield, a territory he manned to near-perfection.

The product of a broken home, Frank was painfully shy as a youth, dividing his time between solo movie outings and sports. He grew up in Los Angeles, the youngest in a family of 10 children, and was an outstanding high school athlete, excelling in baseball, basketball and football. After graduation in 1953, he signed for a $3,500 bonus with the Cincinnati Reds.

From the outset of his pro career, the talented power hitter impressed at the plate, crowding the pay station in a defiant batting stance that invited brushback pitches. Frank was sent sprawling innumerable times, but the "messages" from opposing hurlers only served to heighten his determination as a hitter. He was plunked 20 times in 1956, a league record for rookies, and topped the circuit six times in being hit

by pitches, second all time in the National League behind Ron Hunt (seven). Altogether, Robinson felt the sting of the horsehide 204 times in his career.

As a 21-year-old rookie, Frank cranked out 38 home runs to tie a 26-year-old record for first-year men, led the league in runs scored and was a unanimous selection as Rookie of the Year. Despite recurring cases of blurred vision which hampered him from time to time, Robinson averaged .301 and 32 HRs per year from 1957 through 1960, completing five years of sullen but brilliant performances. He earned a Gold Glove in 1958, and his .595 slugging average in 1960 was tops in the NL.

Insecure and introverted up to this point in his big league career, the moody right fielder emerged dramatically from his shell to become the outspoken thrust in Cincinnati's 1961 pennant push. A pre-season incident, in which the 25-year-old was arrested and fined for threatening a restaurant employee with a gun, lit a fire under Robinson, seemingly speeding up his maturation process.

Determined to atone for the embarrassing event, Robby delivered in style, hitting .323, socking 37 homers and driving in 124 for the pennant-winning Reds. Playing in all but one game during the campaign, Robinson finished second in the league in RBIs and runs (117), third in homers and steals (22), and fourth in total bases (333), leading the NL with an exceptional .611 slugging average.

It was the Reds' first flag since 1940, and for his extraordinary efforts, Frank became the first member of a Cincy team to be named Most Valuable Player since Frank McCormick that same season.

Renewed in confidence, Robinson put together perhaps his finest season in 1962, registering a .342 average, 39 round-trippers and 136 RBIs. Frank's 51 doubles, 134 runs, .624 slugging average and .424 on-base percentage were the best in the league, and the calculated fury he showed on the basepaths earned him 18 stolen bases.

Injuries sent his batting average plummeting 83 points the next season, but the natural-born battler still drove in 91 runs. Then, following a 1965 campaign in which Robinson hit .296 with 33 homers and 113 RBIs, the Reds made one of the worst blunders of all time by trading their most productive player to the Baltimore Orioles.

In return, the Reds received pitchers Milt Pappas and Jack Baldschun, as well as outfielder Dick Simpson. Cincinnati general manager Bill De Witt pointed to his team's pitching needs as the main reason for the swap, but sources close to the club claimed that De Witt had held the 1961 gun incident — as well as yearly salary squabbles — against Robinson right up to the time the superstar was sent packing.

Frank left Cincinnati as the greatest hitter in the history of the franchise, a fact not lost on the angry Reds fandom, who could not comprehend trading the man most responsible for hoisting their last pennant flag.

Robby would go on to play 11 more years, racking up 2,943 hits and a .294 lifetime average in a 21-year career. Before he finished, the man with the violent swing would climb to fourth place all time behind Aaron, Ruth and Mays with 586 home runs, adding eight more in World Series play. Robinson was also sixth all time in extra base hits (1,186), ninth in total bases (5,373), 11th in runs (1,829), 15th in RBIs (1,812), 17th in games (2,808), 20th in walks (1,420), 21st in at-bats (10,006), 26th in doubles (528), and 27th in both hits (2,943) and slugging (.537). He was selected to 12 All-Star Teams.

From 1956 through 1965, National League fans had witnessed the exciting exploits of the aggressive long baller. Now it was time for the junior circuit to give way to the thunder.

Frank Robinson. (Courtesy Cincinnati Reds.)

Top 5 MVP Vote-Getters

1. Frank Robinson, Cincinnati — 219
2. Orlando Cepeda, San Francisco — 117
3. Vada Pinson, Cincinnati — 104
4. Roberto Clemente, Pittsburgh — 81
5. Joey Jay, Cincinnati — 74

1961 AMERICAN LEAGUE — ROGER MARIS

Roger Eugene Maris
B. September 10, 1934, Hibbing, Minnesota
D. December 14, 1985, Houston, Texas

Year	Team	Games	AB	Hits	Avg.	HR	RBI	Runs	SB
1961	NY AL	161	590	159	.269	61	142	132	0

The Season

Changes were rampant in 1961 in the American League, which expanded both its number of teams and games played per club. New franchises were awarded to Los Angeles and Washington, while the Senators were transferred from the nation's capital to Minneapolis-St. Paul and renamed the Twins. AL squads increased their workloads from 154 contests to 162.

But the dominance of the Yankees remained a constant. New York won 109 games for its sixth league crown in seven years, beating out an improved Detroit club by eight games. Under Ralph Houk, who became the third manager to win a World Championship in his initial season, the Bronx Bombers clobbered a major league-record 240 homers, with six players belting 20 or more.

New York eased past Cincinnati in a five-game World Series for its 19th championship in 26 tries. Cy Young Award winner Whitey Ford set a Series record by extending his consecutive scoreless innings streak to 32, and Bobby Richardson enjoyed his second straight sensational Series, collecting nine safeties to tie a record for a five-game set, while hitting .391.

On May 9, Baltimore's Jim Gentile became the first player in major league history to hit grand slams in consecutive innings. Gentile wound up with a record-tying five slams for the season.

On a sad note, Hall of Famer Ty Cobb died of cancer at age 74. At the time of his death, Cobb was still baseball's all-time leader in batting average, hits, runs, total bases, at-bats and games played.

The Asterisk

Of all the men in baseball who could have challenged Babe Ruth's single-season home run record, Roger Maris was perhaps one of the least emotionally suited for the task. The left-handed slugger might have been able to cope with the physical strain of chasing the Babe, but unaccustomed to publicity, he gradually sank under the tremendous weight of hostility emanating from the media, fans, commissioner and even the Yankee organization itself.

The 1961 season started slowly for Roger, who didn't park his first home run until the 11th game. He was well behind Ruth's pace the first 50 games or so, but then came on strong, going ahead of the legend in the 63rd contest with his 25th homer. Maris blasted No. 40 in his 96th game, and when writers noted that the Babe had taken 120 contests to accomplish the same feat, the nation suddenly took interest.

Maris had the distinct advantage of having Mickey Mantle and Yogi Berra surround him in the Yankee batting order and, as a result, never received an intentional walk throughout the campaign. It was becoming apparent that the bland Minnesota native with the crewcut might very well replace Ruth as the best single-season home run hitter of all time, especially with the season extended eight games. And baseball, to its eternal discredit, went berserk with panic.

Deciding Roger Maris was not an acceptable candidate for such a prestigious position, baseball systematically set out to foil his efforts. Among those who sought to derail Maris on his way to 61 homers, or at least lessen the subsequent impact, were:

- Commissioner Ford Frick, who uncharacteristically declared that Roger would not be recognized as the one-season home run champ unless he broke the mark within 154 games, the number of contests played during Ruth's 1927 record year;
- The Yankee front office, which preferring Mantle to break the record rather than Maris, tried to force manager Ralph Houk into altering the lineup by placing Mantle ahead of Maris;
- The media, which cited a lengthier schedule, talent diluted by expansion and the livelier ball as reasons for Maris' outstanding season; and
- The New York fans, many of whom booed Roger even when he homered at Yankee Stadium.

Despite feeling as if he were battling the entire world, Maris kept slugging. Frick's curfew passed with Roger stuck at 58 round-trippers. Undaunted, he tagged homer No. 59 in the Yanks' 155th game, and No. 60 on September 26 against Baltimore's Jack Fisher. Four contests remained. Looking to regroup, he took the first one off to rest, then was shut out the first two days of a three-game series against Boston. Maris finally came through with the record-breaker in his second at-bat on the final day of the season before a small crowd of 23,154 at Yankee Stadium, bopping Tracy Stallard's hanging curve into the right field seats. Fan Sal Durante caught the home run ball and sold it for a then-significant $5,000.

Following the Yanks' World Series victory over Cincinnati, the writers finally acknowledged Roger's performance by announcing his selection as the AL's Most Valuable Player for the second straight year. Maris' league-leading totals in homers, RBIs (142) and runs (132) helped him edge Mantle for the second consecutive season, this time by a 202–198 margin.

The 1961 campaign, complete with its physical and mental strains, left Maris totally drained. Following the stressful season, Maris said, "As a ballplayer, I would be delighted to do it again. As an individual, I doubt if I could possibly go through it again." The next year brought what would normally be considered a productive campaign, with 33 homers and 100 RBIs, but the critics jumped on the deflated figures, calling his previous year's effort a "one-season fluke."

If 1961 and '62 had been torturously painful seasons, then the following four years in New York were merely depressing. Frequent injuries, combined with a dismal mental attitude, caused Roger to average only 16 homers and 48 RBIs in that span.

By this time, the 32-year-old was anxious to leave New York. Resigned to losing Maris, the Yankees dealt him to the Cardinals in December 1966 for journeyman Charlie Smith.

Released from the hotbed of attention in the Big Apple, Maris was much happier in St. Louis, despite hitting only 14 home runs in two years there. Both years the Cards made the World Series. Maris was brilliant in the 1967 classic, which saw St. Louis edge Boston in seven games, hitting .385 with a homer and seven RBIs.

Unlike some players who find it nearly impossible to adjust to postbaseball life, Maris was ready and willing to leave the game after the '68 season. True to form, he stayed away from the lecture circuit, even avoiding speaking engagements on behalf of his beer distributorship business in Gainesville, Florida. Roger passed away of lymphatic cancer in 1985 at the age of 51.

Roger Maris. (Courtesy New York Yankees.)

Thirteen years later, Maris' controversial home run record was shattered when Mark McGwire of St. Louis blasted 70, including the record-breaking 62nd homer September 8 with Maris' sons in attendance. The Maris name surfaced again in 2001 when the family filed a $1 billion defamation lawsuit against Anheuser-Busch a month after the family was awarded $50 million by a jury in another suit against the company.

From mid–1961 to the end of his playing days, baseball minimized Roger Maris' achievements. Today, he is the only two-time MVP winner to be shunned by the Hall of Fame. Although a center field plaque bearing his likeness now resides in Yankee Stadium, the quiet slugger rejected most requests from the Yankees to play in old-timers games. But away from baseball, he was content again, just as in 1959 before being traded to the Yankees. Roger had become his own man again — this time for good.

Top 5 MVP Vote-Getters

1. Roger Maris, New York — 202
2. Mickey Mantle, New York — 198
3. Jim Gentile, Baltimore — 157
4. Norm Cash, Detroit — 151
5. Whitey Ford, New York — 102

1962 National League—Maury Wills

Maurice Morning Wills
B. October 2, 1932, Washington, D.C.

Year	Team	Games	AB	Hits	Avg.	HR	RBI	Runs	SB
1962	LA NL	165	695	208	.299	6	48	130	104

The Season

The Dodgers and Giants ended a sizzling pennant race with 101 wins each in 1962, necessitating a best-of-three playoff. Los Angeles had blown a golden opportunity to win the flag outright by failing to capture any of its three season-ending home games against the sixth-place Cardinals.

The playoffs took an anticlimactic turn in the third and decisive contest when Dodger hurler Stan Williams walked in the game-winner after L.A. again had victory within arm's grasp, leading 4–2 in the ninth.

San Francisco standouts Felipe Alou, Willie Mays, Orlando Cepeda, Willie McCovey, et. al., took the Yankees to the limit in the World Series, finally falling in seven games despite heroics by Chuck Hiller (first NL postseason grand slam) and Jack Sanford (10 strikeouts in a losing Game 5 cause.)

Individual achievements included future MVP Sandy Koufax throwing a no-hitter June 30 after fanning 18 in a nine-inning game April 24; three-time MVP Stan Musial becoming the all-time senior circuit leader in both hits and RBIs; and 1949 MVP Jackie Robinson being enshrined in the Hall of Fame.

It was also a good year for fielders. Ken Hubbs of Chicago established major league records for second basemen with 78 consecutive errorless games and 418 straight chances accepted without an error, while Houston's Bob Aspromonte set an NL mark for third basemen with 57 games in a row without a fielding miscue.

The league expanded to 10 teams for the first time in the 20th century, with the New York Mets losing a record-120 contests (60½ games out of

first), and the Houston Colt .45s managing to finish ahead of the Cubs in eighth with a 64–96 slate.

Renaissance Runner

Maury Wills, an inauspicious wisp of a ballplayer, turned back the clock and breathed life into the lost art of the stolen base. More than 30 years had elapsed since Babe Ruth and his imitators made the running game passé, but by the time Wills retired, the steal ranked right beside the long ball as a viable offensive weapon.

Wills amended the game in his own image, swiping bases at a rate last seen in the turn-of-the-century days of Ty Cobb. Maury wasn't the fastest man in the game, but no one took a bigger leadoff, accelerated faster or slid more effectively than the relentless and daring base thief.

Had he not languished for eight seasons in the minors, where club officials tried him at all nine positions, he would almost certainly have rewritten the record books in the burglary department. As it was, he amassed 586 career swipes, 18th all time. The shortstop's path to the bigs was blocked by the specter of Hall of Famer Pee Wee Reese and the rap that Wills was too small.

One of 13 children of a Washington, D.C., Baptist minister, "Sonny" turned down nine college football scholarship offers for an opportunity to try out with the New York Giants baseball team as a pitcher. Despite performing impressively, the wiry youth was rejected with the phrase, "There's no such thing as a 155-pound pitcher." Next came a shot with the Brooklyn Dodgers, where his ability to out-

sprint all other hopefuls netted a contract. The Dodgers quickly turned him into an infielder.

It was fitting that Wills' speed earned him a baseball opportunity, but the impact "Mouse" would enjoy could not have been imagined at the time. In the preceding three decades, it was not at all unusual for the NL's top base stealer to turn in a total as low as 20–25 thefts. The bowlegged little shortstop more than doubled that amount in 1959, his first full year in the majors, then began filching head-spinning totals, grabbing a record-six straight thievery titles (1960–65) and finishing among the top four in steals from 1966–69. The most exorbitant season of all was the 1962 MVP year in which the 5-foot-11, 170-pounder stole a record-104 bases, eclipsing Cobb's modern-day mark of 96. Wills' total was more than any other major league *team* swiped in '62, and more than any NL squad had pilfered in 13 years.

Maury's stolen base high prior to that campaign was 50 in 1960, the most in the NL since 1923, but two pre-season events immediately put that number in jeopardy. First, the Dodgers moved from the cozy confines of the Coliseum to the more spacious Chavez Ravine, a shift that dictated less reliance on power and more on a balanced offense. Second, manager Walter Alston informed Wills just prior to the season that he could steal at will.

By mid-season, the shortstop had 46 thefts. A steal that did not count toward his 1962 total came in the first of two All-Star Games. Wills earned game MVP honors in that July 10 contest in his hometown of Washington, D.C., with a hit, stolen base and two runs scored. The Dodgers kept winning and leading the pack. Finally, with nine games left in the season, he was within three steals of breaking Cobb's single-season record. Then Commissioner Ford Frick lowered the boom.

Wills, he dictated, must break the record in the next game to officially surpass Cobb's 154-game record, or risk an asterisk a la Roger Maris in 1961. The fleet shortstop stole only one base the next day, finally going beyond Cobb with two steals in the 156th game of the season. What some of Wills' critics failed to note was that Cobb had been thrown out 38 times trying to steal during his 1915 onslaught. Wills would be caught stealing only 13 times in 1962 for a far superior stolen base percentage.

While Wills sparkled, the Dodgers faltered, and the Giants tied them in regular-season play, then beat them in a three-game playoff for the pennant. But the defeat was no fault of Wills, who stole bases No. 102, 103 and 104 in the final playoff game defeat.

Despite the failure of his team, Maury edged San Francisco's Willie Mays for the MVP, 209–202, adding a .299 average, 208 hits (including a league-high 10 triples), 130 runs and a second consecutive Gold Glove to his unbelievable stolen base total. There was nothing fluky about the switch-hitter's solid batting totals during his MVP campaign. A lifetime .281 hitter, he boasted a pair of .300 seasons and two years in the .290s over his career.

Twenty-six-year-old Wills had recently been taught to switch-hit in the minors by Spokane manager Bobby Bragan when he was called up to the Dodgers at the mid-point of the 1959 season. Shortstop Don Zimmer was slumping, and Maury filled the gap, helping the team in its successful bid for a World Championship. Wills then hit .295 and .282 the next two campaigns, racking up NL stolen base titles both years. Dodger coach Pete Reiser had made Wills his special project early in the 1960 season, and the pair's hard work paid dividends. "(Reiser) taught me to believe in myself," Wills said.

Following his amazing personal successes of 1962, Maury's intrepid basepath style spearheaded three more Dodger pennants and two World Championships over the next four years. Wills

Maury Wills. (Courtesy Los Angeles Dodgers.)

stole three bases and hit .367, including a record-tying four-hit contest, in L.A.'s seven-game World Series triumph over Minnesota in 1965. During that period, he was awarded the Dodger captaincy and appeared to be a team fixture until he incensed management by jumping ship during a 1966 post-World Series exhibition tour in Japan. Subsequently, he was traded to Pittsburgh, where at age 34 the veteran hit .302, then followed with a .278 mark. After a brief stint in Montreal, Wills returned to the Dodger fold to finish out the final 3½ years of his career.

Maury was a baseball broadcaster for a short time immediately after his retirement, then served various teams as a pre-season base running coach, and worked as a Dodgers minor league

instructor. Maury took over as manager of the Seattle Mariners near the end of the 1980 season, only to be fired early in the 1981 campaign amidst a deluge of media derision. Wills, who used to benefit from Chavez Ravine groundskeepers' hardening of the dirt near first base where he took his leadoffs, was fined $500 and suspended for two days in 1981 after Oakland manager Billy Martin brought substantiated charges against the Mariners skipper for extending the batters' boxes by a foot to give his hitters an advantage against the Athletics' curveball-throwing pitchers. "That's not cheating," said Wills, who during his playing days had been slowed in some opposing ballparks by overly watered areas near first base. "Just a little gamesmanship."

He resurfaced in an even more negative light in 1983 when he was charged with possession of cocaine. It was later learned that Wills had entered the Dodgers' drug and alcohol counseling program just before the incident, but according to director and former MVP Don Newcombe, had left prior to completion.

But there were also bright spots during this era for Wills, who experienced the pride and joy of seeing his son, Bump, play major league ball for the Rangers and Cubs from 1977–82. Maury, a guest coach for the Expos during spring training 2000 and a base running instructor for the Dodgers in 2001, has earned the right to sit back and watch the speedsters of today bask in the limelight that was once reserved for the man who revolutionized the game in the 1960s by perfecting the art of the stolen base.

Top 5 MVP Vote-Getters

1. Maury Wills, Los Angeles — 209
2. Willie Mays, San Francisco — 202
3. Tommy Davis, Los Angeles — 175
4. Frank Robinson, Cincinnati — 164
5. Don Drysdale, Los Angeles — 85

1962 AMERICAN LEAGUE—MICKEY MANTLE

Mickey Charles Mantle
B. October 20, 1931, Spavinaw, Oklahoma
D. August 13, 1995, Dallas, Texas

Year	Team	Games	AB	Hits	Avg.	HR	RBI	Runs	SB
1962	NY AL	123	377	121	.321	30	89	96	9

The Season

The rest of the junior circuit appeared to be gaining ground on the New York Yankees in 1962, but when the smoke cleared, it was still the Bombers capturing the flag for the 12th time in 14 years.

Two unexpected sources, the Minnesota Twins and Los Angeles Angels, took up the chase, the latter team in only its second year of existence. The Twins, led offensively by future MVP Harmon Killebrew, Bob Allison and Rich Rollins, and on the hill by Camilo Pascual and Jim Kaat, finished only five games back in second place. The Angels were in the running up until the last month, ending up in third, 10 games behind. Leon "Daddy Wags" Wagner and his 37 home runs personified the cocky brashness of that club.

A three-year dry spell for no-hitters exploded this season, when for the first time since 1917, four such gems were uncoiled. The pitchers were Bo Belinsky of L.A., Earl Wilson and Bill Monboquette of Boston, and Jack Kralick of Minnesota.

In the first coast-to-coast World Series, San Francisco took the Yankees the distance before losing. Yankee hurler Whitey Ford's World Series-record consecutive scoreless innings streak finally ended at 33⅔ in Game 1, a 6–2 New York win that marked Ford's record-10th and final Series victory.

The Giants came within inches of victory when with the potential tying and winning runs in scoring position, future MVP Willie McCovey blasted a two-out pitch that nearly eluded the arm-stretching grab of Yankee second baseman Bobby Richardson for the final Series out.

On September 12, Tom Cheney of Washington set a major league record with 21 strikeouts in a 16-inning, 2–1 win at Baltimore.

Acceptance and Decline

Mickey Mantle entered the 1962 season as the most heralded of all American Leaguers. Coming off a resplendent 1961 effort, the massively built center fielder was never more popular in the eyes of baseball fandom, which finally had begun to appreciate his courage in the face of physical trauma. Where it was once demanded that Mantle give more than his aching body would allow, the game's backers were now ready to embrace whatever he could deliver with open arms.

This new acceptance, in retrospect, had much to do with Mantle winning the 1962 MVP. The league lacked an overall dominant force that season; teammate Bobby Richardson and Harmon Killebrew were the only other MVP caliber performers, with Richardson pacing the AL in hits and placing among the top five in several offensive categories, and Killebrew leading the way in homers and RBIs. But neither was the complete player that Mantle was. So, almost by default, the award went to Mantle, whose team again claimed the pennant. In winning, he became the sixth three-time recipient of the MVP.

Moving a bit more gingerly on tentative knees, Mickey was still an awesome physical presence at the plate and in the field in 1962. Burly arms nearly burst out of the pinstripe uniform, and the upper body formed an inverse pyramid which was apparent even in the less than form-fitting garment of the day.

The pleasing sight was, however, deceiving. Aches and pains dragged him down to only 117 starts in '62, and his 123 total appearances were his fewest since breaking in for good in '52. Yet he still led the league in slugging (.605), walks (122) and on-base percentage (.488), and healthy or no, the 30-year-old Mantle's .321 average was the best on the team.

Happily for Mick, MVP votes are not influenced by World Series performances, for Mantle suffered through the most embarrassing post-season affair of his career. New York bested San Francisco in seven games, but did so without help from its No. 1 man. Mantle tallied only three hits, batting .120, and was shut out in the RBI department. It was a foreshadowing of the struggle he was to undergo in the years ahead.

The record distance slams would be less frequent during the final six years of his career. Acknowledging Mantle's physical woes, manager Casey Stengel more than once stated that his center fielder was "the best one-legged player I ever saw."

It was a melancholy conclusion to what was perhaps the most promising beginning of any big leaguer. Nature had seemingly molded the perfect ballplayer; at least that's how it appeared to those who first observed Mantle in his rookie camp in the spring of 1951. A strapping 170-pounder at the time, he generated enormous power from either side of the plate, could drag bunt beyond his years, possessed a cannon-like arm and sped from home to first in a stupefying 3.1 seconds. As the years passed, he tailored his swing to Yankee Stadium dimensions: a level, line-drive cut from the right side to take advantage of the huge acreage in left and center fields, and a slight uppercut when batting lefty to reach the short right field stands.

Had he taken better care of himself, Mantle might have retained this amazing prowess for a longer period of time. Years after he had retired, Mantle expressed regrets about abusing his body with late hours and little sleep, but at the same time defended his actions by saying he had expected to die young of the genetically transferable Hodgkins disease that had killed two uncles and his father.

And so he dragged his aching form through the final six years of his playing days, rarely allowing injuries time to heal properly, and playing on what he considered borrowed time.

Had he retired after the 1966 season, or even after 1967, Mickey would have left the game with a .300 lifetime batting average. But the Yankees begged him to stay and bridge the gap between a now-floundering franchise and a tradition of excellence.

In 1963, he started only 52 games due to a broken ankle, but hit .314 with 15 homers. One of those blasts he considered his most satisfying four-bagger, on the road before an appreciative Baltimore crowd which had just given Mantle one of the most moving ovations of his life.

His final good year was '64 (.303, 35 HRs, 111 RBIs), a season in which he homered from both sides of the plate in the same game for the 10th and final time, a major league record. It also turned out to be his last World Series, and Mickey used the opportunity well, swatting his 16th, 17th and 18th series homers to surpass Babe Ruth's record for the fall classic.

Twenty-three round-trippers in only 108 games followed in 1966; and in 1967, at age 35, he was removed from the center field pastures and relegated to first base, where he hit only .245 with 55 RBIs. Things were no better during the 1968 campaign.

Mantle's career rankings included: sixth all time in walks (1,733), 10th in home runs (536), 19th in slugging (.557), 24th in runs (1,677), 30th in total bases (4,511), 31st in extra base hits (952) and 37th in RBIs (1,509).

When it became painfully apparent that he was embarrassing himself in spring training the following year, a teary-eyed Mantle called a press conference and announced his retirement. Mickey then opened a Manhattan restaurant that still bears his name, and did some announcing on NBC's *Game of the Week*. Mantle was elected to the Hall of Fame in 1974.

Unlike his own debut in 1951, there was no unbounding talent to grasp the Yankee superstar torch and carry it into the 1970s. Even the once bottomless New York farm system had run out of Mantles.

Small wonder. Operating under physical duress, Mickey was among the best in every important phase of the game, especially with a war club in his hands. He did it all, and unlike any before or since, from both sides of the plate.

In that respect, no one can touch "The Mick."

Top 5 MVP Vote-Getters

1. Mickey Mantle, New York — 234
2. Bobby Richardson, New York — 152
3. Harmon Killebrew, Minnesota — 99
4. Leon Wagner, Los Angeles — 85
5. Dick Donovan, Cleveland — 64

1963 NATIONAL LEAGUE — SANDY KOUFAX

Sanford Koufax
B. December 30, 1935, Brooklyn, New York

Year	Team	Games	W	L	ERA	IP	SO	BB	ShO
1963	LA NL	40	25	5	1.88	311	306	58	11

The Season

When the Los Angeles Dodgers began a crucial three-game series in St. Louis on September 16, one word was on their minds: choke. In 1962, the Dodgers had blown a lead down the stretch by losing 10 of their last 13 games, then fell in a best-of-three play-off series to the Giants. Now, the Dodger lead was dwindling again and the Cardinals were nipping at their heels. But the Dodgers not only swept the Cards, they went on to win the National League flag by six games before sweeping the favored New York Yankees in the World Series.

Unlike the powerful Dodger clubs of the early '50s, the 1963 edition won ballgames with speed and pitching. In a 10-team league, the Dodgers were only sixth in runs and seventh in homers, but led the circuit in ERA and stolen bases.

For the second straight year, L.A.'s Tommy Davis paced the majors in hitting, this time with a .326 mark. Milwaukee's Warren Spahn became baseball's all-time winningest left-hander with his 328th victory April 11, and later in the season became the majors' oldest 20-game winner at age 42.

Three-time MVP Stan Musial passed Babe Ruth as the all-time leader in extra base hits with his 1,357th May 8. Only 1957 MVP Hank Aaron would pass Musial in this category.

What could arguably be the all-time best brother act in baseball, the Alous came together on the Giants in 1963 when Jesus joined Felipe and Matty.

King of the Hill

Picture him where he belonged — on the field — breaking off a vicious curve, releasing a blazing fastball, bearing down on a helpless victim formerly known as a hitter or leaping triumphantly off the mound after one of his four no-hitters.

But then envision Sandy Koufax out of his element — in the locker room — his left arm soaking in a bucket of ice and his face wincing in pain. Because that mind's-eye memory, more than any other, graphically illustrates what kept Sandy Koufax from possibly becoming the greatest pitcher of all time.

In 1963, Koufax's MVP year, the left-hander was virtually unhittable. He won 25-of-30 decisions with an ERA of 1.88, struck out 306 batters, hurled 11 shutouts and twirled a no-hitter. He went on to have equally tremendous seasons from 1964 through 1966, and was unquestionably regarded as the best pitcher in the game. But with chronic arthritis in his pitching arm and shoulder that was worsening, the 6-foot-2, 210-pounder was forced into a premature retirement.

Following the 1963 World Series in which the Dodgers swept the Yankees, Yogi Berra was particularly impressed with Koufax, who won two of the games. "I can see how he won 25 games," Berra said. "What I don't understand is how he lost five."

But it wasn't always that way. Koufax was wild and awkward when signed by the Brooklyn Dodgers in 1954 for a $14,000 bonus. As a result of trying to do too much too soon, Sandy's early career was a direct contrast to the later years. In his first six seasons as a Dodger, the hard-throwing lefty lost more games than he won (36–40), and had an ERA in excess of 4.00. But in his final six campaigns (1961–66), Koufax was unparalleled, winning 129 games while losing only 47, with an ERA of just over 2.00.

Not coincidentally, Koufax's six dominant years correlated directly with the Dodgers' consistent success: L.A. won three pennants and finished second twice during those seasons. But in 1967, their first year without him, the Dodgers staggered from first place to eighth.

The winner of three Cy Young Awards, the Dodgers' ace held hitters to a composite batting average of .205 over his career, second best all time. In five consecutive years of total mastery (1962–66), Sandy led the NL in ERA each time. Koufax was the league leader in victories three times, and included among his four no-hitters was a perfect game against the Cubs in 1965.

Considered aloof and ambivalent, Koufax became somewhat of a recluse in the eyes of the fans — a tall, strong, silent lefty. But when the pillar of strength stood 60 feet, six inches away, it was opposing hitters' bats that fell totally quiet.

The youngest (36) player ever to be elected to the Hall of Fame, Sandy Koufax is one of only a handful of pitchers in major league history to be inducted with fewer than 200 wins. The strikeout artist led the league in that department four times, whiffing 269 in 1961, 306 in '63, 382 in '65 (a major league record at the time) and 317 in '66. In the 1963 World Series opener, the K-man fanned the first five Yankees he faced and ended up breaking Carl Erskine's record for strikeouts in a Series game by mowing down 15. The fireballer had fanned 18 San Francisco Giants in front of 82,794 fans at the Los Angeles Coliseum in 1959, and in the fifth game of the World Series that year before 92,206 customers, Koufax gave the White Sox just one run in seven innings.

Born and raised in Brooklyn, Sandy was a Dodger fan from the word *go*, but basketball actually was his first love. He earned a roundball scholarship from the University of Cincinnati, but then impressed Pittsburgh Pirates scout Ed McCarrick with his pitching abilities. McCarrick tried to sign the young phenomenon, but owner Branch Rickey couldn't be persuaded until it was too late. By then, the Dodgers had secured the southpaw's signature.

Sandy began coming into his own in 1961, following a suggestion by batterymate Norm Sherry that he ease up on his fastball. He shared the club leadership in wins with Johnny Podres (18), then followed with a league-leading 2.54 ERA in 1962, setting the stage for more great things to come with his second 18-strikeout effort. But 1963 was the sparkling lefty's dream year. He completed 20-of-40 starts and struck out more than five times as many batters as he walked, while leading the Dodgers to the promised land.

For a while it appeared that 1964 would be as good to baseball's most eligible bachelor as was 1963. During one incredible stretch, the crafty veteran won 15-of-16 decisions, and ended up pacing the senior circuit in ERA (1.74), winning percentage (.792) and shutouts (7). But it also was in 1964 that Koufax banged his left elbow on the ground diving back into second base on a pickoff attempt at Milwaukee in August, the injury eventually leading to his arthritis and retirement at the age of 30.

Although Koufax's mishap kept him out of action the remainder of 1964, he came back to enjoy a sensational season in 1965, hurling an NL-best 27 complete games. His 335-plus innings were the most by a left-hander since 1906, and he posted league bests in wins (26), winning percentage (.765) and ERA (2.04).

Then in 1966, Koufax and teammate Don Drysdale combined for their highly publicized spring holdout. After being offered $100,000 and $85,000, respectively, Koufax and Drysdale decided to join forces and seek a $1 mil-

Sandy Koufax. (Courtesy Los Angeles Dodgers.)

lion pact over several years. The holdout lasted one month and the final terms were never revealed. Koufax was the NL leader that season in wins (27), ERA (1.73), shutouts (5) and innings pitched (323).

Despite pitching for only 12 years, Sandy was 30th all time in strikeouts with 2,396. He was also 11th in winning percentage (.655) and 17th in opponents' on-base percentage (.276). His 382 strikeouts in 1965 were the second highest single-season total since 1900, and his 11 shutouts in 1963 were tied for eighth all time. He compiled a 4–3 record with 61 whiffs and a 0.95 ERA in four World Series.

Following Koufax's retirement after the 1966 season, he tried his hand at broadcasting, but his quiet manner resulted in a rather unsuccessful stint. He returned to Los Angeles in 1979 as a minor league pitching instructor.

Out of his element, whether in the locker room or in the broadcasting booth, Sandy Koufax was an ordinary sight. But where he belonged, on the mound, Koufax was a vision to behold.

Top 5 MVP Vote-Getters

1. Sandy Koufax, Los Angeles — 237
2. Dick Groat, Pittsburgh — 190
3. Hank Aaron, Milwaukee — 135
4. Ron Perranoski, Los Angeles — 130
5. Willie Mays, San Francisco — 102

1963 American League—Elston Howard

Elston Gene Howard
B. February 23, 1929, St. Louis, Missouri
D. December 14, 1980, New York, New York

Year	Team	Games	AB	Hits	Avg.	HR	RBI	Runs	SB
1963	NY AL	135	487	140	.287	28	85	75	0

The Season

This started out looking like the year of the Yankees' fall from grace. Injuries wracked the team throughout the season, and were especially damaging to Mickey Mantle and Roger Maris, who tallied only 484 at-bats between them.

The perennial pennant winners started slowly, but gradually began to move despite their ailments. By mid-June, the Yanks were in first place, forging ahead to a 10½-game margin over the runner-up White Sox.

Long ball hitters were plentiful in the American League, but few junior circuit members registered solid averages. A pre-season expansion of the strike zone resulted in a .247 league batting mark, the lowest since 1910, with only four players managing to exceed the .300 level.

The Yankees were without a regular .300 stick in their lineup, and the team's hitting was nearly non-existent in the World Series. New York dropped four straight to the Dodgers, batting an anemic .171, a record low for post-season play.

Known as "Dr. Strangeglove" for his lack of fielding skills, Boston's Dick Stuart nonetheless set a record for first basemen with three assists in one inning June 23.

Ellie Arrives

The status of New York's inestimable utility player, Elston Howard, evolved from invaluable to most valuable in 1963, as the first black player in the history of the Yankee franchise won the MVP award. And while Howard's achievement was personally gratifying, it represented a much greater turning point in the history of baseball, since such recognition of Ellie marked the first time an African American had been so honored in the American League.

Sixteen seasons had passed since Jackie Robinson integrated the majors, and beginning in 1949 when Robinson won the MVP, 10 of the next 13 winners in the NL were black, while the junior circuit was shut out. As National League teams actively pursued African Americans, AL franchises were infinitely more hesitant in that direction.

The dynastic New York franchise was especially deliberate, and took its time seeking someone it deemed befitting of the Yankee image to become the team's initial non-white member. Elston Howard, who joined the club in 1955, was soft-spoken, well-mannered, gentlemanly and scholarly—everything the team had been looking for in its first black ballplayer.

And, he could hit. Ellie had a wonderful line-drive stroke that sent the ball to all parts of the field. The 6-foot-2, 205-pounder's power was to right center, despite a right-handed stance, and he proved to be extremely productive in the clutch.

Massive hands and wrists were his most striking features. A strong arm complemented the catcher's excellent receiving abilities, particularly in 1963 and '64 when he earned Gold Glove honors. His .998 fielding average in 1964 led all AL backstops.

Despite these latent credentials, it took Elston six years to win the crouch position fulltime. From 1955 through 1960, he alternated between the outfield, first base and catching, averaging more than 100 games per season and playing an essential role on five pennant winners and two World Champion teams. Between 1956 and 1961, he registered a .362 average as a pinch-hitter, and won the Babe Ruth Award as a 1958 World Series MVP.

Finally, at age 32, Howard took over the tools of ignorance from three-time MVP Yogi Berra for the 1961 season, and commemorated the year with a dazzling .348 average and 21 home runs. Nineteen-sixty-two brought 21 more round-trippers and 91 RBIs, but still little in the way of national recognition.

Yet Ellie found nothing about which to complain. The St. Louis native was the only child of a high school principal and a dietician, enjoyed a bountiful childhood and excelled in the high school classrooms and on the athletic fields. Upon graduation in 1947, he turned down 25 collegiate athletic scholarships to pursue a professional baseball career.

Having starred on the Negro League Kansas City Monarchs with roommate Ernie Banks, Elston was signed at age 26 by the Yankees, who converted the outfielder into a long ball–hitting catcher, thanks in part to the tutelage of Yankee coach and former catcher Bill Dickey. Two years in the military were followed by a pair of minor league campaigns with Kansas City of the American Association and Toronto of the International League. By 1955, Howard was a Yankee.

After performing effectively in anonymous fashion through 1962, the hulking backstop took center stage almost by default for the Bombers in 1963. Injuries to Mantle and Maris had the club floundering out of the gate, and as manager Ralph Houk frantically

Elston Howard. (Courtesy New York Yankees.)

platooned his lineup on a daily basis, Howard remained the team's solitary constant. Almost imperceptibly, he took over the leadership role of the ballclub, cajoling not only the pitching staff, but the rest of his mates as well. His clutch hitting won game after game, adding up to a team-high 28 home runs, 85 RBIs and a .287 average. The performance was particularly inspirational because it was accompanied by a torrent of racist hate mail that followed Howard from city to city.

It was Elston's home run that put the Yankees into a first-place tie with the White Sox in an important four-game set at mid-season. After dropping the second contest, New York came back to capture game three behind two Howard round-trippers. The Yanks then took the final contest, buoyed by the receiver's single and triple. And even though the Yankees were swept in the '63 World Series by the Dodgers, Howard rapped out a .333 mark.

When the MVP votes were tallied, runner-up Al Kaline of Detroit was a distant second to Howard, whose 248 to 148 victory made him the 16th Yankee recipient of the award in 33 years, and the fourth straight.

One more exceptional campaign followed in 1964, but various ailments and advancing age dragged down his average the next two seasons. In mid-1967, he was swapped to the pennant-bound Boston Red Sox. The 38-year-old catcher hit only .147 for the Beantown team during the stretch drive, but was a steadying influence behind the plate. He collected two hits and an RBI in the 1967 World Series.

During that '67 season, he was approached by baseball maverick Bill Veeck, who reportedly offered the veteran first crack at managing the Washington Senators if Veeck was successful in purchasing the club. He was not, thus postponing the hiring of baseball's first black pilot.

After a year as a part-timer with the Red Sox in 1968, Elston retired and immediately became the first black coach in AL history, signing on with the Yankees for the 1969 campaign. He waited hopefully for a shot at managing a club, but it never came. He died of heart disease in 1980 at age 51.

The Yankees paid tribute to Ellie in 1984 by including his name with other Bomber greats on a center field plaque. It was a fitting reward for one of the most loyal and talented men ever to play for that proud organization.

Top 5 MVP Vote-Getters

1. Elston Howard, New York — 248
2. Al Kaline, Detroit — 148
3. Whitey Ford, New York — 125
4. Harmon Killebrew, Minnesota — 85
5. Dick Radatz, Boston — 84

1964 NATIONAL LEAGUE — KEN BOYER

Kenton Lloyd Boyer
B. May 20, 1931, Liberty, Missouri
D. September 7, 1982, St. Louis, Missouri

Year	Team	Games	AB	Hits	Avg.	HR	RBI	Runs	SB
1964	SL NL	162	628	185	.295	24	119	100	3

The Season

Philadelphia fans will forever remember 1964 as the year of the "Big Choke." The Phillies held a seemingly insurmountable 6½-game lead with only a dozen contests to play, then dropped 10 in a row to finish in a tie for second with Cincinnati, one game behind St. Louis.

With three days left in the season, four teams had a chance at the pennant. The Cardinals clinched on the final day, whipping the Mets 11–5. Meanwhile, the Phillies aided the Redbird cause by eliminating the Reds with a 10–0 thrashing.

It was the Cardinals' first flag in 18 years, and they followed it by edging the favored Yankees in a seven-game World Series. Immediately after the Series, New York fired rookie manager Yogi Berra, replacing him with, of all people, Cardinal mentor Johnny Keane, who had resigned due to disagreements with owner "Gussie" Busch.

Nineteen-sixty-four was the second consecutive season that saw three NL no-hitters. Philadelphia's Jim Bunning hurled the first perfect game in the league in 84 years, Sandy Koufax of the Dodgers tossed his third no-hitter in as many years and Houston's Ken Johnson baffled the Reds on no hits, but lost 1–0.

Past, present and future MVPs led the National League in eight offensive categories. Roberto Clemente was tops in batting and hits, Willie Mays in homers and slugging, Richie Allen in total bases and runs, Maury Wills in stolen bases, and Ken Boyer in RBIs.

San Francisco and New York set several major league records when they played 32 innings over the course of nearly 10 hours May 31 in a double-header featuring a 23-inning nightcap. The Giants swept the twin bill.

On a tragic note, Chicago's Ken Hubbs, 22, who as a rookie in 1962 set an NL record for second basemen with 78 consecutive errorless games, died when his private plane crashed near Provo, Utah, February 15.

Best of the Bunch

In the Boyer household, it wasn't a matter of which one of the boys would make it to the big leagues, but rather who wouldn't. All six of Ken's brothers played professional baseball, and two — Cloyd and Cletis — made it to the majors. But Kenny was considered the best of the lot, combining a potent bat with a steady glove, good speed and plenty of baseball smarts.

Boyer used those assets to climb from the St. Louis Cardinals' lowest farm team in Lebanon, Pennsylvania, in 1949, all the way to the 1964 World Series. Following the campaign, Kenny was named the National League's MVP, as well as The Sporting News' Player of the Year. He went on to conclude a solid, 15-year career in 1969, prior to several coaching stints and a major league managerial position with the Cards.

Without Ken's brilliant play in 1964, it's doubtful that St. Louis could have edged out three contenders for its first pennant since 1946. Though Boyer ended up hitting a solid .295 with 24 home runs and a major league-leading 119 RBIs, it took a comeback effort in the final two months to post those impressive totals. The team captain since 1959 suffered through a miserable July, and partially as a result, the club dipped to eighth place. But the right-handed hitter snapped out of it late in the month when his two round-trippers and five runs batted in helped defeat first-place Philadelphia. The Cardinals took off from there, winning 33-of-48 games, and nipping the Phils and Reds by a game each in one of the tightest pennant races in history.

With the AL champion Yankees boasting Clete Boyer at the hot corner, the media played up the sibling rivalry prior to and during the '64 World Series. Clete and Ken demonstrated their long ball prowess, becoming the only brothers to both homer in the same fall classic. They combined for three round-trippers and nine RBIs, and made several sparkling fielding plays in the Cards' seven-game triumph. The highlight of the Series came in the sixth inning of Game 4 when Kenny erased a 3–0 New York lead by drilling a grand slam in a 4–3 Card victory. He also homered in the Game 7 clincher.

Despite a decade of service, the Cardinal captain would be gone after the 1965 season. Slumping to .260 with only 13 home runs and 75 RBIs after suffering a spring training back injury in '65, Boyer was dealt to the New York Mets. Definitely past his prime, the 36-year-old Boyer was traded to the White Sox in mid–1967, then to the Dodgers the following year.

Immediately after his retirement, Boyer managed Arkansas of the Texas League in 1970 before returning to St. Louis as a coach for the next two seasons. He was given another head job with the Cards' rookie league club at Sarasota in 1973, then moved on to Tulsa.

The Cardinals, who finished a distant fifth in the NL East's six-team division in 1976, fired skipper Red Schoendienst, and it was speculated that Kenny would get the managerial nod. But Vern Rapp was targeted and a disgruntled Boyer left the organization in a huff, joining the Baltimore Orioles as manager of the Triple A club in Rochester for the '77 season.

St. Louis jumped to third that year, but after a 5–10 start in '78, Rapp was issued his walking papers and Ken accepted an invitation to return, this time as the Redbirds mentor. Though the Cards were 62–82 the rest of the year under Boyer, they vaulted to 10 games over .500 and a third-place finish the following season. When his team dropped 33 of its first 51 contests in 1980, however, Ken was dismissed, remaining as a special assignment scout. Boyer was offered a Triple A top job at Louisville, Kentucky, for the '82 campaign, but was tragically struck down by lung cancer. Brother Clete and Oakland A's manager Billy Martin organized a benefit dinner for Kenny, and many of baseball's greats paid tribute. With Clete at his side, Ken passed away at age 51. The Cardinals honored their fallen star in 1984 by retiring his uniform No. 14.

Growing up near Liberty, Missouri, with a dozen brothers and sisters, Ken played all of the major sports in high school, but preferred baseball — his goal to someday be as good as older brother Cloyd, who signed as a pitcher with the Cardinals in 1945. A strong hitter and solid shortstop for the Alba Aces, a sandlot squad, Kenny was offered athletic scholarships to four large area colleges, but turned them all down to pursue a professional career. Impressed with his rifle-like arm, the Cardinals saw him as a future pitcher and signed the 18-year-old for a $6,000 bonus in 1949.

Boyer's bat soon proved too valuable to sit in a bin three-quarters of the time, so the Cardinals converted him into a third baseman at Hamilton, Ontario, in 1950. He married Kathleen Belle Oliver just prior to being drafted into the Army, then returned to the bushes in 1954, excelling with Houston of the Class AA Texas League and earning a shot with the big club the next year. After a decent freshman campaign in which he paced league third basemen in fielding (.968), Kenny starred in 1956, clubbing 26 round-trippers with 98 RBIs, and leading NL hot corner men in double plays for one of five times in his career. The five-time Gold Glove winner batted .348 in seven All-Star Games.

Boyer proved his versatility in 1957 when manager Fred Hutchinson tried to solidify a shaky "up-the-middle" Cardinal defense by placing the fleet 26-year-old in center field. In the wide open pastures, the novice outfielder led the NL in fielding with a .996 average.

Ken Boyer successfully competed with six brothers to become the family's best ballplayer, consistently producing for 15 years as an aggressive clutch hitter and fielder. Fate robbed him of the opportunity to spend his golden years reminiscing about his days in the sun, but he remains fixed in the minds of St. Louis fans who witnessed his day-in, day-out dedication to the game.

Top 5 MVP Vote-Getters

1. Ken Boyer, St. Louis — 243
2. Johnny Callison, Philadelphia — 187
3. Bill White, St. Louis — 106½
4. Frank Robinson, Cincinnati — 98
5. Joe Torre, Milwaukee — 85

1964 AMERICAN LEAGUE — BROOKS ROBINSON

Brooks Calbert Robinson
B. May 18, 1937, Little Rock, Arkansas

Year	Team	Games	AB	Hits	Avg.	HR	RBI	Runs	SB
1964	Bal AL	163	612	194	.317	28	118	82	1

The Season

In what was to be the dynasty's swan song, the Yankees outlasted the Chicago White Sox by one game and the Baltimore Orioles by two to win the American League pennant, slipping noticeably from their previous years of outright domination.

Regardless, the killer instinct was still apparent in the Bombers, who notched 22 victories in their last 28 contests.

In league action, the era of the relief pitcher had never been more pronounced than in 1964. Three firemen bested the previous AL record for appearances, with Kansas City's John Wyatt coming on 81 times, Dick Radatz of Boston in 79 games and Chicago's Hoyt Wilhelm in 73 contests.

Starting pitchers in the junior circuit were vanquishing free-swinging hitters at unusually high rates. For the first time since 1910, four American League hurlers registered more than 200 K's. Those who turned the trick were Al Downing of New York, Camilo Pascual of the Twins, Dean Chance of the Angels and Gary Peters of the White Sox.

Meanwhile, Luis Aparicio of the Orioles nabbed his ninth straight (and last) stolen base crown, swiping 57; Kansas City rookie Bert Campaneris became the second player since 1900 to hit two home runs in his major league debut, July 23; and Baltimore's Bob Johnson set an AL record with hits in each of six consecutive pinch-hit appearances.

Despite heroics by Bobby Richardson (13 hits, .406 average) and Mickey Mantle (three HRs, eight runs, eight RBIs), the Yankees were edged in seven games by St. Louis in the World Series.

Human Hoover

Baltimore residents proudly refer to him as the greatest player ever to don an Oriole uniform, and for many he ranks as the best in history at holding down the hot corner. There is documented evidence of his brilliance, including films of a stunning 1970 World Series performance, that has even the Pie Traynor and Mike Schmidt backers wavering in their support.

Brooks Calbert Robinson was born in Little Rock, Arkansas, in 1937, and his baseball-crazy father began swatting ground balls in the little tyke's direction as soon as Brooks could walk. The youth's professional baseball ambition was realized immediately after completion of a star-studded high school sports career when the Orioles signed him to a $4,000 bonus.

Twenty-three years later, "Brooksie" had nailed down numerous career records, stroked 2,848 hits and driven in 1,357 runs. His name tops the all-time list for fielding percentage and games played at third base, as well as putouts, assists, double plays and chances accepted as a third sacker, but even those exalted ratings fail to fully impart the dazzling efficiency he exhibited at the position.

At 6-foot-1, 180 pounds, there was nothing in his physical makeup to suggest the radar-like reflexes which tracked down scorching ground balls and sizzling line drives. Perhaps the clue to

the dexterity he displayed is the childhood injury that forced the natural left-hander to learn to throw righty, thereby placing his magic glove on his more authoritative hand.

Robinson shuffled between the minors and majors for four of his first five professional seasons, beginning in 1955 as an 18-year-old. At that time, there was no hint of the clutch RBI and home run potential that would characterize Robinson's prime years. It wasn't until he was shunted back to the minors for the last time in mid–1959 that Brooks brought his hands down to the handle of the bat and elongated his previous lightweight swing. The results were immediately apparent as the third baseman turned into one of the Orioles' most reliable offensive weapons.

Although the wallop took some time to work its way into his bat, Robinson's consistently sunny nature was quickly singled out by teammates. If there were a hall of fame for felicitous outlooks, Robinson and his optimistic attitude would be named on the first ballot. His disposition, as much as his diamond skill, was responsible for the beloved esteem in which Baltimore fans held Brooks. Voted by the faithful as the most popular Oriole of all time, Robinson was extremely accommodating to all who sought his services. When the American League's answer to winsome Ernie Banks became the 14th major leaguer to be elected to the Hall of Fame in his first year of eligibility, in 1983, busloads of Baltimore backers caravanned to Cooperstown.

While this kind of intense ardor was more prevalent among hometown fans, the admiration "Mr. Impossible" garnered with his fielding exploits was universal among baseball zealots. The inconceivable became routine around third base when Brooks manned the post. Robinson led the AL in fielding 11 seasons, including all but one year during the 1960s, and he earned 16 consecutive Gold Gloves from 1960 through '75. In the 1970 World Series, "The Human Vacuum Cleaner" sucked up every ground ball and line drive hit in his general direction. Diving for scintillating shots to either side, Robinson miraculously came up with ball in glove, scrambled to his feet in the

twinkling of an eye and shot down enemy runners time after time. Following the Series, the Hall of Fame laid claim to the incomparable third baseman's glove for permanent display in its archives.

Beginning in 1960, his first year as a bona-fide star, Robinson performed these fielding acrobatics with iron-man efficiency that saw him participate in 98 percent of Baltimore's games for a solid decade. Third in the MVP voting in 1960, he was even better in '62.

At this stage in his career, Robinson was receiving accolades from seemingly everyone connected with baseball, including a couple of retired legends who'd been around the block a few times. "He has exceptional reflexes, and the strongest pull hitters in the game can't seem to get the ball by him," said Hall of Fame third baseman Pie Traynor, with whom Robby was compared on many occasions. "I've been around a long time, but I've never seen anyone make the plays he does," said Yankee manager Casey Stengel.

In 1966, his 100 RBIs helped bring the Orioles their first pennant and World Championship. Following a 23-homer campaign in '69, Brooks hit .500 in the League Championship Series against Minnesota for another pennant. He then batted .583 in a 1970 LCS sweep against the Twins, followed by a .429, two-homer, six-RBI effort in the '70 World Series. He "dipped" to .318 in the '71 fall classic loss to the Pirates after a .364 performance in the ALCS versus Oakland, but helped Baltimore to a couple of additional division titles in 1973 and '74.

In the face of all this team success, it's somewhat ironic that the uncanny defender nabbed his one-and-only MVP award during a third-place campaign. But it's not too surprising when Robinson's numbers from that 1964 effort are considered. The man with the magnetic glove hit .317, second in the league, while topping AL hitters with 118 RBIs and swatting 28 home runs in the process. All were career-high marks for the 27-year-old, who hit a sizzling .464 during the final month of the year as his club fell a pair of victories short of the pennant. Pounding away consistently when it counted most, Robinson delivered 24 of his league-leading RBIs in the final 17 contests.

Robinson, who retired following the 1977 season, was president of the Major League Baseball Players Alumni Association, and an Orioles broadcaster. He also worked for a petroleum company.

Nineteen-sixty-four may have been Brooksie's most productive campaign, but in the eyes of Baltimore fandom, the infield wizard with the alluring personality was worthy of uncommon appreciation for all of his 23 years.

Top 5 MVP Vote-Getters

1. Brooks Robinson, Baltimore — 269
2. Mickey Mantle, New York — 171
3. Elston Howard, New York — 124
4. Tony Oliva, Minnesota — 99
5. Dean Chance, Los Angeles — 97

1965 NATIONAL LEAGUE — WILLIE MAYS

Willie Howard Mays
B. May 6, 1931, Westfield, Alabama

Year	Team	Games	AB	Hits	Avg.	HR	RBI	Runs	SB
1965	SF NL	157	558	177	.317	52	112	118	9

The Season

The 1965 season featured remarkable individual pitching, batting and running feats. Cincinnati's Jim Maloney twirled two no-hitters, while Sandy Koufax of Los Angeles fired a perfect game for his fourth and final no-hit performance on the way to his second Cy Young Award. At the plate, Roberto Clemente hit .329 for his second batting title in a row, and on the basepaths, fleet-footed Maury Wills made it six consecutive stolen base crowns by pilfering 94.

Jumping from a disappointing sixth-place finish the previous year to the pennant were the Los Angeles Dodgers, who hit only 78 homers (lowest in the majors), but edged the Giants by two games. The L.A. mound corps compiled the best ERA (2.81) in baseball, and allowed the fewest runs (521) of any National League team since World War II.

The Dodgers' pitching outdid Minnesota's hitting in a seven-game World Series, despite the Twins winning the first two contests. The victory gave the NL three consecutive world titles, including two by Los Angeles, and made Walter Alston the first National League manager to capture four World Series.

The senior circuit finally obtained a series edge (18–17) in All-Star Game competition by nudging the AL 6–5 at Metropolitan Stadium. Also in 1965, the Houston Astrodome opened, William Eckert was elected the new commissioner and the first free agent player draft was held, with University of Arizona sophomore Rick Monday the No. 1 pick (Athletics). Nolan Ryan was chosen by the Mets in the 10th round.

Hank Aaron and Eddie Mathews became the all-time top home run hitting duo this season, passing the Babe Ruth-Lou Gehrig total of 772.

Not So Instant Replay

It had been more than a decade since Willie Mays was voted the Most Valuable Player, and although the man with the charming, vociferous personality had consistently ripped apart National League pitching both for average and power, and had continued a dazzling display of basket and over-the-shoulder catches in center field, the writers had not seen fit to award him another.

In 1965, however, the scribes looked his way, despite the Giants

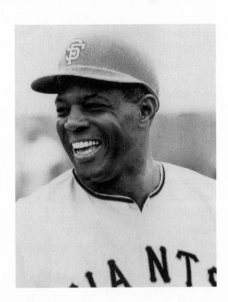

Willie Mays. (Courtesy San Francisco Giants.)

finishing two games in back of the Dodgers in second place. Willie exploded for a career-high 52 homers (most in the league since 1949 when Ralph Kiner blasted 54), and the San Francisco center fielder also led the league in total bases with 360, on-base percentage at .399 and slugging at .645, the latter being the circuit's best effort since his own .659 10 years previously. His 118 runs scored were second in the NL, while a .317 batting average and

112 RBIs were both good for third. Mays also led all outfielders in double plays for the fourth and final time.

While he was magnificent in many of the 24 All-Star Games in which he participated over the years, the 1965 contest was especially gratifying. As the first batter of the game, Willie deposited a Milt Pappas fastball into the seats 420 feet away for a home run. Then in the eighth inning, he took an extra base hit away from Joe Pepitone with a soaring, backhanded stab against the fence. Mays hurt his foot on the play, but the injury couldn't keep him from setting an NL record by homering 17 times in August.

Although well-liked, Mays had developed an overly self-serving attitude by 1965. While a big-name announcer or columnist could get Willie's attention for hours, a small-town writer would be fortunate to receive a polite nod from the superstar. On more than one occasion, the instantly recognizable Mays slipped out the back door of a clubhouse, leaving hopeful autograph hunters waiting in vain.

But Mays was certainly visible enough on the ballfield in the seasons following his initial MVP trophy in 1954. The New York center fielder's league-leading 51 homers in 1955 gave him a staggering two-year total of 92, and his 382 total bases were the most since Stan Musial collected the same number in 1949. Willie was the No. 1 outfielder in double plays at eight and assists with a remarkable 23.

His home run production dropped off slightly in the Giants' final two years in New York (1956 and '57), to 36 and 35, respectively, but Mays scored more than 100 runs both times and batted .333 in the latter campaign. The deceptively quick base runner stole a career-high and league-best 40 bases in '56, and came close to matching that effort the following year when he swiped 38, again tops in the NL. His .626 slugging percentage was the league's highest in 1957, as were the 20 triples. In his personal life, the 25-year-old married Marghueride Chapman in 1956, but the union lasted only six years, causing great sorrow in the normally vivacious Mays.

The Giants' move to San Francisco disappointed New York fans, but did nothing to slow down the on-field performance of the "Say Hey Kid." Willie was also saddened by the relocation, but still hit a personal-best .347 in 1958, pacing the circuit in runs (121) and stolen bases (31), and driving in 96 runs with 29 homers.

As the years rolled along, Willie's bat continued to click. In the five years prior to his second MVP in 1965, Mays averaged more than 40 homers, 116 RBIs and 120 runs scored per campaign, hitting below .300 only once (.296 in 1964, when he was named the first-ever black team captain). His 27 stolen bases in 1959 were tops in the NL, as were his 190 hits in '60, 129 runs in '61, and 47 round-trippers and .607 slugging percentage in '64. He was the ninth player to hit four homers in a game, accomplishing the feat in 1961 while using teammate Joey Amalfitano's bat.

Mays' 1962 effort helped the Giants win their first pennant on the West Coast, nipping the Dodgers in a three-game playoff. A Mays home run against Houston on the final day of the regular season — giving him a league-high 49 — had put San Francisco into a first-place tie. The '62 season took its toll, however. Mays, who knew firsthand from his childhood the agony of a broken home, couldn't keep his first marriage together, and that despair, combined with his exhaustion from playing every day, resulted in fainting spells.

As a payoff for his splendid 1965 MVP season, Mays found himself the highest salaried ballplayer in '66, raking in a then-impressive $125,000 per annum. During that year, he outdistanced all home run hitters, past and present, except for Babe Ruth, whom he'd never catch. By 1967, the 36-year-old outfielder was slowing down.

In his last four years in San Francisco, "The Wonder" averaged 20 homers and 81 RBIs, although he still scared National League pitchers

enough to lead the league in walks (112), as well as on-base percentage (.429), in 1971. In 1969, Mays had become the first member of the 300/300 club (homers and stolen bases), and was named *The Sporting News* Player of the Decade for the '60s.

He collected his 3,000th hit in '70, married Mae Louise Allen in '71, and on May 11, 1972, returned to New York in a trade for Mets rookie pitcher Charlie Williams and $50,000. Mays wasted little time responding to the adulation of the masses, who after 15 years hadn't forgotten Willie's New York Giant exploits. He rekindled past memories by smacking a home run against his former teammates in his first game as a Met, and reached base safely in his first 20 games in a Mets uniform.

In addition to the joys of coming home to New York, Mays was fortunate to end his career with a fourth World Series appearance in 1973. Willie had two hits in three Series contests, but the Oakland Athletics slipped past the Mets in seven games. He went on to coach for the Mets, but after taking a job in an Atlantic City casino, was forced by Commissioner Bowie Kuhn to leave baseball in 1979. Ironically, that was the same year the 12-time Gold Glove winner was elected to the Hall of Fame, making it on the first ballot. In 1985, Commissioner Peter Ueberroth lifted that ban.

Willie Mays was not as fast as Lou Brock, as fluid and graceful as Joe DiMaggio, nor as powerful as Babe Ruth. But he did so many things so exceptionally well, many consider him the best all-around ballplayer in baseball history.

Top 5 MVP Vote-Getters

1. Willie Mays, San Francisco — 224
2. Sandy Koufax, Los Angeles — 177
3. Maury Wills, Los Angeles — 164
4. Deron Johnson, Cincinnati — 108
5. Don Drysdale, Los Angeles — 77

1965 American League—Zoilo Versalles

Zoilo Casanova Versalles
B. December 18, 1939, Veldado, Cuba
D. June 9, 1995, Bloomington, Minnesota

Year	Team	Games	AB	Hits	Avg.	HR	RBI	Runs	SB
1965	Min AL	160	666	182	.273	19	77	126	27

The Season

Although the American League as a whole experienced a power shortage in 1965, the Minnesota Twins used the long ball to cruise to their first pennant in Minneapolis–St. Paul.

Four Twins—Harmon Killebrew, Bob Allison, Don Mincher and Jimmie Hall—clubbed 20 or more homers each as Minnesota ended the Yankees' five-year reign atop the AL, jumping from a sixth-place tie the previous year to outdistance Chicago by seven games.

And speaking of home runs, New York's Mel Stottlemyre became the first pitcher to hit an inside-the-park grand slam in 55 years, during a 6–3 win over Boston July 20.

The powerful Twins were shut out only three times during the regular season, but even though they shelled Don Drysdale 8–2 in the World Series opener and swatted Sandy Koufax 5–1 in Game 2, the AL representatives were blanked three times in the next five contests, suffering a seven-game setback at the hands of the Los Angeles Dodgers.

The aging New York Yankees dipped to sixth place with a 77–85 record, their lowest finish since 1925.

The Kansas City Athletics lost an AL-high 103 games this season, but pulled off a couple of stunts that generated publicity. Fifty-nine-year-old pitcher Satchel Paige made his first major league appearance in 12 years, limiting Boston to one hit in three innings September 25, while Bert Campaneris played all nine positions during a September 8 game against the California Angels.

Following the season, baseball owners unanimously elected retired Air Force Lieutenant-General William Eckert to replace Ford Frick as commissioner.

Zorro Zeroes In

On the outside, Zoilo Versalles appeared to lack nothing in confidence or bravado when he made it to the big leagues for his first full season in 1961. The cocky Cuban had battled his way through 2½ years in the minors, and with only 44 major league games under his belt was already proclaiming himself the No. 2 shortstop in baseball, behind only Luis Aparicio. Teammates and coaches scoffed at the lofty claim, but none questioned his grit or self-assurance.

In reality, however, the 21-year-old was just a scared kid, protecting his ego with brash words. He'd known nothing but poverty while growing up on Fidel Castro's island, and when the skinny 125-pounder came to America to play baseball in 1958, he was completely out of his element. With only a second grade Cuban education, Zoilo found the immense language barrier in the United States extremely frustrating.

By July 1961, the Minnesota Twins middle infielder was a picture of depression—dearly missing his family back in Cuba, and continuing to experience communication problems. At the end of his rope, Versalles went AWOL. Three weeks later, he returned to live with a family who offered him a home away from home, via a newspaper advertisement. Versalles went back to Minneapolis and wound up hitting .280 in his rookie season with 53 RBIs and 16 stolen bases. He then led the AL in triples in both 1963 (13) and '64 (10).

Even though "Zorro" would never exceed his rookie batting mark in a 12-year career, he captured the Most Valuable Player award in 1965 by more than 100 points over his nearest competitor when his inspiring play in the field, at the plate and on the basepaths led the Twins to the American League pennant and just short of the World Championship.

A storybook finish to the Versalles' epic might have included his graceful retirement from the game following several more years of productivity, and peace and prosperity as a family man in his post-baseball life. Unfortunately, such was not the case for the first-ever foreign-born MVP winner. After his 1965 season, the inconsistent right-hander hit below .250 with no more than seven home runs or 50 RBIs in all five of his remaining big league campaigns.

A back injury suffered in 1968 while with the Dodgers continued to plague Zoilo following his retirement, hampering his job-seeking efforts. After a layoff by Northwest Orient Airlines, for which he was cleaning engines, the Cuban reluctantly began collecting workman's disability insurance to pay his bills. As his financial woes worsened, he resorted to selling personal mementos, including his prized MVP trophy. Thirty years after receiving that coveted prize, Zoilo passed away from hardening of the arteries at age 55.

While before-and-after pictures of an unfortunate Versalles are not all that dissimilar, 1965 stands out in sharp contrast. Following the 1964 campaign, recently hired Twins coach Billy Martin made Zoilo his pet project, repeatedly insisting that with a full-fledged effort, both on and off the field, the 5-foot-10, 146-pound shortstop could be the AL's MVP in 1965. On paper, the bespectacled veteran had done little to merit such a prognostication. After a promising rookie season, he'd averaged only about .250 with 16 homers and 62 RBIs per year from 1962 to '64. And while he'd had a standout year defensively in 1962 when he topped league shortstops in putouts, assists and double plays, his fielding had generally been erratic early in his career, thanks in large part to a number of ill-advised throws, and his hustle questionable.

But Martin saw a diamond in the rough, and realized that a shot of confidence could bring out the latent talent. Though Versalles feuded with manager Sam Mele during spring training, and hit only .227 through the first couple of months of the 1965 season, he caught fire and began winning games with his bat, legs and glove. By year's end, Zorro was the league leader in total bases with 308, a remarkable number for a leadoff man. Zoilo was also the AL's best in runs scored (126),

doubles (45), triples (12) and at-bats (666), while placing runner-up in hits (182). A .273 average was his second highest ever, as were his 19 home runs. The dangerous base runner stole 27 times in 32 attempts, and made a habit of scoring from second on an infield hit, accomplishing the feat seven times. On four occasions, he scampered home from first on a single. In the field, the wide-ranging shortstop topped the circuit in double plays with 105, but also committed a league-high 39 errors.

The Twins won the pennant handily, and No. 2 picked up right where he left off, ripping a three-run homer and stealing a base on a pitchout in an 8–2 Minnesota victory over the Los Angeles Dodgers in the first game of the World Series. Zoilo tripled and scored in Game 2, won 5–1 by the Twins, but even his 2-for-3 performance in the third contest couldn't keep the Dodgers from mounting a comeback which sparked a seven-game triumph for the National Leaguers.

Zoilo now possessed a true self-confidence, but the serious-looking, take-charge guy failed to back up that

spunk with equally notable deeds for the remainder of his career. He was dealt to the Dodgers in 1968, played with both Cleveland and Washington in '69, and departed for the Mexican League the next year. Versalles returned to the majors in 1971, appearing in 66 games for Atlanta before retiring.

Zoilo Versalles was the catalyst in his team's drive to the 1965 flag, beating the opposition in a myriad of ways while providing leadership by example to his teammates. But it was a very brief touch with greatness, as potential far outweighed performance for the vast majority of the fiery Cuban's career.

Top 5 MVP Vote-Getters

1. Zoilo Versalles, Minnesota — 275
2. Tony Oliva, Minnesota — 174
3. Brooks Robinson, Baltimore — 150
4. Eddie Fisher, Chicago — 122
5. Rocky Colavito, Cleveland — 89

1966 NATIONAL LEAGUE — ROBERTO CLEMENTE

Roberto Walker Clemente
B. August 18, 1934, Carolina, Puerto Rico
D. December 31, 1972, San Juan, Puerto Rico

Year	Team	Games	AB	Hits	Avg.	HR	RBI	Runs	SB
1966	Pit NL	154	638	202	.317	29	119	105	7

The Season

A stingy pitching staff and solid defense propelled the Los Angeles Dodgers over San Francisco by 1½ games for their second pennant in a row and third in four years. The L.A. mound corps allowed only 490 runs in 1966, and compiled a 2.62 ERA, both the best marks in baseball since World War II.

With Sandy Koufax posting 27

wins and Phil Regan saving 21 games, the Dodgers survived on only 108 homers, second fewest in the league. The lack of offense was costly in a four-game World Series setback against Baltimore, as the Dodgers set dubious Series records for least amount of runs (2), hits (17) and total bases (23), as well as lowest batting average (.142).

The Braves suffered no such lack of punch in their first year in Atlanta,

smacking 207 home runs, the most in the National League in a decade. Sluggers mainly responsible for the long ball onslaught were past and future MVPs Henry Aaron (44) and Joe Torre (36). Also contributing was pitcher Tony Cloninger, who hit two grand slams in the same game — the only player ever to do so — July 3, also setting a major league record for pitchers with nine RBIs in a single contest.

St. Louis celebrated its bicentennial by hosting the 1966 All-Star Game at recently-unveiled Busch Memorial Stadium.

Two-time MVP Willie Mays of San Francisco became the NL's career home run leader May 4 with his 512th circuit clout, passing former Giant Mel Ott.

Unconventional Excellence

Lunging at pitches outside the strike zone and swatting them into the outfield gaps, racing at top speed toward an unrelenting wall to turn a sure-triple into a single, daringly churning his way for that extra base hit … Roberto Clemente was perhaps the greatest unorthodox ballplayer the game has ever seen.

An incredibly strong and accurate arm made him a feared right fielder, but his bat did even more damage, racking up 3,000 career hits, a .317 lifetime average and four batting titles. When he died in a plane crash near his native Puerto Rico on New Year's Eve of 1972, he was the Pirates' all-time leader in five offensive categories. Clemente's herky-jerky form at the plate and his sliding catches on bloop flies—right spike high in the air and left leg tucked beneath him — were not always textbook style, but the results silenced the perfectionists.

Extremely proud of a half-black, half-Puerto Rican heritage, the sensitive Clemente was constantly on the lookout for verbal slights from managers, teammates, fans and the media. Referred to as a showboat for his below-the-waist basket catches and underhand flips to the infield, and as a hypochondriac for numerous ailments that kept him out of a significant number of games, Pittsburgh's unconventional outfielder seethed at the remarks. Roberto's charm could come through like a beacon one moment, but just as suddenly he could turn surly.

In what was perhaps his best overall season, the handsome 32-year-old out-dueled 27-game winner Sandy Koufax for the MVP award in 1966, despite his team's third-place finish. Prior to

Roberto Clemente. (Courtesy Pittsburgh Pirates.)

the campaign, manager Harry Walker asked the 5-foot-11, 175-pounder to sacrifice his average in order to supply more power to an offensive attack that ranked sixth in the NL in home runs in '65. Clemente graciously acquiesced, slugging a career-high 29 homers and driving in a lifetime-best 119 runs. In spite of the altered hitting philosophy, the rifle-armed right fielder's average dipped only a dozen points. Roberto's RBIs and 342 total bases were both good for second in the league, while his 202 hits and 11 triples were third. He also led NL outfielders in assists with 17.

The youngest of seven children of

a sugar field foreman in San Juan, Puerto Rico, Roberto Walker starred in local softball leagues before joining the professional Santurce Cangrejeros ballclub at age 17. The Brooklyn Dodgers gave Clemente a $10,000 signing bonus and $5,000 contract in 1954, immediately assigning him to their top farm club in Montreal. The talent-laden Dodgers weren't quite ready for the strong outfielder, and played him sparingly in an attempt to hide him from enemy scouts. Pittsburgh representative Clyde Sukeforth saw through the ploy, however, and the Pirates used their first choice to draft the swift Clemente.

Bob hit .300 only once during his first five years, but blossomed in 1960, batting .314 with 16 round-trippers and 94 RBIs as the Bucs won the World Championship in seven games over the Yankees. It marked the first of eight consecutive seasons the line-drive hitter with the all-or-nothing swing would be above .300, with phenomenal averages of .351 the next year and .357 in 1967, both NL highs. Clemente also paced the senior circuit in batting in 1964 (.339) and '65 (.329); hits in 1964 (211) and '67 (209); and triples in 1969 (12).

Bothered by a bad back from a 1956 auto accident, the 34-year-old solemnly considered retirement during the 1968 off-season, but decided to give it another shot. Roberto exploded for remarkable averages of .345, .352 and .341 the following three years, leading the Pirates to Eastern Division crowns in 1970 and '71, with a pennant and World Championship the latter campaign.

The Pittsburgh star lacked national exposure throughout most of an 18-year career, but made up for it by putting on one of the most exceptional one-man shows in World Series history when the Pirates edged the favored Baltimore Orioles in 1971. The fall classic's MVP batted .414, collecting a dozen hits, including two homers, one the deciding blow in Game 7.

Although 38 years of age, Clemente was still one of the game's best in 1972. Bob's No. 1 goal that year was to reach the 3,000-hit plateau, and he accomplished it September 30 by drilling a double off of Jon Matlack. Sadly, it would be No. 21's final safety.

Following the '72 season, a devastating earthquake in Managua, Nicaragua, interrupted Clemente's plans to organize a sports city complex for youngsters in his native land. A frantic call from the chief of state there convinced Roberto to put together an impromptu emergency airlift project. He helped load an old DC-7 with food and medical supplies and took off with three others to try to aid the quake's victims. But the craft was two tons overweight, and five minutes after takeoff, an engine exploded. The pilot attempted a return to land, but the plane crashed into the Atlantic Ocean. There were no survivors, and none of the bodies was ever recovered.

Rather than wait the obligatory five years, baseball writers held a special election to make Clemente the first Hispanic member of the Hall of Fame in 1973.

Clemente probably had two or three more good years in him, but as it is, he was among the top 80 players all time in 12 career categories, including hits, 24th with 3,000; triples, tied for 27th with 166; total bases, 31st with

4,492; batting, 57th at .317; runs, 67th with 1,416; and RBIs, tied for 77th with 1,305. He was also a terror in the outfield, placing 18th all time in assists (266), including 27 in 1961; leading the NL in assists a league-high five times; and earning 12 consecutive Gold Gloves. In 1994, the Pirates honored Clemente with a $300,000 statue outside Three Rivers Stadium. And when they constructed PNC Park prior to the 2001 season, they made the right field wall 21 feet high in honor of the man who wore uniform No. 21 proudly for so many years.

Roberto Clemente died in the same manner he lived: helping others less fortunate than himself. His intense love and concern for his fellow human beings are remembered as clearly as his magnificent accomplishments on the ballfield.

Top 5 MVP Vote-Getters

1. Roberto Clemente, Pittsburgh — 218
2. Sandy Koufax, Los Angeles — 208
3. Willie Mays, San Francisco — 111
4. Richie Allen, Philadelphia — 107
5. Felipe Alou, Atlanta — 83

1966 AMERICAN LEAGUE — FRANK ROBINSON

Frank Robinson
B. August 31, 1935, Beaumont, Texas

Year	Team	Games	AB	Hits	Avg.	HR	RBI	Runs	SB
1966	Bal AL	155	576	182	.316	49	122	122	8

The Season

Statisticians had to go back to 1908 to find a more woeful year for hitters, as American League batsmen sputtered to a composite league average of .240 in 1966.

The offensive drought was hardly evident in the lineup of the pennant-winning Baltimore Orioles, who powered their way to a nine-game cushion over runner-up Minnesota. It had been more than two decades since the Baltimore franchise, then the St. Louis

Browns, topped the AL. The Orioles slugged their way to the best team average in the circuit along with the top defense. The left side of the infield, manned by future Hall of Famers Luis Aparicio and Brooks Robinson, was virtually impenetrable.

The dominance of the potent club was even more obvious in the World Series, where the Orioles swept a befuddled Los Angeles Dodger team, registering three consecutive shutouts to wrap up the title.

The Twins set an AL record with five home runs in the same inning June 9. Connecting in the seventh frame of a 9–4 victory over Kansas City were Rich Rollins, Tony Oliva, Don Mincher, and past and future MVPs Zoilo Versalles and Harmon Killebrew.

Other 1966 events included the election of Marvin Miller as the executive director of the Major League Players' Association March 5, and Emmett Ashford becoming the majors' first black umpire in an April 11 game between Cleveland and Washington. Miller was probably the single most influential force in the players eventually achieving unparalleled financial remuneration from big league owners.

Robby's Rampage

Hank Bauer's Baltimore Orioles, already fraught with established stars, had been on the verge of capturing the American League pennant for several years prior to the 1966 season, but had fallen short each time. Brooks Robinson, Luis Aparicio and Boog Powell were the heart of the offense, while Wally Bunker, Milt Pappas and Dave McNally fronted a mound corps that ranked near the top of the heap. But the O's were missing the inner fortitude that turns good teams into exceptional clubs.

It took the down-and-dirty, hustling style of Frank Robinson to ignite the Baltimore bunch. Robinson came to the Baltimore spring training camp with the derisive words of Cincinnati general manager Bill De Witt still ringing in his ears. "Robinson's an *old* 30," De Witt had said, defending the trade. Seething from the remark, Frank turned his rage loose against his new AL opponents in 1966, becoming the first man to net MVP laurels in both major leagues. In fact, his inspired play helped produce four pennants and two World Series titles for the Orioles.

His full-tilt base running style, re-plete with bone-jarring takeout slides, awakened and upset enemy infielders while inspiring fellow Orioles. There were many who questioned his warlike ways, but Frank always demanded, and eventually earned, respect. Between the white lines, he condescended to no one.

With the newcomer leading the way, the Birds soared to the pennant in 1966. His 367 total bases were No. 1 in the circuit by far, and no one in the league seriously challenged the transplanted National Leaguer in any of the Triple Crown categories, where Frank compiled a .316 average, 49 homers and 122 RBIs to become the first to sweep those slots since Mickey Mantle a decade earlier.

That was a golden year for Robinson, who captured his only RBI crown and smacked a career high in the HR department while leading Baltimore to its first pennant. He also led the league in runs (122), slugging (.637) and on-base percentage (.415). In May, the 31-year-old hit the first ball to clear Memorial Stadium — an estimated 451-foot shot that shattered Cleveland pitcher Luis Tiant's 27-inning scoreless streak — then cracked two more round-trippers off Don Drysdale to earn MVP honors in the World Series as the Orioles swept the Dodgers. The awarding of the AL MVP following the campaign was merely a formality, as Robinson was a unanimous selection. His acceptance speech probably should have included a thank-you to catcher Andy Etchebarren, who had saved him from drowning during an August pool party.

A basepath collision in June 1967 brought double vision that plagued him off and on for a year and a half, yet Robby still hit .311 with 30 homers and 94 RBIs. A bad case of the mumps and a shoulder injury kept the right fielder out of the lineup 31 games the following year, and Frank slipped in form.

The 34-year-old came back injury-free in 1969, roaring to a .308 mark with 100 RBIs and 32 round-trippers. The Orioles won 109 games and the AL flag before bowing to the spell of the Miracle Mets in the World Series. In addition to his stellar play, Robby kept the O's clubhouse loose by wearing a mop-style wig while presiding as judge over a "kangaroo court" in which players were tried for minor baseball offenses.

On the way to another pennant in '70, Robinson crushed two grand slams in consecutive at-bats in the same game, tying a major league record, and in '71 became the 11th player in history to reach the 500 mark in four-baggers. The 1971 All-Star Game MVP became the first player to hit a home run for both leagues in the mid-summer classic. In Game 6 of the 1971 World Series loss to Pittsburgh, Robinson forced a seventh game by scoring the winning run from third on a shallow outfield fly ball. Following his trade to the Dodgers prior to the 1972 season, he became the first player to have his uniform number (20) retired by the Orioles.

In the twilight of his career, Robinson smashed 30 homers and drove in 97 runs for the Angels in 1973, but was hitting only .251 late in the next campaign when claimed on waivers by Cleveland. It appeared at the time that the aging star had finished making headlines, but big news was just around the corner.

Between seasons, Frank had quietly gone about the task of acquiring managerial experience in Puerto Rico during the winter leagues, beginning in 1969 when he obscurely became the first American League black man to guide an integrated unit.

The route to a big league skipper post opened with the 1974 shift to Cleveland. On October 3, Frank was named the first black manager of a major league team. The sporting world watched on opening day as Robinson, inserting himself in the lineup, crashed a home run in his first time up and Cleveland went on to win 5–3. Unfortunately, the designated hitter-manager played sparingly in his first two years at the helm due to a bad shoulder.

Two fourth-place Indian finishes were followed by his dismissal a third of the way through 1977, as Cleveland struggled to reach the .500 mark. But in 1981, San Francisco hired Robby as manager, and the Giants came within one game of a division title in 1982, the same year he was elected to the Hall of Fame.

By 1983, the Giants had dipped to fifth place, and when the team hit bottom in '84, Robinson was relieved by third base coach Danny Ozark. But like a cat landing squarely on all fours, the hard-nosed Hall of Famer returned to the front lines a week later, joining the Milwaukee Brewers as their hitting coach. He then signed on as a member of Baltimore's coaching staff in 1985.

Robinson became an assistant to the Orioles' president in 1987, then took over as Baltimore manager six games into the '88 season with the team on its way to a record-21 consec-

utive losses to start a campaign. Frank eventually righted the ship, and was voted AL Manager of the Year in 1989 after piloting the O's to within two games of the East Division title. But the team had peaked, and Robinson was replaced 37 games into the '91 season. He remained in the Orioles' front office through 1995. Although he never hesitated to mix it up as a player on the field, he earned a reputation as a strict disciplinarian in his role as major league vice president of on-field operations, dishing out a number of substantial penalties for fights on the diamonds. In 2002, Robinson was appointed manager of the Montreal

Expos by Major League Baseball, which took over ownership of the franchise.

In all of these roles, Frank Robinson's battling spirit has served him well, as it did during his 21-year playing career.

Top 5 MVP Vote-Getters

1. Frank Robinson, Baltimore — 280
2. Brooks Robinson, Baltimore — 153
3. Boog Powell, Baltimore — 122
4. Harmon Killebrew, Minnesota — 96
5. Jim Kaat, Minnesota — 84

1967 NATIONAL LEAGUE — ORLANDO CEPEDA

Orlando Manuel Cepeda
B. September 17, 1937, Ponce, Puerto Rico

Year	Team	Games	AB	Hits	Avg.	HR	RBI	Runs	SB
1967	SL NL	151	563	183	.325	25	111	91	11

The Season

The 1967 National League race was the least exciting in the past dozen seasons, but only because the dominant St. Louis Cardinals were such an indefectible blend of speed, power, defense and moxie. The Redbirds of Curt Flood, Orlando Cepeda, Lou Brock, Bob Gibson and Roger Maris easily outdistanced San Francisco by 10½ games to nail down the flag.

The Chicago Cubs of Leo Durocher showed the most drastic improvement in the circuit, moving from rock-bottom in 1966 to a comfortable third, but neither the little bears nor anyone else could seriously challenge Red Schoendienst's team.

While the regular season may have been somewhat anticlimactic, the All-Star Game and World Series were both spine-chilling spectacles.

The National League captured the mid-season affair 2–1, the longest in history, on a 15th-inning homer by

Tony Perez after a record-30 batters had struck out. Prime time television consideration had a hand in the hitters' futility, as the game was moved to 4:15 p.m. California time, causing afternoon shadows at Anaheim.

The Cardinals survived a rugged bunch of Boston Red Sox in a seven-game World Series, thanks mainly to the efforts of Brock, Gibson and Maris. Brock's .414 average and eight runs scored were outdone only by his seven stolen bases, which broke a 58-year-old Series mark. Gibson won three games, fanning 26 in 27 innings and registering a miserly 1.00 ERA. Maris hit .385 and drove in seven mates to lead both clubs.

On June 4, Flood's dropped fly ball ended a major league-record streak of 568 consecutive chances without an error, and an NL-record 227 straight games without a fielding miscue.

Cheers for "Cha Cha"

Infectious salsa music bounces loudly off the walls of the team clubhouse. Standing atop the bench in front of his locker, wearing only a towel and a gigantic grin, Orlando Cepeda leads a simple but exuberant cheer that has become the rallying point of the 1967 St. Louis Cardinals.

"El birdos," he screams.

"Yeah," team members answer.

"El Birdos."

"Yeah."

"EL BIRDOS!"

"YEAH!"

The son of Pedro "Perucho" Cepeda, the Babe Ruth of Puerto Rico, had traveled far in distance and maturity to gain the exalted leadership status for the World Champions. His right leg, malformed at birth, was shorter than the other, causing the Latin star no end of troubles since he first signed with the New York Giants in 1955 for a $500 bonus.

It had been a rocky road to the summit. Cepeda's father had died suddenly in '55 during Orlando's first minor league season, and the homesick 18-year-old pondered quitting the game and returning to his native land. But two years and a pair of minor league batting titles later, the strapping youngster was the first hero of the newly located San Francisco Giants.

The "Baby Bull" demonstrated his baseball bloodlines by bashing out a .312 average, 25 home runs, a league-high 38 doubles and 96 RBIs to win the 1958 NL Rookie of the Year award. His April 15 homer off Don Drysdale of Los Angeles was not only his first career home run, but also the first round-tripper on the West Coast in major league history. He upped all of those statistics the following year. Massive Willie McCovey joined the team late in '59, and like Orlando, was a first baseman. This led to Cepeda's shift to the outfield in 1960 and a slight offensive decline.

By the next campaign, Cepeda was splitting his time between first base and the outfield for the most productive season of his 17-year career. The 24-year-old slashed a league-high 46 round-trippers, compiled a commanding NL-best total of 142 RBIs and hit .311, finishing second in the MVP voting. Another stellar year in '62 (.306, 35 HRs, 114 RBIs) helped the Giants to the pennant. There were few who could match the trim-but-muscular athlete's performance from 1961 through '64 when he averaged .309 and 37 home runs per year.

It took an operation on his deformed leg to halt that string, as Cepeda sat out all but 33 games in 1965. When he returned in '66, McCovey was firmly entrenched at first base, and a now-expendable Cepeda was shipped to St. Louis. Welcomed with open arms by the Cardinals and assured of a permanent spot in the lineup, Cepeda hit .303 for St. Louis in 123 games, and was named "Comeback Player of the Year."

Then, in his first full year with the Redbirds, Orlando fronted a machine-like attack, supplying power (25 HRs) and runs (league-high 111 RBIs) while slamming at a .340 pace right up until the time the Cardinals clinched the 1967 pennant. He finally leveled off at .325, the prodigious MVP season vindicating him from criticism that he was unmanageable.

Giant skippers Bill Rigney, Alvin Dark and Herman Franks hadn't quite known what to make of the high-strung talent. Highly emotional, Cepeda's joy was more effusive than the average man's, but his gloomy periods were also more pronounced.

The highly explosive Latin was happiest as a Cardinal, but after an off-season in 1968 (.248, 16 homers), was traded to the Atlanta Braves even-up for Joe Torre in what was the only time two MVPs were involved in a one-for-one swap. There he played on the team's division winner in '69, and at age 33 hit .305 with 34 homers and 111 RBIs the following campaign.

After the third operation on his leg, Orlando was briefly reborn as the first designated hitter in Boston Red Sox history, topping all DHs with 20 four-baggers. But, following a painful 1974, further deterioration of his legs led to retirement at age 37.

In truth, the free-swinging righty had spent a majority of his major league career perched atop less than perfunctory wheels, making his .297 lifetime average over 17 seasons all the more astounding. He hit for power and average, registering nine .300 seasons and as many campaigns with 90 or more RBIs while going over the 20 mark in homers a dozen times. Milwaukee pitcher Lew Burdette once called him "the toughest hitter I ever faced."

The MVP campaign of 1967 was easily his most satisfying, if not the most statistically impressive. He was the first unanimous NL MVP pick under the 20-voter system.

Revered for this and other baseball achievements in his native Puerto Rico, Cepeda made one major mistake that turned his countrymen against him. One year after leaving the major league scene, he was arrested, tried and jailed for smuggling marijuana at the San Juan Airport. The incident devastated his Hall of Fame chances at the time, as well as his psyche.

Following a 10-month prison term, Cepeda returned as batting coach for the Chicago White Sox, then opened a baseball school for the youth of San Juan.

The criticism from past managers pales in comparison to the deep hurt leveled by Cepeda's countrymen, who had made him feel like a social pariah. So, in 1984, he moved to California, hoping that new surroundings would serve as an elixir and help bring back the pride and upbeat persona of the man once called "Cha Cha."

The Veterans Committee finally forgave Orlando his transgression, voting him into the Hall of Fame in 1999. He currently works in community relations for the Giants and speaks to young people about drug abuse.

Top 5 MVP Vote-Getters

1. Orlando Cepeda, St. Louis — 280
2. Tim McCarver, St. Louis — 136
3. Roberto Clemente, Pittsburgh — 129
4. Ron Santo, Chicago — 103
5. Hank Aaron, Atlanta — 79

1967 American League—Carl Yastrzemski

Carl Michael Yastrzemski
B. August 22, 1939, Southhampton, New York

Year	Team	Games	AB	Hits	Avg.	HR	RBI	Runs	SB
1967	Bos AL	161	579	189	.326	44	121	112	10

The Season

The big story in the American League in 1967 was written by the Boston Red Sox. Mired in ninth place the previous year, they became the first team in the 20th century to rebound from next-to-last place to the flag in one season. Rookie manager Dick Williams pulled the strings for the Red Sox, who edged both Minnesota and Detroit on the final day of the season. In a year of overall mediocrity, Boston's .568 winning percentage was the lowest for a pennant winner in AL history.

With the exception of Cy Young Award winner Jim Lonborg, Boston was strictly an offensive ballclub. Fenway Park's inhabitants led the league in runs, batting and slugging, but were ninth in fielding and eighth in ERA. One of Boston's sluggers was Tony Conigliaro, who missed the final 1½ months of the season and the entire 1968 campaign after being hit in the face by a Jack Hamilton pitch. The Red Sox rallied from a 3–1 deficit to even the World Series at three games apiece, but St. Louis prevailed in the finale.

Individual achievements in 1967 included future MVP Rod Carew of Minnesota earning Rookie of the Year honors, and Baltimore's Steve Barber and Stu Miller combining for a no-hitter against Detroit April 30, but losing 2–1.

On July 25, race riots in Detroit caused the postponement of a Tigers-Orioles game, and the next two contests in the series were moved to Baltimore.

Destiny Fulfilled

Groomed by his father to be a big league ballplayer, then touted as the next Ted Williams following a brief but spectacular minor league career, Carl Yastrzemski pursued a course of destiny which eventually led to recognition as one of the all-time greats.

When Yastrzemski completed a stunning 23-year career after the 1983 campaign, he had racked up more than 3,000 hits and 400 home runs (the first American Leaguer to do so), and won three batting titles. Despite a brilliant year-in, year-out performance for the Boston Red Sox, Carl's introverted nature and pensive behavior resulted in a certain amount of alienation from fans and players. But no one did more for his team than Yastrzemski through the 1960s and '70s.

Carl Yastrzemski Sr., a potato farmer in Bridgehampton, Long Island, and avid baseball player and fan, was secure in his belief that his son would be a ballplayer. Young Carl played shortstop for the local amateur teams with dad on his right at third base, and in 1955, the 16-year-old's Bridgehampton Babe Ruth squad rolled to the New York State and Middle Atlantic States titles. Equally successful off the ballfield, Carl Jr. was elected president of his senior class and became renowned for his basketball playing abilities.

But with a slight frame, he showed more potential at the diamond game. The pro scouts liked what they saw of the versatile Yastrzemski, who received 14 solid offers from major league clubs following his graduation. A bright, serious student, Carl turned them all down, choosing to attend Notre Dame on an athletic scholarship. Two semesters into his studies, however, Carl had a change of heart, deciding to take the Yankees up on their offer. But the often moody ballplayer didn't like the way he was treated at the tryout, opting instead for the Red Sox.

Yaz started at the Class B level at Raleigh, North Carolina, tearing up the Carolina League with a .377 average in 1959, but also led league shortstops in errors. He moved all the way to Triple A ball with Minneapolis of the American Association the next season, where he batted .339 and converted to the outfield.

A natural athlete, Carl took well to the switch to left field. His bat and glove were ready in 1961, but pressure from the media and fans to be another Ted Williams was overwhelming. When he hit only 11 home runs and batted .266 in 1961, the rookie felt the severe strain of competing against a legend.

Yaz rebounded his sophomore season, narrowly missing the .300 mark, then batted .321 in 1963 for his first batting crown. He also paced the league in hits (183), doubles (40), walks (95) and on-base percentage (.419) in '63. In 1965, Yastrzemski led the circuit in slugging (.536) and on-base percentage (.398), and he topped AL players in doubles in both '65 (45) and '66 (39). He reached the 20-homer mark only once during his first six years, but even more disturbing to those who anticipated superstar quality was his downcast attitude. Carl had been used to playing with winners, and the Boston teams of the early to mid-'60s were anything but. Unaccustomed to losing, Yastrzemski became uncommunicative with teammates and manager Billy Herman.

But a miraculous turn of events occurred in 1967. Under the spring training tutelage of Ted Williams himself, Carl altered his batting stance and began ferociously pulling the ball. Jamming the helmet down on his head, then squarely facing the pitcher with bat held high, "The Pride of New England" became a slugger overnight, more than doubling his previous one-season home run output with 44, driving in 121 runs and hitting .326 to capture baseball's most recently earned Triple Crown. The port-side swinger also led the AL in total bases (360), slugging (.622), runs scored (112), hits (189) and on-base percentage (.421).

The Red Sox, meanwhile, were conducting a frantic pennant drive with Yaz carrying the offense. In the final two weeks of the '67 campaign, the left fielder hit .522 (23-for-44) with five round-trippers and 16 RBIs. His three-run blast in the next-to-last game pulled the BoSox into a first-place tie, and four straight safeties in the finale helped Boston clinch its "Impossible Dream" flag, and its first pennant since 1946. The obvious choice for the MVP award also starred in the World Series, hitting .400 with three circuit clouts and five RBIs.

Yastrzemski continued to consistently produce with incredible durability over the next 16 years. On six occasions he led AL outfielders in assists (more than any outfielder in league history), playing the caroms off the Green Monster at Fenway Park more efficiently than anyone before or since, and compiling a perfect fielding percentage in 1977. Earning seven Gold Gloves over his career, he was just as sure-handed at first base.

Nineteen-sixty-eight was the year of the pitcher, but Carl was the league's best in batting (.301), walks (119) and on-base percentage (.429). Two years later, he led the American League in runs (125), slugging (.592) and on-base percentage (.453), and in 1974, he scored a league-high 93 runs.

Yastrzemski was named to the AL All-Star Team in 18 of his 23 seasons, and was presented with the Arch Ward Memorial Trophy as the 1970 mid-summer classic's MVP. Five years later, Carl hit .455 in the ALCS sweep of Oakland, then made his second World Series appearance, batting .310. But again the Red Sox were nudged in seven games, this time by Cincinnati. As dismal as two Series losses were, Yastrzemski said his biggest disappointment was the 1978 playoff defeat to the Yankees, in which Yaz ended the game by popping out, then cried openly in front of reporters in the locker room. In fact, although he was known as a clutch hitter, he also made the final out in both the 1967 and '75 World Series.

This display of emotion was rare for Carl, who preferred to keep his thoughts and hurts from the public. At one point late in his career, wrist and back injuries prevented him from keeping both hands on the bat at contact; and later, his Achilles tendons were taped so tightly he could barely feel his feet. Unsympathetic fans at Fenway booed him relentlessly in the early '70s when his hitting slipped noticeably, but the dedicated achiever never let up, eventually passing Hank Aaron as the all-time leader in games played with 3,308. Yaz is now second all-time in that category behind 1973 NL MVP Pete Rose. Carl was also third in career at-bats; fifth in walks; seventh in hits, total bases, doubles and extra base hits; 11th in RBIs; 13th in runs; and 24th in home runs.

Carl Yastrzemski, whose uniform No. 8 was retired by the Red Sox and who was a near unanimous selection for the Hall of Fame in 1989, fulfilled his father's dreams and eventually satisfied the Fenway faithful who were looking for the next Ted Williams. In fact, he surpassed the expectations of even the most demanding fans.

Top 5 MVP Vote-Getters

1. Carl Yastrzemski, Boston — 275
2. Harmon Killebrew, Minnesota — 161
3. Bill Freehan, Detroit — 137
4. Joel Horlen, Chicago — 91
5. Al Kaline, Detroit — 88

1968 NATIONAL LEAGUE — BOB GIBSON

Robert Gibson
B. November 9, 1935, Omaha, Nebraska

Year	Team	Games	W	L	ERA	IP	SO	BB	ShO
1968	SL NL	34	22	9	1.12	304.2	268	62	13

The Season

The St. Louis Cardinals parlayed strong pitching and plenty of speed into their second straight National League pennant, topping the runner-up Giants by nine games.

Leading Detroit by a three games-to-one margin in the World Series, the Cards dropped three in a row, losing their first seven-game fall classic after capturing six in a row. Lou Brock excelled for the losers, batting .464 with six extra base hits and seven stolen bases.

Along with MVP Bob Gibson, Don Drysdale of Los Angeles personified the "Year of the Pitcher." The Dodger right-hander rattled off a remarkable six consecutive shutouts, putting together a major league record-58⅔ scoreless innings streak.

Other pitchers who made history this season were San Francisco's Gaylord Perry and Ray Washburn of St. Louis, who no-hit each other's team on consecutive days late in the season. It was the first time no-hitters were thrown in the same park on two consecutive days. In addition, Houston's Don Wilson tied a major league record July 14 by striking out 18, including a major league record-eight in a row.

Hitting futility was no more evident, nor more in the limelight, than on April 15 when Houston edged New York 1–0 in 24 innings, and when the NL nipped the AL 1–0 July 9 in the All-Star Game. The lone run in the mid-summer classic, which featured only eight hits, was not only unearned, but scored on a double play.

Future two-time MVP Johnny Bench of Cincinnati earned Rookie of the Year honors, and past MVP Joe Medwick was inducted into the Hall of Fame.

A Real Thoroughbred

A relentless, scowling machine of a man on the hill, hard-throwing Bob Gibson blew away hitters like bowling pins, firing strike after strike. No sooner would he receive the ball back from his catcher than the feared pitcher would begin his no-nonsense, rocking-horse windup and release an exploding fastball or hard slider.

During the 1960s and early '70s, batters were at the intimidating right-hander's mercy. Those brave enough to dig in against the menacing figure seldom had time to recuperate from the first blazing pitch before another was on its way. Gibson produced more than 3,000 strikeouts and 251 wins, won two Cy Young Awards and took his place in the Hall of Fame.

Handsome and bright, but also sensitive and moody, the low-key St. Louis hurler nearly always rose to the occasion. The strikeout artist fanned more than 200 batters a record-nine times, and on four occasions led the National League in shutouts, recording 56 over a 17-year career with the Cardinals. The six-time All-Star was also a tough out at the plate, tagging 24

lifetime home runs. Brilliant in the field as well, Gibson earned nine consecutive Gold Gloves (1965–73), thanks to cat-like reflexes and a strong arm.

After reaching a position of acclaim and national recognition, "Hoot" never let it be forgotten that were it not for his baseball skills, he might be like millions of other blacks—poor and downtrodden. A civil rights advocate, Bob was continually speaking out against racial prejudice.

Prior to 1968, his voice was muffled. But it gained considerable volume after perhaps the most sensational effort by a pitcher in the 20th century. The tall, lean smoke-thrower was awesome in '68, winning 22 games and recording a miniscule 1.12 ERA, the best ever by a hurler with more than 300 innings, and the lowest in NL history.

The 32-year-old moundsman was never knocked out of the box that season. Shortly after Don Drysdale's consecutive scoreless innings streak made headlines, Gibby stole the limelight with five straight shutouts, allowing only three runs over a 100-inning stretch. At one point, he won 15 games in a row, and he allowed only two earned runs during a 95-inning span. He shut out the opposition a miraculous 13 times, and was the NL's best in strikeouts with 268.

The unanimous choice as the league's Cy Young Award recipient and the National League's MVP struck out a record-17 batters while twirling a five-hit shutout in the first game of the '68 World Series against Detroit. The Cardinal ace came back to pitch another five-hitter in a 10–1 triumph in Game 4, belting a home run to become the first pitcher with two fall classic round-trippers. But then he tired as the Tigers took the finale 4–1. Still, his 35 strikeouts in one World Series were a record.

Like many African-Americans who eventually made it big in professional sports in his era, Gibson literally fought his way to the top. Bobby grew up in a tough Omaha, Nebraska, neighborhood, never having known his father, who died near the time of his birth. In an "only the strong survive"

atmosphere, he also suffered from numerous ailments, including rickets, a rheumatic heart and asthma.

Snapping back from ill health as a teenager, he was pulled off the streets by older brother LeRoy, who gave Bobby instruction in sports at the local YMCA. He obtained a scholarship from Creighton University, and the school's first black athlete hit .340 as a shortstop and outfielder. Bob quit school to tour with the Harlem Globetrotters; but preferring competitiveness to clowning, he returned to Omaha where he tried out with the St. Louis Cardinals Triple A farm club in 1957. Manager Johnny Keane liked the young man's strong arm, and converted him to a pitcher.

Gibson spent three years in the minors, and although the speedball right-hander was striking out his share of batters, he was also putting too many on base via the walk. The 25-year-old fireballer made the big club to stay in 1961, but walked a league-high 119 in 211 innings during his rookie year, and followed with totals near 100 bases on balls through 1965. But his overall success overshadowed a propensity for wildness. Gibson posted the first of 13 consecutive winning seasons in 1961 (13–12), and his victory total increased every year until he hit the 20 mark in '65 and 21 in '66.

Bob received his first World Series taste in 1964, after helping the Redbirds edge the Phillies and Reds by winning nine of his last 11 starts. Following a loss in Game 2 of the '64 classic, he won the fifth and seventh games against the Yankees, setting a Series record with 31 strikeouts. Gibson was robbed of a third consecutive 20-win season in 1967 when he missed nearly two months after Roberto Clemente's line drive broke his leg. The flame-thrower came back to net the pennant-clinching win, and dominated the World Series with three victories and a 1.00 ERA against Boston.

The unparalleled '68 campaign followed, but Bob was not through yet. He went 20–13 with a magnificent 2.18 ERA and an NL-best 28 complete games in 1969, then won a league-high 23 games with a 3.12 earned run average in '70, capturing his second Cy

Young Award. In 1971, Gibson fired his only no-hitter, baffling the eventual World Champion Pirates 11–0, and led the league in shutouts (five) for the fourth time.

Gibby was suffering from ever-worsening arthritis in his right elbow at this point, and his final outstanding season came in 1972. Personal problems set in as wife Charlene left him with two teenage daughters. He retired following a poor '75 campaign.

Nineteen-eighty-one saw Gibson's return to prominence, as he was elected to the Hall of Fame on the first ballot, and took an assistant pitching coach job with the Mets at the request of former teammate Joe Torre. When Torre

took over the managerial reins in Atlanta the next year, Gibson went with him. He also followed Torre to St. Louis as a coach in 1995.

Gibson never hesitated to brush back a hitter, and sometimes that meant plunking batters who crowded the plate. Speaking of his battery mate, catcher Tim McCarver once said, "Far and away, the meanest, nastiest pitcher I ever saw. There is no second place on this list." Gibson was 11th all time in strikeouts with 3,117, 13th in shutouts with 56, and 40th in both wins with 251 and innings pitched with 3,884.1.

He's mellowed somewhat, but Bob Gibson is still a serious, conscientious competitor. It's doubtful that any

of the pitchers he developed with the Mets, Braves and Cardinals will ever be as outstanding as he was, but hurlers couldn't help but benefit from his vast experience.

Top 5 MVP Vote-Getters

1. Bob Gibson, St. Louis — 242
2. Pete Rose, Cincinnati — 205
3. Willie McCovey, San Francisco — 135
4. Curt Flood, St. Louis — 116
5. Juan Marichal, San Francisco — 93

1968 AMERICAN LEAGUE — DENNY McLAIN

Dennis Dale McLain
B. March 29, 1944, Chicago, Illinois

Year	Team	Games	W	L	ERA	IP	SO	BB	ShO
1968	Det AL	41	31	6	1.96	336	280	63	6

The Season

The performance of American League hitters was so flaccid in 1968 that sixth-place Oakland (replanted from Kansas City) led the league in team batting with a doddering .240 mark. Further evidence of offensive ineptitude could be found in AL hurlers' composite 2.98 ERA, the lowest in nearly half a century.

Pessimistic Tiger fans waited for their team to relinquish its early-season lead, but the Bengals, after falling short by one game the previous year, posted 103 wins to take the flag by a dozen games.

The exultation produced by Detroit's first pennant since 1945 was heightened when the Tigers became the second team in baseball's annals to rebound from a three games-to-one deficit and capture the World Series. Left-hander Mickey Lolich was the De-

troit star, coming out from behind the shadow of teammate Denny McLain to post three victories over St. Louis.

Individual achievements in the junior circuit included a 19-strikeout performance (in 10 innings) by Cleveland's Luis Tiant; the league's first perfect game in 46 years, hurled by Catfish Hunter of Oakland; 10 home runs in a six-game span by Washington's Frank Howard; Hoyt Wilhelm's major league record-907th career appearance; a no-hitter by Tom Phoebus of Baltimore; and a fourth consecutive stolen base crown for the A's Bert Campaneris.

Denny's Dream Year

The roller-coaster existence of Detroit's bad boy, Denny McLain, has been one trip to the summit and screaming descent to near-oblivion after another.

The Chicago-area product was the son of a strict disciplinarian and a firm believer in corporal punishment. Whether Mr. McLain's authoritarianism triggered his son's rebellious nature is more a matter for professional diagnosis, but it's certainly safe to say that Denny held little regard for the straight and narrow. His youth was marked by numerous fights, lackadaisical schoolwork and excellence in sports, especially baseball.

The White Sox signed the hard-throwing McLain immediately upon high school graduation for a $17,000 bonus. But after registering a 5–8 minor league record, the verbose hurler was released in 1963. The Detroit Tigers snapped up Denny, and in his third campaign in 1965, he went 16–6. In a first-inning relief appearance that season, he struck out the first seven batters he faced, a major league record. He then won 20 and 17 games the next two years.

During these efforts, he was unceremoniously dubbed "Mighty Mouth," alternately exhibiting a joyously uninhibited and a disruptively antagonistic personality. Warmth exuded from his relationship with wife Sharyn, daughter of 1948 MVP Lou Boudreau, and adopted son Dennis, but at other times his public persona was inexplicably bizarre. "Super Flake," with his wayward style, was continually quoted and psychoanalyzed in the nation's newspapers.

McLain's gaudiest and most noteworthy performance came in his 1968 MVP season. The mischievous right-hander set the baseball world afire with a 31–6 effort for a league-best .838 winning percentage, becoming the first moundsman in history to unanimously cop both the Cy Young and MVP awards in the same season.

"Denny Detroit" was simply incredible in his fourth full major league campaign, reviving the brag-'n-beat antics of the last hurler to reach the heavenly heights of 30 wins, Dizzy Dean, 34 years before. And no one has done it since.

Starting the season with long, scraggly red hair, McLain accelerated to a 10–2 mark early in June, then switched back to his natural blond, shortly cropped coiffure and proceeded to go 21–4 the rest of the way. Throughout the magnificent year, the garrulous character seemed to draw strength from the national attention that hounded his every step.

Frequently performing on two days' rest, Denny halted a number of short Detroit losing streaks, hauling his Tiger teammates to the top of the AL heap. His 28 complete games and 336 innings pitched were both league highs. Win No. 30 (5–4 over the Oakland A's) was a nationally televised event, and the anticipated head-to-head World Series confrontation between McLain and Bob Gibson of the St. Louis Cardinals loomed.

A troublesome right shoulder muscle and Gibson's stellar mound work thwarted Denny in his first two Series tries. But he took a shot of cortisone in his ailing arm, then allowed only one run in the sixth contest to stave off Detroit's elimination, setting

Dennis McLain. (Courtesy Detroit Tigers.)

the stage for the seven-game World Title clincher.

Riding a wave of success, the tempestuous fireballer went 24–9 in 1969 and shared the Cy Young Award with Baltimore's Mike Cuellar, becoming the first repeat winner of the honor in AL history. McLain was No. 1 in the league in both shutouts (9) and innings (325).

Then came the plunge to ignominy. Early in the '70 season, Commissioner Bowie Kuhn suspended

McLain for three months for alleged 1967 bookmaking activities. When he returned to action, the 26-year-old was overweight and had lost the rhythm in his once-flawless pitching motion. He struggled to a 3–5 record with an ERA that ballooned to 4.65. A reported gun-toting incident brought a second suspension from Kuhn, and the Tigers suspended their troubled right-hander in '70 for dumping a pail of water over the heads of two sportswriters. To top it all off, he declared personal bankruptcy.

The Tigers unloaded their problem child on Washington for the 1971 season, but Senator manager Ted Williams quickly tired of the "individualist," who netted 22 defeats. So it was on to Oakland, where Denny was plagued by a sore shoulder and sudden weight gain (to 218 pounds). By the next year, McLain was out of baseball.

The free spirit fluttered from one profession to another following his retirement, but succeeded in none of them. He headed a musical combo, was general manager of a minor league team, ran a mortgage company and went into the medical clinic business. Along the way, he suffered a heart attack, was left homeless following a fire and filed for bankruptcy again.

In March of 1984, his name was again plastered in headlines as a federal indictment charged McLain with loan sharking, bookmaking and accepting kickbacks; the extortion, possession and distribution of cocaine; and conspiracy to import cocaine. Grossly overweight at close to 300 pounds, the puffy-faced 40-year-old claimed innocence on all fronts. But a conviction resulted in a lengthy prison term.

McLain could have used his time behind bars to take responsibility for his actions and try to get his head on straight, but unfortunately, he's never been one to learn from his mistakes. Following some radio and television gigs in Detroit, the hustler and con artist got caught with his hand in the cookie jar again, and in 1997 began serving an eight-year sentence in a Pennsylvania federal prison for extorting $3 million from a Michigan packing company.

Those who rubbed elbows with McLain during his baseball tenure came forward, following his retirement and problems with the law, with old stories about the pitcher's tendency to gravitate toward get-rich-quick schemes, irresponsible behavior and a head-in-the-clouds attitude.

There were also bittersweet reminiscences about a classic pitching style: the high-kick, textbook follow-through, and the superb assortment of high, hard fastballs, snapping overhand curves, elusive sliders and precise control that once typified a Dennis McLain outing.

There is no doubt, however, that supporters and detractors alike will never forget Denny's dream year of 1968.

Top 5 MVP Vote-Getters

1. Denny McLain, Detroit — 280
2. Bill Freehan, Detroit — 161
3. Ken Harrelson, Boston — 103
4. Willie Horton, Detroit — 102
5. Dave McNally, Baltimore — 78
5. Luis Tiant, Cleveland — 78

1969 NATIONAL LEAGUE — WILLIE McCOVEY

Willie Lee McCovey
B. January 10, 1938, Mobile, Alabama

Year	Team	Games	AB	Hits	Avg.	HR	RBI	Runs	SB
1969	SF NL	149	491	157	.320	45	126	101	0

The Season

Nineteen-sixty-nine was the year of the "Miracle Mets," who came from far behind the Chicago Cubs in the Eastern Division to finish eight games ahead. The New Yorkers specialized in clutch pitching and unlikely heroes, such as Art Shamsky, Al Weis and J.C. Martin performing above capacity at just the right times.

They did so amid a spotlight for the grand old game, celebrating its 100th anniversary with a series of special events. A new commissioner, Bowie Kuhn, took office to preside over the majestic happenings.

While the once-hapless Mets smashed their Eastern Division competition, the Atlanta Braves won that city's first professional sports title, taking the West by three games over San Francisco. Both of the newly formed divisions' expansion franchises, the Montreal Expos and San Diego Padres, finished in the cellar.

Spurred on by the anniversary hoopla, new teams and a winning club in baseball's most populated city, the NL reached an all-time attendance high of 15,094,946.

The Mets wrapped up their Cinderella season by sweeping Atlanta in the first League Championship Series, then besting heavily favored Baltimore in five games in the World Series.

Typifying a season in which nearly everything went right, the Mets edged St. Louis 4–3 September 15, despite the Cards' Steve Carlton striking out a major league record-19 batters.

Also in 1969, three-time National League Most Valuable Players Roy Campanella and Stan Musial were inducted into the Hall of Fame.

"Big Mac" Attack

It's almost impossible to believe that someone of such magnitude and accomplishment as Willie McCovey could play most of his lengthy career in another man's shadow, or that he is remembered for rapping into an out that ended a World Series. Yet the massive McCovey is vividly recalled for his screeching line drive out that concluded the 1962 fall classic. Mere inches robbed him of glory on that occasion; but what kept McCovey out of the national spotlight more than anything else was playing with the highly flamboyant Willie Mays for most of his 22 big league years.

Born in 1938 in Hank Aaron's hometown of Mobile, Alabama, Willie McCovey was one of 10 children, but could hardly be overlooked in the crowd. By age 14, he was starring in basketball and playing baseball on adult teams. He performed so well that after turning 17, Willie was signed by the New York Giants baseball team.

The 20-year-old first baseman was stinging the sphere at a .319 clip in Triple A by 1958. Knee surgery that winter did little to slow his hitting progress, as McCovey powdered the ball at a .372 pace with 29 homers and 92 RBIs in the first 94 games of 1959 at Phoenix.

At 6-foot-4 and fluctuating in weight between 198 and 210 pounds, Willie's reticent personal image contrasted with a striking physical presence. Extremely long legs gave him an almost gangly appearance, but a wide back which accommodated the double-digit 44 more accurately displayed his muscularity.

That forcefulness was unleashed on major league pitching when "Big Stretch" first joined the Giants two-thirds of the way through the 1959 season. The 21-year-old hit baseball's toughest pitchers as if they were Class D pigeons. In 52 games, he compiled a .354 average with 13 round-trippers and 38 RBIs, and was unanimously named the NL Rookie of the Year. His major league debut featured four hits, including two triples.

Pitchers found a chink in his armor in 1960, as Willie flailed unsuccessfully at high and tight pitches all year long, dipping miserably to .238 and being sent back to the minors for a spell. Having 1958 Rookie of the Year

Willie McCovey. (Courtesy San Francisco Giants.)

Orlando Cepeda around didn't help matters either, because the Latin star also played first base. So, Willie occasionally displaced Cepeda, while also playing the outfield and pinch-hitting. He improved steadily in the offensive department, with a batting average that rose to .271 in 1961 and .293 the next year. McCovey played in his lone World Series in '62, bashing a homer against the Yankees before slamming that vicious line drive into the glove of second baseman Bobby Richardson — with the winning run in scoring position — for the final out of the Series.

Playing in the outfield a majority of the time, the pull-hitter captured his first of three home run titles in 1963, ringing up 44 seat-reachers and driving in 102 runs. But 1964 witnessed a return of batting woes. Willie hit his stride for good in '65, pounding 39 homers with 92 RBIs. He took over first base for an injured Cepeda that year, and by 1966, his first base nemesis had departed via the trade route. Permanently anchored, Willie responded with a six-year home run binge that included totals of 39, 36, 31, 36, 45 and 39. He led the league in both RBIs (105) and slugging (.545) in 1968, and in both slugging (.612) and walks (137) in 1970.

The best of these years was 1969, when the giant Giant compiled a mammoth .656 slugging percentage — baseball's highest mark in eight seasons. He also paced the circuit in on-base percentage (.458), and set a major league record with 45 intentional walks. In the 1969 All-Star Game, McCovey slammed two homers.

Even a painful, bleeding right hip didn't deter "Big Mac" during this MVP season. The 11th-year man topped the NL for the second year running in homers (45) and RBIs (126), set off by a splendid .320 average that was fifth in the league. With Willie Mays on the decline, McCovey took over the leadership role offensively for San Francisco, establishing career highs in average, homers, RBIs and slugging.

McCovey had one more year of exceptional productivity in 1970 before an arthritic hip, torn knee cartilage and broken arm lessened his effectiveness. In 1974, he was traded to San Diego, then to Oakland in 1976. The final four years of Willie's career were spent back in San Francisco, where he gained the prestige of an elder statesman at his home field and throughout the league. Still a bona-fide run producer at age 39, he clouted 28 homers

with 86 RBIs and a .280 average in 1977, earning the NL Comeback Player of the Year award. The 42-year-old retired following the 1980 season.

After leaving baseball, McCovey became vice president for a linen manufacturer, still living in his beloved San Francisco and making occasional public relations appearances for the Giants. He was made honorary captain of the 1984 NL All-Star Team.

With 2,588 games played in the big time, the 22-year veteran has certainly earned a rest from the baseball wars. His total of 521 home runs placed Big Stretch tied for 12th on the all-time list. A National League record-18 of those blasts were grand slams, and 16 of his circuit clouts were pinch homers, third best in baseball history. He is the only player to hit two home runs in the same inning twice. McCovey was 26th all time in walks (1,345), 31st in RBIs (1,555), 33rd in games, tied for 37th in extra base hits (920), 47th in both total bases (4,219) and 51st in slugging (.515).

Willie's post-career days have

ranged from the sublime to the devastating. He was elected to baseball's Hall of Fame in 1986, but in 1995 he pleaded guilty — along with fellow Hall of Famer Duke Snider — to tax evasion stemming from unreported promotional fees.

There was a tendency to overlook McCovey's feats when he was absent from the immediate on-field scene, as though only his vigorous presence would awaken the admiration of his fans. "Out of sight, out of mind" is a phrase that fits both the image of the powerful slugger and the baseballs he drove into the stratosphere.

Top 5 MVP Vote-Getters

1. Willie McCovey, San Francisco — 265
2. Tom Seaver, New York — 243
3. Hank Aaron, Atlanta — 188
4. Pete Rose, Cincinnati — 127
5. Ron Santo, Chicago — 124

1969 AMERICAN LEAGUE — HARMON KILLEBREW

Harmon Clayton Killebrew
B. June 29, 1936, Payette, Idaho

Year	Team	Games	AB	Hits	Avg.	HR	RBI	Runs	SB
1969	Min AL	162	555	153	.276	49	140	106	8

The Season

With the top five American League teams in 1968 going to the East in the first year of division play, the Western Division title was ripe for the picking in '69. Under new manager Billy Martin, the Minnesota Twins leaped from seventh place the previous year to a nine-game bulge over Oakland for the division crown.

In his first full year as the Orioles skipper, Earl Weaver brought Baltimore an Eastern Division title and pennant. The O's handled the Twins

in three straight games in the League Championship Series, but then hit only .156 against the Mets, dropping four in a row after an opening game World Series victory.

Making their debuts in 1969 were the Kansas City Royals and Seattle Pilots. Managed by past MVP Joe Gordon, the Royals beat out the Chicago White Sox for fourth place in the West. Seattle was last in the Western Division, but went down running, stealing more bases (167) than any AL team since World War II.

In an effort to beef up the offen-

sive attack after a dismal 1968 season, major league owners lowered the pitching mounds and reduced the strike zone.

Bashful Bomber

Displaying a massive upper torso, sledgehammer arms and powerfully thick wrists, Harmon Killebrew was a scary sight at the plate for American League hurlers in the 1960s and early '70s. But beneath the awesome, intimidating exterior was a quiet, bashful nature which made "The Killer" as loveable off the field as he was feared on it.

When Killebrew stepped into the right-handed batter's box, all fans, regardless of loyalties, sat up and took notice. During a 22-year career, Harmon crunched home runs with more frequency than all but Mark McGwire, Babe Ruth and Ralph Kiner, belting 573 to place fifth on the all-time list, and second in American League annals.

The 13-time All-Star, who played first base, third base and the outfield in rather unspectacular fashion, was the top AL home run hitter in six different seasons, including three in a row from 1962 to '64, and on eight occasions deposited the sphere over the fence more than 40 times. Killebrew led the junior circuit in RBIs three times, and slugging and total bases twice each. The husky gent never hit .300, but tagged 25 or more homers nine years in a row (1959–67) and 13 times in 14 years. His 393 circuit clouts in the 1960s were the most of any player.

Affectionately known as "The Fat Kid," Harmon had established himself as a constant home run threat when the 1969 season rolled along, but his weak '68 campaign (.210, 17 HRs, 40 RBIs) had Twins fans wondering if the 33-year-old's effectiveness might be dwindling.

The modest, soft-spoken Killebrew put those worries to rest in 1969, pacing the AL in home runs with 49 and RBIs with 140. The totals take on added significance when his league-leading 145 walks are considered, which helped account for a league-high .430 on-base percentage. Harmon hit .276, 20 points above his lifetime mark, and was third in total bases (324) and slugging (.584). He even stole a career-high eight bases. Those numbers translated into an MVP award for him and a Western Division championship for the Twins.

Harmon Clayton was born in Payette, Idaho, the last of four children of a professional wrestler. Killebrew was planning to take advantage of a football scholarship at the University of Oregon, when his baseball career took a giant step forward. The right-handed slugger was hitting a mind-boggling .847 in the semipro Idaho-Oregon League, and suddenly the pro scouts began appearing.

At the request of Payette resident and Idaho Senator Herman Walker, Washington Senator owner Clark Griffith sent scout Ossie Bluege to check out the 17-year-old powerhouse. Harmon made the 2,000-mile journey worthwhile, clobbering four home runs and collecting seven other hits in a three-game binge. Bluege quickly signed Killebrew for a $12,000 bonus and $6,000 annual salary for three years.

Harm desperately needed some minor league seasoning, but like many others, he suffered from the rule that stipulated a minimum of two years with the parent club after accepting a large bonus. Not only was his glove work shabby, but unused to major league pitching, Killebrew struck out in nearly half of his at-bats. Following a marriage to childhood sweetheart Elaine Roberts, he gained some much-needed time in the minors from 1956 to '58.

Several Senator bigwigs suggested Killebrew's release, but Calvin Griffith Jr. decided to gamble on the 6-foot, 195-pounder in 1959, trading third base incumbent Eddie Yost and informing new manager Cookie Lavagetto that the hot corner spot belonged to No. 3.

Harmon did not disappoint. He set the stage for what would be a remarkable season by homering on opening day, then belted eight round-trippers in a dozen at-bats soon after. Washington fans had not had much to cheer about in recent years, their team having finished in the second division for the past 12 seasons. But now they came out in droves to see the boy wonder with the bulging muscles.

Killebrew committed a league-high 30 errors at third base in '59, but Griffith Stadium fans overlooked the fielding miscues, pleased with their newfound hero's long ball abilities. Harmon wound up leading the AL in homers with 42, was runner-up in total bases (282) and slugging (.516), and third in RBIs (105).

In spite of the Senators' rise from eighth place in 1959 to fifth in '60, the franchise shifted to Minnesota for the 1961 season. The Killer quickly warmed to the new surroundings, smashing a staggering 188 round-trippers in four years, pacing the AL three times in a row (48 in 1962, 45 in '63 and 49 in '64), and driving in a league-high 126 runs in 1962. He topped the American League in slugging (.555) in 1963, and while a dislocated elbow cut short his '65 campaign, he came back to hit .286 with a home run in the seven-game World Series loss to the Dodgers. He also led the league in walks in both 1966 (103) and '67 (131), and in homers in '67 (44), but suffered a ruptured hamstring in 1968.

Following the MVP season, the 34-year-old showed he still had plenty of pop in his bat by collecting 41 homers in 1970, plus two in the LCS as the Twins were again beaten in three straight by the Orioles. His 28 circuit clouts in 1971 put him above the 500 mark for his career. Also in '71, he paced the AL in both RBIs (119) and walks (114). Harm played three more years in Minnesota, undergoing knee surgery in 1973, then concluded his playing days with the Kansas City Athletics in '75.

Killebrew took a job with E.F. Hutton Financial Services following his retirement, and was also a television broadcaster for the Twins and Oakland A's.

Although his offensive credentials were Hall of Fame material, writers were uncomfortable with the .256 lifetime batting average and lack of fielding prowess, making Harmon wait until his fourth year of eligibility before enshrining him in 1984. Killebrew, whose uniform No. 3 was retired by the Twins, was 13th all time in walks (1,559) and tied for 27th in RBIs (1,584).

Cooperstown is a richer place with the presence of the mellow, hard-working Killer. The big guy's booming drives will be remembered in every American League park where he played, as will his humble, unassuming manner and cheerful demeanor.

Top 5 MVP Vote-Getters

1. Harmon Killebrew, Minnesota — 294
2. Boog Powell, Baltimore — 227
3. Frank Robinson, Baltimore — 162
4. Frank Howard, Washington — 115
5. Reggie Jackson, Oakland — 110

1970 NATIONAL LEAGUE — JOHNNY BENCH

Johnny Lee Bench
B. December 7, 1947, Oklahoma City, Oklahoma

Year	Team	Games	AB	Hits	Avg.	HR	RBI	Runs	SB
1970	Cin NL	158	605	177	.293	45	148	97	5

The Season

The National League unveiled two brand new ballparks in 1970 — Riverfront Stadium in Cincinnati and Three Rivers Stadium in Pittsburgh — and they turned out to be the sites for the League Championship Series.

Under rookie manager Sparky Anderson, the Reds jumped from third place the previous year to dominate the Western Division by 14½ games over Los Angeles. Returning to the helm for the Pirates for his first full season since 1964 was Danny Murtaugh, whose club also rallied from a third-place finish in 1969.

Despite a pitching staff hampered by injuries, Cincy made a three runs-per-game effort stand up in a sweep of Pittsburgh for the NL pennant. The Reds then took 3–0 leads in each of the first two World Series games against Baltimore, but dropped both on the way to a five-game setback.

In a move which eventually had far-reaching effects, Curt Flood refused to report to the Phillies, to whom he'd been traded by St. Louis, challenging baseball's reserve clause with an antitrust suit. Flood was unsuccessful in court, but paved the way for similar suits won by Andy Messersmith and Dave McNally several years later.

Commissioner Bowie Kuhn returned the All-Star Game to the spectators in 1970 by re-instituting fan voting for the first time since 1957. Cincinnati's Pete Rose thrilled the hometown crowd at Riverfront by bowling over Ray Fosse at home plate for the winning run on Jim Hickman's single in the bottom of the 12th inning.

Two pitchers achieved significant feats this season. Jim Bunning of Philadelphia became the first hurler since Cy Young to win 100 games in each league with a 6–5 victory over Houston, while New York's Tom Seaver tied a major league record (since broken) with 19 strikeouts against San Diego. Seaver's 10 consecutive K's in that game were a big league mark.

Three former MVPs reached impressive career milestones in 1970. Hank Aaron and Willie Mays recorded their 3,000th hits May 17 and July 18, respectively, while Ernie Banks belted his 500th home run. Banks' Chicago teammate, Billy Williams, voluntarily ended his NL-record consecutive games played streak at 1,117.

Bench Strength

Shortly after a highly successful rookie season, Johnny Bench approached Washington Senator manager Ted Williams, asking for an autograph. Always an excellent judge of talent, Williams signed the ball, "To Johnny Bench, a sure Hall of Famer."

Considered by many the best all-around backstop in the history of the game, Bench strolled into the Hall in 1989, his first year of eligibility. The all-time leader in home runs among catchers joined fellow MVP standouts Yogi Berra, Mickey Cochrane, Roy Campanella and Gabby Hartnett.

Following a quick ascent through the Reds' farm system, Bench served notice that he was the most gifted young catcher to come along in two decades. He earned Rookie of the Year honors in 1968 with a .275 average, 15 home runs, 82 RBIs and 40 doubles, while catching 154 games, the most ever by a first-year receiver. Bench also was the league's top catcher in putouts and assists.

Poised and self-confident beyond his years, the youngster was unhesitant in ordering veteran infielders to shift positions and telling pitchers what they were doing wrong. The older players resented his brashness at first, but quickly learned the advice was sound, and respected the gritty performer's opinions. Nicknamed "The Little General" by teammates, John was such a heads-up, strong-armed catcher, he could have cracked the starting lineup regardless of his offensive contributions.

His bat was icing on the cake. The 6-foot-1, 197-pounder had a fierce right-handed stroke which resulted in a hearty .293 average his sophomore season, with 11 more homers and eight more RBIs than the previous year. His peers recognized the obvious talent, voting him the starting catcher in the 1969 All-Star Game. Bench responded to the gesture by belting a two-run homer in his first at-bat and later singling and scoring in the NL's 9–3 victory.

Success was no stranger to John, who came to the bigs as a surefire blue-chipper. Raised in Binger, Oklahoma, the one-eighth Choctaw Indian was the youngest of three boys of a former semipro catcher turned delivery truck driver. Ted Bench made no bones about the fact that he wanted one of his sons to be a ballplayer, and Johnny seemed the likely candidate.

A natural at his father's old position, John soon learned to throw a ball 250 feet on the fly from a crouch. He also played first base, third and the outfield for an American Legion team, and batted .675 for Binger High School, winning 29-of-30 decisions as a pitcher. Baseball was the teenager's favorite sport, but the "Binger Banger" also won national honors as a guard on the basketball team. Bench excelled in scholastics as well, and was the valedictorian of his senior class.

Johnny Bench. (Courtesy Cincinnati Reds.)

Immediately after graduation, John was selected in the second round of the 1965 free agent draft by Cincinnati, which assigned him to its Tampa farm team in the Florida State League. Displaying catlike quickness and a bazooka for an arm, Bench advanced to Class A the following year, despite a .248 batting average. The wholesome, vigorous catcher with the round face raised his average to .294 with 22 round-trippers in '66 with Peninsula, and was pushed up at mid-season to Buffalo in the Triple A International League.

The Buffalo fans had to wait until the next spring to get a good look at their new receiver, however, as Bench broke a thumb in his first game and was out for the remainder of the season. Johnny played nearly 100 games for Buffalo in 1967, pounding 23 homers and driving in 68 runs to merit a Minor League Player of the Year citation from *The Sporting News*, and promotion to the Reds for the final month of the campaign. He appeared in 26 games and was five at-bats shy of official rookie status, making his '68 Rookie of the Year award possible.

If Bench was impressive in his first two years in the majors, he was fantastic in 1970 when he became the youngest NL MVP award winner. The 22-year-old pounded the ball to the tune of league highs in home runs (45) and RBIs (148). Three of those homers came in succession July 26 off St. Louis' Steve Carlton. While perfecting the one-handed catching style recently initiated by Randy Hundley, the agile, enthusiastic backstop was runner-up in total bases with 355 and third in slugging at .587. All four totals were career bests, and Johnny matched his top average of .293, collected a third straight Gold Glove and was named *The Sporting News* Major League Player of the Year.

The Reds had finished fourth in 1968 and third in the Western Division the next year. But with Bench as their sparkplug, Cincy ignited to an easy West crown in '70, flying away from the pack at the mid-point of the year and beating out the Dodgers by a wide margin. Squaring off against Pittsburgh in the League Championship Series for the first of four times during John's tenure, Cincinnati won three straight, with Bench clubbing a home run and scoring twice. The power hitter homered again in the World Series and drove in three runs, but Baltimore handled the Reds in nonchalant fashion.

In only three years, the Reds catcher had established himself among baseball's elite, and although Bench and teammates would slump the next season, both would rebound in 1972. But Johnny was to face another crisis in the early 1980s when numerous injuries caused him to relinquish the position he had resurrected, placing him in an unpopular light.

Top 5 MVP Vote-Getters

1. Johnny Bench, Cincinnati — 326
2. Billy Williams, Chicago — 218
3. Tony Perez, Cincinnati — 149
4. Bob Gibson, St. Louis — 110
5. Wes Parker, Los Angeles — 91

1970 AMERICAN LEAGUE—BOOG POWELL

John Wesley Powell
B. August 17, 1941, Lakeland, Florida

Year	Team	Games	AB	Hits	Avg.	HR	RBI	Runs	SB
1970	Bal AL	154	526	156	.297	35	114	82	1

The Season

Alex Johnson of the California Angels and Boston's Carl Yastrzemski went to the wire before a batting champion was crowned in 1970, Johnson earning the title with his .3289 mark, compared to Yaz's .3286. It was Johnson's first and only Silver Bat award, depriving the pride of the Red Sox of his fourth such laurel.

Detroit shortstop Cesar Gutierrez became the first 20th century ballplayer to collect seven hits in one game, June 21 in a 9–8 win over Cleveland. The last to pull off the feat was Wilbert Robinson in 1892. Gutierrez would notch only 128 hits for his career.

These individual sideshows overshadowed divisional races in the American League that were ho-hum affairs. The regular season was a replay of the previous campaign. Both Baltimore and Minnesota won their divisions easily, and as in '69, the Orioles swiftly toppled the Twins three straight in the League Championship Series.

Baltimore's Birds feted a pair of 24-game winners in Mike Cuellar and Dave McNally, and 20-game victor Jim Palmer, along with the No. 1 offense in the league.

The Oriole express made up for its embarrassing defeat at the hands of the Mets the year before by dispatching the "Big Red Machine" from Cincinnati four games to one in the World Series. This particular October showcased the hitting and fielding talents of Baltimore's Brooks Robinson, who posted a .429 Series average and drove Cincy hitters to distraction with his third base play.

Also this season, 1948 MVP Lou Boudreau was inducted into the Hall of Fame, and the Seattle Pilots became the Milwaukee Brewers.

Baltimore Bulwark

The Baltimore Orioles were baseball's most impressive team in the late 1960s and early '70s, and sportswriters almost always extolled the club's virtues with strong references to the Robinsons—Frank and Brooks—and a stingy pitching staff. In the next breath, almost as an afterthought, would usually come the mention of the team's gargantuan first baseman, Boog Powell.

Although "Big John" was generally regarded as third fiddle in this terrifying triumvirate of hitters, his physical magnitude took a back seat to very few throughout the American League. Fluctuating in weight between 230 and 290 pounds, Boog was a furious eater whose trips to an endocrinologist and psychologist did little to deter his penchant for hearty meals.

The Florida native may have looked like the inspiration for the "Beer Barrel Polka," but his .326 batting average through five pressure-packed League Championship Series gained the big lefty a well-deserved reputation for clutch performances. During his two most impressive campaigns, Powell responded with .385 and .429 LCS averages, playing a major part in spurring the O's into the World Series in both 1969 and '70.

Signed for a then-whopping $25,000 bonus by Baltimore in 1959, the first sacker quickly became one of the Orioles' most esteemed properties. After three stellar campaigns in the minors, Boog advanced to Baltimore.

In his rookie year of '62, Boog became an immediate starter. By 1964, he had escalated to a .290 average with 39 homers and 99 RBIs. During Baltimore's first pennant year, 1966, "The Boogeyman" contributed with 109 ribbies, 34 round-trippers and a .287 average. He also batted .357 in the World Series sweep of Los Angeles, and became the first player to compete in a major league World Series after having appeared in the Little League World Series. On July 6, Powell tied an AL record with 11 RBIs in a doubleheader. Boog and the O's slumped the next two years, but returned in '69, with Powell producing an exemplary .304 season with 121 RBIs and 37 home runs in the best effort of his career.

After Baltimore was ambushed by the Mets in the World Series, the full-bodied first baseman and his mates set their sights on demolishing all comers in 1970. For the first time in eight big league seasons, the amiable 29-year-old put superior seasons back to back. While the Orioles ran roughshod over their American League East opponents, Powell was at the head of the charge, slamming 35 homers, driving in 114 runs and hitting .297.

In the LCS sweep of Minnesota, Boog continued his torrential hitting, leading the Birds of Baltimore with a .429 average and topping both teams in RBIs with six. His hot bat continued to smolder in the World Series against Cincinnati, where Boog blasted four-baggers in each of the first two contests, as the Orioles went on to nab the World Championship.

That winter, the 1970 exploits of the powerful port-sider were rewarded when he became the third Baltimore player to win an MVP (after Brooks and Frank Robinson, of course).

At the peak of his game, no one in baseball delivered more distant clouts than the 6-foot-4½-inch powerhouse, with the possible exception of Harmon Killebrew. Powell's titanic blasts included a 469-footer in Baltimore in 1962, and a shot over the Tiger Stadium roof in '69. Three times he blasted three round-trippers in the same game, once in consecutive at-bats. One of baseball's slowest runners, the big guy's whippet-like swing put the hurt on many an AL hurler. Standing deep in the batter's box, Boog would surge forward like a hound on a leash, unloading his Ruthian swat with the force of a gale.

The lumberjack style was not in evidence in 1971, due mainly to a hairline fracture in Boog's right wrist. The next season, Powell was plagued by deteriorating sight in his left eye, and while a temporary attempt at wearing glasses proved unsuccessful, he still managed to connect for 21 circuit clouts.

Flirting with 300 pounds, Boog worked earnestly in the winter of '72, dieting and jogging to get himself down to 250. But a shoulder injury led to a power decline (11 HRs). Powell had one more productive year, playing for ex-teammate Frank Robinson in his Cleveland Indian managing debut in '75, before retiring after the 1977 campaign in a Dodger uniform.

Following baseball, the freckle-faced Boog gained instant notoriety — unmatched since his MVP days — when he became one of many ex-athletes to star in the popular Miller Lite beer commercials. Powell also took great pleasure in owning and operating a marina in his native state. Fishing, like eating, has always been a delight for the fun-loving mountain of a man, who is a survivor of colon cancer. And speaking of food, a popular attraction beyond the right field fence in Oriole Park at Camden Yards is Boog's Barbeque.

It's safe to say that he had a pleas-

ant 17-year hitch in baseball as well. Over that span, Baltimore's all-time home run leader cracked 339 into the seats. Despite this plethora of four-baggers and 1,226 RBIs, Powell amazingly never led the AL in either category. He did, however, pace the junior circuit in slugging in 1964 (.606) and in fielding average (.997) in '75.

When Oriole fans gather to reminisce about their team's first dynastic era, the jumbo outline of the Baltimore Boogeyman casts a giant shadow.

Top 5 MVP Vote-Getters

1. Boog Powell, Baltimore — 234
2. Tony Oliva, Minnesota — 157
3. Harmon Killebrew, Minnesota — 152
4. Carl Yastrzemski, Boston — 136
5. Frank Howard, Washington — 91

1971 NATIONAL LEAGUE — JOE TORRE

Joseph Paul Torre
B. July 18, 1940, Brooklyn, New York

Year	Team	Games	AB	Hits	Avg.	HR	RBI	Runs	SB
1971	SL NL	161	634	230	.363	24	137	97	4

The Season

More than a decade had passed since Bill Mazeroski's dramatic home run gave the Pittsburgh Pirates their startling 1960 World Series championship, and in 1971, the Bucs triumphantly returned to baseball's summit.

This time, the Pirates bested the San Francisco Giants for the pennant, then downed the Baltimore Orioles in a thrilling, seven-game World Series, becoming only the sixth club in history to rally from a two games-to-none deficit.

The 1971 epic was to be dubbed "the Clemente Series," and rightly so,

as the stately 37-year-old right fielder dominated the fall classic with a .414 average, antelope-smooth base running and a powerful, pinpoint throwing arm which kept enemy Orioles at bay.

Individual achievements this season included two-time MVP Willie Mays scoring his 1,950th career run — transcending the National League mark held by three-time MVP Stan Musial — and collecting his major league record-22nd extra-inning home run; 1957 MVP Hank Aaron belting his 600th career homer; 1963 MVP Sandy Koufax being inducted into the Hall of Fame; Montreal's Ron Hunt setting the dubious mark of being hit by a pitched ball

more times (50) in one season than any other player; and Philadelphia pitcher Rick Wise hitting two home runs and throwing a no-hitter June 23 against Cincinnati.

Torre's Time

Fifteen years after Milwaukee Braves scout John "Honey" Russell reported him "too fat, too slow, with absolutely no baseball future," the proud and relentless Joe Torre ripped up the National League.

It was a talismanic season for the Brooklyn native in 1971. His war club was more than just finely honed lumber; it was an enchanted wand. The Cardinal co-captain's .363 average was an astounding 66 points above his eventual .297 lifetime mark. Hits fell in clusters— 230 in all— including 24 round-trippers. The 31-year-old led his second-place club in home runs, topped the NL in four major offensive categories— average, RBIs (137), hits and total bases (352) — and rapped out at least one safety in all but 28 games.

The man had come a long way from the overweight teen his brother had openly criticized in the late 1950s. At that time, Frank Torre was first baseman for the Milwaukee Braves, while 16-year-old Joe was tipping the scales at 240. In spite of his bulk, his short stroke was already groomed for the outfield alleys. But when Russell was summoned for an evaluation, Joe's appearance held more weight in the scout's report than did the youngster's talent.

Afterward, big brother Frank began his derogatory attacks against Joe's overzealous devotion to Mama Torre's pasta. The criticism was harsh, and for an entire year the brothers refused to speak to one another. Despite the anger and bitterness, young Joe perceived the wisdom contained in the taunts. He worked his weight down and began learning the mechanics of catching. It wasn't long before the same Honey Russell was signing him to a Braves contract.

His big break came when Milwaukee's regular catcher, Del Crandall, was felled with an injury. The 21-year-old Torre was quickly called up to the parent club, and hit .278.

In his eight years as a Milwaukee/ Atlanta Brave, the burly signal caller was arguably the best catcher in the game. The swarthy Italian was a model of consistent, high-grade efficiency, both at bat and behind the plate, especially from 1963 through 1967. During that time, his lowest average was a solid .277, with highs of .315 and .321. His RBI totals twice exceeded 100, and for four straight years he drove 20 or more balls into the stands. His first Atlanta season was spectacular, with a .315 average, 36 homers and 101 ribbies.

But financial woes, the serious illness of his daughter, a steady stream of injuries and a tempestuous contract dispute combined for an atypical Torre performance in 1968. Prior to the 1969 season, Torre was sent packing to the St. Louis Cardinals.

Torre greeted the artificial turf expanses of Busch Stadium with talk of rebirth. Manning a new position, first base, he hit .289 and once again reached the elite 100-plus club in RBIs. Slimming down to 200 pounds, he stroked home 100 more teammates in 1970. Another position switch seemed to have little bearing on his productivity that year. Playing third base along with some catching, Torre rapped out what was then a career-high 203 safeties and registered a personal-best .325 average.

But his 1970 excellence was strictly a warm-up for the magical MVP year of 1971. For the first time since becoming a professional, Torre went an entire season without donning the tools of ignorance, fielding the hot corner slot for all but one of the club's games. The freedom from catching, he said, gave him a newfound sense of concentration at bat.

But as quickly as it had appeared, the overwhelming authority in Torre's bat vanished permanently. His average nose-dived 74 points to .289 in 1972, as he drove in 56 fewer runs and hit a feeble 11 home runs. The 1973 season was more of the same (.287, 13 HRs, 69 RBIs), and 1974 was almost a carbon copy.

Earmarking Torre as a future skipper, the New York Mets acquired him prior to 1975, and Joe proceeded to fall promptly on his face before his hometown fans during the following schedule. Embarrassed at his initial showing, he rebounded in 1976 to hit .306 as a 36-year-old in his last full year as a player.

Met management, tiring of last-place finishes, fired manager Joe Frazier 45 games into the 1977 season, replacing him with Torre. Before too long, baseball scribes were wryly noting that the rookie manager and his best ballplayer were probably under the same baseball cap.

The Mets finished dead last in 1977, 1978 and 1979, then managed to move up a notch to fifth during the 1980 and '81 seasons. It was progress, but it was painfully slow, and Torre was ousted after 1981. His old club, the Braves, hired him for the 1982 season. In Atlanta, the triumphs that had so eluded him in New York came instantaneously, as Torre molded his team into Western Division champions.

A bevy of injuries relegated the Braves to second-place finishes in 1983 and '84, and an impatient management fired Torre one day after the '84 campaign concluded.

With no managerial offers on the table, Torre took a job as a sportscaster for the California Angels, spreading his insights and baseball smarts to a wider audience. But after five years behind a mike, Joe was ready to return to the dugout. The last-place Cardinals handed him the reins at the tail end of the 1990 season, and the team vaulted to second place in the National League East in his first full year at the helm. Three consecutive third-place finishes followed, and with St. Louis sitting in fourth place one-third of the way through the 1995 campaign, Torre was shown the door once again.

Torre didn't have to wait long for the phone to ring. George Steinbrenner hired him to be the first New York native to manage the Yankees, and the decision has proven to be a brilliant one. Joe's NL managerial mark was 109 games below .500, and he'd never appeared in a World Series as a player or manager, but his Yankee teams won 582 regular-season games from 1996 through 2001, as well as an amazing four World Championships. The most incredible of those seasons was 1998 when New York won an AL-record 114 games before going 11–2 in post-season play.

Joe, who was baseball's highest paid manager at $3 million a year, took some heat in 2001 for loading up the AL All-Star Team with Yankees. Of the 21 players he was allowed to add to those voted in by the fans, seven were members of his team. The last time that many Yanks made the All-Star Team was in 1942 when nine were selected. But the Yankees won another Eastern Division title and came within one inning of capturing their fifth World Championship in a six-year span. Torre was rewarded with a contract extension through 2004.

Torre, who underwent surgery for prostate cancer in 1999, has received high marks for his fair yet firm treatment of players, as well as for his patience, honesty, intelligence, grit and ability to motivate. All in all, not bad for a guy "with absolutely no baseball future."

Top 5 MVP Vote-Getters

1. Joe Torre, St. Louis — 318
2. Willie Stargell, Pittsburgh — 222
3. Hank Aaron, Atlanta — 180
4. Bobby Bonds, San Francisco — 139
5. Roberto Clemente, Pittsburgh — 87

1971 American League — Vida Blue

Vida Rochelle Blue
B. July 28, 1949, Mansfield, Louisiana

Year	Team	Games	W	L	ERA	IP	SO	BB	ShO
1971	Oak AL	39	24	8	1.82	312	301	88	8

The Season

The virtually invincible Baltimore Orioles, who boasted four 20-game winners in Dave McNally, Jim Palmer, Mike Cuellar and Pat Dobson, won their final 11 regular-season games for a third consecutive Eastern Division title, then swept Oakland in the League Championship Series. Only one other team in major league history — the 1920 Chicago White Sox — fielded four 20-game winners.

But following a pair of victories against Pittsburgh in the World Series, the O's fell in seven. More than 60 million people viewed the first-ever fall classic night game on prime time television, and the successful venture resulted in all future weekday Series games being played at night.

The Athletics had matched Baltimore's 101 regular-season wins in 1971, beginning their dynasty by dethroning two-time defending Western Division champion Minnesota.

Detroit pitcher Mickey Lolich toiled an incredible 376 innings, the most in major league baseball since 1917 and the highest amount in the junior circuit in nearly 60 years.

After dropping eight All-Star Games in a row, the American League finally pulled out a 6–4 decision. A record-tying six home runs — by past and future MVPs Hank Aaron, Johnny Bench, Roberto Clemente, Reggie Jackson, Harmon Killebrew and Frank Robinson — accounted for all of the scoring on a windy night in Detroit. It would mark the AL's only All-Star Game win between 1963 and 1982.

After displaying bizarre behavior resulting in numerous benchings and fines, 1970 batting champion Alex Johnson was suspended by the California Angels June 26. Three months later, Johnson was awarded nearly $30,000 in back pay by an arbitrator who declared that the outfielder should have been treated the same as a physically disabled player because he was "emotionally incapacitated."

Instant Celebrity

Vida Rochelle Blue, who was as colorful as his name, had the world in the palm of his hand by the time he was 22 years old. The sensational instant celebrity burst onto the American League scene in 1971, capturing the imagination of baseball fans across the country in his first full season. Lighthearted yet intelligent, enthusiastic but composed, the flashy left-hander won 24 games with a league-leading 1.82 ERA, guiding the Oakland Athletics to the Western Division championship.

And while the glittering young star drew huge audiences whenever and wherever he performed, his nova was destined to burn out ingloriously in a streaking slide into a black hole. Contract squabbles, a threat to "blow away" a reporter, a three-month prison term for possession of cocaine … all would follow in the next dozen years, permanently tarnishing the image of a man who could have had it all.

As quarterback for DeSoto High School in Mansfield, Louisiana, where he was born and raised, Blue was a "can't miss" football prospect. Representatives from many major colleges begged the hard-throwing signal caller to accept full scholarships. But Vida's father had just passed away and his mother was feebly attempting to support six children. A professional football career was at least four years away, while baseball scouts were willing to provide immediate cash. So to help his family, Blue inked a contract with the Athletics upon graduation in 1967 — despite having signed a letter of intent with the University of Houston — accepting a bonus reported between $28,000 and $50,000.

The first assignment for the strong southpaw was Burlington, Iowa, where the 19-year-old hurled a no-hitter and paced the Midwest League in strikeouts in '68. Vida failed to make the big club in the spring of 1970, but won 12-of-15 decisions with a 2.17 ERA for Iowa of the American Association, earning a return trip to Oakland. His two victories late that year consisted of a no-hitter against the Minnesota Twins and a one-hitter. The former made the 21-year-old the youngest pitcher to toss a no-no in 36 years.

Getting by all season on one basic pitch — a heater — Blue dropped an opening day decision in 1971, then won 10 straight. The AL's starting All-Star Game pitcher gave up two home runs in three innings, but was credited with the victory over the NL. (A decade later, wearing a San Francisco uniform, Vida would become the first moundsman to win All-Star Games for both leagues.)

Eccentric Oakland owner Charlie Finley, who had offered his phenomenon $2,000 to legally change his name to "True Blue," was paying the new sensation less than $14,000 in '71, but reaping the benefits of the youngster's glamour season. Attendance at A's home games shot up 400 percent over the previous year when Blue was on the hill; on the road, Blue's pitching stints nearly always doubled the crowd.

With five weeks remaining in the '71 campaign, the seemingly tireless left-hander had won 21-of-25 decisions and was atop the league charts in ERA, shutouts, strikeouts and complete games. Blue finally wore down, however, losing four of his last seven games. But a 1.82 ERA and eight shutouts paced the circuit, while a 24–8 record resulted in runner-up marks in triumphs and win percentage (.750), so his selection as the AL's MVP and Cy Young Award winner came as no surprise.

The powerhouse with a 95 mph fastball was overwhelmed at his overnight success, demanding a $90,000 contract in 1972; but after a holdout, he settled for much less. A disgruntled, rusty Blue faded on the mound, collecting only six wins but earning saves in Game 5 of the ALCS and Game 1 of the World Series.

Revitalized in 1973, Vida tallied 20 wins against only nine defeats, but was 0–1 in the playoffs and lost his fourth straight post-season game during Oakland's four games-to-three World Series triumph over the Mets. Prior to the 1974 season, Blue announced that he was considering quitting baseball to join the new World Football League. Instead, the southpaw "slipped" to 17 victories in '74, then fired a two-hitter to beat Baltimore in the LCS. Blue enjoyed another splendid campaign in '75 when he racked up a 22–11 record and 3.01 ERA, leading the Athletics to their fifth West Division crown in a row.

Unable to keep pace with the rising salary structure, Finley was twice thwarted in efforts to sell Blue by Commissioner Bowie Kuhn, who declared that such moves would upset the competitive balance. Vida won 18 games in 1976, but skidded to 14–19 in '77 when the A's plummeted to last in the West. Finally, the gifted hurler was traded to San Francisco in 1978 for seven players and $400,000.

Twenty-nine-year-old Blue won 18 games for the resurgent Giants in '78, winning *The Sporting News'* NL Player of the Year award, but averaged only 12 per season the next three years. He battled with the media, threatening a reporter whose story had displeased the struggling pitcher. In 1982,

when he won 13 games, Vida was dealt to Kansas City for three players, including Atlee Hammaker. In '83, he sank to 0–5 before being released while under investigation for drug use. Then, in a shocker to KC fans and the baseball world, four Royals, including Vida, were arrested on drug charges. On January 1, 1984, he donned yet another uniform — this time a prisoner's garb — and entered the Federal Correctional Institute in Fort Worth, Texas, to begin serving a 90-day sentence.

Although not under contract to any ballclub, the left-hander was suspended from baseball by Kuhn in July for the remainder of the 1984 season for "continued use of and involvement with cocaine during the 1982 and 1983 seasons." He was free to sell his services to any team beginning in the 1985 campaign, and wound up his career with two mediocre seasons with the Giants. Blue's attempt to re-join the A's for the 1987 campaign ended when he failed a pre-season drug test.

Vida Blue, a colorful, talented athlete, was given a golden opportunity to combine huge personal gains with overwhelming popularity. He experienced that sweet taste of success, but gave it up, proving that even the most gifted of ballplayers is not immune to self-destruction.

Top 5 MVP Vote-Getters

1. Vida Blue, Oakland — 268
2. Sal Bando, Oakland — 182
3. Frank Robinson, Baltimore — 170
4. Brooks Robinson, Baltimore — 163
5. Mickey Lolich, Detroit — 155

1972 National League — Johnny Bench

Johnny Lee Bench
B. December 7, 1947, Oklahoma City, Oklahoma

Year	Team	Games	AB	Hits	Avg.	HR	RBI	Runs	SB
1972	Cin NL	147	538	145	.270	40	125	87	6

The Season

The 1972 campaign got off to a belated start, thanks to a first-ever general strike which lasted 13 days and forced the cancellation of the first 86 regular-season games. The key issue was an increase in player pensions, and both the owners and ballplayers claimed victory when a raise of $500,000 in the pension fund was finally agreed upon.

The delay nearly upset Roberto Clemente's bid to reach the 3,000-hit plateau, but the Pirates' splendid right fielder finally collected the landmark safety at the close of the season. That final hit of Clemente's career came just three months before his tragic death.

Cincinnati's Big Red Machine was in full force in '72, motoring to a second Western Division title and National League pennant in three years. The Reds outdistanced Houston and Los Angeles by 10½ games each before nipping Pittsburgh in five in the League Championship Series. Oakland then edged Cincinnati in a seven-game World Series.

San Diego's Nate Colbert was glad he didn't call in sick August 1. His 13 RBIs in a double-header sweep of Atlanta set a major league record, and his five home runs tied a big league mark.

For the first time since 1960, two different NL hurlers on the same team threw no-hitters in one season. Chicago's Burt Hooton accomplished the feat against Philadelphia April 16, and teammate Milt Pappas twirled his gem September 2 versus San Diego, missing a perfect game by one pitch.

Other pitchers who stood out in '72 were Philadelphia's Steve Carlton, San Francisco's Jim Barr and Cincy's Clay Carroll. Carlton won nearly half of his last-place team's contests on the way to his first of four Cy Young

Awards, and Barr established a major league record by retiring 41 consecutive batters over two games, including the first 20 St. Louis hitters he faced August 29. With the era of the relief pitcher in full swing, Carroll saved 37 games, the most ever at that time.

Back in the Saddle

A broken thumb, fractured fingers, lower back spasms, six broken bones in one foot and four in the other ... the injuries Johnny Bench suffered while catching read like the medical report of an entire hockey team following a bench-clearing brawl. The dependable receiver tied a major league record by catching 100 or more games in 13 consecutive years, but paid the price for the glory he earned.

Without a doubt, the backstop position is the most demanding job in baseball. Bench once said that he felt more worn out after catching one game than he did playing a full week at first base. The physically and mentally draining occupation can be torturous and debilitating, so it should have come as no surprise when the 32-year-old Cincinnati mainstay told management in 1980 that beginning the following year he would catch only two days a week. John had played sparingly at first base, third and the outfield, but those spots were already well manned, and Reds officials let it be known that No. 5 was putting them on the spot with this declaration. Bench acknowledged his presumptuous attitude, but replied that he'd kept them *off* the spot for 13 years.

Fan reaction was mixed to the veteran's resolution, but the dissenters were more vocal. Spectators with short memories booed the man who had been the heart of the Big Red Machine in the

1970s, but the battered receiver did not relent. He backed up Dan Driessen at first base in the strike-shortened 1981 season, appearing in only 52 games, then took over the third base job the following year after Ray Knight was traded to Houston. Johnny played in more than 100 games in 1983, mostly at third base, before retiring.

The solidly built slugger ended his glorious 17-year career with 389 home runs (top 40 all time). Johnny was named to 14 All-Star Teams, batting .379 in Star competition, and the 10-time Gold Glove award winner paced NL catchers in fielding average in 1976 and double plays in '74. He put together 11 seasons of 20-plus homers, and was ninth all time in putouts by a catcher (9,249). Bench helped propel the Reds to six division titles, four pennants and two World Series victories.

John began this serious assault on the record books back in 1970 when, at age 22, he was recognized as the league's best catcher. He decided to go for all the marbles with a $500,000 contract request over three years, but the Reds offered much less. Johnny finally settled for $80,000 per year after a holdout, and when he slumped to .238 with 61 RBIs in 1971, and the Reds dipped from first in the West to fourth, the fans booed their heroes relentlessly. Bench was one of the crowd's frequent targets, and in response, sarcastically tipped his hat to the crowd, then lashed out against them in the media for their fickle behavior.

Determined to atone for his actions and a bleak season, Bench apologized to the fans, then came back with a vengeance in 1972, wreaking havoc on National League pitchers with his bat and sending fear into the hearts of base runners with a cannon-like arm. Despite a weak start (only five RBIs in

Johnny Bench. (Courtesy Cincinnati Reds.)

April), blamed in part on worry over his mother's poor health, the more mature, charming receiver again led the league in home runs and RBIs (40, 125), and was third in total bases (291), slugging (.541) and walks (100), while hitting a respectable .270. Seven of those homers came in a five-day stretch (May 30–June 3), and Bench wound up hitting round-trippers in all 12 NL parks that season.

The Reds returned to the top of the Western Division in 1972, then received some heroics from their clutch-hitting catcher in the playoffs. Pittsburgh led the fifth and deciding game of the LCS 3–2 heading into the bottom of the ninth inning when Bench homered to tie it, with Cincy scoring the winning run moments later on a

wild pitch. As in 1970, the Reds were thwarted in the World Series, this time by Oakland in seven games, despite Bench's four-bagger in Game 6. The loss did nothing to dampen a banner season for John, who secured a second MVP award in three years.

Off the field, the highly-visible Bench was making a name for himself in the entertainment world. Johnny began singing professionally in nightclubs in the early '70s, and had a cameo role in the "Mission Impossible" television series. Bench also hosted a half-hour show called "MVP Johnny Bench," then began "The Baseball Bunch" series.

Meanwhile, Johnny continued to be a significant force on the field throughout the 1970s, with his team winning division titles four more times, and pennants and World Series in '75 and '76. Bench was named the fall classic's MVP in 1976 when he belted two round-trippers, drove in six runs and hit a remarkable .533 in the Reds' sweep of the Yankees.

Cincinnati's lifetime leader in homers and RBIs survived some stormy

years in the late '70s, highlighted by a marriage to model Vicki Chesser and a bitter, well-publicized divorce less than a year later.

While teammates George Foster, Pete Rose and Joe Morgan went the free-agent route, Bench remained in Cincinnati where he owned a couple of restaurants and a bowling alley. The avid golfer and hunter finally decided that baseball had ceased to be fun, and announced his retirement early in the 1983 season. Going out in style, the Reds star cranked a two-run homer on "Salute Johnny Bench Night." He was elected to the Hall of Fame in 1989, and was voted to baseball's All-Century Team in 1999.

Throughout a 17-year career, Bench was his own man. He played the game with a boundless determination, but when damage to his body began taking its toll, steadfastly stuck to a decision against fulltime catching, despite the subsequent negative reactions. Behind the plate, he ranks as one of baseball's all-time greats, both offensively and defensively.

Top 5 MVP Vote-Getters

1. Johnny Bench, Cincinnati — 263
2. Billy Williams, Chicago — 211
3. Willie Stargell, Pittsburgh — 201
4. Joe Morgan, Cincinnati — 197
5. Steve Carlton, Philadelphia — 124

1972 AMERICAN LEAGUE — DICK ALLEN

Richard Anthony Allen
B. March 8, 1942, Wampum, Pennsylvania

Year	Team	Games	AB	Hits	Avg.	HR	RBI	Runs	SB
1972	Chi AL	148	506	156	.308	37	113	90	19

The Season

The Oakland A's began their impressive reign at the top of the heap in 1972, as owner Charlie Finley's club

brawled its way to the World Championship.

Detroit snared the American League East by one-half game over the Boston Red Sox, who were heavily penalized by a strike-shortened season that robbed them of the opportunity to play as many games as the Tigers.

The Capitol City of the United States lost its franchise in '72, as the

Dick Allen. (Courtesy Chicago White Sox.)

Washington Senators shifted to Arlington to become the Texas Rangers. League officials moved the Rangers from the Eastern to the Western Division, transferring the Milwaukee Brewers to the East. Both clubs finished in the basement.

After besting Detroit in the LCS three games to two, Oakland defeated Cincinnati in a World Series that was a baseball purist's dream affair. All of the contests but one were low-scoring battles, with six of the seven games decided by one run. Oakland's Gene Tenace was the Series batting star, hitting .348, slamming a record-tying four homers and pacing both teams in RBIs (nine) and runs (five).

Other highlights this season included three-time MVP Yogi Berra being inducted into the Hall of Fame and Detroit's Ed Brinkman establishing a major league record for shortstops with 72 consecutive errorless games and 331 total chances without a miscue. For the first time in big league history, two brothers—Tom and Bill Haller—served as the catcher and umpire, respectively, in a game. Tom's Tigers were edged 1–0 by Kansas City in this July 14 contest.

Crashing Out

He loved the game fervently, but only if allowed to play it on his own idiosyncratic terms. Any semblance, real or imagined, of style-cramping authoritarian restrictions or racially slanted injustice was answered with sneering rebuttal or outright disobedience. Dick Allen was given an inordinate amount of leeway in these transgressions because of his immense talent for making the horsehide exit the premises. He paid dearly, however, for the personal freedom that came with bucking the system. Fans booed and bombarded Allen on the field, the media attacked his actions relentlessly, and owners and managers shuttled him about like an unwanted relative. Dick's answer was always increased defiance, until finally his unavailing war against the world became larger than his extraordinary ability.

Raised among nine children by his part-Cherokee mother, Dick was one of four brothers who dominated the rural Pennsylvania sports scene. Two of those brothers, Hank and Ron, wound up playing major league baseball. Dick rejected more than 50 basketball scholarships to sign with the Philadelphia Phillies for the largest bonus ever received by a black ballplayer up to that time: $60,000.

Playing second base, shortstop and the outfield, Allen tore up three minor leagues from 1961 through '63, then joined the Phillies in 1964. By that time, he wore the racial scars of being the first black player to perform in Little Rock, Arkansas, where he was harassed mercilessly with signs, obscene phone calls and vocal abuse. His baseball hero was sunshiny Ernie Banks, but by the time Allen had attained the big time, his experiences had turned him into Ernie's opposite. Allen likened his ballplayer's existence to that of a plantation slave, and he made many enemies spouting off about various rules and regulations.

Richie began his tumultuous journey in the least tolerant of all big league cities—Philadelphia—where unforgiving spectators are legendary. Despite capturing Rookie of the Year honors in '64, the aloof newcomer was blamed for his team's colossal pennant swoon. The following year, a fight with teammate Frank Thomas ended with the latter's banishment, and Philly fans greeted this decision by hurling objects at Allen, who took to wearing a batting helmet as he played third base.

Sportswriters publicly speculated about a serious 1967 hand injury to Allen, all but totally dismissing his explanation involving a car headlight. Management insulted him by offering a conditional contract in '68, based on his hand's recovery. Angered, Richie went out of his way to show his displeasure the next two years, missing team meetings, batting practice, planes and spring training. Determined to get out of the "City of Brotherly Love," he brought the matter to a head by purposely skipping a double-header and getting suspended for a month.

This turmoil was hardly reflected in his superb on-field performances. The assault began with a monstrous rookie season in 1964 when Allen registered 201 hits, averaged .318, poked 29 homers and drove in 91 runs, leading the league in total bases (352), runs scored (125) and triples (13). A .302 batting mark in '65 was followed by a superior 1966 effort when "Thunder" struck for 40 home runs and topped the circuit in slugging (.632). In 1967, he led the way in on-base percentage; in '68, he hit 33 homers and drove in 90 runs; and in '69, he slugged at a .573 pace. The only negatives between the white lines were a propensity to whiff and a lack of fielding skills.

Philadelphia traded its unhappy slugger prior to the 1970 season. During a big statistical campaign as a St. Louis Cardinal, Allen publicly complained about his contractual terms, and the Redbirds swapped him to the Dodgers in 1971. But after one year on the West Coast, it was on to the Chicago White Sox. Three trades in as many years were too much for the fiercely autonomous figure, who insisted he was retiring. But Sox manager Chuck Tanner wooed the controversial 30-year-old, convincing Richie that he need only show up by game-time each day.

Armed with this unprecedented backing, a contented Allen set about the task of thrashing the American League. Wielding a heavy bat, he unloaded a league-high 37 homers; topped the circuit in RBIs (113), slugging (.603), walks (99) and on-base percentage (.422); was runner-up in total bases (305); and hit .308. On July 31, Allen became the first player since 1950 to hit two inside-the-park homers in one game. Less than a month later, he became only the fourth player to hit a home run into Comiskey Park's center field bleachers.

The steel-wristed Allen nearly brought the club into pennant contention single-handedly, with the team finally settling into second place. For one glorious year, he blossomed into an effusive team leader, easily earning the MVP award with 21-of-24 first-place votes.

In a further attempt to inspire their superstar, the White Sox granted Allen a three-year pact for a record $675,000, but the success of 1972 proved short-lived. A fractured left leg virtually aborted the 1973 season. In '74, Allen still pounded the ball to a .301 tune and led the league with 32 homers and a .563 slugging average, but when the Sox tottered from contention, Dick began missing games before going AWOL for the final three weeks of the year.

A seemingly humbled Allen was returned to Philly, staying out of trouble for two years. During that time, his booming bat grew suddenly silent, and although he played on a division winner in '76, Dick's role had been reduced to platoon duty. Oakland acquired his services for 1977, but still struggling at the plate, the 35-year-old retired at mid-season.

Allen titled his autobiography *Crash*, and no one asked why. Following retirement, his uninsured house burned to the ground and his marriage dissolved. The Texas Rangers utilized him as a batting instructor in the early '80s, and he served as a White Sox minor league instructor in 1988.

The six-time All-Star with a lifetime .292 average had battled the system in Don Quixote fashion for 15 campaigns, clouting 351 career four-baggers. Yet, as astonishing as his achievements were, there will always be speculation about the towering heights Dick Allen could have ascended without the excess baggage of total intolerance.

Top 5 MVP Vote-Getters

1. Dick Allen, Chicago — 321
2. Joe Rudi, Oakland — 164
3. Sparky Lyle, New York — 158
4. Carlton Fisk, Boston — 96
5. Bobby Murcer, New York — 89

1973 National League — Pete Rose

Peter Edward Rose
B. April 14, 1941, Cincinnati, Ohio

Year	Team	Games	AB	Hits	Avg.	HR	RBI	Runs	SB
1973	Cin NL	160	680	230	.338	5	64	115	10

The Season

The season-long struggle between the powerful offense of the Cincinnati Reds and the tightly knit defense of the Los Angeles Dodgers ended with Cincy on top of the Western Division by 3½ games in 1973. Looking forward to their third World Series in four years, the Reds were derailed by the "You gotta believe" edition of the New York Mets.

Winners of the East nearly by default, the Mets posted the lowest first-place percentage (.509) of any division- or pennant-winning team ever, and were the only ballclub in their division to finish over .500. The unlikely aggregation from New York then bested the Reds in a five-game League Championship Series. Managed by three-time MVP Yogi Berra, the Mets finally bowed to Oakland in a seven-game World Series.

Legendary Most Valuable Players of the not-too-distant past who made the baseball spotlight in 1973 included Roberto Clemente, inducted into the Hall of Fame following his tragic 1972 death; Willie Mays, who played in his last World Series in his final season, going 2-for-7 for the Mets; and Henry Aaron, finishing the year only one home run short of Babe Ruth's career record of 714.

A couple of obscure records were broken in June of this season. Philadelphia's Ken Brett set a major league mark for pitchers by homering in four consecutive games in which he appeared, while Bobby Bonds of San Francisco hit his National League-record 22nd home run to lead off a game.

Blue Collar Red

To say that Pete Rose hustled when he played baseball is like saying that Beethoven's "Ode to Joy" is an upbeat little ditty. Both the ballplayer's vigorous enthusiasm and the resounding crescendo of the maestro's masterpiece spoke volumes in terms of stirring emotions. In truth, observing Rose's exhilarated fervor on the diamond, Beethoven's "Ode" seemed the perfect background music.

But an apparent refusal to face the music has clouded the incredible persona of the man who many believe belongs in the Hall of Fame despite his status as an outsider from the only game he's ever loved. Banished from baseball for life in 1989 by former Commissioner Bart Giamatti, who was convinced that Rose had bet on baseball games while managing the Cincinnati Reds — including his own team's games — Rose lobbies baseball officials and pleads his case to the fans for reinstatement so that he can take his place in Cooperstown among baseball's other immortals. And even though his public support seems to be growing, he's still outside looking in, like a kid peering through a knothole in a ballyard fence.

Pete's unconstrained style was strongly influenced by his gritty father, a Cincinnati legend who dominated local semipro football games well into his 40s. The elder Rose instilled in young Petey the competitive drive necessary for successfully attaining the baseball career both sought for the youngster. Rose began his long excursion toward stardom after signing a Class D contract with his hometown Reds in 1960. Within three years, the slightly built second baseman had wedged his way into the starting lineup of the parent club.

The 22-year-old came through with a solid .273 average, scored 101 runs and nabbed the league's Rookie of the Year award for 1963. Cynically dubbed "Charlie Hustle" by Whitey Ford during an exhibition game after he ran to first base on a walk, Rose turned the negative sobriquet into a badge of honor in the years to come.

In the next four campaigns, he gained upper body strength, was switched to the outfield and registered a trio of .300-plus seasons, leading the league in hits (209) in 1965 for the first of seven times. His .335 batting average in 1968 topped the circuit at a time when the entire league averaged only .243. A .348 effort and another hitting title immediately followed.

Ironically, Pete's 1973 MVP campaign was the only time a division-winning team for which he played failed to snare the League Championship Series. It was a typical, if not particularly overwhelming, Rose year; but with the "Big Red Machine" in full gear, the time had evidently come for baseball scribes to honor the heart of that club. The switch-hitter nailed down his third and final batting crown (.338), registering a ninth straight .300 average and pacing the league with 230 hits.

Cincinnati faltered in the LCS against the Mets, but the 32-year-old left fielder continued his torrid play, leading both teams with a .381 average. Rising to the fore, Rose delivered two important playoff series homers, including a 12th-inning game winner.

The Reds reached the promised land in '75, with the versatile Pete now positioned at third base. His .370 World Series mark led both teams. Fans with long memories will recall that it was Pete's slide into second that broke up a double play and allowed Joe Morgan to drive in the title-clinching run.

With Rose hitting .323 during the regular season and striking a sizzling

Pete Rose. (Courtesy Cincinnati Reds.)

.429 LCS average, the Reds repeated as baseball's best team in '76. The next two years were devoid of Reds titles, but 1978 featured a grand finale to Rose's first Cincinnati era. That year "Pistol Pete" became the 13th player in history to cross the 3,000-hit barrier. At age 37, the hitting machine also came within a dozen contests of Joe DiMaggio's seemingly unattainable 56-game hitting streak.

But at the end of the season, following 16 years of meritorious service, Pete was turned loose by Cincy. He signed as a free agent with Philadelphia just prior to 1979 for $3.3 million over four years. This contractual windfall shed a ludicrous light on Rose's well-publicized early career goal to be the game's first $100,000 singles hitter. As the oldest member of the team, he helped rally the troops to the 1980 World Championship.

From 1965 through '81, Rose had been the most troublesome out in the game. A picture of coiled intensity at the plate, Pete strangled his war club well up the handle, peeking through the crook of his arm and attacking hurlers' offerings with a purposeful viciousness. Once on the basepaths, his uniform rarely stayed clean for long. Whether it was a head-first dive into a base or a bone-jarring collision with a

fielder, Rose always went all out.

Age finally crept into his performance in '82, and during the 1983 pennant year, Pete found himself in the unfamiliar position of bench warmer during the stretch drive. But when the post-season bell rang, Rose chimed in with a .344 average in the LCS.

After a World Series defeat, the Phils offered Pete a one-year contract as a part-time player. By this time, the 43-year-old Rose had crept within 202 safeties of breaking the once-insurmountable major league record of 4,189 career hits by Ty Cobb. In typical tunnel vision fashion, Pete held out for the opportunity to pursue the all-time hit record with a team that would play him fulltime. Eschewing the Philadelphia offer, he spent three torturous winter months without a contract before signing with Montreal.

In the first month of the 1984 season, Rose stroked hit No. 4,000, joining Cobb as the only players in history to have achieved that lofty plateau. In August, Rose returned to the Reds amidst jubilant headlines proclaiming him as the team's player-manager. In response, he upped his average to .281.

Pete finally broke Cobb's hit record on September 11, 1985, with a line drive single to left field off Eric Show, and Pete Jr. joined his dad for a hug at first base following the 4,190th hit of his incredible career. Rose played one more season for the Reds in 1986, retiring as the all-time leader in hits (4,256), games (3,562) and at-bats (14,053); runner-up in doubles (746); fourth in runs (2,165); sixth in total bases (5,752); 11th in walks (1,566); and 17th in extra base hits (1,041.)

During his 24 years in the bigs,

Rose hit .300 14 times and had 10 seasons of 200-plus hits. In addition to three batting titles, the 17-time All-Star at five different positions led the league in hits seven times, in doubles on five occasions, in runs and fielding percentage four times each, and in on-base percentage once. He also earned Gold Gloves in 1969 and '70, and in 1999 was voted to baseball's All-Century Team.

But Rose has had little opportunity to bask in his success, and his post-playing days have been anything but serene. The Reds teams he managed through 1989 never finished better than second place, but of much greater significance to this fierce competitor was his banishment from baseball in '89, plus a five-month prison sentence in 1990 for tax evasion. And for much of the 1990s, his public appearances consisted of little more than hawking sports memorabilia.

Pete Rose never possessed a great deal of speed, and power was not a regular part of his arsenal. But he may have been the most driven man to ever play the game, and few would argue that he got more out of his abilities than anyone before or since. The very essence of man, it has been said, is his desire. Judged by that standard, and his astonishing achievements in the sport, Rose transcends the realm of ordinary ballplayers and merits a spot as an authentic baseball immortal. Yet the integrity of the game is also at stake. To this day, Rose denies he bet on major league baseball games, but evidence appears strong that he did. The standoff continues.

Top 5 MVP Vote-Getters

1. Pete Rose, Cincinnati — 274
2. Willie Stargell, Pittsburgh — 250
3. Bobby Bonds, San Francisco — 174
4. Joe Morgan, Cincinnati — 102
5. Mike Marshall, Montreal — 93

1973 American League — Reggie Jackson

Reginald Martinez Jackson
B. May 18, 1946, Wyncote, Pennsylvania

Year	Team	Games	AB	Hits	Avg.	HR	RBI	Runs	SB
1973	Oak AL	151	539	158	.293	32	117	99	22

The Season

The controversial Oakland Athletics spent as much time battling with owner Charlie Finley as they did with the opposition, but that didn't prevent them from repeating as the best team in baseball. The A's became the first club in more than a decade to capture two consecutive World Championships, nudging the surprising New York Mets in a seven-game fall classic.

Typical of Finley's meddling with manager Dick Williams and his charges was the owner's attempt to drop Mike Andrews from the roster after the infielder committed two costly errors in a 10–7 World Series loss. An uprising by his teammates and the sporting public led Commissioner Bowie Kuhn to order the second baseman's reinstatement and hand Finley a significant fine. Disgusted with Finley's constant intervention in day-to-day affairs, Williams announced his resignation immediately following the Series.

Both the three-time Western Division champion A's and Baltimore Orioles breezed to their respective loop titles in 1973. Oakland then received some unexpected power from Bert Campaneris, who slugged a couple of homers in a five-game LCS victory over the O's.

California speedball artist Nolan Ryan broke Sandy Koufax's 1965 strikeout mark with 383 K's, and became the first AL hurler in more than 20 years to fire two no-hitters in one season. A record-dozen junior circuit pitchers won 20 games in 1973.

On April 6, New York's Ron Blumberg became the first designated hitter in major league history. In his first at-bat as a DH, Blumberg walked with the bases loaded against Boston's Luis Tiant.

October Opulence

A brash, cocky slugger in Oakland; a disgruntled passer-by in Baltimore; a conceited, self-proclaimed messiah in New York; and finally, a still-confident but subdued contributor in Anaheim and Oakland again … Reggie Jackson ran the gamut through a spectacular but tumultuous baseball odyssey.

Who was Reggie Jackson? Psychologists could fill volumes in response. Ex-teammate Vida Blue nicknamed the left-handed slugger "Mr. Paradox." Self-assured on the surface, yet craving attention, self-promoting and boastful, but frightened to death of failure, Jackson was an enigma. And as with most controversial figures, he was either loved or hated, worshipped or vilified, embraced or scorned.

Regardless of one's opinion of the charismatic ballplayer, Reggie did more to excite baseball fans than any man in the 1970s. Forever etched in baseball history are his three consecutive home run blasts on three straight pitches in the final game of the 1977 World Series … the incredibly smooth and power-laden stroke; the towering, arching trajectory; and most of all, No. 44 standing at home plate, mouth open in awe of his accomplishment. And he knew how to win. During a 12-year period beginning in 1971, Jackson's various teams won the division title 10 times and the World Series on five occasions.

Although the '77 Series was perhaps "Mr. October's" finest hour, Reggie batted a composite .357 in five World Series with 10 home runs and an all-time best .755 slugging percentage.

Jackson's first World Series experience came in 1973 when the Athlet-

ics right fielder followed a unanimous MVP season by batting .310 with six RBIs, including a clutch homer in the seventh-game victory over the Mets, to claim the Series MVP award as well. The aggressive, natural leader had paced the American League in '73 in five offensive categories: home runs (32), RBIs (117), slugging (.531), runs (99) and game-winning hits (18), and finished fourth in total bases with 286.

The 6-foot, 195-pounder concluded an eight-year stay in Oakland by leading the AL in homers in 1975 (36). Reggie had been at odds with owner Charlie Finley for some time, and was traded to Baltimore in 1976, where he was tops in the circuit in slugging at .502. Yankee owner George Steinbrenner then courted the free agent and signed him for $3 million over five years.

Jackson, 31, swaggered into the Big Apple expecting players and fans to bow at his feet, but before long, found himself with few friends and plenty of enemies. Oakland teammates who'd grown up with Jackson in the A's farm system had shrugged off the slugger's arrogance, having learned early on to take his haughty behavior in stride. But the Yankees, established stars with egos of their own, resented Reggie's boasting and taunts.

In five outrageous seasons in New York, the left-hander was rarely out of the headlines. He immediately alienated the team by calling himself "the straw that stirs the drink," and a year later publicly feuded with manager Billy Martin. Jackson was entrenched in more controversy when he skipped the 1978 All-Star Game because of an alleged illness, then was involved in an altercation at a theater that evening. A five-game suspension for disobeying

Martin's signals followed, as did a confrontation on a Manhattan street with a gunman who threw a bottle at Reggie and fired several shots into the air.

Of course, the 14-time All-Star also made news with his bat. Not including the strike-shortened '81 season, he averaged 32 homers and 102 RBIs per year in New York. Mr. October hit .450 with a record-five home runs in the 1977 World Series victory over Los Angeles, then added two homers each in the '78 LCS, '78 Series and '81 Eastern Division playoffs. He also topped the AL in homers (41) in 1980.

Jax re-entered the free agent market following the '81 campaign, signing with Gene Autry's California Angels for $3 million over four years. Reggie ripped a league-high 39 circuit clouts and drove in 101 runs in 1982 as the Angels won the West. But he fell sharply the next year, slumping to .194 and 14 homers. Many speculated the 37-year-old slugger was over the hill, but he proved those contentions wrong with a 25-home run effort in '84, including the 500th of his career. Though still prideful, Jackson toned down his self-proclamations, his confidence now resting comfortably within himself.

Reggie was born in Wyncote, Pennsylvania, in 1946, the fifth of six children of Hispanic and African American descent. When his parents separated, he went to live with his father, who'd played for the Newark Eagles of the Negro League. Jackson starred in sports during high school, then attended Arizona State University on a scholarship.

After his sophomore year, the 20-year-old was chosen second overall in the 1966 free agent draft and signed a contract with the Athletics which included a bonus of about $90,000. Following three solid minor league seasons, Reg joined the A's in 1968. The increasingly egotistical outfielder hit only .250 in his rookie campaign, but displayed the power that would be his meal ticket in years to come by clubbing 29 home runs and driving in 74. Another trademark came into focus that same season: strikeouts. Reggie whiffed a league-high 171 times, and he would fan more than any American Leaguer each of the next three years. He's currently the all-time leader in whiffs with 2,597.

That was acceptable, however, from a powerhouse with an awesome swing, and when Jackson exploded in 1969 with 47 homers and AL bests in slugging (.608) and runs scored (123), the 23-year-old became one of the most talked-about major leaguers. That talk accelerated in 1971 when he blasted a home run off the light tower atop the Tiger Stadium roof during the All-Star Game.

Reggie Jackson was eighth on the all-time home run list with 563. He was also among the top 20 in games (2,820), extra base hits (1,075) and RBIs (1,702); among the top 25 in total bases (4,834), walks (1,375) and at-bats (9,864); and among the top 50 in runs (1,551). Jackson was elected to the Hall of Fame in 1993, the same year he took a short-lived job with the Yankees as a special assistant to Steinbrenner.

In recent years, Reggie has gone digital, hosting an e-radio talk show. He also endorsed an online casino with the understanding that it wouldn't be associated with sports gambling, then joined a lawsuit against the Internet gambling company that was using his name.

Jackson will always be remembered for his nickname, "Mr. October." The moniker is a bit misleading, however, for Reggie was a man for all seasons.

Top 5 MVP Vote-Getters

1. Reggie Jackson, Oakland — 336
2. Jim Palmer, Baltimore — 172
3. Amos Otis, Kansas City — 112
4. Rod Carew, Minnesota — 83
4. John Hiller, Detroit — 83
4. Sal Bando, Oakland — 83

1974 NATIONAL LEAGUE — STEVE GARVEY

Steven Patrick Garvey
B. December 22, 1948, Tampa, Florida

Year	Team	Games	AB	Hits	Avg.	HR	RBI	Runs	SB
1974	LA NL	156	642	200	.312	21	111	95	5

The Season

Record-setting individuals dominated the 1974 season, including:

• All-time home run king Henry Aaron, who broke Babe Ruth's long-standing total of 714 with a blast off Al Downing April 8;

• Lou Brock of the Cardinals, who at age 35 shattered Maury Wills' stolen base record by pilfering 118, and who broke Max Carey's NL career record of 738; and

• Los Angeles pitcher Mike Marshall, whose 106 appearances, 208 innings of relief and 13 consecutive appearances were all the most in the history

Steve Garvey. (Courtesy Los Angeles Dodgers.)

of baseball. The right-hander became the first reliever in the 19 years of the award to earn Cy Young honors.

The Dodgers were the National League World Series representatives in '74, pacing the league in runs, homers and ERA. Pittsburgh clinched its fourth Eastern Division title in five years, nudging St. Louis by 1½ games, but then fell to the Dodgers in a four-game League Championship Series, despite a splendid performance by future MVP Willie Stargell (.400, two HRs, four RBIs).

Los Angeles was then dispatched in the fall classic by Oakland four games to one, with four of the five Series contests being decided by 3–2 scores.

All-American Boy

The most frequently asked question concerning Steve Garvey during his days with the Los Angeles Dodgers was not even remotely connected to his baseball playing abilities. Rather, the fans and media wondered aloud, "Is he *really* as saintly as he seems?"

Those who'd never been close to the squat, muscular first baseman found it difficult to believe that his impeccable "Mr. Nice Guy" image was anything more than an act. But Garvey

not only fit the All-American boy image to a T, he personified it. Arriving early to sign autographs, maintaining a perfect smile — friendly, honest, devoted to his job — Steve was a fan's ballplayer. Although a few blemishes cropped up in the late 1970s and early '80s, including a fistfight with teammate Don Sutton and a highly publicized divorce, the clean-cut, straight-laced gentleman never strayed from his basic tenet that a hard day's work will be rewarded.

The 5-foot-10, 192-pound contact hitter was certainly well remunerated in 1983 when he inked a five-year contract with the San Diego Padres for $6.5 million, plus incentive and attendance clauses. He had spent 15 years as a player in the Dodger organization and had insisted he wished to finish his career in L.A. But the Dodgers' best offer was $5 million over four years, so Garvey, who once claimed that if his arms were cut they'd bleed Dodger blue, donned orange and brown instead.

With the wise 34-year-old veteran shoring up the infield, the Padres quickly became contenders. Garvey hit .294 in 100 games in '83, and his biggest thrill came several days into the season when he broke Billy Williams' National League consecutive games played streak. His 1,118th straight contest occurred, ironically, in Dodger Stadium, where a huge crowd poured

affection on their wholesome hero. Garvey thanked the fans by taking out a $15,000 full-page ad in the *Los Angeles Times.*

Garvey, who combined with Davey Lopes, Bill Russell and Ron Cey to form the longest lasting infield in the history of baseball, was far from the classic mold of the tall, rangy first baseman. But he was a flashy defensive player, leading NL first sackers in putouts five years in a row and topping them in fielding five times.

Steve's physical skills came as naturally as his association with the Dodgers. The youngster served as L.A.'s batboy for several years while his father drove the team bus during spring training. "I sincerely think I was born to be a Dodger," he once said. The all-around athlete starred as a defensive back for the Michigan State University football team before being drafted by Los Angeles in 1968. The "Mr. Perfect" persona took roots when he showed up for rookie league in a suit and tie while other players wore jeans and t-shirts.

It was his bat, not his clothing, that persuaded Dodger management to give Steve, a scatter-armed third baseman, a chance with the big club. In '72 with the Dodgers, Garvey made more errors than any third sacker in baseball, despite playing only 85 games at the position. Relegated to back-up duty at first base in 1973, Steve hit .304 with 50 RBIs. The Dodgers moved Bill Buckner to left field the following season, giving the 25-year-old Garvey a make-or-break opportunity at first base.

With his career on the line, the right-hander responded magnificently in 1974, batting .312, clubbing 21 homers, collecting 111 RBIs (third in NL) and accumulating 301 total bases (fourth). His 95 runs scored were a lifetime best, and his 200 hits were third in the circuit. He also earned his first of four consecutive Gold Glove awards. Because he'd never been a full-time first baseman, Garvey's name was not included on the '74 All-Star ballot. But more than 1 million fans voted for the seemingly angelic newcomer as a write-in candidate. The choice turned out to be a smart one, as Steve earned the Arch Ward Trophy as the game's MVP for the first of two times. He was also selected as an All-Star in nine of the next 11 seasons.

The Dodgers won the Western Division, then whipped Pittsburgh three games to one in the League Championship Series. Garvey was exceptional in the finale, smashing two home runs, singling twice and driving in four runs. Oakland handled the Dodgers in a five-game World Series, but Steve's .381 average was unmatched. For his season-long efforts, the sturdy first baseman was named the National League's Most Valuable Player.

Garvey began his consecutive games played streak in 1975, continuing the remarkable consistency that defined him as a man and a player. In 10 full years as a Dodger, his batting average was always between .282 and .319, and he was almost always good for 20 homers and 80-plus RBIs. He also led the league in hits in both 1978 (202) and '80 (200), and enjoyed six 200-hit seasons overall.

By 1980, life seemed to be a bed of roses for the 31-year-old celebrity. But then a national magazine article appeared, detailing the alleged emotional and sexual frustrations of his television star wife. The Garveys were devastated by the revelations, which they contended were taken out of context. After suing for $11.2 million, they accepted a $100,000 out-of-court settlement. A year later, the couple separated.

Meanwhile, Steve was also becoming disillusioned with the Dodgers, who were making no effort to extend the reliable veteran's contract beyond 1982. Pressured by the fans, L.A. finally made an offer, but the first baseman elected to go with the Padres.

The decision paid dividends in 1984 when he hit .284, drove in 86 runs and played flawlessly in the field while leading San Diego to its first pennant in the 16-year history of the club. Steve's .200 average in the five-game World Series loss to the Tigers was a disappointment, but he had led the charge against the Cubs in the LCS. Batting .400 and driving in seven runs, including five in one contest, Garvey was selected as the League Championship Series MVP as the Padres rallied to win in five games.

In 2001, Garvey won a $3.1 million labor settlement stemming from a collusion suit brought against the team owners during the late 1980s. But the Supreme Court overturned the decision after baseball's players' union argued that giving Garvey the money would upset a careful system for handing out labor settlements to the players based on an arbitrator's findings.

Garvey never asked to be labeled "perfect," only "consistent." But some L.A. and San Diego teammates struggled to cope with him and his image. If showing up every day, performing to the best of his ability, showing kindness to everyone he met, contributing to numerous charities and being a winner are all crimes, then Steve Garvey stands guilty as charged.

Top 5 MVP Vote-Getters

1. Steve Garvey, Los Angeles — 270
2. Lou Brock, St. Louis — 233
3. Mike Marshall, Los Angeles — 146
4. Johnny Bench, Cincinnati — 141
5. Jim Wynn, Los Angeles — 137

1974 AMERICAN LEAGUE — JEFF BURROUGHS

Jeffrey Alan Burroughs
B. March 7, 1951, Long Beach, California

Year	Team	Games	AB	Hits	Avg.	HR	RBI	Runs	SB
1974	Tex AL	152	554	167	.301	25	118	84	2

The Season

Although the surprising Texas Rangers battled Oakland through most of the 1974 regular season, the defending World Champion A's once more persevered to come out on top in the Western Division by five games for their fourth straight divisional title. And for the third time in four years, this aggregation met the Baltimore Orioles in the League Championship Series. After dropping the first contest, Oakland went on to win the next three.

In a World Series that was much closer than a five-game set might indicate, the A's bested the L.A. Dodgers, with four of the five contests decided by one run. The Series difference was future MVP Rollie Fingers, who saved three of the games and won another as the A's captured their third consecutive World Championship.

Individual league highlights included the second no-hitter in as many years for Kansas City's Steve Busby. Nolan Ryan of California did Busby one better, hurling his third gem in the same time frame. Cleveland's Dick Bosman registered his first hitless contest, and had he not made a throwing error in the fourth inning, would have thrown a perfect game.

Rod Carew's league-leading .364 average nailed down his third straight hitting title and was the best AL mark since Ted Williams batted .388 in 1957. Detroit Tiger Al Kaline became the 12th player in baseball history to swat 3,000 career hits, and three-time junior circuit MVP Mickey Mantle took his rightful place in the Hall of Fame.

Baffling Bruiser

Somewhere within Jeff Burroughs lurked a superstar waiting to be released. The broad-shouldered California native originally seemed destined to become one of baseball's most imposing figures. Those grandiose plans withered to nothingness — vanquished, it would seem, by Jeff's wavering ego that could not accept the media's glowing references to his vast potential.

It would be easier to accept Burroughs as the run-of-the-mill performer he became were it not for the flashes of pure brilliance previously displayed. Playing only his second full year in the majors, the immense outfielder earned the 1974 American League MVP award hands down.

He admitted on occasion to be lacking in self-assuredness, despite being labeled in 1972 by baseball's greatest batting authority, Ted Williams, as "the best hitting prospect I've ever seen at his age." Burroughs had the game's higher-ups scratching their heads at his inability to consistently fulfill that early promise.

Jeff was the No. 1 pick in the 1969 major league draft, signing with the expansion Washington Senators for an $88,000 bonus. Never having been particularly enthralled with the prospect of playing baseball as a career, the hulking youth was actually disappointed at having to miss a fishing vacation in order to join the Senators.

Five years later, Burroughs was in a more positive frame of mind as he pasted junior circuit pitching for a .301 average, a league-leading 118 RBIs and 25 home runs (fourth in the league) to become the first member of the new Texas franchise and the third-youngest AL player to win the MVP award. In a fashion reminiscent of 1972's winner, Dick Allen, big Jeff virtually carried the 1974 Texas Rangers up the standings, moving them from a last-place finish the previous campaign to second.

Media gushed with enthusiasm about his future. He hit for power and average, and did so in the clutch, spraying the ball to all fields. The right-hander's distant clouts usually were directed to right-center field, which cut down on his round-tripper total but upped his average.

The right fielder, not normally noted for his ball-hawking ability, even topped league fielders in double plays during his MVP campaign. But his forté was driving teammates across the pay station — and this he accomplished at a rate that outdistanced the team's next closest hitter by 44 RBIs.

Jeff's growth as a big leaguer had been gradual and somewhat discouraging in his four previous years as a professional. He struggled with frequent strikeouts, a tendency to overswing and an explosive temper, all of which had him traipsing back and forth between the Rangers and their minor league clubs. Everything came together in 1973 when Burroughs popped 30 homers, hit .279 and drove in 85 runs. Ranger fans claimed the only reason their new hero wasn't named AL Rookie of the Year was because winner Al Bumbry played for the highly visible Baltimore Orioles. Everyone waited in excited anticipation for the slugger to rectify that slight in the future.

They didn't have long to wait, as the powerfully constructed 6-foot-1, 200-pounder pieced together his MVP effort the very next campaign.

In 1975, however, tired of battling the Arlington Stadium wind that blew in from right field and robbed him of numerous four-baggers, Burroughs made a crucial mistake, deciding to become a pull-hitter. His batting average promptly plummeted to .226, with no discernible increase in circuit shots, although he still registered 94 RBIs. The once-smooth stroke having vanished, Burroughs flailed at a .237 pace in '76, and his power decline continued. As Jeff's performance depreciated, so did the Rangers' fortunes in the standings. In a desperate move to halt the skid, Texas traded Burroughs to Atlanta for five players and $250,000.

The change in scenery did wonders for Burroughs' hitting, immediately resulting in a career-high 41 homers, a .271 average and 114 RBIs. He also led the league in walks (117) and on-base percentage (.436). Deciding to go for a higher average, Jeff leveled his swing in '78; he reached .301, but his round-trippers dropped to 23.

His hitting prowess disappeared early in '79, and the tenuous confidence, which had been steadily on the rise, declined to an abysmal state. The deflated star was eventually benched, finishing at .224 with a paltry 11 home runs. His woes continued into the next campaign, and just before the '81 season, he was swapped to Seattle.

After an uneventful year, Burroughs signed as a free agent with the Oakland A's, who turned Jeff into a part-time designated hitter. And although he initially improved his average to around the .270 level, 1984 was a verifiable disaster. The following winter, Jeff was unceremoniously purchased by the Toronto Blue Jays, where he concluded his career in '85.

The Burroughs talent may not have fully resurfaced in the 1980s, but it was passed along in the genes. Son Sean, who played for the Long Beach, California, team that advanced to consecutive Little League World Series, was selected in the 1998 draft by the San Diego Padres, making Jeff and Sean only the second father-son duo to be picked in the first round of baseball's amateur draft. Another son, Scott, played Triple A ball in 2001.

Jeff Burroughs wound up playing the part of a small cog where he once powered an entire machine. Every time one of his infrequent fence-busters rocketed off his bat late in his career, a tiny ember of hope glowed in the hearts of his fans: "Is the real Jeff Burroughs coming back?" But like the title figure in Samuel Beckett's *Waiting for Godot*, the subject of this waiting game never showed up again.

Top 5 MVP Vote-Getters

1. Jeff Burroughs, Texas— 248
2. Joe Rudi, Oakland —161½
3. Sal Bando, Oakland —143½
4. Reggie Jackson, Oakland —119
5. Fergie Jenkins, Texas—118

1975 NATIONAL LEAGUE—JOE MORGAN

Joe Leonard Morgan
B. September 19, 1943, Bonham, Texas

Year	Team	Games	AB	Hits	Avg.	HR	RBI	Runs	SB
1975	Cin NL	146	498	163	.327	17	94	107	67

The Season

The awesome Cincinnati Reds tangled with a splendid Boston Red Sox club in the 1975 World Series, finally coming out on top after a memorable seven-game tussle. Five of the contests were decided by one run, with Cincy's Big Red Machine winning the finale on a ninth-inning bloop single off the bat of National League MVP Joe Morgan.

Cincy had fewer problems in the League Championship Series, sweeping the three-game set against Pittsburgh with none of the games ever being in doubt.

The LCS and World Series victories capped one of the most successful NL seasons ever by any ballclub. Cincinnati decimated the Western Division by 20 games over a good Dodger team, posting 108 wins, the most in the senior circuit in 66 years. The Reds' .667 winning percentage (only 54 losses) was the highest in the NL since Brooklyn's 1953 powerhouse.

A number of noteworthy achievements highlighted this season, including:

- Rennie Stennett of Pittsburgh tying an 83-year-old major league record by going 7-for-7 in a nine-inning game;
- New York's Tom Seaver, who won his third Cy Young Award this season, setting a major league record with his eighth consecutive season of 200-plus strikeouts (he'd do it again in 1976);
- Davey Lopes of Los Angeles breaking a 53-year-old major league mark by stealing 32 consecutive bases without being caught;
- Rick and Paul Reuschel of Chicago

becoming the first-ever brother duo to combine for a shutout; and
- Houston's Bob Watson scoring the 1 millionth run in major league history.

Class Menagerie

Never in baseball history has one so small completely dominated the outcome of as many contests as the multitudinously talented Joe Morgan. His speed, fielding prowess and long ball wallop, tightly packed in a diminutive 5-foot-7-inch frame, was both deceiving and deadly.

"Little Joe's" varied skills fueled the fires of seven divisional title teams, four pennant winners and two World Championship squads, and it's no mere coincidence that this connection with victors was so consistent.

Morgan's MVP campaigns of 1975 and 1976 rank as shining examples of all-around play unmatched in versatility by other winners of the award. During those two seasons, he was among the league's top batsmen, hitting for power, stealing and fielding. "Pound for pound," the saying went at the time, "he's the best player in the game."

The gutsy little second baseman was a major run producer in his prime—scampering around the basepaths and generating tremendous power with a vicious swing that was always preceded by the vigorous flapping of his left arm. At second base, he made up for a lack of range with sure hands and an unequaled ferocity in standing his ground against barreling sliders.

Born in Bonham, Texas, Joe moved with his family to Oakland, California, when he was 4 years old. Like many

MVPs before him, Morgan's interest in baseball was whetted by his father's love for the sport, and the youngster set his mind on a baseball career early in life.

A graduate of the same Oakland high school as another two-time MVP—Frank Robinson—Morgan's early hero was 1949 award winner Jackie Robinson; later, Morgan became a big Nellie Fox booster, emulating "Little Nel's" hustle throughout his career. Coincidentally, it was Joe—upon his fulltime arrival in Houston in 1965—who forced Fox to the bench. Fox later suggested that his replacement adopt the "chicken flap" arm movement that reminded Joe to keep his upper appendages extended during his swing.

The left-handed hitter came to the big time having recently completed a superior season at San Antonio. Joe's multifaceted play during his final minor league campaign was a harbinger. He hit .323, stole 47 bases, scored 113 runs and drove in 90.

Those consummate skills blossomed at the major league level a dozen campaigns later, as Morgan captured his first MVP award while playing with the World Champion Cincinnati Reds. During that memorable season, the 32-year-old whirlwind was the top hitter (.327) on one of the more talented assemblages ever to grace the same squad. The Reds, spearheaded by Joe, sprinted from the starting block and were out of the reach of the rest of the West by mid-season, setting a record for the earliest clinching date (September 7).

Little Joe topped the league with career highs in walks (132) and on-base percentage (.471), was second in steals (67) and fourth in average. Additionally, he led all second sackers in fielding percentage (.986), and won his third of five consecutive Gold Glove awards. Seventeen homers, 107 runs and his highest RBI output to date (94) rounded out the banner 1975 campaign, which concluded with Joe becoming the fourth Reds MVP in six years. Emulating his childhood idols, Morgan was the first second baseman in either league to win the most valuable honor since Nellie Fox in 1959, and the first National Leaguer at his position since Jackie Robinson 26 years earlier.

The dynamo went on to pilfer four bases in a three-game LCS sweep of the Pirates, then provided ninth-inning, game-winning singles in both the third and the final World Series games against Boston. The anticlimactic MVP balloting made Joe the most lopsided winner in the history of the award, as he outdistanced runner-up Greg Luzinski 321½ points to 154.

The previous decade of Morgan's major league career showed Little Joe improving in all facets of his varied game as the years progressed. He was *The Sporting News* NL Rookie of the Year for Houston in 1965, hitting .271, scoring 100 runs, stealing 20 bases and leading the league in walks (97) for the first of four times. A fractured kneecap placed a dark cloud over an otherwise

excellent sophomore campaign, and an early-season knee injury sidelined Joe for all but 10 contests in 1968. But he came back to lead the circuit in triples (11) in 1971.

A blockbuster eight-player trade sent Joe to Cincinnati in 1972, and the flashy performer came into his own with a .292 average, 58 steals, 16 homers and league highs in runs (122), on-base percentage (.419) and fielding average (.990) as the Reds won the pennant. Morgan added more power to his already vast arsenal the next two seasons, poking a surprising total of 48 homers while maintaining his usual output in other departments. In '74, he was voted the Reds' MVP, and again was tops in the league in on-base percentage (.430).

The team honor was followed by the league laurel for his extraordinarily diverse efforts in 1975. But as amaz-

Joe Morgan. (Courtesy Cincinnati Reds.)

ing as Joe Morgan's exploits were during that campaign, an even more spectacular year was about to begin.

Top 5 MVP Vote-Getters

1. Joe Morgan, Cincinnati — 321½
2. Greg Luzinski, Philadelphia — 154
3. Dave Parker, Pittsburgh — 120
4. Johnny Bench, Cincinnati — 117
5. Pete Rose, Cincinnati — 114

1975 American League — Fred Lynn

Fredric Michael Lynn
B. February 3, 1952, Chicago, Illinois

Year	Team	Games	AB	Hits	Avg.	HR	RBI	Runs	SB
1975	Bos AL	145	528	175	.331	21	105	103	10

The Season

For the fifth consecutive year, the Oakland Athletics captured the Western Division crown, but for the first time in four seasons, they were ousted in the League Championship Series.

The Boston Red Sox, led by veterans Carl Yastrzemski and Luis Tiant,

and rookies Fred Lynn and Jim Rice, snapped Baltimore's two-year hold on the East title, then whipped the A's three straight in the playoffs.

The 1975 World Series featured the pinch-hitting prowess of ex-Cincinnati Red Bernie Carbo and the famous body English of Carlton Fisk. Carbo came back to haunt his old club

by cracking two pinch home runs, including a three-run shot to tie the sixth game. Fisk's blast off the left field foul pole, accompanied by his memorable "body English" dance down the first base line, won that contest in the 12th inning. But the Reds shattered Beantown's dream with a seventh-game victory.

For the first time in the history of baseball, four pitchers combined to hurl a no-hitter. Oakland moundsmen Vida Blue, Glenn Abbott, Paul Lindblad and Rollie Fingers collaborated to thwart California September 28. Earlier in the season, Nolan Ryan of the Angels fired a record-tying fourth career no-hitter.

Surprising absolutely no one, Rod Carew of Minnesota won his fourth batting title in a row with a .359 average.

Rookie Magic

A fluid, graceful outfielder with the rare ability to hit for power as well as average, Fred Lynn entered the major leagues in dramatic fashion. The 23-year-old from Southern California not only dominated his Boston Red Sox teammates—featuring Carl Yastrzemski, Carlton Fisk, Rico Petrocelli and Jim Rice — but also the entire American League in a brilliant 1975 rookie campaign.

Utilizing a compact yet beautiful swing, the confident left-hander smacked the ball with authority all year. Lynn ended up leading the AL in runs scored with 103 and doubles at 47, and was the first rookie slugging champ (.566). Fred was also second in hitting (.331), third in RBIs (105) and fourth in total bases (299). His average was the best by a rookie since 1948, and his RBI total the highest by a first-year man in 25 years.

Lynn was nearly as proficient patrolling the green pastures. Diving, sprawling grabs on short flies, as well as leaping, wall-crunching catches on deep ones, became regular occurrences for the Gold Glove winner. Those defensive gems, combined with good speed and a mighty left arm, prodded many a sportswriter to project No. 19 as the game's next superstar.

The Red Sox center fielder enjoyed the most spectacular day of his career in 1975, smashing three home runs, a triple and a single; driving in 10 runs; and collecting a record-tying 16 total bases in a June game against Detroit.

In accordance with Lynn's splendid campaign, the Red Sox rose from seven games behind the Orioles in 1974 to the Eastern Division crown, outlasting Baltimore by 4½. They swept Oakland in the League Championship Series, with Fred batting .364 and driving in three runs, before being nudged in seven by Cincinnati in a World Series many consider the finest ever played. He hit .280 with a homer and five RBIs against the Reds, and quickly the accolades came rolling in. Lynn was selected by both the Associated Press and United Press International as Athlete of the Year, and was the only Rookie of the Year and Most Valuable Player in the same season until Ichiro Suzuki of Seattle pulled off the same feat in 2001.

Born in Chicago, Freddie was raised by a diligent father in El Monte, California, following his parents' separation. After excelling in prep sports, the 18-year-old declined a Yankees offer, entering USC on a football scholarship. The gifted athlete played only one year on the gridiron, however, devoting himself to baseball and contributing to three national collegiate championship teams.

The two-time All-American was chosen by the Red Sox in the second round of the 1973 free agent draft and assigned to Bristol, Connecticut. Quiet and innocent when he first arrived in the bigs, Lynn gradually loosened up, though he maintained a placid exterior throughout his career. Seldom commenting on controversial issues, the 6-foot-1, 185-pounder kept his emotions inside.

Following his sensational rookie campaign, Fred held out during spring training, eventually signing a five-year, $2.1 million contract late in the season. Lynn suffered a slight case of the sophomore jinx in '76, but still hit .314 and was fourth in the league in slugging at .467. The next two years were dismal for the BoSox center fielder, who tore ligaments in an ankle in '77, missing 33 games, and was made the scapegoat for the Red Sox dive in '78. Lynn blamed nagging injuries and overall fatigue for his collapse, vowing to come back in 1979 in the best shape of his life.

Nautilus workouts three times a day during the off-season added only a couple of pounds to the now-sculpted athlete, but teammates marveled at his vastly increased upper body strength. The newfound power suddenly made the port-side swinger a home run threat. His previous round-tripper high was 22, but he blasted 39 in 1979. Freddie's .637 slugging mark was the AL's best in 13 years, and his .333 average was also tops in the circuit.

Nineteen-eighty saw the slugger's playing time dwindle considerably, thanks to a pulled hamstring and broken toe, but he earned his fourth and final Gold Glove. Though management contended that 1981 constituted the option year of contracts signed by their center fielder and Fisk, Boston missed the deadline for mailing new pacts to both players by two days, inadvertently allowing them to file for free agency.

Trying to cover their blunder, the Red Sox attempted to trade Lynn to the Dodgers, but Fred negated the deal when L.A. refused to give him a one-year contract. Boston finally exchanged its hot property, along with Steve Renko, to the Angels for Joe Rudi and pitchers Frank Tanana and Jim Dorsey.

Back home in California, the 29-year-old signed a four-year pact worth $5.25 million, but was a flop in '81, hitting only .219. Freddie rebounded by batting .299 with 21 homers and 86 RBIs as the Angels captured the Western Division title the next season. Despite a 1982 LCS loss to Milwaukee, Lynn was the dominant force, batting .611 with a homer, five RBIs and four runs. More injuries limited the outfielder to 117 games in '83; but Lynn still cracked 22 round-trippers and was named MVP of the All-Star Game at Comiskey Park in Chicago, where he belted the first grand slam in All-Star history.

Chronic knee problems and speedy Gary Pettis combined to push Fred over to right field in 1984. He clouted 23 homers and drove in 79 runs while batting .270 as the Angels contended for the West crown. In December of '84, the free agent signed a five-year, $6.8 million contract with Baltimore.

Lynn never regained his rookie magic in six final seasons with the

Orioles, Detroit Tigers and San Diego Padres, but he was a model of consistency during a seven-year stretch (1982–88), hitting between 21–25 homers and driving in between 56–86 runs each season.

A natural athlete with a classic swing and graceful gait, Fred Lynn was one of the best all-around ballplayers in the mid-to-late 1970s, hampered only by a propensity toward injury. Many major leaguers would be thrilled to retire with more than 300 home runs and 1,100 RBIs as Lynn did in 1990 following a 17-year effort, but some consider his overall career a bit of a disappointment when contrasted with its prodigious beginning.

Top 5 MVP Vote-Getters

1. Fred Lynn, Boston — 326
2. John Mayberry, Kansas City — 157
3. Jim Rice, Boston — 154
4. Rollie Fingers, Oakland — 129
5. Reggie Jackson, Oakland — 118

1976 NATIONAL LEAGUE — JOE MORGAN

Joe Leonard Morgan
B. September 19, 1943, Bonham, Texas

Year	Team	Games	AB	Hits	Avg.	HR	RBI	Runs	SB
1976	Cin NL	141	472	151	.320	27	111	113	60

The Season

After threatening for the last two years, the Philadelphia Phillies finally broke through to the top in 1976, winning 101 games and the National League East by nine over the Pittsburgh Pirates.

But the Phils met up with the Reds in the League Championship Series and were swept. Cincinnati won the final LCS contest in the ninth inning on back-to-back homers by future MVP George Foster and Johnny Bench, a two-time past winner.

The defending World Champion Reds had secured another playoff berth by posting 102 triumphs in the regular season, outdistancing the Dodgers by 10 games. The Big Red Machine successfully defended its World Championship with a sweep of the Yankees, becoming the first team to record a perfect 7–0 post-season slate.

An exciting batting crown contest substituted for the lack of drama in the divisional races, with Chicago's Bill Madlock (.339) winning his second consecutive title on the final day of the season over Cincy's Ken Griffey (.336). Madlock grabbed the championship with a four-hit finale, while Griffey, who entered the last game in the lead,

sat. When word of the Cub third baseman's charge to the fore reached Griffey, he hurriedly entered the Reds' contest, but came up empty in two at-bats.

Pitchers who accomplished noteworthy feats this season included San Diego's Randy Jones, who tied a 63-year-old NL record on the way to a Cy Young Award by tossing 68 consecutive innings without allowing a walk, and Houston's Joe Niekro, who belted his only home run in a 22-year career, off brother Phil of Atlanta.

Encore Extraordinaire

Only once in National League history prior to 1976 had a senior circuit player managed to reap back-to-back Most Valuable Player honors, and it had been 17 seasons since Ernie Banks turned the trick as a Chicago Cub.

Joe Morgan vanquished the odds stacked against him in '76 by managing to supercede his own superb efforts of the previous year, capturing his second consecutive MVP. In doing so, the 33-year-old tightened the stranglehold Cincinnati players had established on the prestigious honor, becoming the fifth Reds winner in the past seven seasons.

His second MVP campaign is probably the finest example of total baseball execution by an individual in any one year, and certainly the second baseman's best. Morgan finished in the top five of eight offensive categories during another Cincinnati World Championship effort. The league's smallest No. 3 hitter outpolled the Schmidts, Fosters and Kingmans to win the slugging title with a mighty .576 percentage. He was tops in the circuit in on-base percentage (.453); runner-up in RBIs (111), runs (113), walks (114) and steals (60); and fifth in total bases (272), home runs (27) and batting average (.320).

With their one-man wrecking crew razing a broad path through the opposition, the Reds easily outdistanced Western Division rival Los Angeles by a comfortable margin. Philadelphia carefully evaded Morgan's bat in the LCS, giving him only seven official at-bats, but Cincy still swept. Morgan then crafted his finest World Series, busting away at a .333 clip and stealing a pair of bases in a sweep of the Yanks.

In a sport where batteries continually run down, Little Joe's energy level was undying. It was fueled to a great degree by what he referred to as a "necessary arrogance" essential to all

Joe Morgan. (Courtesy Cincinnati Reds.)

would-be superstars. Quick to smile, with an easy, high-pitched giggle, he both relaxed and inspired those around him.

Morgan had more going for him than merely positive vibrations and exceptional natural talent. He was an unrelenting student of the game, as reflected in the painstaking way he approached the art of base thievery. Years of study evolved this part of his game into an art form. And although his plan to steal only in "game" situations kept him from securing a larceny title, nobody swiped more clutch bases than Joe in his prime. Watching this potent peewee bound around a ballfield was like following a silver sphere carom from bumper to bumper on a pinball grid. The chubby-cheeked game-

breaker was a model of compact resolution, dedicated to triumph wherever he played.

After a productive '77 season that included a third and final fielding title (.993) and began a 91-game errorless streak, Joe suffered through four sub-par years, failing to hit higher than .250. But in 1978, his 200th career home run made him the first player in major league history to accumulate 200 round-trippers and 500 stolen bases. At age 36, he was set loose by Cincy, signing with his old Houston team for the 1980 campaign. Slightly overweight, two steps slower and lethargic at the plate, he hit only .243 for the Astros, but answered the bell late in the season to lead the team to its first division title. He moved on to San Francisco the next year, but his performance standard continued to decline, and he seriously contemplated retiring.

At the strong urging of Giants manager Frank Robinson, Morgan recaptured his "Little Joe" physique by dropping 10 pounds, and at age 39, the gamer was back. With Morgan posting a .289 average, San Francisco stayed in the pennant race until the waning days of the campaign. And when his club was finally eliminated, Joe made sure the Dodgers would be denied as well, smashing L.A.'s pennant dreams with a game-winning four-bagger on the final day of the year.

Morgan's market value shot up with his return to form, and he signed

with Philadelphia for 1983. Along with a couple of old running mates from dynasty days gone by — Pete Rose and Tony Perez — No. 8 returned to the World Series a fourth time. Again he sizzled down the pennant stretch, offsetting a weak .230 season average with a .341 September that included five homers.

That was to be the final hurrah for the 10-time All-Star, until Oakland A's President Roy Eisenhardt convinced the veteran to end his career with a season in front of the hometown folks. So, after 21 stellar campaigns in the NL, Morgan joined the junior circuit, bringing his leadership, charisma, emotion and stabilizing presence to a third team in as many years. Early in 1984, the graying 40-year-old surpassed the immortal Rogers Hornsby as the most prolific home run hitting second baseman of all time, swatting his 265th.

Morgan, who was inducted into the Hall of Fame in 1990, ranked fourth all time in bases on balls (1,865), and in fact walked 850 more times than he struck out. He was 11th in career stolen bases (689), among the top 30 in both runs (1,650) and games (2,649), and among the top 50 in at-bats (9,277). For second basemen, Morgan was third all time in assists (6,967), fourth in putouts (5,742) and sixth in double plays (1,505). Since 1990, he has shared his baseball expertise with a national television audience as an ESPN announcer.

For two decades, Joe Morgan spearheaded countless success stories. And for two consecutive MVP campaigns, the 5-foot-7-inch wunderkind was among the most powerful forces the game has ever seen.

Top 5 MVP Vote-Getters

1. Joe Morgan, Cincinnati — 311
2. George Foster, Cincinnati — 221
3. Mike Schmidt, Philadelphia — 179
4. Pete Rose, Cincinnati — 131
5. Garry Maddox, Philadelphia — 98

1976 American League — Thurman Munson

Thurman Lee Munson
B. June 7, 1947, Akron, Ohio
D. August 2, 1979, Canton, Ohio

Year	Team	Games	AB	Hits	Avg.	HR	RBI	Runs	SB
1976	NY AL	152	616	186	.302	17	105	79	14

The Season

The most significant baseball personality in 1976 never stroked a timely base hit, chased down a long fly ball or pitched out of a bases-loaded jam. Yet he flexed his muscles more than any home run hitter or 20-game winner during that season. Making the decision which had a more profound long-term effect on baseball than any plays on the field was arbitrator Peter Seitz.

In ruling in favor of free agency in the landmark cases of Andy Messersmith and Dave McNally prior to the 1976 season, Seitz put a dent in baseball's sacred reserve clause. The arbitrator's decision helped give players a freedom of movement they'd never known, and set the stage for bidding wars for the rights to such stars as Catfish Hunter and Reggie Jackson.

Another man of authority who made a controversial decision in '76 was Commissioner Bowie Kuhn. Citing "the best interests of baseball," Kuhn negated Oakland Athletics owner Charlie Finley's sales of Vida Blue, Rollie Fingers and Joe Rudi.

Back in renovated Yankee Stadium after a two-year hiatus at crosstown Shea, the New York Yankees returned to the World Series following a 12-year absence, the longest drought in the history of the franchise.

For Minnesota's Rod Carew, this season meant an interruption in his seemingly endless string of batting titles. The sharp-eyed Panamanian had a lock on the American League hitting crown from 1972 to '75, and again in 1977 and '78. But in 1976, it was Kansas City's George Brett (.333) edging teammate Hal McRae (.332) and Carew (.331) on the final day of the season. Brett, who in May set a major league record by stroking three hits in each of six consecutive games, earned the title with an inside-the-park homer.

While the batting crown went to Brett, the basepaths belonged to Oakland's Bill North, who stole 75 bases, the most by an American Leaguer in 61 years.

Gritty Competitor

A myriad of emotions surrounds the aura of Thurman Munson: pride, for his fierce, competitive spirit; exhilaration, for his vast accomplishments; frustration, for his inability to fully enjoy what he attained; and sadness, for his early, tragic death.

Emotions always played a big part in the Yankee captain's career, from his intense rivalry with Boston catcher Carlton Fisk to his embittered feud with Reggie Jackson. Those emotions which revealed his combative nature were easy for Munson to display, but the halcyon, engaging aspects of Thurman's personality rarely showed through. As a result, he was viewed as standoffish, his gruff appearance adding to that impression.

Jackson and Fisk, the latter of whom perennially outpolled the Yankee catcher in All-Star balloting, seemed more at home with their star status than did Munson. Had the gritty performer dealt with media recognition and fan admiration with the same adroitness he used in handling fastballs and curves behind the plate, he might have been an even more popular figure with the fans.

The New York catcher certainly did his best to please the pennant-hungry Yankee faithful in 1976 when he batted .302, clubbed 17 home runs and drove in 105 base runners while leading his team to the American League flag. The writers perceived the stocky backstop as the key ingredient in the Yankee recipe for success, christening him the league's Most Valuable Player.

As well as Munson played during the 1976 season, the line drive hitter with home run power was even more unstoppable in post-season play. He collected 10 safeties in the five-game playoff series victory over the Kansas City Royals, then batted .529 in the World Series. The 5-foot-11, 195-pounder, who went 4-for-4 in the final World Series contest, had the highest average ever for a player on the losing team, and his six straight hits set a Series record. Despite Munson's efforts, the powerful Cincinnati Reds needed only four games to retain their World Championship status.

Immediately prior to the 1976 season, Yankee owner George Steinbrenner broke with 35 years of tradition by naming Thurman Munson the first Yankee captain since Lou Gehrig. The man who ably filled the shoes of past Yankee catcher greats such as Bill Dickey, Yogi Berra and Elston Howard was elected to the starting All-Star Team in 1976, one of seven mid-season classic selections for Munson. By that time, the Yanks were 20 games over .500 and well on their way to winning the Eastern Division by 10½ games over the Orioles. Thurman more than pulled his weight, contributing 17 game-winning hits and never falling below .300.

Following his 1976 MVP season, Munson hit .308 with 18 homers and

Thurman Munson. (Courtesy New York Yankees.)

100 RBIs in 1977 to help lead New York to the second of its three consecutive Eastern Division and AL titles. But it was not a particularly happy year for Thurman, whose character and leadership qualities had been maligned by newly acquired free agent Jackson, who called himself "the straw that stirs the drink," and who said that Munson "could only stir it bad."

Munson hit safely in all six World Series games to end another fine season, but the first Yankee MVP since Howard (1963) couldn't quite seem to enjoy it. Bitter at Steinbrenner over an incentive clause dispute, and still angry with Jackson over his caustic remarks, the disgruntled Munson began requesting a trade to the Cleveland Indi-

ans, which would have put him closer to his wife and three children in Canton, Ohio.

The trade never materialized, and although Thurman entered the '78 campaign in a foul mood, he hit .297 and drove in 71 runs as the Yankees won the division over Boston in a one-game playoff. His two-run homer won Game 3 of the LCS versus Kansas City. The post-season wonder wound up hitting .373 in three World Series and .339 in League Championship Series play.

Like the last Yankee captain, Lou Gehrig, Thurman Munson was destined to die young. While practicing touch-and-go landings in his recently purchased Cessna Citation on a clear August afternoon in 1979, fate took

over. Neither of his passengers was seriously injured when the plane came down 900 feet short of an Akron-Canton Airport runway, but the 32-year-old pilot sustained massive impact injuries and was helplessly pinned between his seat and the controls when fire erupted.

Munson had come into major league baseball almost as abruptly as he left it. A fourth pick of the Yankees in the 1968 free agent draft, the youngster quickly outgrew the New York farm system. As a rookie in 1970, Munson led the club in hitting at .302 and ran away with Rookie of the Year honors. After tying a team record by committing a league-low one error in 1971, the sure-handed receiver won three consecutive Gold Glove awards beginning in 1973.

Following a mediocre 1974 season, Munson had what was in many ways a more productive season in 1975 than in his 1976 MVP year. The Ohio native hit a career-high .318, 16 points above his '76 mark, and drove in 102 runs, the most by a Yankee in 11 years.

Thurman Munson is gone, his uniform No. 15 retired, along with those of such Yankee immortals as Babe Ruth and Mickey Mantle. But the impassioned, emotional spirit he brought to Yankee Stadium lives on.

Top 5 MVP Vote-Getters

1. Thurman Munson, New York — 304
2. George Brett, Kansas City — 217
3. Mickey Rivers, New York — 179½
4. Hal McRae, Kansas City — 99
5. Chris Chambliss, New York — 71½

1977 National League—George Foster

George Arthur Foster
B. December 1, 1948, Tuscaloosa, Alabama

Year	Team	Games	AB	Hits	Avg.	HR	RBI	Runs	SB
1977	Cin NL	158	615	197	.320	52	149	124	6

The Season

The Los Angeles Dodgers started strong and never looked back in 1977, racing to a 10-game bulge over Cincinnati, which saw its two-year hold on the Western Division broken.

Nailing down their second Eastern Division title in a row, the offensive-minded Philadelphia Phillies outlasted Pittsburgh by five games. The Phils were tops in the National League in runs, batting and slugging.

L.A., which paced the circuit in home runs and ERA, whipped the Phillies three out of four in the League Championship Series, thanks in part to two homers and eight RBIs from Dusty Baker. But the Dodgers fell short against the Yankees, who took the World Series in six games.

Although Cincinnati tumbled from atop the West, the defense certainly could not be blamed. The Reds' 95 errors were the fewest in league history.

Capturing individual attention in 1977 were Lou Brock, whose 893rd career stolen base broke Ty Cobb's seemingly unattainable mark, and two-time MVP Ernie Banks, who was inducted into the Hall of Fame.

Ted Turner now manages a media conglomerate, but for one day, he also managed a ballclub. On May 11, the Braves owner inserted himself as skipper after Atlanta dropped 16 games in a row. The team lost again, and NL President Chub Feeney invoked a rule prohibiting a manager from owning any part of his club.

Down the Stretch

Like a powerful stretch-running racehorse, George Foster was always at his best with the wire in sight. The tall, sinewy slugger's career mirrored his 1977 MVP season: a slow start, built-up speed and a ferocious gallop down the stretch.

A solid but unspectacular player at El Camino Junior College in California, the outfielder was signed for a small bonus in 1968 by the San Francisco Giants, who gave up on him after only 54 major league games. Seeing a potential big stick to complement their already formidable lineup, Cincinnati traded shortstop Frank Duffy and a minor league pitcher for Foster in 1971. The newcomer gave no indication for the first couple of years that the trade would turn out to be ridiculously lopsided in the Reds' favor.

George saw little action in Cincy's 1972 pennant year, then was demoted to Triple A Indianapolis for the '73 campaign. Deathly afraid of inside pitches, outfield walls and sliding into bases, Foster was an overly tentative player whose chances of making it back to the big leagues were rapidly fading. But a visit to a hypnotist while at Indianapolis cured him of his fear of the pitched ball, and suddenly he began displaying the offensive skills for which he had been acquired.

The quiet, unassuming ballplayer received his big break in '75. Reds manager Sparky Anderson, believing that George would produce with a chance to play every day, asked Pete Rose to move from left field to third base, opening up a position for the 25-year-old Foster. Batting coach Ted Kluszewski showed the new left fielder the benefits of a closed stance, and before long, he was authoritatively spraying the ball to all fields.

With Anderson's vote of confidence, George began coming into his own in 1975. The following year, Foster smashed 29 homers, drove in a league-leading 121 runs, was third in total bases with 298 and runner-up in slugging at .530, while hitting .306. He was also tops in fielding in '76 with a .994 mark.

Not surprisingly, the 27-year-old's campaign started slowly in 1977. By the time the season was nearly a quarter of the way along, Foster had poked only four home runs. Then "The Destroyer" came alive. Beginning in late May, Big George used his black bat to tag seven round-trippers in six contests, and added a dozen homers apiece in July and August. Although the Reds finished 10 games behind the Dodgers in the West, Foster topped the league in nearly every significant offensive category, including homers (52), RBIs (149), total bases (388), slugging (.631) and runs scored (124). Always scowling at the plate, the left fielder also hit for average, finishing third with a splendid .320 mark.

"Mr. Clean-up's" home run total, a record-31 hit on the road, was the highest in baseball since Willie Mays collected the same number in 1965, and the third best in NL history. His RBIs were the most since 1962 when Tommy Davis accumulated 153, and his total bases were the top number since Hank Aaron's 400 in 1959. When the MVP votes rolled in, Foster had outpolled Greg Luzinski of the East Division champion Phillies 291–255.

A casual glance at Foster did not reveal the awesome power of which he was capable. Long, thin legs blended unobtrusively into a 30-inch waist; his upper torso was muscular, but not imposing; while his jutting jaw and long, L-shaped sideburns belied an inner sensitivity. A deeply religious man,

George Foster. (Courtesy Cincinnati Reds.)

George was more apt to return home or to his hotel room to read his Bible following a game than to go out for drinks with the boys.

While his sessions with a hypnotist gave him confidence at the plate, he was frequently criticized for "playing it safe." Foster only once stole more than seven bases in a season, and he freely acknowledged a hesitation to slide — particularly into home plate — and rarely left his feet for a fly ball. His fielding also left much to be desired.

The long ball hitter seldom needed to slide between 1976 and '79 when he connected for more home runs (151) and totaled more RBIs (488) than any other major leaguer, while still batting an amazing .303. His 40 homers and 120 RBIs in 1978 were tops in the league.

Foster's $750,000-a-year contract was due to expire following the 1982 season. Unwilling to meet the slugger's $1.5 million-a-year request and not anxious to lose their big gun to free agency, the Reds dealt George to the Mets for catcher Alex Trevino and pitchers Jim Kern and Greg Harris. New York more than fulfilled its new left fielder's demands with a guaranteed five-year pact worth at least $10 million.

Foster was hyped as the Mets' savior, but sagged miserably in 1982, tallying only 13 homers and hitting .247. The media blasted him for his failure to earn the bulky salary, but in addition to aging, Foster was now playing in a more pitcher-friendly park than what he'd been used to in Cincinnati, and there were far fewer men on the basepaths for him to drive in.

He more than doubled that round-tripper output the next year with 28, but the 33-year-old managed only a .241 average as New York finished last in the East for the second straight time. The Mets miraculously rose to contention in 1984 as Foster bashed 24 HRs, collected 86 RBIs and hit .269, his best average as a Met. He hit 21 homers with 77 ribbies in 1975, then saw limited action with the Mets and Chicago White Sox in '86 before hanging it up.

During an 18-year career, Foster slugged 348 home runs and drove in 1,239 runs. He was named to NL All-Star Teams in five seasons, and performed well in post-season play for the Reds. He hit .364 in the 1975 League Championship Series win over Pittsburgh, then rapped out a team-high eight hits in the World Series triumph over Boston. In '76, he stroked two home runs and drove in four teammates in the LCS victory over Philadelphia, before batting .429 with four RBIs in the World Series sweep of the Yankees. And in 1979, Foster had a homer and two RBIs in an LCS loss to Pittsburgh.

George Foster was not a charismatic ballplayer who could carry a team with his clubhouse leadership. But in the mid-to-late 1970s, he was an awesome force at the plate and a vital cog in a team that made post-season play a regular habit.

Top 5 MVP Vote-Getters

1. George Foster, Cincinnati — 291
2. Greg Luzinski, Philadelphia — 255
3. Dave Parker, Pittsburgh — 156
4. Reggie Smith, Los Angeles — 112
5. Steve Carlton, Philadelphia — 100

1977 AMERICAN LEAGUE — ROD CAREW

Rodney Cline Carew
B. October 1, 1945, Gatun, Panama

Year	Team	Games	AB	Hits	Avg.	HR	RBI	Runs	SB
1977	Min AL	155	616	239	.388	14	100	128	23

The Season

Fifteen years after registering the last World Championship of their dynasty era, the refurbished New York Yankees returned to the pinnacle. They did so dramatically, the final victory in their World Series triumph bearing the flourishing signature of 1973 MVP Reggie Jackson, who clouted three home runs on three straight pitches.

The Yanks advanced to post-season play by surviving a hot three-way race in the Eastern Division that saw both Baltimore and Boston fall 2½ games short. The six-game Series win over the Dodgers was preceded by a second consecutive League Championship Series triumph over the Kansas City Royals, who had put together a 16-game winning streak — longest in the majors in 24 years — during the regular season.

Expanding from 12 to 14 teams this season, the league added the Toronto Blue Jays and returned a franchise to Seattle, which became the Mariners. More than 19½ million fans, a league record, visited American League ballparks.

Some of those folks saw 1964 MVP Brooks Robinson wind down his glorious career and establish records in six lifetime categories: most games at third base, best fielding percentage, and highest number of assists, chances, putouts and double plays.

Two pitchers who sparkled this season were Seattle's John Montague, who tied an AL record by retiring 33 batters in a row over two games, and California's Nolan Ryan, who struck out 19 hitters in a game for the fourth time in his career.

Fireworks were prevalent at Fenway Park July 4, with Boston belting a major league record-eight home runs in a 9–6 win over Toronto. Two and a half months later, Boston's Ted Cox established a big league mark for consecutive hits at the beginning of a career with safeties in his first six at-bats.

Magic Wand

Ghosts of .400 hitters past haunted American League ballparks in 1977, as Rod Carew turned the clock back 36 years and challenged the mystical figure last attained by Ted Williams.

Maintaining a .400-plus pace for a majority of the campaign, the sleek Panamanian finished at a still-astounding .388 in a season overflowing with personal highs. The 32-year-old topped the league in average, hits (239), runs (128), triples (16) and on-base percentage (.452), while finishing third in doubles with 38 and knocking in 100 runs — all lifetime bests.

A throwback to the singles-conscious days of Ty Cobb and Wee Willie Keeler, Carew adjusted the might of his cut according to the hurler's delivery. Pitchers came at him in a myriad of ways, and he countered with an unusual assortment of stances and strategies uncommon to most hitters.

The easygoing stylist's love affair with baseball could be traced to youthful days in Panama where he wandered the barrios alone, bat in hand at all times. Rod was 15 when his family moved to New York, and he experienced great difficulties in communicating and avoiding low-life temptations of the inner city.

A father of one of his teammates discovered Rodney dominating a sandlot ballgame, and phoned in a glowing report to his favorite team, the Twins.

The next time the Minnesota club came to town, Carew was given a special tryout at Yankee Stadium, and the 18-year-old was quickly signed.

Carew joined the Twins in 1967, earned a starting second base post and went on to win the AL's Rookie of the Year award. Two years later, he nailed down the first of seven batting championships (.332) and tied an American League record by stealing home seven times. The Twins won their division that year, but "Junior" failed miserably in the playoffs, hitting only .071 in the League Championship Series loss.

Extremely sensitive to bigoted remarks in his early days with the Twins, Rod was easily driven to anger or aloofness. But after marrying a Jewish woman in 1969, a newfound tolerance seemed to restore his composure and earn him the eventual distinction as one of the game's most even-tempered players.

A torn cartilage limited him to only 51 games in '70, and his robust .366 average was thus denied qualification for the batting title. Following a .307 effort in '71, Carew racked up four consecutive hitting crowns, starting with .318, then zooming to uncontested heights of .350, .364 and .359. He led the AL in hits (203) and triples (11) in 1973, hits (218) and on-base percentage (.435) in '74, and on-base percentage (.428) in '75.

In 1976, he was moved to first base and denied a fifth straight title by two percentage points (.333 to .331) by George Brett. Despite this consistent output, national acclaim remained somewhat subdued by his Minnesota locale, and monetary rewards were even less satisfactory.

During this period, Carew was enhancing his value with stealing exploits that ranked him among the league's best. Extremely daring on the basepaths, Rod's 16 swipes of home plate were a major league record. Combined with an uncanny knack for dragbunting, Carew's fleetness afoot served him well, as leg hits and bunt singles kept the speedy veteran out of prolonged slumps.

There were few dry spells in 1977 when the MVP set an American League record for most games with one or more safeties (131). Pandemonium in the nation's media corps took a toehold three months into the season after Rod put together an amazing .486 June to put him just over .400. By mid-July, he was still over that exulted mark, but despite hitting in all but six games in August, dropped to .374 at the end of the month. In September, Carew pumped out a bevy of hits (.439 for the month), but Minnesota dropped to fourth in the standings and their star ended the season eight hits shy of the .400 mark.

Still, Carew's .388 was the loftiest big league average in two decades. And an unusually power-laden campaign saw the Twins headliner drive 14 homers and finish second in the league in slugging percentage. Baseball writers awarded Carew the MVP by a 273 to 217 margin over Kansas City's Al Cowens, marking the first time an American Leaguer from a second-division team had won.

Rod picked up his seventh batting championship in 1978 with a .333 mark, as well as his fourth on-base percentage title (.415). Big money awaited on the free agency market, but the underpaid superstar was still on the fence as his contract was expiring in 1978. However, owner Calvin Griffith made it easy for Rod to leave. Griffith's speech at a Lions Club luncheon on the final day of the '78 season reportedly included outrageous racial jabs at blacks, and a vicious swipe at Carew, calling him a "damn fool" for playing for less than he was worth.

Rod's career with the Twins was over, and all concerned knew it. After the veteran negated a trade to San Francisco, he agreed to a four-for-one swap with the California Angels.

A painful wrist kept Carew on the disabled list for more than a month in '79, and pulled his average down to a still-exceptional .318 for the season. California's divisional championship brought fervent hopes of a World Series trip, but the Angels fell to Baltimore despite Rod's .412 LCS.

Another division title in '82 brought more post-season heartbreak for the 37-year-old, who hit .319 in the AL playoff series loss to Milwaukee. Frightened by rumors that Carew was seeking a three-year, $4.5 million pact, opposing teams stayed away when the consummate batsman went the free agent route after the 1982 season. The

Angels then signed Rod for another two-year stint.

Nineteen-eighty-four witnessed the usual Carew excellence, but Rod's incredible string of 15 consecutive .300-plus efforts was halted by an injury. In 1985, the 39-year-old joined the 3,000-hit club, then decided to call it quits.

Among Carew's activities following his playing days was serving as a batting coach for the Milwaukee Brewers. But after the team set a single-season major league record for strikeouts in 2001, he resigned.

During his 19-year career, Carew won seven batting titles (only Ty Cobb won more), collected 3,053 hits (20th all time) and posted a .328 batting average. He was elected to the Hall of Fame in 1991. Critics claimed that his bat lacked the punch required of a first baseman, but few players wielded a magic wand with better dexterity and results than Rod Carew.

Top 5 MVP Vote-Getters

1. Rod Carew, Minnesota — 273
2. Al Cowens, Kansas City — 217
3. Ken Singleton, Baltimore — 200
4. Jim Rice, Boston — 163
5. Graig Nettles, New York — 112

1978 NATIONAL LEAGUE — DAVE PARKER

David Gene Parker
B. June 9, 1951, Calhoun, Mississippi

Year	Team	Games	AB	Hits	Avg.	HR	RBI	Runs	SB
1978	Pit NL	148	581	194	.334	30	117	102	20

The Season

The Grand Old Game prospered as never before in 1978, as for the first time in history, the National and

American Leagues each drew more than 20 million fans, setting all-time attendance marks.

The Los Angeles Dodgers again proved to be the best senior circuit

entry, leading the NL both offensively and defensively to capture their second pennant in a row, by 2½ games over Cincinnati.

Things were even tighter in the

Dave Parker. (Courtesy Pittsburgh Pirates.)

gold early, then proceeded to shrivel in stature until his gigantic future all but disappeared. Following a change of uniforms, the sizeable package of talent recaptured his standing as a game-breaker, and had he not been his own worst enemy at times, there's no telling what heights he might have climbed.

At the top of his game, Parker prevailed in all facets of play, pounding shots to all parts of the park and firing out enemy runners from his right field post. Dave's running speed was startling in view of his mammoth size. He transported his sinewy, 230-pound frame along the bases with the dispatch of a gazelle and the ferocity of a tank.

The son of a foundry worker and undisputed leader of the local Cincinnati youths, he was a terror on the high school gridiron as a running back until a knee injury persuaded him to point his varied talents in baseball's direction. The knee damage and an already prolific reputation as a brash troublemaker made major league teams wary, and it wasn't until the 14th round of the 1970 draft that Pittsburgh decided to take a chance.

The first order of business was refining the newcomer's atrocious outfield play, and through many hours of hard work, Dave gradually made himself into a superb glove man. His cannon-like right arm gained accuracy that would take the nation's breath away in the 1979 All-Star Game, an affair in which the right fielder uncorked two monstrous throws to snuff out base runners at third base and home plate, and was named the game's MVP.

Parker alienated many who came in contact with his steady stream of self-serving verbiage. Supremely confident, the ringleader of the rowdy Pirates prophesied near-impossible deeds for himself, then went out and achieved them. He further defied the game's traditionalists by wearing a single gold earring and a brazen, unkempt beard.

"Every team needs a foundation, and I'm it," he would exclaim to all within shouting distance. Commandeering a free-swinging band of Buccos from his No. 3 spot in the lineup, "The Cobra" smote baseballs for average and

East race, which was not decided until a season-ending four-game set between the Phillies and Pirates. The Bucs needed a sweep to win it all, but could net only three victories.

Cincinnati's Pete Rose mounted a magnificent 44-game hitting streak to tie an NL record, coming within a dozen games of Joe DiMaggio's all-time mark. The 1973 MVP also registered the 3,000th hit of his illustrious career.

For the second year running, the Dodgers bested the Phils three games to one in the League Championship Series, with Steve Garvey smashing four home runs and driving in seven. But after winning its first two World Series games, L.A. dropped a second straight coast-to-coast confrontation

by losing the next four games to the New York Yankees.

No one in the history of the major leagues had ever hit two pinch grand slams in the same year, but two players — Davey Johnson of Philadelphia and Mike Ivie of San Francisco — did it during June of this season.

Gaylord Perry became the first pitcher to win the Cy Young Award in both leagues, capturing the honor with San Diego after earning the accolade with Cleveland in 1972.

The Cobra Strikes

Dwarfing the competition in both size and skill, the outrageously vociferous Dave Parker claimed his pot of

distance. His hitting philosophy was simple: "I see something I like and attack it."

Pittsburgh's prize property was an immediate sensation upon joining the franchise in 1970. The 1972 Carolina League MVP was a willing pupil, and after three campaigns in the bushes, appeared ready to fill the right field vacuum left by the untimely passing of Roberto Clemente. Physical ailments impeded Dave during his first two years with the Pirates, but the 24-year-old finally unleashed his fury in an injury-free 1975 campaign. He hit .308, poked 25 homers, drove in 101 mates and posted an NL-best .541 slugging percentage as the club took the Eastern Division crown before stumbling in the League Championship Series. Parker was over .300 again the next year — along with 19 steals — and in '77 conducted a breakneck late-season Pittsburgh charge that fell just short of another division title.

During that '77 campaign, he shrugged off a bad knee strain to nab his first batting title (.338), slugged 21 four-baggers and tallied 107 runs while earning a Gold Glove. His 215 hits and 44 doubles were both league highs.

His true mettle, however, surfaced in 1978. It was a season that could have easily been a throwaway, but the indomitable Parker transformed it into an MVP effort. The Pirate ruffian suffered a severely shattered cheekbone in a home plate collision, but instead of taking a long recuperative period as expected, was back in the Pittsburgh lineup 11 games after the accident. Wearing a football face guard for protection, the resolute indestructo piled up the best numbers of his career. Lifetime highs were achieved in homers (30), RBIs (117) and steals (20), and a second consecutive batting crown (.334)

was accentuated with league-topping marks in total bases (340), intentional passes (23) and slugging percentage (.585), as well as another Gold Glove.

A five-season, million-dollar-per-year contract was Parker's reward for the valiant effort, but the milestone pact turned out to be too overwhelming for even "D.P." to handle. Pittsburgh's fandom, steeped in blue collar work ethic tradition, had trouble relating to a millionaire athlete. The booing, object throwing and mindless vandalism of Dave's personal property began almost immediately.

The turmoil was temporarily forgotten in the World Championship campaign, during which the right fielder was his usual brilliant self, chipping in with a .345 World Series for the victors. But the abuse returned in 1980 when Parker, suffering from knee pain that would require surgery, posted atypical statistics. The 1981 players' strike did him no favors either; Parker reported overweight and out of shape, and promptly careened to a paltry .258 average as death threats, hate mail and an increasing array of garbage were hurled his way from the paying customers. The wounded veteran retaliated with derogatory comments about the fans to the media. Eventually, it was revealed that Parker had also gotten involved in drug abuse.

Meanwhile, he was flailing wildly at a barrage of off-speed deliveries and was reduced to a platoon role in his last two years in Pittsburgh. When Parker offered free agency services in the winter of '83, only Seattle and Cincinnati showed interest. The Reds signed the hometown alum, and Dave willingly shed his excess weight, shaved his beard and gave up the gold earring to conform to the team's conservative dress code policies.

Only 32 going into the 1984 campaign, Parker was convinced he could regain his once-awesome powers in the more friendly surroundings of Cincy. Subdued in attitude almost beyond recognition, the rejuvenated outfielder stroked a solid .285 with a team-high 94 ribbies, his best effort in five years.

He came back even stronger in '85, batting .312 with 34 round-trippers and league highs in RBIs (125) and doubles (42). In 1986, he was named to his sixth of seven All-Star teams, clubbing 31 homers and driving in 116 runs.

Parker enjoyed another productive season in Cincinnati before spending the final four years of his career as a very effective designated hitter with Oakland, Milwaukee, California and Toronto. In both 1989 and '90, he went over the 20-homer, 90-RBI marks.

Dave Parker put up some enormous numbers over 19 years, and at one time was the epitome of the complete 20th century athlete, adroitly combining size, power and speed. Only *he* could slow himself down, and unfortunately that's what temporarily derailed his career. But Dave demonstrated a willingness and ability to bounce back, and that's why baseball fans remember the Cobra in a positive light.

Top 5 MVP Vote-Getters

1. Dave Parker, Pittsburgh — 320
2. Steve Garvey, Los Angeles — 194
3. Larry Bowa, Philadelphia — 189
4. Reggie Smith, Los Angeles — 164
5. Jack Clark, San Francisco — 107

1978 AMERICAN LEAGUE—JIM RICE

James Edward Rice
B. March 8, 1953, Anderson, South Carolina

Year	Team	Games	AB	Hits	Avg.	HR	RBI	Runs	SB
1978	Bos AL	163	677	213	.315	46	139	121	7

The Season

The Bronx was a hotbed of controversy in 1978, as Yankee manager Billy Martin battled with owner George Steinbrenner and slugger Reggie Jackson before resigning nearly 100 games into the season. But the electricity only served to spark the New Yorkers to 35 victories in their final 47 contests.

The Yanks wound up in a first-place tie with Boston in the Eastern Division, and in the second playoff in AL history, bounced the Red Sox on a three-run homer by normally light-hitting shortstop Bucky Dent. In the West, Kansas City repeated, then lost its third straight League Championship Series to New York, three games to one.

Becoming the first team in World Series history to rally from a 2–0 deficit and win in six games, the Yankees ousted the Dodgers for the second consecutive year. Graig Nettles' fielding wizardry initiated the comeback in the third contest, and the unlikely Dent captured Series MVP honors by hitting .417 with seven RBIs.

The most dramatically improved ballclub in '78 was offensive-minded Milwaukee, which led the league in hitting, runs and homers. Enjoying the first winning season since their inception eight years before, the Brewers posted 26 more victories than in the previous campaign. Three of those wins came in a season-opening sweep of Baltimore that featured a grand slam by the Brewers in each game—by Sixto Lexcano, Gorman Thomas and Cecil Cooper—a major league record.

A second straight batting title and seventh overall went to Minnesota's Rod Carew, who hit .333.

Boston Strongboy

A Rock of Gibraltar both on and off the field, Jim Rice wasn't just a powerful man who clobbered home runs for a living—he was the very source of strength. Bulging, muscular biceps and rock-hard thighs enabled him to crush baseballs out of sight, while an intense, competitive spirit revealed a sturdy toughness emanating from within.

A quiet man who could hush an entire room with merely a piercing glare, the Boston Red Sox left fielder was known to flare up at invasions of his personal space. Not surprisingly, an inquiring media became an instant enemy once Jim put himself in the limelight with his miraculous on-field deeds. Reporters who crossed that thin line between the ballplayer and the person had good reason to feel as intimidated by the cold, icy stare as did opposing pitchers.

Although the Boston strongboy never manhandled a media member, he shook up his share of hurlers. Rice belted 382 home runs in 16 seasons, but his greatest show of brawn did not involve ripping the cover off a ball, but in checking his swing. In 1975, he decided at the last moment to hold back on a pitch just outside the strike zone. With his mighty wrists, Jim halted what would have been a typically frightening cut. The amazing result was the bat snapping in half, with the thick end whistling over the head of the third base coach.

Without a doubt, Rice was one of the most productive AL hitters from the mid–1970s to the mid–1980s. From 1977 to '79, he blasted an incredible 124 home runs and led the American League in total bases all three years, tying a record set by Ty Cobb. In seven seasons beginning in '77, the virile slugger was the major league's overall leader in RBIs and total bases. True, the power hitter benefited from playing half of his games in Fenway Park with its shallow left field porch, but a .298 lifetime batting average is proof positive of his overall hitting abilities. In addition to three home run and total bases crowns, Rice also topped the AL in RBIs and slugging twice each. For two straight years, the nimble athlete legged out 15 triples, a remarkable feat for a right-handed pull hitter in Fenway.

James Edward Rice was the fourth of nine children of a factory supervisor, and was known as Ed through high school. He was such an impressive athletic prospect that previously all-white Hannah High School in Anderson, South Carolina, changed its integration plan to include him. Following graduation and faced with the choice of four years in college prior to a possible pro football career or instant gratification in the form of a hefty Boston Red Sox bonus, Rice willingly chose the latter.

The strong right-hander enjoyed one of the finest rookie campaigns ever in 1975, and had it not been for the even more exceptional season of first-year man and teammate Fred Lynn, Jim would have been a shoe-in for Rookie of the Year honors. As it was, he finished third in the league MVP balloting, hitting .309 with 22 home runs and 102 RBIs. An arm injury kept Rice out of the seven-game World Series loss to Cincinnati.

Rice's average fell off slightly in 1976, but he was runner-up in the AL in slugging at .482 and third in total bases with 280. With Carl Yastrzemski firmly entrenched in left field in '77, big Jim was the fulltime designated hitter, a role he openly detested. His hitting, however, wasn't affected, as Rice dominated the league in home runs (39), slugging (.593) and total bases (382).

But that was just the prelude to a fantastic 1978 MVP season. Playing more than 100 games in left field and appearing in every Red Sox contest, Jim pounded the ball at an almost unheard of rate, becoming the first player to lead the American League in homers (46), RBIs (139) and triples (15) in the same season. His round-tripper and ribbie tallies were AL highs dating back to 1969, and his 406 total bases were the most in baseball in 30 years and the best in the league since 1937, when three-time MVP Joe DiMaggio accumulated 418. Rice also led the junior circuit in hits (213) and slugging (.600), was runner-up in runs scored (121) and third in batting (.315).

The Red Sox started '78 with an incredible 55–24 surge, but faded down the stretch and were caught by the Yankees, who captured a one-game playoff victory. No one dared blame

the clutch-hitting left fielder for the club's demise. He hit .339 with men on base and paced Boston with 16 game-winning RBIs. Rice was the choice as the league's Most Valuable Player, despite a phenomenal season by New York pitcher Ron Guidry, who posted a 25–3 record, a 1.74 earned run average, nine shutouts and 248 strikeouts. Rice was rewarded for his efforts with a seven-year, $5.4 million contract.

An astigmatism in his right eye contributed to a poor defensive year in 1979, but Jim was still a dominant force at the plate, where his 39 homers and 130 RBIs were both second in the AL. His .325 batting average was a career best. The power hitter fell off the next two seasons, but came back to hit .309 in 1982 and .305 in '83, with league highs in home runs (39) and RBIs (126). Despite persistent rumors that he would be swapped to Atlanta, Jim came through with another fine effort in 1984, knocking out 28 homers and collecting 122 RBIs.

Possessing a swing well suited for Fenway Park, Rice continued to dis-

play power with 20-plus homers and 100-plus RBIs in both 1985 and '86, batting a stellar .324 the latter year. He reached double figures in circuit clouts two more times, then wound down his 16-year career in 1989. Eight years later, he began a four-year stint serving as the Red Sox batting coach.

Jim Rice's prodigious swats and high batting averages influenced a significant number of Hall of Fame voters to pencil him in the last few years, but he's never quite made it over the top. If he is enshrined some day, he'll be one of the few players whose body was as hard as his Hall of Fame bust.

Top 5 MVP Vote-Getters

1. Jim Rice, Boston — 352
2. Ron Guidry, New York — 291
3. Larry Hisle, Milwaukee — 201
4. Amos Otis, Kansas City — 90
5. Rusty Staub, Detroit — 88

1979 NATIONAL LEAGUE
WILLIE STARGELL / KEITH HERNANDEZ

Wilver Dornel Stargell
B. March 6, 1940, Earlsboro, Oklahoma
D. April 9, 2001, Wilmington, North Carolina

Year	Team	Games	AB	Hits	Avg.	HR	RBI	Runs	SB
1979	Pit NL	126	424	119	.281	32	82	60	0

* * * * *

Keith Hernandez
B. October 20, 1953, San Francisco, California

Year	Team	Games	AB	Hits	Avg.	HR	RBI	Runs	SB
1979	SL NL	161	610	210	.344	11	105	116	11

The Season

The Pittsburgh Pirates broke Philadelphia's three-year hold on the Eastern Division, wreaked revenge against Cincinnati in the League Championship Series and rallied from a 3–1 deficit to defeat the Baltimore Orioles in the World Series. The Reds had ousted the Pirates from post-season play in 1970, '72 and '75, but the Bucs swept Cincy in '79.

Individual achievements included Pete Rose of the Phillies collecting 200 hits for a record-10th time; J.R. Richard of the Astros striking out 313 batters, the most in the league since 1966; and Pittsburgh's Omar Moreno stealing 77 bases for a second straight theft title.

Two pitching brother duos came into prominence this season. The knuckleballing sibling act of Joe (Houston) and Phil (Atlanta) Niekro posted a league-high 21 triumphs each, and became the first 20-game winning brothers in the same NL season.

Houston's Ken Forsch fired the earliest season no-hitter ever when he blanked Atlanta 6–0 April 7, joining brother Bob of St. Louis as the only sibling combination to toss no-hitters.

For the first time, balloting for the Most Valuable Player award ended in a dead heat, with Pittsburgh's Willie Stargell and Keith Hernandez of St. Louis sharing the honor.

On September 28, St. Louis short-stop Garry Templeton became the first player in major league history to stroke 100 hits from both sides of the plate in the same season. Normally a switch-hitter, he batted right-handed exclusively down the stretch in order to set the record.

Inducted into the Hall of Fame in 1979 was two-time MVP Willie Mays.

Pirate Patriarch

Huge but tender, imposing yet benign, Willie Stargell was the Pittsburgh Pirates' spiritual guru, using a quick bat and emotional inspiration to catapult his team to a World Championship in 1979.

The brawny first baseman came through with clutch hits time and again during the '79 pennant drive, and rewarded teammates for similar heroics by handing out gold "Stargell Stars" to attach to their caps. Victories were raucously celebrated in the locker room as Sister Sledge's "We Are Family" blared from Willie's tape player. And blacks and whites on the most integrated team in baseball looked to "Pops" as the unifying force and heart of the ballclub.

Statistically, the 39-year-old fa-

Willie Stargell. (Courtesy Pittsburgh Pirates.)

ther figure did not experience an overwhelming season; only his 32 home runs placed in the top five in any offensive category. But the team captain's timely slugging helped Pittsburgh outlast Montreal by two games for the Eastern Division title, and his postseason play was phenomenal. The man with the windmill practice swings made short work of the Reds in the League Championship Series, clubbing two round-trippers, driving in six runs and batting .455.

Willie also excelled in the seven-game World Series victory, tagging Baltimore pitching for a .400 average with three circuit clouts and seven RBIs. After being named MVP of both the LCS and World Series, No. 8 was

selected as co-Most Valuable Player in the National League. The only player to sweep all three awards in one season was also the oldest (39 years, eight months) to be named a league MVP.

Throughout his career, it was often hit or miss, as Stargell retired with the highest number of strikeouts in baseball history (1,912, now second behind Reggie Jackson). But his 475 lifetime homers made him a terror to NL pitchers, and the .282 career batting average was impressive for a long ball hitter.

Many of those home runs were absolute moon shots. He was the first player to hit a ball out of Dodger Stadium, in 1969, and he repeated the incredible feat four seasons later. (It would be 24 years before it was done again.) Stargell also smashed seven baseballs over the right field roof of Forbes Field in Pittsburgh — then the biggest park in the majors — and he was the only one to hit four shots into the upper deck at Three Rivers Stadium. Off the field, Willie was equally noticeable. His relentless campaign to stamp out sickle-cell anemia was acknowledged worldwide.

Wilver Dornel Stargell was born of African-American and Seminole Indian descent in Earlsboro, Oklahoma, and grew up in Alameda, California. Knee injuries forced him out of football at Encinal High School, but he continued to play baseball and went on to star at Santa Rosa Junior College before fracturing a pelvic bone. He returned to baseball, however, and was signed by the Pittsburgh Pirates in 1959.

The hulking 19-year-old with the lumbering gait played four years in the minors before being brought to Pittsburgh in '62. The left-handed outfielder and first sacker narrowly missed MVP awards in both 1971 and '73. He blasted a league-high 48 home runs and drove in a runner-up 125 in '71, then singled and scored the winning run in the seventh game to give Pittsburgh a World Series victory over Baltimore. In 1973, Willie paced the league in homers with 44, RBIs with 119, doubles with 43 and slugging percentage at .646.

By the time the 1977 season was complete, it appeared the Pirates' spiritual leader was on the way out. Bad wheels, an inner ear ailment and pinched nerve in his left elbow weakened Pops physically, while worry over his hospitalized wife, Dolores, affected his concentration. But his spouse recovered and he snapped back to earn Comeback Player of the Year honors in 1978, setting the table for his stalwart '79 MVP campaign. Never really known for his glove work, Stargell led NL first basemen with a .997 fielding average.

Over the next three years, a series of injuries limited Stargell to an average of 60 games per year, and he retired following the 1982 season. In 1984, the Pirates hired Willie as a minor league batting instructor. He also was a Braves coach before returning to Pittsburgh in 1997.

Stargell was elected to the Hall of Fame in 1988, but tragically, the man who had spent so much time and effort battling other people's diseases was now himself a victim of poor health. He did not return in the spring of 2001 to his job as a special assistant to Pirates General Manager Cam Bonifay following several hospitalizations and undergoing dialysis for failing kidneys several times a week for more than five years. The 61-year-old finally died of an acute stroke April 9, 2001, ironically on the very day that the Pirates opened PNC Park. A 12-foot bronze statue honoring Pops had been unveiled two days earlier.

Respected and loved, Willie Stargell's supreme play and exemplary behavior made him a natural leader — one whose actions spoke louder than his words.

The Silken Scoop

Every resplendent movement Keith Hernandez executed on a baseball field — both at first base and in the batter's box — was pure textbook. Unsurpassed in digging errant throws out of the dirt, charging bunt attempts and ranging far and wide to snare grounders, he was as fluid as they come.

The port-side hitter always had an impeccable stroke, even as far back as early minor league days when the safeties came less frequently. His strength as a batsman was line drives to the power-alley gaps, limiting his home run production but making Keith one of the game's most prolific two-base hit artists.

Hernandez's baseball development was guided by his father, Tony, whose advancement in the St. Louis Cardinals farm chain had been halted by a career-ending head injury. As the son excelled on the diamonds around San Francisco, it appeared that the father's dashed dreams would be vicariously fulfilled. But after the youngster was booted off the high school team his senior year for quarreling with the coach, once-eager scouts backed off, fearing potential attitude problems.

Consequently, it wasn't until pick No. 783 that St. Louis matter-of-factly drafted its future MVP. However, the Cardinals didn't offer the 18-year-old a $30,000 bonus until after he'd absolutely burned up a local summer league.

Publicized far and wide as the second coming of Stan Musial, the flashy-fielding first baseman bombed in his initial shot with the big club in '75, and was returned for another half-season in the minors before coming up to stay the next campaign.

A solid .289 effort was followed by an even better 1977 season that saw Keith reach the seats a career-high 15 times. This sudden surge of home run power had the lefty unconsciously abandoning his usual straight-away stroke in '78 as he searched in vain for even more four-baggers. The result was a ragged year at the plate, and profound self-doubt.

But after that horrible sputter, Hernandez redefined himself as a gap hitter, raised his average a whopping 89 points and shared the 1979 Most Valuable Player award. He began the campaign hitting only .237 through April, but successive months of .340, .369 and .333 soon made it apparent that Keith was experiencing a career year.

On the strength of a .384 August, the 25-year-old sailed to the sole batting title of his life (.344), becoming the first senior circuit infielder to win a hitting crown and Gold Glove in the same year. Additionally, he finished first in runs scored (116), doubles (48) and on-base percentage (.421); second with 210 hits; and fifth with 105 RBIs.

The production continued the next two campaigns, as he led the league in both runs (111) and on-base percentage (.410) in 1980. In 1982, his .299 average, 94 RBIs and league-high 21 game-winning ribbies played a major role in the Redbirds' World Championship. Hernandez batted .333 in the League Championship Series win over Atlanta that year, then contributed a home run and a World Series-high eight RBIs in the thrilling fall classic victory over Milwaukee.

But with the team slumping terribly in '83, Cardinal officials looked to upgrade their pitching, and traded Keith to the Mets for hurler Neil Allen early in the season. St. Louis fans are still grousing about the deal. It wasn't until early in 1984 that Cardinal manager Whitey Herzog stated that Hernandez was deemed expendable when he allegedly took to working crossword puzzles on the bench during practices.

After netting a five-year, $8.4 million contract prior to 1984, Keith was the epitome of dedicated professionalism on a surprising young Mets team that mounted a serious assault on the National League East title. With Hernandez leading the way, New York was on top of the division at mid-season, and the first baseman was prominently mentioned as an MVP candidate once more.

The New York charges eventually fell short of a division crown by 6½ games, but few could argue that the '84 season was anything but spectacularly rewarding for both the Mets and Hernandez. The team's new leader had stroked his way to a .311 pace, driving

in 94 runs and bringing his lifetime average to an even .300, while finishing second in the MVP voting to Ryne Sandberg.

Keith batted .309 with 91 RBIs in 1985, but the Mets fell three games shy of the NL East championship. They rectified the situation the following season with a 108-win effort in a campaign that saw Hernandez bat .310 with a league-high 94 walks and 83 RBIs. The first sacker punched out seven hits and three RBIs in an LCS win over Houston, then drove in four runs in the seven-game World Series triumph over Boston. He hit .290 with 89 RBIs in 1987, then drove in 55 runs in 95 games in '88 as the Mets won another division title. Hernandez produced five RBIs, as well as a homer, among his seven hits in the LCS loss to Los Angeles. He played another season for New York in 1989, then finished his 17-year career in '90 in a Cleveland uniform.

Keith Hernandez was an impressive hitter, as evidenced by his .296 career batting average and 1,000-plus to-

tals in RBIs and runs. But he'll always be best known for his classy fielding skills which earned him 11 consecutive Gold Gloves (1978–88), as well as a No. 2 all-time ranking in assists for first basemen (1,682) and a No. 6 ranking in double plays (1,654). He'll also be remembered in pop culture for a 1992 appearance in a *Seinfeld* episode, "The New Friend: The Boyfriend," in which he dated Elaine (but was held up by the third base coach). Few pitchers were able to deny him, however, when Keith stood in the batter's box in the 1970s and '80s.

Top 5 MVP Vote-Getters

1. Willie Stargell, Pittsburgh — 216
1. Keith Hernandez, St. Louis— 216
3. Dave Winfield, San Diego—155
4. Larry Parrish, Montreal —128
5. Ray Knight, Cincinnati — 82

1979 AMERICAN LEAGUE—DON BAYLOR

Don Edward Baylor
B. June 28, 1949, Austin, Texas

Year	Team	Games	AB	Hits	Avg.	HR	RBI	Runs	SB
1979	Cal AL	162	628	186	.296	36	139	120	2

The Season

The American League, which had suffered through seasons of horrendous offensive drought in the 1960s, suddenly came alive in the hitting department in 1979. Junior circuit bats pounded the ball at a .270 average, while league hurlers combined for an uncommonly inflated 4.22 ERA. Both marks were highs dating back to the early 1950s.

Heading the hit parade were the Western Division champion California Angels, who scored more runs than

any major league club. Baltimore, led by skipper Earl Weaver, was anchored by the league's best pitching and commanded the East with 102 wins.

The No. 1 pitching team in the league then ousted the premiere AL offensive club in the League Championship Series, three games to one. But after winning three of the first four World Series contests, the O's succumbed to the Pirates in seven.

Considering the increased run production, it was a fitting year for 1967 MVP Carl Yastrzemski to become the first AL player to record both 400

homers and 3,000 safeties. He joined past National League MVPs Willie Mays, Hank Aaron and Stan Musial in that elite group.

On successive days in September, a couple of players raced around the basepaths in style. Bob Watson became the first player to hit for the cycle in both leagues when he turned the trick against Baltimore September 15. The next day, Willie Wilson of Kansas City hit his fifth inside-the-park homer of the season, the most in 54 years.

On a tragic note, 1976 MVP Thurman Munson died when the small plane he was piloting crashed in Canton, Ohio. The following day, more than 50,000 attended a memorial tribute at Yankee Stadium.

The Angel Soars

With virtually the entire American League engaged in an offensive barrage of unusually productive proportions, more than the usual handful of lumber-wielding principals delighted in 1979 statistical yields of MVP magnitude. Jim Rice and Fred Lynn rocked Beantown in an effort to recapture that lofty status, while Kansas City's George Brett and Ken Singleton of Baltimore were also in the hunt. A case could easily be made for each of their efforts, but in the end, the most deserving of the lot was the prodigious run producer of the California Angels: Don Baylor.

Despite a debilitating succession of injuries that included a pulled hamstring, sprained right wrist, separated shoulder and dislocated right thumb, the rampaging right-hander outdistanced them all, leading the league in RBIs (139) and runs (120). While injured Angel teammates dropped like felled warriors around him, Baylor remained grimly in the California lineup, playing every game and leading his club to its first Western Division title.

This was the kind of season the Austin, Texas, native had dreamed of a dozen years before when he turned down a University of Texas football scholarship to pursue a baseball career with the Baltimore Orioles. He'd known pain in varying forms as a pigskin star, playing with a dislocated shoulder that often popped out of joint. There had never been room for the word *surrender* in Don's vocabulary.

Five minor league campaigns, beginning in 1967 when he earned Appalachian League Player of the Year honors, had honed his winning instincts. Baltimore's classy farm chain bred victory-minded thoroughbreds, and Baylor was one of its premiere stallions. In 1970 at Rochester, the 21-year-old won *The Sporting News* Minor League Player of the Year honor with a 22-homer, .327-average, 127-run effort.

Don Baylor. (Courtesy California Angels.)

But with the parent club deep in outfield talent and the designated hitter rule not yet a reality, Don was reluctantly returned to the farms for another brilliant season in 1971.

Earmarked as the recently traded Frank Robinson's successor, Baylor's apprenticeship in the big time began in '72 when the muscular fly-chaser managed a lukewarm .253 in 102 games. His stats improved in 1973 as the budding ballplayer participated in his first League Championship Series, posting a .273 average in a losing cause. The progress continued as Baylor was promoted to a fulltimer. The O's won another division title in '74, aided by Don's .272 average, but suffered an LCS setback again.

Don was unexpectedly traded prior to '76 to the Oakland A's as part of a deal that brought Reggie Jackson to the Orioles. Dumbstruck and discouraged, he played out a sub-par year in Oakland before moving as a free agent to the Angels in 1977. Two campaigns later, he was a serious MVP contender for owner Gene Autry's charges, pounding 34 homers.

Despite obvious talents, Don was often overlooked by the media and fandom. Passively calculating on a ballfield, the 6-foot-1, 190-pound assemblage of strength possessed a qui-

etly efficient, upright disposition, although he could also light up a room with his beaming smile. Not many realize how highly regarded Baylor's contributions were in the inner circles of the game. An enterprising baserunner with excellent speed, Don swiped 52 sacks in 1976, and he was one of only 12 players to have accumulated 250 home runs and 250 steals.

Nagging problems associated with his high school football injury made throwing a chore, however. As a result, the proud Texan was shunted between the outfield and a designated hitter's role.

Keeping a bat such as Baylor's out of a lineup altogether would have been ludicrous. The former all-time leading Angel home run hitter was an enigma among free-swingers, rarely taking a free pass, yet hardly ever striking out. Utilizing a straight-up stance and crowding the dish, the line-driver's name was always mentioned with those batters most feared when the game was on the line. That challenging posture at the plate resulted in Baylor being hit by pitches a major league record-267 times, including an AL-record 35 times in 1986.

Clutch situations were plentiful in Baylor's MVP year, and Don responded with as many RBIs as had been seen in the AL since Harmon Killebrew's 1969 MVP effort. Splitting his time between the outfield and DH, the one-man run factory led the Angels to an 88–74 record and a spot in the playoffs.

Besides leading the league in RBIs and runs, the 30-year-old was fourth in both homers (a career-high 36) and total bases (333), while hitting .296 and pilfering 22 bases, all while playing hurt. A monstrous July in which he unloaded 11 circuit shots and hit .349 spurred California to the front.

The momentum came to a screeching halt in the LCS, however, when Don dipped to .188 against his former team from Baltimore, and for the third time in as many tries was a member of a losing team. But the defeat was somewhat smoothed when baseball's writers named the eighth-year man as the first MVP in the history of the Angels.

The glory was fleeting, however, and the newly crowned king of the AL was beset by hard times in the next two seasons. His 1982 record helped California to another division crown, but Don's team was again bounced in the LCS.

Yankee owner George Steinbrenner eyed Baylor's league-leading 21 game-winning RBIs and made him a Big Apple ballplayer prior to 1983. The 34-year-old did the pinstripes proud, going over .300 for the first time in his

career (.303). Although Don's average dipped to .258 the next season, his 27 HRs represented his best long ball effort in five years.

Baylor provided the Yankees with 23 homers and 91 RBIs in 1985, and was named the winner of the annual Roberto Clemente Award for combining on-field skills with civic responsibility. Over the next three years, he managed to reach post-season play with three different teams. The two-time winner of the Outstanding Designated Hitter award batted .346 for Boston in the 1986 LCS, after contributing 31 round-trippers and 94 RBIs during the regular season. He then batted .400 in the 1987 LCS for Minnesota, followed by a .385 effort in the World Series, including a homer and three RBIs. Baylor concluded his playing days in 1988 with Oakland, which also made it to the World Series.

Don wound up with 338 home runs, 1,276 RBIs, 1,236 runs scored and 285 stolen bases over his 19-year career. Always possessing an astute baseball mind, Baylor did not stay inactive for long following his retirement. He was an assistant to the Milwaukee Brewers' general manager in 1989 and served for two years as the team's batting coach, then worked in the same capacity for the St. Louis Cardinals in

1992. He became the first manager in Colorado Rockies history, and the squad won more games (67) in 1993 than any expansion team in modern NL history. Baylor was named 1995 NL Manager of the Year after Colorado earned a Wild Card spot, and the following year the Rockies became the first team in major league history to reach the 200 mark in both home runs and steals. After six years in Colorado, Baylor was named the Atlanta Braves batting coach for the 1999 season, and in November of '99, he signed a four-year deal to manage the Chicago Cubs.

Post-season play eluded Baylor on the north side of Chicago, although his 2001 team's 23-game improvement from 2000 was the best in baseball. He was dismissed in mid–2002, but if history is any indicator, it won't be long until he steers another club to the winner's circle as he's done with so many teams in so many ways.

Top 5 MVP Vote-Getters

1. Don Baylor, California — 347
2. Ken Singleton, Baltimore — 241
3. George Brett, Kansas City — 226
4. Fred Lynn, Boston — 160½
5. Jim Rice, Boston — 124

1980 NATIONAL LEAGUE — MIKE SCHMIDT

Michael Jack Schmidt
B. September 27, 1949, Dayton, Ohio

Year	Team	Games	AB	Hits	Avg.	HR	RBI	Runs	SB
1980	Phil NL	150	548	157	.286	48	121	104	12

The Season

The 1980 season began on a very precarious note, with players having struck exhibition games and threatening to sit out the year if a new basic agreement was not decided upon. On April 1, the 27-player executive board

voted to skip the 92 remaining pre-season games, start the campaign on time, then strike at midnight May 22 if a settlement had not been reached.

But federal mediator Kenneth Moffett helped avert a work stoppage with the strike date fewer than 48 hours away, with all issues settled ex-

cept free agent compensation, which was tabled for a year.

With play on for good, the Philadelphia Phillies earned their fourth Eastern Division title in five years, edging Montreal by one game. Houston dropped its final three contests of the regular season to Los

Angeles to fall into a tie with the Dodgers for the top spot in the West. The Astros then won a one-game playoff.

In a thrilling LCS, the Phils nipped Houston three games to two with the last four meetings requiring extra innings. Philadelphia took the finale 8–7 in 10 frames after trailing 5–2 in the eighth. The Boys from Broad Street followed their first pennant in 30 years with their initial World Championship in a 98-year history, beating Kansas City in six games.

An ex-Phillie also earned long overdue recognition, as former MVP Chuck Klein was inducted into the Hall of Fame in 1980.

Two NL pitchers experienced opposite fates this season. Montreal's Bill Gullickson set a major league rookie record by striking out 18 batters in a game during a 4–2 win over visiting Chicago. Houston's J.R. Richard, who had led the league in strikeouts in 1978 and '79, and in ERA the latter year, suffered a stroke July 30 due to a blood clot in his neck, and never pitched in the majors again.

Prior to the season, 1957 MVP Hank Aaron made a striking statement that baseball was not treating black ballplayers fairly when he refused an award from commissioner Bowie Kuhn intended to honor the all-time home run king for his 715th homer.

Faithful Phillie

His torso rigid and muscular, his menacing war club held aloft, he waited patiently, deep in the batter's box. It was more than just his formidable reputation that made hurlers quiver before delivering a pitch to Mike Schmidt. His notoriety as a Philadelphia powerhouse was well-earned, with every at-bat a potential home run. The most prolific hitter in Philly history swatted 548 home runs over an 18-year career on the way to Cooperstown, but he was much more than a power hitter.

A private person, Mike is a deep thinker who takes life seriously. The devout Christian is a family man, and was known by former teammates as "Captain Cool." When the pressure of baseball became too intense, he retreated to his attic and the model trains on which he spent thousands of dollars.

As a ballplayer at Fairview High School in Dayton, Ohio, Michael was only slightly above average. A .250 hitter, the teenager showed considerably more promise as a football quarterback and a sharpshooting forward on the hardcourt. But two knee operations limited his abilities in those sports, and baseball became the focal point at Ohio University, where he twice achieved All-America honors.

Schmidt hoped to be an architect, but rapid improvement on the diamond led him in another direction. The Phillies came calling with a $37,000 bonus in 1971, and by the next year the right-hander was up with the big club for the tail end of the season. The 23-year-old could have used another year in the minors, but the Phils needed immediate help.

Touted as a future superstar, Mike fell flat on his face in 1973, batting lower (.196) than any major league regular, and striking out 136 times in 367 at-bats. Mike's confidence took a dive, but manager Danny Ozark stuck with Schmidt.

The 6-foot-2, 195-pounder justified Ozark's faith and came through above and beyond expectations. From 1974 to '77, he averaged more than 37 homers and nearly 105 RBIs per season, topping the NL in circuit clouts three consecutive years. In a game at Wrigley Field in 1976, he ripped four round-trippers in a row, the first NL

Mike Schmidt. (National Baseball Hall of Fame Library, Cooperstown, N.Y.)

player to accomplish the feat since 1894.

As Schmidt's star rose, so did the Phillies, climbing to third place in '74 and second the next campaign before capturing the division title in 1976. Mike hit .308 in the League Championship Series, but Cincinnati swept the Phils in three.

Although overshadowed by his offensive production, Schmidt's defense was always exceptional. Displaying excellent range and a cannon-like arm, he set a still-standing National League record for assists by a third baseman with 404 in 1974, and led the circuit in assists again in '76 and '77. His 396 assists in 1977 were the second highest NL total ever.

Deservedly, the solidly constructed athlete became the league's highest paid player prior to the 1977 season, signing a six-year pact at $565,000 annually. He earned every penny in '77, but slumped terribly in '78 when

Philadelphia lost its third consecutive LCS. Fickle Phillie fans made their displeasure known by booing their hot corner man. Mike took the abuse in stride, then rebounded in 1979 with another remarkable season.

By the time 1980 rolled around, the big bopper was being hailed as one of baseball's utmost all-around performers. Between 1973 and '79, he amassed 234 home runs and 663 RBIs, more than any major leaguer, and won five Gold Gloves while making four All-Star Teams. He won NL home run titles in 1974 (36), 1975 (38) and 1976 (38); led the league in slugging (.546) in '74; and topped the circuit in walks (120) in '79. But, he still had not garnered the MVP.

The long ball hitter rectified that situation in 1980 with career highs in homers (48) and RBIs (121), both tops in the NL, and an improved .286 batting average. Mike led the National League in total bases with 342 and slugging at .624, while placing runner-up in runs scored with 104.

Schmidt had come to spring training a dozen pounds heavier in 1980, and the added weight apparently helped his power. He cracked five circuit clouts during a nine-day stretch in May, then blasted nine more in September as the Phillies battled Montreal for the East crown. In a crucial series in early October, the clutch hitter homered to give Philadelphia a 2–1 win over the Expos, then tagged a two-run shot in the 11th inning the following day as the Phils grabbed another division title. Mike finished the campaign with 17 game-winning hits, and led third sackers in assists for the fourth time and in double plays for the third occasion.

His .208 average notwithstanding, Philadelphia edged Houston in a highly contested LCS. Then Schmidt got hot. A key double paved the way for a 6–4 win over Kansas City in the second game of the World Series, and a solo homer contributed to the 4–3 third game defeat. The Phillies captured Game 5 as Mike belted a two-run round-tripper and scored the tying run in the ninth inning. In the sixth and final contest, he drove in two runs, then was selected the Series MVP for his .381 average, two homers and seven RBIs. Schmidt became the first unanimous MVP in the NL since Orlando Cepeda in 1967.

Mike had already accomplished more in eight full seasons than most players do in an entire career, but he wasn't through yet. Nineteen-eighty-one would bring more heroics and a second straight MVP, with still another such honor on the horizon.

Top 5 MVP Vote-Getters

1. Mike Schmidt, Philadelphia — 336
2. Gary Carter, Montreal — 193
3. Jose Cruz, Houston — 166
4. Dusty Baker, Los Angeles — 138
5. Steve Carlton, Philadelphia — 134

1980 AMERICAN LEAGUE — GEORGE BRETT

George Howard Brett
B. May 15, 1953, Glen Dale, West Virginia

Year	Team	Games	AB	Hits	Avg.	HR	RBI	Runs	SB
1980	KC AL	117	449	175	.390	24	118	87	15

The Season

Both the Kansas City Royals and New York Yankees captured their fourth division titles in five years, but this time K.C. finally shook the monkey off its back by slamming the New Yorkers three straight to win the League Championship Series. Kansas City had won Western Division crowns in 1976, '77 and '78, but was thwarted each time by the Bronx Bombers.

The Yankees, who posted the most wins (103) in the Eastern Division in a decade, outdistanced Baltimore by three games, while the Royals romped to a 14-game advantage over Oakland in the West. Kansas City took a team batting average of .286, highest in baseball in 30 years, into the World Series, but suffered a six-game setback at the hands of the Philadelphia Phillies.

Oakland's Rickey Henderson went wild on the basepaths in '80, pilfering an all-time American League-high 100 bases. Scoring 133 runs, the most in the AL since Ted Williams' 150 in 1949, was Kansas City's Willie Wilson.

In a bizarre spring training incident outside a Mexico City hotel, Cleveland rookie Joe Charboneau was stabbed by a crazed fan with a ball point pen that penetrated one inch and struck a rib. Charboneau was sidelined for only four days, and wound up winning the Rookie of the Year award.

One of the Boys

Success never spoiled George Brett. Some ruggedly handsome bachelors with hefty salaries might choose to sip Perrier water by day and champagne at night. They might also elect to don expertly tailored suits and Gucci shoes. But Kansas City's gifted third

George Brett. (Courtesy Kansas City Royals.)

But then a renewed Brett went on a rampage. Four-for-four days became common occurrences for the port-side swinger, and on August 17, he stroked four hits against Toronto to reach the .400 mark. A week later, the amazing batsman collected five hits in one game in Milwaukee to reach .407.

A tender right hand caused George to miss nine games that month, but he was able to meet the plate appearance quota. Taking an even greater toll than the injuries was the intense pressure. The instant celebrity's life was one continuous media circus, and as the nation eagerly watched Brett attempt to become baseball's first .400 hitter since Ted Williams nearly 40 years before, the dream exploded in a 3-for-19 skid with only two weeks remaining. George collected 10 hits in his final 19 at-bats to raise the average to a still-incredible .390, the best of the century by an AL third baseman. The consistent performer was first in the league with a .664 slugging average, the highest figure in the American League in 19 years; first in on-base percentage (.461); and tied for second in RBIs. His 118 RBIs in 117 games made him the first player since Joe DiMaggio in 1948 to drive in more than one run per game in a season.

George's bat kept Kansas City atop the Western Division all season. Competing in a fourth League Championship Series against the Yankees in the past five years, the 27-year-old finally tasted victory, clinching the finale with a tremendous three-run homer off fireballer Goose Gossage and ensuring the Royals' first-ever pennant.

Brett then suffered an extremely painful and embarrassing hemorrhoid condition, forcing him out of the second World Series contest. Following surgery, he came back to smash a round-tripper in the Royals' 4–3 third-game win, but the Phillies triumphed in six. For the Series, he hit .375 with nine hits and three RBIs. Post-season laurels included the Most Valuable Player award, and Major League Player of the Year awards from *The Sporting News*, *Sport Magazine* and the Associated Press.

The youngest of four boys, all of whom eventually played professional baseball, George decided he wanted to

baseman was far more likely to pull on a pair of jeans and cowboy boots, and enjoy a beer or two with the boys after the game, than he was to put on any airs.

Which is not to say the down-to-earth, perennial All-Star was without his faults. He graphically proved his humanity in 1981 when outside pressures and a sub-par season caused him to erupt violently several times. The sandy-haired competitor apologized for the outbursts, and reverted to the lovable figure so much in evidence during the magical 1980 campaign

when all America backed his quest for the elusive .400 batting average.

The way Brett's 1980 season began, a *.300* average looked like a lofty goal. After a month and a half, George was batting only .247, having missed nine games because of a bruised heel. When he finally got untracked, a torn right ankle ligament sidelined him for 26 contests, and despite his .337 average by the All-Star break, it appeared the contact hitter might not have enough plate appearances to qualify for the batting title.

be a major leaguer while watching brother Ken pitch for Boston in the 1967 World Series.

Remarkably, the third baseman never hit .300 in three minor league campaigns. George unsuccessfully tried to copy the stance and swing of Carl Yastrzemski, forever attempting to pull the ball out of the park, but in mid–1974, renowned K.C. batting coach Charley Lau changed Brett into a line drive hitter who used all fields.

The 6-foot, 185-pounder led the league in hits (195) and triples (13) in 1975, then was a terror in '76, pacing the AL in four offensive categories: batting (.333), hits (215), triples (14) and total bases (298). His average fell off slightly the following two campaigns, but the Royals continued to win, capturing their second and third consecutive West Division titles. Rising to the occasion, Brett slugged an AL-record three home runs in one game of the '78 LCS, batting .389 with three RBIs for the series. His 20 triples in 1979 were the most in the majors in 22 years, and the highest in the AL in 30 seasons. He also paced the junior circuit with 212 hits that year.

Nineteen-eighty-one was a bleak year for Kansas City's star, despite a .314 average. The 28-year-old and his team slumped drastically in the first half, and with the media hounding him constantly, George became less tolerant and open. He flew off the handle several times, demolishing two toilets and a sink in a Minnesota clubhouse, poking a photographer with a crutch and scrapping with a reporter in an Anaheim hotel lobby.

Brett came back with a fine '82 campaign, but embroiled himself in more controversy by wearing a Cardinals cap at Busch Stadium during the World Series, sparking trade rumors. But Brett was soon back in good graces, leaping to a sparkling start which included his finest day as a pro on April 20 when he drilled three homers and collected seven RBIs in a game at Detroit.

One of his 25 round-trippers in '83 resulted in a highly unusual confrontation. With two outs and a runner on base in the top of the ninth inning, George clobbered a homer off Gossage to apparently give the Royals a 5–4 lead. But when Yankee manager Billy Martin argued that pine tar went too far up the barrel of Brett's bat, the home run was disallowed and George was called out to end the game. The third baseman exploded out of the dugout and charged at the umpires before being restrained by coaches and teammates. Four days later, AL President Lee MacPhail reversed the decision, and the Royals won the continued game. Brett was the league's top slugger in '83 with a .563 mark.

Knee surgery kept Brett out of the lineup early in 1984, but he returned to hit .284 and drive in nearly 70 runs on the way to a West Division crown.

Brett signed a contract extension which would pay him a then-impressive $1.78 million a year through 1989, but it certainly didn't make him complacent. He enjoyed one of his best seasons in 1985, batting .335 with a career-high 30 home runs, 112 RBIs, 108 runs scored, a league-best .585 slugging percentage and a Gold Glove, while leading the Royals to another Western Division title and a seven-game World Series victory over St. Louis. Brett batted .348 with eight hits, three home runs and five RBIs during the LCS against Toronto, and .370 with 10 hits versus the Cardinals.

He would never return to post-season play, but led the AL in doubles (45) and batting (.329) in 1990 — becoming the only player to win batting titles in three decades — and stroked 19 homers with 75 RBIs in his 21st and final season in '93. Brett batted .300 11 times, including five years in a row (1979–83); slugged at a .500 clip eight times; belted 20 homers on eight occasions; and drove in 80 runs 10 times. In nine post-season series, he hit .349, and his nine playoff homers were a record. He was fifth all time in doubles (665), 14th in hits (3,154), tied for 24th in RBIs (1,595) and 41st in runs (1,583).

Despite his tremendous success in baseball, including induction into the Hall of Fame in 1999, George Brett never let it go to his head. On the field or off, he was always just one of the boys.

Top 5 MVP Vote-Getters

1. George Brett, Kansas City — 335
2. Reggie Jackson, New York — 234
3. Rich Gossage, New York — 218
4. Willie Wilson, Kansas City — 169
5. Cecil Cooper, Milwaukee — 160

1981 NATIONAL LEAGUE—MIKE SCHMIDT

Michael Jack Schmidt
B. September 27, 1949, Dayton, Ohio

Year	Team	Games	AB	Hits	Avg.	HR	RBI	Runs	SB
1981	Phil NL	102	354	112	.316	31	91	78	12

The Season

The credibility of baseball suffered a severe blow in 1981, as a seemingly endless, terribly costly player strike threatened to wipe out the entire season.

The major issue at stake was free agent compensation. Owners, demanding replacements for lost free agents, and players, afraid that enforced compensation would reduce their value on the open market, failed to reach an agreement after months of negotiations. At 12:30 a.m. on June 12, players' union chief Marvin Miller announced, "The strike is on."

By the time the two sides reached a compromise and play resumed August 10, 712 games had been lost, as well as an estimated $100 million in players' salaries and owners' revenue.

In an effort to create renewed interest in the tarnished game, owners set up a split season format whereby the division leaders at the point when play was halted were declared the first-half winners. Those teams would face the second-half victors in a best-of-five playoff series at the end of the campaign to determine the division winner. The big loser in this system was Cincinnati, which posted the best overall record in the majors for the season, but failed to make the playoffs.

In the Eastern Division, second-half victor Montreal nudged Philadelphia in five games, while in the West, first-half winner Los Angeles came back from a 2–0 deficit to defeat Houston. But the Dodgers' come-from-behind efforts were only beginning. L.A. trailed the Expos 2–1 in the LCS, but rallied to win it, then fell behind the Yankees two games to none in the World Series before storming back with four straight victories.

Nineteen-sixty-eight may have been the year of the pitcher, but 1981 wasn't far off. Nolan Ryan of Houston became the only major league pitcher to throw five no-hitters with his fifth this season; Tom Seaver of Cincinnati and Philadelphia's Steve Carlton became the fifth and sixth moundsmen, respectively, to reach the 3,000-strike-out plateau; Fernando Valenzuela of Los Angeles became the first player to win both the Cy Young and Rookie of the Year awards in the same season; and 1968 MVP Bob Gibson was inducted into the Hall of Fame.

Abbreviated Bombardment

After establishing himself as one of the game's premiere power hitters, Mike Schmidt aired a secret desire to someday win a batting title. The closest the affable redhead came to that goal was in his 1981 MVP year when he finished fourth in the hitting race with a .316 mark. The ruddy-complexioned third baseman struck out far too many times to be a serious batting crown threat; but more important, the fans came out to see him smack the ball out of sight, and the Phillies counted on him for run production.

Repeating the domination he displayed in 1980 when he earned his first Most Valuable Player award was no easy task, but the heady third sacker did just that in strike-shortened 1981, ripping 31 home runs, driving in 91, collecting 228 total bases, slugging at a .644 clip, scoring 78 runs, walking 73 times, compiling a .439 on-base percentage and notching 249 assists, all league highs. The Phillies won the first-half crown, but it was Schmidt's second-half surge (.356, 17 HRs, 50 RBIs in 51 games) that made him the

third National Leaguer to be voted MVP two years in a row, following in the footsteps of Ernie Banks and Joe Morgan. In the Eastern Division playoffs, Schmidt tagged a two-run homer to help the Phils stay alive in the fourth game, but they faltered in the finale. He also had a double in that series, and hit .250.

The well-conditioned infielder remained relatively injury-free through his first decade of big league ball, but in 1982, ailments began cropping up. After signing a six-year contract at close to $2 million a year, he broke a toe in spring training, damaged his rib cage in April and suffered a pulled left hamstring just before the All-Star break. Still, Schmidt appeared in 148 games and totaled 35 round-trippers and 108 runs, both third in the league. His .547 slugging average was the NL's best, and he also topped the circuit in walks with 107 and on-base percentage with a .407 mark.

The next year, Mike bolted out of the gate, depositing seven pitches into the seats and driving in 23 runs during the first month, while batting .353. But by June 2, he'd slipped to .252, adding only two home runs and four RBIs. Despite the slump, he wound up leading the league in homers (40) and walks (128), and placing third in RBIs (109) and runs (104). His .402 on-base percentage was the best in the NL, giving him his third and final title in that department. Schmidt's ability to excel in the on-base percentage category despite a large number of strikeouts illustrates that he had a keen eye, and that when he picked out a pitch to hit, it often found a hole—or a bleacher seat.

Although they appeared to possess the necessary talent, the Phillies were flailing helplessly until Labor Day when, with a blast at management, Schmidt said the club had no sense of direction. From that point on, Philadelphia won 21 of its final 25 games to capture the 1983 Eastern Division title and pennant before bowing meekly to Baltimore in a five-game World Series. Following the season, Mike was presented with the Lou Gehrig Memorial Award, an honor granted to the player who best exemplifies Gehrig's character both on and off the field.

Schmidt was a tiger in the '83 LCS, batting .467 with seven hits, including two doubles and a homer, and driving in a pair of runs. The fair-weather Philadelphia fans who had booed Mike when he slumped in 1978

voted him the all-time greatest Phillie several years later. The boo birds were at it again in the '83 Series when Schmidt managed only one broken-bat single in 20 at-bats. The 35-year-old third baseman came back strong in 1984, tying Dale Murphy for the league home run title with 36, and driving in an NL-best 106 runs while batting .277.

Schmidt enjoyed yet another impressive season in 1985, pounding 33 home runs (tied for third in the league), slugging at a .532 pace (fourth), racking up 292 total bases (fifth) and collecting 87 bases on balls (tied for second).

Despite the inevitable catcalls from unappreciative spectators, Mike

Schmidt continued to lash the ball out of National League parks and play a sparkling third base. And only one year away was an honor that only a handful of ballplayers would ever achieve — a third Most Valuable Player trophy.

Top 5 MVP Vote-Getters

1. Mike Schmidt, Philadelphia — 321
2. Andre Dawson, Montreal — 215
3. George Foster, Cincinnati — 146
4. Dave Concepcion, Cincinnati — 108
5. Fernando Valenzuela, Los Angeles — 90

1981 AMERICAN LEAGUE — ROLLIE FINGERS

Roland Glen Fingers
B. August 25, 1946, Steubenville, Ohio

Year	Team	Games	W	L	ERA	IP	SO	BB	Saves
1981	Mil AL	47	6	3	1.04	78	61	13	28

The Season

The 1981 season witnessed an anticipated shrinkage of statistical exploits due to the strike which erased 38 percent of the campaign. Four players tied for first place in the home run derby, while the same number of pitchers was bunched at the top in the wins department.

Bobby Grich of California, Baltimore's Eddie Murray, Dwight Evans of Boston and Oakland's Tony Armas all tagged 22 round-trippers, while Milwaukee's Pete Vukovich, Dennis Martinez of the Orioles, the A's Steve McCatty and Jack Morris of Detroit earned 14 victories each.

The split season format enabled the New York Yankees to return to the fall classic despite a 25–26 record and sixth-place finish in the second half. Winners of the first session, the Yanks edged the second-half victors from

Milwaukee three games to two in the Eastern Division playoffs.

In the West, Kansas City rallied from a weak first session (20–30) to earn the second-half crown by one game over Oakland, which had copped first-half honors. The A's then whipped the Royals three straight in the playoffs.

The Yankees made short work of the A's in the League Championship Series, taking three in a row while outscoring their opponents 20–4. But after jumping to a 2–0 lead in the World Series, New York was stunned by the Dodgers' four-game rampage.

Firing the first perfect game since Catfish Hunter's in 1968, Len Barker of Cleveland blanked Toronto 3–0 May 15. Barker's gem was the first AL no-hitter in nearly four years.

On May 25, former MVP Carl Yastrzemski became only the fourth major leaguer to play in 3,000 games.

R-O-L-L-I-E Spells Relief

Often, Rollie Fingers' job consisted of watching and waiting. As one of baseball's special breed — the relievers — he usually spent the first six or seven innings observing opposing hitters, carefully studying their habits and diligently searching for weaknesses. Then, when the contest would become close, he psyched himself up for that inevitable call that would bring him onto the mound for a classic confrontation between pitcher and batter with the game on the line.

Fingers became a bullpen specialist, ironically, because he couldn't handle the anxiety he experienced as a member of the Oakland Athletics' rotation in 1970. Unable to sleep the night before a start, Rollie would usually be exhausted by the fourth inning. But the prospect of storming in to quell a potential rally appealed to the fierce competitor, who became a full-time fireman in 1971.

A reliever ordinarily has little chance of winning the Cy Young Award, let alone a Most Valuable Player trophy. But two situations—a strike-shortened 1981 season and the increased importance of the relief specialist—provided a unique opportunity for Fingers to garner both accolades, becoming the first reliever to win the AL MVP award.

In his first season in Milwaukee, Fingers experienced his best campaign of a 17-year career. The power-laden Brewers, who finished a distant third in the AL East in 1980, were desperate for a top-notch reliever, and so acquired Fingers in a seven-player deal with St. Louis, which had traded for the relief artist four days previously.

The lanky right-hander wasted no time proving his worth to the Brew Crew. Then, shortly after signing a four-year contract estimated at $600,000 per year, Fingers walked out with the rest of the players. Rollie, who later said the strike helped him stay fresh down the stretch, was the losing pitcher in the All-Star Game. But then the hard-throwing 35-year-old caught fire, blanking the opposition in his next nine outings. The Brewers' bullpen ace entered September with 20 saves, and his final win of the campaign came in a 2–1 decision over Detroit, clinching the second-half crown and giving Fingers an AL-leading 28 saves. He placed runner-up in appearances with 47, while posting a brilliant 1.04 earned run average, and was involved in 13 of Milwaukee's last 15 victories.

The Brewers were bounced by the Yankees in a five-game Eastern Division playoff, despite a win and save by Rollie, who was showered with post-season laurels. His MVP trophy, won by a narrow margin over Oakland's Rickey Henderson, marked the first time in more than three decades that a relief pitcher had been so honored. Fingers also became the fourth late-inning hurler to earn a Cy Young plaudit, and he captured a record-fourth Fireman of the Year award.

Sporting a villainous handlebar mustache giving off an Old West aura of roughness, Fingers was a surly,

Rollie Fingers. (Courtesy Milwaukee Brewers.)

chronic complainer who often won half the battle by snarling at the hitter. With long, gangling arms, the 6-foot-4, 190-pounder came at the batter with a variety of motions and pitches. Rollie was effective enough to post NL-leading save totals of 35 and 37 for the San Diego Padres in 1977 and '78, respectively, while throwing a sinking fastball and hard slider. But in '81, he perfected a forkball, causing batsmen additional distress.

Born in Steubenville, Ohio, the youngster grew up on the West Coast, starring in American Legion ball. But his professional career almost ended before it started. While pitching for Birmingham of the Southern Association in

1967, a line drive shattered Rollie's jaw and cheekbone. Fingers recovered from the setback and joined the A's late in 1968. The next three years, the skinny moundsman appeared in approximately one-third of Oakland's games.

Under eccentric owner Charlie Finley, who paid $300 to each of his players who would grow a mustache, the A's won three consecutive World Championships, beginning in 1972. Rollie was dominant in nearly every one of those post-season experiences, copping a World Series MVP in '74 for his 1.93 ERA, two saves and a win in Oakland's five-game triumph over the Dodgers. His six saves in three World Series were a record.

Midway through the '76 season, Finley tried to break up his squad of aging stars, which he could no longer afford; but a sale of Fingers and Joe Rudi to the Red Sox for $1 million apiece was negated by Commissioner Bowie Kuhn. Rollie became a free agent following the 1976 season and was signed by San Diego to a four-year, $1.6 million pact.

Following his magnificent 1981 MVP effort, the fiery right-hander accumulated 29 saves for the awesome Brew Crew, but tore a muscle in his right forearm and was unable to pitch again that season. Fingers was sidelined by tendonitis for the entire 1983 campaign.

The rugged athlete appeared ready to make a comeback in 1984, regaining his fireman position with 23 saves until a herniated disc ended his season in late July. That final save was his 216th in the AL. Fingers saved 17 more games in 1985, retiring with 341 (sixth best all time) and 107 relief wins (fourth). In 2001, Fingers announced the launch of his Web site—www.fingers34.com—where sports memorabilia collectors can submit questions and purchase collectibles. The site also includes a Fingers biography, events page, trophy showcase and a statistics page.

Recognizing Rollie's mastery in the role of reliever, the voters elected him to the Hall of Fame in 1992. A handful of relievers have passed his career save total since Fingers retired, but Rollie's name will always be spelled R-E-L-I-E-F by his fans.

Top 5 MVP Vote-Getters

1. Rollie Fingers, Milwaukee—319
2. Rickey Henderson, Oakland—308
3. Dwight Evans, Boston—140
4. Tony Armas, Oakland—139
5. Eddie Murray, Baltimore—137

1982 NATIONAL LEAGUE—DALE MURPHY

Dale Bryan Murphy
B. March 12, 1956, Portland, Oregon

Year	Team	Games	AB	Hits	Avg.	HR	RBI	Runs	SB
1982	Atl NL	162	598	168	.281	36	109	113	23

The Season

The Atlanta Braves started the season with a modern-day major league record-13 consecutive victories, taking a commanding lead in the NL Western Division, but lost 19-of-21 in August to fall into a tie with the charging Dodgers. The Braves regained their composure to edge L.A. by one game. Two-time MVP Joe Morgan of San Francisco aided the Atlanta cause with a dramatic home run that defeated L.A. on the final day of the season.

Meanwhile, a different kind of excitement was unfolding in the East, with St. Louis and Philadelphia slugging it out all season. The Cardinals finally ended on top by three games, then went on to bop Atlanta three straight in the LCS.

Past MVP winners fared well in 1982, with Pete Rose becoming only the fifth player in history to reach the 3,000 games played plateau, and passing Hank Aaron for the No. 2 spot in the all-time hit parade. Steve Garvey moved within 10 of Billy Williams' senior circuit record of 1,117 consecutive games played, and Frank Robinson and Aaron were both elected to the Hall of Fame in their first year of eligibility.

In perhaps the most interesting accomplishment of the season, Joel Youngblood became the first player in major league history to play for two teams in two cities on the same day. After playing for the Mets in Chicago in an August 4 afternoon game, Youngblood was traded to Montreal. He immediately flew to Philadelphia and entered the Expos lineup in the sixth inning. To top it off, Youngblood collected one hit in each game, both against eventual Hall of Fame pitchers (Ferguson Jenkins and Steve Carlton).

After winning their first pennant in 14 years, the Cardinals came back from a three games-to-two deficit against the Milwaukee Brewers in the World Series to grab the championship. Future MVP Willie McGee, who never hit more than 11 homers in any season, belted a pair of dingers and drove in five runs for the winners in the fall classic, while Joaquin Andujar won two games with a 1.35 ERA.

Brave in Bloom

Nineteen-eighty-one was an appalling season for Dale Murphy. The big outfielder groped and struggled at the plate, never really getting untracked, and finished with a .247 average. It took all the bargaining abilities of Dale's agent to convince Atlanta Braves management not to cut "Murf's" salary the maximum 20 percent. It was eventually agreed that the center fielder would play for less money, but numerous incentive clauses were added to the pact. And in 1982, the Prince Charming of the Cinderella Braves collected on all of them.

That season, the fifth-year man became only the third Braves player to earn the MVP award, an honor last gleaned by Henry Aaron while playing for Milwaukee 25 years earlier. Murphy's ascendance coincided with Atlanta's first division title since 1969. The converted catcher played in every game in '82, tied for the National League RBI crown with 109, hit a solid .281 and captured his first of five consecutive Gold Gloves.

The difference between the "Gentle Giant" of 1982 and the Dale Murphy of the four previous years centered on a sudden realization that it was not necessary to swing from the heels in order to smack a baseball out of the park. Glimpses of MVP magic had surfaced occasionally in the past, especially in the four-bagger department, where Dale slugged 23, 21 and 33 in three consecutive years. But during that time, he had twice led the league in strikeouts and was shuttled from catcher to first base, failing to suffice at either position. An encouraging note was the steady rise in Murphy's batting average, but when that nose-dived during the strike-shortened 1981 campaign, there were serious doubts that Dale would ever become the player for whom Atlanta fans yearned.

Back in 1974, the Braves made him their first pick in the draft, drawn by magnificent abilities that resulted in mammoth home runs and deer-like speed that dominated his Portland, Oregon, high school competition. The middle-class youth quickly reversed a decision to attend Arizona State University's baseball factory on a scholarship, joining the Braves' farm system at age 18.

The youngster was the epitome of wide-eyed innocence and strong puritanical values, both of which have been retained to this day. The deeply religious man spurned smoking, drinking, cursing and carousing. Soft-spoken and polite beyond reasonable expectation (he even called reporters "sir"), big No. 3 humbly chalked up his good fortune to luck, his manager, teammates and God. Gary Cooper had nothing on Dale in the "aw shucks" school of sincere uprightness.

Unsullied amidst the usually rau-

Dale Murphy. (Courtesy Atlanta Braves.)

cous atmosphere of a baseball clubhouse, Murphy was a natural target for friendly gibes from fellow players, the eager-to-please attitude often fair game for practical jokes. Dale's even temper helped keep everything in perspective, however, and the Atlanta star rested secure in the knowledge that he was one of the most popular players on the team.

He was a notch above the competition in the diamond game in 1982 when at age 26 he spearheaded Atlanta's successful divisional drive. Besides topping the circuit in RBIs,

"John-Boy" was second in runs scored (113) and home runs (36), and fourth in walks (90) and total bases (318). He also swiped 23 sacks while covering center field like a tarpaulin.

Dale and Bob Horner provided their club with the most potent dual power punch around, and riding on the strength of its two musclemen, Atlanta shot from the gate with 13 straight wins. Things were going smoothly until Horner was downed by an injury, and with league hurlers pitching around Murphy, the center fielder began reaching for less desirable offerings. The result was a dreadful August, in which he hit only .177 in 21 games. The Braves managed to hang on for the division title against the onrushing Dodgers, but were swept by St. Louis in the League Championship Series, with Murf hitting .273.

In the post-season MVP balloting, Dale outpolled Lonnie Smith of the Cardinals 283 points to 218, placing first on 14 of 24 ballots.

Numerous articles were written during the trying month of August concerning the relatively young outfielder's composure in the face of personal and team failings. It was duly noted that while struggling with the stick, Dale was saving many a contest with leaping nabs, diving catches and strong throws from his middle outfield post. Power hitters, it was observed by Atlanta manager Joe Torre, are often a hindrance when they're going bad, but in Murphy's case, the opposite was true. A gangly physical makeup belied the remarkable coordination he displayed in running down fly balls with deceivingly quick, loping strides.

Finally it appeared that after four big league years, the promising colossus had found a position at which he could excel, and had mastered the fine art of playing within his limitations. As Dale's mighty deeds multiplied, it became harder for the virtuous new MVP to shrug off his frequent heroics to mere chance or luck. But if Dale Murphy were to be believed about his successes of 1982, it could only be assumed that Lady Luck took up permanent residence in the strongboy's hip pocket during the very next campaign.

Top 5 MVP Vote-Getters

1. Dale Murphy, Atlanta — 283
2. Lonnie Smith, St. Louis — 218
3. Pedro Guerrero, Los Angeles — 175
3. Al Oliver, Montreal — 175
5. Bruce Sutter, St. Louis — 134

1982 AMERICAN LEAGUE — ROBIN YOUNT

Robin R Yount
B. September 16, 1955, Danville, Illinois

Year	Team	Games	AB	Hits	Avg.	HR	RBI	Runs	SB
1982	Mil AL	156	635	210	.331	29	114	129	14

The Season

Two exciting division races, a controversial batting title competition and several outstanding individual achievements highlighted this season.

In the Eastern Division, a torrid stretch run by the Baltimore Orioles resulted in a first-place tie with Milwaukee going into the last day of the campaign. But the Brewers came through with a convincing 10–2 victory over the O's for Harvey Kuenn, who took over the managerial reins June 2. California placed second in the majors in home runs behind the Brew Crew, and outlasted the top hitting team in baseball, Kansas City, by three games in the West Division.

The Angels jumped to a 2–0 lead in the League Championship Series before the Brewers rallied for three straight to capture their first pennant. Milwaukee then fell in a seven-game World Series to the St. Louis Cardinals.

Kansas City's Willie Wilson held on for a batting crown by sitting out the final game of the season while Milwaukee's Robin Yount tried desperately to catch him with a 3-for-4 effort. In a controversial move, Royals skipper Dick Howser and Yankee manager Billy Martin conspired to delay K.C.'s last game in the late innings while word of Yount's progress was being received from Baltimore. The American League's MVP had a chance to garner the hitting title in a later at-bat, but was hit by a pitch.

Oakland's Rickey Henderson stole an incredible 130 bases to easily shatter Lou Brock's major league mark of 118; Gaylord Perry of Seattle became the 15th pitcher to win 300 games; Rollie Fingers of Milwaukee became the first pitcher to collect 300 saves; and Kansas City's Duke Wathan set an all-time record for stolen bases by a catcher with 36.

Force-Fed Phenomenon

The most important defensive position on the ball diamond is shortstop, and most managers would be happy to possess a slick gloveman with a strong arm, even if he didn't have much power. Rare is the athlete who combines superb fielding skills at the middle infield spot with slugging prowess. Two-time MVP Ernie Banks and the immortal Honus Wagner were such players, but the most proficient at the dual role from the mid–1970s to the mid–'80s was the fierce competitor from Milwaukee, Robin Yount.

All his life Yount played to win, whether flying around corners on his

Robin Yount. (Courtesy Milwaukee Brewers.)

Although he raised his average to .288 in 1977, some were beginning to write off the "Boy Wonder," failing to take into consideration that unlike players who advanced through the farm system, the force-fed 22-year-old was learning his craft at the big league level. The criticisms, poor Brewer finishes through '77 and his injured ankles dragged Robin's spirits down to the point where he left Sun City, Arizona, during spring training of 1978 amid rumors that he wished to join the pro golf tour.

Brewer President Bud Selig tried to talk the young man into returning, but it took more than a month for the infielder to rejoin the team. Following the "semi-retirement," Yount hit .293 and Milwaukee jumped to third place in the Eastern Division.

Dissatisfied with a lack of power, Robin spent the 1979–80 off-season lifting weights; and with a newfound strength, he pounded the ball with authority in '80. Moved from eighth in the batting order to second behind double play partner Paul Molitor, Yount was tops in the AL in doubles (franchise-high 49) and fourth in total bases (317, third highest by a shortstop at that time). His 23 homers equaled the number he had accumulated in the past four years combined.

"Rockin' Robin" came into his own as a shortstop in 1981, his eight errors as few as any major leaguer at the position; and though his average dipped slightly, he hit .438 down the stretch to help give the Brewers a second-half title. He then batted .316 in the division playoffs against the Yankees.

Then came the season that resulted in a Most Valuable Player award, a Major League Player of the Year honor from *The Sporting News* and seven other prestigious accolades. Yount began quickly in 1982, and remained hot all year. The starting All-Star was one of many powerful cogs in the Brew Crew's machine, becoming the third shortstop in history — and the first in the AL — to lead the league in both slugging (.578) and total bases (367). He stroked an American League-best 210 hits, including an AL-high 46 doubles, finished runner-up in

first dirt bike, firing passes as quarterback of a Pop Warner football team or gobbling up grounders and smacking baseballs as the American League's starting All-Star shortstop in the early '80s.

Born in Danville, Illinois, in 1955, the youngest of three boys grew up on the West Coast. By age 13, Robin was competing in motorcycle races, as well as excelling in football, baseball and golf. After being named the most outstanding high school ballplayer in Los Angeles, Yount was the Brewers' first-round draft choice in 1973. Assigned to the Class A Newark club, his minor league career was destined to be brief. The shortstop, whose older brother, Larry, played Triple A ball and appeared in one game for the Houston

Astros, hit .285 in 64 games, then was given a look-see at Milwaukee's spring training camp.

The Brewers were so weak at shortstop, and "The Kid" so impressive during his trial, that manager Del Crandall made the 18-year-old the youngest regular position player in major league history. Robin appeared in 107 games for the fifth-place club in '74, batting .250, then fell apart defensively in 1975, committing a major league-high 44 errors. His fielding a prime concern, Yount improved dramatically and wound up pacing AL players at his position in both putouts and double plays the next year when he became the youngest major leaguer ever to appear in 161 games.

batting (.331) and runs scored (129), third in triples (12), and fourth in RBIs (114), while winning a Gold Glove. Yount also became the first league shortstop to hit over .300 with at least 20 homers and 100 RBIs in a season.

Milwaukee held a seemingly comfortable three-game lead over the Orioles in the East going into Baltimore for a final four-game set, but the Birds struck for three quick victories. Robin then took matters into his own hands, homering in his first two at-bats and adding a triple as Harvey's Wallbangers clinched with a 10–2 triumph.

Yount then starred in the World Series, becoming the first player to collect four hits in each of two games in the same fall classic, and batting .414 for the Series with three doubles, a homer and six RBIs. But the Cardinals came back from a 3–2 deficit to spoil Milwaukee's dream season. Late in the

campaign, Brewer fans had screamed "MVP, MVP" each time Robin stepped to the plate, and their chants proved prophetic as he garnered all but one first-place vote. True to form, Yount rode a motorcycle across County Stadium during a post-season celebration.

Although now a veteran, Yount maintained a boyish appearance, with curly blond hair and a wispy mustache offsetting bright blue eyes. Lean but muscular, Robin produced amazing power with a quick bat, slapping balls into both alleys with regularity. Excellent range at short blended well with good hands and a strong arm.

Yount was bothered by a ruptured disc much of 1983, but still posted impressive numbers, including a league-high 10 triples, and was the leading All-Star Game vote-getter. Anxious to remain in Milwaukee, the shortstop signed a multi-year contract in '83 es-

timated at more than $1 million per annum. The Brew Crew slipped to fifth place in '83 on their way to the cellar in '84, despite Robin scoring 105 runs, driving in 80 and hitting nearly .300.

No longer "The Kid" or "Boy Wonder," the model husband and father of three had emerged as a leader on the Milwaukee squad, his winning attitude rubbing off on Brewer rookies and established veterans alike. And it would only be a few years before Yount would claim his second MVP award.

Top 5 MVP Vote-Getters

1. Robin Yount, Milwaukee — 385
2. Eddie Murray, Baltimore — 228
3. Doug DeCinces, California — 178
4. Hal McRae, Kansas City — 175
5. Cecil Cooper, Milwaukee — 152

1983 National League — Dale Murphy

Dale Bryan Murphy
B. March 12, 1956, Portland, Oregon

Year	Team	Games	AB	Hits	Avg.	HR	RBI	Runs	SB
1983	Atl NL	162	589	178	.302	36	121	131	30

The Season

The Philadelphia Phillies, despite a ninth-place team batting average, won their fifth Eastern Division title in eight seasons on the strength of a pitching staff that was runner-up in the ERA department. Manager Pat Corrales had the dubious distinction of being the first skipper in baseball annals to be relieved of his post with his team in first place, when on July 18, General Manager Paul Owens took over the Philadelphia reins. Two months later, the "Wheeze Kids," buoyed by veterans Mike Schmidt (age 34), Joe Morgan (39) and Pete Rose (42), emerged from a four-team fracas to triumph over the runner-up Pirates by six games.

In the West, the Dodgers overtook a struggling Atlanta club in August, then limped home the rest of the way (15–19) for the division crown.

Phillies ace Steve Carlton became the 16th 300-game winner in baseball history this season, and fans also watched "Lefty" battle with Nolan Ryan for all-time strikeout supremacy. Houston's Ryan was first to pass the 3,508 K-mark of the immortal Walter Johnson, but Carlton soon followed suit.

Former Most Valuable Player Steve Garvey surpassed Billy Williams' NL record by playing in his 1,118th consecutive game before giving way to injuries later in the campaign, the streak ending at 1,207.

The Phillies surprised a favored L.A. squad, taking the League Championship Series in four games, but then bowed to the Orioles in a five-game World Series after winning the first outing.

Indisputably "Murf"

Dale Murphy spent nearly 15 years of his career as an Atlanta Brave, and his fans recognize him as one of the most noble and worthy knights their club has ever produced. Henry Aaron, after all, was originally a Milwaukee treasure, but "Murf" was developed and nurtured through the Atlanta farm system, the southern-based

Dale Murphy. (Courtesy Atlanta Braves.)

city's first MVP and the initial star of the transplanted franchise.

The long-spun power broker unlocked the secrets of his hitting genius beginning in 1980, and the unassuming slugger never let up throughout the decade. Once a wild-swinging pull-hitter, Dale found his more natural strength to center and right fields. And the pleasant 1983 discovery that this ability could be matched with a .300-plus average brought a collective groan from opponents around the league.

Murphy's elegant swing was a decade in the refining process. From 1974 through 1976, he played in four different minor leagues without lifting his batting average above .267. But the Braves saw enough raw skill to bring the 20-year-old up.

During that time, Dale had avowed himself to the Mormon faith and its strict moral principles. The church's teachings so enamored Murphy that worried Atlanta executives had to talk him out of a two-year leave to become a missionary.

The Oregon native's distant clouts were already sending future pennant flags dancing in the heads of Braves' honchos. His arm was as powerful (although inaccurate) as any around, and he could fly with speed practically unmatched throughout the Atlanta system.

Packaged in a lithe, 6-foot-5-inch, 220-pound frame, the prospect was given every opportunity to succeed. Yet even after making it to the bigs, Dale's only claim to fame was that he ate food like a coal-burning locomotive devours fuel. As a catcher, strong-armed throws sailed futilely into center field. At first base, the friendly Goliath seemed equally out of place, practically tripping over his gargantuan size-13 shoes. Finally, in near-desperation, Dale was placed in the outfield in 1980, and wonder of wonders, he took to the position as if it were his own. Thirty-three homers rang off his bat that year, and after a sharp decline in '81 came the brilliant 1982 campaign.

So what would the reigning MVP do for an encore in 1983? Only this:

- A .302 average, sixth in the league and 21 points better than in 1982;
- A league-leading 121 RBIs, an increase of a dozen over his previous peak figure;
- A second consecutive 36-homer campaign;
- 131 runs scored, second best in the NL and a modern-day Braves record;
- A circuit-commanding .540 slugging average;
- An increase in the stolen base department from 23 in '82 to 30; and
- A second straight Gold Glove award.

The center fielder chased the Triple Crown for much of the 1983 season, and from mid–August on, propelled the Braves almost single-handedly, as fellow slugger Bob Horner was again lost to the team due to injuries. The Braves fell short of the Dodgers by three games in the NL West, but Murphy had resoundingly answered the question, "How do you improve on an MVP year?" The glowing 1983 statistics prompted another query from ex-Cincinnati manager Russ Nixon: "Is there something *above* MVP?"

Dale was an overwhelming 318–213 winner over Andre Dawson of the Expos in the MVP balloting in 1983, earning 21-of-24 first-place votes. Only five other players in baseball history had put together 30-homer, 30-stolen base seasons; and at age 27, the sixth-year man became only the ninth back-to-back MVP winner.

A familiar burden accompanied the 1984 campaign, as once more Horner fell victim to hurts early in the season, laying the full production responsibilities squarely on Murf. The Braves finished in a distant tie for second, but along the way Dale clouted 36 four-baggers (tying for the HR crown), reached 100 RBIs and played in every game, all for the third year in a row. He also paced the league in slugging (.547) for the second consecutive season.

Murphy continued on a tear for the next three seasons despite playing for non-contenders. He led the NL in home runs (37), runs (118) and walks (90) in 1985, while batting .300 with league runner-up totals in RBIs (111) and total bases (332), and a third-best .539 slugging percentage. The Atlanta stalwart cracked 29 homers with 83 RBIs in 1986, then exploded the following season with career highs in round-trippers (44), slugging (.580) and walks (115), while batting .295 with 328 total bases, 115 runs and 105 ribbies.

At this point in his splendid career, Dale's average starting slipping, but he maintained enough gusto in his bat to sandwich a couple of 24-homer campaigns around a 20-home run season from 1988 to 1990. Murphy was traded to Philadelphia late in the 1990 season, and drove in 81 runs for the

Phils in '91 before knee injuries slowed him down. He concluded his 18-year career in 1993 with Colorado, and the Braves retired his uniform No. 3 in '94.

Dale Murphy, who enjoyed 12 seasons of 20-homer output, five 100-RBI campaigns and six .500-slugging efforts, wound up with 398 career circuit clouts and 1,266 RBIs. Unfortunately, the seven-time All-Star only made it into post-season play once (1982). He held 13 Atlanta franchise records, including home runs, RBIs, hits, runs and games. Although many feel he is deserving, Murphy has not yet received that Hall of Fame call. But he is content with himself and his faith, and with the knowledge that he was one of the upper echelon of stars during the decade of the '80s.

Top 5 MVP Vote-Getters

1. Dale Murphy, Atlanta — 318
2. Andre Dawson, Montreal — 213
3. Mike Schmidt, Philadelphia — 191
4. Pedro Guerrero, Los Angeles — 182
5. Tim Raines, Montreal — 83

1983 American League — Cal Ripken, Jr.

Calvin Edwin Ripken, Jr.
B. August 24, 1960, Havre de Grace, Maryland

Year	Team	Games	AB	Hits	Avg.	HR	RBI	Runs	SB
1983	Bal AL	162	663	211	.318	27	102	121	0

The Season

The Baltimore Orioles and Chicago White Sox exploded in the second half of 1983 to win their divisions by comfortable margins. The O's, under rookie manager Joe Altobelli, wound up with a six-game bulge over Detroit in the Eastern Division, while the Pale Hose snapped back from a 16–24 start to run away from Kansas City by a record-20 games in the West.

The "Winning Ugly" Sox took the League Championship Series opener, but Baltimore came back with three straight triumphs, limiting its opposition to one run over the final 31 innings. The Orioles also dropped the first World Series contest to Philadelphia, but stormed back with four victories in a row for their first World Championship in 13 years.

Commissioner Bowie Kuhn's job was in jeopardy all year. But owners who voted to oust him from office persuaded the beleaguered commissioner to remain until a successor could be found. As his final, most dramatic act in '83, Kuhn nailed three Royals players — Willie Wilson, Willie Aikens and Jerry Martin — with one-year suspensions for drug involvement.

Individual highlights included 1967 MVP Carl Yastrzemski becoming the all-time leader in games played with 3,308; Oakland's Rickey Henderson stealing 100 bases for a record-third consecutive season; and Dan Quisenberry of Kansas City setting a big league mark by saving 45 games.

After 11 years of frustration, the American League finally won an All-Star Game, pounding the NL 13–3 in the 50th anniversary contest. Aiding the AL cause was 1975 MVP Fred Lynn, who connected for the first grand slam in All-Star competition.

Following the season, former Yankees third baseman Dr. Bobby Brown was elected president of the American League.

Box Office Hit

Like an actor whose first movie performance results in an Academy Award, Calvin Edwin Ripken, Jr. was an overnight box office smash. The tall, well-built leading man took center stage in the drama which opened in Baltimore in 1982, and has received rave reviews across the country ever since.

In only two full seasons (1982–83), the Orioles shortstop collected a Rookie of the Year trophy, a Most Valuable Player award and a World Series ring. But the polite, unassuming young man did not allow the honors to go to his head.

The son of former Baltimore third base coach and manager Cal Ripken, Sr., who joined the Orioles organization as a catcher in 1957, was a self-taught athlete due to his father being on the road during most of Cal's early years. He was shuffled between shortstop and third base by minor league coaches, and at one time was highly regarded as a pitching prospect.

Although his long-time desire was to wear the Orioles colors, a myriad of emotions flooded the 17-year-old when he was drafted by Baltimore in 1978, for he feared charges of nepotism. Whatever hesitation the fans might have originally felt was completely dispelled very quickly.

Calvin began his minor league career in 1979 in Bluefield, West Virginia, where he was given the option of pitching or manning an infield spot. Preferring to play every day, and figuring he could always return to the mound if he failed at the plate, the baseball-hungry lad selected shortstop.

Cal Ripken, Jr. (National Baseball Hall of Fame Library, Cooperstown, N.Y.)

The next two seasons were spent at Charlotte, and as he grew to 6-foot-4 and 200 pounds, the long ball became a significant part of an impressive offensive arsenal. Ripken cracked 25 home runs in '80, then added 23 the following campaign at Triple A Rochester.

Cal struggled in his first major league stint, but Oriole management was so convinced he would succeed that they traded third base incumbent Doug DeCinces prior to the '82 season. Amid much fanfare, Ripken started slowly his freshman year. But following a beaning by Seattle's Mike Moore, a father-to-son talk with Cal Sr. and a word of encouragement from Reggie Jackson, Ripken caught fire, breaking club rookie records with 28 round-trippers and 93 RBIs. A move to short-

stop July 1 had set him back temporarily, but he went on to hit .264 and earn Rookie of the Year honors.

No top first-year man had ever vaulted to Most Valuable Player the following season, but in 1983, Cal became the first, playing every inning of every game at shortstop. The gap hitter again began slowly, but destroyed the sophomore jinx by excelling in the second half, hitting close to .400 over the final 43 games.

The slugging shortstop wound up leading the American League in hits (211), runs (121), doubles (47), extra base hits (76) and at-bats (663); was runner-up in total bases (343); and tied for third in game-winning RBIs (17). His .318 batting average was good for fifth in the junior circuit, as was the

.517 slugging percentage, while 27 homers and 102 RBIs rounded out the awesome figures.

Despite possessing a shotgun arm, Cal's range had been questioned prior to '83. Those doubts were put to rest during the MVP season when he led major league shortstops in assists, and placed first in the AL in total chances and double plays.

Ripken followed his splendid season with a remarkable effort in the League Championship Series, hitting .400 with two doubles and five runs scored in the O's three games-to-one victory over the White Sox. He then managed only a .167 mark against Philadelphia in Baltimore's five-game World Series triumph. His Series performance notwithstanding, Cal beat out teammate Eddie Murray for the MVP award 322 points to 290. The second consecutive AL shortstop to be so named was also *The Sporting News* Major League Player of the Year.

After earning $40,000 in 1982 and $180,000 the following campaign, Ripken was rewarded with a four-year pact at just over $1 million per year. In keeping with his generous spirit, Cal used part of his newfound wealth to purchase a block of 25 season tickets for youths and senior citizens in his home county, and also agreed to provide a physical therapist at a day care center for retarded citizens near Aberdeen.

Anxious to show the people of Baltimore he deserved the big bucks, Ripken shot out of the gate quickly in 1984, homering in his first at-bat and becoming only the second player in Oriole history to hit for the cycle. Though the Orioles faded to fifth place in the East, Cal enjoyed another banner season, matching his 1983 home run total of 27 and batting .304.

Ripken was a model of consistency over the next six years, even if the Orioles weren't. Baltimore finished dead last in the Eastern Division twice — falling 22½ games behind the pace in 1986 and 34½ behind in '88 — contending only in 1989 when the O's came within two games of division-winning Toronto. But Ripken placed second in the AL in runs scored in 1985 with 116, and was third in walks in '88 with 102. He batted .282 in both 1985 and '86, and from 1985 through '90 tagged at least 20 home runs per season, scored at least 78 runs and drove in 80 runs or more, with a high of 110 ribbies in 1985.

And, on the verge of Cal's second

MVP award in 1991, people starting saying, "Hey, this guy hasn't missed a game for a while, has he?"

Top 5 MVP Vote-Getters

1. Cal Ripken, Jr., Baltimore — 322
2. Eddie Murray, Baltimore — 290
3. Carlton Fisk, Chicago — 209
4. Jim Rice, Boston — 150
5. Cecil Cooper, Milwaukee — 123

1984 NATIONAL LEAGUE — RYNE SANDBERG

Ryne Dee Sandberg
B. September 18, 1959, Spokane, Washington

Year	Team	Games	AB	Hits	Avg.	HR	RBI	Runs	SB
1984	Chi NL	156	636	200	.314	19	84	114	32

The Season

Even George Orwell would have been hard pressed to create a more exciting script than the 1984 scenario played out in the National League. A team that had not won a championship of any kind in 39 years, and another that tasted victory for the first time in its 16-year existence claimed division titles.

The Chicago Cubs, laughingstocks of the senior circuit for close to four decades, shocked the baseball world with the most dramatic turnaround in the sport's history, rallying from 20 games under .500 in 1983 to 31 above, and winning the NL East by a comfortable 6½ games. The San Diego Padres, a team which had never finished higher than fourth in the West Division, enjoyed a 12-game bulge over Atlanta and Houston.

The two virgin playoff squads then squared off in the League Championship Series, and after the Cubs won the first two contests in Chicago, the Padres roared back to capture three straight for the NL flag.

Three past MVPs experienced varying emotions in 1984 due to managerial changes. Two-time Most Valuable Player Frank Robinson was fired as San Francisco's pilot August 4, while 1973 MVP Pete Rose was named Cincinnati's player-manager a dozen

days later. Following the season, Atlanta skipper and former MVP Joe Torre was also canned.

Bowie Kuhn's stormy reign as commissioner finally ended when Los Angeles Olympic Organizing Committee President Peter V. Ueberroth took over October 1. His first action was to settle an umpire strike.

A couple of pitchers who stood out this season were veteran Rick Sutcliffe and rookie Dwight Gooden. Sutcliffe came over to the Cubs immediately prior to the June 15 trading deadline and won 16-of-17 decisions to capture the Cy Young Award. Gooden struck out 276 batters for the Mets to lead the league and break Herb Score's major league rookie record.

In the most frightening scene of the season, 19 players, two managers and two replacement managers were ejected from a 5–3 Atlanta win over San Diego featuring two bench-clearing brawls, the second also involving several fans. Five players and both managers were suspended for their part in the fracas, which began on the first pitch of the game when Atlanta's Pascual Perez plunked Alan Wiggins in the back.

Kid Natural

Fluid as a running stream at the plate, in the field and on the basepaths,

Ryne Sandberg performed every aspect of the game with an effortless grace that left envious onlookers amazed. Referred to by teammates as "Kid Natural" during his early years for an incredible ability to make the difficult plays appear simple, the 25-year-old became baseball's best all-around player practically overnight in 1984.

Quiet and reserved, the steady Chicago Cub second baseman found himself in a raucous, circus atmosphere that season when his team stupefied the nation with an unlikely chase for its first pennant in 39 years. And while the Northsiders had to settle for the Eastern Division crown, Sandberg came away with nothing less than a well-deserved MVP award, becoming the first Cub to cop the honor since Ernie Banks in 1959 (the year Ryne was born).

Second sackers are not generally known for their power, and neither was "Ryno" prior to the '84 campaign. But after working with Nautilus equipment during the off-season and heeding the power-stroking advice of new manager Jim Frey, Sandberg rapidly transformed from a mild-mannered Clark Kent to a heavy-hitting Superman.

Thankfully, the 6-foot-2, 185-pounder did not allow his newfound, nationwide popularity to affect his modest demeanor and pleasant attitude.

Following in the clean-cut, low-key image of the winner of the NL's previous two MVP laurels, Dale Murphy, Ryne let his actions do the talking throughout a marvelous 16-year career.

Born to baseball-conscious parents, who named their sons "Del," after Philadelphia slugger Del Ennis, and "Ryne," in honor of Yankee pitcher Ryne Duren, Sandberg was all-state in baseball, football and basketball at North Central High School in Spokane, Washington, and many major colleges sought his services. But while older brother Del selected college over baseball, Ryne chose a $30,000 bonus from the Phillies and reported to Helena, Montana, in 1978.

After hitting .311 there, Sandberg moved up to Spartanburg, South Carolina, in '79, pacing the Western Carolina League's shortstops in double plays and stealing 21 bases. In 1980, the smooth glove man demonstrated a quick bat, hitting .310 with a dozen triples and 79 RBIs at Reading.

With Julio Franco touted as the Phillies' future shortstop, Ryne was shifted to second base the next year at Oklahoma City. Then, the Phillies committed what President Bill Giles called "my biggest mistake," trading the budding star, along with Larry Bowa, to the Cubs for Ivan DeJesus. On the surface, Sandberg was an unknown throw-in, but Chicago General Manager and ex-Philly mentor Dallas Green insisted that the 22-year-old be part of the deal, and his persistence paid off handsomely for the Cubs. A superb spring training performance in 1982 had the multi-talented rookie earmarked as Chicago's center fielder, but when third baseman Ken Reitz failed to make the club, Ryne switched to the hot corner.

Despite a lack of experience at the new position, the uncomplaining, nearly flawless fielder committed fewer errors than all but two NL third basemen. He began the '82 season with a horrendous 1-for-32 slump which might have completely deflated most rookies. But Green and manager Lee Elia showed confidence in the youngster, who wound up leading the Cubs in runs scored with 103.

Apparently set at third base, Ryno was forced to make another move the next year when Ron Cey was signed as a free agent. Not surprisingly, the sure-handed Sandberg adapted immediately to second base, and became the first National Leaguer to earn a Gold Glove in his initial year at a position. His batting fell off slightly to .261, but he stole 37 bases and scored 94 runs.

Then came "The Kid's" dream year. The normally slow starter had driven in only two runs in April of 1983, but he bolted out of the gate in '84, ripping two home runs and a triple while collecting eight RBIs in the first five games.

Wrigley Field crowds had already learned to anticipate Sandberg's heroics, but even they were shocked when he treated a national television audience to an overwhelming display of clutch power hitting in a 12–11, extra-inning Cub win over St. Louis. Ryne went 5-for-6 in that contest, including two game-tying home runs off relief ace Bruce Sutter in the ninth and 10th innings. The sensational effort prompted Cardinal manager Whitey Herzog to call the fourth-year infielder "the best baseball player I've ever seen."

The starting second baseman in the '84 All-Star Game had signed a six-year, $3.85 million contract prior to the campaign, and he was earning every penny of it. Finishing the year with a .314 batting average (third in NL), 114 runs (first), 200 hits (second), 36 doubles (third) and 19 triples (first), Ryne also slugged 19 home runs, drove in 84 runs and stole 32 bases. His 74 extra base hits were the most by an NL second baseman since 1929. In the field, he was equally outstanding, making only six errors all season, setting a record with 61 consecutive errorless games and garnering another Gold Glove.

The Cubs' dreams of their first pennant since 1945 were shattered by the San Diego Padres in a thrilling five-game League Championship Series, despite Sandberg's .368 average, two doubles and a pair of RBIs.

Heading into the 1985 season, hopes were high in Chicago for a return to post-season play. But the Cubs faltered badly, failing to reach the .500 mark in any of the next four years. No one could point a finger at Ryno, who placed fourth in the league in four departments in '85: runs (113), hits (186), stolen bases (54) and total bases (307). In 1986, the man with the sticky glove committed only five errors in 153 games, setting an NL record with a .994 fielding percentage.

Sandberg and his teammates rallied in 1989, however, and the Cubs made a 16-game improvement to win the NL East by six games over New York. Ryne tied for league leadership in runs scored with 104, and placed fifth in home runs (30), hits (176) and total bases (301). And despite another splendid post-season performance, including a .400 average, three doubles, a triple, a homer and four RBIs, Sandberg's Cubs fell 4–1 to San Francisco in the NLCS.

The Cubs would not make it back to the playoffs during Sandberg's tenure, but the steady second baseman continued to carve out a Hall of Fame plaque for himself with his stellar play at the plate and in the field. Ryne's power went up a notch in 1990 when his league-leading 40 home runs were the third highest single-season total for a second baseman in baseball history. The 40 dingers made him the first second baseman in history with 30 or more homers in consecutive seasons, and gave him the distinction of being the first player with both 40-homer and 50-steal campaigns in a career.

Sandberg also paced the circuit in runs (116) and total bases (344), while finishing second in slugging (.559) and third in hits (188); he placed fourth in MVP voting for the second year in a row. His glove work also received national attention in '90 as he set a major league record by playing errorless ball for 123 consecutive games at second base (June 21, 1989, through May 17, 1990). For his career, Sandberg is tied for the best fielding percentage (.989) of all time by a second baseman.

He scored 100-plus runs again in both 1991 and '92, and in the latter year placed second in the league in total bases (312), third in hits (186) and fifth in slugging (.510) after signing a $7 million-per-annum contract. The leading All-Star Game vote-getter three years running (1990–92), Sandberg was limited to 117 games during an injury-plagued 1993 season, but still managed to hit .309. Following a slow start in 1994, Sandberg made a stunning retirement announcement at age 34. He returned to the Cubs in 1996 and played two more seasons, connecting for 25 home runs and 92 RBIs in '96, before retiring for good with the most homers as a second baseman (277).

Ryne Sandberg is a cinch for the Hall of Fame. Possessing good range and a strong arm, he earned nine consecutive Gold Glove awards from 1983 through 1991, and led NL second basemen in fielding average four times, and in assists on seven occasions. The 10-time All-Star was even more impressive at the plate, knocking out 282 home runs and driving in 1,061 while scoring 1,318 times and stealing 344 bases, a huge total for a guy with power.

Once he became a veteran, Sandberg lost the title of "Kid Natural." But he never quit hustling, and his fluid motions in the field, bat speed and ability to run the basepaths made him one of the greatest second basemen in the history of the game.

Top 5 MVP Vote-Getters

1. Ryne Sandberg, Chicago — 326
2. Keith Hernandez, New York — 195
3. Tony Gwynn, San Diego — 184
4. Rick Sutcliffe, Chicago — 151
5. Gary Matthews, Chicago — 70

1984 American League — Willie Hernandez

Guillermo Hernandez
B. November 14, 1954, Aguada, Puerto Rico

Year	Team	Games	W	L	ERA	IP	SO	BB	Saves
1984	Det AL	80	9	3	1.92	140.1	112	36	32

The Season

It was the year of the Tigers. Sparky Anderson's charges roared out of the gate to a phenomenal 35–5 start and became the first American League team since the legendary 1927 Yankees to lead wire to wire. The Detroit bunch racked up 104 wins, most in the majors.

Bengal hurler Jack Morris won 19 and fired an early-season no-hitter to lead the staff, as the Tigers finished 15 games ahead of a good Toronto ballclub in the Eastern Division. Detroit then swept the Kansas City Royals in the League Championship Series and handed the San Diego Padres a convincing 4–1 setback in the fall classic to earn the Motor City's first major league title in 16 years. The Tigers' 7–1 post-season mark made Anderson the first manager in big league history to post World Championships in both leagues.

The Royals had captured the West, a division that seemingly nobody wanted, by finishing only six games over .500.

Mike Witt of the Angels uncorked a perfect game on the last day of the campaign against Texas, the 13th such outing in major league annals.

Yankee teammates Dave Winfield and Don Mattingly were first and second in hitting most of the year, and entered the last game of the season in a virtual dead heat. Mattingly responded to the challenge with a 4-for-5 day to win the batting championship, .343 to .340.

Past MVPs reached personal milestones in 1984, with Harmon Killebrew gaining entry to the Hall of Fame, Joe Morgan surpassing Rogers Hornsby as the all-time leading second baseman in homers and Reggie Jackson joining the elite ranks of the 500-homer club.

In the longest game in AL history, Harold Baines' 25th-inning home run gave Chicago a 7–6 victory over Milwaukee, ending an eight-hour, six-minute marathon begun May 8, suspended for the evening and concluded May 9. Winning pitcher Tom Seaver also notched a victory in the May 9 regularly scheduled contest.

Bengal Bonanza

Prior to the 1984 season, a gambler would have had to search high and low to obtain betting odds of any kind on Willie Hernandez winning the Most Valuable Player award. The low-key southpaw wasn't only a long shot for the prestigious laurel, he wasn't even in the picture.

But Hernandez turned virtual obscurity into national prominence by posting a statistic that belied his rather ordinary track record and made the crafty relief pitcher the American League's top player: 32 saves in 33 save opportunities.

Perfecting two pitches — a wicked screwball that handcuffed left-handed hitters and a "cut" fastball that veered in on righties — Detroit's first-year star turned the tide for a talented Tiger club that leaped to baseball's summit.

The ability to change his fortunes for the better was apparent in Hernandez's personal history, dating back to his origins. The seventh child of nine, born to a poor Puerto Rican family in

Willie Hernandez. (Courtesy Detroit Tigers.)

Upon coming from Philadelphia to Detroit only weeks prior to the start of the season, he was told by Tigers manager Sparky Anderson that he was the No. 1 closer in the bullpen. By season's end, the lefty had so mystified his new opponents in the junior circuit that he garnered both the Cy Young and MVP awards, becoming only the seventh hurler to reap both honors in the same year, and only the second reliever to do so.

Somewhat of an unknown quantity in the new "door-slamming" role, Willie had toiled for 6½ years as a middle reliever for the Cubs, setting up ace finishers Bruce Sutter and Lee Smith. The Cubs dealt Willie to Philadelphia for pitcher Dick Ruthven early in the 1983 campaign, and another fine effort by Hernandez (9–4, eight saves, 3.28 ERA) was again overshadowed, this time by Al Holland. Four no-hit innings of work in the World Series were also virtually unheralded in light of a Philadelphia defeat.

Phillie management all but declared Willie a loafer when intolerable back spasms rendered him unable to give 100 percent in the spring of 1984. An insulted Hernandez welcomed the subsequent trade to Detroit with open arms. The Tigers had silently coveted Willie's services for several years, but his 1984 performance exceeded even his new club's wildest expectations.

After registering only 27 saves over seven previous campaigns, the Puerto Rico native blew past that total in his first year as a Tiger. Only three years earlier he'd been demoted to Chicago's farm system, and was perilously close to dropping completely out of sight. But during Detroit's machine-like march to the championship, Hernandez came through in one extraordinarily successful outing after another. Willie's confidence soared to such a degree that he was perfect during the divisional title run, going 32-for-32 in save opportunities. Only after the AL East crown had already been sewn up did the budding star falter for the first time and allow a late-game lead to slip away. He led the league in appearances with 80, then went out and nailed down three more saves in post-season play, including

Aguada, Willie did odd jobs as a young-ster to help make ends meet. His primary release from the impoverished condition was baseball. An excellent batsman as a youth, the left-hander played third base and the outfield, until one day in 1973 his semipro team found itself without a pitcher. Hernandez volunteered, tossed seven shutout frames and within six weeks had signed with the Philadelphia Phillies for $25,000.

The mustachioed hurler was getting by with a crackling fastball that neared the 100 mph mark in his first two minor league campaigns. Though the 21-year-old was still very raw in the intricacies of pitching, the Chicago Cubs were impressed enough to draft him out of the Phillies system in 1976.

Willie's Chicago stint was work-manlike yet practically invisible to baseball fandom. Despite averaging more than 50 appearances yearly from 1977 through 1980, he was probably more recognized for the huge chaw of tobacco bulging from his cheek than for his pitching accomplishments on the lowly Cubs.

The articulate relief pitcher, whose wild, natural hairdo sprung out from the sides of his baseball cap, was a slim piece of background music at Wrigley Field. It wasn't until 1984, with the Tigers, that Hernandez would know the more intense joys of the spotlight, as he was finally given the chance to show what he could do as a game-ending relief specialist on a pennant contender.

two in the World Series dismantling of San Diego.

The 6-foot-2, 180-pounder had progressed masterfully since the days when his repertoire consisted of one pitch: the fastball. A devastating screwball, picked up from ex-major league star Mike Cuellar in 1983, was the most hailed of Willie's pitches in '84, but an inside-veering fastball helped paralyze enemy hitters almost as frequently. Preceded by a purposeful, menacing visage that oozed bravado, the mixed bag of offerings was delivered in three-quarters and straight sidearm styles in rapid, unsettling fashion.

The Tigers had frittered away 27 late-game leads in 1983, but with Hernandez on the hill, the '84 Detroit bunch put away opponents with calculated regularity. In addition to a 9–3 record and a miniscule 1.92 ERA, Willie posted saves in his team's division, pennant and World Series clinchers.

Hernandez enjoyed two more exceptional seasons for Detroit, posting 31 saves and a 2.70 ERA in 1985, and 24 saves with a 3.55 ERA in '86. He then garnered 33 saves over the final three years of his career to wind up with 147.

Willie Hernandez does not have a plaque in Cooperstown, but he'll al-

ways be remembered for his nearly perfect performance in 1984 when he helped the Tigers put together one of baseball's most dominant performances of all time.

Top 5 MVP Vote-Getters

1. Willie Hernandez, Detroit — 306
2. Kent Hrbek, Minnesota — 247
3. Dan Quisenberry, Kansas City — 235
4. Eddie Murray, Baltimore — 197
5. Don Mattingly, New York — 113

1985 NATIONAL LEAGUE — WILLIE MCGEE

Willie Dean McGee
B. November 2, 1958, San Francisco, California

Year	Team	Games	AB	Hits	Avg.	HR	RBI	Runs	SB
1985	SL NL	152	612	216	.353	10	82	114	56

The Season

With sluggers such as Albert Pujols and Jim Edmonds as threats to hit the ball out of the park every time they stepped to the plate, St. Louis fans in the early 2000s may have found it difficult to fathom how few and far between the home runs were in 1985 when the Cardinals won 101 games and advanced to the World Series. St. Louis scored runs in a variety of ways, leading the league in batting average, walks, steals, runs scored and stolen bases, but hit fewer homers (87) than all but one major league team.

The Cardinals connected for three home runs in a four games-to-two National League Championship Series victory over Los Angeles, which featured the batting exploits of Ozzie Smith (.435, one home run, three RBIs) and Jack Clark (.381, one homer, four RBIs). Despite a fine offensive effort from Tito Landrum (.360) and two wins by John Tudor, St. Louis al-

lowed a three games-to-one lead over Kansas City to slip away in the World Series.

The biggest highlight of the season came September 11, when Cincinnati's Pete Rose became baseball's all-time hits leader. Rose's line drive single to left field off Eric Show of San Diego in the first inning of a 2–0 Reds win was his 4,190th hit, breaking Ty Cobb's long standing mark in front of 47,237 fans at Riverfront Stadium.

This was also a year for pitchers to shine. When Dwight Gooden of New York struck out 16 batters in a 5–0 win over San Francisco August 20, he became only the second pitcher of the century to fan 200 hitters in each of his first two seasons. Gooden went on to earn the Cy Young Award by pacing the league in wins, earned run average, strikeouts, complete games and innings pitched. Another right-hander, Houston's Joe Niekro, posted his 200th career win July 2 over San Diego. The triumph enabled Joe and Phil Niekro

to join Jim and Gaylord Perry as the only brothers to win at least 200 games each in the major leagues.

The Rookie of the Year award went to St. Louis speedster Vince Coleman, who stole 110 bases and joined former MVPs Orlando Cepeda, Willie McCovey and Frank Robinson as the only unanimous winners of the rookie accolade.

In a game which established a major league record for the latest finish, the New York Mets celebrated Independence Day by defeating the Atlanta Braves 16–13 in 19 innings. The six-hour, 10-minute contest featured two rain delays before mercifully concluding at 3:55 a.m. July 5.

Slashing Speedster

When St. Louis baseball fans sit around talking about the best trades the Cardinals have made through the years, Lou Brock for Ernie Broglio is always mentioned first. Little did the Cubs know that when they sent the raw, 25-year-old outfielder to St. Louis in mid–June 1964 that Brock would blossom into a star, batting .293 lifetime, stealing a then-record 938 bases and entering the Hall of Fame in his first year of eligibility. Broglio, a right-handed pitcher who had won 21 games for the Cardinals in 1960, won only eight in a Cub uniform over three years.

Another shrewd trade that deserves consideration as one of the Cards' best occurred in late 1981. The New York Yankees, well-stocked with promising young outfielders but low on left-handed pitchers, sent 22-year-old Willie Dean McGee to St. Louis for veteran reliever Bob Sykes. One of six children born to a deacon in a Pentecostal church, McGee enjoyed a remarkable 18-year career, played in 11 post-season series with three different clubs and was on four World Series teams. Sykes never wore a Yankees uniform.

And it wasn't as if the Cardinals had to wait several years for McGee to develop. He had been doing that quite nicely in the Yankees farm system for several years, and by the time he joined the St. Louis parent club in early 1982, he was ready for prime time. McGee's rookie campaign was nothing short of sensational. His .296 batting average was the top mark for National League first-year men that season, and he was third in Rookie of the Year balloting. His first major league home run, July 20 against Atlanta at Busch Stadium, was a grand slam. An inside-the-park homer later in the season came during the game in which the Cardinals clinched the Eastern Division title.

But the youngster's impressive influence on his team didn't end in the regular season. The switch-hitter batted .308 with two triples, a home run, five RBIs and four runs scored in a three games-to-none League Championship Series victory over the Braves, then hit a pair of homers, drove in five runs and scored six times in the 4–3 World Series triumph over the Milwaukee Brewers. If typical baseball fans were unaware of McGee's presence prior to the Series, they certainly took notice in Game 3. Two home runs, in-

cluding a three-run shot, accompanied two leaping catches in which he robbed Brewer hitters of homers. The right-handed throwing McGee wound up tying a World Series record for outfield putouts with 24, and set a Series record for most chances accepted.

It was during Game 3, when the camera zoomed in on McGee's face, that ABC announcer Howard Cosell blurted out, "He looks like E.T." It was not among Cosell's more sensitive comments, but it became a nickname for the ballplayer who, while gangly, performed other-worldly feats on a regular basis. Unlike a silky smooth Devon White, the 6-foot-1, 175-pounder was all arms and elbows and legs, flailing about every time he toured the bases or raced toward a fly ball. Stooped forward when he ran, the pigeon-toed McGee never fit the mold of a slick athlete, but he certainly got the job done right.

Willie showed that his rookie season was no fluke when he rattled off a 19-game hitting streak, was successful in 17 consecutive stolen base attempts and led St. Louis in hits while batting .286 in 1983, despite starting the year on the disabled list with a slight separation of his right shoulder. In 1984, the slash hitter with deceptive speed hit for the cycle in one game, stroked five hits in another, batted .291 and drove in 82 runs while stealing 43 bases.

But those first three campaigns turned out to be merely a tune-up for an amazing 1985 performance that resulted in McGee being named the NL's Most Valuable Player and the Cardinals returning to the World Series. The aggressive hitter sprayed baseballs to all parts of the ballpark, winning the batting title with a .353 mark, the highest ever by a National League switch-hitter. He placed first in hits (216) and triples (18), and finished third in total bases (308), runs (114) and steals (56). He and Vince Coleman combined to pilfer the most bases (166) in a season by teammates.

As with the calendar, Willie's hottest month of 1985 was August, when he batted .436, but he was a terror throughout the season, especially in the clutch. McGee batted .391 with runners in scoring position and .377

with runners in scoring position and two outs. His batting average dipped somewhat in post-season play, but he contributed six runs and three RBIs in the four games-to-two LCS win over Los Angeles, and a home run, two doubles and a pair of RBIs in the 4–3 World Series loss to Kansas City.

A few NL players enjoyed better statistical years than McGee in '85, including Cincinnati's Dave Parker, the league's MVP in 1978 while a member of the Pittsburgh Pirates. Parker led the league in RBIs (125), total bases (350) and doubles (42); placed second in home runs (34), hits (198) and slugging percentage (.551); and was fifth in batting average (.312). But the writers saw McGee as the catalyst who drove the Cardinals to 101 wins and into the playoffs by three games over New York, giving him 14-of-24 first-place votes. The swift center fielder also earned his second Gold Glove award and was named *The Sporting News* NL Player of the Year.

A pulled hamstring in his right leg and a left knee injury limited McGee to 124 games in 1986, but he still managed to collect a third Gold Glove. Moved from second in the St. Louis batting order to the fifth spot, he helped the team return to post-season play in 1987 by batting .285 with career highs in homers (11) and RBIs (105). His 11 triples tied for third in the league. Once again, McGee excelled in the post-season, batting .308 with two extra base hits and two RBIs in the Cardinals' 4–3 LCS win over San Francisco, and hitting .370 with a team-high 10 hits, two doubles and four RBIs in the 4–3 World Series loss to Minnesota.

McGee's 1,000th career hit came in 1988 when he boosted his average to .292, increased his stolen base total to 41 and made his fourth All-Star Team. But more injuries, including a painful one to his wrist, limited him to 58 games the following season.

Willie made it back to the playoffs and World Series in 1990, but not as a Cardinal. Despite an NL-leading batting average of .335, he was traded to the Oakland A's August 29. Because he had the required number of plate appearances and no one overtook him, McGee became the first player in big league history to win a batting title in one league after being traded to a team in the other. He hit .322 for the year with 99 runs scored and 77 driven in. He was limited to only a few hits in the A's LCS sweep of Boston, and in their World Series loss to Cincinnati.

McGee tested the free agency waters following the '90 season and wound up across the bay with San Francisco. He played for the Giants for four seasons, placing fourth in the '91 batting race with a .312 mark, and batting .343 with runners in scoring position. The fleet outfielder moved to right field in 1992, where he placed fourth in the league with 11 assists, and went over the 300 mark in thefts for his career. He batted .301 in 1993, but a torn Achilles tendon and a player strike limited him to 45 games in '94.

Returning to the American League,

McGee signed a minor league contract in 1995 with Boston, moving up from Triple A Pawtucket to bat .285 in 67 games for the Red Sox. Willie batted .250 in the three games-to-none LCS loss to Cleveland.

Always a popular player in St. Louis where his line drive hitting style and excellent speed were a natural for spacious Busch Stadium, McGee returned in 1996 for the final four years of his career. He batted .307 and .300 in 1996 and '97, respectively, then slipped to around the .250 mark for his last two years before retiring at age 41. In his 11th and final post-season series, Willie batted .333, but St. Louis was edged 3–2 by Atlanta in the 1996 LCS.

Willie McGee's herky-jerky running motions and awkward appearance did not win him any style points dur-

ing his 18-year major league career. But his ability to hit to all fields, race around the bases and track down drives into the alleys made him a sought-after commodity by a number of ballclubs following the Yankees' ill-advised decision to let him go just as he was about to sprout into a bona-fide star. And his 1985 MVP season is one that Cardinal fans will remember for many years to come.

Top 5 MVP Vote-Getters

1. Willie McGee, St. Louis — 280
2. Dave Parker, Cincinnati — 220
3. Pedro Guerrero, Los Angeles — 208
4. Dwight Gooden, New York — 162
5. Tommy Herr, St. Louis — 119

1985 AMERICAN LEAGUE — DON MATTINGLY

Donald Arthur Mattingly
B. April 20, 1961, Evansville, Indiana

Year	Team	Games	AB	Hits	Avg.	HR	RBI	Runs	SB
1985	NY AL	159	652	211	.324	35	145	107	2

The Season

The Kansas City Royals were the comeback kids this season, falling behind three games to one in both the American League Championship Series and the World Series, only to rally for seven-game victories in both to earn the franchise's first and only World Championship.

Former MVP George Brett provided many of the heroics in the LCS win over Toronto, batting .348 with two doubles, three home runs and five RBIs. The Blue Jays had won the AL East by two games over New York, while Kansas City slipped past California in the West by a single contest. Brett also hit .370 with 10 safeties in the World Series triumph over St. Louis, but it was pitcher Bret Saberha-

gen who earned Series MVP honors with two wins (Games 3 and 7) and a 0.50 earned run average. The Cy Young Award winner and his fellow moundsmen held the Cardinals to a World Series record-low .185 batting average.

Several players posted numbers in 1985 that had not been witnessed in decades. Wade Boggs of Boston knocked out 240 hits, the most in the major leagues in 55 years and the highest total in the AL since 1928. New York's Rickey Henderson's 146 runs scored were the top big league total since two-time MVP Ted Williams scored 150 times in 1949, while Willie Wilson's 21 triples for the Royals were the most in baseball in 36 seasons.

On October 6, Phil Niekro, 46, of New York became the oldest pitcher to throw a complete game shutout with

an 8–0 blanking of Toronto. It was Niekro's 300th career win, and it came on the final day of the season. Continuing a seemingly annual tradition, Billy Martin was fired October 27 as Yankees manager for the fourth time, and was replaced by Lou Piniella.

Intensity Personified

Prior to the 1987 season, a statistic was published revealing that Don Mattingly was a rather ineffective hitter with the bases loaded. In 47 career at-bats with the bags juiced, the New York Yankees first baseman was batting only .255 with just one extra base hit, a double. This came as a surprise to the many baseball fans who had witnessed Mattingly tear apart American

Don Mattingly. (Courtesy New York Yankees.)

field—as seriously as possible. This was a guy who never wasted a chance, whose every at-bat was life or death and whose every fielding play was crucial. Mattingly's deep intensity in all areas of his game help explain his amazing ability to excel in so many different aspects of a multi-faceted sport.

At the plate, the picture of concentration got his bat on the ball nearly every time he swung, as indicated by a nearly 1½-to-1 walk-to-strikeout ratio. Most hitters with home run power strike out frequently, but Mattingly crushed 222 homers in his career, including 160 during a six-year span, while never fanning more than 43 times in a season. Batters who consistently go deep seldom hit .300, but Don reached that lofty plateau in each of his first six full years, and seven times altogether, including two seasons of .340-plus.

As if his hitting weren't enough, Mattingly was also a magician with the glove. The naturally ambidextrous ballplayer had played shortstop and third base in Babe Ruth League ball, so fielding was a solid component of the resumé he brought to the big leagues. Now wearing his mitt on the right hand, he earned nine Gold Gloves during a 10-year span (1985–94) at first base for the Yankees, and was the AL's top first sacker in fielding percentage seven times from 1984 to '94. His .996 fielding average was third all-time in baseball annals at his position.

The only thing that kept the humble, unassuming Mattingly from posting even more impressive numbers over a longer career was a series of debilitating injuries, including a bad back, hamstring pulls and a wrist problem, most of which began kicking in after a tremendous flurry that resulted in him being voted the top player in baseball by his peers in 1986. And the only hurdles keeping the gritty competitor from deriving even more enjoyment from his success were a lack of post-season play and a number of contract disputes with owner George Steinbrenner, whose public criticism of his club's best player served to erode team chemistry.

Baseball was merely a game to Don while growing up in Evansville, Indiana, as well as a way of bonding

League pitching over the past three seasons. The left-handed hitter with the nearly flawless swing was not only hitting for high averages, but was producing plenty of power and playing a slick first base to boot. Apparently batting well with three runners aboard was the one thing he couldn't do. Until 1987, that is.

Whether the determined 26-year-old took the matter to heart, or if it was merely a coincidence doesn't really matter. What is significant is that Mattingly responded by belting six grand slam home runs during the '87 campaign, breaking the all-time, single-season, major league record previously shared by Ernie Banks and Jim Gentile, who had smacked five each in 1955 and '61, respectively. For the season, Mattingly was 9-for-19 (.474) with 33 RBIs in bases-loaded situations, and that majestic answer to an apparent chink in his armor is one of many things that set Don Mattingly apart from other players during his 14-year career.

Described by teammates as one of the most intense competitors they'd ever encountered, the mustachioed perfectionist took every opportunity to perform — both at the plate and in the

with his father and older brothers. His dad worked 12-hour shifts as a postal employee in order to receive time off to play ball with his sons. This sports-minded atmosphere paid off for Randy, a quarterback in the Canadian Football League for five years, and for Jerry and Michael, who played basketball at the University of Evansville. Don excelled in three sports in high school, but it eventually became evident that his best shot at turning pro was in baseball. He batted .500 his junior year at Reitz Memorial High School, then raised his average to .575 the following season.

Concerned about a lack of power and speed, scouts did not rank Mattingly particular high, and the anxious youngster was forced to wait until the 19th round of the 1979 free agent draft before his name was called by the Yankees. Among the more than 400 players selected ahead of him were three eventual NFL quarterbacks: Dan Marino, John Elway and Jay Schroeder. Mattingly signed for a $22,500 bonus, and following his first year in the minors, the 18-year-old married 16-year-old Kim Sexton, the daughter of a high school football coach. He spent the next three seasons climbing the minor league ladder, and while his batting averages were impressive, the 6-foot, 175-pounder was still not displaying the type of power normally associated with a first baseman.

Mattingly played in a few games for the parent club at the tail end of the 1982 season after a good year at Columbus, Ohio, in the International League, then made the Yankees roster following spring training in '83. He was demoted to Columbus after a slow start — for which he would become known during his big league career — but came back in June to fill the roster spot of the retired Bobby Murcer. Mattingly hit .283 with four homers in 91 games for New York in his rookie campaign, setting the tone for what would be a marvelous career.

To prepare for the 1984 season, Mattingly played winter ball in Puerto Rico, where he led the league in batting with a .368 mark. Disappointed when he learned that Yankee manager Yogi Berra did not plan to start his young first baseman, Mattingly gritted his teeth and worked extra hours to be ready when the opportunity opened up. Before long, batting coach Lou Piniella was quoted as saying, "Don Mattingly is by far the most talented young batter to come up through this organization in the 11 years I've been here."

Mattingly earned that praise in 1984 by winning the AL batting title (.343), going 4-for-5 on the final day of the season to edge teammate Dave Winfield. Mattingly also paced the league in hits (207) and doubles (44), and placed second in slugging (.537) and fourth in total bases (324). Just as encouraging to the Yankee brass was seeing Don match his uniform number (23) in home runs, and drive in 110 base runners, while striking out only 33 times. *The Sporting News* American League Player of the Year committed only five errors all season, none of which came in the second half.

Following his first salary dispute — he ended up receiving less than one-third of the $1 million contract he'd hoped for — Mattingly was a man on a mission in 1985. Already intense by nature, "Donnie Baseball" was even more focused than usual as he sought to draw additional greenbacks out of Steinbrenner's wallet. The first baseman went wild on the way to claiming the American League Most Valuable Player award, driving in a stunning total of 145 runs, the most by an AL player in 32 years; cracking a league-high 48 doubles; leading the junior circuit in total bases with 370; finishing runner-up in the AL in hits (211) and slugging (.567); and batting .324 (third) with 35 homers (fourth) and only 41 strikeouts.

A clutch hitter, he batted .354 with runners in scoring position and two outs in '85, and became the first player since Ted Williams (1957) to belt more than 30 home runs in a season while striking out fewer than 50 times. Mattingly's doubles total was the second highest in team history, while his hits total was the most by a Yankee in 46 years. Despite the amazing season, New York fell short of Toronto in the East Division race.

After signing a $1.375 million contract, Mattingly went to work in 1986 determined to show he was worth every penny. The hits came fast and furious this season — 238 of them to be exact — and the result was an incredible .352 batting average. Among the safeties he recorded were a league-high 53 doubles. He also led the circuit in slugging percentage (.573) and total bases (388), scored 117 runs and drove in 113 (both third in the AL), and placed fifth with an on-base percentage of .399 while finishing second in the MVP voting. New York again failed to win its division, and feeling he needed a scapegoat, Steinbrenner chose Mattingly to blame.

Yet another salary battle was decided in Mattingly's favor by an arbitrator, and the slick first baseman came back in 1987 to hit .327 with 30 round-trippers and 115 RBIs, despite being sidelined for three weeks early in the season with a back injury. In addition to his six grand slams, Mattingly also tied Dale Long's major league record by hitting at least one home run in eight consecutive games. Don also held the major league mark for most homers in seven consecutive games (nine) and in nine consecutive contests (10).

Frustrated with a fourth-place finish, Steinbrenner's reaction to his most productive player's performance was to say that Mattingly had been playing "selfishly" in the midst of the home run streak. During the All-Star break in 1988, the Yankees owner called him "the most unproductive .300 hitter in baseball." A rib cage injury had stymied Don in '88, but he managed to hit .311 with 18 homers and 88 RBIs while scoring 94 runs. Finally tired of Steinbrenner's lack of appreciation for his contributions, Mattingly said that the owner's negativity had produced a clubhouse of unhappy players.

Mattingly regained some of his power in 1989, climbing back to 23 homers and 113 RBIs, and he used a 17-game hitting streak to reach the .300 mark (.303) for the sixth year in a row. He celebrated his 1,000th career game by going 4-for-4 with a home run and four RBIs against the Angels. Still, the Yankees continued to slide, and Mattingly was the fall guy in Steinbrenner's mind. He was even benched for one game during the 1991 season for refusing to get his hair cut.

The still brilliant glove man played six more seasons, but a variety of injuries limited his effectiveness. He did manage to post team highs in most offensive categories in 1992, driving in 86 runs and recording his fourth 40-double season, the third most in Yankee history. Mattingly slugged his 200th career homer in 1993, then established an AL record for first basemen in 1994 by leading the league in fielding for the seventh time.

The Yankees finally made it to post-season play in 1995 during Mattingly's final season, and the 34-year-old veteran came through by batting .417 with a team-high 10 hits, four doubles, a homer and six RBIs. But New York fell three games to two to Seattle in the divisional playoffs. The long-time Yanks star retired with a .307 lifetime batting average, 1,099 RBIs and 1,007 runs scored. He was the 14th Yankee to have his uniform number retired. Following the 2001 season, reports had the Yankees pursuing Mattingly as a batting coach, but he was hesitant to accept a fulltime position.

A private individual, Mattingly kept a low profile throughout his career in the Big Apple. But the fans loved him and teammates appreciated him. Hall of Fame voters may show their appreciation as well someday.

Hopefully, those who design the Hall of Fame busts will be able to capture the intense look that Don Mattingly wore while he was sculpting a masterful career both at the plate and in the field.

Top 5 MVP Vote-Getters

1. Don Mattingly, New York — 367
2. George Brett, Kansas City — 274
3. Rickey Henderson, New York — 174
4. Wade Boggs, Boston — 159
5. Eddie Murray, Baltimore — 130

1986 NATIONAL LEAGUE — MIKE SCHMIDT

Michael Jack Schmidt
B. September 27, 1949, Dayton, Ohio

Year	Team	Games	AB	Hits	Avg.	HR	RBI	Runs	SB
1986	Phil NL	160	552	160	.290	37	119	97	1

The Season

They were called the "Miracle Mets" in 1969, but this year's edition of the New York National League franchise was no less miraculous. Using a potent mixture of skill and luck — mostly skill — the Mets claimed their first World Championship since 1973 in dramatic fashion.

The regular season was a cakewalk for the Mets, whose 21½-game margin of victory over East Division runner-up Philadelphia was the largest in the majors in 84 years. New York won 108 games while pacing the senior circuit in earned run average, but it was the Mets' bats that did most of the damage, posting league bests in runs, hits, batting average, slugging, walks and on-base percentage. Over in the West, Houston strolled to a 10-game victory over Cincinnati. The Astros did it mainly with pitching, leading the league in least runs and hits allowed, shutouts, strikeouts and saves.

The Mets' bats versus the Astros' arms produced a thrilling League Championship Series, with four of the six games decided by one run and another by two runs. It appeared that Houston would send the series to a seventh game when it led 3–0 heading into the ninth inning of Game 6, but New York rallied for three runs in the ninth, and eventually won 7–6 in 16 innings in the longest game in post-season history.

The Mets needed an even greater miracle to win the World Series over Boston. Down three games to two and trailing 5–3 with two outs in the ninth inning and nobody on base, New York rallied for three runs to win 6–5, the final run coming on Mookie Wilson's grounder which skidded under first baseman Bill Buckner's glove. The Mets then overcame a 3–0 deficit in the sixth inning to win Game 7, 8–5.

Houston's Mike Scott was the NL's dominant pitcher this year, leading the league in ERA and becoming only the third hurler in league history to reach 300 strikeouts in a season. Scott's 2–0 no-hitter over San Francisco September 25 marked the first time that a title of any kind was clinched by a no-hitter.

A couple of former MVPs, Willie McCovey (1969) and Ernie Lombardi (1938), were honored with induction into the Hall of Fame. Following the season, Yale University President A. Bartlett Giamatti became the NL president after Chub Feeney's retirement.

Still Slugging

When baseball fans huddle to discuss rankings of the greatest players in the history of the game at each position, there is usually plenty of friendly disagreement. Some place more emphasis on a player's batting average or earned run average, some on his power, others on his fielding abilities. Some believe leadership skills should weigh heavily, while others look at post-season contributions. Due to these different perspectives and areas of emphasis, it's difficult enough to compare players of the same era, let alone those who played in far different times and conditions.

It's also difficult to argue against Mike Schmidt being the best third baseman in baseball history.

Schmidt was a one-man wrecking crew during many of his 18 years in a Philadelphia Phillies uniform. The mustachioed power hitter led the National League in home runs a league-record eight times, smacking 48 in 1980, 45 in 1979 and 40 in 1983. During a 14-year stretch beginning in 1974, Schmidt hit 30 or more homers 13 times, averaging more than 36 per season. He also topped the league in RBIs four times to tie an NL record, passing the 100 mark on nine occasions, and led the way in slugging five times, including a .644 percentage in 1981 and .624 in 1980. Mike also posted NL-best marks in walks four times, on-base percentage on three occasions and runs scored once.

When compared to players at all positions for his career, Schmidt stands out. He was eighth all time in home runs with 548, 15th in walks (1,507), 21st in extra base hits (1,015), tied for 24th in RBIs (1,595) and among the top 40 in both slugging (.527) and total bases (4,404). The only downside to Schmidt's incredible power was a propensity to strike out. He was among the top five all time in that category (1,883), but the runs he produced with a potent bat far outweighed the K's.

Schmidt was hardly a one-dimensional player. A heady base runner, he produced double figures in stolen bases eight times, and his fielding was almost unparalleled. Utilizing a rifle

for an arm, Schmidt gobbled up ground balls and threw out batters more consistently than any slugger throughout baseball history. He won nine consecutive Gold Gloves from 1976 to '84, and added a 10th in '86. He was third all time among third basemen in assists with 5,045, and fourth in double plays with 450.

Yet another of Schmidt's many assets was his durability. He was fifth all time in games played by a third baseman at 2,212, and was never really slowed down by injury until he tore a rotator cuff, limiting him to 108 games in 1988. But in 1986 at age 36, Michael Jack Schmidt was still going strong.

The right-handed power source won his eighth and final home run crown with 37 dingers, and also led the league in RBIs with 119 and slugging at .547. Schmidt was runner-up in total bases with 302 and walks with 89, third in on-base percentage with a .395 mark, and tied for third in runs with 97. He also batted an impressive .290 and topped league third basemen in fielding percentage (.980). The Phillies finished 11 games over .500 in '86, but were a distant second in the East Division to the New York Mets. Still, the writers saw fit to reward Mike with the Most Valuable Player award, as he outpolled first baseman Glenn Davis of the West Division-winning Houston Astros 287–231.

The accolade made Schmidt only the third player in NL history to garner three Most Valuable Player trophies, the others being Roy Campanella of the Brooklyn Dodgers (1951, '53 and '55) and Stan Musial of the St. Louis Cardinals (1943, '46 and '48). Interestingly, all three stars spent their entire careers with one franchise.

By the time the 1987 season rolled along, baseball fans wondered if Schmidt would ever become mortal. After all, he had celebrated his 37th birthday toward the end of his 1986 MVP season, and the artificial turf at Veteran's Stadium could not have been

doing his knees any favors. But he produced yet another Schmidt-like season in '87 with 35 home runs to reach the magical 500 plateau, and drove in 113 runs (third best in the NL). Perhaps even more impressive, Mike batted .293, his career high when one discounts his .316 average in the strike-shortened 1981 campaign.

As the Phillies slipped in the standings the next two seasons, so too did the aging Schmidt. He batted .249 with 12 homers and 62 RBIs in 1988 before sustaining the season-ending rotator cuff injury, then finished his career in 1989 with six home runs and 28 ribbies. It was an inglorious end to a magnificent career, but that is not what he will be remembered for. In recent years, Schmidt has enjoyed hitting a smaller ball great distances. The avid golfer earned more than $100,000 per year playing on fringe golf circuits before making his PGA Senior Tour debut.

A 12-time All-Star, Mike Schmidt led the Philadelphia Phillies to post-season play during six different seasons in the late 1970s and early 1980s, then shined like a beacon in the darker days. His induction into the Hall of Fame was a mere formality in 1995. Needing 345 points from voters, he received 444.

Who was the greatest third baseman of all time? Arguments could be made for several candidates, including Pie Traynor and Brooks Robinson. But no one ever combined power, fielding and base running the way Mike Schmidt did.

Top 5 MVP Vote-Getters

1. Mike Schmidt, Philadelphia — 287
2. Glenn Davis, Houston — 231
3. Gary Carter, New York — 181
4. Keith Hernandez, New York — 179
5. Dave Parker, Cincinnati — 144

1986 AMERICAN LEAGUE — ROGER CLEMENS

William Roger Clemens
B. August 4, 1962, Dayton, Ohio

Year	Team	Games	Won	Lost	ERA	IP	SO	BB	ShO
1986	Bos AL	33	24	4	2.48	254	238	67	1

The Season

The Boston Red Sox pulled off what was arguably the most dramatic comeback in League Championship Series history, only to execute perhaps the biggest choke in the history of the World Series.

Only one loss away from elimination in the 1986 LCS, and trailing 5–2 in the ninth inning of Game 5 at California, Boston received a two-run homer by former MVP Don Baylor to pull within one, followed by a two-out, two-strike, two-run home run by Dave Henderson to take a 6–5 lead. The Angels tied it in the bottom of the ninth, but Henderson's sacrifice fly in the 11th gave the Red Sox a 7–6 win to stay alive. Boston then won the sixth and seventh games handily for its first American League pennant in 11 years.

The Red Sox were one out away from winning the World Series for the first time since 1918, but blew a two-run lead in the 10th inning of Game 6 to the New York Mets to lose the game, then dropped Game 7.

With the crucial role of the relief pitcher being emphasized in the intense post-season spotlight this year, it was apropos that New York reliever Dave Righetti would set a major league record by recording 46 saves. A former starter, Righetti broke the single-season record of 45 previously shared by Dan Quisenberry and Bruce Sutter when he saved both ends of a double-header on the next-to-last day of the season. Another hurler who received well-deserved recognition was California's Don Sutton, whose 300th career win came June 18 when he tossed a three-hitter at Texas.

A rule change was instituted in 1986 allowing the use of the designated hitter in the home park of the AL team during the World Series. Since 1976, the DH had been used in the fall classic in all parks in alternate years.

In one of the most surprising events of the year, Heisman Trophy winner Bo Jackson signed with the Kansas City Royals despite being the Tampa Bay Buccaneers' No. 1 selection in the NFL draft.

Rocket Man

Two Cy Young Awards, one Most Valuable Player trophy, a major league record for strikeouts in a nine-inning game … most pitchers would be thrilled to list those significant achievements on their resumé following a lengthy career. Roger Clemens had accomplished all of this and more by the age of 25, and he was just getting started on a phenomenal run.

Nolan Ryan was Roger's boyhood hero, so it's fitting that Clemens would eventually take over Ryan's role as the hardest throwing right-hander in the game. And while Clemens' mound brilliance has experienced a few ebbs and tides over the years, his intensely competitive spirit has always been at the forefront.

Entering the 2002 season, Clemens had spent 13 years in Boston, two in Toronto and three in New York, demonstrating an uncanny ability to bounce back from injury with a resurgent arm, and fooling those who had declared him finished as an effective pitcher. The uniforms have changed a couple of times, but his basic pitching philosophy has not. His method is simple: throw the horsehide at high speeds, knock guys off the plate when necessary and bear down in the late innings.

That strategy has resulted in an amazing set of credentials. Through an 18-year career, Clemens has:

- Earned six Cy Young Awards, two more than any other pitcher in baseball history;
- Struck out 3,717 batters, tops in the American League and third all time;
- Posted 280 wins, 27th all time;
- Fanned a major league-record 20 batters in one game — twice;
- Led the AL in earned run average and shutouts six times each, strikeouts on five occasions, wins four times and complete games three times.

Even as recently as the last two years, the aging yet brilliant pitcher has been dominant. Clemens placed second in the AL with a 3.70 ERA, and fired a one-hitter against Seattle in Game 4 of the 2000 League Championship Series to give the Yankees a three games-to-one advantage. In 2001, he placed second in wins with 20 and third in strikeouts with 213 on the way to earning his sixth Cy Young Award and nearly leading the Yankees to another World Series championship.

Clemens, who has won 20 or more games six times, put together a number of sensational seasons warranting MVP consideration, including 1990 when he won 21-of-27 decisions with a 1.93 ERA for the Red Sox, 1997 when he went 21–7 with a 2.05 ERA and 292 strikeouts for the Blue Jays, and 2001 with the Yankees. But the season in which Rocket Man claimed his MVP award was 1986, a campaign in which Boston narrowly missed capturing its first World Series title in 68 years.

The 6-foot-4, 225-pound hurler was nearly unhittable in '86, starting strong with a 14–0 record after 15 starts

Roger Clemens. (National Baseball Hall of Fame Library, Cooperstown, N.Y.)

and ending impressively by winning his final seven decisions. His most dominating game of the season came April 29 at Fenway Park when he struck out 20 Seattle batters for a major league record in a nine-inning game, allowing only three hits and no walks in a 3–1 Boston victory. Clemens kept the Red Sox in position to nab the East Division title by posting 14 of his wins immediately following Boston losses.

The strong right-hander, who did not suffer his first defeat in '86 until July 2, started the All-Star Game and was declared the winning pitcher for his three perfect innings. Eight times Roger struck out 10 or more batters in a game this season, including four games in a row in late April and early May, and he pitched three two-hitters. Clemens earned the victory in Game 7 of the LCS over California, tossing four-hit ball over seven innings despite battling the flu. He then threw no-hit ball for four innings of Game 6 of the World Series against the Mets, and allowed only one earned run in seven innings before being lifted for a pinch-hitter due to a blister on his pitching hand. Clemens wanted to enter Game 7 with the score tied 3–3, but manager John McNamara opted for Calvin Schiraldi, who was tagged with the loss.

For the year, Clemens' statistics were mind-boggling. He went 24–4 with a 2.48 earned run average and 238 strikeouts, with league bests in wins, winning percentage (.857) and ERA. He also placed second in strikeouts and fifth in innings pitched (254). The unanimous Cy Young Award winner and the AL MVP's 24 wins were the highest Red Sox total since 1949, and his 238 K's were the third highest mark in club history.

The joy did not last long, however.

Clemens reported to spring training in 1987 without a contract following a bitter salary battle with General Manager Lou Gorman, then left camp March 6. Commissioner Peter Ueberroth brought the two parties together, and the young pitcher signed a contract in early April for $500,000 for '87 and $1.2 million for '88. The lack of preparation was a factor in a slow start which saw him lose six of his first 10 decisions, but the power pitcher snapped back to go 16–3 the rest of the way, and wound up with a 20–9 mark, leading the league in complete games (18) and shutouts (7), tying for first in wins, placing second in strikeouts (256) and finishing third in ERA (2.97). The stunning comeback resulted in Clemens earning a second consecutive Cy Young Award.

The Red Sox, who faltered in 1987, used a second-half rally in '88 to win their second East title in three years. Clemens' fortunes went the opposite way. A 15–5 start was soured by a 3–7 finish, but he still wound up with AL highs in shutouts (eight) and strikeouts (291) while tossing 14 complete games and crafting a 2.93 ERA. Roger did not have a decision in his only start of Oakland's LCS sweep of Boston.

At this point in his career, Clemens had developed a reputation as a ruthless competitor between the lines, but he was also becoming known as a generous soul off the field. The regular visitor to Children's Hospital in Boston, sometimes in full uniform, was also a strong proponent of anti-drug campaigns, speaking on the subject at local high schools.

In 1989, the flame-thrower registered his 1,000th career strikeout among the 230 he posted (second in the league), and won 17 games with a 3.13 ERA for the third-place Red Sox. Boston came back with its third East title in five years in 1990, and despite a 21–6 record with a miniscule 1.93 ERA, Clemens failed to garner the Cy Young Award. He did, however, pass the legendary Young in career strikeouts by a Red Sox pitcher, and won eight consecutive starts while allowing three or fewer earned runs in 29 of his 31 starts. He led the AL in ERA, tied for the top spot in shutouts (four), placed third in wins and finished fourth in strikeouts (209). Clemens was 0–1 in another LCS sweep by the Athletics, losing his cool in Game 4 and being ejected by umpire Terry Cooney in the second inning for arguing balls and strikes.

The Boston ace stormed back in 1991, despite a five-game suspension for his LCS ejection, to cop his third Cy Young Award with an 18–10 season featuring a 2.62 ERA. His 241 strikeouts, four shutouts, 271⅓ innings pitched and ERA figure were all league bests, and his 13 complete games were runner-up. He rattled off 30-plus consecutive innings of scoreless ball early in the season, and had seven 10-plus strikeout games.

Clemens enjoyed his final dominating season in a Red Sox uniform in 1992, becoming the first pitcher to earn three consecutive ERA (2.41) and shutout (five) titles since Grover Cleveland Alexander in 1915–17. His 208 strikeouts (third in AL) marked the seventh year in a row that he fanned 200 or more, tying a league record, and he made the All-Star Team for the fifth time.

Four mediocre years — at least by Clemens' standards—followed for the big right-hander, who began experiencing some right shoulder problems. He did manage to put together a 28-inning scoreless streak in 1996, and matched his major league record by striking out 20 Detroit batters in a game that same season.

Believing his best years were behind him, the Red Sox allowed Clemens to escape via the free agency route. But Clemens made his former team regret the decision by returning to his dominating form with Toronto. Clemens won his fourth and fifth Cy Young Awards in 1997 and '98, going 21–7 with a 2.05 ERA in '97, and 20–6 with a 2.65 ERA in '98.

The former year, Roger was the AL's best in wins, ERA and strikeouts (292), while tying for the top spot in shutouts (three), complete games (nine) and innings pitched (264). In the latter campaign, he led the way in ERA and strikeouts (271), tied for the lead in wins and tied for second in shutouts (three). His first season in a Blue Jays uniform witnessed an 11–0 start, 14 games with 10 or more strikeouts and his 200th career victory. In his first return to Fenway Park, Clemens whiffed a Toronto-record 16 batters in a 3–1 win. In 1998, he threw three consecutive shutouts, recorded his 3,000th career strikeout, became the first pitcher to win five Cy Young Awards and became only the fourth moundsman to capture the pitching triple crown (wins, ERA, strikeouts) two years in a row. His sixth ERA title placed him second all time behind only 1931 MVP Lefty Grove.

A stunning trade in February 1999 between the Blue Jays and New York Yankees resulted in Clemens changing uniforms again. Swapped for left-handed pitcher and New York fan favorite David Wells, Graeme Lloyd and Homer Bush, Roger donned pinstripes at age 36. He had ended the '98 season with 15 consecutive wins, and he extended the streak to 20 on June 1 with an 11–5 triumph over Cleveland, tied for third best all time.

Despite his renowned pitching prowess through the years, Clemens had never been overly impressive in post-season play. After accumulating a 14–10 mark with a 4.60 ERA for the Yanks in '99, he tried to alter that flaw by winning the clinching game of both the divisional playoff series against Texas and the World Series versus Atlanta. At age 37 and 2 months, Clemens became the oldest starter to win a deciding game of a World Series since 1953, posting his first Series win after 247 regular season victories. In 2000, Clemens' 3.70 ERA was the second best in the AL, and he again rose to the occasion in the post-season by firing a one-hitter against the Mariners in Game 4 of the LCS, and winning Game 2 of the World Series against the Mets with eight shutout innings. The first inning of that contest featured a bizarre incident involving Clemens and the man he'd beaned during the regular season, Mike Piazza. When a Clemens pitch shattered Piazza's bat, the barrel rolled toward Clemens, who inexplicably threw it toward Piazza, later saying he'd thought it was the ball.

Even Clemens' most ardent supporters could not have predicted the phenomenal season the right-hander would enjoy in 2001 at age 39. The AL's oldest starter won 20 of his first 21 decisions — the first major leaguer to do so — including a league record-tying 16 in a row, and finished with an incredible 20–3 record. Earning an unprecedented sixth Cy Young Award, he moved into third place all time in strikeouts and fashioned a 3.51 ERA.

He was unable to pitch more than 4⅓ innings in either of his Division Series starts, being tagged with a loss to Oakland in Game 1, and lasted only five frames in an ALCS outing versus Seattle. But he posted a win in Game 3 of the World Series against Arizona, and gave the Yankees a chance to win Game 7 by allowing only one run over 6.1 innings.

William Roger Clemens did not get off to a great start in life. The youngest of five children, his mother left his father when he was 3½ months old, and his stepfather died when he was 9. With his mother frequently at work, Roger was raised mostly by his grandmother, Myrtle Lee, in Vandalia, Ohio, and he began showing promise of things to come by picking grapes off her vine and hurling them at passing cars. Older brother Randy, a college basketball star who had tryouts with two NBA teams, was a father figure to Roger, as well as an advisor when the youngster starting making career decisions.

Roger won 24-of-27 decisions as a high school hurler, then pitched for a junior college and the University of Texas. He lost the final game of the 1982 College World Series to the University of Miami on a pair of unearned runs, then won the deciding game in the 1983 Series over the University of Alabama. Boston took him 19th overall in the '83 free agent draft, and after a couple of years of seasoning in the minors, Clemens overcame right shoulder and forearm injuries to make the big club for good in his 1986 MVP campaign.

Regardless of how much longer Roger Clemens decides to pitch in the big leagues, he will go down in baseball history as one of the greatest of all time. Overpowering yet possessing control, the Rocket has proven that counting him out is a dangerous mistake to make.

Top 5 MVP Vote-Getters

1. Roger Clemens, Boston — 339
2. Don Mattingly, New York — 258
3. Jim Rice, Boston — 241
4. George Bell, Toronto — 125
5. Jesse Barfield, Toronto — 107

1987 NATIONAL LEAGUE — ANDRE DAWSON

Andre Nolan Dawson
B. July 10, 1954, Miami, Florida

Year	Team	Games	AB	Hits	Avg.	HR	RBI	Runs	SB
1987	Chi NL	153	621	178	.287	49	137	90	11

The Season

The St. Louis Cardinals experienced both the thrill of victory and the agony of defeat this season, rallying from a three games-to-two deficit to win the National League Championship Series 4–3 over San Francisco, but losing a seven-game World Series to the Minnesota Twins despite being up 3–2. It was the third World Series appearance in six years for the Cardinals, who beat Milwaukee in 1982 but fell to Kansas City in '85. The Giants qualified for post-season play for the first time since dropping the 1971 LCS to Pittsburgh.

San Francisco outfielder Jeff Leonard, who won NLCS MVP honors, rocked St. Louis pitchers for a home run in each of the first four games, and batted .417 for the series. But it was Cardinal hurlers who had the last word, shutting out the Giants for the final 22 innings, an NLCS record. St. Louis received sterling World Series performances from catcher Tony Pena (.409 with four RBIs) and former NL MVP Willie McGee (.370, four RBIs), but couldn't salvage a Metrodome victory in four tries.

Several offensive-minded players enjoyed stellar seasons in 1987. New York's Darryl Strawberry and Howard Johnson became the first teammates to both produce 30 home runs and 30 steals in the same season; Tony Gwynn of San Diego batted .370, the highest league mark since three-time MVP Stan Musial hit .376 in 1948; and Jack Clark of St. Louis walked 136 times, the most since former MVP Willie McCovey was issued 137 free passes in 1970.

The top pitchers in the NL battled down to the wire for the Cy Young Award. Once the smoke cleared, Steve Bedrosian of Philadelphia nudged Chicago's Rick Sutcliffe 57–55 in the voting, with San Francisco's Rick Reuschel right behind with 54. Bedrosian, who led the league with 40 saves, was the third reliever to earn the award.

Baseball fans who love a pitcher's duel were glued to their seats during the All-Star Game at Oakland. The contest was scoreless until Tim Raines ripped a two-run triple in the top of the 13th inning for a 2–0 NL triumph.

In other news this season, the Los Angeles Dodgers parted company with Vice President Al Campanis April 8, two days after his remarks regarding race on ABC-TV's *Nightline*, and the Rookie of the Year award was renamed the Jackie Robinson Award.

Fan Favorite

In the final season before Wrigley Field installed lights, the Chicago Cubs acquired a ballplayer who wanted nothing more than to play every day on natural grass and in the daylight. And that's exactly the kind of throw-back to the past that Cubs fans longed to embrace. The relationship between Andre Dawson and his new fans was love at first sight in 1987, and that attraction did not fade when the original passion waned. Day after day, week after week, month after month, Dawson proved himself worthy of the crowd's acclamation, and the fans responded with unabashed adoration.

Many of Chicago's left field bleacher bums abandoned their customary seats by moving to right field that season in order to be closer to the man they nearly worshipped. Animated "we're not worthy" bowing tributes were offered by right field bleach-erites to Dawson when he would trot out to his right field position before each game and between innings, especially following a frame in which "The Hawk" cranked out one of his many prodigious blasts over the ivy-covered walls.

The Cubs were far from competitive in 1987 — they finished in last place in the NL East, 18½ games out of first place — but Dawson never let up. His vicious swing from the right-hander's batter's box produced 49 home runs, 137 RBIs and 353 total bases, all National League highs. The man with the new lease on life played in 153 games, the first time he'd reached that mark in four years; batted .287 with 24 doubles among his 178 hits; and scored 90 runs. It was a tremendous season for the 33-year-old slugger, everyone acknowledged, but no player from a cellar-dwelling team had ever been presented with the Most Valuable Player award.

Fortunately for Dawson and the many Chicago fans who loved him, no individuals from any of the contending clubs put together overwhelming seasons such as Andre had, and the baseball writers rewarded him for his "second life" effort this season. He accumulated 269 points in the MVP balloting to outpoll Ozzie Smith (193) and Jack Clark (186) from the pennant-winning St. Louis Cardinals in an election that sparked renewed debate regarding the true meaning of "Most Valuable."

Dawson may not have immediately lifted his teammates to new heights after coming to the Cubs as a free agent in 1987, but he certainly renewed his career. The 6-foot-3, 190-pound outfielder was 32 when he joined the Cubs, but his knees felt like they were about 80. Ten full seasons of pounding from the artificial turf of Olympic Stadium in Montreal had taken his toll, and while he excelled for the Expos and helped lead them into post-season play in 1981, one knee operation after another was wearing him down and limiting his productivity.

When he became a free agent following the 1986 campaign, Dawson didn't even bother to start a bidding war for his services. In fact, he signed a blank contract and mailed it to Cubs officials, telling them to fill in whatever amount they considered fair. This unprecedented move was big news, and while Andre's agent may not have been thrilled with the deal, Cubs fans who had admired him from afar for so many years were impressed by the competitor's willingness to play for their team regardless of the financial remuneration.

Later it was learned that Dawson was taking only $500,000 out of the Cubs' coffers for the year, and considering the season he enjoyed, it might have been the steal of the year. The power hitter had deposited well over 200 baseballs beyond outfield walls during his career, but only once had he hit as many as 32 in a season; so the 49 he recorded in '87 were a pleasant surprise to even his more ardent fans. After striking four of those round-trippers in nine at-bats, he was hit in the left check by an Eric Show pitch, igniting a benches-clearing incident featuring Dawson frantically trying to get at the retreating pitcher.

Dawson followed a fourth All-Star Game appearance, in which he doubled, with a red-hot August, earning NL Player of the Month honors with 15 home runs and 28 RBIs. The attacking swinger had hit for the cycle April 29 for the fifth time in his career, and he homered in three consecutive at-bats August 1. In addition, the aggressive outfielder had 12 assists and nabbed his seventh Gold Glove.

The Cubs dramatically improved Dawson's salary in 1988, and while he was unable to repeat his incredible MVP performance, he still hit 24 homers with 79 RBIs, and finished among the top four NL players in hits (179, second), total bases (298, second), batting (.303, third) and slugging (.504, fifth), as Chicago moved up to fourth place. Wearing uniform No. 8 and a scowling visage at the plate, he led the league in multi-hit games with 57, became the first major league player to have at least 10 home runs and 10 stolen bases in each of 12 consecutive seasons, and collected his eighth and final Gold Glove.

Having competed in post-season play only once during a 13-year career, Dawson was ecstatic to be part of the Cubs' rise to first place in the Eastern Division in 1989. Right knee problems limited him to 118 games, but he belted 21 homers and collected 77 RBIs, reaching milestones with his 300th career homer and his 2,000th hit. Unfortunately, Andre managed only a .105 batting average and three runs batted in during the four games-to-one NLCS loss to San Francisco.

Dawson would turn 36 during the 1990 season, but he was still playing like a brash rookie eager to prove himself in the bigs. His career-high .310 batting average was fifth in the senior circuit, and his 16 stolen bases were his highest total in a Cubs uniform. He cracked 27 home runs and drove in 100 runs while scoring 72 times. Apparently the Cincinnati Reds were impressed because they enabled him to set a major league record with five intentional walks in one game. The Hawk wasn't finished yet. In 1991 and '92, he combined for 53 homers and 194 RBIs, hitting above .270 in both campaigns. He hit a home run off Roger Clemens in the '91 All-Star Game, the NL's first dinger in All-Star competition since 1984 and the first by a Cub player since 1964. His 2,500th career hit came late in the '92 season.

Dawson went to the Boston Red Sox as a free agent in 1993, tagging his 400th career homer early in the season, and becoming only the second major league player to reach 2,000 hits, 200 home runs and 300 stolen bases. More knee problems and a fractured wrist cost the designated hitter time and power, and '94 proved to be another injury-riddled season. The eight-time All-Star finished his career in his native Miami with a couple of seasons playing for the Florida Marlins.

Young Andre Nolan Dawson, a nephew of Theodore Taylor, an outfielder in the Pirates organization in the late 1960s, played ball at Southwest Miami High School and Florida A&M University. A total of 250 players was chosen ahead of Dawson in the 1975 free agent draft, but he moved up the minor league ladder quickly before the Expos brought him to the big club late in the 1976 season.

The promising youngster got off to a slow start in 1977, but after manager Dick Williams gave him a shot of confidence by announcing that he was the team's permanent center fielder, Dawson responded by batting .282 with 19 home runs (a Montreal rookie record), recording 65 RBIs and 21 stolen bases, and claiming the league's Rookie of the Year trophy. He showed off a rifle for an arm in 1978 when he posted a career-high 17 outfield assists; tied for second in triples in 1979 with 12; and tied for second in doubles (41) and finished fourth in runs (96) in '80. The Expos fell just short of the NL East crown in the latter two years.

Dawson really started coming into his own in 1981 when he hit .302 with 24 home runs and 64 RBIs, placing second in the MVP voting and being named *The Sporting News* Player of the Year. In this strike-shortened season, Montreal won the second-half title, then edged Philadelphia three games to two in the league divisional series, with Dawson batting .300. But he managed only a .150 mark in a five-game, heart-breaking loss to Los Angeles in the LCS.

Now clearly among the game's elite, his star shone brightly in the early to mid–1980s. Dawson placed among the top four players in hits, doubles, total bases and runs in 1982, and led league outfielders in putouts and total chances. He soared even higher in '83, placing first in total bases (341), tying for first in hits (189), finishing runner-up in both RBIs (113) and slugging (.539), and tying for third in homers (32), runs (104) and triples (10). In a *New York Times* player poll, Dawson was voted the best all-around player in the majors, and was second in NL MVP voting.

Andre's final three years in Montreal included an 86-RBI effort in 1984,

23 homers and 91 RBIs in '85, and a .284 batting average in '86. Perhaps his greatest game as an Expo came on September 24, 1985, when he hit three homers, including two during a 12-run fifth inning, and tied a club record with eight RBIs in a slugfest with Chicago. That game made Dawson one of only three major leaguers to hit two home runs in the same inning twice (he also accomplished the feat in 1978). Not surprisingly, when he left the Expos following the 1986 season, it was as the franchise's leader in many offensive departments.

For his 21-year career, Dawson ranked among the top 30 in baseball in numerous categories, including career home runs (438), RBIs (1,591), total bases (4,787) and extra base hits (1,039), plus games, at-bats and outfield putouts. He also stole 314 bases.

Dawson, who in 1997 became only the third former Expo to have his uniform number retired by the team, put up some awesome numbers through the years, despite being hampered by bad knees that required eight operations. An all-around star who hit for average and power, ran the bases well and patrolled the outfield expertly, Dawson is a prime candidate for the Hall of Fame in the not-so-distant future. After all, Cubs fans aren't the only ones who had a love affair with Andre Dawson.

Top 5 MVP Vote-Getters

1. Andre Dawson, Chicago — 269
2. Ozzie Smith, St. Louis — 193
3. Jack Clark, St. Louis — 186
4. Tim Wallach, Montreal — 165
5. Will Clark, San Francisco — 128

1987 American League — George Bell

George Antonio (Mathey) Bell
B. October 21, 1959, San Pedro De Macoris, Dominican Republic

Year	Team	Games	AB	Hits	Avg.	HR	RBI	Runs	SB
1987	Tor AL	156	610	188	.308	47	134	111	5

The Season

Home is where the heart is, and for the Minnesota Twins, home was also where the victories were this season. The Twins, who beat out Kansas City by two games in the American League West Division, won both Metrodome games during a four games-to-one League Championship Series triumph over Detroit, then took all four home contests in a thrilling, seven-game World Series victory over St. Louis.

Gary Gaetti (two homers, five RBIs) and Tom Brunansky (.412, two homers, nine RBIs) starred for Minnesota in the LCS, as the team won its first league championship since 1965. The Tigers, whose 225 home runs were the most in the majors in 24 years, hit seven more in a losing cause in the five-game set. Kirby Puckett (.357, three RBIs) and Series MVP Frank Viola (2–1, 3.72 ERA) stood out for the Twins in the World Series, the first ever World Championship for the franchise in Minnesota. Game 1, the first fall classic night game, featured a grand slam by Minnesota's Dan Gladden.

Several individuals performed eye-opening feats in 1987. Former MVP Don Mattingly, who had never hit a grand slam in his career, belted six of them, breaking a major league record shared by Ernie Banks (1955) and Jim Gentile (1961), who had five each. New York's Mattingly also tied Dale Long's major league record when he recorded at least one home run in eight consecutive games.

Paul Molitor of Milwaukee brought back memories of Joe DiMaggio's 56-game hitting streak when he hit safely in 39 consecutive contests before the streak ended. Puckett was on fire in late August, going 4-for-5 with two home runs on August 29, then tying an AL record for most hits in a nine-inning game August 30 with a 6-for-6 performance, including two more round-trippers.

Boston's Roger Clemens became the first pitcher to win back-to-back Cy Young Awards, posting a 20–9 record with a 2.97 ERA, 18 complete games, seven shutouts and 256 strikeouts. Mark McGwire of Oakland showed signs of things to come by belting 49 home runs — the most in the league since Harmon Killebrew's 49 in 1969 — and earning Rookie of the Year honors.

Suspicious Slugger

There are those who believe that had George Bell's defensive attitude not clashed with his offensive prowess, he could have accomplished so much more. The slugging right-hander played only 10 full seasons in the major leagues, yet hit 265 home runs and drove in more than 1,000 runs. An inability to get a firm grip on the English language caused communication problems for the Dominican Republic native, who often remained silent rather than risking embarrassing himself with ineffective speech. A hot temper and a persecution complex also limited Bell's efforts to win friends and influence people, and he was often portrayed in a negative light by the media.

But when it came time to step into the batter's box during the 1980s and early '90s, Bell communicated one thing very clearly to the man on the mound: fear. The 6-foot-1, 200-pound package of muscle would rock back just prior to the hurler's delivery, then burst into the pitch with his entire body, frequently sending the white sphere sailing into distant corners of the ballyard, or quite often, into the bleachers.

Bell was a key cog in the Toronto Blue Jays' rapid rise to the top of the American League East during the early stages of the franchise's existence. And while he played only seven full seasons with the club, and has now been gone for more than a decade, he still ranked among its top five all-time in a variety of offensive categories. In Blue Jays annals, Bell was first all time in RBIs, total bases and extra base hits; second in home runs and sacrifice flies; third in hits, runs, doubles and at-bats; fourth in games; fifth in batting average; and seventh in triples.

Tightly wound, both physically and emotionally, Bell earned a reputation as a hothead following a questionable brush-back pitch in 1985, his second full season in the majors. Bell's response to the perceived purpose pitch was to charge the mound and karate kick Boston pitcher Bruce Kison. Three years later, manager Jimy Williams announced that Bell would be removed from the outfield and inserted into the designated hitter's spot. The official reasoning was the continued deterioration of Bell's knees, but more likely, it was a reaction to his less than stellar fielding capabilities. Regardless, Bell complained loudly. Fans and teammates were well aware and appreciative of Bell's stunning abilities with the stick, but now they were questioning his interest in being a team player.

Bell's impressive work with the bat remained approximately the same after what he considered a demotion to the DH role, but he left the club following the 1990 season via the free agent route, then played for the two Chicago ballclubs before retiring at age 34 after the 1993 campaign.

Born George Antonio Mathey Bell in San Pedro De Macoris in the Domincan Republic, he preceded two of his brothers into professional baseball (Juan was a major league infielder from 1989–95, while Rolando was a minor league infielder from 1985–87), and made a name for himself in the local leagues as a big-time pounder of baseballs. He helped the Escogido team win a pair of professional league titles in the early 1980s; led the league in slugging, total bases and doubles in the 1983–84 season; and contributed to another league title and a Caribbean Series crown for the Licey club in 1984–85.

Much of this action came in winter ball after George had signed a contract with the Blue Jays. Bell appeared in 60 games for Toronto in 1981, placing eighth in Rookie of the Year balloting, then came back for 39 more games in 1983 before earning the starting right field position in '84 with a splendid spring training camp. Bell had platooned with outfielders Dave Collins and Barry Bonnell in 1983 as the Blue Jays became contenders in their seventh season, but he played in 159 games the following year. More than 2 million fans came out in '84 to see the Jays, who won 89 games and finished second behind Detroit in the East. Bell was one of the draws in his first full season, batting .292 with 26 home runs and 87 RBIs, and placing third in the league in doubles with a franchise-high 39.

Toronto made it into post-season play for the first time in 1985, winning 99 games to capture the AL East. Bell was a major contributor again, smacking 28 circuit clouts, driving in 95 runs and scoring 87 times. Beginning to show incredible power for his size, Bell twice launched balls over Chicago's Comiskey Park roof in the same series. He continued to lead the club in the League Championship Series against Kansas City by batting .321 with four runs and nine hits, including three doubles. But the Royals won a seven-game series over the Jays.

Hopes were high in Toronto entering the 1986 season, as many felt the team was ready to take the next step. And while the hitters came through in fine fashion, pitching let the team down. The Blue Jays finished in fourth place in the Eastern Division with an 86–76 mark. Bell reached the .300 plateau for the first time in his brief career, batting .309 with 198 hits and tying for third in the league in total bases with 341, and placing fourth in slugging with a .532 percentage. Bell drilled 31 homers, scored 101 runs and led the junior circuit in game-winning hits (15), while he and fellow outfielder Jesse Barfield shared a franchise record with 108 RBIs each. Bell's efforts did not go unnoticed, as evidenced by his fourth-place status in the Most Valuable Player award voting.

Many players reach their primes in their late 20s, and Bell was no exception. He put together a career year at age 27 in 1987, blasting the horsehide to all fields, and building a reputation as a clutch hitter. Bell led the American League in RBIs with 134 and total bases with 369, and was runner-up in home runs with a career-high 47, slugging at .605 and runs with 111. He had nine multi-homer games, including four in a three-week stretch in late May and early June, enabling him to hit 11 home runs in both months. Bell also contributed a franchise-best 83 extra base hits and made his first of two All-Star Teams, becoming the first Blue Jay to be voted to the starting lineup. Surprisingly, he led AL left fielders in assists with 14.

Bell and teammates Barfield (28 homers) and Lloyd Moseby (26) helped Toronto record the sixth highest home run total (215) in AL history in 1987. Ten of those blasts came September 14 when the Jays set a major league record in an 18–3 dismantling of Baltimore. Ernie Whitt cracked three of those dingers, while Bell added two. Other major contributors to the Jays' run at the East title were Jimmy Key (17–8 with a 2.76 ERA), Tom Henke (AL-high 34 saves) and Tony Fernandez (.322 with 32 stolen bases).

The awards came pouring in for Bell following the 1987 season, including the AL Most Valuable Player award, which made him the first Dominican Republic native to earn the honor, as well as the first player from a Canadian team. He was also named *The Sporting News* Major League Player of the Year.

But it was a bittersweet season for Bell and Jays fans. The team held a one-game lead over Detroit heading into a final three-game series, but dropped each affair by one run — including a painful 1–0 defeat in the regular-season finale — to fall two games short of the East championship, despite posting the second highest win total (96) in the majors. And Bell's MVP award proved to be controversial, not unlike his career, as some felt Detroit shortstop Alan Trammell was more deserving. Trammell batted .343 with 28 home runs and 105 RBIs for the division-winning Tigers, but Bell won by a 332–311 margin.

Bell got off to a rousing start in 1988 in a bid to prove his MVP award was no fluke, becoming the first player in major league history to hit three home runs on opening day. But he hit only 24 round-trippers for the season and took some of the heat for the Jays' slide to a third-place tie, despite playing nearly every game and driving in 97 runs.

Toronto came back to qualify for post-season play in 1989 after moving from Exhibition Stadium into the Sky-dome, winning the East Division by two games over Baltimore. Bell, who placed fourth in the MVP balloting, was first in the AL in sacrifice flies (11) and fourth in doubles (41), and raised his average nearly 30 points from the previous season to .297, thanks in part to a 22-game hitting streak. He had a home run among his four hits in the ALCS, but Oakland defeated the Jays four games to one. In his final season in Toronto, Bell hit .265 with 21 homers and 86 ribbies despite increasing problems with his knees and shoulder.

In nine seasons with the Blue Jays, Bell was the team's MVP four times. He hit .286 with 237 doubles, 32 triples and 202 home runs, drove in 740 runs, scored 641 times, stroked 1,294 hits and stole 59 bases. George did not walk much (255), but he didn't strike out all that much either (563). Bell led Toronto in RBIs five times; in doubles and sacrifice flies on four occasions; in homers, hits and at-bats three times each; and in batting average and slugging percentage once each.

Bell was considered a clutch hitter throughout his career. He smacked at least one extra-inning homer per season five times during a six-year span (1985–90), and is the Toronto franchise leader in grand slams with seven, including two each in 1985 and '87. On five occasions he had five hits in a game, and five different times he contributed four hits in a contest.

Bell's bat picked up some steam again in 1991 after he signed as a free agent with the Cubs. He batted .285, clubbed 25 home runs, drove in 86 runs and appeared in his third All-Star Game. The Cubs then pulled off what turned out to be one of their best trades ever when they acquired Sammy Sosa from the cross-town White Sox for Bell. The 32-year-old newcomer showed Sox fans a few things in 1992 with 112 RBIs — fourth in the league, and his highest total since his MVP season in '87 — and 25 homers. Bell concluded his career in 1993 with a 13-homer, 64-RBI effort, and did not appear in Chicago's 4–2 ALCS loss to his former teammates in Toronto.

George Bell was a highly competitive, high-strung batsman who proved year after year that he could pound the ball and drive in runs with the best of them. Had he been blessed with a sturdier pair of knees, and had he been better able to put a variety of perceived slights behind him, his career statistics probably would have been even more impressive. As it is, Bell was one of the top sluggers of the 1980s, as well as a major cog in the Blue Jay teams which provided their fans with so much excitement.

Top 5 MVP Vote-Getters

1. George Bell, Toronto — 332
2. Alan Trammell, Detroit — 311
3. Kirby Puckett, Minnesota — 201
4. Dwight Evans, Boston — 127
5. Paul Molitor, Milwaukee — 125

1988 NATIONAL LEAGUE — KIRK GIBSON

Kirk Harold Gibson
B. May 28, 1957, Pontiac, Michigan

Year	Team	Games	AB	Hits	Avg.	HR	RBI	Runs	SB
1988	LA NL	150	542	157	.290	25	76	106	31

The Season

If there was one team the Los Angeles Dodgers did not want to meet in the League Championship Series this season, it was the New York Mets. But there wasn't much choice. The Mets, who had beaten Los Angeles 10-of-11 times during the regular season, cruised to the National League East title by 15 games over Pittsburgh, while the Dodgers won the West by a comfortable seven-game margin over Cincinnati.

L.A. blew late leads in two of the first three LCS games, then was in danger of falling behind three games to one before rallying in Game 4. The Dodgers went on to win the series in seven games before upsetting Oakland four games to one in the World Series for the franchise's seventh championship. Catcher Mike Scioscia hit .364 with a homer and two RBIs for the winners in the LCS, while Tim Belcher won a pair of games. Outfielder Mickey Hatcher was the Dodgers' hitting hero in the World Series, batting .368 with two homers and five RBIs.

But the MVP of both series was Orel Hershiser, whose unanimous Cy Young Award season included NL bests in wins (23), shutouts (eight), complete games (15) and innings pitched, plus a 2.26 earned run average. The tall right-hander, who ran off a scoreless streak of 59 regular-season innings to break the major league record of former Dodger Don Drysdale, was 1–0 with a 1.09 ERA over 24-plus innings during the LCS, then went 2–0 with a 1.00 ERA and 17 strikeouts in the World Series.

The end of an era came in 1988 when night games were played in Wrigley Field for the first time ever. The Cubs received permission from city aldermen to add lights to the historic ballpark for up to 18 games per season after fearing the loss of the 1990 All-Star Game and future playoff and World Series games. In the first official night game, played August 9 (the 8-8-88 night game was rained out), the Cubs defeated New York 6–4.

St. Louis infielder Jose Oquendo became the first position player to be credited with a decision in 20 years. He shut out Atlanta for three innings before giving up the winning runs in a 7–5, 19-inning Cardinal loss May 14.

On September 8, NL President Bart Giamatti was elected baseball's seventh commissioner, officially succeeding Peter Ueberroth in 1989.

True Grit

You could call him a bull in a china shop, but bulls have no idea where they're going. He could be compared to a caged leopard, but few were able to corral him. He may have resembled a stampeding stallion at times, but he never followed the crowd.

Pinning a label on Kirk Gibson is an elusive occupation at best. Big and strong, he possessed incredible speed and base-running smarts. Yet he spent an inordinate amount of time sidelined by injury, and was considered a defensive liability with a less than adequate arm. But in one respect, Gibson was predictable and consistent: he played the game of baseball with an intensity almost unheard of in the current era, and was one of the best clutch hitters the game has ever known.

Gibson had made a name for himself during the 1980s as a prominent member of the Detroit American League conglomeration that put on one of the most dominating performances ever in a World Championship season in 1984. As one of seven players in early 1988 to be declared "no-risk free agents" by arbitrator Thomas Roberts, as a result of the Major League Baseball Players Association collusion suit against the owners three years earlier, Gibson signed a three-year contract with the Los Angeles Dodgers.

Gibby was well aware of the franchise's rich history when he joined the club in spring training, but it didn't take long for him to discover that some of the Dodgers players seemed to be more interested in enjoying the Florida sun than in preparing to improve on their fourth-place finish the previous season. When prankster Jesse Orosco applied black eye to the inside brim of Gibson's hat, the high-strung newcomer exploded, letting his teammates know in no uncertain terms that he hadn't come to this club to goof around, but rather to win a title.

The statement angered some and impressed others, but once his new teammates saw the day-in, day-out grit and determination Gibson brought to his game, they all agreed that this kind of rare intensity could jump-start a previous lethargic ballclub and bring out the best in dormant talents.

Perhaps Gibson's volcanic response that memorable spring day was fueled by an incident five years earlier when Tigers manager Sparky Anderson verbally spanked the cocky outfielder for failing to live up to his potential. Gibson had displayed flashes of brilliance during the early 1980s when he wasn't injured, and was entering the '83 season with some onlookers still raving about his potential to be another Mickey Mantle, but he'd developed a few bad off-the-field habits. Anderson benched his right fielder for the opener, telling him that he was

Kirk Gibson. (Courtesy Los Angeles Dodgers.)

turned things around in '84 with a marvelous season featuring a .282 average, 27 homers, 91 RBIs, 92 runs, 10 triples and 29 stolen bases. And he wasn't even close to being finished for the year. Gibson won the American League Championship Series MVP award by batting .417 with a home run and two RBIs in the Tigers' 3–0 sweep of Kansas City, then helped Detroit trounce San Diego 4–1 in the World Series with a .333 average, two homers, seven RBIs, four runs, four walks and three stolen bases. Both of his round-trippers—a two-run shot in the first inning and a three-run blow in the eighth—came in the fifth and final game.

The intense competitor would play three more seasons with the Tigers, including 1987 when he moved from right field to left, and the team returned to the playoffs. During those three years, he averaged .278, 27 homers, 87 RBIs and 30 steals. He batted .286 with four runs, six hits, a homer and four RBIs in the four games-to-one loss to Minnesota in the '87 ALCS.

Gibson surprised the baseball world when he left his native Michigan for the West Coast in 1988, delighting the Dodger faithful who had witnessed two consecutive 73–89 campaigns. Gibson's stats in his first season in Dodger blue—.290 average, 25 home runs, 76 RBIs, 28 doubles, 106 runs (second in the NL), 31 stolen bases, 73 walks and .381 on-base percentage (fourth)—were not all that much superior to what he'd been producing in the Motor City, but his clutch hitting (.348 in the late innings) and determined spirit were contagious as the Dodgers drove toward the West Division title.

The right fielder started slowly in '88, and tailed off during the final month, but in between he was a man on a mission, batting .324 with seven homers and 17 RBIs in May, then averaging .298 with five homers and 14 RBIs per month from June through August. Los Angeles beat out Cincinnati by seven games for the division crown, and the fun was only beginning.

The Dodgers outlasted the New York Mets in a thrilling seven-game

"acting like an idiot," and that he was heading for a fall if he didn't get his act together.

Gibson wasn't yet ready to change for Anderson — or anyone else, for that matter — and he struggled in 1983 with a .227 average, 15 home runs and 51 RBIs in 128 games. These were unacceptable figures for a guy who'd come to the major leagues with much fanfare after being the Tigers' No. 1 selection in the June 1978 draft. Gibson, an

All-America flanker at Michigan State, opted for baseball over football because he felt it offered more longevity and money, with less chance of serious injury.

The Pontiac, Michigan, native broke in with the big club in 1979, hit .263 in 51 games in '80, batted .328 in a half-season the following year, then dropped to .278 in 69 games in 1982. Following the dismal 1983 campaign, the 6-foot-3, 215-pound left-hander

LCS, and while a hobbled Gibson batted only .154, he managed two clutch homers and drove in six runs (including the game-winning RBI in Game 7), while teammate Orel Hershiser posted a 1.09 ERA over nearly 25 innings.

Gibson may have thought that he could never top his 1984 World Series heroics, but he was about to produce one of the most dramatic moments in fall classic history. A leg injury figured to sideline the gutsy performer for the entire Series, but he told manager Tom Lasorda that he probably had at least one good at-bat left in him. Lasorda selected just the right time to utilize it.

With the favored Oakland Athletics leading Game 1 by a 4–3 margin and relief ace Dennis Eckersley on the hill in the bottom of the ninth, it appeared that L.A. was going to fall behind in the Series. But Gibson limped to the plate with two outs and Mike Davis on base. After fouling off several pitches and working the count to 3–2, he recalled advance scout Mel Didier telling him that Eckersley would probably throw a backdoor slider in this type of situation. Sure enough, that's what the reliever delivered, and Gibson turned on the pitch, driving it into the right field stands for a 5–4 Dodger victory

and one of the most exciting moments in World Series history. It would be his only at-bat in a Series that L.A. captured four games to one, and it made him just the third player in baseball annals to homer in his only Series at-bat.

Following the season, Gibson was named the National League's Most Valuable Player, outpolling New York's Darryl Strawberry 272–236. These two players were the only ones who had 20 homers and 20 steals each year from 1984 through '88. The honor made Gibson only the second player in history to earn an MVP award before being selected to an All-Star Team.

Injuries limited Gibson to 71 games in 1989 and 89 contests in '90, and he moved to the Kansas City Royals for the 1991 season, where he played in 132 games but hit only .236 with 16 homers. It appeared that the gritty, 35-year-old outfielder was finished after participating in only 16 games as a Pittsburgh Pirate in 1992, but he came back to the Tigers in '93 and turned a few heads.

Gibson played in 116 games in '93, batting .261 with 13 homers, 62 RBIs and 15 stolen bases, then clubbed 23 circuit clouts in only 98 games in '94,

adding a .276 average, 72 RBIs and 71 runs to an already impressive resumé. He hit .260 in his final season in 1995, retiring as a Tiger with 255 lifetime homers, 870 RBIs, 985 runs scored and 284 stolen bases.

Gibson took some time off from baseball to work as an environmental activist and play some recreational hockey in northern Michigan. He became a Detroit Tigers broadcaster in 1997, wrote an autobiography with sportswriter Lynn Henning titled *Bottom of the Ninth* and turned down a Tigers bench coach job.

By his own admission, Kirk Gibson had a good career, not a great one. But what he'll always be remembered for will be his all-out effort, fierce determination and an uncanny ability to come through in the clutch.

Top 5 MVP Vote-Getters

1. Kirk Gibson, Los Angeles — 272
2. Darryl Strawberry, New York — 236
3. Kevin McReynolds, New York — 162
4. Andy Van Slyke, Pittsburgh — 160
5. Will Clark, San Francisco — 135

1988 American League — Jose Canseco

Jose (Capas) Canseco
B. July 2, 1964, Regla, Cuba

Year	Team	Games	AB	Hits	Avg.	HR	RBI	Runs	SB
1988	Oak AL	158	610	187	.307	42	124	120	40

The Season

A pair of teams that were mediocre at best the previous year came on strong to win their divisions this season. Oakland rebounded from a .500 effort in 1987 to win 104 games and capture the West Division by 13 games over Minnesota. After finishing 20 games out of first place the year before,

Boston rallied to outlast Detroit by one game in the East.

The Red Sox's offense was no match for the A's pitching in the League Championship Series, won in a sweep by Oakland. Dennis Eckersley earned an ALCS-record four saves, Dave Stewart posted a 1.35 earned run average over 13-plus innings and league MVP Jose Canseco belted three

homers in the four-game set. The Athletics' joy faded quickly, however, after being upset four games to one by the Los Angeles Dodgers in the World Series.

A couple of AL clubs experienced lengthy streaks of an opposite nature this year. Baltimore established a league record with 21 consecutive losses in April, while the Red Sox set a junior circuit mark with 24 consecutive home victories, only two shy of the major league record. Not to be outdone, the Athletics broke a franchise record with their 14th win in a row, the longest streak in the majors in 11 years.

Several individuals prospered in 1988, including Boston's Wade Boggs. The third baseman earned his fourth consecutive league titles — and fifth in the past six years — in batting (.366) and on-base percentage (.480), and his 125 walks were the most in the AL since 1970. Teammate Roger Clemens posted eight shutouts and 291 strikeouts, the highest totals in the league in 10 and 11 years, respectively.

In less than a month's time, two pitchers made names for themselves without touching a baseball. On June 11, Rick Rhoden of New York became the first pitcher to start a game as a designated hitter since the rule was adopted in 1973, and his sacrifice fly helped the Yankees beat the Orioles. Oakland's Gene Nelson, who in a few months would win two ALCS games in relief, became the first AL moundsman to steal a base in 15 years when he swiped a sack while pinch-running during a 16-inning, 9–8 victory over Toronto July 3.

Another hurler, Minnesota reliever Jeff Reardon, became the first pitcher in major league history to save 40 games in a season in both leagues. Reardon, who notched 42 saves for the year, had posted 41 saves for Montreal in 1985.

Catcher Terry Steinbach of Oakland wreaked a bit of revenge in the July 12 All-Star Game, smacking a solo homer and lifting a sacrifice fly in the American League's 2–1 triumph at Riverfront Stadium in Cincinnati. Steinbach had been portrayed as unworthy of All-Star starting status by some media prior to the game, but wound up as the contest's MVP.

Big Boomer

Big and handsome, he could pound the baseball mercilessly, sending it skyrocketing into the stratosphere. Possessing a rifle for an arm and amazing speed for a 6-foot-4, 240-pounder, he could go get 'em in the outfield and race around the bases with the quickness and ferocity of a tiger. Suffice it to say that Jose Canseco had the world at his feet in 1988 when he was a unanimous selection as the American League's Most Valuable Player.

But some chinks in the armor were to be discovered only a few months later, and while he continued his impressive battery of assaults on the horsehide over the next dozen years, his glorious accomplishments often took a back seat to frequent injuries and various controversies that flared up for this flamboyant athlete.

Born in 1964 in Regla, Cuba, a Havana suburb, to a once-prominent family that lost everything in the 1959 Communist revolution, Jose and twin brother Ozzie moved to the Miami area in 1965. Neither their mother, Barbara, who never enjoyed good health after contracting hepatitis from an infected blood transfusion during the twins' birth, nor their father, Jose Sr., were interested in sports, instead encouraging the boys to focus on academics. But once Jose picked up a baseball for the first time at age 13, he and Ozzie were hooked.

Jose Jr. was unable to make his Coral Park High School varsity team until his senior year, but then hit .400 as a third baseman and was selected by the Oakland Athletics in the 15th round of the 1982 draft after being scouted by former American League pitcher Camilo Pascual. Ozzie was signed by the New York Yankees in '82, later playing in the A's organization and in Japan.

Jose Canseco got off to a sluggish start in rookie league ball, then slowly made his way up to Class A in 1983. He moved to the outfield in the Arizona Instructional League, where he started demonstrating a propensity for the distant shot and the strikeout. After taking a month off in April 1984 when his mother passed away, Canseco returned to the A's farm team in Modesto, California, where he clubbed 15 home runs, but also fanned 127 times.

He conducted a serious weight training program during the off-season, and really began coming into his own in 1985 as a powerhouse. The beefed-up slugger pounded 25 homers with 80 RBIs in a half-season with the Double A Huntsville, Alabama, team, and was named the Southern Association's MVP. He also put on a show later that year at Triple A Tacoma, Washington, batting .348. *The Sporting News'* Minor League Player of the Year brought in fans early for batting practice with his mighty clouts, and was the first player in 26 years to tattoo a ball out of Tacoma's Cheney Stadium.

Canseco made his major league debut with the A's late in the '85 season and quickly made a name for himself by smacking a ball onto the roof at Comiskey Park in Chicago. He also laid the groundwork for his other trademark — the dramatic whiff — by fanning 31 times in only 96 at-bats. The big outfielder was selected for the All-Star Team, and placed second in the league in RBIs (117) and tied for fourth in homers (33) while earning Rookie of the Year honors in 1986. Jose also set a rookie record for strikeouts with 175 and committed 14 errors as the A's tied for third in the West Division.

In 1987, Canseco became the first A's player to drive in 100 runs in two consecutive seasons with a total of 113 to augment his 31 homers. Both his fielding and batting averages improved as the big bopper started to become a complete ballplayer. The strikeouts were still frequent — 157 this season — but his overall excellent play was pushing that dubious statistic to the back burner in the eyes of A's fans.

The table was set for the A's and their long ball game to thrive in 1988, and that's exactly what happened. Canseco put together a phenomenal season, becoming the founding member of the 40-homer, 40-steal club. He led the majors in home runs (42), RBIs (124) and slugging (.569), while batting .307, collecting 347 total bases (second in the AL), scoring 120 runs (second) and stealing 40 bases (fourth), as Oakland won 104 games and the West title.

The first player in major league history to hit at least 30 round-trippers in each of his first three full seasons, Canseco continued his batting barrage in the League Championship

Series, posting a .313 mark and stroking three homers in the four-game sweep of Boston. Canseco walloped a grand slam in the first game of the World Series, but the A's were manhandled four games to one by the Los Angeles Dodgers. The next month, Canseco was named the first unanimous AL MVP since Reggie Jackson in 1973, and was chosen the Major League Player of the Year by both *The Sporting News* and the Associated Press.

Things were looking up for Canseco, who had recently married former Miss Miami, Esther Haddad, and signed a $1.64 million contract, but a series of events would quickly remove the luster from his spectacular 1988 campaign. Canseco had said in a *Sports Illustrated* article that he sometimes felt like the gorilla in the zoo that everybody stares at and points at. But if that were the case, it could be argued that Jose put himself in that cage and locked the door. Rumors of steroid use preceded Canseco being taken to task by the media in early 1989 for failing to fulfill his commitments to a charity fund-raiser and a sports collectibles show. He was arrested in February for driving his Jaguar in excess of 125 miles per hour, reported to spring training late for the third year in a row, and injured his left wrist and went on the disabled list. Canseco was arrested again while on the disabled list, this time on the University of California-San Francisco campus for having a semiautomatic pistol in his car.

He rejoined the team in mid–July, clobbered five homers in his first nine games and helped lead the team to another West Division title. The A's won the LCS 4–1 over Toronto, with Canseco crushing a Game 4 home run 540 feet into the fifth deck of the Skydome, then went on to sweep San Francisco in the World Series, as Jose went 3-for-5 with a three-run homer and three runs scored in Game 3.

Canseco got back into the fulltime swing of things in 1990 with a 37-homer, 101-RBI effort that featured another highlight reel circuit clout at the Skydome, his May 22 grand slam banging off the window of a restaurant over the center field wall. The following month, Canseco signed a five-year contract worth $23.5 million, making him baseball's highest compensated player. Back problems that would become chronic also made themselves felt in June for the All-Star Game's leading vote-getter. Jose hit only .182 in the LCS sweep of Boston, then just .083 in the World Series loss to Cincinnati

The A's dipped to fourth place in 1991, but no one could blame Canseco. Wielding a heavy war club, he tied for the AL home run leadership with 44, drove in 122 runs (second), scored 115 times (tied for second) and slugged at a .556 pace (third). Finishing fourth in the MVP balloting, he became the first A's player since Jimmie Foxx to hit 40 or more homers in two different seasons, but also struck out 152 times. In '92, he tied a major league record with seven consecutive walks before being traded to Texas August 31 for Ruben Sierra, two other players and cash.

Rangers fans might have found it amusing when Canseco was used as a relief pitcher during a 15–1 loss at Boston May 29, 1993, but manager Kevin Kennedy's ill-advised decision resulted in Canseco injuring his elbow and needing season-ending surgery in July. He became a fulltime designated hitter in 1994 and was named *The Sporting News'* AL Comeback Player of the Year for his 31 homers and 90 RBIs.

Canseco moved to the Red Sox for the 1995 season, homering in five consecutive games and collecting his 300th career homer. He was hitless in Boston's division playoff series loss to Cleveland. In '96, two more stints on the DL did not deter him from joining Foxx as the only Red Sox players to homer at least 10 times in consecutive months (11 in May, 10 in June). The 1997 season saw a return to Oakland, where back problems limited him to 108 games, but did not deter him from being arrested for hitting his second wife in the head, for which he was ordered to undergo battery counseling. Five years earlier, he had been charged with aggravated assault for ramming his vehicle into a new car driven by his first wife.

Jose rebounded in 1998 with Toronto, clouting a career-high 46 homers, third in the AL and the second highest total in Blue Jays history.

On July 26, he became the all-time leading home run hitter among those born outside the U.S., but in keeping with his all-or-nothing swing, also set a club record with a league-high 159 strikeouts.

Canseco joined the Tampa Bay Devil Rays in 1999, and along with teammate Fred McGriff became the only players to hit 30 homers in a season with four different teams. Canseco was leading the AL in homers — tying a league record with 21 road shots prior to the All-Star break — before undergoing back surgery July 11. The first Devil Ray to be elected an All-Star, he homered in five consecutive games in mid–May for the second time in his career. He had one World Series at-bat, a strikeout, in 2000 after going from Tampa Bay to the Yankees.

Canseco signed with the Anaheim Angels during the off-season, but was released prior to opening day 2001. He tried to convince major league personnel that he was healthy by playing with brother Ozzie for the Newark Bears in the Atlantic League, but received no takers for a while. Then his comeback opportunity arrived. Needing some punch following a season-ending injury to Frank Thomas, the Chicago White Sox employed the 37-year-old slugger as a designated hitter in late June. Limited to 256 at-bats in an ongoing lobbying effort for more playing time, Canseco hit .258 with 16 homers and 49 RBIs for the South Siders for a salary of $135,000. With two stolen bases, he became only the ninth player in major league history to hit 400 home runs and steal 200 bases.

Following the 2001 season, Canseco's 462 career home runs were 22nd all time, while his 1,942 strikeouts were second. On eight occasions he bashed 30 or more homers, and six times he notched 100 or more RBIs. The six-time All-Star also slugged at a .500 or better clip in nine different seasons. Canseco had said that with the opportunity to play every day, he could reach the 500 mark in homers and dramatically increase his Hall of Fame chances. But voters may take into account his brushes with the law, including a November 2001 arrest following a nightclub fight in which he and "Bash Brother" Ozzie sent a couple of patrons to the hospital with facial injuries. Jose, who retired prior to the 2002 season, has promised to write a tell-all book about his career.

Jose Canseco was a very visible and outspoken star who brought notoriety to himself through a variety of deeds, both positive and questionable. Some loved him, others disliked him, but all agree that had he stayed healthy, his already lofty statistics would have been even more gargantuan than the ones he tallied over 16 very interesting and rocky years.

Top 5 MVP Vote-Getters

1. Jose Canseco, Oakland — 392
2. Mike Greenwell, Boston — 242
3. Kirby Puckett, Minnesota — 219
4. Dave Winfield, New York — 164
5. Dennis Eckersley, Oakland — 156

1989 National League — Kevin Mitchell

Kevin Darnell Mitchell
B. January 13, 1962, San Diego, California

Year	Team	Games	AB	Hits	Avg.	HR	RBI	Runs	SB
1989	SF NL	154	543	158	.291	47	125	100	3

The Season

Two fourth-place ballclubs in 1988 leap-frogged their way to division titles this season, with San Francisco claiming its second Western Division crown in three years by three games over San Diego, and Chicago earning its second East Division championship in six years by six games over New York.

The National League Championship Series smiled favorably on left-handed first basemen. Will Clark of the Giants and Mark Grace of the Cubs combined to hit .649, belt three home runs, drive in 16 runs, stroke six doubles and score 11 runs. Four Giants hit two homers each as San Francisco won several close games and the series, 4–1.

Several past NL MVPs experienced a variety of emotions in 1989. Two-time MVP Johnny Bench was named on 96.4 percent of the Hall of Fame ballots in his first year of eligibility, the third highest mark in history; three-time MVP Mike Schmidt announced his retirement May 29; and Pete Rose was permanently banned from baseball by Commissioner Bart Giamatti August 24 for allegedly gambling on major league games.

Future three-time MVP Barry Bonds stroked a home run July 5 to give he and his father, Bobby, the all-time leadership in father-son home runs with 408, passing both the Berras (Yogi and Dale) and Bells (Gus and Buddy), who had shared the mark with 407 each.

It was also a significant year for pitchers. Defending Cy Young Award winner Orel Hershiser, who became baseball's first $3 million man with a new contract, saw his major league record-consecutive scoreless innings streak of 59 snapped in his first inning of the season. San Diego's Mark Davis won the Cy Young Award with 44 saves and a 1.85 earned run average.

Changes at the top also highlighted this season. Six-time All-Star and long-time New York Yankees broadcaster Bill White broke new ground when he became the highest ranking black official in American professional sports. White was elected the National League president February 2. In mid–September, Fay Vincent became baseball's eighth commissioner following the death of Giamatti.

After nine years, baseball dropped the game-winning RBI as an official statistic. Keith Hernandez of New York, the 1979 co-NL MVP, was the all-time leader with 129.

Malcontented Man-Child

In the movie *Big*, Tom Hanks is a boy in a man's body, using his first paycheck to fill a big apartment with countless toys to amuse himself and entertain his best friend. Give Hanks a troubled past and a major league baseball uniform, and you've got Kevin Mitchell.

Mitchell was a 5-foot-11, 210-pound hitting machine on the outside during a tumultuous 13-year major league career, but on the inside, he was merely a little boy who never really grew up. Almost totally devoid of stabilizing influences as a child, then dropping out of school in 10th grade, Kevin Darnell Mitchell escaped the rough streets of San Diego for one reason: he had the uncanny ability to effectively swing the hickory and crush a baseball.

Were it not for that skill, and the watchful eye of a grandmother, Mitchell probably would have wound up in jail or dead ... just like the friends he continued to associate with well into his professional baseball career. Conflicts with authority figures, a propensity for injury and a nearly total disregard for team unity caused Mitchell numerous problems throughout a career that saw

Kevin Mitchell. (Courtesy San Francisco Giants.)

him play in fewer than 100 games in half of what could otherwise have been full seasons.

San Francisco Giants manager Roger Craig once said that Kevin was like a little kid about a lot of things, and that he didn't think about how his actions would affect his team. Cincinnati Reds and New York Mets skipper Davey Johnson, who once had a physical confrontation with Mitchell, said that the ballplayer was still a boy at heart. Over and over again, Mitchell blew off scheduled appearances, team flights and practices, causing no end of consternation to his employers and teammates.

But Mitchell had another side as well. On game day, he was usually one of the first players at the ballpark, and he put in considerable time working on his hitting. Although his fielding was less than average at third base and in the outfield, he never loafed after a ball. As a general rule, he was friendly and accessible to media. He once bought a tombstone for a woman friend whose son had been killed, then purchased a car for her. He also served as the devoted big brother he never had to

rookie teammates, inviting them to his home and buying them meals.

Regardless of one's opinion of Kevin Mitchell the man, few could question the hitting skills of Kevin Mitchell the ballplayer, especially during the 1989 season. Mitchell, who had come to the Giants in a trade with San Diego during the 1987 campaign, had proven to be a better-than-average player, but had never put it altogether since entering the majors at the tail end of the '84 season with the Mets.

But in 1989, Mitchell slugged his way to the National League's Most Valuable Player award, helping lead the Giants to their first pennant in 27 years. Mitchell paced the majors in five power departments—home runs (47), RBIs (125), slugging (.635), total bases (345) and extra-base hits (87)—becoming only the eighth player in history to accomplish the feat. His slugging average was the highest in the NL during a full season since 1973. He batted .291 with 34 doubles, six triples and a .392 on-base percentage, while tying for fourth in the league in runs with 100. Few of his stats were padded during lopsided affairs. He batted .362

with nine homers in 69 at-bats when San Francisco trailed by a run, and hit .366 with the score tied and runners in scoring position. Twenty-three of his round-trippers either tied a game or gave the Giants a lead.

Consistency was also a trademark for the right-handed batsman in 1989. He never hit fewer than six nor more than 10 home runs in any month, and never drove in fewer than 15 nor more than 25 runs in a month. He was walked intentionally 32 times, a major league record for a right-handed batter, and he made the All-Star Team for the first time. Despite a chronically sore knee, he missed only eight games and grounded into only six double plays to tie for the lowest rate on the team. His April 26 bare-handed catch of a drive to the left field corner at St. Louis has been seen on countless highlights shows.

Mitchell's MVP award would have come regardless of his post-season play, but the left fielder contributed mightily there as well. Mitchell batted .353 with two homers, seven RBIs, five runs and three walks in San Francisco's 4–1 LCS victory over Chicago, then hit .294 with a circuit clout and a pair of ribbies in the Giants' 4–0 loss to Oakland in the World Series.

Any negative influence Mitchell may have had on the Giants clubhouse during the regular season was kept quiet, but once the team came close to entering the bright glare of the post-season, it became obvious that Kevin did not play by the same rules as everyone else. While his teammates huddled in the locker room to listen to a ballgame between San Diego and Cincinnati in late September, then poured champagne on each other's heads in celebration of their subsequent Western Division title, Mitchell was long gone from the ballpark.

He also blew off a celebration party at Craig's ranch the following day, skipped a chartered team flight to Chicago for the playoffs and missed a mandatory workout several days prior to the World Series. During the off-season, Mitchell failed to show up for a Candlestick Park news conference announcing him as the league's MVP, then missed a flight to Nashville for a ceremony honoring him as *The Sporting News*' Major League Player of the Year. Craig often wanted to discipline his problem child, but had his hands tied by Giants General Manager and former American League MVP Al Rosen, who declared that he had acquired Mitchell for his skills on the diamond, not for his ability to win friends and influence people.

Mitchell came back with another superb season in 1990, contributing a team-high 35 home runs and a .544 slugging percentage, both good for third in the senior circuit. A second consecutive All-Star selection was added to his resumé, as was a May 8 homer that soared completely out of Shea Stadium in New York.

In 1991, he started off with a bang, blasting six home runs in his first five games, and eventually finished ninth in the league with 27. But he was unable to avoid controversy; a friend who picked up a ticket left by Mitchell at Candlestick Park was arrested on the spot in connection with a police officer's murder. The Giants wound up 19 games out of first place, and Mitchell was traded during the off-season to Seattle for reliever Norm Charlton, where he hit .286 with only nine homers and 67 RBIs in 99 games in '92.

Cincinnati was Mitchell's home in 1993 and '94, and as was his custom, he hit well when healthy, but spent considerable time on the disabled list. Kevin batted .341 with 19 round-trippers in 1993, but did not have enough plate appearances to qualify for the batting title. In '94, he stroked the ball at a .326 pace (fifth in the league) with an impressive 30 homers (sixth), 77 RBIs, a .681 slugging average (second) and a .438 on-base percentage (third) in 95 games. Trouble was brewing again, however. One evening after begging out of a game in 1994, he was hit above the eye by a thrown glass in a bar.

Mitchell avoided the continuation of the player strike in 1995 by joining the Fukuoka Daiei Hawks of Japan's Pacific League, where he cracked a grand slam on the first pitch of his season. Following a dispute regarding the severity of a knee injury, he walked out on the team for two months, proving that he was perfectly capable of clashing with authority figures on more than one continent.

The 1996 season saw Mitchell playing for both Boston and Cincinnati. Typifying his career, he sat out 10 consecutive Red Sox games with a hamstring injury, returned to belt a two-run homer among three hits in his first game back, but re-injured the hamstring in the same contest and spent six weeks on the DL. Shortly after being acquired by the Reds July 30 for a second stint, he went on a tear, batting .486 with 25 RBIs before missing a game with a sore hip. After twisting an ankle the next day, Mitchell missed a full week with a fever and sore throat, then failed to report for a mid–September game in Pittsburgh and was suspended for the season.

Cleveland decided to give the troubled 35-year-old a chance in 1997, signing him to an incentive-laden contract that included a weight clause, but true to form, he came into camp 30 pounds overweight. After sounding off about preferring to play paintball in the desert — an activity he enjoyed with former gang member friends during the off-season — over sitting on the bench, he got into a clubhouse altercation with outfielder Chad Curtis and was released from the team. Mitchell's final major league hurrah came with Oakland in 1998 when he played in 51 games and batted .228.

How many of Mitchell's problems can be traced to his difficult childhood? It's impossible to say, of course. His parents split up when he was 2 years old, and his mother was often ill and moved frequently. His grandmother, Josie Whitfield, spent the most time with him. His father, who eventually pawned Mitchell's 1986 Mets World Series ring for drug money, was a cocaine dealer and an addict, and Kevin's brother, Donald, died in a gang war.

Surely a lack of niceties as a child influenced his adult decision to stock up on whatever "toys" appealed to him. At one point, he owned more than 20 vehicles, including 11 all-terrain vehicles, a Humvee and a couple of dune buggies. He also wore crocodile-skin combat boots worth close to $2,000, loved to don his night-vision goggles, and installed a voice-activated stereo system in one of his trucks that set him back nearly $20,000.

Those kinds of accoutrements must have seemed nothing more than a pipedream for the teenager when he was signed to a minor league contract by the Mets in 1980. Mitchell placed fourth in batting (.335) in the Appalachian League in 1981, the same year he got into a fight with teammate Darryl Strawberry during a basketball game. Two years later, Kevin was an All-Star with Jackson in the Texas League, then helped Tidewater win the Triple A World Series. In '84, he was talked out of returning to San Diego to avenge the death of a stepbrother, and responded positively to the mentoring of coach Bill Robinson.

He played a few games with the Mets late in the '84 season, then batted .290 for Tidewater in '85 before coming up to the show for good in 1986. He played six different positions and placed third in Rookie of the Year balloting in '86, helping the Mets win the World Series with a single in the amazing Game 6 rally against Boston. Mitchell was traded to San Diego for Kevin McReynolds following the season, and after some struggles at the plate, was sent to San Francisco, where he hit two home runs in his first game. Mitchell batted .251 with 19 homers and 80 RBIs for the Giants in 1988, but was accused of beating a former girlfriend and threatening her with one of his three guns.

Mitchell, who has a teenage daughter and a cousin, Keith, who played in the majors for parts of four seasons, has had a few years to mellow since his retirement from a roller-coaster career, but as recently as 2000, he was expelled from the independent Western Baseball League for punching the owner of an opposing team during an on-field, benches-clearing incident.

Kevin Mitchell was robbed of his childhood by a dysfunctional family and a dangerous neighborhood. But he robbed himself of the chance to take full advantage of a talent that most athletes can only dream of by his refusal to submit to authority and be a team player. Considering he never played in 70 consecutive games over 13 years due to injuries and suspensions, it's amazing what he accomplished between the white lines, including 234 career homers, 760 RBIs and a .284 batting average. What may be more remarkable with Kevin Mitchell, however, is

what he could have accomplished had he ever really grown up.

Top 5 MVP Vote-Getters

1. Kevin Mitchell, San Francisco — 314

2. Will Clark, San Francisco — 225
3. Pedro Guerrero, St. Louis — 190
4. Ryne Sandberg, Chicago — 157
5. Howard Johnson, New York — 153

1989 AMERICAN LEAGUE — ROBIN YOUNT

Robin R Yount
B. September 16, 1955, Danville, Illinois

Year	Team	Games	AB	Hits	Avg.	HR	RBI	Runs	SB
1989	Mil AL	160	614	195	.318	21	103	101	19

The Season

The Oakland Athletics won their first World Championship in 15 years with a sweep of the San Francisco Giants, but the World Series will be best remembered for the devastating earthquake which struck a half-hour before Game 3 and delayed the Series by 10 days. Only minor damage occurred at Candlestick Park, where power was lost, but 67 people throughout the Bay Area were killed by the quake October 17.

The A's, who had lost the 1988 World Series to Los Angeles, returned with the league's best pitching and a 4–1 rout of Toronto in the League Championship Series. Outfielder Rickey Henderson earned ALCS MVP honors by batting .400 with two homers and five RBIs, while pitcher Dave Stewart won two games with a 1.69 ERA to nab the World Series MVP award. Oakland never trailed in any of the four Series games versus San Francisco.

"Hard luck pitcher of the year" honors went to Toronto right-hander Dave Stieb, who lost a perfect game with two outs in the ninth inning August 4 when New York's Roberto Kelly doubled. It marked the third time that Stieb had pitched no-hit ball for 8⅔ innings, only to fall short of immortality. On April 10, Stieb's one-hitter against the Yankees gave him three one-hitters

in his past four starts, dating back to September 1988.

The batting title race came down to the final day of the season, with Minnesota's Kirby Puckett going 2-for-5 to outlast Carney Lansford of Oakland .339 to .336. It was Puckett's fourth consecutive season hitting .328 or higher, but his first and only batting crown.

At age 25, Kansas City's Bret Saberhagen became only the fourth pitcher to win a second Cy Young Award (he also garnered the prize in '85). The right-hander led the AL in wins (23), earned run average (2.16), complete games (12), winning percentage and innings pitched.

Giving Robin Yount a serious run for his money in the MVP race was Texas outfielder Ruben Sierra, who paced the junior circuit in RBIs (119), total bases (344), slugging (.543) and triples (14), and tied for third in runs scored (101).

Former MVP Carl Yastrzemski of Boston was elected to the Hall of Fame in 1989.

Big Fish in a Small Pond

Playing in a state where they love their fishing, Robin Yount was a big fish in a small pond in the mid–1980s. Of course, with an MVP under his belt

and a long string of excellent seasons behind him, Yount would have been a big fish in just about any pond. A rare combination of speed, power, fielding prowess and grit, Robin not only wore the Milwaukee Brewers' blue and gold proudly, he was golden in a blue-collar city.

Yount's popularity was well earned, but a shoulder injury was making the demanding position of shortstop increasingly difficult for the man who had literally grown into the position, having been named the starter there at age 18 in 1974.

In 1985, Yount moved to the greener pastures of center field, and it didn't take him long to adjust. The following season, the sure-handed gloveman led the league in fielding with a .997 mark, making him the first player to pace the American League in fielding in both the infield and outfield. He also collected his 2,000th career hit in 1986, and at age 31 figured to have a number of good years remaining in what was shaping up as a splendid career. As it turned out, Yount had much more to offer than most suspected.

In a topsy-turvy 1987 campaign, in which the Brewers stunned the baseball world by starting out with 13 consecutive victories and 17 wins in their first 18 games, only to drop 12 contests in a row in May, Yount was a model of consistency. The slightly built but rugged competitor stroked 198 hits to finish fifth in the National League in that category, among them nine triples (fourth in the circuit) and his 400th career double.

In 1988, Milwaukee finished in third place in the AL East for the second year in a row, but Yount tied for the top spot in triples with 11, collected 190 hits and became only the third player in Brewers history to hit for the cycle, in a 16–2 win over Chicago June 12.

It seemed difficult to believe, but the Danville, Illinois, native was still improving as he entered the 1989 season at age 33. Yount put on a display of his versatility this campaign, hitting for average and power, running the bases with abandon and playing an exciting center field. His 314 total bases were good for second in the league, his .511 slugging average and 101 runs third, his .318 batting average and 195 hits fourth, and his 38 doubles fifth. His ability to spray the ball evidenced itself in 10 of his 21 homers going to the opposite field.

The Brewers dropped to fourth place in '89, eight games out, but Yount outpolled Texas slugger Ruben Sierra in the MVP voting 256–228 in a season where no individuals on pennant contenders stood head and shoulders above the competition. It was the second MVP honor for the deserving Yount, making him one of only three players to be named MVP at two different positions.

Frustrated with the fact that he still did not own a World Series ring, Yount declared his free agency following the 1989 campaign, negotiating with several teams. But he responded to a letter-writing initiative from Brewers fans by signing a three-year contract for $9.6 million with Milwaukee.

Rockin' Robin was not finished turning opposing pitchers' deliveries into base hits and tearing around the basepaths like a kid on the sandlots. Although his batting average would never again approach the .300 mark, he was still showing up every day and driving in his share of teammates. Yount was fourth in the AL in runs (98) in 1990 and tied for third in doubles (40) in '92. He collected exactly 77 RBIs each year from 1990 through '92, and scored 60-plus runs in each of his final three seasons (1991–93).

One of the biggest thrills in Yount's career came September 9, 1992, when he lined a single off Jose Mesa of Cleveland at Milwaukee County Stadium for his 3,000th career hit. At that time, Yount was only the 17th major leaguer to accomplish this feat, and the third youngest behind a couple of guys named Cobb and Aaron. On April 20, 1993, Robin's 200th career hit against Minnesota gave him the distinction of being the only player to have at least 200 hits versus every team he played against.

Unfortunately for Yount and his fans, the Brewers were unable to make another post-season appearance following their 1982 World Series loss to St. Louis, although they finished just four games out of first place in the East Division in 1992.

Yount retired following the 1993 campaign as the Brewers' all-time leader in an amazing eight offensive categories: games played (2,858), at-bats (11,008), hits (3,142), runs (1,632), home runs (251), RBIs (1,406), doubles (613) and triples (126). He was also second all time in stolen bases (271) and fifth in batting average (.285). Compared to all major leaguers in baseball history, he was seventh in at-bats, and among the top 20 in games, doubles and hits.

The Brewers honored their long-time sparkplug on May 29, 1994, by retiring his uniform No. 19. In his first year of eligibility (1999), Yount became the first player to be inducted into the Hall of Fame wearing a Brewers cap. Of course, what other cap could he have worn? At a time when it's unusual to see any player spend more than 10 years with one club, Yount served Milwaukee faithfully for 20 seasons on the field, as well as nearly 10 others under a personal services contract.

But he finally did don another uniform in 2002 as the defending World Champion Arizona Diamondbacks first base coach, and a tutor for the team's outfielders.

Robin Yount will always be remembered not only for how well he played the game, but also for *how* he played the game. Never afraid to get his uniform dirty, Yount leaped, dived, thrashed and plunged his way to success like a bruising running back, despite possessing a place kicker's 6-foot, 170-pound frame. A blue-collar ballplayer in a working class town, Yount continues to be revered by the Brewers faithful. Spanking new Miller Park opened in Milwaukee in 2001, but the memories that Robin Yount and his teammates provided at old County Stadium for so many years will live on indefinitely in the fans' minds.

Top 5 MVP Vote-Getters

1. Robin Yount, Milwaukee — 256
2. Ruben Sierra, Texas — 228
3. Cal Ripken, Jr., Baltimore — 216
4. George Bell, Toronto — 205
5. Dennis Eckersley, Oakland — 116

1990 NATIONAL LEAGUE — BARRY BONDS

Barry Lamar Bonds
B. July 24, 1964, Riverside, California

Year	Team	Games	AB	Hits	Avg.	HR	RBI	Runs	SB
1990	Pit NL	151	519	156	.301	33	114	104	52

The Season

Neither Pittsburgh nor Cincinnati had won a division crown since 1979 when they had squared off against each other in the League Championship Series, but both earned titles in '90 to forge a long-awaited rematch. Cincinnati, which was the first National League team to lead wire to wire since the league expanded its schedule to 162 games, wreaked revenge against the Pirates for its '79 setback with a four games-to-two triumph in the LCS. Outfielder Paul O'Neill propelled the Reds toward their first pennant since 1976 by batting .471 with a homer, three doubles and four RBIs in the victory over the Bucs.

Cincinnati then pulled off a stunner by sweeping Oakland in the World Series, ending the A's 10-game postseason winning streak in Game 1 and earning its first World Championship in 14 years. Pitcher Jose Rijo captured World Series MVP honors with a 2–0 record, 0.59 ERA, 14 strikeouts and 20 consecutive batters retired in Game 4. Teammate Billy Hatcher established a Series record with seven consecutive hits while batting .750 for the Series.

It may have been a good year for the Reds, but it was not a particularly enjoyable one for former Cincinnati manager and all-time hits king Pete Rose, who in April pled guilty to two felony counts of filing false income tax returns. Three months later, the 1973 NL MVP was sentenced to five months in prison and fined $50,000.

Chicago was unable to repeat its division title, but three Cubs players were in the limelight this season. Former MVP Ryne Sandberg became the first second baseman to hit at least 30 home runs in two consecutive seasons, and increased his major league record-

errorless streak to 123 games and 584 chances. On April 29, Greg Maddux set a big league mark for pitchers with seven putouts in a game, while Andre Dawson established a major league record when he was walked intentionally five times in a game May 22.

Pittsburgh hurler Doug Drabek (22–6) secured the Cy Young Award with 23 of a possible 24 first-place votes, while NL Rookie of the Year honors went to future star David Justice of Atlanta. Not surprisingly, two-time MVP Joe Morgan was inducted into the Hall of Fame in his first year of eligibility.

Bred for Success

If ever a child were bred to be an athlete, it was Barry Bonds. Both his father, Bobby Bonds, and cousin, Reggie Jackson, were outstanding major league ballplayers, while an aunt, Rosie Bonds, was a member of the 1964 U.S. Olympic women's track team. Breeding doesn't always produce the desired results, but in this case, the end product was even more remarkable than anticipated.

Barry Bonds was clearly the best all-around baseball player during the 1990s, and he has shown no signs of slowing down since the new century began. His ability to hit for both average and power, spray the ball to all fields, reach base safely an inordinate percentage of the time for a slugger, run the bases swiftly and smartly, and man his left field position expertly while displaying a strong and accurate arm led *The Sporting News* to declare him the Major League Player of the Decade for the '90s.

On the other hand, Bonds has not led the majors in cultivating friends

throughout his career, mainly due to a surly disposition and a propensity for self-absorption. A sense of entitlement apparently became ingrained in the young man as he grew up in an upper class neighborhood in San Carlos, California, and spent many hours hanging out at San Francisco's Candlestick Park with his dad and godfather, Willie Mays. Teammates — going as far back as his college days — have sometimes found him to be rude, inconsiderate and self-centered.

Personality conflicts aside, it's difficult to argue with the generosity of the United Way board member. He has renovated a home for autistic children and donated funds to the Adopt-A-Special-Kid Foundation. He also contributed to the United Negro College Fund, and his Barry Bonds Family Foundation supports, among other initiatives, a program to raise the technology skills of low-income children and their families.

Of course, it's also impossible to dispute his prowess on the ball diamond. Although he did not bolt out of the gate when he came up to the Pittsburgh Pirates in 1986 following a three-year college career and a brief stint in the minors, Bonds placed sixth in Rookie of the Year voting for the last-place Pirates that season.

Some believed he deserved a better standing in the balloting after leading all National League first-year men in home runs with 16, RBIs with 48, walks with 65 and stolen bases with 36. But Barry was already beginning to gain a reputation for a less-than-stellar attitude. Pittsburgh gained some ground in 1987, climbing to a tie for fourth place in the NL Eastern Division — 15 games out after being 44 behind the previous year — and Bonds showed a glimpse of things to come in

Barry Bonds. (Courtesy Pittsburgh Pirates.)

the power department by smacking five home runs in a four-game stretch in mid–August.

Bonds, who had clubbed 25 homers with 59 RBIs, 99 runs and 32 stolen bases in '87, had a nearly identical statistical season in 1988, despite injuring his left knee in mid–June and needing arthroscopic surgery in late September. He batted .283 in '88 while clouting 24 circuit blasts with 58 runs batted in, scoring 97 times and swiping 17 sacks. He was particularly adept at leading off the first inning, batting .347 with eight homers in those situations.

The Pirates, who rose to second place in the East in '88, faltered to fifth in 1989. Bonds had a decent year by most standards after reluctantly signing a $360,000 contract following a lengthy and acrimonious negotiation, but it was a step back from the progress he had been making. His batting average dipped to .248 and his homers to 19, although he did boost his stolen base total back up to 32, tied for third in the league in walks with 93 and was second among league outfielders with 14 assists.

Following the salary dispute, the Pirates planned to unload the player they were beginning to suspect would never live up to his potential. They picked up outfielder Billy Hatcher in an August '89 trade, assuming he'd replace Bonds in left field the following season. But other general managers had the same doubts about this discontented ballplayer, and refused to offer as much in trade as Pittsburgh was demanding.

Bonds, who was awarded an $850,000 salary for 1990 by an arbitrator rather than the $1.6 million he sought, was not ignorant regarding what was going on around him, and he decided that the only way he could "stick it" to the Pirates and acquire the type of monetary compensation he felt he deserved was to weave together a few monster seasons. He hooked up with team conditioning coach Warren Sipp prior to the season, and his savage campaign to dominate began in earnest in 1990 when he garnered the first of an unprecedented three NL Most Valuable Player awards over a four-year span.

Bonds absolutely exploded in '90, enjoying one of the most well-rounded seasons in recent history. He led the senior circuit in slugging with a .565 mark, tied for first in outfield assists with 14, placed second in walks with 93, was third in stolen bases with 52 and finished fourth in both RBIs (114) and on-base percentage (.410). He also tied for fourth in home runs with 33, becoming only the second player in baseball history with 30-plus homers and at least 50 steals in the same season.

Managerial strategies did little to slow the left-handed batter with the short stroke and the powerful punch. He batted .304 against southpaws (.301 overall), and more than half of his round-trippers (17) came versus lefties, despite nearly 40 fewer at-bats. Being on the road didn't bother Barry, either. He batted .321 with 19 homers, 68 ribbies and a .607 slugging percentage away from Three Rivers Stadium. And in the clutch, Bonds was even more impressive, with a .344 average with runners on base and a .377 mark with runners in scoring position.

In addition to claiming his first All-Star berth and initial Gold Glove in 1990, Bonds was named the NL's MVP and *The Sporting News*' Major League Player of the Year. The Pirates responded to the charge led by their coming-of-age left fielder, beating out the New York Mets by four games and returning to the playoffs for the first time in 11 years. Unfortunately, a flaw in the Bonds mystique that would plague him for the entire decade first surfaced in the '90 post-season: an inability to produce when it counts most. He was held to a .167 average and one RBI in a four games-to-two loss to Cincinnati in the League Championship Series.

But a series of superb seasons — including two more MVP efforts over the next three years — was right on the horizon.

Top 5 MVP Vote-Getters

1. Barry Bonds, Pittsburgh — 331
2. Bobby Bonilla, Pittsburgh — 212
3. Darryl Strawberry, New York — 167
4. Ryne Sandberg, Chicago — 151
5. Eddie Murray, Los Angeles — 123

1990 AMERICAN LEAGUE — RICKEY HENDERSON

Rickey Henley Henderson
B. December 25, 1958, Chicago, Illinois

Year	Team	Games	AB	Hits	Avg.	HR	RBI	Runs	SB
1990	Oak AL	136	489	159	.325	28	61	119	65

The Season

It's a well-known axiom that good pitching will stop good hitting, and the 1990 American League Championship Series was a prime example.

The Boston Red Sox led the AL in batting with a .272 mark on the way to their third East Division title in the past five years — by two games over Toronto — but they were no match for the pitching-rich Oakland Athletics, who captured the West for the third consecutive year, by nine games over Chicago.

Boston scored first in each of the first three LCS games, but never tallied more than once in any of the four contests. The A's, who paced the junior circuit in earned run average with a 3.18 mark, swept Boston in the LCS for their third pennant in a row. Leading the Oakland playoff charge were Carney Lansford with a .438 average and two RBIs, Harold Baines at .357 with three ribbies, and Dave Stewart with two wins and a 1.13 ERA. Boston's Wade Boggs hit .438 and had the series' lone home run. The A's were then flattened 4–0 by Cincinnati in the World Series.

This was the year of the no-hitter. When Toronto's Dave Stieb twirled a no-no against Cleveland September 2,

it marked the ninth such major league gem of the season. The no-hitter was so prevalent in '90 that two occurred on the same day, as Stewart blanked Toronto and Fernando Valenzuela of Los Angeles stymied St. Louis June 29. Earlier that month, Nolan Ryan tossed his sixth no-hitter, striking out 14 in Texas' shutout of Oakland.

Two other pitchers who achieved prominence this season were former Baltimore hurler Jim Palmer, who was inducted into the Hall of Fame in his first year of eligibility, and Oakland's Bob Welch, who earned the Cy Young Award with 27 wins, the most in baseball in 18 years and the top total in the AL since Denny McLain notched 31 during his 1968 MVP campaign.

On August 31, 40-year-old Ken Griffey, Sr. and 20-year-old Ken Griffey, Jr. made baseball history by playing in the same game as teammates. Both had a base hit in Seattle's 5–2 win over Kansas City. In another oddity, the Minnesota Twins established a major league record by pulling off two triple plays in the same game July 17. Both began with ground balls to third baseman Gary Gaetti.

Individuals who stood out this year included 1980 MVP George Brett, whose .329 average gave him batting crowns in three different decades; 1986

MVP Roger Clemens, whose 1.93 ERA was the best in the American League in 12 years; Chicago's Bobby Thigpen, whose 57 saves demolished the major league record; and Detroit's Cecil Fielder, whose 51 homers were the most in the AL since Roger Maris clubbed 61 in 1961.

Energizing Force

It's official — the Energizer Bunny can take his sorry, bushy tail into retirement. The drum-beating rabbit has been replaced by a guy who not only never stops, he rarely even slows down. Despite more than 25 years of professional baseball pounding on a body he regularly submits to top-speed headfirst slides and breakneck wall-banging leaps, Rickey Henderson keeps on going and going and going.

Henderson's status as the greatest leadoff hitter in the history of baseball is etched in stone. No man at the top of the lineup has ever come close to his abilities to hit for average and power, reach via the base on balls, and turn his singles and walks into virtual doubles and triples through an unparalleled aptitude for stealing bases ... even when pitchers know he's going to be running.

Manager Bobby Valentine once said of Henderson that he's the type of guy who keeps pitchers awake the night before they have to pitch to him. Hurlers know that if they groove a pitch to him, he'll smack it out of the park, as evidenced by his major league-record 79 home runs leading off a game. Moundsmen also realize that with his keen eye, he's likely to coax a walk out of them if they don't throw strikes. Henderson has collected more bases on balls than any player in the history of baseball. And finally, pitchers understand that allowing the disruptive force to walk or poke a single is paramount to giving up a leadoff two- or three-bagger to anybody else. Rickey stole more bases during a 12-year span (1980–91) than any player has ever pilfered during an entire career.

The knock on Rickey is that he's full of himself and more concerned with personal statistics than wins. It's true that he celebrates his accomplishments a little too ostentatiously for some people's tastes — pulling out a base and waving it triumphantly over his head after setting a record, for example — and he occasionally breaks into a home run trot on a drive that fails to clear the fence. Boyhood friend and fellow major leaguer Lloyd Moseby said that Henderson could strut before he could walk. But it's obvious that the more successful he is at his job, the better off his team is. And it's certainly no coincidence that Henderson's teams have reached the postseason in eight of his 23 big league years.

Besides, it's tough to criticize a guy for getting excited about his successes when you consider from where he came. Before the age of 8, Rickey and his seven siblings were abandoned by their father, then moved from Chicago to Arkansas to Oakland. No wonder he's been so kind to kids at the ballpark during his career. It didn't take long for the teenager to discover that sports could provide the positive feedback he desperately required. The All-America football player rushed for more than 1,000 yards during his senior year at Oakland Technical High School, but on the advice of his mother, Bobbie, turned down close to 25 college football scholarships to sign with the Oakland Athletics in 1976.

The A's converted the 5-foot-10, left-handed throwing first baseman into an outfielder during his Rookie League year at Boise, Idaho, where he hit .336. Henderson swiped a league-record 95 bases at Class A Modesto, California, in 1977, then stole 81 sacks to break an Eastern League mark at Class AA Jersey City, New Jersey, in '78. A strong start at Triple A Ogden, Utah, in '79 was followed by his graduation to the parent club in June.

Henderson stole 33 bases during the second half of the 1979 season for the A's, who posted the second worst record in baseball. But new manager Billy Martin turned things around in 1980 with his spirited brand of "Billy Ball." In only his first full year, Rickey broke Ty Cobb's 65-year-old American League steals record with 100, and walked 117 times as Oakland leaped to second place in the West.

Enjoying an MVP-caliber season in '81, Henderson led the junior circuit in runs (89), hits (135) and stolen bases (56), tied for second in triples (seven), placed third in on-base percentage (.411), was fourth in batting (.319) and walks (64), and earned his only Gold Glove. After the A's took the 1981 first-half AL West title in a strike-shortened season, he batted .364 with a pair of doubles and two steals in a 3–0 ALCS loss to New York. But Henderson was edged 319–308 in MVP voting by Milwaukee reliever Rollie Fingers, prompting the outspoken outfielder to say, "No way is a relief pitcher more valuable than an everyday player."

It would be nine years before Henderson owned that elusive MVP trophy, but he provided plenty of dramatics along the way. Crouching low in the right-hander's batter's box with his left leg extended out toward the pitcher, Rickey offered a small target, but swatted the ball like a big man when he viciously uncoiled. From 1982, when he stole 51 bases in the first 51 games on the way to an incredible 130 thefts to shatter Lou Brock's record of 118, to 1989 when he collected a career-high 126 walks, was unanimously named the ALCS MVP and batted .474 in the A's four-game World Series

sweep of San Francisco, Henderson was nothing less than miraculous as the consummate leadoff man.

He walked a league-high 116 times in 1982, tied the AL record for most stolen bases in two consecutive games with seven and became the youngest player to reach the 400-steal plateau in '83. He led the circuit in steals for the fifth consecutive year in '84, despite being restrained on the basepaths by manager Steve Boros.

Rickey was dealt to the Yankees during the off-season, and in 1985 the speedster became the first AL player to hit 20-plus home runs (matching his uniform number with 24) and steal 50-plus bases (league-high 80). Scoring 146 runs, the highest total in the majors since 1949, he finished third in the MVP balloting.

In 1986, Henderson earned his seventh consecutive steals title with 87, stroked 28 homers — including an AL-record nine leading off a game — and drove in a career-high 74 runs. His league-best 130 runs scored made him the first American Leaguer to lead the circuit in runs in consecutive seasons since Mickey Mantle did it in 1960–61.

Henderson's last two full seasons with the Yanks, 1987 and '88, were sometimes controversial, as manager Lou Piniella and owner George Steinbrenner raised doubts regarding the severity of Rickey's injuries, which limited him to 95 games the former year. New York sent him back to Oakland in June 1989, where he helped the A's defeat Toronto 4–1 in the ALCS with a .400 average, eight runs, two homers and eight steals. Henderson's World Series-high nine hits, including a homer, and his three steals aided the A's in their sweep of the Giants.

After signing a four-year, $12 million contract in late '89, Henderson was at the top of his game at age 31 in 1990 when he earned the league's Most Valuable Player award in a close vote over Detroit slugger Cecil Fielder. Leading the A's to their third consecutive AL West title, Henderson was the league's best in runs (119), steals (65) and on-base percentage (.441); runner-up in batting (.325) and slugging (.577); and fourth in walks (97). He topped off a phenomenal campaign with clutch performances in the post-season, batting .294 with three RBIs and two steals in Oakland's ALCS sweep of Boston, and .333 with a homer and three thefts in a 4–0 World Series loss to Cincinnati.

Henderson broke Brock's all-time steals record with his 939th May 1, 1991. He co-authored *Off Base: Confessions of a Thief* following the season, then collected his 1,000th career steal in '92 while helping the A's win the West. He returned to the post-season in 1993, this time in a Blue Jays uniform, after becoming the first player in 80 years to open both games of a double-header with a home run (July 5 versus Cleveland.)

His third tour of duty with Oakland (1994-95) was followed by his National League debut in 1996 with San Diego, where he hit .333 with a homer in the 3–0 NLDS loss to St. Louis. He was traded to Anaheim in August 1997 the day after hitting his 250th career round-tripper. Returning in 1998 to Oakland yet again, Rickey became the oldest player to lead his league in steals (66 at age 39), and paced the junior circuit in both walks and stolen bases for the fourth time in the same season. Only three other players have done it once in major league history.

After signing with the New York Mets, Henderson hit .340 over the final 88 regular-season games and led NL leadoff men in on-base percentage in 1999. He also helped the Mets defeat Arizona 3–1 in the NLDS with a .400 average, five runs and a record-six steals, before tying an LCS single-game record with two outfield assists in Game 3 of the Mets' 4–2 loss to Atlanta.

Henderson's days as a Met became numbered following an alleged ill-timed clubhouse card playing incident, and in May 2000, he was traded to Seattle. Once again, he wound up in the post-season, batting .400 in the Mariners' 3–0 ALCS victory over Chicago after enjoying his 21st season of 30-plus steals.

One of only two major leaguers to steal bases in four decades, Henderson added to his major league-leading total of home runs leading off a game in 2001 with San Diego, belting No. 79. After starting the year in Triple A ball, the 42-year-old became the all-time leader in walks with his 2,063rd early in the season, passing Babe Ruth, and in runs with his 2,246th late in the campaign. Henderson's record-breaking run came on a homer, and he fulfilled a promise to teammates by sliding into home plate in celebration. On the final day of the season, he became the 25th member of the 3,000-hit club with a bloop double. Rickey's Padres did not come close to the post-season, but the veteran was selected to throw out the ceremonial first pitch of Game 2 of the World Series. Despite having reached three incredible milestones in 2001, he said he wanted to come back and play again in 2002.

Over his simply amazing career, the 10-time All-Star placed among the top five in his league in stolen bases 15 times (including 12 top spots), walks on a dozen occasions, runs 11 times, on-base percentage 10 times, batting average on three occasions, and hits, triples and slugging once each. In 14 post-season series, he batted .284, scored 47 runs, walked 37 times, stole 33 bases, hit five homers and drove in 20 runs.

Some day, the greatest leadoff hitter ever will be handed a Hall of Fame plaque on a platform in Cooperstown. It would only be fitting if he leads off the procession.

Top 5 MVP Vote-Getters

1. Rickey Henderson, Oakland — 317
2. Cecil Fielder, Detroit — 286
3. Roger Clemens, Boston — 212
4. Kelly Gruber, Toronto — 175
5. Bobby Thigpen, Chicago — 170

1991 NATIONAL LEAGUE — TERRY PENDLETON

Terry Lee Pendleton
B. July 16, 1960, Los Angeles, California

Year	Team	Games	AB	Hits	Avg.	HR	RBI	Runs	SB
1991	Atl NL	153	586	187	.319	22	86	94	10

The Season

The Atlanta Braves began a decade of prominence in 1991 by earning their first division title in nine years, outlasting Los Angeles in the West by one game. Over in the East, Pittsburgh made it two consecutive division crowns with a comfortable 14-game cushion over St. Louis, thanks to National League-high marks in runs, hits and batting average.

The Pirates headed home from Atlanta with a 3–2 NLCS lead, but failed to score in the final two games. In fact, Pittsburgh was shut out three times in the series — all at home — and managed only seven runs over the final six games. The Braves' 4–3 series victory gave them their first National League pennant since moving to Atlanta in 1966.

Terry Pendleton. (Courtesy Atlanta Braves.)

Hockey and baseball were briefly connected when superstar Wayne Gretzky and Los Angeles Kings owner Bruce McNall combined to purchase a 1909-10 mint-condition tobacco trading card featuring Honus Wagner during a Sotheby's auction in New York.

Brave New World

When one looks back at the career of Terry Pendleton, it's easy to assume that the St. Louis Cardinals gave up on him too quickly. But that assessment is not entirely fair. Pendleton wore the Cardinal red for seven years, and while he showed flashes of brilliance, such as a .324 batting average during his rookie season of 1984 and 96 RBIs in 1987, he was mostly mediocre at the plate and was often hobbled or sidelined by pesky hamstring injuries.

But the Atlanta Braves saw something they liked in this clutch-hitting, sure-handed third baseman, signing the free agent to a four-year contract in December 1990. At 5-foot-9 and 180 pounds, Terry hardly looked the type to turn a sixth-place ballclub into a contender, but that's exactly what he helped do during a stunning 1991 season.

A significant factor in the Braves' worst-to-first season, Pendleton hit only .234 in April, but exploded in May with a .410 average and .651 slugging mark. He batted .360 with five home runs and 21 RBIs in July, and .336 with six round-trippers and 19 RBIs over the final month. Thanks in large part to his leadership and the winning attitude he'd developed in St. Louis, Atlanta won 29 more games in '91 than it had the previous season, edging Los Angeles by a single game in the West.

Establishing Braves franchise records for third basemen with a .319 average (Bob Elliott hit .317 in his 1947 MVP campaign) and 187 hits (Tony Boeckel had 185 in 1921), Pendleton led the National League in both categories. He also tied for the top spot in both total bases (303) and multi-hit games (52), was third in slugging (.517), tied for fifth in extra base hits (64), tied for sixth in triples (eight), tied for seventh

Steve Avery (0.00 ERA) and John Smoltz (1.76) both won a pair of LCS games for the Braves, while Brian Hunter and Greg Olson each hit .333 with a homer and four RBIs. Jay Bell batted .414 with a series-best 12 hits for the Pirates. Despite the offensive heroics of Atlanta's Terry Pendleton and Mark Lemke, Minnesota edged the Braves 4–3 in the World Series. Lemke's three triples were the most in a World Series since 1947, and the highest total by an NL player in 88 years.

A couple of pitchers who excelled this season were St. Louis' Lee Smith, who set a league record for saves with 47, and Montreal's Dennis Martinez, who threw the 13th perfect game in major league history. Catching the 2–0 gem against Los Angeles July 28 was Ron Hassey, who was also behind the plate when Len Barker of Cleveland

tossed a perfect game versus Toronto 10 years earlier.

Chicago outfielder Doug Dascenzo's NL-record errorless streak to begin a career finally ended after 242 games August 25 in a loss to San Diego. Also coming to an end nearly three weeks later was any home field advantage Montreal might have been enjoying. A 55-ton block collapsed in Olympic Stadium September 13, forcing the Expos to play the remainder of this season's games on the road.

The Pirates engineered the greatest extra-inning comeback in major league history April 21 by scoring six runs in the bottom of the 11th inning to wipe out a five-run Chicago lead built on a grand slam by 1987 MVP Andre Dawson. The Cubs had also blown a five-run lead prior to extra innings.

in doubles (34) and placed ninth in runs scored (94). Pendleton also added a career-high 22 home runs, 86 RBIs, a .367 on-base percentage, 43 walks and 10 stolen bases.

Although his .319 average was the second lowest mark ever to lead the NL — San Diego's Tony Gwynn won a batting title at .313 in 1988 — Pendleton became the first player in big league history to improve his average by at least 80 points and his home run total by at least 15 from the previous year (minimum 400 at-bats).

Terry had already built a reputation as a clutch hitter, and he didn't disappoint in '91, batting .361 in late-inning situations with runners on base and .400 in the late going with runners in scoring position. The switch-hitter did most of his damage from the left-hander's batter's box this season, batting .328 against righties with 18 homers. The first Braves player to earn a batting crown or pace the circuit in hits since Ralph Garr in 1974 was also very effective in front of the home fans, hitting .340 with a .561 slugging average in Atlanta. A team player in every respect, Pendleton's seven sacrifice bunts were the most by an MVP (not counting pitchers) since 1964. In the field, his 2.45 assists per nine innings at third base was the highest rate in the majors.

Playing in the post-season for the third year, the stocky third sacker struggled offensively during the Braves' 4–3 NLCS victory over Pittsburgh, but came alive in the World Series loss to Minnesota with a .367 average, six runs, three doubles, two homers, three RBIs and three walks. Following the season, in which he collected his 1,000th career hit and 500th career RBI, Terry not only won a close battle with Pittsburgh's Barry Bonds for the MVP trophy, but also was named Comeback Player of the Year.

It could be argued that Pendleton's 1992 season was superior to 1991, although this time Bonds surpassed him in the MVP voting. The Atlanta spray hitter forged career bests in hits (199, tied for first in the NL), RBIs (105, second) and runs (98, tied for sixth); was fourth in total bases with 303; tied for fifth in doubles with 39; tied for sixth

in batting (.311); and tied for ninth in homers (21). Despite a variety of physical ailments, the third baseman picked up the third and final Gold Glove of his career. The first Brave voted to the All-Star Team since Dale Murphy in 1986 was also the first Braves third baseman to hit .300 in consecutive seasons, and only the third Atlanta player to do it.

Pendleton's second splendid season in a row helped his team repeat in the NL West, this time by eight games over Cincinnati. His 1992 post-season performances were somewhat below par — .233 in the 4–3 NLCS triumph over Pittsburgh and .240 in the World Series loss to Toronto — but he led off the dramatic three-run rally in the bottom of the ninth inning in Game 7 against the Pirates with a double, moving to third on an error and scoring on a Ron Gant sacrifice fly. In Game 3 of the fall classic, however, Terry was called out for passing Deion Sanders on the basepaths during a potential rally in a pivotal contest that the Blue Jays won 3–2.

Pendleton enjoyed a solid if not spectacular season in 1993, aiding the Braves' third consecutive successful West Division title drive with nine homers over a 25-game span and 17 for the season to go along with a .272 average, 84 RBIs and 81 runs. He then hit safely in all six games of the NLCS, batting .346 with four runs, a homer, double and five RBIs, but Atlanta fell 4–2 to Philadelphia. The hot corner-man's 1994 season featured his 1,500th career hit, but also saw an end to his 187 consecutive games played streak at third base due to a lower back strain that placed him on the disabled list, and an overall drop-off at the plate.

Immediately prior to the 1995 season, Pendleton was signed as a free agent by Florida, where his career was revived by a .290 average, 14 homers, 78 RBIs and 70 runs scored. He homered in his first at-bat as a Marlin, placed second on the team with 47 extra base hits, tied his career high with five hits in a game and set a club record with 32 doubles. The first suspension of the normally mild-mannered gentleman's career occurred after he bumped umpire Bill Hohn during a May 16 argument.

Terry split his time between Florida and Atlanta in 1996, driving in 75 runs for the year and appearing in his fifth World Series (all losses), a 4–2 setback to the Yankees. Pendleton played in 50 games in 1997 for Cincinnati and in 79 games in '98 for Kansas City before retiring.

Pendleton was born in Los Angeles in 1960 and graduated from Channel Island (California) High School in '78. He attended Oxnard Junior College for two years, then played baseball at Fresno State, hitting .397 with 12 homers as senior. The Cardinals selected him in the seventh round of the June 1982 draft.

Once in the show, he made a good first impression, going 3-for-5 in his debut and batting .324 over 67 games in 1984. St. Louis jumped from third place to first in the Eastern Division in 1985, despite the first of two consecutive disappointing seasons for the third baseman. Pendleton, who had two grand slams during the '85 regular season, hit only .208 in the NLCS victory over Los Angeles, but stroked a game-winning, three-run double in the ninth inning of Game 2 of the World Series loss to Kansas City, and added a triple in Game 4. The Cardinals fell off dramatically in 1986, but Terry led league third sackers in putouts, assists, total chances and double plays.

His fielding prowess was recognized with his first Gold Glove in 1987, as he again paced NL players at his position in assists and total chances. Pendleton also improved at the plate, conducting a 19-game hitting streak and posting a .286 average with 12 home runs, 82 runs and 19 stolen bases. His 96 RBIs were the most by a Cardinal third baseman since Joe Torre drove in 137 in his 1971 MVP season. St. Louis stormed back to win the East and the NLCS, and although injuries limited his effectiveness in the NLCS, Pendleton batted .429 with two runs, three hits, an RBI and two steals in pinch-hitting and designated hitter roles in the 4–3 World Series defeat at the hands of Minnesota.

A pulled right hamstring and torn cartilage in his left knee kept Pendleton at only 110 games in 1988, and St. Louis slipped to fifth place. Terry led

NL third basemen with a career-high .971 fielding average in 1989, winning his second Gold Glove and being selected by *Baseball America* as the league's top player at his position. In his final year with the Cardinals, he had a five-hit game versus New York in June, but batted only .230 for the year, showing very few signs of the excellence about to be unleashed.

For his 15-year career, Pendleton hit .270 with 1,897 hits, 140 homers, 946 RBIs, 851 runs and 127 stolen bases. In 66 post-season games, he batted .252 with 26 runs, 12 doubles, three triples, three circuit clouts, 23 RBIs, 12 walks and a pair of steals. Following the 2001 season, it was announced that Terry, 41, would become the Braves hitting coach for 2002. Although it was his first coaching position since his retirement, there's no reason to believe that Pendleton won't be able to instill his batting expertise into Atlanta's hitters

Terry Pendleton may never be enshrined in the Hall of Fame, but he took full advantage of his days in the sun in the early to mid–1990s, and was a significant cog in the return to power of the proud Braves organization.

Top 5 MVP Vote-Getters

1. Terry Pendleton, Atlanta — 274
2. Barry Bonds, Pittsburgh — 259
3. Bobby Bonilla, Pittsburgh — 191
4. Will Clark, San Francisco — 118
5. Howard Johnson, New York — 112

1991 AMERICAN LEAGUE — CAL RIPKEN, JR.

Calvin Edwin Ripken, Jr.
B. August 24, 1960, Havre de Grace, Maryland

Year	Team	Games	AB	Hits	Avg.	HR	RBI	Runs	SB
1991	Bal AL	162	650	210	.323	34	114	99	6

The Season

The 1991 regular season and American League Championship Series may have been lacking in drama, but the World Series more than made up for it. The Toronto Blue Jays and Minnesota Twins won the Eastern and Western Division titles, respectively, by comfortable margins, followed by a 4–1 rout by the Twins in the ALCS.

Minnesota then fell behind the Atlanta Braves three games to two in the World Series. But the Twins came back to win Game 6 by a 4–3 margin in 11 innings, and Game 7 by the slimmest of margins, 1–0 in 10 innings, marking the first time in 67 years that a fall classic Game 7 had gone to extra innings. Kirby Puckett, who ripped Toronto pitching for a .429 average with two home runs and six RBIs in the LCS, added two more homers and four ribbies in the World Series. Right-hander Jack Morris won two games each in the LCS and the World Series for the Twins.

May 1 was a big day in baseball history. Oakland's Rickey Henderson stole third base in the fourth inning of a 7–4 win over New York for his 939th career theft, breaking Lou Brock's all-time record. Age was never a barrier for hard-throwing right-hander Nolan Ryan, 44, who threw his seventh career no-hitter, blanking the Blue Jays 3–0.

A pitcher who excelled all season was Boston's Roger Clemens, who earned his third Cy Young Award by leading the AL in earned run average, strikeouts, shutouts and innings pitched. Frank Thomas of Chicago looked at a lot of bad pitches this season, walking 138 times, the most in the major leagues since 1969.

For the first time in seven years, three players were elected to the Hall of Fame, and none of them ever played in a World Series. Former MVP Rod Carew entered the Hall with seven batting titles, while pitchers Gaylord Perry with 314 wins and Fergie Jenkins with seven 20-win seasons also were enshrined.

A Real Gamer

It has been said that 75 percent of life is showing up, and if so, Cal Ripken, Jr. has life down pat. Of course, Baltimore's favorite son did so much more than merely punch the clock nearly every day since joining the Baltimore Orioles in 1981. Retiring after the 2001 season, the 41-year-old infielder had lashed 3,184 hits, belted 431 home runs, driven in 1,695 runs and scored 1,647 times.

Despite those miraculous numbers produced over a 21-year career, Ripken will always be remembered for one accomplishment above all else: shattering an "unbreakable" record.

When Cal laced up his spikes on May 30, 1982, during his Rookie of the Year season, little did he know that it would become a daily habit surpassing even the most wild of imaginations. Of all baseball's long-standing records, including Hank Aaron's 755 career home runs, Joe DiMaggio's 56-game hitting streak and Roger Maris' single-season mark of 61 round-trippers, it was believed that Lou Gehrig's streak of 2,130 consecutive games played would never be broken. Athletes may be bigger, faster and stronger than they were decades ago, but they are just as susceptible to injury. Thirteen-plus seasons without missing a game seemed too much to fathom.

Considering the aches and pains that Ripken suffered during the lengthy streak, the biggest threat to his surge toward Gehrig's mark came only a few months before the climax, and had nothing to do with his durability. During spring training of 1995, with the previous season's strike having yet to be settled, baseball officials were preparing to open the campaign with replacement players. If the Orioles had played even one official game without Cal in the lineup, the streak would have ended in an inglorious fashion. But Ripken announced that he'd rather lose his streak — now more than 2,000 games — than cross a picket line. Further intensifying the situation was Orioles owner Peter Angelos' assertion that he would forfeit games before using replacement players. Fortunately, the strike was finally settled, and a 144-game season began.

Excitement grew all season as the day approached, and O's fans were thrilled when they learned that Ripken was scheduled to break the consecutive games played record at home. On September 5, Ripken tied the record, celebrating with a home run. The next night, in front of a packed house and a national television audience, Cal Ripken, Jr. went into the history books as the most durable player in the game's history, playing in his 2,131st consecutive game. Once the game became official after 4½ innings, play was halted to acknowledge Ripken's incredible achievement. When it became apparent that the ovation would not end on its own, teammates persuaded the humble ballplayer who had homered earlier in the game to take a victory lap around Camden Yards, waving to the fans and shaking hands with those crowded near the railings.

This was just the shot in the arm that baseball needed, after having cancelled the second half of the 1994 season, including the playoffs and World Series, due to the player strike. While that unspeakable crime against baseball fans may never be completely forgiven, and certainly won't be forgotten, Ripken's tremendous accomplishment was a soothing ointment on a festering wound.

Not surprisingly, Ripken's workman-like attitude did not disappear from view once the arduous task of breaking Gehrig's record was achieved. Not content with merely establishing the record, Ripken continued to play every game for several more years. Finally, after 2,632 consecutive games played, Cal took himself out of the lineup for the Orioles' last home game of the 1998 season on September 20. It was the first O's game in which Ripken did not play in 17 years.

Beginning in the late 1980s, when fans were starting to talk about the possibility of Ripken reaching this out-of-sight record, there were those who criticized Ripken's insistence on playing every day. From 1987 through 1990, he was unable to hit higher than .264, and his power appeared to be slipping slightly as well. Some felt that the streak had become more important to Cal than maximizing his performance, and that he should voluntarily take a day off now and then to regroup.

But Cal felt that he was merely going through a down time, and that he would get back into the groove at any time. And that wasn't going to happen with him on the bench. So, he kept plugging away, and Oriole managers Cal Ripken, Sr. and Frank Robinson continued writing Ripken's name on the lineup card every day during those years. Then came the 1991 season, when the 30-year-old shortstop put on an awesome display that silenced all of his critics and brought his fans back to life.

Playing all 162 of his team's game, as usual, Ripken was a man on a mission, stroking an amazing 210 hits for the runner-up mark in the AL, batting .323, leading the league in total bases with 368, smacking a career-high 34 home runs (third in the circuit) and driving in 114 runs (fourth). He also placed second in both doubles (46) and slugging percentage (.566), led AL shortstops in fielding with a .986 percentage, and earned his first of two consecutive Gold Gloves. Adding to his season's resumé, he hit a three-run homer in the 1991 All-Star Game to give the American League a 4–2 victory. The Orioles suffered through another brutal season, finishing in sixth place in the Eastern Division, 24 games out, but Ripken outpolled Detroit's Cecil Fielder for his second Most Valuable Player award.

Ripken was unable to keep up the 1991 pace over the remainder of the decade, but he continued to put up some impressive numbers, especially for a guy who never sat out to rest. He hit 24 home runs with 90 RBIs and 87 runs scored in 1993, batted .315 in the strike-shortened 1994 season, and powered 26 circuit clouts with 102 RBIs in 1996 to lead Baltimore into post-season play for the first time since his initial MVP season in '83.

Cal hit .444 with three doubles and two RBIs in the O's three games-to-one win over Cleveland in the '96 Division Series, then batted .250 in the 4–1 ALCS loss to New York. Ripken moved to third base in 1997 to make room at shortstop for Mike Bordick, and Baltimore returned to the playoffs after a season in which Cal hit .270 with 84 RBIs. Ripken was sensational in post-season play in '97, batting .438 with two doubles in the three games-to-one Division Series win over Seattle, and .348 with his first-ever post-season home run and three RBIs in the 4–2 LCS defeat at the hands of the Indians.

Ripken continued to produce in the late 1990s, batting .271 with his fifth fielding crown in 1998, and .340 with his 400th career homer in a limited role in '99. He then collected his 3,000th career hit in 2000. With his retirement looming in 2001, Ripken owed baseball fans nothing, but that didn't stop him from offering such treasured gifts as a home run and an MVP effort at the All-Star Game in Seattle. He hit 14 homers for the season to reach double figures in that category for the 20th consecutive year, adding 68 RBIs. NASCAR honored the Iron Man in 2001 by renaming its September race in Dover, Delaware, the Cal Ripken MBNA 400.

Ripken concluded his career as the Orioles franchise leader in games, at-bats, runs, hits, doubles, homers, RBIs, total bases and extra base hits. The 19-time All-Star was among the top 40 ballplayers all time in numerous categories, including games (sixth with 3,001), at-bats (fourth with 11,551), hits, doubles, home runs, total bases, RBIs and extra base hits. He held 11 major league and AL fielding records. Following his retirement, Cal was focused on his family and building a $38 million Cal Ripken, Jr. Youth Baseball Academy on 50 acres near his home in Aberdeen, Maryland. One million of that price tag was contributed by the Orioles during a final game ceremony in which Cal's No. 8 jersey was retired.

Cal Ripken, Jr. proved himself to be a man for all seasons. A 21-year career was filled with personal triumphs, including several that set him apart from many of his contemporaries. The man demonstrated beyond a shadow of a doubt that showing up every day is only the first step to greatness. The only people who are happy he retired are the ones who wished to hasten his inevitable enshrinement in baseball's Hall of Fame.

Top 5 MVP Vote-Getters

1. Cal Ripken, Jr., Baltimore — 318
2. Cecil Fielder, Detroit — 286
3. Frank Thomas, Chicago — 181
4. Jose Canseco, Oakland — 145
5. Joe Carter, Toronto — 136

1992 NATIONAL LEAGUE—BARRY BONDS

Barry Lamar Bonds
B. July 24, 1964, Riverside, California

Year	Team	Games	AB	Hits	Avg.	HR	RBI	Runs	SB
1992	Pit NL	140	473	147	.311	34	103	109	39

The Season

The Atlanta Braves and Pittsburgh Pirates featured a number of household names, including past MVPs Terry Pendleton and Barry Bonds, but it was a little known pinch-hitter by the name of Francisco Cabrera who came up with the biggest hit of the season. The Pirates, who had lost a seven-game NLCS the previous year to these same Braves, appeared to be in great position to exact revenge, leading 2–0 heading into the bottom of the ninth of Game 7.

The Braves rallied, thanks in part to a crucial error by second baseman Jose Lind, and Cabrera stroked a two-out, two-run single to give Atlanta a 3–2 victory and its second consecutive National League pennant. It was the third NLCS setback in a row for Pittsburgh, which paced the senior circuit in runs and won the East Division by a comfortable nine games over Montreal. Atlanta led the league in homers and slugging percentage on the way to an eight-game bulge over Cincinnati in the West.

John Smoltz, who topped the NL in strikeouts (215), won two of the LCS games for the Braves with a 2.66 ERA and 19 strikeouts, while Steve Avery extended his LCS-record scoreless innings streak to 22⅓ before it was snapped in Game 2. Outfielders Ron Gant and David Justice provided a chunk of the offense for Atlanta with two home runs and six RBIs each. Tim Wakefield earned two victories for the Pirates.

The Braves were unable to sustain their good fortune in the World Series, however, dropping a six-game decision to Toronto despite outscoring the Blue Jays 20–17.

On June 6, Eddie Murray of the New York Mets became the all-time RBI leader among switch-hitters. His 1,510th ribbie enabled him to pass three-time MVP Mickey Mantle. Another man who played for the Mets, pitcher Tom Seaver, was inducted into baseball's Hall of Fame.

The Houston Astros gave new meaning to the phrase "road warriors" when they conducted a 26-game road trip, the result of the Republican National Convention being held in the Astrodome.

Patience Is a Virtue

Barry Bonds is one of only 17 players in the history of the major leagues to hit 500 home runs. But unlike some all-or-nothing home run hitters, Bonds is a complete ballplayer who exercises patience to reach base, hits for average and plays an exceptional left field. Yes, Bonds drilled 30-plus homers in 10 consecutive seasons (1992–2001), and is almost always among the National League slugging leaders, but he is also at or near the top of the heap when it comes to walks and on-base percentage, and has stolen close to 500 bases over his 16-year career.

Pitch selection is the key for Bonds, who likes to crowd the plate and choke up on the bat. Every time he steps up to the dish, the left-handed batter determines exactly where a delivery must be for him to offer at it, and if the pitch is even slightly outside that zone, he'll let it pass. As a result, he gets called out on strikes more than most long ball hitters, but he also receives more than his share of walks, and puts up on-base percentages that are far superior to the typical big bopper.

Through 2001, the 37-year-old was among the upper echelon of all-time major league leaders in a variety of statistical categories, including slugging percentage, walks, homers, extra base hits, on-base percentage, stolen bases, runs scored, total bases and RBIs.

From 1989 through 2001, Bonds placed among the top five NL players in the following categories:

- Walks—12 times, including league-high totals in seven of those years;
- On-base percentage—11 times, including league bests in five seasons;
- Slugging—on 10 occasions, including NL highs in four years;
- Home runs—eight times, including a league best twice;
- Runs batted in—six times, including one circuit topping season;
- Stolen bases—on four occasions;
- Total bases—four times, including one league high total; and
- Batting average—once.

Although he has been with San Francisco only since 1993, he was fourth in franchise history in home runs entering the 2002 season with 391, fourth in extra base hits with 689, fifth in RBIs with 986, fifth in total bases with 2,835 and sixth in runs with 1,041. In the 1990s alone, Bonds produced more than 350 homers, 1,000 RBIs, 1,000 runs and 340 stolen bases.

Bobby Bonds, Barry's father who played 14 years for San Francisco and seven other teams, was the first major league player to hit 30 home runs and steal 30 bases in the same season in both leagues. But Barry did him one better by becoming only the second player in big league history with 30 homers and 50 stolen bases in the same campaign (1990). Barry was the first NL player with 40 homers and 40 steals in the same season (1996), and the first major leaguer to compile 40 round-

Barry Bonds. (Courtesy Pittsburgh Pirates.)

trippers and 30 swipes in two different seasons (1996–97). He is the only player in history to accumulate 400 homers and 400 thefts over a career, and was the 25th player to record 2,000 hits and 400 homers. Bobby and Barry are the top father-son combination not only in home runs with 899 through the 2001 season, but also in stolen bases with 945.

Pitching around Barry has been the modus operandi for many pitchers; he holds the major league record for intentional walks in a career with 355 through the 2001 season. During the decade of the '90s, he was one of only two players to hit at least 20 home runs each year, the only player to receive MVP points each season, and was

third in the majors in both circuit clouts and RBIs. A well-rounded athlete, Bonds is a 10-handicap golfer, and he enjoys weight lifting and dancing. He has been in two movies—*Rookie of the Year* and *Jane's House*—and has had roles in a variety of television shows, including *Beverly Hills 90210, Bridges, Renegade* and *In Living Color.*

Is there anything this guy can't do? Unfortunately, yes. Despite posting regular-season stats that a vast majority of big leaguers could only dream of, he has not fared particularly well in late-inning situations throughout his career, and his post-season efforts were less than spectacular through 2001. In two Division Series totaling seven games, Bonds batted .207 with no home runs and only three RBIs, while in three League Championship Series encompassing 20 games, he hit .191 with only one homer and three RBIs. Not coincidentally, his teams were 0–5 in post-season series. Unlike his cousin, Reggie Jackson, Barry Bonds has not earned the nickname "Mr. October."

Barry's fielding is often overlooked due to his incredible abilities with the bat, but not by appreciative Giants fans. He earned Gold Gloves every year except for two during the 1990s, and collected 146 outfield assists through 2001. Only once did his fielding percentage dip below .980.

With a diamond-studded gold crucifix dangling from his left earlobe, the martial arts practitioner who works out five hours a day during the off-season presents an ominous sight for pitchers. The 10-time All-Star has also found a way to compete off the field, and once he retires, should be in good shape to tackle the business world. Along with business partner Skip Marsh, Bonds founded Digital Interiors, a San Jose-based company that installs state-of-the-art technology in homes. Although he doesn't use it often, Bonds can sit with his laptop at Pacific Bell Park and, via the Internet, alter the air conditioner/heater, lighting and security in his Los Altos home 25 miles away.

Bonds' high-tech house, which he shares with wife Liz, features 19 television sets, eight computers, a video library including every one of his major league at-bats and a hallway housing his numerous awards, plus memorabilia from Muhammad Ali, Julius Erving, Dan Marino, Elvis Presley and Elton John.

Bonds was the one providing the star power in his initial MVP season of 1990, and he arguably should have been bestowed that same honor in '91. He was first in on-base percentage (.419), runner-up in walks (107), tied for second in RBIs (116), third in outfield assists (13), fourth in slugging (.514) and fifth in stolen bases (43), leading the Pirates to their second consecutive NL East crown. Bonds faltered in the post-season with a .148 average in a 4–3 LCS loss to the Braves, and placed second in the 1991 MVP balloting to Atlanta's Terry Pendleton, whose stats were clearly inferior. Prior to the '91 campaign, Bonds had been awarded a one-year, $2.3 million contract by an arbitrator, rather than the $3.25 million he had requested. Taking his frustrations out on manager Jim Leyland, Bonds' well-publicized, obscenity-filled spring training tirade didn't exactly earn him any admirers. A couple of years later, a USA Today baseball writer suggested that some 1991 MVP votes for Pendleton may in reality have been votes against Bonds.

But as in the past, Barry gritted his teeth and determined to prove his worth on the field. It certainly didn't hurt his attitude when he inked a $4.7 million contract for 1992, the highest one-season figure in baseball history at the time. Bonds made it virtually impossible to not vote him the National League's Most Valuable Player for the second time in three years in '92. Guiding the Pirates to a nine-game bulge over Montreal and a third straight NL East title, Bonds was the league's best in runs (109), slugging (.624), extra base hits (75), walks (127, including a franchise record-32 intentional passes)

and on-base percentage (.461). He placed second in home runs with 34, fourth in RBIs with 103, sixth in batting at .311 and ninth in stolen bases with 39.

Despite spending three weeks on the disabled list with a strained rib cage muscle, Bonds became the first player to average 30 homers, 100 RBIs and 40 steals over a three-year span (1990–92), and was the only batter to drive in more than 35 percent of runners from scoring position in each of those three seasons. Barry tried to shake the post-season monkey off his back with a .261 effort that included a homer, two RBIs and five runs scored, but the Pirates again fell in a seven-game LCS to the Braves.

The Associated Press Player of the Year finally got his wish when he became a free agent following the 1992 season, and in less than two months had signed a lucrative contract with the San Francisco Giants, who also hired his father as a coach. If Giants fans were worried that this controversial slugger may have already peaked, their fears were quickly alleviated in 1993 when Bonds became the first ballplayer to earn three Most Valuable Player awards in a four-year period.

Top 5 MVP Vote-Getters

1. Barry Bonds, Pittsburgh — 304
2. Terry Pendleton, Atlanta — 232
3. Gary Sheffield, San Diego — 204
4. Andy Van Slyke, Pittsburgh — 145
5. Larry Walker, Montreal — 111

1992 AMERICAN LEAGUE — DENNIS ECKERSLEY

Dennis Lee Eckersley
B. October 3, 1954, Oakland, California

Year	Team	Games	W	L	ERA	IP	SO	BB	Saves
1992	Oak AL	69	7	1	1.91	80	93	11	51

The Season

Opponents of Toronto and Oakland were shedding 96 tears after the two division winners both won that exact number of games. The Blue Jays earned their third Eastern Division crown in the past four years and their fourth in the last eight, by four games over Milwaukee, while the Athletics claimed their fourth West championship in five years by a six-game margin over Minnesota.

Toronto's first pennant resulted from a 4–2 League Championship Series victory, avenging a 4–1 ALCS loss to the Athletics three years earlier. Roberto Alomar provided plenty of offense for the Blue Jays in the series, batting .423 with two home runs, four RBIs and five stolen bases. Teammates Candy Maldonado and Dave Winfield contributed two homers each, John Olerud and Devon White both hit .348, and Juan Guzman won two games with a 2.08 ERA and 11 strikeouts.

The Blue Jays then made Canada proud with a 4–2 World Series triumph over Atlanta. All of the Jays' wins were one-run affairs, including the Game 6 clincher in 11 innings. Jimmy Key and Duane Ward won two games each for Toronto, while Pat Borders hit .450 with three doubles, a homer and three RBIs, and Joe Carter smacked two round-trippers.

Two former AL MVPs collected their 3,000th hits in the same month this season. Two-time winner Robin Yount stroked his landmark safety against Cleveland at County Stadium in Milwaukee September 9, while Kansas City's George Brett joined the exclusive club with his fourth hit of the game September 30 versus California.

Twelve years after his father, Ken Griffey, Sr., was named MVP of the All-

Star Game, Seattle's Ken Griffey, Jr. received the same accolade following a 3-for-3 performance, including a homer, in the American League's 13–6 victory over the National League at Jack Murphy Stadium in San Diego July 14. In another family affair, the Boone clan became the first to spawn three generations of major leaguers when Bret played second base for Seattle August 19. Father Bob played for the Phillies, Angels and Royals for 19 years (1972–90), while grandfather Ray suited up for the Indians, Tigers and four other clubs for 13 seasons (1948–60).

It was fitting that in the same year that Oakland ace reliever Dennis Eckerlsey earned the AL MVP, former A's fireman and 1981 MVP Rollie Fingers was inducted into the Hall of Fame. Another pitcher who made it to Cooperstown this season, albeit through the veteran's committee, was two-time Most Valuable Player Hal Newhouser.

Other hurlers who enjoyed the limelight in 1992 were Nolan Ryan of Texas, who struck out 100-plus batters for a major league-record 23rd consecutive year; Boston's Roger Clemens, who claimed the AL ERA title (2.41) for the third straight season; and Jeff Reardon of the Red Sox, who set the career saves record with his 342nd June 15.

A couple of sluggers also made names for themselves this season by driving in runs. Winfield became the oldest player (40) in major league history to collect 100 RBIs in a season, accomplishing the feat in his 2,700th career game September 24, while Detroit's Cecil Fielder was the junior circuit's RBI leader (124) for the third year in a row.

Bullpen Battler

The tragic stories of superb talents going to waste due to immaturity

and addictions are far too plentiful in the world of sports, even among some of the players gifted enough to have earned baseball's Most Valuable Player award. The Dennis Eckersley saga, on the other hand, is a fragrant deviation from that unfortunate pattern. Here was a man with a blossoming career and tremendous potential for additional prosperity, but who was on the verge of losing everything, including a loving wife and children.

A serious drinking problem was manifesting itself in 1986, and had Dennis not vowed to seek help and stop the imminent carnage after seeing himself behave drunkenly on a home video following a party, it's a virtual certainty he would not have continued to enjoy either the sweet smell of success or the joy that comes from the love and support of a family.

Dennis kicked the alcohol habit after checking into a treatment center in 1987, and within two years was one of baseball's top relief pitchers. One habit Eckerlsey never shed was a fiercely demonstrative, competitive spirit that endeared him to teammates but occasionally irritated his strikeout victims and their teammates. Dark, penetrating eyes, a curled mustache and straight black hair flapping well below the back of his hat gave the tall right-hander a rugged, Old West look, and his confident stride and cocky look added to the effect and made hitters think twice about digging in against the long-armed enemy on the hill.

Although he was a moderately successful starter for the first dozen years of his career — including seasons of 20–8 in 1978 and 17–10 in '79 — it was only after A's manager Tony LaRussa turned Eck into a relief specialist, at first against the pitcher's will, that he really found his niche. Eckersley eventually accepted this new role, and from 1988 through 1997, averaged 37 saves. In those first five seasons of strolling in from the bullpen, his ERA always ended up below 3.00, and three times it was below 2.00.

While Eckersely holds neither a single-season nor career record for saves — he was third all time with 390 — he did have the most saves in major league history over two-, three-, four-, five- and six-year spans, and he possessed four of the top 30 single-season save totals. A master of control, Eckersley was frequently among the league leaders in fewest walks per game throughout his career, and also vied with the league's leading hurlers in fewest hits allowed and lowest opponents' on-base percentage. In addition, he fielded his position impeccably.

This type of promise was revealed early in the lanky moundsman, a three-sport athlete at Washington High School in Fremont, California. Selected by the Cleveland Indians in the third round of the 1972 draft, Eckersley posted five shutouts and 218 strikeouts in the California League in 1973, then was named Texas League Right-Handed Pitcher of the Year in 1974 after winning 14 games and fanning 163.

Dennis, whose father had been an Idaho state boxing champion, earned a reputation as a battler early on, beginning his big league career in 1975 with a major league-record 28.2 innings pitched without allowing an earned run. He tossed a three-hit shutout in his first major league start — May 25 against Oakland — and claimed *The Sporting News'* American League Rookie Pitcher of the Year award with 13 wins and a 2.60 earned run average, third best in the AL.

In his next two seasons with the Tribe, Eckersley fired a no-hitter at California, a one-hitter against Milwaukee and a two-hitter versus Oakland; became only the eighth pitcher ever to strike out 200-plus batters in a season before the age of 22; led the junior circuit in lowest opponents' on-base percentage; and made the All-Star Team. Despite a world of potential wrapped up in his right arm, Eckersley was traded to Boston just prior to the 1978 season.

Eck used the trade as incentive to post his only 20-win campaign, striking out 162 batters (fifth best in the league) and placing fourth in the Cy Young Award voting. The Red Sox rode their new hurler to a tie for first place in the AL East, but lost a one-game playoff to the Yankees. Another exceptional season followed in '79 for the long-haired righty, who won 17 games, tied for second in complete games (17) and placed third in ERA (2.99)

But the next four years in Boston were mediocre at best — although he tossed a one-hitter in 1980 and was the AL's starting pitcher in the 1982 All-Star Game — and Dennis' ERA ballooned to 5.61 in 1983. Believing his best days were over, the Red Sox swapped Eckersely for Cubs first baseman Bill Buckner in late May 1984. Eck provided his new squad with 10 wins, and Chicago advanced to the post-season for the first time in 39 years. But he was tagged with a loss in the 3–2 National League Championship Series defeat to San Diego.

The 6-foot-2, 190-pounder went on the disabled list for the first time in his career in 1985, with tendonitis in his right shoulder, and could manage only 17 wins over two more years in a Cubs uniform. More importantly, Dennis' life was unraveling. His excessive drinking resulted in his wife moving back to Boston in 1986, but he wasn't yet ready to quit. Finally, in January 1987, he was admitted to a rehab center, and has been sober ever since. He was traded to Oakland in April and immediately became a reliever.

The 1988 season may be best remembered for Kirk Gibson's dramatic home run off Eckersley that propelled the Los Angeles Dodgers to the World Championship over the Athletics, but A's fans will recall it as the year Dennis finally came into his own. His 45 saves shattered the club record and were tops in baseball, and his four-save effort made him the ALCS MVP. The All-Star pitcher finished second in the Cy Young Award balloting, and was named AL Fireman of the Year by *The Sporting News.*

Eckersley missed one-fourth of the 1989 season with a shoulder problem, but still posted 33 saves, striking out 55 and walking only three. He had a 1.59 ERA with three saves in the ALCS victory over Toronto, and earned his first World Series ring with a save and a 0.00 ERA in the sweep of San Francisco. Dennis' 48 saves in 1990 (second in the league) included his franchise-record 137th. He also posted a 0.61 regular-season ERA, as well as two saves and a spotless ERA in the ALCS sweep of Boston. He then saved 43 games in 1991 for the runner-up mark in the circuit, and registered his 2,000th career strikeout.

At age 37, Eckersley still had some outs remaining in his right arm, but nobody could have guessed how many. He cut loose in 1992, winning seven of eight decisions and fashioning a 1.91 ERA. In 54 save opportunities, he came through 51 times, the second highest save total in baseball history at the time. His 51st save of the season was the 239th of his career, breaking the American League mark. Thirty-six of those saves came in succession at the start of the season, setting a major league record, and he allowed only two of 31 inherited base runners to score. He walked only 11 hitters all season, and earned at least one save against every AL team. The only negative this year was a 6.00 ERA in the 4–2 ALCS loss to Toronto.

The first pitcher to record 40-plus saves in four different seasons and the third moundsman to save 200 games and win 100 over a career, Eckersley became only the ninth player to win both the Most Valuable Player and Cy Young accolades in the same year.

Dennis pitched six more seasons, including two with St. Louis where he was reunited with skipper LaRussa, and one with Boston, continuing to post impressive save totals through 1997. He was fifth in the AL in saves in 1993 (36) and fourth in '94 (19, all in a row). In 1995, he saved 29 games and became the sixth pitcher to record 300 saves for a career, while also extending an error-less games streak to 470. He saved 30 games in '96 for the Cardinals, plus four more in the post-season. He then racked up 36 more saves in '97 to move into second place on the all-time list, and became the fifth pitcher in major league history to appear in 1,000 games.

A vivid image of Dennis Eckersley pumping his fist following a key strikeout sticks with many of his fans following the ace reliever's retirement in 1998 at the ripe age of 44. A true warrior who never let down, the six-time All-Star amassed 390 saves, as well as 197 wins, 2,401 strikeouts and a 3.50 ERA. He was the only pitcher to accumulate both 100 complete games and 100 saves. Had Eckersley ignored his alcohol problems in the 1980s, he'd probably be remembered as just another talented athlete who gave it all away. But his determination to battle that demon as fiercely as he did his opponents over a 24-year career is a stirring tribute to one of the all-time great relievers in baseball history.

Top 5 MVP Vote-Getters

1. Dennis Eckersley, Oakland — 306
2. Kirby Puckett, Minnesota — 209
3. Joe Carter, Toronto — 201
4. Mark McGwire, Oakland — 155
5. Dave Winfield, Toronto — 141

1993 NATIONAL LEAGUE — BARRY BONDS

Barry Lamar Bonds
B. July 24, 1964, Riverside, California

Year	Team	Games	AB	Hits	Avg.	HR	RBI	Runs	SB
1993	SF NL	159	539	181	.336	46	123	129	29

The Season

The National League's leading run producers — the Philadelphia Phillies — and the circuit's top ERA club — the Atlanta Braves — won the Eastern and Western Divisions, respectively, with Philadelphia beating out Montreal by three games and Atlanta outlasting San Francisco by one.

It was the third consecutive division title for the Braves, while the Phillies earned their first division crown in 10 years. The Giants became the first team since the 1954 New York Yankees to win 103 games but not play in the post-season.

Atlanta outscored the Phillies by 10 runs and outhit them by 12, but Philadelphia won three one-run games, including two in extra innings, to capture the League Championship Series four games to two. Lenny Dykstra and Dave Hollins contributed two home runs each in the series for the winners, while starter Curt Schilling and reliever Mitch Williams both posted ERAs of 1.69. The Phils' luck ran out, however, in a 4–2 World Series loss to Toronto.

The National League expanded from 12 to 14 teams in 1993, with the Florida Marlins playing in Miami and the Colorado Rockies in Denver. Less than two months into the season, two-time MVP Dale Murphy of the Rockies announced his retirement, only two home runs shy of the 400-mark.

What if St. Louis manager Joe Torre had benched Mark Whiten in the second game of a double-header September 7 after Whiten's misplay of a fly ball led to the winning runs in a 14–13 loss to Cincinnati in the opener? Well, the outfielder would not have experienced the single greatest day of his baseball career. Whiten hit a grand slam in his first at-bat of the nightcap, stroked three-run homers in both the sixth and seventh innings, and pounded a two-run dinger in the ninth to tie the major league record for homers in a game at four. Whiten had not reached double figures in round-trippers in any of his three big league seasons prior to '93.

Chicago reliever Randy Myers recorded 53 saves this season, the most in NL history, while Dykstra's 143 runs were the highest league total since another Phillie — Chuck Klein — scored 152 times during his 1932 MVP season. San Francisco's Darren Lewis played in his 267th consecutive error-less game July 16 to break the major league record for outfielders that Don Demeter set from 1962–65 with Philadelphia and Detroit. New York pitcher Anthony Young's infamous 27-game losing streak mercifully ended July 28 when the Mets rallied for a 4–3 win over Florida after a Young error allowed the Marlins to take the lead.

The award for the most creative vantage point from which to watch a ballgame was won by Cincinnati pitcher Tom Browning, who walked across the street from Chicago's Wrigley Field during a July 7 game to view the action from the rooftop of a building where fans regularly congregate. The "seat" cost him $500 in the form of a fine.

Still Smokin' After All These Years

Not everybody who hangs out at a ballpark as a kid eventually becomes a great baseball player. Barry Bonds enjoyed the boyhood thrill of shagging flies at Candlestick Park with his father, Bobby Bonds, and his godfather, Willie Mays, during the late 1960s and early '70s, but it soon became apparent that Barry would be providing much

Barry Bonds. (Courtesy San Francisco Giants.)

more excitement on the diamond than he ever received by watching others perform.

The eldest of three sons of Bobby and Pat Bonds, and the brother of Bobby Jr., who would play in the San Diego Padres organization, Barry was a superb athlete at Serra High School, an all-boys Roman Catholic school in San Mateo, California, that also produced Lynn Swann and Gregg Jefferies.

Sensing a potential star, the San Francisco Giants dangled $70,000 in front of Barry after selecting him in the second round of the 1982 draft, but he opted for a baseball scholarship at Arizona State University. In three years with the Sun Devils, Bonds hit .347 with 45 home runs and 175 RBIs, was named an All-America and tied an NCAA record with seven consecutive hits in the College World Series as a sophomore.

Bonds concluded his college career following his junior year when he was selected by the Pittsburgh Pirates in the first round (sixth pick overall) of the June 1985 draft. After a short stay in the minors, he joined the parent club in 1986. Following a number of decent but hardly awe-inspiring seasons with the Pirates, Bonds turned it up a couple of notches, earning National League MVP awards in 1990 and '92.

Following the 1992 campaign, his new agent, Dennis Gilbert, connected with a group that was purchasing the Giants, and soon Bonds had the type of deal he'd been futilely seeking for several seasons: a six-year, $43.75 million contract with an incentive package worth an additional $11 million. The port-side swinger could have rested on his laurels at this point, but instead acted like a man on a mission, putting together yet another MVP season in 1993 to make him the first player in history of the award to claim it three times in a four-year period.

Choking up on his bat and shortening his stroke even more than in previous years, Bonds dominated the league in '93, finishing more than 100 points ahead of his nearest competitor in the MVP balloting. Bonds' league-leading home runs (46) and RBIs (123), and his .336 batting average (fourth in the NL) would have been good enough to garner a rare Triple Crown award in five of the previous seven years. His 365 total bases were the most in the league since 1977, his .677 slugging average the highest mark in the majors since 1961 and the NL since 1948, and his .463 on-base percentage the best in the senior circuit since 1975.

Bonds placed second in runs with 129, was runner-up in walks (126, including 43 intentional passes, the sec-

ond highest total in major league history), finished seventh in hits with 181 and was eighth in doubles with 38. The leading All-Star vote-getter matched a major league record with a pair of doubles in the mid–summer classic, and tied a franchise mark with five runs scored in a single game August 4.

The driving force on this Giants squad, under the direction of first-year manager Dusty Baker, led his team to an incredible total of 103 wins, but with Atlanta winning 104 times to capture the West Division title, San Francisco was denied post-season play. Still, the awards poured in for the deserving catalyst, including the *Associated Press* Major League Player of the Year, the S. Rae Hickok Award as the nation's top professional athlete and the coveted NL MVP accolade.

Bonds continued to shine throughout the decade and into the new century, and was clearly the player of the 1990s and beyond. Despite an elbow spur in May and surgery following the strike-shortened season, he finished fourth in the MVP balloting in 1994 with top-five marks in walks (74), homers (37), slugging (.647), runs (89), outfield assists (10), on-base percentage (.429) and total bases (253), plus 29 steals. The Giants were second in the NL West when the strike ended the season.

The leading NL vote-getter for the 1995 All-Star Game became the first Giant to hit 30 homers and steal 30 bases in the same season since his dad did it 17 years earlier. Barry led the league in both walks and on-base percentage, and again was among the top five in homers, runs, total bases and slugging. But the Giants slipped to last place in the West, 11 games out.

Another phenomenal year followed in 1996 for Bonds, despite his team languishing in the West cellar. Although his 357 consecutive games played streak ended, he placed among the top four NL hitters in an amazing seven significant statistical categories, including RBIs (career high-129), walks (a then league record-151), home runs (42), runs (122), stolen bases (40), slugging (.615) and, of course, on-base percentage (.465). The first NL player — and the second overall —

with a 40-homer, 40-stolen base season tied a major league record with 11 homers in April.

The Giants finally returned to the playoffs in 1997, but Bonds was limited to a .250 average with two RBIs in the 3–0 Division Series loss to the Florida Marlins. During the regular season, he hit 40 home runs, scored 123 times and again led the league in walks (145) while placing second in on-base percentage (.450) on the way to a second consecutive fifth-place standing in the MVP voting. He also tied his father's major league record with a fifth 30-homer, 30-steal season.

Bonds celebrated his eighth All-Star selection by homering at Coors Field in the 1998 game, but the next month was suspended for several games for charging the mound in Philadelphia after being hit by a Ricky Bottalico pitch. Bonds established a league record by reaching base in 15 consecutive plate appearances from late August through early September, and reached the 100-plus mark in RBIs, runs and

walks for the fourth year in a row. He reached a career high with 44 doubles, and received the ultimate compliment with a bases-loaded intentional walk May 28. The Giants tied for the Wild Card spot, but were beaten by Chicago in a one-game playoff.

His 102 games in 1999 — due to a variety of injuries — represented the lowest figure in his big league career, and San Francisco finished second in the West, 14 games out. Still, Bonds managed a 16-game run-scoring streak, stroked his 2,000th career hit and set a league record with his 290th career intentional walk.

At age 36, Bonds figured to be slowing down, but apparently nobody bothered to tell him. Finishing second to teammate Jeff Kent in the 2000 MVP voting, Bonds was an incredible presence in a Giant lineup that produced the most regular-season wins in baseball (97). He pounded a then-career high 49 home runs, slugged at a .688 clip and posted a .445 on-base percentage — all good for second in the

league — while leading the NL in walks (117) and scoring 129 runs. True to form, Bonds was awesome in the regular season, but impotent in the postseason, hitting only .176 with one RBI in a 3–1 NLDS setback to the New York Mets, although he did smack a clutch triple in Game 1. The 3-for-17 effort dropped his career playoff batting average to .196.

But just on the horizon was a 2001 campaign that made even his detractors shake their heads in amazement as he became the first player in the history of baseball to garner a fourth Most Valuable Player award.

Top 5 MVP Vote-Getters

1. Barry Bonds, San Francisco — 372
2. Lenny Dykstra, Philadelphia — 267
3. David Justice, Atlanta — 183
4. Fred McGriff, San Diego/Atlanta — 177
5. Ron Gant, Atlanta — 176

1993 AMERICAN LEAGUE — FRANK THOMAS

Frank Edward Thomas
B. May 27, 1968, Columbus, Georgia

Year	Team	Games	AB	Hits	Avg.	HR	RBI	Runs	SB
1993	Chi AL	153	549	174	.317	41	128	106	4

The Season

The Toronto Blue Jays kept the World Series trophy out of the United States for the second consecutive year, defeating the Philadelphia Phillies in a six-game, high-scoring affair. Series MVP Paul Molitor hit .500 with six extra base hits and eight RBIs for the winners, while teammates Roberto Alomar (.480), Joe Carter (two homers) and Tony Fernandez (nine RBIs) provided plenty of offensive support. The Blue Jays' 15–14 Game 4 win was both the longest (four hours, 14 minutes)

and highest scoring contest in World Series history. Carter's three-run homer in Game 6 ended the entertaining Series.

Toronto had earned its third consecutive Eastern Division title — as well as its fourth in the past five years and fifth in nine years — by seven games over the New York Yankees, thanks to American League highs in batting, slugging, stolen bases and saves. The Chicago White Sox captured the West crown for the first time in 10 years, by eight games over Texas.

Molitor was also a significant fac-

tor in the Jays' 4–2 League Championship Series victory over Chicago, batting .391 with five RBIs, while Devon White (.444), John Olerud (.348), Juan Guzman (2–0, 2.08 ERA) and series MVP Dave Stewart (2–0, 2.03) contributed mightily as well.

Former and future MVPs were in the limelight in 1993. Reggie Jackson, the 1973 MVP, was elected to baseball's Hall of Fame in his first year of eligibility, while Ken Griffey, Jr. (1997 MVP) tied a major league record with a home run in eight consecutive games.

Other highlights included New

York's Jim Abbott throwing a no-hitter against Cleveland September 4; Dave Winfield of Minnesota collecting his 3,000th career hit, off 1992 MVP Dennis Eckersley, September 16; Toronto's Olerud lashing 54 doubles, the most in baseball in 16 years; and future two-time MVP Juan Gonzalez of Texas posting the highest slugging average (.632) in the AL in 13 years.

On a tragic note, a March 22 boating accident at Little Lake Nellie in Clermont, Florida, killed Cleveland pitchers Steve Olin and Tim Crews, while seriously injuring Bob Ojeda, who would return to pitch for the Indians in '93.

Big Hurt Emerges

Frank Thomas is a big man. No, make that a *huge* man. At 6-foot-5 and 270 pounds, he is a behemoth who crushes baseballs for a living. There have been large sluggers before, of course, with 6-foot-7 Frank Howard and 6-foot-6 Dave Kingman coming immediately to mind. But there's a significant difference between Thomas and other over-sized bruisers. For a guy with a strike zone roughly the size of a luxury Buick, Thomas not only drives the ball with frightening power, but also has a keen eye, strokes the ball for incredibly high averages and is difficult to strike out.

When Thomas won the 1997 American League batting title with a magnificent .347 mark, he was the largest man ever to do so, outdistancing his closest competitor by 17 points. Amazingly, he had already topped that titanic average twice in his career. Most managers would kill for a player who could produce a .300-plus batting average with 40 or more home runs in a season. Frank has done it FOUR times! In three other years, he pounded 30-plus homers and hit over .300. In 10 full seasons, the all-around hitter has batted .300-plus, driven in 100-plus runs, scored 100-plus runs and collected 100-plus walks nine times each.

Put simply, Frank Thomas is an awesome offensive force, and while the Chicago White Sox designated hitter

and first baseman lacks defensive skills and hasn't always chosen the best way to express himself, he has never gotten himself into serious trouble or disrespected the game of baseball that has made him wealthy.

And yet, Thomas falls well below other Chicago sports heroes in popularity. Michael Jordan, Gale Sayers, Ernie Banks, Ryne Sandberg, to name a few, all enjoyed more esteem and respect from Chicago sports fans and media through the years. While all were quickly forgiven any shortcomings, Thomas has been forced to pay for his personal and on-field letdowns by a tough group of media and demanding fans.

As recently as May 2001, Frank was being called on the carpet for not playing with a right arm injury sustained April 27 while diving for a ground ball in a game against Seattle. The original MRI had revealed no tear, and a muscle strain was suspected. New Sox pitcher David Wells took Thomas to task on a radio show, telling listeners that anybody who can't play hurt should find a new place to play. Shortly thereafter, Frank's father passed away, and when he returned from the funeral, a second MRI revealed a tear in the right triceps muscle that required surgery.

The incident was reminiscent of another two years previously when Chicago manager Jerry Manuel angrily sent Thomas home from a late-season road trip in Texas because he refused to pinch hit in the second game of a double-header after fanning ingloriously as a pinch batsman in the opener. Thomas insisted that the pain in his right foot and ankle were so severe that he could barely walk, let alone dig in at the plate with his back foot to give himself a chance. One week later, team podiatrist Scott Weil removed from Frank's ankle a spur the size of a golf ball that had been rubbing on a tendon, as well as a large corn from the little toe on his right foot.

Both times the enormous slugger with the friendly face and the fade haircut was exonerated by the medical findings, but still couldn't get the respect he felt he deserved; and he was deeply distressed by his father's death

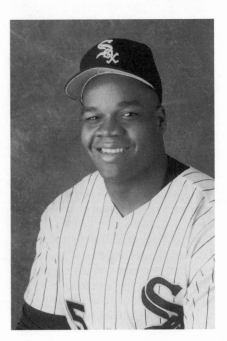

Frank Thomas. (Courtesy Chicago White Sox.)

and the subsequent lost season in 2001. Back in 1990, there was little to grieve for the 22-year-old kid who was called up to the White Sox after earning *Baseball America*'s Minor League Player of the Year for batting .323 with 71 RBIs and a league-best 112 walks with the Class AA Birmingham Barons.

Born and raised in Columbus, Georgia — the fifth of six children of bail bondsman and Baptist deacon Frank Sr. and textile worker Charlie Mae — Thomas led his high school baseball team to the state championship in 1984, and made the all-state team his senior year. Because he had signed a letter of intent to accept a football scholarship at Auburn University, he was not chosen in the June 1986 amateur baseball draft. He played a few games at tight end for the Tigers, but it was in baseball that he made a name for himself, garnering a pair of Southeastern Conference batting titles; establishing Auburn school marks for home runs (21) and walks (73) in a season, as well as for homers (49) in a career; and being named the SEC's MVP in 1989.

The seventh overall selection in the 1989 draft by the White Sox needed only 180 minor league games to reach the big time. And he made an impressive showing once in Chicago in 1990, batting .330 (the highest average by a White Sox with 200-plus plate appearances since 1942) with seven round-trippers and 31 RBIs in 60 games. His stick certainly gained the attention of Chicago broadcaster and former AL slugger Ken "Hawk" Harrelson, who pinned him with the nickname "The Big Hurt" for the pain he inflicted on baseballs.

White Sox fans prayed during the off-season that this basher's debut was no fluke, and their prayers were quickly answered. Thomas helped Chicago to its second consecutive runner-up finish in the Western Division in 1991 by placing among the top 10 AL players in nine offensive categories, including walks (138, a franchise record and the 26th highest total in baseball history), slugging (.553), home runs (32), RBIs (109) and on-base percentage (.454). Earning a $120,000 salary, Thomas was called "the biggest bargain in baseball" by *The New York Times.* He placed second in the AL Most Outstanding Designated Hitter voting and third in the league Most Valuable Player balloting. Following the season, it was learned that Thomas would undergo surgery for a right shoulder injury he had suffered in spring training. If The Big Hurt could play that well while injured, just think how he might fare with a completely sound body, his fans speculated.

The 1992 season at least partially answered that question. Frank put together an even more spectacular effort in his second full year, finishing among the top five in nine important offensive departments. He was first in on-base percentage (.446); tied for first in walks (122) and doubles (46); placed runner-up in runs (108); was third in RBIs (115), batting (.323) and slugging (.536); fourth in total bases (307); and fifth in hits (185). Somehow he found the time to appear in the '92 film *Mr. Baseball,* starring Tom Selleck, two years prior to showing up in an episode of *Married ... With Children.* Thomas was eighth in the MVP voting, but the Sox slipped to third place, 10 games out.

Heading into the 1993 season, Thomas was being heralded as a superstar in the making, but the mature young man refused to let it go to his head. Taped above his locker, the initials "DBTH" were a constant reminder to the prodigy to keep his new-found celebrity status in perspective. "Don't Believe the Hype" was a phrase Frank employed to stay focused on the work at hand. And that he did. Thomas not only produced another phenomenal season individually, he also helped lead Chicago to its first division title in 10 years. The White Sox outlasted Texas by eight games in the Western Division before bowing 4–2 to Toronto in the AL Championship Series.

Batting third in the lineup, playing 150 games at first base and serving as a DH in four others, Thomas was a one-man wrecking crew in 1993. Of his franchise-record 41 homers (third in the AL), 15 came in the first inning to get the Sox off on the right foot, and 22 tied the score or put his team ahead. The steam-rolling Mack truck also established a then-club mark with 77 extra base hits, drove in 128 of his teammates to place second in the junior circuit, was third in total bases (333) and slugging (.607), and finished fourth in walks (112) and on-base percentage (.434). In only 15 games did the .317 hitter fail to reach base via a walk or base hit, and never in consecutive contests. The first-time All-Star managed a hit in his only at-bat in the mid–summer classic, and was the 10th most difficult AL player to fan.

Although the Sox fell short in their World Series bid, Thomas did his part, batting .353 in the six-game ALCS with a home run, three RBIs and a record-10 walks. His round-tripper tied the score at 3–3 in a Game 4 that Chicago went on to win. Following the season, the 25-year-old became only the 10th player selected unanimously for the MVP, and also earned *The Sporting News'* Player of the Year award. The White Sox rewarded their bona-fide star with a four-year, $29 million contract.

In only three full seasons, Frank Thomas had established himself as one of the game's top players, and there would be many more heroics in the years to come. Hard times on and off the field were also in store for the unsuspecting phenom, but on the immediate horizon was another tremendous season and a second consecutive MVP accolade.

Top 5 MVP Vote-Getters

1. Frank Thomas, Chicago — 392
2. Paul Molitor, Toronto — 209
3. John Olerud, Toronto — 198
4. Juan Gonzalez, Texas — 185
5. Ken Griffey, Jr., Seattle — 182

1994 NATIONAL LEAGUE — JEFF BAGWELL

Jeffery Robert Bagwell
B. May 27, 1968, Boston, Massachusetts

Year	Team	Games	AB	Hits	Avg.	HR	RBI	Runs	SB
1994	Hou NL	110	400	147	.368	39	116	104	15

The Season

The 1919 World Series, in which eight Chicago White Sox allegedly participated in throwing the Series in exchange for money from gamblers, is generally considered the darkest moment in baseball history. But at least there *was* a World Series that season.

In 1994, the inability of wealthy players and owners to share the profits from a sport steeped in tradition and financially supported by an adoring public led to an August 12 players' strike that eventually resulted in the cancellation of post-season play. It represented the eighth work stoppage in baseball in the past 22 years. Nineteen-ninety-four will forever live in infamy as the first season without a World Series in 90 years.

Especially affected by the strike were the fans of the division leaders when play halted, including the Montreal Expos, who posted a major league-high 74 wins and sat atop the Eastern Division by six games over Atlanta. Los Angeles led the West by 3½ games over San Francisco, while Cincinnati held a one-half game advantage over Houston in the Central.

Individuals whose fine seasons were cut short included Barry Bonds of San Francisco, who was among the top five National League players in six categories; teammate Matt Williams, Atlanta's Fred McGriff, San Diego's Tony Gwynn and Colorado's Dante Bichette, each of whom was among the league leaders in four departments; and, of course, MVP Jeff Bagwell of Houston.

Perhaps Ryne Sandberg had the right idea. Ten years after earning the MVP award, the Chicago second baseman avoided the upcoming strike by announcing his surprise retirement June 13. Two years later, he would rejoin the Cubs.

Despite the shortened season, several milestones were reached in 1994. St. Louis shortstop Ozzie Smith broke Luis Aparicio's major league record for assists with his 8,017th July 14, New York's John Franco established a saves record for left-handers with his 253rd June 22 and Williams became the first NL player to hit 40 home runs by the end of July.

On the same day, April 8, Kent Mercker's no-hitter against Los Angeles came in the Atlanta left-hander's first-ever complete game and Dodgers hurler Chan Ho Park became the first Korean-born player to participate in a major league game. Darren Lewis' record of errorless games came to an end at 392 June 30 when the San Francisco outfielder finally booted one.

Prior to the season, the Hall of Fame opened its doors for pitcher Steve Carlton (329 wins, four Cy Young Awards) in his first year of eligibility, while former manager Leo Durocher was tabbed by the veteran's committee.

It's in the Bag

There is a tendency among some baseball purists to undervalue individual and team accomplishments that were achieved during seasons deviating from the norm in one manner or another. The prime example is Roger Maris' 61 home runs in 1961. Some, including Commissioner Ford Frick, believed that an asterisk should have accompanied the new home run record because Babe Ruth's 60 homers in 1927 were hit during a 154-game schedule, while Maris clubbed 61 dingers in a 162-contest season.

Statistics compiled during shortened seasons can also be viewed as suspect, especially those involving percentages. Skeptics may conclude that the astronomical batting and slugging averages a player posted during a season cut short by a players' strike surely would have come back to earth had the hitter played in a full slate of contests.

Jeff Bagwell put together a phenomenal campaign in 1994 prior to the player strike, and while he played in only 110 games, there is reason to believe that he might have established full-season marks rivaling those of some of the top players in baseball history had the strike not so rudely interrupted. The Houston first baseman, who would have been delayed in that hypothetical effort after breaking a bone in his left hand two days prior to the August 12 strike, was only the third National League unanimous selection for the Most Valuable Player award, and even a cursory look at his statistics shows why.

The 26-year-old bomber led the league in RBIs (116), total bases (300), slugging (.750), runs (104) and on-base percentage (.461); placed second in batting (.368) and home runs (39); tied for the runner-up spot in hits (147); finished third in sacrifice flies (10); was fifth in walks (65); and tied for fifth in multi-hit games (41). His incredible slugging percentage was the ninth best single-season mark in major league history, and his batting average remains a franchise record.

Voted Player of the Year by the *Associated Press*, *The Sporting News*, *USA Today Baseball Weekly* and *Baseball Digest*, Bagwell's 1994 season can be favorably compared to many of the great ones in history, despite the shortened campaign. He was the first NL player since Willie Mays in 1955 to

Jeff Bagwell. (Courtesy Houston Astros.)

finish either first or second in batting, runs, homers and RBIs, and the first major leaguer since 1980 to average more than one RBI per contest while playing in 100-plus games. Jeff was only the third senior circuit player to win both the Rookie of the Year and MVP award in a span of four or fewer years, and the first batter to lead his league in both runs and RBIs in a season since Mike Schmidt during his 1981 MVP campaign.

Bagwell, who fashioned an 18-game hitting streak, led major league first basemen with 120 assists on the way to his first Gold Glove, and also made his initial All-Star Game appearance, going 2-for-4 with a run scored. His biggest day of the season, however, came June 24 against Los Angeles when he tied a major league mark with two homers in the same inning, adding another round-tripper later in the game and tying a club record with 13 total bases.

Jeff's breakout season must have sent shivers down the spines of Red Sox officials, whose only solace from having traded the future star in 1990 was that at least they'd had the foresight to dispatch him to the other league. Boston selected Bagwell in the

fourth round of the June 1989 draft after he'd starred at the University of Hartford for three years, posting a .413 career average and twice being named East Coast Athletic Conference Player of the Year. The Boston native played third base in the Gulf Coast and Florida State leagues in '89, then earned MVP honors in the Eastern League in 1990 after batting .333 for Double A New Britain and pacing the circuit in hits, total bases and doubles.

Inexplicably, the Red Sox traded Bagwell to Houston for middle reliever Larry Andersen August 31, 1990, and have regretted it ever since. Andersen appeared in only 15 games for Boston, while Bagwell would become one of the game's best players. The right-handed slugger has five of the top six single-season home run marks in Astros history, including 47 in 2000, and the top four single-season RBI efforts for Houston, including 135 in 1997. The 6-foot, 195-pounder has belted 40 or more homers three times, driven in 100-plus runs on seven occasions, scored 100-plus runs seven times and walked 100 or more times in six seasons.

The four-time All-Star became only the fifth player in baseball history to reach 300 home runs, 1,000 RBIs,

1,000 runs and 1,000 walks in his first 10 seasons. Bagwell's only blemish in an otherwise outstanding career has been an inability to perform in the post-season. The Astros had one of the majors' best teams in the late 1990s, but still have not garnered a pennant since their 1962 inception. Bagwell must foot some of the blame for the failures in three consecutive division series (1997–99). In those 11 post-season games, he batted .128 with three runs and five hits (none of the extra base variety), four RBIs, seven walks and 15 strikeouts.

Bagwell didn't waste any time making the Red Sox pay for their blunder, garnering 23-of-24 first-place votes in National League Rookie of the Year balloting in 1991. After switching from the hot corner to first base just prior to the season, he batted .294 in 156 games, poking 15 home runs and driving in 82 runs. The first-year man struck out 116 times, but also led the Western Division cellar dweller in homers, RBIs, slugging, walks and on-base percentage. Showing the type of power that would soon become his trademark, the *Baseball America* Major League Rookie of the Year slammed a 456-foot homer in Pittsburgh.

Houston moved up a couple of notches to fourth place in 1992, thanks in part to Bagwell's 96 RBIs (sixth in the NL), 84 walks (seventh) and 87 runs (tied for ninth). In '93, Jeff hit .320 (sixth in the league), but saw his 304 consecutive games played streak end in September when a pitch broke a bone in his left hand. It was the first of three such occurrences for Bagwell, whose crowding of the plate has resulted in several visits to the disabled list. More unorthodox is No. 5's batting stance. Instead of stepping into the pitch like most hitters, he begins with his feet planted wide apart and goes into a bobbing crouch, then lessens his foot-spread as the pitch approaches.

Nobody has questioned his batter's box idiosyncrasies since the 1994 performance. Bagwell followed the MVP season with a sub-par effort, for him, batting .290 with 21 homers and 87 RBIs. He placed fifth in the NL in both walks and on-base percentage, produced back-to-back four-hit games in July, and became the first player in club history to lead the team in RBIs for five consecutive years. The Astros were second in the Central Division in '95, but for the third consecutive season, a pitch shattered a bone in Jeff's hand.

Bagwell rebounded in 1996, placing among the top five in four categories, including doubles (first with 48), extra base hits (fourth with 81) and walks (third with 135). Four of those two-baggers came in one game, tying a major league record. The second-time All-Star failed to reach base in only 11-of-162 games, and joined Willie Stargell as the only players to belt a homer into the upper deck of Three Rivers Stadium more than once with a 459-foot shot.

The Astros, who had finished runner-up in the Central in '96, finally broke through with a division title in 1997, with Bagwell playing a huge role. He became the first player in major league history to hit 30 homers and steal 30 bases in a season while playing exclusively at first base, and one of only six players all time to hit 40-plus homers and steal 30-plus bases. Bagwell, who placed third in MVP balloting, was among the top five NL hitters in seven departments, including homers (43), RBIs (135), slugging (.592), total bases (335), runs (109) and walks (127). But Jeff managed only one hit in a division series sweep at the hands of Atlanta.

In 1998, he was limited to a .143 average in a 3–1 Division Series loss to San Diego after placing third in both runs (124) and walks (109) during the regular season. A right knee injury in May put him on the disabled list, but

he came back to become the first Astro with 30-plus homers in four different seasons, and the first with at least 100 RBIs in three consecutive years.

The Astros made it three division titles in a row in 1999, with Bagwell leading the league in runs (143) and walks (149, a franchise record), while hitting .304 and driving in 126 runs. He also clouted 42 homers and stole 30 bases, becoming only the seventh player in major league history to join the 40–30 club in two different seasons. He also became the 13th player ever to have a pair of three-homer games in one year, and tied a big league mark with six walks in one contest. But once again Jeff's prowess ended with the regular season; he hit .154 with only two safeties, three runs and five walks in the Astros' 3–1 Division Series loss to the Braves.

The move from the Astrodome to Enron Field in 2000 did wonders for many of the players' bats, as the Astros set an NL record with 249 homers. Bagwell was one of the beneficiaries of the cozy ballpark's outfield dimensions, becoming the first National Leaguer to collect 45-plus home runs, 100-plus RBIs and 150-plus runs in a season. He hit 28 of his career-high 47 round-trippers at home, drove in 132 runs and walked 107 times (all third in the NL), while leading the way in runs (152, the most in the majors since 1936) and placing fourth in total bases (363). His 295 runs scored in 1999 and 2000 set an NL record for two seasons, and his 528 runs over four years (1997–2000) are the most by a major leaguer in more than half a century. But the team's offensive surge at home did little for its overall fortunes, as Houston

slipped to fourth place in the Central Division.

Prior to the 2001 season, Bagwell signed a five-year, $85 million contract extension. His batting average (.288) then dipped below .300 for the first time in four years, but he swatted 39 homers, drove in 130 runs, scored 126 runs (fifth in the NL) and drilled 43 doubles as the Astros won another division title. He hit for the cycle for the first time in his career in a game against St. Louis, homering and doubling in one inning. On September 30, he became the first player ever with 30 home runs, 100 RBIs, 100 runs and 100 walks in six consecutive seasons. Atlanta didn't give Bagwell much to swing at during its three-game sweep in the NLDS, walking him five times, but Jeff managed to hit .429 in seven at-bats.

Jeff Bagwell is at or near the top of the Houston franchise's career leader list in nearly every offensive department, and among the majors' top 25 all time in slugging percentage. At 34 years of age in 2002, Bagwell is likely to add to his legacy over the next few years. And if the Astros continue to make a habit of post-season play, perhaps he can excel there as well so that Hall of Fame voters will have no choice but to pencil him in during his first year of eligibility.

Top 5 MVP Vote-Getters

1. Jeff Bagwell, Houston — 392
2. Matt Williams, San Francisco — 201
3. Moises Alou, Montreal — 183
4. Barry Bonds, San Francisco — 144
5. Greg Maddux, Atlanta — 133

1994 AMERICAN LEAGUE—FRANK THOMAS

Frank Edward Thomas
B. May 27, 1968, Columbus, Georgia

Year	Team	Games	AB	Hits	Avg.	HR	RBI	Runs	SB
1994	Chi AL	113	399	141	.353	38	101	106	2

The Season

The 1994 season will be best remembered for the strike that wiped out one-third of the schedule and all of the post-season, but American League baseball fans can also look back on a few interesting oddities that made up this cursed campaign, including home run records, pitching gems and triple plays.

Cleveland's Eddie Murray hit a home run from both sides of the plate April 21 for the 11th time in his career, breaking the record of three-time MVP Mickey Mantle. On June 19, Detroit matched a major league mark by homering in its 25th consecutive game, while the Orioles and Angels tied a big league standard by combining for 11 home runs in a July 1 contest.

Scott Erickson may have believed he had pitched the game of the year April 27 when he provided Minnesota with its first no-hitter in 27 years during a 6–0 victory over Milwaukee, but Kenny Rogers of Texas went him one better by tossing the 14th perfect game in major league history July 28 in a 4–0 win against California.

Boston shortstop John Valentin recorded only the 10th unassisted triple play ever July 9, two months after Minnesota third baseman Gary Gaetti participated in his seventh career triple play.

When the strike stopped play August 12, the New York Yankees were sitting atop the AL East by 6½ games over Baltimore with an AL-best 70 wins, while Chicago and Texas held one-game leads in the Central and West divisions, respectively.

The strike cut short impressive seasons by a number of players, including Cleveland's Albert Belle, who placed among the top five AL hitters in nine important categories; teammate

Kenny Lofton, who was among the top four in six departments; and Seattle's Ken Griffey, Jr., who was among the top three in four categories. New York pitcher Jimmy Key led the majors in wins with 17, while Seattle's Randy Johnson was tops in strikeouts (204), shutouts (4) and complete games (9), and fifth in earned run average (3.19).

Finally, 1994 can be remembered for the professional baseball debut of Michael Jordan, who went 0-for-3 for the Birmingham Barons April 9 in a 10–3 loss to Chattanooga, and for the replacing of AL President Bobby Brown by University of Kansas Chancellor Gene Budig June 8.

Repeat Performance

Roberto Clemente may have been the best unorthodox hitter the game of baseball has ever seen, but Frank Thomas isn't too far behind. Most sluggers like to tee off on pitches up in their wheelhouse, but Frank prefers the low ball, frequently diving into the plate when he swings. Seemingly off-balance at the point of contact, Thomas will sometimes hit the ball with his back foot off the ground and his right hand slipping off the bat. The average hitter might have trouble getting the ball past an infielder under those circumstances, but Thomas is so big and strong that he still manages to whack line drives that often don't slow down until they've rattled a bleacher seat.

The White Sox designated hitter and first baseman distinguishes himself from other unconventional hitters in a couple of other significant ways. While it's all or nothing for most batters who lunge at pitches in and out of the strike zone, Thomas not only hits for high averages, but is also very dis-

cerning about which pitches he selects to greet with his lumber. The 6-foot-5, 270-pounder decided early on that he would never see the pitches he liked if he swung at the ones he didn't. Patience at the plate has provided the enormous boomer with more than 100 walks per year in nine of his 10 full seasons, and has forced pitchers to feed him strikes when they can't afford to put him aboard via the base on balls.

Thomas has also been the beneficiary of a number of calls through the years on offerings in the vicinity of the inside corner of the plate due to his pitcher-exasperating habit of jumping away from the deliveries at the last moment. This tactic was particularly effective through the first seven or eight years of his career, but those same pitches began being called strikes after Frank made the foolish mistake of publicly complaining about umpires' ball-strike calls. In fact, some attribute his 1998 and 1999 drop-off at the plate to this factor.

Another decision that Thomas wound up paying for—this time in the public forum—was skipping the first six days of voluntary full-squad workouts prior to the 2001 season. The White Sox were coming off a campaign in which they did everything right until their sorry performance in the American League Championship Series, and anticipation was high that the team's 2001 odyssey could lead them to the World Series for the first time since 1959.

Despite the fact that he was under contract—$9.9 million per year from 2001 through 2006—the man who'd represented Reebok, Wendy's and Pepsi stayed away from Tucson because he was upset that his salary trailed those of other players of his caliber. But he was messing with the wrong guy in the wrong town. Jerry Reinsdorf, owner of the White Sox and Chicago Bulls, had emphatically declared many times that he would not renegotiate contracts, a painful lesson learned by forward Scottie Pippen during the Bulls' 1990s NBA reign. And while Thomas did not miss any required workouts, his absence stirred the wrath of blue-collar Sox fans who found it difficult to relate to the "tribulations" of a superstar having to settle for approximately $10 million a year.

Thomas showed up in time to avoid breaking any rules, but struggled for his first 20 games of the regular season before tearing a triceps muscle in his right arm while diving for a ground ball, and was lost for the season.

Back in 1994 when he was coming off an MVP season, the only pain associated with The Big Hurt was what he was meting out to the opposition. Those who might have been waiting for Thomas to show some chinks in his armor after three of the best seasons to start a career that Sox fans had ever seen were still waiting when the player strike aborted the campaign in mid–August.

Frank became the first American League player since Roger Maris in 1960–61 to win two consecutive Most Valuable Player awards, outdistancing his nearest competitor by 139 points in the voting. He was first in the league in slugging (a franchise-record .729, the highest mark in the AL since 1957 and the 17th best in baseball history), runs scored (106), walks (109), and on-base percentage (.494, 24th highest in major league history); tied for first in extra base hits (73); second in home runs (38); third in batting (.353) and total bases (291); tied for third in RBIs (101) and doubles (34); and fourth in hits (141).

He pounded a White Sox franchise-record 32 homers by the All-Star Game break, the seventh most in major league history, and in only nine games did he fail to reach base with a hit or walk. The big guy cranked the longest clout of the All-Star Game home run derby with a 519-footer prior to his second All-Star appearance. Thomas was hoping to lead Chicago to its second consecutive post-season

berth, but the strike destroyed that aspiration with the White Sox one game ahead of Cleveland in the Central Division.

In 1995, Thomas became the first player ever to combine 100-plus RBIs and 100-plus walks in five consecutive years. While his team slipped to third place, 32 games out, Frank kept right on hacking. He led the junior circuit in walks with 136 (including 29 intentional, tying an AL record for right-handed batters) and sacrifice flies with a dozen; placed second in on-base percentage at .463; tied for second in home runs with 40, one shy of his club record; placed third in slugging at .606; and drove in 111 runs while accumulating 299 total bases. He also won the All-Star Game home run derby competition and placed eighth in MVP balloting.

Thomas had been free of serious injury for the first half of the decade, but he went on the disabled list for the first time in his career with a stress fracture in his left foot in 1996 while sitting atop the league in RBIs with 85. He wound up with 134 ribbies — a career high at the time and now fourth most in club history — and his .95 RBI per game was the best ratio ever by a Sox player. He also smacked 40 homers with 330 total bases in yet another exceptional season, placing among the top five AL hitters in batting (.349), on-base percentage (.465) and walks (109). As impressive as his batting average was, the clutch hitter fared even better when it really counted, hitting .351 with men on base and .363 with runners in scoring position.

Off the field, Thomas was enjoying the fruits of his labor, moving with his wife, Elise, and their three children into an eight-bedroom, 13-bathroom, $8.1 million mansion on three acres in an affluent Chicago suburb. The 24,000-square-foot palace featured an 83-foot by 23-foot indoor batting cage.

The beat went on for Thomas in 1997 when he became the only player in major league history with seven consecutive seasons of reaching the .300 mark with 20 homers, 100 RBIs, 100 runs and 100 walks. To give this phenomenal performance some perspective, only Lou Gehrig and Ted

Williams had accomplished that feat as many as four years in a row. The Big Hurt not only won the batting title (.347), but led the league in hitting with men on base (.383) and was second with runners in scoring position (.417).

Chicago finished second in the Central Division in '97, six games behind Cleveland, and Thomas was third in the MVP voting after leading the league in on-base percentage (.461), placing runner-up in slugging (.611), fourth in both total bases (324) and walks (109), and fifth in RBIs (125). He signed a contract extension in September, but separated from his wife in December. Those marital difficulties would eventually culminate in divorce, and were definitely a factor in a couple of sub-par seasons, at least for him, in 1998 and '99.

Accused by teammate Robin Ventura of devoting too much of his attention and intensity to his music business, Un-D-Nyable Entertainment, Thomas slipped dramatically to a .265 batting average in 1998, although he still managed 110 walks (second in the league), 29 round-trippers and 100-plus RBIs and runs. In 1999, his Big Hurt Enterprises sports marketing company and his marriage were eroding, agent Robert Fraley was killed in the plane crash that claimed the life of golfer Payne Stewart, and Thomas was hobbled much of the year with a bone spur in his ankle which required surgery in September. He managed to hit over .300 for the eighth time in nine full seasons, but could produce only 15 homers and 77 RBIs, and was booed emphatically by the home crowd after an 0-for-8 effort in a late August double-header.

While healing from surgery during the off-season, Thomas worked with former White Sox hitting instructor Walt Hriniak to help him get back on track, and apparently the strategy worked. Following a spring training verbal battle with manager Jerry Manuel over Frank's refusal to participate in a running drill, The Sporting News' AL Comeback Player of the Year helped lead the White Sox to their first division title in seven years by placing among the top five AL hitters in six categories in 2000, including home runs (43), RBIs (143), slugging (.625) and total bases (364). Thomas and his teammates were impotent in a three-game AL Division Series sweep at the hands of Seattle, and Thomas soon learned that he'd lost out on a third MVP award by a mere 32 points to Oakland's Jason Giambi.

Frank was expecting to come back strong from his arm injury, and there was no reason to believe he wouldn't as the 2002 season approached. Thomas not only is the all-time White Sox

leader in a number of offensive departments, including home runs and RBIs, but is also among baseball's career hitters in slugging and on-base percentage. Incredibly, Thomas has walked 351 more times than he's struck out in a 12-year career through the 2001 season.

Despite all he's accomplished on the diamond in a relatively short period of time, Frank Thomas will never be the most popular athlete in Chicago. But the 34-year-old still has a number of years left to convince the

skeptics of his worth and leadership, and once this awesome slugger's career dies down, he's a virtual lock for the Hall of Fame.

Top 5 MVP Vote-Getters

1. Frank Thomas, Chicago — 372
2. Ken Griffey, Jr., Seattle — 233
3. Albert Belle, Cleveland — 225
4. Kenny Lofton, Cleveland — 181
5. Paul O'Neill, New York — 150

1995 NATIONAL LEAGUE — BARRY LARKIN

Barry Louis Larkin
B. April 28, 1964, Cincinnati, Ohio

Year	Team	Games	AB	Hits	Avg.	HR	RBI	Runs	SB
1995	Cin NL	131	496	158	.319	15	66	98	51

The Season

After seeing 1½ months of the regular season and the entire post-season cancelled in 1994 due to a players' strike, baseball fans watched nervously as spring training camps remained empty in 1995. But on March 31, a U.S. District court forbade owners from forcing new working conditions on the players, which meant that old rules from the previous season went back into effect. The players immediately ended their strike, and 18 games were deleted from the schedule as the players rushed to prepare in an accelerated spring training.

Many fans were slow to forgive and forget, but Colorado supporters were given added incentive to return to the ballparks. The Rockies posted a 77–67 season for the best percentage (.535) by a third-year franchise, and became the first major league team to qualify for the post-season before its eighth year.

The Wild Card team was able to garner only one playoff win, however,

as Eastern Division champion Atlanta whipped Colorado 3–1 in the National League Division Series. Outfielder Marquis Grissom was one of the Braves' offensive heroes in the series, batting .524 with three home runs and four RBIs. Chipper Jones and Fred McGriff homered twice each for the winners, while reliever Alejandro Pena managed to win two games with only three innings of work. Vinny Castilla hit .467 with three homers and six RBIs for the Rockies.

Cincinnati, which won the Central Division by nine games over Houston, made short work of West Division winner Los Angeles, sweeping the Dodgers 3–0 in an NLDS. Barry Larkin batted .385 and teammate Mark Lewis drove in five runs in only two at-bats. Atlanta then stifled the Reds 4–0 in the League Championship Series, outscoring Cincinnati 19–5.

The Braves became the first franchise to win a World Series in three different cities (Boston, Milwaukee and Atlanta) with a 4–2 triumph over Cleveland in a rematch of the 1948 fall

classic. Contributing to the Braves' first world title since 1957 were Tom Glavine, who won two games while posting a 1.29 earned run average and 11 strikeouts; Ryan Klesko, who batted .313 with three home runs; and McGriff, who belted two round-trippers.

Individuals who helped draw fans back to the game that had spurned them in 1994 included Colorado's John Vander Wal, who established a major league record with his 26th pinch hit of the season; future MVP Ken Caminiti of San Diego, who became the first player to hit home runs from both sides of the plate three times in four games; Chicago's Mark Grace, whose 51 doubles were the most in the NL since 1978; and Dante Bichette of Colorado, whose 128 RBIs were the highest league total in eight years.

Prior to the season, three-time Most Valuable Player Mike Schmidt was elected to the Hall of Fame. At the mid-point of the campaign, the NL defeated the AL 3–2 in the All-Star Game despite going hitless in the first 5⅔

Barry Larkin. (Courtesy Cincinnati Reds.)

Barry. Well, his voice, anyway. Good move by the Reds. They know that Larkin is the symbol for this organization, and they want his voice to be the first one callers hear when they contact the team.

It's difficult to imagine Barry wearing the threads of any other organization. A star in baseball, football and basketball at Cincinnati's Moeller High School, Barry's lone extended venture outside the southwestern Ohio area came in 1983–85 when he played baseball for the University of Michigan. He batted .361 during his three-year tenure with the Wolverines, becoming the first Big Ten player to be named MVP twice. Larkin also hit .311 for the 1984 U.S. Olympic Team that won the silver medal.

Barry was hardly the only family member to make a name for himself in sports. Brothers Mike, Byron and Stephen all excelled in one arena or another, with Mike playing football at Notre Dame, Byron suiting up for the Xavier University basketball team and Stephen playing professional baseball in the Texas Rangers and Cincinnati Reds organizations.

Barry, a 6-foot, 185-pounder, made his major league debut in August 1986 after claiming American Association MVP and Rookie of the Year honors at Triple A Denver, where he was also voted the league's best defensive shortstop. A slow start in 1987, exasperated by a hyperextended left knee that placed him on the disabled list in mid–April, was offset when he hit .270 during the second half of the season.

The Reds finished second in the Western Division for the fourth consecutive year in 1988, and if Larkin's teammates had matched his output, they might have made it to the postseason. Larkin showed what he could do over the course of a full season by leading the team in hits (174) and batting average (.296), ending the campaign with a 21-game hitting streak, leading major leaguers by striking out only 24 times in 652 plate appearances and stealing 40 bases. Following the season, he hit .476 during a Japan tour and was voted MLB's Most Valuable Player for the series.

Larkin continued his strong play through the first half of the 1989 season, hitting .340 at the All-Star break. But a torn medial collateral ligament in his right elbow, suffered during a skills competition prior to the All-Star Game, landed the lanky shortstop on the disabled list for seven weeks, and the team plummeted to fifth place. Still, he wound up hitting .342 in 97 games.

In 1990, Larkin was again blessed with a full season of play—a rarity during an injury-plagued career — and he responded with a .301 batting average, a team-high 185 hits (tied for fourth in the NL), 30 steals and a fine playoff effort. He stroked six hits, including a pair of doubles, and stole three bases in Cincinnati's four games-to-two NLCS win over Pittsburgh, then batted .353 with six hits, an RBI and two walks in the Reds' World Series sweep of Oakland. Larkin finished seventh in the MVP voting after leading league shortstops in RBIs (67).

The wiry right-handed hitter's home run high had been 12 through his first five seasons in the majors, but he developed a power stroke in 1991 that saw him notch 20 seat-reachers to go along with a .302 average, 69 RBIs, 88 runs and 24 stolen bases. Five of those homers came in a two-game span, tying a major league record. Although the Reds dipped to fifth place in the West, Larkin was fifth in the league in slugging (.506) and among the top 10 in batting and on-base percentage (.379).

From 1992 through '94, Larkin's newfound power appeared to diminish, and while he still hit for average

innings. And at the end of the season, David Justice turned boos to cheers after questioning Braves fans' loyalty by hitting a home run in Atlanta's 1–0 Game 6 World Series-clinching victory.

Red-Blooded Ballplayer

Playing an entire career with one team is the exception rather than the rule in baseball these days, and that's one of the reasons that ballplayers who wear the same uniform year after year become indelibly linked with both their team and the city.

Few athletes are as intricately intertwined with a ballclub and town as Barry Larkin and the Cincinnati Reds. Not only was Larkin born in Cincinnati, he has played his entire 16-year career in a Reds uniform. Need more proof? Call the Cincinnati Reds administration telephone number and listen to who answers. That's right, it's

(including a .315 mark in 100 games in '93), his runs and stolen base totals dropped off. In 1993, he became the first shortstop in 40 years to hit at least .300 in five consecutive seasons, and was voted the starting shortstop for the NL All-Star Team to snap Ozzie Smith's string of 10 consecutive starts. He also led league shortstops in putouts and earned his first Gold Glove in 1994.

With baseball back in full force in 1995 following the players' strike, Larkin lit up NL pitchers to the tune of a .319 average, clubbing 15 homers (his highest total in four years) and scoring 98 runs (fifth in the league). He was seemingly even more dangerous once on base, stealing a career-best 51 bases in 56 attempts—including 18 in a row—and becoming only the fourth player in major league history to swipe at least 50 sacks with a 90 percent success ratio. This season also featured a couple of career milestones: his 500th RBI and 200th stolen base.

Larkin's prowess and his team's West Division title led voters to select him as the league's Most Valuable Player. The ninth Cincinnati Red to corral the award won a close vote over Colorado's Dante Bichette. Barry, who earned his second Gold Glove, continued to carry his team in the post-season. He batted .385 with five hits and four stolen bases in the Division Series sweep of Los Angeles, then hit .389 with two doubles and a triple in a four-game League Championship Series loss to Atlanta.

In what would prove to be his most impressive slugging campaign, Larkin blasted 33 homers, drove in 89 runs and stole 36 bases in 1996, becoming the first shortstop in major league history with 30 round-trippers

and 30 steals in the same season. He wound up placing among the top 10 NL players in numerous categories, including walks, on-base percentage, runs, slugging and steals, while garnering a third consecutive Gold Glove.

Reds management recognized that the 33-year-old Larkin was developing into one of the league's best all-around players in 1997, naming him the team's first captain since 1988. But the injury bug struck again. He managed to play in only 73 games due to a variety of left leg and foot injuries, with season-ending surgery performed on an Achilles tendon. Prior to the physical setbacks, Larkin hit safely in a club-record 13 consecutive plate appearances in late May.

Despite preseason neck surgery, Larkin came back strong in 1998, leading senior circuit shortstops in batting (.309), homers (17) and RBIs (72); stealing 26 bases; and placing runner-up in the league in triples with 10. In an August 7 game against Milwaukee, he tied a modern NL record by scoring two runs in an inning.

Larkin played a career-high 161 games in 1999, leading his team in runs (108) and walks (93), compiling a 16-game hitting streak, stroking an RBI single in the All-Star Game and collecting his 1,000th career run. But the Reds finished second in the Central Division, missing out on the Wild Card by one game.

Cincinnati was second in the Central Division again in 2000, as Larkin batted .313 for his ninth .300 season and posted his 2,000th career hit, becoming the fourth player in Reds history to reach that plateau. He was off to another great beginning, batting .355 in his first 17 games, when injuries to a finger and left knee cost him 59 starts.

In 2001, the frustrated 37-year-old batted .256 in only 45 games, thanks to pulled groin muscles and season-ending surgery for a hernia, as the Reds dropped to fifth place in the Central Division. But he got a monkey off his back by ending the longest streak among active major leaguers when he hit his first grand slam after 6,734 at-bats.

Frequently on the verge of stardom during his career, each time Larkin would get a taste of it, an injury would slow him down. Still, the sure-handed shortstop is among the top 10 in franchise history in a variety of departments, including games, at-bats, hits, runs, extra base hits, doubles, homers, RBIs, total bases and stolen bases. The 11-time All-Star is the only shortstop in major league history to collect 2,000 hits, 170 homers and 350 stolen bases, and he is vying to become the first player at his position to average .300 over his career since 1950.

In the twilight of his career, Barry Larkin hopes to stay injury free in order to boost his career totals and eventually impress Hall of Fame voters. And unlike many other players of his era, if he does get the coveted call, he certainly won't have to concern himself with which team's hat to wear during the induction ceremony.

Top 5 MVP Vote-Getters

1. Barry Larkin, Cincinnati — 281
2. Dante Bichette, Colorado — 251
3. Greg Maddux, Atlanta — 249
4. Mike Piazza, Los Angeles — 214
5. Eric Karros, Los Angeles — 135

1995 AMERICAN LEAGUE — MO VAUGHN

Maurice Samuel Vaughn
B. December 15, 1967, Norwalk, Connecticut

Year	Team	Games	AB	Hits	Avg.	HR	RBI	Runs	SB
1995	Bos AL	140	550	165	.300	39	126	98	11

The Season

If there was one thing that baseball needed in 1995 to recapture its fans' hearts, it was a touching yet profound human interest story. Fortunately for baseball, Cal Ripken, Jr. was there to provide it. Of course, he was always there, and his presence in the Baltimore lineup, day after day and season after season, is what made this great moment possible.

By ignoring everything from nagging discomfort to searing pain over the course of 14 seasons, Ripken shattered what was long considered an unbreakable record — Lou Gehrig's consecutive games played streak. On September 6, the new Iron Man played in his 2,131st straight game, belting a home run in a 4–2 victory over California to make it a perfect night. Basking in the glow of a 22-minute ovation, Ripken trotted out a victory lap while shaking hands with fans and opponents alike prior to the bottom of the fifth inning when the game became official.

Although the National League won the World Series, it was also a magical season for both the Cleveland Indians and Seattle Mariners. Making its first post-season appearance in 41 years, Cleveland won the American League Central Division by a record-30 games, while Seattle claimed its first West Division crown in its 19-year existence by winning a one-game playoff against California. The Indians then swept East Division champion Boston in a Division Series, with Eddie Murray batting .385. The Mariners edged Wild Card entry New York 3–2 in the other Division Series, thanks in large part to Ken Griffey, Jr. (five homers), Edgar Martinez (.571, 10 RBIs) and Cy Young Award winner Randy Johnson (2–0, 16 strikeouts).

Cleveland cut Seattle's dream season short with a 4–2 League Championship Series victory on the strength of Orel Hershiser (2–0, 1.29 ERA), Carlos Baerga (.400, four RBIs) and Kenny Lofton (.458, five stolen bases). Seattle's Jay Buhner, who had hit .458 in the Division Series, slammed three homers in the LCS.

While their milestones did not gain the fanfare of Ripken's, Albert Belle of Cleveland became the first player ever with 50 home runs and 50 doubles in the same season, while teammate Murray collected his 3,000th career hit. Belle's 377 total bases were the most in the major leagues since 1986, despite a season shortened to 144 games.

Chicago and Detroit touched a few bases in a May 28 game, setting a major league record by combining for 12 home runs (seven by the Tigers) in a 14–12 White Sox win. Seattle's Johnson, on the other hand, kept runners off base by producing the best winning percentage (.900, 18–2) in the AL since 1937.

Finally, the Bells joined the Boones as the only three-generation families in big league history when David Bell made his major league debut for Cleveland May 3. Father Buddy Bell and grandfather Gus Bell played for four organizations each over 18 and 15 years, respectively. Gus passed away four days after David's debut.

Hit or Be Hit

No one would have the nerve to tell 6-foot-1, 268-pound Mo Vaughn that he swings like his mother, but if he ever heard such a remark, he'd probably respond by saying, "Thanks for the compliment." Many major league

ballplayers through the years have attributed some of their success to devoted fathers who played ball with them at every opportunity, and while Maurice Samuel also had such a dad, it was mom who taught him how to smack the horsehide with the hickory.

A former standout softball player, Shirley Vaughn used her skills as a hitter and teacher to show Mo how to bat from the left side while he was growing up in Norwalk, Connecticut. This was truly a family affair, however, as sisters Donna and Catherine would chase down the baseballs Mo sent hurtling to all parts of the neighborhood. Hoping to save his neighbors' windows and improve his son's batting eye, father Leroy — a former semipro football player — constructed a backyard device with 20 baseballs hanging on the ends of ropes that Mo would pound into submission regularly. Leroy also used an old Knute Rockne trick by making his son dance by himself to better coordinate his feet as they grew to gargantuan size early on.

"Bigfoot" was soon terrorizing opponents in baseball, football and basketball at Trinity Pawling Prep school in Pawling, New York, before his 1986 graduation. Then it was the Seton Hall University rivals' turn to take abuse from the huge left-handed slugger, who set a school single-season freshman record with 28 home runs. Over three years with the Pirates, Vaughn batted .417 with school records in homers (57) and RBIs (218).

The big-chested thumper was selected in the first round (23rd pick overall) of the 1989 free agent draft by the Boston Red Sox and assigned to Double A New Britain, where he hit .278 with eight home runs in 73 games. Vaughn enjoyed a splendid season at Triple A Pawtucket in 1990, slamming

22 round-trippers, driving in 72 runs and hitting .295 in 108 games. The first baseman began the '91 season at Pawtucket, then made his major league debut in June, providing a taste of things to come by blasting a 438-foot shot at Baltimore for his first big league circuit clout. He started the 1992 season in Boston, homering in his first two games of the campaign, but wound up splitting his time between Beantown and Pawtucket.

Vaughn made it to the show for good in 1993, demonstrating why he belonged with 29 homers, 101 RBIs, a .297 batting average, .525 slugging mark and .395 on-base percentage. Boston was fifth in the Eastern Division in '93, moving up a notch in the revamped division in 1994 when Vaughn led the Red Sox in batting (.310) and hits (122), belted 26 homers, slugged at a .576 clip, led the league in intentional walks (20) and tied a major league record with two doubles in one inning. He was hampered by left knee and hamstring problems over the last two months of the season, and underwent arthroscopic surgery in late October.

Apparently the surgery was just what the doctor ordered, because Mo came out with a vengeance in 1995. He paced the Sox in virtually every important offensive category, including RBIs (126, tied for first in the league), homers (39, tied for fourth), extra base hits (70, fifth), total bases (316, fifth), slugging (.575, sixth) and hits (165). The first-time All Star even stole a career-high 11 bases in 15 attempts and legged out three triples.

Fortunately for Mo, MVP voting was conducted prior to the post-season. Boston won the East by seven games over New York, but his big bat went silent in a three-game sweep at the hands of the Indians in an AL Division Series. Vaughn went 0-for-14 with seven strikeouts. In November, it was announced that he had garnered 12 first-place votes to narrowly defeat Cleveland's Albert Belle for the Most Valuable Player award.

It was a fitting tribute for the man who while only 27 years of age, was giving so much back to the community that embraced him more lovingly than any black athlete before him. Vaughn once said that a number of African American athletes frequently asked him how he could stay in an area not known for its ethnic tolerance, and while he did eventually leave as a free agent, it wasn't before he'd spent eight years serving both the ballclub and the area's youth.

Instead of taking for granted his healthy, family-oriented upbringing, Vaughn repeatedly reached out to those whose beginnings in life were much less stable. In addition to his Mo Vaughn Youth Development Program, Vaughn stayed visible in Boston through numerous charity fund-raisers and youth-oriented programs, conveying the importance of establishing character and self-esteem. Liberal in his thinking regarding the black man's plight in society, yet conservative in his work-ethic methods of problem solving, Mo was respected and admired in the town where he lived year-round.

The only on-field flaws that have tainted Vaughn's superstar status throughout his career have been a propensity to strike out and a less than golden glove. Vaughn has whiffed approximately once every four at-bats through his 10 years in the majors, including 181 times in 2000 to establish the dubious all-time, single-season, major league mark for a left-handed batter. Crowding the plate has taken its toll on Mo's body, as he approaches the 100-mark in being hit by pitches.

Vaughn's stick came back to life in 1996 when he enjoyed a season clearly superior to his '95 MVP campaign. He batted .326 with 44 home runs, 143 RBIs, 118 runs, 207 hits and a .583 slugging percentage — all career highs at the time — to place fifth in the balloting as the Red Sox slipped to third place in the East. The big portside swinger became the first major league player since Jim Rice (1978) to collect 40-plus homers and 200-plus hits in the same season, and started in the All-Star Game for the first time, contributing a double.

Starting every game but one, he fashioned a 16-game hitting streak in '96, posted his first career three-homer game, was named AL Player of the Month in May and became the first Red Sox player to win the Thomas A. Yawkey Award (team MVP) for a fourth consecutive season. His round-tripper total tied for third all-time in Red Sox history, while his RBI mark tied for seventh.

Vaughn had stayed off the disabled list for the first six years of his career, but that ended in 1997 when he tore the lateral meniscus in his left knee in June. He still managed to crank out 35 homers and drive in 96 runs while finishing fifth in the junior circuit in on-base percentage (.422).

In what would turn out to be his final season in Boston, Mo produced another stellar effort in 1998, becoming the third player in Red Sox history with more than one 40-homer season and with four consecutive 30-homer campaigns. He reached the 200-hit mark for the second time in his career, and posted career bests in batting (.337, second in the AL) and slugging (.591). His 205 hits were runner-up in the league and his 360 total bases were fifth. Tying for fourth in the MVP voting, Vaughn led the team in home runs for the sixth consecutive year, then excelled in Boston's 3–1 Division Series loss to Cleveland by batting .412 with two homers and seven RBIs.

Even if Mo's ties to the Boston community had not been so strong, his defection to the Anaheim Angels via free agency in 1999 would have been a huge disappointment to Red Sox fans. But his enormous popularity — gained over the years in large part to the class and grace he displayed off the field — made it that much more difficult to stomach. And as if fate itself was offended by his departure, Vaughn injured his left ankle in the first inning of his first regular-season game as an Angel while chasing a pop foul.

The sprained ligaments and bone bruise put him on the disabled list, but he came back to power 33 home runs and drive in 108 runs (both among the top eight totals in Angels history). Vaughn split time between first base and designated hitter, and while his average (.281) was his lowest in seven years, he was very effective in the clutch, batting .343 with runners in scoring position and .388 with runners in scoring position and two outs. All this did little to inspire his teammates, however, as the Halos finished last in the West, 25 games out.

The Angels put on a power fest in 2000, setting a franchise record for home runs (236), but 62 percent of those dingers came with the bases empty, and Anaheim placed third. Playing in all but one game, Vaughn's 36 home runs helped the Angels become the first team in American League history to boast four players with 30-plus homers. His 117 RBIs made him the second player in franchise annals with consecutive 100-plus RBI seasons, and his homer total made him the third player with back-to-back 30-homer seasons.

Still wearing uniform No. 42 in honor of Jackie Robinson, the bald-shaven and earring-wearing first sacker and DH was looking forward to another exceptional season in 2001, but fate reared its ugly head again. In February, he had surgery to repair a distal biceps tendon rupture in his left arm — the result of a late-season swing in 2000 — and missed the entire campaign.

Despite having signed a six-year, $80 million contract with the Angels prior to the 1991 season, Mo caused waves following the 2001 campaign by saying that he'd like to play for Boston again. Right coast, wrong team. The Red Sox did not express interest in bringing him back, but the New York Mets traded pitcher Kevin Appier for Vaughn late in 2001, putting him in the National League for the first time.

Vaughn was anxious to get back into the swing of things with the Mets as the 2002 season approached, with a few career milestones in sight, including 1,500 hits, 300 home runs and 1,000 RBIs. Not bad for a guy who's unafraid to admit he swings like his mother.

Top 5 MVP Vote-Getters

1. Mo Vaughn, Boston — 308
2. Albert Belle, Cleveland — 300
3. Edgar Martinez, Seattle — 244
4. Jose Mesa, Cleveland — 130
5. Jay Buhner, Seattle — 120

1996 NATIONAL LEAGUE—KEN CAMINITI

Kenneth Gene Caminiti
B. April 21, 1963, Hanford, California

Year	Team	Games	AB	Hits	Avg.	HR	RBI	Runs	SB
1996	SD NL	146	546	178	.326	40	130	109	11

The Season

The Atlanta Braves once again proved to be the best team in the National League, claiming their fifth consecutive division title (not including the 1994 strike season), by eight games over Montreal, breezing through a Division Series over Wild Card Los Angeles and outlasting St. Louis in the League Championship Series before bowing to the Yankees in the World Series.

While some players ran hot and cold, Atlanta pitcher John Smoltz was a mainstay throughout the regular season and post-season. The Cy Young Award winner led the senior circuit in wins (24), strikeouts (276), winning percentage, innings pitched and opponents' on-base percentage during the season. The right-hander then with a 1.00 earned run aver-age in the Division Series sweep, 2–0 with a 1.20 ERA and 12 strikeouts in the 4–3 NLCS triumph, and 1–1 with a 0.64 ERA and 14 whiffs in the 4–2 World Series defeat.

The Cardinals, under new manager Tony LaRussa, rebounded from 19 games under .500 the previous season to win the Central Division by six games over Houston. St. Louis swept San Diego — a West Division winner for the first time since 1984 — in the other Division Series, with Ron Gant batting .400 with four RBIs. But the Cards went flat at the wrong time. Leading the NLCS three games to one, St. Louis was outscored 32–1 over the final three games as Javy Lopez (.542, two homers, six RBIs) and the Braves stormed back. Atlanta's Andruw Jones became the youngest player (19½) to hit a home run in a World Series game, smacking two in a 12–1 Braves win in Game 1.

In the first full season following two campaigns shortened by the strike, several individuals posted stats that had not been seen for quite a while. Lance Johnson of New York legged out 21 triples, the most in the NL since 1930, and collected 227 hits, the best league mark in 23 years; San Francisco's Barry Bonds walked 151 times, the highest major league total in 40 years and the top mark ever in the NL; Colorado's Andres Galarraga drove in 150 runs, the most impressive big league figure in 34 years; Ellis Burks of Colorado accumulated 392 total bases, which had not been accomplished in the league since 1959; and Florida's Gary Sheffield had the highest NL on-base percentage (.469) since 1975.

The Dodgers may not have won a post-season game, but they had a very interesting year. Todd Hollandsworth became the fifth consecutive Dodger to earn Rookie of the Year honors, Hideo Nomo fired a no-hitter September 17 against the Rockies in hitter-heaven Coors Field and 20-plus-year manager Tommy Lasorda retired July 29 following a heart attack and angioplasty surgery.

Over on the other coast, New York's Todd Hundley broke three-time MVP Roy Campanella's single-season major league record for home runs by a catcher with 41. And down south, Major League Baseball played its first official game in Mexico, with San Diego outslugging the Mets 15–10 August 16. An apparent conflict with the Republican National Convention was the cause for the relocation.

The Survivor

What a long, strange trip it's been for Ken Caminiti. Undoubtedly grateful that he's not dead following battles with alcoholism, a painkiller addiction, a crack cocaine bust, a smokeless tobacco habit and a myriad of injuries that include a broken back, the gritty third baseman is a survivor who has kept on truckin' while continuing to produce on the ballfield as he approaches 40 years of age.

In 2001, the hobbled warrior latched on with Atlanta in mid-season after a brief stint with the Texas Rangers that featured yet another visit to the disabled list. Caminiti had already performed admirably for Houston in two tours of duty totaling 10 years prior to joining the Rangers in 2001, but his glory days were from 1995 to '98 when he was the driving force on the Padres' two division-winning clubs. Many players have worn the San Diego uniform in far more games than Caminiti, yet the switch-hitter was among the all-time top 10 players in franchise history in seven categories when he left following the 1998 campaign: batting average (.295), home runs (121), extra base hits (250), RBIs (396), doubles (127), runs (362) and total bases (1,086).

Ken had never hit more than 18 home runs in a season for the Astros through his initial eight-year tenure with the club, but following an off-sea-

Ken Caminiti. (Courtesy San Diego Padres.)

son trade to San Diego, he bulked up prior to the 1995 campaign with what he said was a conditioning program and found his power stroke. Caminiti blasted 26, 40, 26 and 29 homers in his four years with the Padres, reaching 90-plus RBIs in three of those seasons and batting .300 or better twice.

It's fair to say that Caminiti came into his own in 1995 following a series of decent but unspectacular years with the Astros. In his ninth season, he posted then-career bests in home runs (26), batting (.302), hits (159), RBIs (94), doubles (33), walks (69) and stolen bases (12), placing among the top 10 NL hitters in six offensive departments. Finishing third in the West Division, the Padres were led in almost every offensive category by the third sacker, who earned his first Gold Glove and led the National League in assists, double plays and total chances at his position.

It was also in 1995 that Caminiti became known for an unusual feat: belting a home run from both sides of the plate in the same game. In fact, he set a major league record by doing it in consecutive games (September 16 and 17). If that wasn't enough, two days later he turned the trick for the third time in four games. He is tied with Mickey Mantle and Chili Davis for second place all time in this unique category with 10, the career leader being Eddie Murray with 11. Caminiti holds the NL record for most homers by a switch-hitter in two consecutive seasons (66).

If Houston was having any regrets for including Caminiti in an 11-player deal following the 1994 season, that remorse intensified during the 1996 campaign when he became only the fourth unanimous selection for the senior circuit's Most Valuable Player award, and the first-ever Padre MVP. "The Gun" clobbered 40 home runs— second most in San Diego history — drove in a franchise-high 130 runs to tie Mantle's 1956 record for a switch-hitter, and posted an all-time club-best .621 slugging average. His 40 circuit clouts made him the third switch-hitter ever to reach that mark.

Ken wound up third in the league in RBIs and slugging, fifth in total bases (339), tied for fifth in both homers and extra base hits (79), sixth in batting (.326), tied for seventh in on-base percentage (.408) and tied for first in sacrifice flies (10). He set a single-season, major league record for most games with switch-hit homers (four, including three in August), earned NL Player of the Month accolades in both August and September, and became only the third hot corner man ever — and the first in 43 years— to hit .300 with 40 round-trippers and 130 ribbies.

The Padres, who claimed their first division title since 1984, were swept by St. Louis in a Division Series, but Caminiti smacked three home runs with the same number of runs and RBIs while batting .300. All this plus a second consecutive Gold Glove, despite being bothered by a wide variety of ailments, including an abdominal strain, groin and hamstring pulls,

chronic pain in his back, a partly torn biceps tendon and a left elbow injury that resulted in surgery following the season. In an August game against the Mets in Mexico, he ripped two homers after conquering dehydration and nausea.

The 1997 season saw the third baseman voted to start in the All-Star Game for the first time (his third All-Star appearance overall), and the honor must have pumped him up because he hit .331 with 20 homers and 55 RBIs in the second half. The clutch hitter batted .444 with the bases loaded and .345 with a runner at third base. He became the first NL third baseman since 1984 to win three Gold Gloves in a row, batted .290, bopped 26 homers and drove in 90 runs, but San Diego plummeted to last in the West.

In his final season in San Diego, Caminiti shot out of the gate with five homers and 12 RBIs in an eight-day stretch in April, and enjoyed a three-homer game in July. His 29 homers and 82 RBIs were both runner-up on the club for the year. The Padres cruised to the West title in 1998, won a Division Series over Houston and defeated Atlanta in the NLCS before bowing to the Yankees in the World Series. Ken struggled with .143 averages in the first and third of those series, but had two home runs, four RBIs and five walks in the LCS. In November, he signed as a free agent with Houston.

Caminiti made the move at the right time, as Houston won the Central Division in 1999. He came back from a lengthy stay on the DL with a torn calf muscle to hit .471 with three homers and eight RBIs in the Division Series loss to the Braves. Later that fall, he fractured three bones in his lower back from a fall during a Texas hunting expedition. He was on his way to a very productive 2000 season for the Astros (.303, 15 homers, 45 RBIs through 59 games), but a ruptured tendon in his right wrist ended his year in June. He admitted to a relapse with alcohol abuse, and underwent evaluation for chemical dependency. In 2001, he batted .228 with 15 homers for Texas and Atlanta, then went hitless in two Division Series pinch-hitting appearances before being left off the Braves' NLCS

roster. One month later, he filed for free agency, then was arrested on crack cocaine possession charges. In 2002, he admitted to using steroids during his 1996 MVP season.

Born in Hanford, California, Caminiti was a star at San Jose State University, batting .327 with a school-record 29 doubles over two years and being named a second team All-America by The Sporting News in 1984. He was chosen by the Astros in the third round of the June '84 free agent draft, then tried out for, but did not make, the U.S. Olympic Team. That didn't deter the 22-year-old third baseman, who was a Florida State League All-Star in '85 after batting .284 with 73 RBIs for Osceola. In 1986, Ken hit .300 with 82 RBIs to help Double A Columbus capture the Southern League crown, and in '87, he earned a berth on the league All-Star team with a .325 mark before being called up to the Astros.

In his major league debut, the 6-foot, 200-pounder tripled and homered, scoring the game-winning run in the bottom of the ninth inning. In fact, Caminiti claimed NL Player of the Week honors in his first big league week, batting .500 with two homers and three RBIs in his first four games. He began the 1988 campaign at Triple A Tucson, then was brought back up to the big club for good in July.

Caminiti's first full season in the majors was impressive. In 1989, he hit safely in 22 of his first 28 games; led the Astros in games, at-bats and doubles (31); and placed second in RBIs (72), runs (71) and hits (149). Baseball America called him the infielder with the best-throwing arm in the league after he placed second in putouts and assists, and third in fielding. His ascension in the professional ranks had been steady, but he fell back in 1990 with a .242 average, nearly 100 strikeouts, only four home runs and 51 RBIs despite playing in 153 games.

He boosted those totals in 1991 while continuing to play a solid third base, then rallied to bat a team-high .294 in '92 and score a then-career high 75 runs in '93. Ironically, it was a separated shoulder in 1992 that Caminiti credited with his improvement from the left side of the plate because it forced him to stop trying to always pull the ball. He cranked out 18 home runs during the strike-shortened 1994 season, put together a 14-game hitting streak, placed second among league third basemen in fielding and earned his first All-Star berth. Following the season, Houston traded Caminiti to San Diego with four other players, including Steve Finley and Andujar Cedeno, for six players, including Derek Bell and Ricky Gutierrez.

Caminiti, who is among the top 10 in five offensive categories in Astro franchise history, has battled a variety of demons throughout his career, but has survived each time. The man who rebuilds cars for show and has the names of his three daughters tattooed on his chest, would love nothing better than to go out on his own terms. That would include contributing to another division title and finally earning that elusive World Series ring.

Top 5 MVP Vote-Getters

1. Ken Caminiti, San Diego—392
2. Mike Piazza, Los Angeles—237
3. Ellis Burks, Colorado—186
4. Chipper Jones, Atlanta—158
5. Barry Bonds, San Francisco—132

1996 AMERICAN LEAGUE—JUAN GONZALEZ

Juan Alberto (Vazquez) Gonzalez
B. October 20, 1969, Arecibo, Puerto Rico

Year	Team	Games	AB	Hits	Avg.	HR	RBI	Runs	SB
1996	Tex AL	134	541	170	.314	47	144	89	2

The Season

Major League Baseball remained in image-shaping mode in 1996 following two seasons affected by a strike, and up until late September, the plan was working pretty well. Two long-time stars—Eddie Murray and Paul Molitor—collected their 500th home run and 3,000th hit, respectively; 1986 MVP Roger Clemens tied his major league record with 20 strikeouts in a game; Dwight Gooden's comeback effort featured a no-hitter against Seattle; races in two of the three divisions were close; and the Wild Card competition was fierce.

But then Roberto Alomar went and acted like a 12-year-old, forgetting that his saliva belonged inside his mouth, while a real 12-year-old—fan Jeff Maier—tried to act like a major league ballplayer, forgetting that his glove belonged outside the playing field.

In a fit of rage during a September 27 argument, Alomar spit in umpire John Hirschbeck's face. With his five-game suspension appealed, the Baltimore second baseman homered

the next night to clinch the Wild Card berth for the Orioles. Only a court order kept the umpires from striking the Orioles-Indians Division Series, in which Baltimore used the bats of B.J. Surhoff (.385, three homers, five RBIs), Cal Ripken, Jr. (.444), Bobby Bonilla and Brady Anderson (combined four homers, nine RBIs), and the arm of Armando Benitez (two wins) to upset the Central Division champions three games to one.

Over in the other ALDS, Juan Gonzalez was belting everything in sight (five home runs, nine RBIs) for West Division champ Texas, but New York took the series 3–1, thanks to a bullpen that allowed only one earned run in nearly 20 innings of work, and the sticks of Rookie of the Year Derek Jeter (.412), Bernie Williams (.467, three home runs, five ribbies) and Cecil Fielder (.364, four RBIs).

The Yankees then earned their first pennant since 1981 with a little help from Maier, who reached over the wall and drew in Jeter's deep fly to right in Game 1 of the American League Championship Series. New York went on to defeat the O's 5–4 in that

game, and took the series four games to one, thanks to three wins at Camden Yards where the Yanks were 9–0 for the season. Series MVP Williams batted .474 with a pair of round-trippers and six runs batted in, Darryl Strawberry hit .417 with three homers and five RBIs, and Fielder contributed two circuit clouts and eight RBIs.

The Atlanta Braves outscored the Yankees 16–1 in the first two games of the World Series, but New York bounced back to win the next four games and claim its first World Championship since 1978. John Wetteland posted four saves for the winners, while Fielder batted .391.

Individual highlights during the season included Alex Rodriguez of Seattle scoring 141 runs, the most in the league since 1985, and accumulating 379 total bases, the highest AL total since '86; Oakland's Mark McGwire slugging at a .730 clip, the best AL mark in 39 years, and tagging 52 homers, the most in the majors since 1977 and the highest junior circuit total since 1961; and Albert Belle of Cleveland driving in 148 runs for the best league effort since 1949.

Juan Gonzalez. (Courtesy George Brace Photo.)

Coming to an end were Kirby Puckett's career and a Ripken streak. Puckett announced his retirement July 12 after the veteran Minnesota outfielder and eventual Hall of Famer damaged his retina, while Ripken's 2,216 consecutive games streak of starting at shortstop concluded when he started a July 15 game at third base.

Icon with Deep Roots

"Igor, Igor," the adoring throngs chant when they see his car approaching. They rush toward him at full tilt, desperately hoping for a close-up look at their fabled hero, some with aspirations of actually touching this legend, or perhaps being on the receiving end of his famous smile.

Juan Gonzalez is an icon in Puerto Rico, where he returns during each off-season to live with his family. After he beat out Mark McGwire for the American League home run title on the final day of the 1992 season, he was greeted by 5,000 screaming fans at the San Juan airport. Fifteen police officers on motorcycles were needed to escort him to his Vega Baja home, more than 100,000 admirers lined Baldorioty Expressway to watch the motorcade pass and another 3,000 were awaiting his arrival in the main plaza near his home.

Locals say that nothing close to this type of hero worship has been observed since the days when Puerto Rico native Roberto Clemente would return after yet another exceptional season of playing baseball in the United States.

Why is Gonzalez so popular in his homeland? First and foremost is the huge amount of success he has enjoyed and the acclaim he has received for his abilities on the diamond. The big right-handed slugger has been blasting baseballs in and out of American League ballparks since 1989, most notably for the Texas Rangers and Cleveland Indians. Through the 2001 season, he had accumulated 397 home runs and driven in 1,282 runs while maintaining an impressive batting average (.297) for a long ball hitter.

But nearly as important to the fervor surrounding Juan is his intense love for the people of this land, demonstrated through his generous gifts and annual pilgrimages back to his roots. He has been known to pay the utility bills and prescription costs for some of the poor in Alto de Cuba, and his annual Christmas party brings joy to a number of people who otherwise might have empty stockings. Many professional athletes establish charitable foundations benefiting the unfortunate, but how many return to live among the poverty-stricken with whom they might have grown up? Former Rangers teammate Ivan Rodriguez is also a huge hero in Puerto Rico, but even he chooses not to venture into the crime-ridden area where Gonzalez walks the streets.

These are the same types of streets as those in Alto de Cuba where little Juan would use a broomstick for a bat and a bottlecap for a ball, running the imaginary bases in full view of very real drug dealers and prostitutes. His father, a high school math teacher, saved enough money to move the family across Highway 2 to a somewhat safer neighborhood when Juan was 13 years old. When he could scrounge up enough pennies to buy candy, he'd use the tiny brown paper bags as boxing gloves to emulate professional boxers, but his real passion was for a professional wrestler named The Mighty Igor. That's how Juan acquired the nickname that his Puerto Rican devotees use when serenading him. Many of those same shops where Juan once purchased gum and candy now feature shrines to the Zeus-like icon, who along with wife Jackie named their firstborn son Juan Igor Gonzalez.

Eventually, Juan traded his broomstick for a real bat, and began showing signs at an early age of an incredible talent about to be unwrapped. At 16, he received a $75,000 bonus while being signed by Rangers scout Luis Rosa. He topped the Gulf Coast League in at-bats and tied for third in RBIs at Sarasota in 1986 before graduating from Vega Baja High School in 1987, then was named to the South Atlantic League All-Star Team while playing for Class A Gastonia. In 1988, torn cartilage in his left knee and subsequent arthroscopic surgery limited Gonzalez to 77 games at Class A Charlotte, but he rebounded the following season by leading the Double A Texas League in total bases and placing among the top four in home runs, hits and slugging, claiming both mid- and post-season All-Star honors while at Tulsa.

Gonzalez struggled in his initial big league stint with the Rangers at the tail end of the 1989 season, then earned the franchise's Minor League Player of the Year award and the American Association's MVP and Rookie of the Year laurels in 1990 while at Triple A Oklahoma City. Another slow start in the majors later that year was offset by a hot streak which gave him a .289 average over 25 games.

There wasn't much left for Gonzalez to prove on the minor league level, so the Rangers threw him into the fray in 1991 following another knee surgery. He responded by leading Texas in home runs (27) and placing second in RBIs (102) in his first full season, appearing in 142 games, the majority in center field. The Rangers slipped from third place to fourth in 1992, but couldn't lay the blame at their 22-year-old star's feet. Gonzalez smacked 43 homers to lead the league, placing third in total bases (309), fourth in extra base hits (69), fifth in slugging (.529) and seventh in RBIs (109). The well-sculpted 6-foot-3, 210-pounder was displaying power beyond his years. He became the sixth player ever to hit 40-plus home runs in a season prior to his 23rd birthday, and was the youngest to produce a three-homer game in more than 20 years.

Having cracked 75 round-trippers in just over two full seasons, Igor was pitched carefully by AL hurlers in 1993. But it didn't matter. He still muscled 46 offerings over the fences to lead the junior circuit for the second consecutive season, and posted his first .300 batting average (.310) to boot. His slugging average (.632) was No. 1 in the league, his 339 total bases second, his 80 extra base hits tied for second and his 118 RBIs fourth. At 23 years and 11 months, Gonzalez became the second youngest player ever with back-to-back 40-homer seasons, and the sixth youngest to reach 100-plus RBIs three times. The second Ranger to earn the team's Triple Crown (highest average, home runs and RBIs) was named to the AL All-Star Team for the first time — winning the home run hitting contest the day before — and finished fourth in the league MVP voting, as Texas rose to second place.

The Rangers were first in the West Division when play was halted by the players' strike in 1994, and although he played well in left field with only two errors in 234 total chances (career-best .991 fielding average), Gonzalez saw his batting average dip 35 points. The news got worse in 1995 when a herniated disk in his lower back caused him to miss 33 games. Limited to designated hitter duty for most of the season, and placed on the disabled list again in August with a bone spur in his neck, he still managed to hit .295, rip 27 home runs (second among DHs) and drive in 82 runs, including an RBI every 3.8 at-bats, second best in the majors. One of those dingers was his all-time club-record 154th.

Texas had finished third in the West in '95, but claimed the division crown in 1996 by 4½ games over Seattle, thanks in large part to a phenomenal season from Gonzalez, who earned the AL Most Valuable Player award by three points over Seattle's Alex Rodriguez in the second-closest league voting ever. Juan was an absolute terror at the plate, blasting a career-high 47 homers and collecting 348 total bases, both fifth in the league. He placed runner-up in the circuit in RBIs (144) and slugging (.643), and was fourth in extra base hits (82), despite missing 28 games with a partial tear of his left quadriceps muscle.

Yet another outfield move — from left to right — did not break his concentration either in the field (only two errors in 171 total chances) or at the plate, where he put together a pair of career-best 21-game hitting streaks. The AL July Player of the Month tied a major league record for home runs that month with 15, collecting the most RBIs (38) in any month by an AL player since 1983. He set single-season, Texas Rangers franchise records for homers, runs batted in, slugging, total bases and extra base hits; posted the best RBI-per-game ratio (1.07) in baseball since Jimmie Foxx's 1.17 mark in 1938; and tied Jeff Burroughs' 1974 club record with 28 RBIs in August.

The Rangers were no match for the New York Yankees in an AL Division Series, falling three games to one, but Gonzalez did everything he could to keep his team competitive. He hit a scintillating .438 in the series with five home runs among his seven hits, and added nine RBIs, five runs and three walks. He became only the second player ever to hit at least one home run in four consecutive games of a single post-season series, tied the record for total bases (22) in a four-game post-season series and accumulated a 1.375 slugging percentage to tie for the second highest in a playoff series.

The thought of a 27-year-old slugger about to enter his prime with more than 200 home runs and 650 RBIs already under his belt was a scary one for American League pitchers, and Juan Gonzalez was just about to fulfill those nightmares, including the fashioning of another MVP campaign only two years later.

Top 5 MVP Vote-Getters

1. Juan Gonzalez, Texas — 290
2. Alex Rodriguez, Seattle — 287
3. Albert Belle, Cleveland — 228
4. Ken Griffey, Jr., Seattle — 188
5. Mo Vaughn, Boston — 124

1997 National League — Larry Walker

Larry Kenneth Robert Walker
B. December 1, 1966, Maple Ridge, British Columbia, Canada

Year	Team	Games	AB	Hits	Avg.	HR	RBI	Runs	SB
1997	Col NL	153	568	208	.366	49	130	143	33

The Season

A fifth-year expansion team, the Florida Marlins finished nine games behind Atlanta in the East Division and were outscored and outhit in two of their three post-season series. But they still managed to win the World Series and bring an unlikely championship to south Florida.

Boasting 101 wins and the best ERA in the major leagues (3.19), the Braves captured a division title for an unprecedented sixth consecutive time (not including the strike-shortened 1994 season). They manhandled Central Division-winning Houston 3–0 in one National League Division Series, while Wild Card entry Florida whipped Western Division champ San Francisco 3–0 in the other.

Atlanta outscored the Marlins 21–20, outhit them 49–36 and out-homered them 6–1 in the League Championship Series, but Florida prevailed in six games. Moises Alou and Charles Johnson batted a combined .094 for the Marlins, but drove in half of their team's runs with clutch hitting. Kevin Brown and Livan Hernandez both won a pair of games for Florida.

The Marlins were then outscored 44–37 and outhit 72–68 in the World Series, but outlasted the Cleveland Indians 4–3 to become the first expansion franchise to win a fall classic in only its fifth season. The second-longest Game 7 of a World Series ended with a bases-loaded, 11th-inning single by Edgar Renteria. Series MVP Hernandez posted two wins, Alou hit three home runs and drove in nine, and Johnson batted .357. For Cleveland, Sandy Alomar hit .367 with 10 RBIs and Chad Ogea won a pair of games.

In honor of the 50th anniversary of Jackie Robinson breaking the color barrier, acting commissioner Bud Selig declared that uniform No. 42 would be retired in perpetuity for every team, although players currently wearing that number could continue to do so.

Showing signs of even greater things to come, Mark McGwire tied Jimmie Foxx for the most home runs (58) in a season by a right-handed hitter after being obtained by St. Louis from Oakland July 31. Astro Craig Biggio's 146 runs were the top NL total since 1932, Expo Mark Grudzielanek's 54 doubles were the most in the league since 1937, Johnson of Florida became the first catcher in history to go an entire season errorless, Andres Galarraga of Colorado led the senior circuit in RBIs (140) for the second year in a row and Scott Rolen of Philadelphia was a unanimous Rookie of the Year selection.

Pitchers were in the limelight as well in 1997. Phil Niekro was elected to the Hall of Fame 10 years after retiring; Florida's Brown tossed a no-hitter at San Francisco June 10; Pittsburgh teammates Francisco Cordova and Ricardo Rincon combined for a 10-inning no-hitter against Houston; Curt Schilling of Philadelphia struck out 319, the most in baseball in 20 years and the top mark in the NL since 1965; and San Francisco's Julian Tavarez appeared in 89 games, the most in the majors in 10 seasons.

Icing the Competition

How good of a hitter is Larry Walker? Well, consider that he rattled off a 20-game hitting streak in May 1998 — batting an impressive .342 during the stretch — but saw his average fall, from .350 to .347.

Walker has been swinging a piece of wood in front of rapidly moving objects with great precision for nearly as long as he can remember. The Maple Ridge, British Columbia, native grew up idolizing New York Islanders goalie Billy Smith, and served as a young netminder for teams that included eventual Boston Bruins All-Star Cam Neely. Larry's dream of making it to the National Hockey League never materialized, but fate had other plans. The superstitious athlete's raw skills were ultimately honed on the baseball diamond, where he has become a big-time star for the Colorado Rockies after performing well for the Montreal Expos.

That 1998 season was key for Walker, who was coming off a 1997 campaign in which he'd won the National League Most Valuable Player award with a batting average (.366) so far above his career mark (.285 prior to '97) that many couldn't help but think it was a fluke. But the left-handed hitting outfielder not only won the batting title in 1998, his .363 average was nine points higher than that of his closet competitor.

Although Colorado finished in fourth place, 21 games out, Walker became only the third player in the past 60 years to hit .360 or better in two consecutive seasons, and the first Canadian-born player in the 20th century to earn a batting crown. (Tip O'Neill of St. Louis won the American Association batting title in 1887.) Walker finished third in slugging (.630) and on-base percentage (.446), fourth in doubles (46, tying a career high), and eighth in runs (113) while making his third All-Star Team and claiming his fourth Gold Glove.

He hit .350 or better against eight NL clubs, and batted .528 during September. His .402 batting average following the All-Star break was the best in the league, and he also slugged at a .699 clip in the second half. The only personal disappointments in '98 were a home run total (23) less than half of his MVP season, and only 67 RBIs. He was limited to 130 games due to one stint on the disabled list with an elbow problem, back spasms and a sprained finger. Still, Walker's .333 average over five seasons (1994–98) was third highest in the majors.

The Rockies fell even further in 1999, placing fifth in the West Division, despite Walker's continuing incredible hitting demonstrations. After signing a six-year contract extension, he put together a 21-game hitting streak from late April through late May, batting .506 in the process, then added an 18-game streak later in the season. Topping his previous two seasons' batting averages was considered virtually impossible, but he did it with a phenomenal .379 mark that led the league and was the fifth highest average in 58 years. His .461 average at home is believed to be a major league record. Injuries kept him out of 35 games and eventually resulted in knee surgery, but he cranked out 37 home runs and drove in 115 runs, placed first in slugging (.710) and on-base percentage (.464), earned his fifth Gold Glove, and made his fourth All-Star Team. Walker was the first player to win the percentage Triple Crown (batting, slugging, on-base) since 1980, and the first NL player to do it since 1948.

The injury bug bit again in 2000, this time more severely. He missed 23 games due to a stress reaction irritation in his right elbow, and eventually went on the 60-day DL with inflammation that required surgery. The elbow problems dropped his home run total to nine, but he still posted a .309 average — hitting .391 with runners in scoring position and .359 at home — and led his team in outfield assists (10). "Walk" became the all-time Canadian-born leader this season in both hits and RBIs, and concluded the year as Canada's all-time top man in homers, doubles and runs as well.

Finally experiencing a relatively injury-free season in 2001, Walker was his old self again. He hit a robust .350 for his third batting title in four years

Larry Walker. (Courtesy Colorado Rockies.)

and his seventh .300 campaign in the past eight. The five-time All-Star also blasted 38 home runs, drove in 123 runs, scored 107 times and posted a .662 slugging average (fifth in the NL) for the fifth-place Rockies. For his career, Walker went over the 300 mark in round-trippers, past the 1,000 plateau in both RBIs and runs, and over the 200 mark in stolen bases.

In addition to hockey, Larry probably learned rhymes at an early age. His parents, Larry and Mary, named their boys Gary, Cary, Barry and Larry. The youngest child, Larry was born in 1966 and inherited a pair of well-used goalie pads from Cary, who was drafted by the Montreal Canadiens as a goaltender in 1977. Larry invested 13 years in his first love — switching from a fiberglass mask molded by his father to a birdcage style after the former split in half from the force of a slapshot to the forehead — and earned a tryout with the Regina (Saskatchewan) Pats at age 16. The last goalie cut from the squad, Walker gave baseball a shot after graduating from Maple Ridge Senior Secondary School. He was playing for the Canadian National Junior Team when Montreal Expo scouts decided to take a chance on this raw talent.

Pitchers quickly learned that although Walker could hit a fastball great distances, he couldn't handle other pitches and was a sucker for offerings outside the strike zone. He batted .223 with only two homers in 62 games for the Utica Blue Sox in 1985 under manager and former major league pitcher Ken Brett. Pitching coach Ralph Rowe successfully lobbied for Walker to remain in the organization, and his pleas paid off. Walker hit .289 with 29 homers and a league-high 74 RBIs in only 95 games at Burlington in 1986, and .283 in 38 games with West Palm Beach. He clubbed 26 round-trippers with 83 RBIs and 24 stolen bases in 1987 with Class AA Jacksonville, earning Southern League postseason All-Star honors and winning the prestigious James "Tip" O'Neill Award as the top Canadian-born baseball player.

Walker's career was put in jeopardy in 1988 when he suffered a right knee injury while playing winter ball in Mexico. After being in a cast for eight weeks, he needed seven months of rehabilitation. But he came back well in 1989, playing 114 games for Triple A Indianapolis and stroking a base hit in his major league debut in August with the Expos. In 1990, Walker tied for seventh in Rookie of the Year balloting after hitting .241 with 19 homers, 51 RBIs, 59 runs and 21 stolen bases.

Larry started to come into his own during the second half of the 1991 season, batting an NL-best .338 following the All-Star break and finishing with a .290 mark and 64 ribbies. He earned his initial All-Star selection and Gold Glove in '92 after reaching the .300 mark for the first time, belting 23 homers and driving in 93 runs. Leading the league with 16 outfield assists, Walker committed only two errors in 287 total chances. He placed fifth in the MVP voting and was named to Associated Press and *The Sporting News* All-Star squads.

The Expos finished in the runner-up position in the East Division for the second consecutive season in 1993, as Walker corralled his second Gold Glove and enjoyed his first 20/20 campaign with 22 home runs and 29 steals. In 1994, Montreal was first in the East before a strike wiped out the season. He hit .322 in 103 games and tied for the league lead in doubles with 44, playing first base for part of the season to limit the wear and tear on a right shoulder that needed surgery in October.

A free agent, Walker went to Colorado for the 1995 season, and it didn't take him long to adjust to the thin air. In his Rockies debut and the inaugural game at Coors Field, he pounded three doubles. He wound up second in the league in slugging (.607), total bases (300) and extra base hits (72), and tied for second in homers (36). Batting .306 and driving in 101 runs, Walker was one of the major cogs for the team that qualified for the post-season in only its third year of existence. Larry, who finished seventh in the MVP balloting, batted only .214 in the 3–1 NL Division Series loss to Atlanta, but launched a game-tying three-run homer in Game 2. He also had three runs, three hits and three walks in the series.

All those "threes" must have warmed Larry's heart. Three has always been the favorite number of the man who wears uniform No. 33. He was married at 3:33 p.m. on November 3, and his phone number has as many threes as he could acquire. He always takes three (or a multiple of three) practice swings in the batter's box.

Speaking of threes, Colorado slipped to third place in 1996, and their 6-foot-3, 237-pound outfielder played in only 83 games, thanks to a broken clavicle suffered when he ran into the Coors Field wall. Prior to the June 9 injury, he set a franchise record with a career-high 13 total bases in a game against Pittsburgh, then tied a club mark with two triples the next day, establishing an NL record for consecutive extra base hits with six.

Any doubts regarding Larry's ability to come back in 1997 were quickly erased. He won the April Player of the Month award by tying an NL record with 11 homers, and before this MVP campaign was over, had established a variety of franchise records. Walker led the league in home runs with 49 (the most in the senior circuit in 10 years), total bases with 409 (the highest mark in either league in nearly 50 years), slugging at .720 (the seventh highest percentage in NL history) and on-base percentage at .455.

He placed runner-up in batting (.366), hits (208) and runs (143), and third in RBIs (130) and doubles (46). He came within four hits and 10 RBIs of winning the league's first Triple Crown in 60 years, becoming only the fifth major leaguer ever with 40 homers and 30 steals in a season, and only the third to add 200 hits to the mix. Setting a club record with 132 consecutive errorless games, the second-time All-Star claimed his third Gold Glove. Garnering 22-of-28 first-place votes, he became the first Rockie and native Canadian to win the MVP award. Through 2001, Walker was among the top four players in Rockies franchise history in a dozen categories.

Larry Walker never envisioned himself as a baseball player while growing up in Canada. In fact, he couldn't imagine any career that did not involve hockey. But natural athletic skills allowed him to shift gears at the proper time, and now it's difficult to picture him anywhere except a baseball diamond, where he continues to lash away at National League pitches like pucks sitting on a frozen pond.

Top 5 MVP Vote-Getters

1. Larry Walker, Colorado — 359
2. Mike Piazza, Los Angeles — 263
3. Jeff Bagwell, Houston — 233
4. Craig Biggio, Houston — 157
5. Barry Bonds, San Francisco — 123

1997 AMERICAN LEAGUE—KEN GRIFFEY, JR.

George Kenneth Griffey, Jr.
B. November 21, 1969, Donora, Pennsylvania

Year	Team	Games	AB	Hits	Avg.	HR	RBI	Runs	SB
1997	Sea AL	157	608	185	.304	56	147	125	15

The Season

The Cleveland Indians had not won a World Series since 1948, but were determined to change that situation this season. And they almost did. Capturing their third consecutive American League Central Division title — by six games over Chicago — the Indians held off Wild Card entry New York three games to two in a Division Series, despite being outscored (24–21) and out-homered (6–4). Sandy Alomar (two homers, five RBIs) and Omar Vizquel (.500) led the offensive charge for Cleveland, while Jaret Wright won two games. Paul O'Neill (.421, two home runs, seven RBIs) starred for the Yankees.

Seattle led the majors in runs, homers and slugging percentage while claiming its second West Division crown in three years (by six games over Anaheim), but Baltimore, which earned its first division title since 1983, knocked off the Mariners 3–1 in the other Division Series. Excelling for the Orioles against Seattle were Geronimo Berroa (.385, two homers), Cal Ripken, Jr. (.438), Brady Anderson (.353, four RBIs) and Mike Mussina (2–0, 1.93 ERA).

The Indians advanced to the World Series for the second time in three years by outlasting Baltimore 4–2 in the AL Championship Series. Manny Ramirez had a pair of home runs for the winners, while teammate Jose Mesa posted two saves. Anderson (.360, two home runs) and Ripken (.348, three RBIs) kept the O's close. The fifth-year National League franchise Florida Marlins then edged Cleveland in a seven-game World Series.

Former MVP Roger Clemens won a fourth AL Cy Young Award, his first with Toronto, while Boston's Nomar Garciaparra became the sixth unanimous AL Rookie of the Year selection. On the day he was named AL Manager of the Year, Davey Johnson announced his resignation as Orioles skipper.

Randy Johnson of Seattle struck out 19 Chicago batters August 8 to become the first pitcher to fan 19 twice in one season. New York's David Wells won a Division Series game for the third straight year — each with a different team — and Mussina set an LCS record with 15 strikeouts in a game. In the first regular-season interleague game, San Francisco defeated host Texas 4–3 June 12.

Finally, 1959 MVP Nellie Fox was elected to the Hall of Fame by the veteran's committee.

Ahead of His Time

One of the most frequently used yet infrequently accurate phrases that comes out of athletes' mouths these days is, "It's not about the money." We've heard far too many athletes utter that statement, even after leaving a team and a community where they had established deep roots in order to take another club's more lucrative contract offer. We even hear it when a player departs from a contender to play for an also-ran. "It's not about the money."

But every once in a while, a player will speak those words and really mean them. Ken Griffey, Jr. is a classic example. After spending 13 years in the Seattle Mariners organization, setting numerous franchise records and becoming one of the best all-around players in the game, Griffey turned down a more financially rewarding offer from Seattle to return to his roots in Cincinnati for the 2000 season. Shunning even more bucks that he would have received had he chosen to become a free agent, Griffey came back to the town he'd grown up in and the team whose clubhouse and outfield lawn were his childhood home-away-from-home while his father played for the Big Red Machine in the 1970s.

Still, Griffey was lambasted nationally and in Seattle for "deserting" the up-and-coming Mariners, then criticized when he failed to live up to expectations and lead the Reds to postseason play during his first two years with the club. Some players are able to ignore negative feedback, but Griffey has always taken such things to heart. For inside that fun-loving exterior and boyish appearance is a man who desires to be wanted and appreciated.

Ken Jr. not only followed in his dad's footsteps as a major league baseball player, he far surpassed Ken Sr.'s accomplishments early on, and is still amazing fans with his awesome hitting and brilliant fielding. Though he was tagged with an immature label early on in his career, Ken Jr. grew up quickly. Through the 2001 season, he had blasted 460 home runs; driven in and scored well over 1,200 runs; and hit nearly .300. Voted a starter in the All-Star Game 11 consecutive seasons, he led major leaguers in All-Star voting five times, earned 10 Gold Gloves, garnered seven Louisville Silver Slugger awards and won the 1997 American League Most Valuable Player honor.

Griffey has always been ahead of his time. He began his professional baseball career as a 17-year-old, and in 1989 at the age of 19 was the youngest player in the major leagues. Kenny was the second youngest player to win a Gold Glove and start in an All-Star Game (both in 1990), the youngest since 1956 to produce 100 RBIs in a season (1991), sixth youngest to hit 100

Ken Griffey, Jr. (National Baseball Hall of Fame Library, Cooperstown, N.Y.)

to wear his cap backward was so impressive that he earned a spot on the opening day roster, joining dad as the first father-son duo to play in the majors at the same time.

The Mariners finished 24 games out of first place in the AL West in 1989, but the left-handed hitting and throwing Griffey played well, finishing third in Rookie of the Year balloting with a .264 average, 16 home runs, 61 RBIs, 61 runs scored and 16 stolen bases in 127 games. He doubled in his first career plate appearance, drilled the first pitch he saw at the Kingdome into the seats, tied a club record with eight consecutive hits, set a franchise mark by reaching base 11 times in a row and cracked a game-winning, two-run homer in his first pinch-hitting assignment. Ken Jr. led all league outfielders with six double plays, and was fifth with a dozen assists. The only downside to this season was a one-month disabled list stint due to a broken finger.

Griffey started ferociously again in 1990, earning Player of the Month honors in April. He led the club in hits (179), homers (22) and RBIs (80); placed among the top 10 in the junior circuit in total bases (fourth, 287), hits (fifth), batting (seventh, .300), triples (tied for eighth, seven) and slugging (ninth, .481); and earned his first Gold Glove. When dad came to the Mariners in August, the pair became the first father-son combination to play in the same lineup, and celebrated September 14 by connecting for back-to-back homers against the Angels.

The MVP of the Major League Baseball team that toured Japan during the off-season, Griffey continued his exceptional play in 1991, establishing franchise records for batting (career-high .327), doubles (42), slugging (.527), grand slams (3) and intentional walks (21). He was ninth in MVP voting, but Seattle placed fifth, 14 games out.

Although the Mariners were a non-factor again in 1992, Griffey stayed in the limelight by earning the All-Star Game MVP award with a home run and a double in the AL's 13–6 win, joining his dad as the only father-son duo to both claim mid-summer classic

home runs in a career (1993), third youngest with 150 homers (1994), seventh youngest to record his 1,000th hit (1995), fourth youngest to collect 1,000 RBIs (1998), and the youngest to hit his 350th (1998), 400th (2000) and 450th (2001) homers. He is also the junior member of baseball's All-Century Team, named in 1999.

Ken was born in 1969 in Donora, Pennsylvania, birthplace of his father and three-time MVP Stan Musial. He felt no pressure to play ball, but adapted to it quickly. After starring as a left-handed Little League pitcher, as well as in both football and baseball at Moeller High School, he was the first overall selection in baseball's 1987 free agent draft. While playing for Seattle's

Bellingham (Washington) club, his first professional hit was a homer. Griffey wound up batting .313 with 14 home runs and 40 RBIs and was named to the Northwest League All-Star Team.

Nineteen-eighty-eight was a rough year for the youngster, who prior to the season swallowed more than 200 aspirin tablets while battling depression. After recovering, he hit .338 with 11 round-trippers and 42 runs batted in for Class A San Bernardino, and missed two months with a strained lower back before playing in the Class AA Eastern League. The Mariners invited him to spring training in 1989, fully expecting to assign him to their Triple A team. But the exuberant young man who loved

MVP accolades. For the season, he led his team in homers (27) and RBIs (103), placed second among league outfielders with a .997 fielding percentage, and was third in the league in extra base hits (70), fourth in slugging (.535), fifth in doubles (39) and sixth in total bases (302).

His 1993 campaign was even more impressive. Griffey tied a major league record by homering in eight consecutive games (July 20–28), and established franchise records for homers (45, second in the AL), total bases (359, first), runs (113), slugging (.617, second) and intentional walks (25), while batting .309. He also set a league mark for consecutive errorless chances for outfielders with 573 over 240 games.

Like everybody else, Griffey's 1994 season was cut short by the strike, but he still produced statistics that would have looked impressive over a full campaign. Finishing second in MVP balloting, he hit .323, belted 40 home runs (first in the league), scored 94 runs (third) and accumulated 292 total bases (second). His 22 homers through May broke Mickey Mantle's major league record, and his 32 dingers through June surpassed Babe Ruth's league mark.

Junior was limited to 72 games in 1995, fracturing his wrist as he crashed into an outfield wall on May 26, but came on strong to help Seattle win the AL West. Griffey was phenomenal in the playoffs, tying Reggie Jackson's major league record for homers in a single post-season series with five in the Mariners' 3–2 Division Series victory over New York. Griffey batted .391 in that series with nine runs and seven RBIs, and scored the winning run in the deciding game. He then hit .333 with another homer in the M's 4–2 ALCS loss to Cleveland.

The 26-year-old became baseball's highest-paid player in January 1996 when he inked a four-year, $34 million contract extension. Not willing to rest on his laurels, Griffey placed among the top five AL players in homers (49), RBIs (140), runs (125) and slugging (.628), finishing fourth in MVP voting despite missing 20 games following wrist surgery.

By 1997, Griffey was considered the best active player without a league MVP trophy on his shelf, but he changed that situation with yet another stellar performance. Blasting 56 home runs — the most in the majors since Roger Maris' 61 in 1961 — the 6-foot-3, 205-pounder led the AL in RBIs with 147, runs with 125, total bases with 393 (highest league total in 19 years) and slugging at .646. He broke his own league record for homers through May (24), earned his eighth consecutive Gold Glove and was the ninth unanimous AL selection for MVP. Seattle won the West, but Griffey (.133) and the Mariners were beaten three games to one by Baltimore in a Division Series.

Seattle slipped to third place in 1998, but again Griffey was sensational, leading the junior circuit in homers (56); placing second in total bases (387); and third in RBIs (146), slugging (.611) and extra base hits (92). The slugging port-side swinger really shared the wealth this season, homering against all 18 opponents and tying an AL record for home runs in the most ballparks in one year (16).

In his final year with Seattle, Griffey became the first player since Harmon Killebrew (1962–64) to pace the league in homers in three consecutive seasons, clubbing 48. Driving in 134 runs, collecting 349 total bases, scoring 123 runs, stealing a career-high 24 bases and garnering his 10th consecutive Gold Glove, Griffey added to his legacy by winning the 1999 All-Star Game home run contest for the third time. Fittingly, he hit the final home run at the Kingdome (June 27) and the first round-tripper at Safeco Field (July 18).

Accepting $40 million less than he could have made by staying in Seattle, Griffey approved a trade to his hometown of Cincinnati where he signed a nine-year, $116.5 million contract in February 2000. Although he smacked 40 homers (including the 400th of his career on April 10, his father's 50th birthday), drove in 118 runs and was voted an All-Star starter for the 11th consecutive season, hamstring injuries limited his effectiveness, and the Reds

won 11 fewer games than they had the previous year. Griffey was criticized for not living up to his reputation, as well as for not always running out ground balls.

The 2001 season was even more frustrating for Junior, who suffered a partially torn left hamstring during spring training and didn't come off the disabled list until mid–June. With the Reds struggling again and beginning to unload veteran players, Griffey hinted at calling it quits in late July. Wearing No. 30 in honor of his father, the Reds batting coach, he ripped his 450th career homer in August. He wound up batting .286 and slugging at a .533 clip in 111 games, but was limited to 22 home runs and 65 RBIs.

Regardless of what occurs during his remaining time with the Reds, Griffey has already put up Hall of Fame numbers. He was one of only three players with 140-plus RBIs in three consecutive seasons, and with 50-plus homers and at least 20 stolen bases in a year. He was also one of only four men to hit 40 homers in a season seven different years, in five consecutive campaigns and in both leagues. He left the Mariners organization as its all-time leader in seven key offensive categories, including homers (398) and RBIs (1,152), and had the top five single-season home run totals in franchise history.

Ken Griffey, Jr. may not be the most thick-skinned ballplayer in the game, but his fluid motions, spectacular catches in the outfield and consistent pounding of the baseball to all fields make him one of the greatest in the history of baseball. A sensitive man, he just wants to be appreciated. Considering all he's done between the white lines through the years, is that so much to ask?

Top 5 MVP Vote-Getters

1. Ken Griffey, Jr., Seattle — 392
2. Tino Martinez, New York — 248
3. Frank Thomas, Chicago — 172
4. Randy Myers, Baltimore — 128
5. David Justice, Cleveland — 90

1998 NATIONAL LEAGUE — SAMMY SOSA

Samuel Peralta Sosa
B. November 12, 1968, San Pedro de Macoris, Dominican Republic

Year	Team	Games	AB	Hits	Avg.	HR	RBI	Runs	SB
1998	Chi NL	159	643	198	.308	66	158	134	18

The Season

While 1968 will always be remembered as the year of the pitcher and 1994 as the year of the strike, 1998 will be recalled as the season that hosted the great home run derby. Sluggers Mark McGwire and Sammy Sosa allowed a nation of fans to set aside their troubles for a few brief moments this summer as they witnessed one of the all-time great races for baseball immortality.

While Roger Maris' 61 home runs in 1961 never seemed the insurmountable record that Joe DiMaggio's 56-game hitting streak does, no one could have anticipated that two batsmen in the same season would engage in such a vicious attack on the 37-year-old standard, and absolutely demolish it in the process. McGwire of St. Louis ripped his 62nd round-tripper September 8 off Chicago's Steve Trachsel in front of a huge throng at Busch Stadium that included the deceased Maris' sons. Five days later, the Cubs' Sosa cranked his 62nd. McGwire wound up with an incredible sum of 70 homers — more than half the total of five National League teams — knocking out two on the final day of the regular season, while Sosa finished with an amazing 66.

The long ball competition came at an opportune time, taking the spotlight off three nonexistent division races. Atlanta won the Eastern Division by 18 games over New York, Houston the Central by 12½ contests over Chicago and San Diego the West by 9½ over San Francisco. The only excitement for post-season positioning came in the form of the Wild Card race, with three teams — the Mets, Giants and Cubs — sputtering down the stretch. San Francisco and Chicago avoided losing just often enough over the final two weeks to tie for the privilege of facing the Braves and their franchise-record 106 victories in the playoffs. Trachsel and the Cubs won the playoff 5–3 against the Giants.

As expected, Atlanta made short work of the Cubs in a Division Series. The three games-to-none victory featured four RBIs each from Ryan Klesko and Eddie Perez, and a staff ERA of 1.29. San Diego knocked off Houston 3–1 in the other Division Series, with Kevin Brown posting a win, a 0.61 ERA and 21 strikeouts, and Jim Leyritz connecting for three homers and five RBIs.

For the second year in a row, the Braves claimed the league's best regular-season record but could not advance to the World Series. The Padres took the NL Championship Series 4–2, thanks to a pair of wins and a 0.90 ERA from Sterling Hitchcock, and two home runs and four RBIs from former MVP Ken Caminiti. San Diego's celebration was quelled quickly, however, in a World Series sweep at the hands of the Yankees.

McGwire did more than merely hit home runs in 1998. His 162 walks were the most ever in the league, his .752 slugging percentage was the highest in baseball in 71 years and his .473 on-base percentage was the league's top mark since 1935. Then three-time MVP Barry Bonds made history by becoming the first major leaguer with 400 home runs and 400 stolen bases in a career.

Several pitchers also managed to enjoy their day in the sun. Cubs hard-throwing right-hander Kerry Wood (13–6, 3.40 ERA, 233 strikeouts) set an NL record and tied a major league mark with 20 whiffs against Houston May 6 on his way to Rookie of the Year honors, Atlanta's Tom Glavine notched his second Cy Young Award, Trevor Hoffman of San Diego tied a senior circuit standard with 53 saves, Curt Schilling of Philadelphia fanned 300-plus for the second consecutive year, and Don Sutton (324 wins) was elected to the Hall of Fame.

Finally, Milwaukee housed a National League team for the first time in 33 years when the Brewers moved over from the AL, and the Diamondbacks gave Arizona its first-ever major league team when they entered the NL, playing in Phoenix.

Superstar Makeover

When the dancer for a Dominican Republic television show strolled into the ballpark in 1990 to meet the man who had shown interest in her at a disco in San Pedro de Macoris and given her tickets to a game, she expected to spend the afternoon sitting with him. But Sammy Sosa was not the flashy traveling salesman Sonia had assumed he was, but rather a ballplayer who wanted her to watch him play.

Back in the early 1990s, there weren't all that many people who came to the park strictly to watch Sammy perform — either in the Dominican Republic or the United States — with the obvious exception of Sonia, who became his wife and the mother of their four children. In his first full season in the major leagues, the Chicago White Sox outfielder was the only American League player to reach double figures in doubles, triples, home runs and steals, but he hit only .233, struck out 150 times in 153 games and was an erratic fielder.

Fast forward to the tail end of the 1998 season, one month before Sosa would be announced as the National League's Most Valuable Player by a

Sammy Sosa. (National Baseball Hall of Fame Library, Cooperstown, N.Y.)

landslide vote despite a 70-homer season by Mark McGwire. More fans came to the Astrodome to see Sosa and the Cubs on the final weekend of the regular season than attended an Astros' playoff game against the San Diego Padres a few days later.

Attendance is up everywhere Sammy goes these days, as baseball's goodwill ambassador eases his way into the role of one of the best all-around players in the game. In the course of just the past few seasons, Slammin' Sammy has managed to dramatically alter the way he is perceived by management, teammates, opponents and fans. Once possessing a reputation for being one-dimensional and self-centered — to the point of being accused of padding his statistics at the expense of the team — he is now considered the consummate team player, an all-around star and a compassionate philanthropist. Sosa's ability to hit for average and power, run the bases swiftly and smartly, and field his position and throw have made him not only one of today's top players, but one of the best ever. His unprecedented three seasons of 60-plus home runs are breathtaking, and nearly unmatched are his four years in a row of powering 50-plus dingers. Nearly all of these circuit clouts featured his patented hop

out of the batter's box, and heart taps and blown kisses after he reached the dugout.

As radical as Sosa's transformation from a talented but sometimes shaky outfielder to the American and Dominican Republic icon that he is today, is his road from poverty to riches. One of seven children in a poor family in San Pedro de Macoris, his father died when Sammy was 5, and his mother tried to make ends meet by selling food to factory workers. The family was jammed into a two-bedroom apartment, and Sammy helped out by selling oranges, shining shoes and washing cars.

The youngster's first love was boxing — he would wrap his hands in socks stuffed with rags and pretend they were boxing gloves — but he took quickly to baseball after beginning to play in an organized league at age 14. One scout said he looked malnourished, but a Texas Rangers scout saw a diamond in the rough, signing Sosa to a $3,500 bonus at 16. A wild, undisciplined swinger and fast but limited outfielder, Sosa led the Gulf Coast Rookie League in doubles and total bases in 1986, then scored a team-high 73 runs at Class A Gastonia and was a mid-season South Atlantic League All-Star in 1987. The 19-year-old right-

handed batter and thrower paced the Florida State League with 12 triples and stole 42 bases in 1988 while with Class A Charlotte (Florida). He made his major league debut with the Rangers in 1989 and hit his first homer off eventual MVP Roger Clemens, but was demoted to the minors before being traded to the White Sox.

His White Sox debut featured a home run, two RBIs and two runs, but the next two seasons (1990–91) were bleak ones. Fortunately for Sosa — who compared his departure from the White Sox to being released from jail — former White Sox General Manager Larry Himes, now in that same capacity with the Cubs and one of the few who saw the potential in a player others were calling "Sammy So-So," traded George Bell for the future star. Bell retired following the 1993 season, while 10 years later, Sosa is still blasting away at everything in sight. After an injury-plagued 1992 campaign, Sosa started to come into his own in 1993, becoming the first player in Cubs history to hit 30-plus homers and steal 30-plus bases in a season.

Some raised their eyebrows when he stole 20 of those bases in the last two months of a fourth-place season, then held their noses when he began wearing a gold chain with a gem-encrusted pendant marking the 30–30 feat, and ordering an "SS 30–30" license plate for his sports car. Sosa claimed the Cubs Triple Crown with a .300 batting average, 25 homers and 70 RBIs in the strike-shortened 1994 season, then produced another 30–30 effort in '95 (the sixth player all-time to do it twice) as the Cubs came within five wins of a Wild Card berth. The first player in the 20th century to lead the Cubs in both homers and steals in three consecutive seasons, he was second in the league in RBIs (119), tied for second in round-trippers (36) and seventh in stolen bases (34).

After signing a two-year, $10.25 million contract, the new U.S. citizen enjoyed remarkably similar seasons in 1996 and '97 as he continued to round into form as one of the game's elite. The July 1996 Player of the Month was leading the NL in home runs (40) on August 20 when his season ended with a broken right hand, but he still finished fifth in that category, and drove in 100 runs. In 1997, he placed among the top seven in homers (36) and RBIs (119). But Chicago finished fourth in the former year and fifth in the latter, and some figured the team couldn't do much worse by acquiring some young talent for its top commodity, who had struck out a franchise-high 174 times in '97. One of those might have been manager Jim Riggleman, who chastised his outfielder in the dugout during a nationally televised game after Sosa ignored a hold sign and stole a base. Despite a .246 average with runners in scoring position, and an anemic on-base percentage (.300), Sosa was granted a four-year, $42.5 million contract.

Sammy was still displaying the raw skills that brought him to the majors, and was putting up some impressive numbers, but was considered an incomplete ballplayer with a self-serving attitude. All that changed during the 1998 season when Sosa and McGwire staged a storybook battle for the home run title, both shattering Roger Maris' 37-year-old record. McGwire finished with 70 dingers, but Sosa, who all along called McGwire "The Man," put together a better all-around season and won the MVP vote handily. Sosa, who drilled his 66th and final circuit clout when McGwire still had 65, received 30-of-32 first-place MVP votes (only the two St. Louis writers voted McGwire first), shared the *Sports Illustrated* and *The Sporting News* Sportsman of the Year award with McGwire, and captured Major League Baseball's Roberto Clemente Man of the Year honor.

Sosa had started slowly, but really turned it up a notch beginning in late May. He pounded 21 homers during a 30-day stretch (May 25–June 23), and earned the Player of the Month accolade in June when he set a major league record with 20 round-trippers and tied an NL mark with eight home runs in a week. He clobbered his 60th home run September 12, and his 61st and 62nd the following day in his 150th game. (Babe Ruth hit No. 60 in his 154th contest). Sosa's 416 total bases were the most in baseball since 1948, and his 158

RBIs were the highest total since 1949 and the best National League figure in 68 years.

Leading the majors in runs (134) and finishing second in the league in slugging (.647), he paced the Cubs in hits (196) and batted (.307) while leading them to a Wild Card berth. Both his 35 round-trippers at home and 31 road homers were club records, as were his 11 multiple-homer games, tying Hank Greenberg's 1938 major league record. He also set a franchise mark by homering in 15 consecutive series.

This was one of those seasons where little could go wrong for Sammy. The 6-foot, 220-pound package of muscle had held the record for most home runs (246) to begin a career without a grand slam, but after ending that streak July 27, he belted another granny the following night. The only downside for the second-time All-Star was a .182 effort in an NL Division Series sweep at the hands of Atlanta. Sosa was the MVP of the Major League Baseball team that played in Japan following the season, and after his selection as the senior circuit's MVP, headed to the Dominican Republic to assist victims of Hurricane Georges.

What to do for an encore? Incredibly, Sosa was nearly as impressive in 1999 with a 63-homer, 141-RBI effort. Mentioned by President Bill Clinton in his State of the Union address, the league's leading vote-getter for the All-Star Team placed first in the NL in total bases (397) and extra base hits (89), second in homers, and third in both RBIs and slugging (.635). The first player in baseball history to reach 60 homers in two different seasons, he put together an 18-game hitting streak and collected his 300th career home run.

But all was not well in Cubbyville. Cubs manager Don Baylor, whose team had plummeted to sixth place in the Central Division in his 1999 debut with the club, called Sosa a selfish troublemaker early in the 2000 season. Sammy retaliated by saying Baylor was showing a lack of respect for him, and over the summer trade rumors had the superstar going to the New York Yankees. Thankfully for Cubs fans, Sosa continued to produce despite the tumult. Although a lower back muscle

strain ended Sosa's major league-longest consecutive games played streak at 388, he earned his first home run crown with 50, and produced then-career highs in batting (.320) and walks (91).

Placing second in the league in both RBIs (138) and total bases (383), sixth in slugging (.634) and seventh in hits (193), he became the third major leaguer in history to hit 50-plus homers more than twice (Ruth and McGwire being the others), and produced only the eighth 50-homer, 190-hit season in big league history. The first-ever Cub to collect 100-plus RBIs in six consecutive seasons, and the second player in franchise history to reach 120 RBIs three straight years, his three-year RBI total of 437 was second in baseball annals to Boston's Vern Stephens. The fourth-time All-Star won the home run derby contest prior to the midsummer classic with 26 long balls in 56 swings.

Sosa, who over the past few years had learned to lay off pitches outside the strike zone, and who had gradually improved his right field capabilities and base-running decisions, enjoyed what many considered his best all-around season in 2001. After signing a four-year, $78.5 million contract extension, he surpassed even his own lofty standards, logging career highs in batting (.328), RBIs (160) and runs (146), while exploding for another 64 homers. His league-leading RBI total was the third highest in NL history, and was 94 more than any teammate accumulated, establishing the biggest differential in major league history. Sosa's run total was also a league best, while his home runs and slugging percentage (.737) were runner-up marks.

The first Cubs outfielder to start three consecutive All-Star Games came through with his seventh 35-homer, 100-RBI season in a row; Ruth and Jimmie Foxx were the only other players to do it. He also set single-season franchise records for total bases (425) and extra base hits (103), and became the first player in major league history to hit three home runs in a game three times in the same season. Sosa is the only player since World War II to hit 50 home runs and drive in 150 runs in the same year, and he's done it twice.

He smacked the longest home run in Atlanta's Turner Field history—a 471-foot shot off Greg Maddux September 1—joined Ruth and McGwire as the only men to clobber 50-plus homers in four different seasons, and set a major league record for intentional walks by a right-handed batter with 37. The August Player of the Month (.385, 17 homers, 36 RBIs) carried the Cubs all season. His 59th homer came in the first game at Wrigley Field following the September 11 terrorist attacks, and he paid tribute to the U.S. by waving a small American flag as he rounded the bases. Unfortu-nately, his 60th homer came in the game that Chicago was eliminated from playoff contention after leading the Central Division for much of the year. Sosa finished second in MVP balloting, marking four years in a row in the top 10.

Sammy Sosa had the natural talent all along. He was born with it. But it took a number of years for him to hone his skills and become the hitting machine that has terrorized National League pitchers like perhaps no one before him. With his ears sticking out from under his cap, a friendly, boyish smile and his charismatic approach to the game, he's become a fan favorite at Wrigley Field and across the country. At age 33, Sosa entered the 2002 season poised to obliterate even more records and carve out his almost certain position in the Hall of Fame.

Top 5 MVP Vote-Getters

1. Sammy Sosa, Chicago—438
2. Mark McGwire, St. Louis—272
3. Moises Alou, Houston—215
4. Greg Vaughn, San Diego—185
4. Craig Biggio, Houston—163

1998 AMERICAN LEAGUE—JUAN GONZALEZ

Juan Alberto (Vazquez) Gonzalez
B. October 20, 1969, Arecibo, Puerto Rico

Year	Team	Games	AB	Hits	Avg.	HR	RBI	Runs	SB
1998	Tex AL	154	606	193	.318	45	157	110	2

The Season

The New York Yankees were all about winning games in 1998—125 of them to be exact. The Yanks established an American League record with 114 regular-season victories, although their .704 winning percentage was not an AL high, then fashioned an 11–2 post-season mark to capture the franchise's 24th World Series title.

New York, which led the junior circuit in both runs and earned run average, moved into the post-season by claiming the AL Eastern Division by 22 games over Boston, while Cleveland was winning the Central by nine games over Chicago, and Texas the West by three over Anaheim.

The Indians made short work of Boston in one Division Series, shaking off an 11–3 opening game loss to emerge with a 3–1 series triumph. Outfielders Kenny Lofton (.375) and Manny Ramirez (.357) combined for four home runs and seven RBIs, while Mike Jack-son posted three saves. Nomar Garciaparra contributed three homers and 11 RBIs to the losing cause, while teammate Mo Vaughn hit .412 with a pair of round-trippers and seven ribbies.

In the other Division Series, the Yankees swept Texas 3–0, limiting the Rangers to one run and 13 hits. Shane Spencer belted two homers and drove in four runs, and Mariano Rivera collected two saves. New York then withstood a power onslaught from Jim Thome (four homers, eight RBIs) and Ramirez (two homers, four RBIs) to beat Cleveland 4–2 in the ALCS and garner the club's 35th AL pennant. David Wells earned MVP honors by winning two games and striking out 18 batters, while Bernie Williams, Scott Brosius and Chili Davis combined for 16 runs batted in.

World Series MVP Brosius batted .471 with a pair of circuit clouts and six RBIs, and Rivera saved three games as the Yanks swept San Diego. Tino Martinez (.385) and Chuck Knoblauch (.375) also contributed at the plate for the winners.

This was a milestone year for several big names, including three former MVPs. Toronto pitcher Roger Clemens reached the 3,000-strikeout plateau on his way to an unprecedented fifth Cy Young Award; Alex Rodriguez became only the third player in baseball history to join the 40-home run, 40-stolen base club; Cal Ripken, Jr. voluntarily ended his incredible consecutive games played streak at 2,632; Ken Griffey, Jr. (28 years, five months) became the second youngest player ever to reach 300 home runs, smacking 56 for the second year in a row; and Wells tossed the 13th perfect game in major league annals.

In other news, the American League's first black player, Larry Doby, was elected to the Hall of Fame; the Tampa Bay Devil Rays joined the league; Bud Selig was unanimously elected baseball's commissioner; the AL won the highest scoring All-Star Game,

13–8 at Colorado's Coors Field; and Chicago's Albert Belle accumulated 399 total bases, the most in the AL in 20 years.

Dangerous Ranger

When one focuses attention on the Texas Rangers, a handful of players come to mind who have put their personal imprint on this franchise since its 1972 relocation from Washington, D.C. Those stars include Rafael Palmeiro, Jeff Burroughs, Ivan Rodriguez, Charlie Hough and Nolan Ryan, but the one with perhaps the strongest link to the team's history—especially since he again wears the Rangers uniform—is Juan Gonzalez.

For nine full seasons, Gonzalez provided Rangers fans—and all of baseball, for that matter—with a nonstop lesson in hitting for both power and average, and fielding a variety of outfield positions with dexterity. From 1991, when he became a fulltimer after a few minor league seasons, to 1999, when he played the final campaign of his first stint in Arlington, Gonzalez repeatedly ripped the cover off the ball while wearing Rangers blue.

Gonzalez was the franchise's all-time No. 1 hitter in six significant offensive categories: home runs (340), RBIs (1,075), runs scored (791), total bases (2,761), extra base hits (641) and at-bats (4,831). He was also second in hits (1,421) and doubles (282), fourth in games (1,248) and eighth in batting (.294). He had six of the top eight single-season home run totals in Texas Rangers franchise history, and four of the top five RBI totals. Through 2001, he had slugged at a .500 clip or better nine times, scored 75-plus runs and driven in 100 or more runs eight times each, stroked 150-plus hits and legged out 30 or more doubles on seven occasions each, drilled 40-plus homers five times, and batted .300 or better five times.

Although his Ranger teams were never able to make it past the first round of the playoffs, he had six home runs and 10 RBIs in 10 post-season games, and scored seven runs with 10 hits and four walks.

One of the reasons the Cleveland Indians decided to wrestle Gonzalez away from Detroit for the 2001 season was the incredible performances the big right-handed batter had put on at Jacobs Field. A career .344 hitter in 131 at-bats at the Jake prior to 2001, his 12 homers there were the most by a visiting player, and his 36 RBIs were second. The Indians did not regret the move. In 2001, Gonzalez put on an amazing display of batsmanship with a .325 average, 35 home runs, 140 RBIs and a .590 slugging percentage. He became an instant hero with Indians fans by belting two home runs on opening day. The All-Star Game starter also homered in the August 8 win that put Cleveland in first place to stay on the way to its sixth Central Division crown in seven years. The Indians lost a five-game Division Series to Seattle, but Juan hit .348 with two homers and five RBIs, then received a $100,000 bonus for placing fifth in the MVP voting.

Following the 1999 season, the Detroit Tigers had gone after the Puerto Rican star, acquiring him and two other Rangers in exchange for six players. But Comerica Park and its distant fences were not a good match for the long ball hitting Gonzalez. Twenty-two homers were his lowest figure in any full, non-strike season since he broke into the league, and he was limited to 115 games due to hamstring, foot and back problems. Juan did manage to hit the first home run in Comerica Park's regular-season history, spending close to half of the year in the DH role as the Tigers finished third in the Central Division, 16 games outs. Gonzalez, who had complained about the park's dimensions, turned down a huge offer (eight-year, $140 million contract) to remain in Detroit, responding instead to the Indians' courtship.

Anyone who thought that "Igor" might rest on his laurels following his initial MVP award in 1996 was quieted when he produced yet another superb campaign in 1997. While Texas was sliding to third place in the West, Gonzalez was leading the majors with an RBI for every 4.07 at-bats. Despite missing all of spring training and the first 24 games of the regular season

with a torn ligament in his left thumb—suffered while diving for a ball in a Puerto Rican League championship series in late January—he placed among the top 10 AL hitters in five offensive categories, including homers (third, 42), RBIs (third, 131) and slugging (fourth, .589). The AL's Player of the Month for September divided his 133 games nearly evenly between the outfield and DH.

Various injuries had limited Gonzalez to only one season with more than 142 games through 1997, but he played in 154 games in '98 and the results were spectacular. A tremendous first half of the season—featuring 101 RBIs at the All-Star break (second most in major league history and the highest total since 1935)—paved the way for an effort featuring league bests in RBIs (157) and doubles (50), a runner-up .630 slugging percentage, 45 home runs (tied for fourth) and 382 total bases (fourth). He hit .318, fashioning a 20-game hitting streak and establishing franchise records with his RBI, double and total base totals.

His runs batted in figure was the most in the league since 1949, he became the first Ranger and the fifth major league player ever with 40-plus homers and 50 doubles in the same season, and he was the 12th player to hit 40-plus homers in five or more years. His 300th career round-tripper September 19 made him the sixth youngest to reach that plateau. Gonzalez was an All-Star starter for the first time in '98, and Texas captured the Western Division by three games over Anaheim. Unfortunately, the Rangers were completely stymied in a three games-to-none loss in a Division Series against New York, with Juan's performance (.083, one hit, one run) mirroring that of his team's.

Gonzalez received 21-of-28 first-place votes to capture the MVP award for the second time in three years, becoming the first Latin American to garner this prestigious honor more than once. He also received similar awards from *USA Today* and *USA Today Baseball Weekly*.

Juan continued his assault on American League pitchers in 1999 in what would be his final season in

Arlington until 2002. He was among the top 10 hitters in six departments, including slugging (.601, fourth), RBIs (128, fifth), total bases (338, sixth) and home runs (39, seventh), and batted a career-high .326 as the Rangers won the West Division for the third time in four years. Juan was thwarted (.182, one homer) in yet another Division Series loss to the Yankees, but not before he had reached 30 home runs and 100 RBIs for the fourth consecutive season and sixth overall, and had become the first Ranger with 100-plus runs and 100-plus RBIs in the same season for a third time.

Named the AL's second best power hitter by *Baseball America*, Gonzalez shook off a right hamstring strain that caused him to miss a dozen games, scoring a career-high 114 runs and lifting 12 sacrifice flies (second in the majors), including a big league record-tying three in one game. He also clouted three round-trippers in a game, becoming the 13th player in AL history to accomplish that feat for a third time in his career. From his first full season in 1991 through '99, Gonzalez had averaged 37 home runs and 117 RBIs.

As he enters the 2002 season — as a Texas Ranger once again — with nearly 400 home runs and 1,300 RBIs, it's difficult to believe that he is only 32 years old. Juan Gonzalez still has plenty of baseball left in him, and if he can limit his time on the disabled list, has a chance to put some numbers on the board that will be impossible for Hall of Fame voters to ignore.

Top 5 MVP Vote-Getters

1. Juan Gonzalez, Texas — 357
2. Nomar Garciaparra, Boston — 232
3. Derek Jeter, New York — 180
4. Mo Vaughn, Boston — 135
4. Ken Griffey, Jr., Seattle — 135

1999 NATIONAL LEAGUE — CHIPPER JONES

Larry Wayne Jones
B. April 24, 1972, DeLand, Florida

Year	Team	Games	AB	Hits	Avg.	HR	RBI	Runs	SB
1999	Atl NL	157	567	181	.319	45	110	116	25

The Season

In only their second year of existence, the Arizona Diamondbacks improved by 35 games, won 100 times and earned the West Division title by 14 games over San Francisco. The Diamondbacks led the National League in runs, but it was a pitcher who stood head and shoulders above his teammates.

Despite posting five fewer wins than Houston's Mike Hampton, newcomer Randy Johnson became one of only three pitchers to win a Cy Young Award in both leagues. The Big Unit notched a 17–9 record and paced the senior circuit in ERA (2.48), strikeouts, complete games (12) and innings pitched. His 364 whiffs were the most in baseball since 1974 and the highest total in the NL in 34 years, while his 271⅔ innings were the top mark in the league in 13 years.

Johnson and the Diamondbacks did not last long in the post-season, however. The Wild Card New York Mets saw to that with a 3–1 Division Series victory that featured the long ball prowess of Edgardo Alfonzo (three homers, six RBIs), the batting of John Olerud (.438, six ribbies) and the speed of Rickey Henderson (Division Series-record six stolen bases).

In accumulating 100-plus wins for the third consecutive season, Atlanta captured the East Division by 6½ games over the Mets for its eighth division title in a row (not counting the 1994 strike season). Leading the majors in ERA (3.63), the Braves defeated Central winner Houston 3–1 in the other Division Series. Brian Jordan (.471, seven RBIs) and Bret Boone (.474) led the way over the Astros, who received three round-trippers and eight runs batted in from 1996 MVP Ken Caminiti.

An extremely tense League Championship Series featuring five one-run games culminated with Atlanta claiming a 4–2 decision over the Mets,

thanks to an 11-inning, 10–9 victory in Game 6. Series MVP Eddie Perez batted .500 with two homers and five RBIs, while Jordan clubbed two home runs and drove in five runs. The Braves' hopes for their second World Series triumph in five years were dashed in a four-game sweep by the New York Yankees.

Grand slams were in vogue this season. On April 13, Fernando Tatis of St. Louis became the first player in major league history to hit two grand slams in the same inning, connecting both times off Chan Ho Park of Los Angeles, while New York's Robin Ventura became the first major leaguer to belt a granny in both games of a double-header, May 20 against Milwaukee.

Individually this season, Houston's Craig Biggio drilled 56 doubles, the most in baseball since 1950 and the highest NL total in 62 years; Mark McGwire of St. Louis topped Roger Maris' 1961 homer output for the

Chipper Jones. (Courtesy Atlanta Braves.)

second consecutive season, this time with a league-leading 65; the Cubs' Sammy Sosa also passed the 60-mark in back-to-back years with 63 round-trippers; and San Diego's Tony Gwynn reached the 3,000-hit plateau August 6 at Montreal.

The season's biggest tragedy occurred July 14 in Milwaukee, where a 567-foot crane lifting a 400-ton section of Miller Park collapsed and killed three workers. As a result, the opening of the stadium was postponed from 2000 to 2001.

Finally, 1967 MVP Orlando Cepeda was inducted into the Hall of Fame by the veteran's committee.

The Right (-Handed) Stuff

Chipper Jones never had a problem looking himself in the mirror. He was one of the best players on a very good Atlanta Braves team in the late 1990s, hitting for both average and power and performing well in the post-season. All in all, this tall, well-built young man from Florida felt pretty good about himself and his accomplishments as he approached his 27th

birthday — revealed in a confident swagger and an "I'm better than you" look — and figured he had plenty of great things in his future.

But one day the face staring back at him was a scowling one. On the first day of spring training in 1999, new Braves batting coach and former American League Most Valuable Player Don Baylor introduced himself to Chipper, not with a smile or a pat on the back, but with a serious visage and a challenging question regarding Jones' hitting philosophy. When the switch-hitter, who was being compared by the media to Mickey Mantle, responded by saying his goals were to continue to hit .300 from both sides of the plate and drive in runs, Baylor lit into him. Proclaiming that as the No. 3 hitter, Jones' responsibilities included knocking the sphere out of the ballyard more often, especially from the right side of the plate where he had generated very little power during his first few seasons, the intense hitting coach gave his protégé a wake-up call.

Baylor, who said he wanted his new project to be feared as a right-handed hitter, not merely admired, insisted that Jones put more weight on his back foot and move his hands back and away from his chest. The student complied, and the results came swiftly. Jones, who had hit only 12 right-handed homers from 1995 through '98, powered 15 from the right side in 1999 and set a National League record for a switch-hitter with 45 dingers altogether.

Chipper not only led the Braves in batting (.319), hits (181), extra base hits (87, an Atlanta record) and homers (tied for third in the NL), but also placed among the top four in the league in total bases (359), slugging (.633), walks (126) and on-base percentage (.445), and was seventh in runs (116) and tied for seventh in doubles (41) while stealing a career-high 25 bases. The first player in major league history to hit .300 with 100 runs, 40 doubles, 40 homers, 100 RBIs,

100 walks and 20 stolen bases helped his team overcome a number of injuries to win the East Division.

A month and a half into the season, Jones was batting .259 and was an unlikely candidate for any type of post-season award. But he took off from there and wound up garnering 29-of-32 first-place votes in the Most Valuable Player award balloting, winning the coveted honor in a landslide. He reached base safely in an Atlanta-record 39 consecutive games, tied a league record with a walk in 16 straight contests, batted .367 from the seventh inning on, hit .349 over the final three months, and smacked four extra-inning, game-winning home runs.

Prior to the '99 season, Jones' 12 right-handed round-trippers over four years had come in 678 at-bats. This year, he had 15 homers from the right side in only 142 at-bats. May 1 was the first time in his career that Chipper had homered from both sides of the plate in the same game, and he twice repeated the feat over the next four months. Baseball writers were already leaning toward making Jones their top MVP pick in late September, but he made it easy for them by belting four homers in a crucial three-game series sweep of the challenging New York Mets. Fittingly, two of those circuit clouts came right-handed, one breaking a 1–1 tie in the eighth inning, and the other a three-run poke that snuffed out a 2–1 Mets lead.

Jones was unable to keep up the pace in the post-season, however. He batted .231 in both the Division Series victory over Houston and the World Series loss to the Yankees, sandwiched around a .263 effort with two doubles and nine walks in the NLCS win over the Mets. But he certainly impressed any doubters in the final year of a four-year, $8.75 million contract.

No one in Jones' tiny hometown of Pierson, Florida, questioned Chipper's ability to rise to this level of play. He began switch-hitting at age 5 when his father, Larry, a high school baseball coach, threw tennis balls that the youngster would loft onto the top of the hay barn with a piece of PVC pipe. Larry didn't need his position as an algebra teacher to figure out that size plus strength plus skill equals success. Well on his way to a 6-foot-4, 210-pound frame, Chipper batted .448 and led The Bolles High School in Jacksonville, Florida, to a 2A state championship as the 1990 Florida High School Player of the Year. Jones was selected by the Braves as the nation's No. 1 overall pick in the '90 amateur draft, receiving a $275,000 signing bonus.

Actually, Todd Van Poppel was Atlanta's first choice, but the highly-touted pitcher made it clear he didn't want to play for a non-contender. The Braves went on to win eight division titles during the 1990s, and Jones proved to be a big part of it, while 11 years later, Van Poppel has yet to appear in a post-season game. Through the 2001 season, the switch-hitter was fifth in franchise history in both homers (227) and extra base hits (487). In seven Division Series, Jones batted .329 with six homers and 16 RBIs; in six League Championship Series, he hit .315 with three home runs and 15 ribbies; and in three World Series, he batted .273 with six doubles and a half-dozen RBIs.

The shortstop began his professional career in the Gulf Coast League with Bradenton in 1990, then made the South Atlantic League All-Star Team with Class A Macon after compiling some very impressive stats in '91. He played for Class A Durham in 1992 before graduating to AA Greenville, where he was named the Southern League's top prospect in a *Baseball America* poll. Jones continued to improve in 1993, setting Richmond club records in at-bats, hits and total bases; being named Rookie of the Year and the No. 2 prospect in the International League; and being selected as the Braves Triple A Minor League Player of the Year. A well-earned call-up to the parent club came in September when the Braves outlasted San Francisco by one game for the West Division title.

Chipper was chomping at the bit to earn a starting spot in left field for the 1994 campaign when fate dealt a cruel blow. Running out a ground ball in a spring training game against the Yankees in Ft. Lauderdale, he tore the anterior cruciate ligament in his left knee. The broadcast booth was as close as Jones came to the field following surgery during a season that ended prematurely for others as well, due to the strike.

Following a successful rehab, Jones replaced the departed Terry Pendleton at third base and came within an eye-lash of the 1995 NL Rookie of the Year award as the Braves won the East Division by 21 games on the way to their first World Series title in 38 years. *The Sporting News* Rookie Player of the Year led all first-year men in games, runs (87) and RBIs (86), and was runner-up in homers (23), hits (139) and walks (73). Seldom is a rookie given the responsibility of batting third for a defending division champion, but such was manager Bobby Cox's trust in this poised youngster. Jones proved his mettle on many occasions, including the three times he provided a game-winning homer in the ninth inning. Jones hit .389 with two homers and four RBIs in the Division Series, .438 with a home run and three RBIs in the NLCS, and .286 with three doubles in the World Series triumph over Cleveland.

The fly in the ointment for Jones in 1995 was his 25 errors at the hot corner, and although he will never be a Brooks Robinson, he cut that total to 13 in 1996 while enjoying another splendid season at the plate and finishing fourth in MVP voting. The switch-hitter missed the first few games after having a bone chip removed from his right knee, then became an All-Star for the first time on the way to placing among the top 10 in the senior circuit in several offensive categories. The first Braves third baseman with 30-plus doubles and 30-plus homers in a season since 1953 put together an 18-game hitting streak, reached base safely in 34 consecutive games, scored 114 runs and drove in 110. He homered in the Division Series, batted .440 and drove in four runs in the NL Championship Series, and hit .286 with three doubles and three RBIs in the World Series loss to the Yankees.

Chipper led his team in numerous offensive departments again in 1997, including RBIs (111), runs (100) and hits (176), and set an Atlanta single-season record with 41 doubles. He also established a league mark with three grand slams in a 13-game span, hit .500 with a homer in the Division Series and .292 with two round-trippers and four RBIs in the NLCS. An All-Star for the second time, Jones finished ninth in MVP voting.

The consistent third sacker posted a career-best .971 fielding average in 1998, and tied for fourth in the league in runs (123, most ever by a Braves third baseman) and walks (96), and was among the top 10 in total bases (329) and on-base percentage (.408). Disparity between his left-handed and right-handed power stroke — 32 of his 34 homers came from the left side — led to opposing managers bringing in southpaws to face him in late-inning situations. October proved to be a dreadful month for Jones, who not only hit just .200 in the Division Series and .208 in the NLCS, but also came forward with an admission of an affair and illegitimate fatherhood that eventually led to a divorce.

Following his 1999 MVP season, Jones became only the second third baseman in major league history with five consecutive 100-RBI seasons, and the first since Pie Traynor in 1927–31. He clubbed 36 homers in 2000, matched his career high with 111 RBIs, batted .311, slugged at a .566 clip and walked 95 times. Jones collected three hits, including a homer, in the NL's 6–3 All-Star setback at Turner Field, and batted .333 in the Division Series loss to St. Louis. The 28-year-old's error count jumped back up to 23, but he lowered his strikeout total to 64. Jones, who had been eligible to become a free agent following the 2000 season, signed a six-year deal reported to be worth $90 million.

Jones showed no signs of slowing down in 2001 as the Braves won their 10th consecutive division title. His 102 RBIs made him the first third baseman in major league history to drive in 100-plus runs in six consecutive seasons. Jones batted a career-high .330 (fifth in the NL), belted 38 homers, scored 113 runs and slugged at a .605 pace. The All-Star Game starter hit .444 with two homers and five RBIs in the Division Series sweep of Houston, then .263 with a pair of RBIs in the 4–1 NLCS loss to Arizona.

Heading into the 2002 season, Chipper Jones was one of the game's best, and the versatile ballplayer's willingness to switch from third base to left field should pay dividends for the Braves. He has proven to possess the right stuff, and thanks to Baylor's challenge, is a powerful force from both sides of the plate, and a big headache for National League pitchers.

Top 5 MVP Vote-Getters

1. Chipper Jones, Atlanta — 432
2. Jeff Bagwell, Houston — 276
3. Matt Williams, Arizona — 269
4. Greg Vaughn, Cincinnati — 121
5. Mark McGwire, St. Louis — 115

1999 AMERICAN LEAGUE — IVAN RODRIGUEZ

Ivan (Torres) Rodriguez
B. November 27, 1971, Manati, Puerto Rico

Year	Team	Games	AB	Hits	Avg.	HR	RBI	Runs	SB
1999	Tex AL	144	600	199	.332	35	113	116	25

The Season

The 1999 American League races were eerily similar to the previous year's, with New York, Cleveland and Texas all repeating as division winners, and Boston again claiming the Wild Card spot by exactly seven games. Almost identical as well was the Yankees' three-game sweep of Texas in a Division Series. For the second consecutive year, New York pitchers limited the Rangers to exactly one run in three games, despite the fact that Texas had led the league in regular-season batting for the second straight year. Derek Jeter (.455) and Bernie Williams (.364, six RBIs) helped extend the Yanks' post-season domination of Texas to nine wins in a row, dating back to 1996.

The Indians won the Central Division for the fifth straight year — by 21½ games over Chicago — their 1,009 runs scored the most in baseball since 1950. But Boston, which led the AL in ERA, shutouts, saves and several other pitching categories, rallied from a 2–0 deficit to capture the other Division Series 3–2. Following that second-game loss, the Red Sox had dropped 18 of their last 19 post-season contests. But an offensive barrage featuring a 23-run outburst in Game 6 enabled Boston to reach the ALCS. Leading the way in the ALDS victory over Cleve-

land were Nomar Garciaparra (.417, two homers, four RBIs), John Valentin (three home runs, 12 RBIs) and Troy O'Leary (two homers and seven RBIs in Game 5). Jim Thome paced the Indians with four round-trippers and 10 ribbies.

The error-prone Red Sox held a lead in each of the first four games of the League Championship Series, but the Yankees tied their own mark with a 12th consecutive post-season win (Game 2) — last accomplished in 1927–32 — and took the series 4–1. Series MVP Orlando Hernandez was 1–0 with a 1.80 ERA and 13 strikeouts, Scott Brosius hit two homers and Jeter batted .350 with three RBIs. Jose Offerman (.458) and Garciaparra (.400) led the Red Sox.

The Yankees then captured their second consecutive World Series title and 25th overall with a four-game sweep of Atlanta, giving them wins in their last dozen World Series games. Chad Curtis, who had only five regular-season homers, swatted a pair in Game 3, including a game-winning shot in the 10th inning, while Brosius (.375) and Jeter (.353) also contributed. Series MVP Mariano Rivera was 1–0 with a 0.00 ERA and two saves.

This was a stunningly successful year for Boston hurler Pedro Martinez, who became one of only three pitchers

to win Cy Young Awards in both leagues. The MVP of the All-Star Game at Fenway Park fanned 313 batters in 1999, the most in the AL since 1977, and allowed no earned runs in 17 innings of post-season play, striking out 23 batters along the way.

Other standouts this year were 1997 MVP Ken Griffey, Jr., who won the home run title (48) for the third year in a row and earned his 10th consecutive Gold Glove; Cleveland's Manny Ramirez, whose 165 RBIs were the highest major league total since 1938; Baltimore moundsman Mike Mussina, who claimed his fourth straight Gold Glove; New York's David Cone, who tossed the 15th perfect game of the modern era, July 18 versus Montreal; and Tampa Bay's Wade Boggs, who smashed a home run August 7 for his 3,000th career hit. In an obvious case of voting on past performance, Rafael Palmeiro of Texas won his third consecutive Gold Glove despite serving as a designated hitter in 135 games and playing only 28 games at first base.

On July 14, Richie Phillips of the Major League Umpires Association announced the mass resignation of umps, effective September 2, in an attempt to raise salaries. But the move backfired as baseball accepted the resignations and the union split up.

Finally, three all-time greats —

George Brett, Nolan Ryan and Robin Yount — were enshrined in the Hall of Fame.

At the Crossroads

With very few exceptions, baseball experts agree that the most physically and mentally demanding and debilitating position on the diamond, day in and day out, is that of catcher. Responsible at all times to keep his teammates prepared and alert, the catcher must also simultaneously serve as his pitcher's mentor, confidante, babysitter and psychologist.

Crouched in an unnatural position, equipment weighing heavy in sometimes frigid, sometimes sweltering temperatures, the backstop must repeatedly field a rock-hard sphere hurtling toward him at 90-plus miles an hour, skid to his knees to block pitches in the dirt and occasionally leap from his prone position to fire the ball to an infielder in order to cut down an enemy runner. If that were not enough, the catcher must also stand his ground at home plate, waiting on an unpredictable throw from a teammate as a 200-pound runner charges toward him from his blind side with hopes of separating him from the ball.

It's no wonder that many major league catchers through the years have either seen their days cut short by wear and tear, or have extended their careers to a normal length only by eventually switching to a less rigorous position such as first base or the outfield. It's also not surprising that while many backstops have excelled in either the defensive or offensive skills, few have prospered in both.

This brings us to Ivan Rodriguez, who after eight years of nearly unparalleled success — both behind the plate and at bat — recently became susceptible to the relentless physical requirements of his position. From 1992 through 1999, the Texas Rangers catcher averaged 135 games played, but a variety of ailments limited him to 91 contests in 2000 and 111 in 2001. The 30-year-old entered the 2002 campaign and the final year of his contract with something to prove: that he still possessed the physical strength and mental fortitude to continue donning the tools of ignorance and demonstrating the kind of quality play he showed during the 1990s.

Rodriguez impressed scouts early on in his native Puerto Rico, starring for the Lino Padron Rivera High School team in Vega Baja and signing with the Rangers as a non-drafted free agent at age 16 in 1988. The 5-foot-9, 205-pounder led South Atlantic League catchers in assists and was second in both putouts and total chances while clouting 22 doubles for Gastonia in 1989. The next season, Ivan led Charlotte in hitting (.287) and RBIs (55), while pacing Florida State League catchers in putouts and chances. Cutting down runners with the audacity to test his arm would become Rodriguez's forté, and he began proving it this season by throwing out a league-best 39.1 percent of runners attempting to steal.

Baseball America's Class A All-Star Team catcher in 1990 figured to benefit from another year of seasoning in the minors, but after excelling for Tulsa in the Texas League during the first couple of months of the 1991 season, the Rangers promoted him to the big club June 20, the same day he married Maribel Rivera. The precocious youngster, who had thrown out nearly half of the Texas League runners trying to steal on him, became one of only two catchers in major league history to lead his team in games caught (88) at the age of 19. The youngest Ranger ever to hit a home run (19 years, nine months), Rodriguez finished fourth in Rookie of the Year balloting, while his team was third in the American League West.

The major's youngest player in 1992 played 116 games behind the plate, the fourth most in baseball history by a catcher 20 years or younger. The only player ever to lead his team in games caught at both age 19 and 20, he was third among AL catchers in batting (.260).

In 1993, the Rangers moved up to second place, thanks in part to the steady improvement of their young and maturing catcher. Rodriguez pushed his batting average to .273, reached double figures in home runs for the first time and drove in 66 base runners. He tied a team record with hits in eight consecutive at-bats (July 26 and 28), and doubled at Baltimore in his second All-Star Game appearance.

Ivan led junior circuit backstops in hitting (.298, second on the team) in 1994, and his 16 homers were a team record for catchers and a career-high at the time, despite the season being cut short by the strike. "Pudge" was 2-for-5 with a run scored in the All-Star Game, and helped Texas gain a one-game lead in the AL West before the strike.

Batting .300 or better in 1995 for the first time in what would be at least seven consecutive seasons, Rodriguez drove in 67 runs and enjoyed a 15-game hitting streak and his first two-homer effort (July 13 at Boston), both round-trippers coming off 1986 MVP Roger Clemens. The Texas Rangers Player of the Year led the club in batting (.303), doubles (32) and total bases (221), but the team slipped to third place.

Baseball fans across the country were already taking note of this exciting ballplayer, but in 1996, Rodriguez fully entered the spotlight with an exceptional season. The 24-year-old set major league records for catchers in doubles (47, third in the league) and at-bats (639, fourth), tied a major league mark for most runs (116) by a player serving primarily as a catcher, and tied for the third most hits (192) by a player who caught at least 100 games. Batting .300 with 19 home runs and 86 RBIs, he put together a 19-game hitting streak and finished seventh in the circuit in hits, helping lead the Rangers to their first-ever division title.

Ivan then batted .375 in a 3–1 Division Series loss to New York, stroking six hits and collecting two RBIs and a pair of walks. Following the post-season, Rodriguez was a member of the Major League Baseball team that played a series in Japan.

The 1997 season saw the Rangers drop to third place in the West, but Rodriguez topped AL catchers in batting (.313), hits (187) and runs (98), while placing second in homers (20), RBIs (77) and doubles (34). Featured on the cover of the August 4 issue of *Sports Illustrated*, he was fifth in the league in hits, tied for fifth in singles (129), tied for eighth in multi-hit games (53) and 10th in batting. Three of his homers came in successive plate appearances September 11 against Minnesota, only the eighth three-homer game in history by an AL catcher.

Rodriguez got off to a sensational start in 1998, earning April AL Player of the Month honors by batting .446 in 23 games and setting a club record for hits (41) in the season's first month. He led the majors in batting for 41 consecutive days (May 21–July 1) and was hitting .350 at the All-Star break. Starting an AL-high 137 games behind the plate, Rodriguez's 40 doubles were the seventh-best mark ever by a catcher, and he became the first major league backstop to collect 40 doubles in two different seasons.

The right-handed hitter wound up leading the Rangers in batting (.321, eighth in the league), placing seventh in the AL in multi-hit games (55) and ninth in hits (186) in '98. He recorded his 1,000th career hit in May; went 3-for-4 with a run, an RBI and a stolen base in the All-Star Game; collected his fifth consecutive Silver Slugger Award; and helped Texas win the West Division by three games. Rodriguez batted only .100 in the Division Series sweep at the hands of New York, but further endeared himself to his homeland by donating thousands of dollars to assist Puerto Rican victims of Hurricane Georges.

What to do for an encore? How about winning the American League Most Valuable Player award? Rodriguez did just that in 1999 in an exceptionally close vote. The top four players finished within 26 points of each other, and runner-up Pedro Martinez of Boston actually received one more first-place vote than Rodriguez. Nonetheless, Rodriguez was a worthy winner, with an all-around effort that ranked among the best all time for any position.

Before it was over, Rodriguez had become the first catcher in AL history with a 30-plus homer (35), 100-plus run (116) and 100-plus RBI (113) season, and the first catcher ever with at least 20 homers and 20 stolen bases.

Among catchers, his 199 hits and his run total were second all time, his 25 stolen bases the sixth highest mark in history, his .332 batting average the seventh best ever and the best for an AL catcher since 1937, and his 600 at-bats the 10th highest total. His RBI output was the most by a league backstop since 1983. He placed among the top seven in the league in batting, hits, runs, total bases and multi-hit games.

The third Rangers MVP in the past four seasons, Ivan set a league record for homers by a catcher, and threw out an amazing 54.2 percent of runners attempting to steal, the highest percentage since those records began to be kept in 1989. His one passed ball was the fewest ever by a league catcher with more than 130 games, and he extended an errorless streak from the previous season to 57 games. The *Baseball Digest* Major League Player of the Year was the co-Player of the Month in August (shared with teammate Rafael Palmeiro), homering a dozen times that month and hitting .349 in his final 43 games.

Hitting streaks of 20 and 14 games enabled Pudge to wind up fifth in the league in hits, five of which came in a single August game. Rodriguez had a club-record nine RBIs in an April contest — only the third catcher in major league history to do it — and joined Mickey Cochrane as the only catchers to score 100-plus runs more than once. The only drawbacks for Ivan this season were grounding into a club-record 31 double plays, and yet another Division Series loss to the Yankees.

The Rangers plummeted from first to fourth in 2000, at least partly due to Rodriguez appearing in only 91 games. In late July, his right thumb was broken by the bat of 1995 MVP Mo Vaughn as Rodriguez attempted to gun down a base runner following a swinging strike. Ivan, who led AL catchers in fielding average (.996), hit a club-best .347 with a .667 slugging percentage, 27 doubles and four triples, with a pair of four-hit games and four multi-homer games.

The 2001 season also was shortened by injury. Rodriguez began having knee problems in August, and in early September was diagnosed with patellar tendonitis in his left knee. A section of damaged tendon was removed, and there were questions regarding his ability to mend by spring training 2002. The All-Star Game starter hit .308 in 111 games in 2001, ripping 20-plus doubles (24) for the seventh consecutive year, belting 25 home runs and driving in 65. But it was an off-year, and some attributed it to his frustration over the lack of an extension on a five-year, $42 million contract running through 2002. Trade rumors were floating this season, although owner Tom Hicks assured his perennial All-Star that he was the heart and soul of the team and wasn't going anywhere.

Hicks' comment was right on target. Through the 2001 season, Rodriguez was among the top Rangers all time in eight categories, including hits, runs, RBIs, doubles, total bases, extra base hits, games and at-bats. From 1992 through 2001, he won an AL-record 10 consecutive Gold Gloves (tying Johnny Bench for the Major League record), and was an All-Star in 10 straight years (1992–2001).

From 1989 through 1999, he posted six of the top eight caught-stealing percentages in the majors, including 52.5 percent in 1998, 51.9 in '97 and 49 in '92. Through the 2001 season, he is the only Ranger with seven consecutive .300 seasons.

Rodriguez was at the crossroads of what had been an outstanding career as he entered the 2002 season. Now in his 30s, will he bounce back from recent injuries and return to his glory years as a multi-talented catcher, or will the aches and pains associated with his demanding position limit his effectiveness? Only time will tell. Regardless of what happens, Ivan Rodriguez accomplished much more on the field of play during the 1990s than most catchers do in their careers.

Top 5 MVP Vote-Getters

1. Ivan Rodriguez, Texas — 252
2. Pedro Martinez, Boston — 239
3. Roberto Alomar, Cleveland — 226
3. Manny Ramirez, Cleveland — 226
5. Rafael Palmeiro, Texas — 193

2000 NATIONAL LEAGUE—JEFF KENT

Jeffrey Franklin Kent
B. March 7, 1968, Bellflower, California

Year	Team	Games	AB	Hits	Avg.	HR	RBI	Runs	SB
2000	SF NL	159	587	196	.334	33	125	114	12

The Season

The Atlanta Braves won their ninth consecutive division title, but it was the Wild Card New York Mets who advanced to the World Series for the first time in 14 years. The Mets, who finished one game behind Atlanta in the East Division, bounced West Division champion San Francisco 3–1 in a National League Division Series. Edgardo Alfonzo drove in five runs during the series, while Bobby J. Jones tossed a one-hit, complete-game shutout in the clinching game.

Central Division champion St. Louis, which won 20 more games than it had in 1999, shocked the Braves with a three-game sweep in the other Division Series. Jim Edmonds paced the Cardinals in the series with a .571 average, two home runs and seven RBIs.

League Championship Series MVP Mike Hampton, in his first year with the Mets, won two games with a spotless ERA and 12 strikeouts during the 4–1 victory over St. Louis. Leading the way for New York were Mike Piazza (.412, two homers, four RBIs), Todd Zeile (.368, eight RBIs), Alfonzo (.444, four ribbies), Benny Agbayani (.353, three RBIs) and Timo Perez (NLCS record-tying eight runs scored). The Mets' miracle season ended in a 4–1 World Series loss to the cross-town Yankees, despite Zeile hitting .400 and Piazza drilling two round-trippers and driving in four runs.

Individually, Colorado's Todd Helton made a run at the magical .400 mark and wound up leading the NL in batting (.372), hits (216), RBIs (147), total bases (405), doubles (59, the most in baseball since 1936), slugging (.698) and on-base percentage (.470). Chicago's Sammy Sosa, the 1998 MVP, finished atop the league home run leaders with 50, making him only the second player in baseball history to hit 50-plus homers in three consecutive seasons.

Randy Johnson of Arizona claimed his second Cy Young Award in a row, and third overall, while San Diego's Tony Gwynn collected his 3,000th career hit. Dave Hansen of Los Angeles set a major league record with seven pinch-hit homers, while 1994 MVP Jeff Bagwell of Houston scored 152 runs, the highest total in baseball since 1936 and the most in the NL since '32.

After moving into cozy Enron Field, the Houston Astros set a league record by hitting 249 home runs. This 2000 campaign also marked the first time since 1942 that no manager in either league was fired during the regular season.

Finally, former Cincinnati Reds star Tony Perez was inducted into the Hall of Fame, while Braves reliever John Rocker made himself a candidate for the Hall of Goofballs. Rocker served an early-season suspension for published comments made during the off-season that offended virtually every minority who'd ever set foot in New York.

Late Bloomer

In an age of self-promotion and glorification, Jeff Kent is a breath of fresh air. When the telephone call came, informing him that he had won the 2000 National League Most Valuable Player award, Kent marked the occasion by taking a seat on his tractor and mowing the lawn at his Texas ranch. That evening, he continued this raucous celebration by going out for a barbeque dinner and finalizing plans for a weekend hunting trip.

In many ways, Kent is the antithesis of his flamboyant and sometimes controversial San Francisco Giants teammate, Barry Bonds, and the two are not exactly the best of buds away from the ballpark. A guy who prefers to ride his cycle or quietly raise funds for various women's causes over basking in the limelight of athletic success, Kent has transformed himself from a pretty good ballplayer to a very good player over the past five years.

After bouncing around from Toronto to the New York Mets to Cleveland during his first five seasons in the majors, this late bloomer has found a home in San Francisco, where he has established franchise and big league hitting and RBI records. In doing so, the second baseman has been a wonderful complement to Bonds in driving the Giants to post-season contention nearly every season.

The biggest of those campaigns for Kent, of course, was in 2000 when he put together an all-around season that rivaled the best ever by a second sacker. Batting at a .334 clip—nearly 50 points higher than his career average—stroking 33 home runs and driving in 125, Kent helped push the Giants to the majors' best record and an 11-game bulge over their nearest competitor in the West Division. He then batted .375 with three runs scored and an RBI in the 3–1 Division Series loss to the Mets.

Kent began his serious assault on senior circuit pitchers in May by batting .365, then really let loose in June with a .424 average, 34 RBIs and an .808 slugging percentage to garner NL Player of the Month honors. Two separate August hitting streaks of 12 and 10 games helped the All-Star Game starter bat .366 that month, and he wound up fourth in the league in RBIs, fifth in both hits (196, most by a Giant in 30 years) and on-base percentage (.430), sixth in batting, tied for sixth in both extra base hits (81) and multi-hit games (57), seventh in total bases (350), eighth in runs (114), tied for eighth in doubles (41), and 10th in slugging (.596).

It was Jeff's clutch hitting in the first half of the season — his 85 RBIs before the All-Star break led the NL and were tops in franchise history — that kept slow-starting San Francisco (4–11) from falling out of the race in the early going. Playing in brand new Pacific Bell Park, the Giants rallied to score 925 runs, second most in team history, and finish with baseball's best record for the first time since 1962. Kent led the team in seven key offensive categories, including batting, total bases, RBIs and triples (seven).

Playing 150 games at second base, he was fourth in fielding average (.986) among NL players at his position. He became the fourth second baseman ever with more than one 30-homer season (he had belted 31 in 1998) and the fourth player in franchise history with four consecutive 20-homer, 100-RBI seasons. Only 14 times has a Giants player had 30-plus homers and 125-plus RBIs in the same year, but none did it with a higher batting average and more hits than Kent.

The 32-year-old second sacker received 22-of-32 first-place votes in MVP balloting, becoming the eighth player at his position to win the award, and the first in 16 years. The clean-up hitter also received a $100,000 bonus to augment his $6 million salary. Bonds, who finished second in the voting, benefited from Kent batting behind him, while Kent's RBI total was enhanced by frequently having Bonds on base when he came to the plate. This season marked the first time teammates had finished 1–2 in MVP voting since 1990, when the Pirates duo of Bonds and Bobby Bonilla were first and second, respectively. And with Jason Giambi of Oakland capturing the AL MVP, it was the first time since 1959 that both MVPs came from the same geographic region.

In addition to enjoying an exceptional individual season in 2000, Kent

Jeff Kent. (Courtesy San Francisco Giants.)

was a catalyst during key games for the Giants. Following the 4–11 start and a players-only meeting, the 6-foot-1, 215-pounder helped spark a three-game sweep at Arizona with a 3-for-5 effort, including a home run, double and five RBIs. And in a 6–5 early July victory over Los Angeles that keyed an eight-game winning streak, he slugged two round-trippers and scored three times.

Jeff had always possessed home

run power, as evidenced by 11 dingers during his rookie season of 1992 and 21 in his sophomore campaign. But it wasn't until 1997 after he'd been traded from the Indians to San Francisco — along with several players and cash for Matt Williams — that his power stroke became finely honed. Kent placed eighth in MVP voting that season after helping lead the Giants to the West title with 29 home runs (a franchise high for second basemen) and 121 RBIs (fifth in the NL), both career bests at the time. He was particularly effective with the bases loading, batting .500 (10-for-20) with two doubles, three grand slams and four sacrifice flies. Kent also hit .300 with a pair of homers in the post-season, but his team was swept by Florida in a Division Series.

Proving that this newfound power was no fluke, Kent blasted 31 home runs and drove in 128 runs (fourth in the NL) in 1998, raising his batting average (.297) by nearly 50 points from the previous season in the process. Establishing a franchise RBI record for second basemen (Rogers Hornsby had 125 in 1927), Kent also posted the fourth highest RBI total by a major league second sacker since 1920, despite missing 24 games due to a right knee sprain. He had set the tone for this season with a 5-for-7 performance in the opener, including a three-run homer, and he went on to earn August Player of the Month honors with a .355 average, 11 homers and 32 RBIs. Kent, who posted a career-high 13-game hitting streak and batted .332 with runners in scoring position, was among the top 10 in MVP voting once again, but San Francisco finished second in the West, losing out on the Wild Card spot in a one-game playoff with the Cubs.

In 1999, Kent battled a chronic toe injury all season, missed 14 games while on the DL and saw his power numbers (23 homers, 101 RBIs) dip slightly. But he earned his first All-Star berth, and enjoyed some individual success, including hitting for the cycle at Pittsburgh, a five-hit game at Seattle, 40 doubles and a career-high 13 stolen bases. He also turned more double plays per game than all but three NL second basemen. On the heels of his MVP season, Kent batted .298 with 22 homers and 106 RBIs, slugged at a .507 clip and was an All-Star starter in 2001, but the Giants again finished second in the West.

Jeffrey Franklin Kent gave early indications that he had baseball talent, setting a record at Edison High School in Huntington Beach, California, by batting .500 in his junior year in 1985. He was a second team All-America freshman squad member in 1987 at the University of California-Berkeley, and was the starting shortstop for the Golden Bears in 1988 when they won the NCAA Central Regional and advanced to the College World Series.

Selected by Toronto in the 20th round of the 1989 June draft, the shortstop and third baseman led the New York-Penn League in home runs (13) while playing for Class A St. Catharine's. The Class A Dunedin MVP moved to second base in 1990, placing second in the Florida State League in home runs, doubles and total bases, and was named to both mid- and post-season All-Star Teams. In 1991, Kent was the team MVP at Double A Knoxville, leading the Southern League in games and doubles, and pacing his squad in several offensive categories.

Kent played 65 games with the Blue Jays in 1992 before being traded to the Mets with another player for pitcher David Cone. Toronto went on to win the World Series, while New York finished 24 games out of first place in the NL East. Overall, Jeff was second among big league rookies with 50 RBIs and third in homers (11). Nearly half of his 73 hits were of the extra base variety, and he showed versatility by playing all four infield positions.

The up-and-coming 25-year-old established then-Mets franchise records for home runs (21) and RBIs (80) by a second baseman in 1993, and really picked up his game in the second half of the season, batting .303 with 16 homers and 55 RBIs. In the strike-shortened 1994 campaign, he started quickly, going 4-for-5 in the opener, hitting two home runs in an April 17 contest and tying a then-Mets record with an RBI in eight consecutive games. He batted .385 with runners in scoring position for the year, but the Mets were 18½ games out when the season ended prematurely.

A 20-homer campaign followed in 1995, but he could manage only 65 RBIs as New York finished 21 games out of first place. In July 1996, Kent was traded to Cleveland, which rolled to the American League Central title. After batting .290 for the Mets earlier in the year, he was limited to a .265 mark with the Indians, although he stepped up the pace with a .348 average in 18 September games. Jeff was unable to make much of an impression in the post-season, batting only .125 in the 3–1 Division Series upset loss to Baltimore, and a month later he was traded again.

Jeff Kent has proven himself to be a rare commodity: a power hitter in a non-power hitting position. Through 2001, his 475 RBIs were the most ever over a four-year span by a major leaguer playing primarily as a second baseman. He is the only second baseman in the past 51 years to collect 120 RBIs for a season, and he did it in both 1997 and 1998. (Only 117 of his RBIs in 2000 came when he was playing second base.) He has hit 20-plus homers with at least 100 RBIs and 80 runs scored in each of the past five seasons through 2001. The lifetime .285 hitter through 2001 is over the 200-mark in career homers, and was one RBI shy of 900 entering the 2002 season.

Many players begin slowing down at his age, but the 34-year-old still sports an all-around solid game. It's only the rare fastball that gets past him, and he has proven to be a savvy base runner and a sure-handed fielder who knows how to turn the twin killing. Most importantly, Kent appears to have a number of productive seasons ahead of him, and at the rate he's going, may just establish some all-time batting marks for second basemen.

Top 5 MVP Vote-Getters

1. Jeff Kent, San Francisco — 392
2. Barry Bonds, San Francisco — 279
3. Mike Piazza, New York — 271
4. Jim Edmonds, St. Louis — 208
5. Todd Helton, Colorado — 198

2000 American League — Jason Giambi

Jason Gilbert Giambi
B. January 8, 1971, West Covina, California

Year	Team	Games	AB	Hits	Avg.	HR	RBI	Runs	SB
2000	Oak AL	152	510	170	.333	43	137	108	2

The Season

The way the New York Yankees limped into the post-season — losing 15 of their last 18 regular-season games — few believed they would become the first team since the Oakland Athletics in 1972–74 to capture three consecutive World Series titles. But the club that almost always finds a way to win did it again this year.

The Yankees, who claimed the American League East title by 2½ games over Boston, edged a soaring Oakland team 3–2 in an exciting AL Division Series. Tino Martinez paced the Yanks with a .421 average and four RBIs in the series, Luis Sojo drove in five runs and Mariano Rivera recorded three saves. The Athletics won 22 of their final 29 games to garner the AL West title for the first time since 1992.

Over in the other Division Series, Seattle swept Central Division champ Chicago 3–0, with David Bell and Edgar Martinez both batting .364 in the series. The White Sox notched their first division championship since 1993, while the Mariners came on strong down the stretch to nudge Cleveland for the Wild Card spot.

The first subway series in 44 years resulted in the Yankees wearing their fourth World Series crown in five years. The 4–1 Series triumph over the Mets featured MVP Derek Jeter batting .409 with two homers, Paul O'Neill hitting .474, Mike Stanton winning two games and Rivera saving a pair.

The best pitcher in the majors this year was Boston's Pedro Martinez, who won his second consecutive Cy Young Award and third in four years. His 1.74 earned run average was the best in the American League since 1978, and he tossed a one-hitter and a two-hitter, fanning 15 or more three times.

Toronto's Carlos Delgado put together a brilliant season, his 57 doubles the high mark in the junior circuit since 1936. Nomar Garciaparra of Boston won his second consecutive batting title, his .372 average the best league mark in two decades. Minnesota's Cristian Guzman legged out 20 triples, while Darin Erstad of Anaheim collected 240 hits; both were the most in the AL in 15 years.

Other individual highlights included two-time MVP Cal Ripken, Jr. collecting his 3,000th hit early in the season, and former catcher Carlton Fisk being enshrined in the Hall of Fame.

Extreme Excellence

He loves professional wrestling, heavy metal music and riding motorcycles. He sported wild black hair, a goatee and a large tattoo of a melting skull surrounded by a swirling sun. He describes his diet as "the worst in the world." In other words, he's the poster child for the young extreme sports fan that baseball is trying to woo.

But Jason Giambi, who lists tough hombre Clint Eastwood as his favorite actor and *Gladiator* as his top movie, can't be fully comprehended by what one sees on the surface. Substance is what it's all about, and Giambi's inner drive and fierce, competitive nature are what truly define this emerging superstar.

Wielding a mighty stick from the left-handed batter's box, Giambi has been powering the ball to all parts of the ballpark and beyond since his first full season with the Oakland Athletics in 1996. The only knock on the gruff-looking first baseman was his tendency to experience almost as many cold spells as hot streaks during his first few years in the bigs. But his year-by-year improvement — evident even through a cursory glance at his statistics — has also included a much greater consistency, culminating in a couple of absolutely stellar seasons beginning with the turn of the century.

Giambi's dedication to baseball began at an early age. While many school kids dream of summer vacations, Jason said he never took one as a child because he preferred to play ball on a team. A New York Yankees fan growing up on the West Coast, he earned letters in three sports — baseball, football and basketball — through three years at South Hills High School in West Covina, California, including two as a quarterback, and was the hoops MVP of his league as a senior. Baseball talent obviously ran in the family, as younger brother Jeremy was drafted by the Royals organization and joined Jason in Oakland in 2000.

Selected by the Milwaukee Brewers in the 43rd round of the June 1989 free agent draft, Jason opted for college instead, playing baseball and majoring in business at Long Beach State. The league's Freshman of the Year led the Big West Conference in batting (.407) as a sophomore, hit .397 for his college career and earned all-league First Team honors twice.

A member of the 1991 All-College World Series team, Giambi helped the U.S. squad capture a bronze medal at the '91 Pan Am Games in Havana, Cuba, and also played with the U.S. Olympic team in Barcelona in 1992. When Oakland called his name in the second round of the June '92 draft, he decided to go pro, batting .317 with three home runs and 13 RBIs in only 13 games for Southern Oregon in the Class A Northwest League.

Jason was the starting third baseman for the North squad in the California League All-Star Game in 1993, driving in 60 runs in 89 games for Class A Modesto. He split his time in 1994 between Double A Huntsville and Triple A Tacoma, showing signs of the clutch hitting he would become known for in the big leagues with a .346 average with runners in scoring position and two outs at Tacoma.

He bounced back and forth between Triple A Edmonton and the parent club in Oakland in 1995, playing both third base and first. His .342 average for the Trappers through early July earned Giambi a permanent home in the majors, where he homered in three consecutive games at Kansas City in mid–August. A series of injuries—hamstring, concussion and rib cage—kept the 6-foot-3, 235-pound bruiser out of 20 games down the stretch for the A's, who finished last in the AL West Division.

Giambi performed admirably in his first full major league season in 1996, batting .291 with 20 home runs, 79 RBIs and 84 runs scored for the third-place Athletics. His streakiness evidenced itself in this rookie campaign with a .323 average prior to the All-Star break and a .245 mark after it. Giambi fashioned a 19-game hitting streak in April, homered in four consecutive games in June, tied a club record by stroking five hits in a game in July and established a single-season franchise mark with 40 doubles. But he did not homer after July 26. He divided his time evenly between the outfield, third base and at first—becoming the first Oakland player to start at least 30 games at three different positions—struggling only at the hot corner.

In a virtual carbon copy of his 1996 season, Giambi hit .293 with 20 round-trippers, 81 ribbies and 41 two-baggers in '97. Again playing both the infield and outfield, and now serving as an occasional designated hitter as well, he batted only .248 for the first month and a half before putting together an Oakland-record 25-game hitting streak. The thumping port-side swinger rang up a .364 average in June, set a franchise record with seven con-

Jason Giambi. (Courtesy George Brace Photo.)

secutive multi-hit games beginning in late August and hit .366 in September, but Oakland dropped to last place again.

With personal friend and mentor Mark McGwire having been traded to St. Louis, Giambi now had first base to himself. Although he committed 14 errors in 1998, his bat was more consistent. Moving from fifth in the order to third, he crafted hitting streaks of 16 and 17 games, batted .340 in July, drove in 27 runs in August, reached base via a hit or walk in 39 consecutive contests, and wound up leading the last-place A's in batting (.295), home runs (27), RBIs (110) and multi-hit games (45). He also batted .385 with a homer during the Major League Baseball All-Star Team's tour of Japan.

Giambi continued to climb the ladder in 1999, and his efforts helped the Athletics jump to second place in the West. His .315 average was an Oakland record for a lefty, and he upped his home run total to 33 and his RBIs to 123 (one shy of Jose Canseco's Oakland record) while scoring a career-high 115 runs and walking 105 times (second in the AL). Jason was one of only two junior circuit players to finish among the top 10 in walks, RBIs, extra base hits, on-base percentage and runs. He was particularly effective after the All-Star break, hitting .361 with 18 homers and 72 RBIs. The right-handed throwing first baseman also cut his error total in half and tied for second in fielding average (.995) among AL first sackers.

A's fans who were interested to see if Giambi could continue his amazing year-to-year improvement were not disappointed in 2000. The emerging team leader raised the bar in almost every offensive category, including batting average (.333), homers (43, tied for second in the league) and RBIs (137, tied for fourth), while piloting Oakland to its first West Division crown in eight years. The A's had been seven games behind Seattle August 11, but the September AL Player of the Month guided his club to a 22–6 finish by hitting .400 over the final month. Giambi led the majors in walks (137) and on-base percentage (franchise-record .482), and paced his team in batting, runs (108), hits (170), total bases (330), home runs, RBIs and slugging (.647, third in the AL).

The first-time All-Star hit two homers on opening day, belted four grand slams, hit .356 with runners in scoring position, was 7-for-11 in bases loaded situations, extended an errorless games streak to 78 and notched another .995 fielding percentage. Giambi was the player his teammates carried off the field when the A's clinched the division title on the final day of the regular season, but his .286 average was not enough to carry the club past New York in a five-game Division Series setback.

The heart and soul of the Athletics was seen as the team's catalyst by the writers, who gave him a narrow victory over Chicago's Frank Thomas in the MVP balloting. Giambi collected 14 first-place votes to nudge the two-time winner by 32 points. Jason's 2000 effort was one of the best in franchise history. His RBIs were the most by an A's player since 1933 when three-time MVP Jimmie Foxx drove in 163, his walks were second to Eddie Joost's 149 in 1949, and his batting and slugging averages were both runner-up marks in Oakland history.

Giambi built a 2001 season that was every bit as worthy of an MVP award, but fell just short in the voting to Ichiro Suzuki of Seattle. He led the team in batting for a record-fifth consecutive year with a career-best and league runner-up .342 mark, and although his home run and RBI totals slipped slightly (38 and 120), Giambi lashed a league-high 47 doubles, slugged at an AL-best .660 clip, produced a league-high .477 on-base percentage, scored 109 times and made his second All-Star Team. Although he collected four hits in Game 5 of the ALDS loss to the Yankees, he had only two safeties in his first 13 at-bats and may have cost his team a Game 3 victory when he failed to slide on a seventh-inning play in which shortstop Derek Jeter came out of nowhere to flip a relay toss to catcher Jorge Posada and protect a 1–0 New York lead.

A free agent following the 2001 season, Giambi had been close to signing a six-year deal worth $91 million, but by the time the A's were willing to add a no-trade clause to the mix, Jason had begun shopping his wares elsewhere. In December, he signed a seven-year, $120 million pact with the Yankees, whose deep pockets and shallow right-field porch were apparently too enticing to pass up. His departure as Oakland's all-time leading hitter (.308) marked a huge loss for the club that drafted him and harnessed his numerous skills through the years.

A talented package of braun and baseball smarts, the 31-year-old Jason Giambi should be a fan favorite in New York, where fans demand an all-out effort and will get nothing less from their new slugger. And if Giambi continues to improve every year, he'll eventually be banging on the front door in Cooperstown, probably with his motorcycle idling in the driveway.

Top 5 MVP Vote-Getters

1. Jason Giambi, Oakland — 317
2. Frank Thomas, Chicago — 285
3. Alex Rodriguez, Seattle — 218
4. Carlos Delgado, Toronto — 206
5. Pedro Martinez, Boston — 103

2001 NATIONAL LEAGUE — BARRY BONDS

Barry Lamar Bonds
B. July 24, 1964, Riverside, California

Year	Team	Games	AB	Hits	Avg.	HR	RBI	Runs	SB
2001	SF NL	153	476	156	.328	73	137	129	13

The Season

The year 2001 was a bittersweet one for Major League Baseball, which saw one week's worth of games postponed following the September 11 terrorist attacks in New York City and Washington D.C., then witnessed one of the most exciting World Series of all time.

Everything — sports, entertainment and even major news stories — took a backseat to the devastation that occurred in the country's most significant financial and political centers. What had seemed vitally important to baseball fans on September 10, including division races, batting averages and earned run averages, now seemed trivial compared to the loss of life and the preparation for war in Afghanistan.

Bent but not broken, United States citizens rallied behind President George Bush and followed his admonition to return as much as possible to their normal routines. One of those activities was going to the ballpark, where heightened security measures could not dampen a wave of patriotism unseen since World War II. And once the sport had its followers' attention again, it flourished like a spring bloom.

The Atlanta Braves, who became the first team to qualify for the postseason with a losing record at home (40–41), established a mark believed to be unmatched in any sport with their 10th consecutive division title, coming back from an eight-game deficit to win the National League East by two games over Philadelphia. Arizona captured the West by a pair of games over San Francisco, while Houston earned its fourth Central Division crown in the past five years by virtue of a tie-breaker over Wild Card St. Louis.

The Astros made yet another early exit from post-season play when they were swept by Atlanta 3–0 in one Division Series, while Arizona knocked off the Cardinals 3–2 in the other. Continuing to rely on the mighty left and right arms of Randy Johnson and Curt Schilling, respectively, the Diamondbacks crushed the Braves 4–1 in the League Championship Series to advance to the World Series in only their fourth year of existence.

Featuring two incredible come-from-behind victories by the New York Yankees, who were seeking their fourth consecutive World Championship, the World Series ended with an equally dramatic comeback by Arizona, which scored two runs in the bottom of the ninth inning of Game 7 to earn a 3–2 victory and the ultimate prize in baseball.

There were many individual achievements in 2001, but none greater than the record-shattering season fashioned by Barry Bonds, who slammed 73 home runs, demolished longstanding marks for slugging percentage and walks, and garnered an unprecedented fourth Most Valuable Player award.

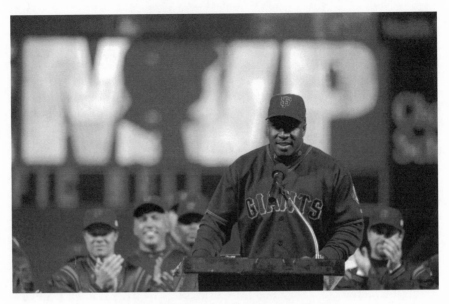

Barry Bonds. (Courtesy San Francisco Giants.)

Another player who earned the spotlight was San Diego's Rickey Henderson. He established major league career highs in walks (2,141) and runs (2,248) — passing a guy named Babe Ruth in both categories — and collected his 3,000th hit on the final day of the regular season. The 42-year-old had already stolen more bases than any player in history (1,395 through 2001), and he added to his major league-leading total of home runs leading off a game with No. 79.

Johnson, who tied a major league record with 20 strikeouts in a game, posted 21 regular-season victories, plus league bests in ERA (2.49) and strikeouts (372) to claim his third consecutive Cy Young Award and fourth overall. The Big Unit then won three World Series games, including No. 6 and 7. Schilling won 22 games, led the league in complete games (six) and innings pitched (256.2), and placed second in ERA (2.98) and whiffs (293), giving Arizona a 1–2 pitching punch reminiscent of Spahn and Sain, and Koufax and Drysdale.

Chicago right fielder Sammy Sosa became the first player in major league history to record three 60-homer seasons when he belted a runner-up total of 64. The NL leader in RBIs (160), runs (146) and total bases (425) finished second in slugging (.737) and in the MVP balloting.

Atlanta pitcher Greg Maddux es-

tablished a major league record for most innings without issuing a walk (72.1) and earned his 12th consecutive Gold Glove, while San Diego's Trevor Hoffman became the first pitcher to record four straight 40-save seasons and five career 40-save seasons. Albert Pujols of the Cardinals set NL rookie records for RBIs (130), extra base hits (88) and total bases (360), and Colorado's Todd Helton became the first player with 100-plus extra base hits in consecutive seasons. Helton's teammate, Jason Jennings, became the first pitcher in the modern era to hit a home run and toss a shutout in his major league debut.

Cubs pitchers set a record for strikeouts in a season with 1,344, while their batters made the Cubs the first team in major league history to avoid having a complete game thrown against them. On the other hand, Milwaukee Brewers batsmen established a single-season record for strikeouts (1,399) and became the first team to have more whiffs than hits (1,378).

Finally, Tony Gwynn of the Padres and Mark McGwire of St. Louis hung up their cleats for the last time after producing 3,141 hits and 583 home runs, respectively.

Seventy-Three

They say that records are made to be broken. But not this kind of record, and certainly not this quickly. It took 34 years following Babe Ruth's 60-homer effort in 1927 for a player named Roger Maris to come along and establish a new one with 61 home runs in 1961. Another 37 years lapsed before Maris' single-season record was eclipsed by Mark McGwire in 1998. But McGwire did not merely break Maris' standard, he obliterated it with 70 round-trippers, and baseball experts were claiming that here was a record that would stand the test of time, just as Ruth's and Maris' had over a combined 71 years.

But something simply amazing occurred only three years later. Barry Bonds shocked the baseball world by upping the ante with 73 homers in 2001, and now the pundits are wondering if 80 circuit clouts in a season is just around the corner.

Although he possessed tremendous power, and had already drilled 494 seat-reachers over a 15-year career, Bonds seemed an unlikely candidate to attain the most acclaimed record in baseball prior to the 2001 season. The San Francisco Giants left fielder would be turning 37 in just a few months—10 years past most players' prime—and had never stroked more than 49 homers in a season.

But Bonds, who weighed 185 pounds when he earned his initial National League MVP award in 1990, and who had filled out to 210 in 2000, bulked up even more during the off-season through a rigorous weight-training program, coming to camp with a 228-pound frame and virtually no body fat. Wearing his pants legs all the way down to his shoes, choking up on a 34-inch, 31½-ounce bat and adding elevation to his swing, Barry was a sight to behold in 2001. Any pitchers who figured he was past his prime were in for a rude awakening.

The left-handed slugger homered on opening day, and never let up. His sixth homer of the season — which he called his greatest baseball thrill — came April 17 at Pacific Bell Park in San Francisco against Los Angeles. It was the 500th of his illustrious career, making him one of only 17 players to reach that magical plateau.

Standing close to the plate and utilizing a short, compact power stroke with his hand-made maple bat, Bonds was not only hitting home runs at a frightening pace, he was jacking them for great distances, including a significant number which splashed into McCovey Cove beyond the right field seats at Pac Bell. But he was even more impressive away from home during the first half of the season, hitting 16 of his first 25 homers in road games. The veteran smacked 25 round-trippers in the Giants' first 47 games, and 35 of his first 45 hits went for extra bases.

Although the clean-up hitter had some protection around him in the lineup — Rich Aurilia enjoyed a breakout season batting in the No. 3 spot and defending NL MVP Jeff Kent was solid in the fifth slot — Bonds was still pitched very cautiously this season, as indicated by 89 walks in his first 85 games. But even when he would see only one decent pitch per at-bat, Bonds took advantage of his opportunities, making hurlers pay big time for their strike zone offerings.

Several multi-homer games for the port-side swinger, including the three-homer day he crafted May 19 at Atlanta, helped boost what was becoming an impressive long ball total prior to the All-Star break. In fact, his five home runs over two consecutive games (May 19–20) tied a major league record. Media were beginning to take note that Bonds was ahead of McGwire's 1998 home run pace, but always with the caveat that Barry's mission would become much more difficult in the latter part of the season, especially if the Giants were in a race for the division title.

Wisely, Bonds downplayed his quest for baseball immortality, repeatedly saying he was astonished at what was happening, but possessed no illusions of reaching the lofty heights McGwire had climbed so recently. The National League Player of the Month in May was the NL All-Star Game's leading vote-getter, but he received a scare July 18 when back spasms sent him to the clubhouse after he had connected for a pair of homers against Colorado. Following a one-week dry spell, he walloped two circuit clouts, including a grand slam, against Arizona for his 43rd and 44th of the season in his team's 103rd game, moving ahead of three-time American League MVP Mickey Mantle into ninth place on the career homer list.

Bonds launched his career-high 50th home run August 11 at Chicago's Wrigley Field, then hit three in a home series against Florida for a total of 53 through 121 games. With 41 games remaining, he seemed a cinch to reach the once-prized pinnacle of 60, and talk of his odds of reaching 70 was increasing rapidly. Bonds clubbed his 58th homer, a 435-foot shot to center field, September 3 against Colorado, then drilled a pair in a series with Arizona to match Ruth's 60 mark.

Even before the terrorist attacks of September 11, there was considerable speculation regarding why Bonds' incredible march toward the major league home run record was not receiving nearly the attention that McGwire's feat had in '98. Among the theories were how recently the new standard had been established, the proliferation of the long ball over the past several years, beefed-up athletes, the increased number of hitter's parks being built, diluted pitching, a smaller strike zone and Bonds' overall lack of popularity among the media and much of the public.

All no doubt contributed, but perhaps the most plausible reason was that in 1998, the nation's attention had focused on a wonderful home run derby between McGwire and Sammy Sosa. This soothing ointment being poured over a baseball fandom still smarting from the 1994–95 strike was a pleasant distraction to everyday problems. But Bonds was going it alone, chasing a number rather than a person.

And speaking of alone, that's what Barry preferred to be left. Never having sought out the limelight, this was a role he did not cherish. He tried to be as accommodating to the media as possible before and after most games, but sometimes chose to slip out the back door rather than answer the same questions about his home run pace day after day. A *Sports Illustrated* column defining Bonds as a self-absorbed individual playing a team game only added to the recalcitrant athlete's reputation.

Despite the pressure surrounding him at every turn, Bonds kept on slugging. On September 9 at Colorado, he pounded his longest homer of the season, 488 feet to center field, then laced two more shots to the right field seats for a total of 63 in the Giants' 144th game. The events of September 11 put baseball on hold for a week, and it took Barry a few games to get untracked again. He later linked this drought to a lack of concentration due to death threats he had received.

Bonds launched his 64th homer September 20 against Houston, then hit four versus San Diego and one against Los Angeles during a seven-day stretch late in the month. He now had 69 — tying Reggie Jackson for seventh place in career homers — with seven games to play. The only thing that could seemingly keep the September NL Player of the Month from reaching his goal was a lack of pitches to hit, and that's exactly what he got. In his next 19 plate appearances, he was walked 10 times and hit by two pitches, prompting his daughters to hold up a sign at Houston's Enron Field that read, "Please pitch to our Daddy." Finally, in the ninth inning of an October 4 game at Houston, Wilfredo Rodriguez served up a high fastball that Bonds tattooed 454 feet for his record-tying 70th homer, sending the Enron Field crowd into a frenzy.

Returning to Pac Bell Park for a season-ending series with Los Angeles, Bonds wasted little time setting the all-time single-season home run record. A first-inning blast off Chan Ho Park sailed 442 feet to right-center field for his 71st homer, and two innings later, Park was the victim of a 404-footer to left-center for No. 72. Ironically, the Giants were eliminated from playoff contention in an 11–10 loss that evening. After taking the next day off, Bonds connected for his 73rd and final homer in the first inning of the season finale off Dennis Springer, a 385-foot

drive to right field that set off a mad scramble in the bleachers. Fan Patrick Hayashi emerged with the ball, but was later ordered by a San Francisco judge to refrain from selling it until an ownership suit was settled with another fan, Alex Popov.

The oldest player to lead the majors in home runs hit at least one dinger in every NL park in 2001. Twenty-four of those clouts gave the Giants a lead, seven tied the game, 10 extended a one-run lead and six brought San Francisco within a run of its opponent. He hit 36 of his homers on the road and 37 at home, with 57 coming off right-handed pitchers and 16 off southpaws. San Diego was tagged with 11 of the round-trippers, Colorado with 10 and Arizona nine. Bonds clobbered 12 homers each in the first and fourth innings of his games, and his 73 blasts traveled a combined distance of 29,468 feet, or 5.6 miles.

His home run total will be what is remembered most fondly this season, but Bonds did so much more than provide souvenirs for bleacherites. Two major league records that Ruth had established some eight decades earlier were erased by Bonds in 2001. Barry's .863 slugging percentage was 16 points higher than Ruth's in 1920, and his 177 walks topped Ruth's 170 total in 1923. A .515 on-base percentage was the highest in the NL since 1899, and he reached base via a hit, walk or hit by pitch in 143 of 153 games, including his last 42 contests. Bonds, who batted an impressive .328, was third in the league in both runs (129) and total bases (411), and fourth in RBIs (137).

While much of the media might not be overly fond of Bonds on a personal level, they certainly respect his abilities on the diamond. Receiving 30 of 32 first-place votes, Barry captured his fourth Most Valuable Player award, the only player in baseball history to do it. The honor finally set him apart from three-time winners Jimmie Foxx,

Joe DiMaggio, Stan Musial, Yogi Berra, Roy Campanella, Mickey Mantle and Mike Schmidt. In addition to his $10.3 million salary for 2001, Bonds received a $100,000 bonus for his award, the same amount he donated to the United Way to aid victims of the terrorist attacks ($10,000 per homer beginning with his 64th.) He was also named the Male Athlete of the Year by the Associated Press.

Through the 2001 season, Bonds was the lone member of the 400-homer, 400-stolen base club, and was only 16 steals shy of creating an exclusive 500-500 club. That lethal combination of power and speed, as well as an ability to hit for average and field his position so flawlessly, puts Bonds in a class by himself among current players. Bonds took himself out of the soft free agent market in December 2001, accepting the Giants' offer of salary arbitration. Agent Scott Boras reportedly had been seeking a five-year, $100 million deal.

A shoe-in for the Hall of Fame five years after he retires, Barry Bonds will not go down in history as the greatest player in baseball, despite his vast accomplishments. An inability to guide his teams to post-season glory — at least through the 2001 season — will always represent a smudge on his resumé. But he is definitely one of the best to ever don a major league uniform, and his four Most Valuable Player awards are proof positive of that.

Top 5 MVP Vote-Getters

1. Barry Bonds, San Francisco — 438
2. Sammy Sosa, Chicago — 278
3. Luis Gonzalez, Arizona — 261
4. Albert Pujols, St. Louis — 222
5. Lance Berkman, Houston — 125

2001 AMERICAN LEAGUE—ICHIRO SUZUKI

Ichiro Suzuki
B. October 22, 1973, Kasugai, Japan

Year	Team	Games	AB	Hits	Avg.	HR	RBI	Runs	SB
2001	Sea AL	157	692	242	.350	8	69	127	56

The Season

What could possibly be expected from a team that loses players with the caliber of Randy Johnson, Ken Griffey, Jr. and Alex Rodriguez over a 2½-year period? How about the most regular-season wins in American League history? The Seattle Mariners defied all the odds in 2001, winning a major league record-tying 116 games, winning the West Division by 14 games over Oakland and qualifying for post-season play for the second year in a row.

The eighth team in history to win its league or division going wire to wire, the Mariners featured the table-setting talents of Rookie of the Year and Most Valuable Player Ichiro Suzuki; the run-producing skills of Bret Boone, Edgar Martinez, John Olerud and Mike Cameron; and the pitching of Jamie Moyer, Freddy Garcia, Paul Abbott and Kazuhiro Sasaki to lead the junior circuit in runs scored and fewest allowed. After a poor start, the Athletics closed with a 29–4 run and became the first Wild Card team with 102 wins.

The New York Yankees helped the nation recover from terrorist attacks that destroyed the World Trade Center towers by bearing down to win their fourth consecutive division title, outdistancing Boston by 13½ games in the East, while Cleveland claimed its sixth Central crown in seven years, by six games over Minnesota.

In a pair of exciting five-game Division Series, the Yankees came back from a 2–0 deficit to eliminate Oakland, while Seattle rallied from a 2–1 hole to edge the Indians. New York continued to illustrate its resiliency, bouncing the Mariners 4–1 in the AL Championship Series to advance to the World Series for the fifth time in a half-dozen years.

Special baseballs featuring a stars and stripes pattern were used in the fall classic, and President George Bush threw out the ceremonial first pitch prior to Game 3 at Yankee Stadium. Julie Ruth Stevens, 84, the daughter of Babe Ruth and a part-time Phoenix resident, attended the Series, rooting for the Arizona Diamondbacks. Heading into the ninth inning of Game 7, it appeared that the Yanks would capture yet another World Series title, but reliever Mariano Rivera's streak of 23 consecutive post-season saves ended when the Diamondbacks stormed back for a pair of runs in the bottom of the ninth. It marked the first time since 1947 that the Yankees lost a post-season game they led after eight innings.

Individual standouts this season included Texas shortstop Rodriguez, who after signing a record-$252 million contract, established a major league mark for home runs by a shortstop with 52. Seattle's Boone set records for homers (37) and RBIs (141) by a second baseman, while New York's Paul O'Neill became the oldest player (38) with 20-plus home runs and 20-plus steals in a season.

In the Gold Glove department, Texas catcher and 1999 MVP Ivan Rodriguez earned his 10th in a row, while the Cleveland double play combination of second baseman Roberto Alomar and Omar Vizquel continued to dominate. Alomar claimed his record-10th in the past 11 years, while Vizquel won for the ninth consecutive season.

While the World Series produced a tremendous buzz for baseball, a couple of events following the season put a damper on the sport. With rumors of another work stoppage on the horizon and owners decrying huge financial losses—the average player salary during 2001 was a record-$2,138,896—

Commissioner Bud Selig announced that two major league teams would be eliminated in 2002. Legal efforts by the players association to thwart that contraction were taken immediately, and the eventual settlement resulted in the Minnesota Twins and Montreal Expos franchises remaining intact.

Shortly after the owners pled poverty, the Yankees signed free agent and 2000 AL MVP Jason Giambi to a seven-year contract worth $120 million, and the Boston Red Sox were sold for a mind-boggling $660 million to a group led by Florida Marlins owner John Henry and former San Diego Padres owner Tom Werner. The sale more than doubled the previous record-$323 million that was paid for the Cleveland Indians in 2000.

Also, Toronto assistant general manager Dave Stewart accused baseball of having racist hiring policies when he was bypassed for the GM job in favor of J.P. Ricciardi, then took a job as a Milwaukee Brewers pitching coach. Kenny Williams of the Chicago White Sox was the only African-American GM during the 2001 campaign.

Finally, Cal Ripken, Jr. retired after 21 seasons featuring 3,001 games, 3,184 hits and a consecutive games played streak of 2,632 that should endure through the ages. Elected to the Hall of Fame in 2001 were outfielders Kirby Puckett and Dave Winfield.

Japanese Sensation

A breath of fresh air from the Far East swept across the United States in 2001, and his name was Ichiro Suzuki. Fully modern, yet harkening back to a time when singles, base running and defense were the key ingredients to success, the "Michael Jordan" of Japan took baseball back to its roots by putting on a brilliant display of the game's basics seldom seen since the first few decades of the 1900s.

Many baseball writers in recent years had settled into the comfortable habit of selecting Most Valuable Players based mainly on their abilities to crank the ball out of the park and drive in base runners. But conjuring up images of MVPs such as Frankie Frisch, Marty Marion, Nellie Fox, Dick Groat and Maury Wills — ballplayers who made their living off reaching base, taking the extra base, stealing a base and playing superb defense — the scribes gave the nod for the American League 2001 Most Valuable Player to a slashing-style right fielder who demonstrated both a masterful knowledge of the game and an uncanny skill at executing the fundamentals.

Possessing lightning speed, a potent arm, an ability to spray the ball to all fields and base running smarts, Suzuki was the catalyst for a Seattle Mariners squad which set an all-time American League record for regular-season wins with 116, tying the Chicago Cubs' 1906 big league mark.

Utilizing a quick bat that more often resembled a magic wand this season, "The Wizard" slapped an amazing total of 242 hits, the most in baseball since Bill Terry stroked 254 in 1930 and the largest number in the AL in 76 years. The 5-foot-9, 160-pounder led the majors in batting (.350) and stolen bases (56), and scored 127 runs (second in the league). He led the junior circuit in multi-hit games with 75, tied for seventh in triples with eight and was ninth in total bases with 316. In one of the closest votes in the 81 years of MVP balloting, Suzuki edged defending AL MVP Jason Giambi 289–281, with Seattle teammate Bret Boone a close third at 259.

This type of season would have been considered phenomenal if produced by any player, but for an athlete competing in his first major league season, it was even more remarkable. Twenty-seven-year-old rookies are few and far between, but Suzuki was hardly a rookie in the traditional sense. He'd already torn up the Pacific League in Japan for nine years before coming to the U.S.

One week prior to being named the AL's MVP, Suzuki captured 27-of-28 first-place votes for the league's Rookie of the Year honor. Although admittedly "embarrassed" to be called a rookie, the precedent had already been set, with Mariners relief pitcher Kazuhiro Sasaki claiming the 2000 Rookie of the Year honor after becoming the all-time saves leader in Japan.

Suzuki broke the rookie record for hits that had been established by Shoeless Joe Jackson of Cleveland (233) in 1911, and became the first rookie to win the batting title since Tony Oliva of Minnesota turned the trick with a .323 mark in 1964. Ichiro was the first player to lead the majors in both batting and steals in the same season since another pioneer, Jackie Robinson, pulled off the feat during his 1949 MVP campaign.

Suzuki's 192 singles shattered Harvey Kuenn's 1953 rookie record of 167, and came within six of Lloyd Waner's all-time mark. He was only the seventh rookie to surpass 200 hits with no prior major league experience, and his 692 at-bats were a league record for first-year players. Suzuki joined Fred Lynn (1975) as the only players to garner both the MVP and Rookie of the Year awards in the same season.

Over in Japan, where Ichiro Suzuki enjoys the popularity of a rock star, they know he is no rookie by any stretch of the imagination. His father encouraged him to bat left-handed when he was a youngster, and he excelled as a right-handed pitcher in high school. He won seven consecutive Pacific League batting titles while playing for the Orix Blue Wave, earned seven Gold Gloves and was a three-time league MVP (1994–96). Japan's most popular player, to whom a museum with baseball memorabilia and childhood toys and bikes is dedicated in Nagoya City, was a league "Best Nine" member seven years in a row, including in 2000 when he hit a career-high .387 and led the circuit in on-base percentage (.460) for the fifth time.

The Mariners had invited Suzuki to spring training in 1999, and following the 2000 season, paid his team $13.125 million for the right to offer

him a contract. The free agent gladly accepted, signing a three-year deal for $14.088 million. His only perk? An English teacher for he and his wife, Yumiko, an anchor for Toyko Broadcasting at the 1998 Nagano Winter Olympics.

Even in smaller Japanese ballparks, Suzuki had fewer than 60 career home runs over nine seasons, so eight round-trippers during his rookie year with the Mariners were icing on the cake. With the exception of pitchers, no MVP had hit fewer than 10 homers since Wills in 1962, and no AL MVP had been under that mark since Fox in '59. But the writers looked closely at this sparkplug's flashy fielding, superb base running and an ability to set the table for his slugging teammates.

Though he had not learned English, and always spoke to reporters through an interpreter, this Japanese import adjusted quickly to life in the States, enjoying hip-hop music, wearing dark sunglasses and utilizing pop culture phrases such as "Wassup?" as well as his personal favorite, "Thanks, dogg." Although the first Japanese position player to play for a major league team did not fare well in spring training, Suzuki broke out of the gate quickly once the real deal began. Rookie of the Month for the first of four times, he hit .336 in April. An on-the-fly throw to gun down Oakland jackrabbit Terrence Long trying to advance from first to third on a single that month gave notice that this was no one-dimensional ballplayer. Using a large, black Mizuno outfielder's glove, Ichiro wound up committing only one error in 344 total chances for the year, was third among league outfielders with a .997 fielding percentage and tied for the team high with eight outfield assists.

With another Rookie of the Month honor coming in May, the All-Star Game votes started pouring in. Suzuki ended up collecting a major league-high 3,373,035 votes, thanks in part to worldwide online support and paper ballots that were cast in Japan for the first time. Fittingly, the surging Mariners hosted the All-Star contest, where Suzuki was the first elected rookie starter in 11 years.

The outstanding "rook" slumped

immediately following the mid-summer classic, going 1-for-20 and batting only .268 in July. But he charged back to hit .429 in August with 51 hits (matching his uniform number), then batted .349 in September–October. A 23-game hitting streak tied for the longest in the majors this season (he also had streaks of 21 and 15 games), and his .445 average with runners in scoring position was a big-league best.

Seattle, which had won the AL West Division by a wide margin over Oakland, struggled to eliminate Cleveland in a five-game Division Series, then ran out of gas in a disappointing 4–1 League Championship Series setback to New York. Suzuki hit safely in nine of the 10 Mariners' post-season games, batting .600 in the Division Series with a trio of three-hit contests, but being limited to a .222 mark in the LCS.

In addition to the Rookie of the Year and MVP accolades, which earned him an extra $225,000 in bonuses, Suzuki claimed a Gold Glove and a Silver Slugger award, and was named *The Sporting News* American League Rookie of the Year.

Ichiro's name means "First Boy" in Japanese, and that was certainly a fitting moniker for the Mariners' very effective leadoff hitter in 2001. Rumors surfaced following the season that Seattle would move the only U.S. major leaguer to wear his first name on the back of his jersey down in the lineup if they could acquire another speedy leadoff man, but the MVP vowed he would not change his style of play despite his place in the order. "If I start trying to hit for more power, I will lose what I do as a baseball player," he said.

And nobody wants that.

Top 5 MVP Vote-Getters

1. Ichiro Suzuki, Seattle — 289
2. Jason Giambi, Oakland — 281
3. Bret Boone, Seattle — 259
4. Roberto Alomar, Cleveland — 165
5. Juan Gonzalez, Cleveland — 156

Appendix A:
Listing by Positions

Outfielders have been chosen 52 times as Most Valuable Player, making them, in general, the most likely to be voted MVPs. But if the award is broken down into specific positions, first basemen top the list. Pitchers are second overall, but are rare winners these days; only nine have been selected since the inception of the Cy Young Award in 1956. Second base is the toughest position from which to capture the laurel.

Position	*Times Selected MVP*
First Baseman	23
Pitcher	20
Left Fielder	19
Right Fielder	19
Catcher	14
Center Fielder	14
Third Baseman	13
Shortstop	12
Second Baseman	9

Appendix B:
Best Marks Achieved by
MVPs During Their MVP Seasons

Category	Statistic	MVP	Team (League)	Year
Batting Average	.390	George Brett	Kansas City (AL)	1980
Hits	242	Ichiro Suzuki	Seattle (AL)	2001
Home Runs	73	Barry Bonds	San Francisco (NL)	2001
RBIs	175	Jimmie Foxx	Boston (AL)	1938
Runs	167	Lou Gehrig	New York (AL)	1936
Stolen Bases	104	Maury Wills	Los Angeles (NL)	1962
Wins	31	Lefty Grove	Philadelphia (AL)	1931
ERA (Starter)	1.12	Bob Gibson	St. Louis (NL)	1968
ERA (Reliever)	1.04	Rollie Fingers	Milwaukee (AL)	1981
Innings Pitched	336	Denny McLain	Detroit (AL)	1968
Strikeouts	306	Sandy Koufax	Los Angeles (NL)	1963
Shutouts	13	Bob Gibson	St. Louis (NL)	1968
Saves	51	Dennis Eckersley	Oakland (AL)	1992

Appendix C:
Listing by Teams

NATIONAL LEAGUE

St. Louis Cardinals — 14

Frankie Frisch (1931)
Dizzy Dean (1934)
Joe Medwick (1937)
Mort Cooper (1942)
Stan Musial (1943)
Marty Marion (1944)
Stan Musial (1946)
Stan Musial (1948)
Ken Boyer (1964)
Orlando Cepeda (1967)
Bob Gibson (1968)
Joe Torre (1971)
Keith Hernandez (1979)
Willie McGee (1985)

Cincinnati Reds — 11

Ernie Lombardi (1938)
Bucky Walters (1939)
Frank McCormick (1940)
Frank Robinson (1961)
Johnny Bench (1970)
Johnny Bench (1972)
Pete Rose (1973)
Joe Morgan (1975)
Joe Morgan (1976)
George Foster (1977)
Barry Larkin (1995)

Brooklyn/Los Angeles Dodgers — 10

Dolph Camilli (1941)
Jackie Robinson (1949)
Roy Campanella (1951)
Roy Campanella (1953)
Roy Campanella (1955)
Don Newcombe (1956)
Maury Wills (1962)
Sandy Koufax (1963)
Steve Garvey (1974)
Kirk Gibson (1988)

New York/San Francisco Giants — 9

Carl Hubbell (1933)
Carl Hubbell (1936)
Willie Mays (1954)
Willie Mays (1965)
Willie McCovey (1969)
Kevin Mitchell (1989)
Barry Bonds (1993)
Jeff Kent (2000)
Barry Bonds (2001)

Chicago Cubs — 8

Gabby Harnett (1935)
Phil Cavarretta (1945)
Hank Sauer (1952)
Ernie Banks (1958)
Ernie Banks (1959)
Ryne Sandberg (1984)
Andre Dawson (1987)
Sammy Sosa (1998)

Boston/Milwaukee/Atlanta Braves — 6

Bob Elliott (1947)
Hank Aaron (1957)
Dale Murphy (1982)
Dale Murphy (1983)
Terry Pendleton (1991)
Chipper Jones (1999)

Pittsburgh Pirates — 6

Dick Groat (1960)
Roberto Clemente (1966)
Dave Parker (1978)
Willie Stargell (1979)
Barry Bonds (1990)
Barry Bonds (1992)

Philadelphia Phillies — 5

Chuck Klein (1932)
Jim Konstanty (1950)
Mike Schmidt (1980)
Mike Schmidt (1981)
Mike Schmidt (1986)

Colorado Rockies — 1

Larry Walker (1997)

Houston Astros — 1

Jeff Bagwell (1994)

San Diego Padres — 1

Ken Caminiti (1996)

AMERICAN LEAGUE

New York Yankees — 18

Lou Gehrig (1936)
Joe DiMaggio (1939)
Joe DiMaggio (1941)
Joe Gordon (1942)
Spud Chandler (1943)
Joe DiMaggio (1947)
Phil Rizzuto (1950)
Yogi Berra (1951)
Yogi Berra (1954)
Yogi Berra (1955)
Mickey Mantle (1956)
Mickey Mantle (1957)
Roger Maris (1960)
Roger Maris (1961)
Mickey Mantle (1962)
Elston Howard (1963)
Thurman Munson (1976)
Don Mattingly (1985)

Philadelphia/Oakland Athletics — 10

Lefty Grove (1931)
Jimmie Foxx (1932)
Jimmie Foxx (1933)
Bobby Shantz (1952)
Vida Blue (1971)
Reggie Jackson (1973)
Jose Canseco (1988)
Rickey Henderson (1990)
Dennis Eckersley (1992)
Jason Giambi (2000)

Boston Red Sox — 9

Jimmie Foxx (1938)
Ted Williams (1946)
Ted Williams (1949)
Jackie Jensen (1958)
Carl Yastrzemski (1967)
Fred Lynn (1975)
Jim Rice (1978)
Roger Clemens (1986)
Mo Vaughn (1995)

Detroit Tigers — 8

Mickey Cochrane (1934)
Hank Greenberg (1935)
Charlie Gehringer (1937)
Hank Greenberg (1940)
Hal Newhouser (1944)
Hal Newhouser (1945)
Denny McLain (1968)
Willie Hernandez (1984)

Baltimore Orioles — 5

Brooks Robinson (1964)
Frank Robinson (1966)
Boog Powell (1970)
Cal Ripken, Jr. (1983)
Cal Ripken, Jr. (1991)

Chicago White Sox — 4

Nellie Fox (1959)
Dick Allen (1972)
Frank Thomas (1993)
Frank Thomas (1994)

Texas Rangers — 4

Jeff Burroughs (1974)
Juan Gonzalez (1996)
Juan Gonzalez (1998)
Ivan Rodriguez (1999)

Milwaukee Brewers — 3

Rollie Fingers (1981)
Robin Yount (1982)
Robin Yount (1989)

Minnesota Twins — 3

Zoilo Versalles (1965)
Harmon Killebrew (1969)
Rod Carew (1977)

Cleveland Indians — 2

Lou Boudreau (1948)
Al Rosen (1953)

Seattle Mariners — 2

Ken Griffey, Jr. (1997)
Ichiro Suzuki (2001)

California Angels — 1

Don Baylor (1979)

Kansas City Royals — 1

George Brett (1980)

Toronto Blue Jays — 1

George Bell (1987)

Appendix D:
Missing MVPs

The Missing MVPs

Baseball writers have taken excellent care of the Most Valuable Player award in both leagues since 1931, but the irregular status of the honor in the early days of the game's "modern era" leaves room for much speculation. Who, for example, might have captured MVP honors prior to the short-lived Chalmers Award, which was presented from 1911 through 1914? And what of those campaigns between 1915 and 1921, before the League Awards were established, when the most valuable laurel was in limbo?

The presumptuous premise of this appendix is to fictionally fill in those gaps with MVP winners (in bold) and deserving runners-up. No doubt, the delving into this unopened can of worms will lead to much disagreement, but such is the nature of the game and its MVP award. Here then are the "Missing MVPs," along with the Chalmers Award and League Award winners, from 1900 to 1930.

1900 NL

Honus Wagner, Pittsburgh

Shortstop led the league in batting (.381), slugging (.573), total bases (302), doubles (45) and triples (22), and was third in both RBIs (100) and hits (201).

- Joe McGinnity, Brooklyn, pitcher — 28 wins, 343 innings, .778 win percentage.
- Elmer Flick, Philadelphia, right fielder — .367, 11 homers, 110 RBIs, 297 total bases.

1901 NL

Jimmy Sheckard, Brooklyn

Left fielder topped the circuit in slugging (.534) and triples (19), and was second in batting (.354), homers (11) and total bases (296), while placing third in RBIs (104) and hits (196).

- Jesse Burkett, St. Louis, left fielder — .376, 226 hits, 10 homers, 142 runs, 306 total bases.
- Ed Delahanty, Philadelphia, left fielder — .354, 108 RBIs, 38 doubles, .528 slugging average.

1901 AL

Napoleon Lajoie, Philadelphia

Second baseman dominated the league in batting (.426), homers (14), RBIs (125), total bases (350), runs (145), hits (232), doubles (48) and slugging (.643).

- Cy Young, Boston, pitcher — 33 wins, 1.62 ERA, 158 strikeouts, five shutouts, 38 complete games, .767 win percentage.
- Buck Freeman, Boston, first baseman — .339, 12 homers, 114 RBIs, .520 slugging average.

1902 NL

Honus Wagner, Pittsburgh

Outfielder/infielder led the league in a shortened season in RBIs (91), runs (105), slugging (.463), doubles (30) and steals (42), while accumulating 247 total bases (second) and a .330 batting average (fourth).

- Tommy Leach, Pittsburgh, third baseman — 85 RBIs, 22 triples, six homers.
- Sam Crawford, Cincinnati, right fielder — .333, 256 total bases, 22 triples, .461 slugging percentage.

1902 AL

Cy Young, Boston

Pitcher paced the AL in wins (32), complete games (41), innings (384.2) and appearances (45), while compiling a 2.15 ERA (third).

- Charles "Piano Legs" Hickman, Boston/Cleveland, first baseman — .361, 11 homers, 110 RBIs, 193 hits, 288 total bases.
- Ed Delahanty, Washington, left fielder — .376, 43 doubles, .590 slugging average.

1903 NL

Honus Wagner, Pittsburgh

Shortstop was the NL's best in batting (.355) and triples (19), while placing second in RBIs (101) and slugging (.518), and third in total bases (265) and stolen bases (46).

- Christy Mathewson, New York, pitcher — 30 wins, 2.26 ERA, 267 strikeouts, 37 complete games.
- Joe McGinnity, New York, pitcher — 31 wins, 2.43 ERA, 44 complete games, 171 strikeouts.

1903 AL

Cy Young, Boston

Pitcher was No. 1 in the junior circuit in victories (28), win percentage (.757), innings (341.2), complete games (34) and shutouts (seven), while posting a 2.08 ERA (second).

- Buck Freeman, Boston, right fielder —104 RBIs, 13 homers, 281 total bases.
- Napoleon Lajoie, Cleveland, second baseman — .344, .518 slugging average, 41 doubles.

1904 NL

Joe McGinnity, New York

Pitcher produced circuit-topping marks in wins (35), ERA (1.61), saves (five), win percentage (.814), innings (408) and appearances (51).

- Honus Wagner, Pittsburgh, shortstop — .349, 255 total bases, .520 slugging average, 44 doubles, 53 steals.
- Christy Mathewson, New York, pitcher — 33 wins, 212 strikeouts, 367.2 innings.

1904 AL

Jack Chesbro, New York

Pitcher rang up league bests in wins (41), win percentage (.774), complete games (48), innings (454.2) and appearances (55), while fanning 239 (second) and crafting a 1.82 ERA (fifth).

- Napoleon Lajoie, Cleveland, second baseman — .376, 102 RBIs, 208 hits, 49 doubles, 302 total bases, .546 slugging average.
- Rube Waddell, Philadelphia, pitcher — 25 wins, 1.62 ERA, 349 strikeouts, eight shutouts, 383 innings.

1905 NL

Christy Mathewson, New York

Pitcher topped the statistical charts in wins (31), ERA (1.28), strikeouts (206) and shutouts (eight), while appearing in 43 games over 338.2 innings (both third).

- Cy Seymour, Cincinnati, center fielder — .377, 121 RBIs, 325 total bases, .559 slugging average, 219 hits, 40 doubles, 21 triples.
- Honus Wagner, Pittsburgh, shortstop — .363, 101 RBIs, .505 slugging percentage.

1905 AL

Harry Davis, Philadelphia

First baseman was the AL's most productive in homers (eight), RBIs (83), runs (93) and doubles (47), while placing second in total bases (256) and hits (173).

- Rube Waddell, Philadelphia, pitcher — 27 wins, 1.48 ERA, 287 strikeouts, seven shutouts.
- Sam Crawford, Detroit, right fielder — .297, 75 RBIs, 38 doubles.

1906 NL

Honus Wagner, Pittsburgh

Shortstop produced league-leading totals in batting (.339), runs (103), total bases (237) and doubles (38), while slashing 175 hits and slugging at .459 (both second).

- Harry Steinfeldt, Chicago, third baseman — .327, 83 RBIs, 176 hits, 232 total bases.
- Frank Chance, Chicago, first baseman —103 runs, 57 steals, .419 on-base percentage.

1906 AL

George Stone, St. Louis

Left fielder was the league's leader in batting (.358), total bases (291), slugging (.501) and on-base percentage (.417), while placing runner-up in hits (208) and triples (20).

- Napoleon Lajoie, Cleveland, second baseman — .355, 214 hits, 48 doubles, 280 total bases, .465 slugging average.
- Harry Davis, Philadelphia, first baseman —12 homers, 96 RBIs, 253 total bases, 42 doubles, .459 slugging percentage.

1907 NL

Honus Wagner, Pittsburgh

Shortstop paced the NL in batting (.350), slugging (.513), total bases (264), doubles (38) and steals (61), while adding 82 RBIs and 180 hits (both second).

- Sherry Magee, Philadelphia, left fielder — .328, 85 RBIs, 46 steals, .455 slugging percentage.
- Christy Mathewson, New York, pitcher — 24 wins, 178 strikeouts, eight shutouts, 31 complete games.

1907 AL

Ty Cobb, Detroit

Right fielder grabbed two legs of the Triple Crown with a .350 average and 119 RBIs, also pacing the league in steals (49), hits (212), slugging (.468) and total bases (283).

- Sam Crawford, Detroit, center fielder — .323, 102 runs, 268 total bases, .460 slugging average.
- Ed Walsh, Chicago, pitcher — 24 wins, 1.60 ERA, 206 strikeouts, 422.1 innings.

1908 NL

Christy Mathewson, New York

Pitcher crafted one of the greatest seasons ever with league bests in wins (37), ERA (1.43), strikeouts (259), shutouts (11), complete games (34), innings (390.2), saves (five) and appearances (56).

- Honus Wagner, Pittsburgh, shortstop — .354, 109 RBIs, 201 hits, 100 runs, 39 doubles, 19 triples, 10 homers, 308 total bases, .542 slugging average.
- Mordecai Brown, Chicago, pitcher — 29 wins, 1.47 ERA, nine shutouts, five saves.

1908 AL

Sam Crawford, Detroit

Center fielder was a run-producing machine, leading the senior circuit in homers (seven), and fashioning runner-up marks in RBIs (80), total bases (270), slugging (.457), runs (102), hits (184) and batting (.311).

- Ty Cobb, Detroit, right fielder — .324, 108 RBIs, 20 triples, 276 total bases, .475 slugging average, 39 steals.
- Ed Walsh, Chicago, pitcher — 40 wins, 1.42 ERA, 42 complete games, 11 shutouts, six saves, 464 innings.

1909 NL

Honus Wagner, Pittsburgh

Shortstop led the way in batting (.339), RBIs (100), slugging (.489), total bases (242), doubles (39) and on-base percentage (.420).

- Mordecai Brown, Chicago, pitcher — 27 wins, 1.31 ERA, 32 complete games, eight shutouts, seven saves, 342.2 innings.
- Larry Doyle, New York, second baseman — .302, 239 total bases, 172 hits.

1909 AL

Ty Cobb, Detroit

Right fielder won the Triple Crown with a .377 average, nine homers and 107 RBIs, also nabbing the No. 1 spot in hits (216), slugging (.517), total bases (296), runs (116) and steals (76).

- Sam Crawford, Detroit, center fielder — .314, 97 RBIs, 266 total bases, .452 slugging percentage, 35 doubles.
- George Mullin, Detroit, pitcher — 29 wins, 29 complete games, .784 win percentage, 303.2 innings.

1910 NL

Sherry Magee, Philadelphia

Left fielder claimed the top spot in batting (.331), RBIs (123), slugging (.507), runs (110), total bases (263) and on-base percentage (.445), while posting runner-up stats in doubles (39) and triples (17), and stealing 49 bases (fourth).

- Christy Mathewson, New York, pitcher — 27 wins, 1.89 ERA, 184 strikeouts, 27 complete games.
- Mordecai Brown, Chicago, pitcher — 25 wins, 1.86 ERA, 27 complete games, seven saves.

1910 AL

Jack Coombs, Philadelphia

Pitcher won a league-best 31 games with a runner-up 1.30 ERA, leading the league with 45 appearances and 13 shutouts, while placing third in both strikeouts (224) and innings (353).

- Ty Cobb, Detroit, center fielder — .383, 106 runs, 65 steals, .551 slugging average, 279 total bases.
- Napoleon Lajoie, Cleveland, second baseman — .384, 227 hits, 304 total bases, 51 doubles, .514 slugging percentage.

CHALMERS AWARD

National League	Year	American League
Frank Schulte, Chicago, RF	1911	Ty Cobb, Detroit, CF
Larry Doyle, New York, 2B	1912	Tris Speaker, Boston, CF
Jake Daubert, Brooklyn, 1B	1913	Walter Johnson, Washington, P
Johnny Evers, Boston, 2B	1914	Eddie Collins, Philadelphia, 2B

1915 NL

Gavvy Cravath, Philadelphia

Right fielder set a 20th century major league home run record with 24 wallops, also leading the league in RBIs (115), runs (89), total bases (266), slugging (.510), walks (86) and on-base percentage (.393).

- Grover Cleveland Alexander, Philadelphia, pitcher — 31 wins, 1.22 ERA, 12 shutouts, 36 complete games, 376.1 innings.
- Larry Doyle, New York, second baseman — .320, 261 total bases, 189 hits, 40 doubles.

1915 AL

Ty Cobb, Detroit

Center fielder captured his ninth consecutive batting crown with a .369 effort and stole a record-96 bases while scoring a league-high 144 times, and also led the way with 208 hits, 274 total bases and a .486 on-base percentage.

- Walter Johnson, Washington, pitcher — 27 wins, 1.55 ERA, 203 strikeouts, seven shutouts, 35 complete games, 336.2 innings.
- Eddie Collins, Chicago, second baseman — .332, 118 runs, 46 steals, 119 walks.

1916 NL

Grover Cleveland Alexander, Philadelphia

Pitcher posted league bests in wins (33), ERA (1.55), shutouts (16), complete games (38), strikeouts (167) and innings (389), while compiling a runner-up .733 win percentage.

- Zack Wheat, Brooklyn, left fielder — .312, 262 total bases, .461 slugging average.
- Dave Robertson, New York, right fielder — 12 homers, 250 total bases, 180 hits, 88 runs.

1916 AL

Tris Speaker, Cleveland

Center fielder won the batting title with a .386 average and also topped the junior circuit with a .502 slugging percentage, 211 hits, 41 doubles and a .470 on-base percentage, while placing second with 274 total bases.

- Joe Jackson, Chicago, left fielder — .341, 293 total bases, 40 doubles, 21 triples, 202 hits, .495 slugging percentage.
- Babe Ruth, Boston, pitcher — 23 wins, 1.75 ERA, nine shutouts, 323.2 innings.

1917 NL

Grover Cleveland Alexander, Philadelphia

Pitcher again was the NL's best in wins (30), ERA (1.83), shutouts (eight), complete games (34), strikeouts (200) and innings (388), while averaging slightly more than one walk per game.

- Rogers Hornsby, St. Louis, shortstop — .327, 253 total bases, .484 slugging average, 17 triples.
- Gavvy Cravath, Philadelphia, right fielder — 12 homers, 83 RBIs, 16 triples, 70 walks, .473 slugging average.

1917 AL

Ed Cicotte, Chicago

Pitcher led the league in wins (28), ERA (1.53) and innings (346.2), while placing second in strikeouts (150) and appearances (49), third in complete games (29), and fourth in shutouts (seven).

- Ty Cobb, Detroit, center fielder — .383, 225 hits, 107 runs, 55 steals, 44 doubles, 24 triples, 335 total bases, .570 slugging average.
- Bobby Veach, Detroit, left fielder — 103 RBIs, eight homers, 261 total bases.

1918 NL

James "Hippo" Vaughn, Chicago

Pitcher topped the circuit in a shortened season in wins (22), ERA (1.74), strikeouts (148), innings (290.1) and shutouts (eight), while tossing 27 complete games (second).

- Heinie Groh, Cincinnati, third baseman — .320, 86 runs, 158 hits, 28 doubles.
- Wilbur Cooper, Pittsburgh, pitcher — 19 wins, 2.11 ERA, 26 complete games, 117 strikeouts.

1918 AL

Ty Cobb, Detroit

Center fielder won his 11th batting crown with a .382 mark and also led the way in triples with 14 and on-base percentage at .440, while placing runner-up in slugging at .515, runs with 83, hits with 161 and total bases with 217.

- Walter Johnson, Washington, pitcher — 23 wins, 1.27 ERA, eight shutouts, 162 strikeouts, 29 complete games.
- George Burns, Philadelphia, first baseman — .352, 236 total bases, 178 hits, 70 RBIs, .467 slugging average.

1919 NL

Rogers Hornsby, St. Louis

Third baseman finished runner-up in batting (.318), RBIs (71), total bases (220) and hits (163) in a shortened season.

- Hy Myers, Brooklyn, center fielder — .307, 73 RBIs, 223 total bases, .436 slugging average.
- Edd Roush, Cincinnati, center fielder — .321, 71 RBIs, 216 total bases.

1919 AL

Babe Ruth, Boston

Left fielder was the league's top man in homers (29), RBIs (114), runs (103), total bases (284), slugging percentage (.657) and on-base percentage (.456).

- Bobby Veach, Detroit, left fielder — .355, 101 RBIs, 279 total bases, 191 hits, 45 doubles, 17 triples, .519 slugging percentage.
- Ed Cicotte, Chicago, pitcher — 29 wins, 1.82 ERA, 306.2 innings, 30 complete games.

1920 NL

Grover Cleveland Alexander, Chicago

Pitcher had league leadership totals of 27 wins, 1.91 ERA, 173 strikeouts, 363.1 innings and 33 complete games, while twirling seven shutouts (second).

- Rogers Hornsby, St. Louis, second baseman — .370, 94 RBIs, 218 hits, 44 doubles, 20 triples, 329 total bases, .559 slugging average.
- Burleigh Grimes, Brooklyn, pitcher — 23 wins, 2.22 ERA, .676 win percentage, 131 strikeouts, 25 complete games.

1920 AL

Babe Ruth, New York

Right fielder outhomered every other AL team with 54, and posted other league highs in runs with 158, RBIs with 137, walks with 150, slugging at .847 and on-base percentage at .532, while batting .376 (fourth).

- George Sisler, St. Louis, first baseman — .407, 257 hits, 122 RBIs, 42 steals, 137 runs, 49 doubles, 18 triples, 399 total bases, .632 slugging percentage.
- Jim Bagby, Cleveland, pitcher — 31 wins, 2.89 ERA, 30 complete games, 339.2 innings.

1921 NL

Rogers Hornsby, St. Louis

Second baseman achieved top NL honors in batting (.397), RBIs (126), runs (131), hits (235), doubles (44), triples (18), total bases (378) and slugging (.639), while belting 21 homers (second).

- George Kelly, New York, first baseman — .308, 23 homers, 122 RBIs, 42 doubles, 310 total bases, .528 slugging percentage.
- Burleigh Grimes, Brooklyn, pitcher — 22 wins, 2.83 ERA, 136 strikeouts, 30 complete games, 302.1 innings.

1921 AL

Babe Ruth, New York

Left fielder outdid even himself, finishing No. 1 in homers (59), RBIs (171), runs (177), walks (145), slugging (.846), total bases (457) and on-base percentage (.512), while cracking 44 doubles (second) and batting .378 (third).

- Carl Mays, New York, pitcher — 27 wins, 3.05 ERA, .750 win percentage, 30 complete games, 336.2 innings, seven saves.
- Harry Heilmann, Detroit, right fielder — .394, 237 hits, 139 RBIs, 365 total bases, .606 slugging percentage.

1922 NL

Rogers Hornsby, St. Louis

Second baseman was the Triple Crown winner with a .401 average, 42 homers and 152 RBIs, while also leading the league in runs with 141, hits with 250, doubles with 46, total bases with 450, slugging at .722 and on-base percentage at .459.

- Wilbur Cooper, Pittsburgh, pitcher — 23 wins, 3.18 ERA, 27 complete games, four shutouts, 294.2 innings, 129 strikeouts.
- Irish Meusel, New York, left fielder — .331, 132 RBIs, 314 total bases, 17 triples.

1923 NL

Dolf Luque, Cincinnati

Pitcher led in wins with 27, ERA at 1.93, win percentage at .771 and shutouts with six, while posting runner-up totals of 151 strikeouts and 28 complete games.

- Frankie Frisch, New York, second baseman — .348, 223 hits, 111 RBIs, 116 runs, 311 total bases, 29 steals.
- Jack Fournier, Brooklyn, first baseman — .351, 22 homers, 102 RBIs, 303 total bases, .588 slugging percentage.

LEAGUE AWARD

National League	Year	American League
No selection	1922	George Sisler, St. Louis, 1B
No selection	1923	Babe Ruth, New York, RF
Dazzy Vance, Brooklyn, P	1924	Walter Johnson, Washington, P
Rogers Hornsby, St. Louis, 2B	1925	Roger Peckinpaugh, Washington, SS
Bob O'Farrell, St. Louis, C	1926	George Burns, Cleveland, 1B
Paul Waner, Pittsburgh RF	1927	Lou Gehrig, New York, 1B
Jim Bottomley, St. Louis, 1B	1928	Mickey Cochrane, Philadelphia, C
Rogers Hornsby, Chicago, 2B	1929	No selection

1929 AL

George Earnshaw, Philadelphia

Pitcher posted an AL-best 24 victories, while placing second in strikeouts (149), win percentage (.750) and appearances (44), and fashioning a 3.29 ERA (fourth).

- Al Simmons, Philadelphia, left fielder — .365, 34 homers, 157 RBIs, 373 total bases, 212 hits, .642 slugging average.

- Lefty Grove, Philadelphia, pitcher — 20 wins, 2.81 ERA, .769 win percentage, 170 strikeouts.

1930 NL

Chuck Klein, Philadelphia

Right fielder was the league's No. 1 hitter in total bases (445), runs (158) and doubles (59), while finishing second in homers (40), RBIs (170), slugging percentage (.687) and hits (250), and third in batting (.386).

- Hack Wilson, Chicago, center fielder — .356, 56 homers, 191 RBIs, 423 total bases, .723 slugging percentage, 105 walks.

- Babe Herman, Brooklyn, right fielder — .393, 35 homers, 130 RBIs, 241 hits, 48 doubles, 416 total bases, .678 slugging percentage, 18 stolen bases.

1930 AL

Al Simmons, Philadelphia

Left fielder slashed his way to league-leading marks in batting (.381) and runs (152), while placing runner-up in RBIs (165) and total bases (392), and third in slugging (.708) and hits (211), and adding 36 homers (fifth).

- Lou Gehrig, New York, first baseman — .379, 41 homers, 174 RBIs, 220 hits, 419 total bases, .721 slugging percentage.

- Lefty Grove, Philadelphia, pitcher — 28 wins, 2.54 ERA, 209 strikeouts, .484 win percentage, nine saves.

Appendix E:
Career Statistics for Each MVP

1931 National League — Frankie Frisch

Year	Team	Games	AB	Hits	Avg.	HR	RBI	Runs	SB
1919	NY NL	54	190	43	.226	2	24	21	15
1920		110	440	123	.280	4	77	57	34
1921		153	618	211	.341	8	100	121	49
1922		132	514	168	.327	5	51	101	31
1923		151	641	223	.348	12	111	116	29
1924		145	603	198	.328	7	69	121	22
1925		120	502	166	.331	11	48	89	21
1926		135	545	171	.314	5	44	75	23
1927	SL NL	153	617	208	.337	10	78	112	48
1928		141	547	164	.300	10	86	107	29
1929		138	527	176	.334	5	74	93	24
1930		133	540	187	.346	10	114	121	15
1931		**131**	**518**	**161**	**.311**	**4**	**82**	**96**	**28**
1932		115	486	142	.292	3	60	59	18
1933		147	585	177	.303	4	66	74	18
1934		140	550	168	.305	3	75	74	11
1935		103	354	104	.294	1	55	52	2
1936		93	303	83	.274	1	26	40	2
1937		17	32	7	.219	0	4	3	0
19 yrs		2311	9112	2880	.316	105	1244	1532	419

1931 American League — Lefty Grove

Year	Team	Games	W	L	ERA	IP	SO	BB	ShO
1925	Phil AL	45	10	12	4.75	197	116	131	0
1926		45	13	13	2.51	258	194	101	1
1927		51	20	13	3.19	262.1	174	79	1
1928		39	24	8	2.58	261.2	183	64	4
1929		42	20	6	2.81	275.1	170	81	2
1930		50	28	5	2.54	291	209	60	2
1931		**41**	**31**	**4**	**2.06**	**288.2**	**175**	**62**	**4**
1932		44	25	10	2.84	291.2	188	79	4
1933		45	24	8	3.20	275.1	114	83	2
1934	Bos AL	22	8	8	6.50	109.1	43	32	0
1935		35	20	12	2.70	273	121	65	2
1936		35	17	12	2.81	253.1	130	65	6
1937		32	17	9	3.02	262	153	83	3
1938		24	14	4	3.08	163.2	99	52	1
1939		23	15	4	2.54	191	81	58	2
1940		22	7	6	3.99	153.1	62	50	1
1941		21	7	7	4.37	134	54	42	0
17 yrs		616	300	141	3.06	3940.2	2266	1187	35

1932 National League — Chuck Klein

Year	Team	Games	AB	Hits	Avg.	HR	RBI	Runs	SB
1928	Phil NL	64	253	91	.360	11	34	41	0
1929		149	616	219	.356	43	145	126	5
1930		156	648	250	.386	40	170	158	4
1931		148	594	200	.337	31	121	121	7
1932		**154**	**650**	**226**	**.348**	**38**	**137**	**152**	**20**
1933		152	606	223	.368	28	120	101	15
1934	Chi NL	115	435	131	.301	20	80	78	3
1935		119	434	127	.293	21	73	71	4
1936	Chi NL/Phil NL	146	601	184	.306	25	104	102	6
1937	Phil NL	115	406	132	.325	15	57	74	3
1938		129	458	113	.247	8	61	53	7
1939	Phil NL/Pit NL	110	317	90	.284	12	56	45	2
1940	Phil NL	116	354	77	.218	7	37	39	2
1941		50	73	9	.123	1	3	6	0
1942		14	14	1	.071	0	0	0	0
1943		12	20	2	.100	0	3	0	1
1944		4	7	1	.143	0	0	1	0
17 yrs		1753	6486	2076	.320	300	1201	1168	79

1932 American League — Jimmie Foxx

Year	Team	Games	AB	Hits	Avg.	HR	RBI	Runs	SB
1925	Phil AL	10	9	6	.667	0	0	2	0
1926		26	32	10	.313	0	5	8	1
1927		61	130	42	.323	3	20	23	2
1928		118	400	131	.328	13	79	85	3
1929		149	517	183	.354	33	118	123	9
1930		153	562	188	.335	37	156	127	7
1931		139	515	150	.291	30	120	93	4
1932		**154**	**585**	**213**	**.364**	**58**	**169**	**151**	**3**
1933		149	573	204	.356	48	163	125	2
1934		150	539	180	.334	44	130	120	11
1935		147	535	185	.346	36	115	118	6
1936	Bos AL	155	585	198	.338	41	143	130	13
1937		150	569	162	.285	36	127	111	10
1938		149	565	197	.349	50	175	139	5
1939		124	467	168	.360	35	105	130	4
1940		144	515	153	.297	36	119	106	4
1941		135	487	146	.300	19	105	87	2
1942	Bos AL/Chi NL	100	305	69	.226	8	33	43	1
1944	Chi NL	15	20	1	.050	0	2	0	0
1945	Phil NL	89	224	60	.268	7	38	30	0
20 yrs		2317	8134	2646	.325	534	1922	1751	87

1933 National League — Carl Hubbell

Year	Team	Games	W	L	ERA	IP	SO	BB	ShO
1928	NY NL	20	10	6	2.83	124	37	21	1
1929		39	18	11	3.69	268	106	67	1
1930		37	17	12	3.87	241.2	117	58	3
1931		36	14	12	2.65	248	155	67	4
1932		40	18	11	2.50	284	137	40	0
1933		**45**	**23**	**12**	**1.66**	**308.2**	**156**	**47**	**10**
1934		49	21	12	2.30	313	118	37	5
1935		42	23	12	3.27	302.2	150	49	1
1936		42	26	6	2.31	304	123	57	3
1937		39	22	8	3.20	261.2	159	55	4
1938		24	13	10	3.07	179	104	33	1
1939		29	11	9	2.75	154	62	24	0
1940		31	11	12	3.65	214.1	86	59	2
1941		26	11	11	3.57	164	75	53	1
1942		24	11	8	3.95	157.1	61	34	0
1943		12	4	4	4.91	66	31	24	0
16 yrs		535	253	154	2.98	3590.1	1677	725	36

1933 American League — Jimmie Foxx

Year	Team	Games	AB	Hits	Avg.	HR	RBI	Runs	SB
1925	Phil AL	10	9	6	.667	0	0	2	0
1926		26	32	10	.313	0	5	8	1
1927		61	130	42	.323	3	20	23	2
1928		118	400	131	.328	13	79	85	3
1929		149	517	183	.354	33	118	123	9
1930		153	562	188	.335	37	156	127	7
1931		139	515	150	.291	30	120	93	4
1932		154	585	213	.364	58	169	151	3
1933		**149**	**573**	**204**	**.356**	**48**	**163**	**125**	**2**
1934		150	539	180	.334	44	130	120	11
1935		147	535	185	.346	36	115	118	6
1936	Bos AL	155	585	198	.338	41	143	130	13
1937		150	569	162	.285	36	127	111	10
1938		149	565	197	.349	50	175	139	5
1939		124	467	168	.360	35	105	130	4
1940		144	515	153	.297	36	119	106	4
1941		135	487	146	.300	19	105	87	2
1942	Bos AL/Chi NL	100	305	69	.226	8	33	43	1
1944	Chi NL	15	20	1	.050	0	2	0	0
1945	Phil NL	89	224	60	.268	7	38	30	0
20 yrs		2317	8134	2646	.325	534	1922	1751	87

1934 National League — Dizzy Dean

Year	Team	Games	W	L	ERA	IP	SO	BB	ShO
1930	SL NL	1	1	0	1.00	9	5	3	0
1932		46	18	15	3.30	286	191	102	4
1933		48	20	18	3.04	293	199	64	3
1934		**50**	**30**	**7**	**2.66**	**311.2**	**195**	**75**	**7**
1935		50	28	12	3.04	325.1	190	77	3
1936		51	24	13	3.17	315	195	53	2
1937		27	13	10	2.69	197.1	120	33	4
1938	Chi NL	13	7	1	1.81	74.2	22	8	1
1939		19	6	4	3.36	96.1	27	17	2
1940		10	3	3	5.17	54	18	20	0
1941		1	0	0	18.00	1	1	0	0
1947	SL AL	1	0	0	0.00	4	0	1	0
12 yrs		317	150	83	3.02	1967.1	1163	453	26

1934 American League — Mickey Cochrane

Year	Team	Games	AB	Hits	Avg.	HR	RBI	Runs	SB
1925	Phil AL	134	420	139	.331	6	55	69	7
1926		120	370	101	.273	8	47	50	5
1927		126	432	146	.338	12	80	80	9
1928		131	468	137	.293	10	57	92	7
1929		135	514	170	.331	7	95	113	7
1930		130	487	174	.357	10	85	110	5
1931		122	459	160	.349	17	89	87	2
1932		139	518	152	.293	23	112	118	0
1933		130	429	138	.322	15	60	104	8
1934	Det AL	**129**	**437**	**140**	**.320**	**2**	**76**	**74**	**8**
1935		115	411	131	.319	5	47	93	5
1936		44	126	34	.270	2	17	24	1
1937		27	98	30	.306	2	12	27	0
13 yrs		1482	5169	1652	.320	119	832	1041	64

1935 National League — Gabby Hartnett

Year	Team	Games	AB	Hits	Avg.	HR	RBI	Runs	SB
1922	Chi NL	31	72	14	.194	0	4	4	1
1923		85	231	62	.268	8	39	28	4
1924		111	354	106	.299	16	67	56	10
1925		117	398	115	.289	24	67	61	1
1926		93	284	78	.275	8	41	35	0
1927		127	449	132	.294	10	80	56	2
1928		120	388	117	.302	14	57	61	3
1929		25	22	6	.273	1	9	2	1
1930		141	508	172	.339	37	122	84	0
1931		116	380	107	.282	8	70	53	3
1932		121	406	110	.271	12	52	52	0
1933		140	490	135	.276	16	88	55	1
1934		130	438	131	.299	22	90	58	0
1935		**116**	**413**	**142**	**.344**	**13**	**91**	**67**	**1**
1936		121	424	130	.307	7	64	49	0
1937		110	356	126	.354	12	82	47	0
1938		88	299	82	.274	10	59	40	1
1939		97	306	85	.278	12	59	36	0
1940		37	64	17	.266	1	12	3	0
1941	NY NL	64	150	45	.300	5	26	20	0
20 yrs		1990	6432	1912	.297	236	1179	867	28

1935 American League — Hank Greenberg

Year	Team	Games	AB	Hits	Avg.	HR	RBI	Runs	SB
1930	Det AL	1	1	0	.000	0	0	0	0
1933		117	449	135	.301	12	87	59	6
1934		153	593	201	.339	26	139	118	9
1935		**152**	**619**	**203**	**.328**	**36**	**170**	**121**	**4**
1936		12	46	16	.348	1	16	10	1
1937		154	594	200	.337	40	183	137	8
1938		155	556	175	.315	58	146	144	7
1939		138	500	156	.312	33	112	112	8
1940		148	573	195	.340	41	150	129	6
1941		19	67	18	.269	2	12	12	1
1945		78	270	84	.311	13	60	47	3
1946		142	523	145	.277	44	127	91	5
1947	Pit NL	125	402	100	.249	25	74	71	0
13 yrs		1394	5193	1628	.313	331	1276	1051	58

1936 National League — Carl Hubbell

Year	Team	Games	W	L	ERA	IP	SO	BB	ShO
1928	NY NL	20	10	6	2.83	124	37	21	1
1929		39	18	11	3.69	268	106	67	1
1930		37	17	12	3.87	241.2	117	58	3
1931		36	14	12	2.65	248	155	67	4
1932		40	18	11	2.50	284	137	40	0
1933		45	23	12	1.66	308.2	156	47	10
1934		49	21	12	2.30	313	118	37	5
1935		42	23	12	3.27	302.2	150	49	1
1936		**42**	**26**	**6**	**2.31**	**304**	**123**	**57**	**3**
1937		39	22	8	3.20	261.2	159	55	4
1938		24	13	10	3.07	179	104	33	1
1939		29	11	9	2.75	154	62	24	0
1940		31	11	12	3.65	214.1	86	59	2
1941		26	11	9	3.57	164	75	53	1
1942		24	11	8	3.95	157.1	61	34	0
1943		12	4	4	4.91	66	31	24	0
16 yrs		535	253	154	2.98	3590.1	1677	725	36

1936 American League — Lou Gehrig

Year	Team	Games	AB	Hits	Avg.	HR	RBI	Runs	SB
1923	NY AL	13	26	11	.423	1	9	6	0
1924		10	12	6	.500	0	5	2	0
1925		126	437	129	.295	20	68	73	6
1926		155	572	179	.313	16	112	135	6
1927		155	584	218	.373	47	175	149	10
1928		154	562	210	.374	27	142	139	4
1929		154	553	166	.300	35	126	127	4
1930		154	581	220	.379	41	174	143	12
1931		155	619	211	.341	46	184	163	17
1932		156	596	208	.349	34	151	138	4
1933		152	593	198	.334	32	139	138	9
1934		154	579	210	.363	49	165	128	9
1935		149	535	176	.329	30	119	125	8
1936		**155**	**579**	**205**	**.354**	**49**	**152**	**167**	**3**
1937		157	569	200	.351	37	159	138	4
1938		157	576	170	.295	29	114	115	6
1939		8	28	4	.143	0	1	2	0
17 yrs		2164	8001	2721	.340	493	1995	1888	102

1937 National League — Joe Medwick

Year	Team	Games	AB	Hits	Avg.	HR	RBI	Runs	SB
1932	SL NL	26	106	37	.349	2	12	13	3
1933		148	595	182	.306	18	98	92	5
1934		149	620	198	.319	18	106	110	3
1935		154	634	224	.353	23	126	132	4
1936		155	636	223	.351	18	138	115	3
1937		**156**	**633**	**237**	**.374**	**31**	**154**	**111**	**4**
1938		146	590	190	.322	21	122	100	0
1939		150	606	201	.332	14	117	98	6
1940	SL NL/Bkn NL	143	581	175	.301	17	86	83	2
1941	Bkn NL	133	538	171	.318	18	88	100	2
1942		142	553	166	.300	4	96	69	2
1943	Bkn NL/NY NL	126	497	138	.278	5	70	54	1
1944	NY NL	128	490	165	.337	7	85	64	2
1945	NY NL/Bos NL	92	310	90	.290	3	37	31	5
1946	Bkn NL	41	77	24	.312	2	18	7	0
1947	SL NL	75	150	46	.307	4	28	19	0
1948		20	19	4	.211	0	2	0	0
17 yrs		1984	7635	2471	.324	205	1383	1198	42

1937 American League — Charlie Gehringer

Year	Team	Games	AB	Hits	Avg.	HR	RBI	Runs	SB
1924	Det AL	5	13	6	.462	0	1	2	1
1925		8	18	3	.167	0	0	3	0
1926		123	459	127	.277	1	48	62	9
1927		133	508	161	.317	4	61	110	17
1928		154	603	193	.320	6	74	108	15
1929		155	634	215	.339	13	106	131	27
1930		154	610	201	.330	16	98	144	19
1931		101	383	119	.311	4	53	67	13
1932		152	618	184	.298	19	107	112	9
1933		155	628	204	.325	12	105	103	5
1934		154	601	214	.356	11	127	134	11
1935		150	610	201	.330	19	108	123	11
1936		154	641	227	.354	15	116	144	4
1937		**144**	**564**	**209**	**.371**	**14**	**96**	**133**	**11**
1938		152	568	174	.306	20	107	133	14
1939		118	406	132	.325	16	86	86	4
1940		139	515	161	.313	10	81	108	10
1941		127	436	96	.220	3	46	65	1
1942		45	45	12	.267	1	7	6	0
19 yrs		2323	8860	2839	.320	184	1427	1774	181

1938 National League — Ernie Lombardi

Year	Team	Games	AB	Hits	Avg.	HR	RBI	Runs	SB
1931	Bkn NL	73	182	54	.297	4	23	20	1
1932	Cin NL	118	413	125	.303	11	68	43	0
1933		107	350	99	.283	4	47	30	2
1934		132	417	127	.305	9	62	42	0
1935		120	332	114	.343	12	64	36	0
1936		121	387	129	.333	12	68	42	1
1937		120	368	123	.334	9	59	41	1
1938		**129**	**489**	**167**	**.342**	**19**	**95**	**60**	**0**
1939		130	450	129	.287	20	85	43	0
1940		109	376	120	.319	14	74	50	0
1941		117	398	105	.264	10	60	33	1
1942	Bos NL	105	309	102	.330	11	46	32	1
1943	NY NL	104	295	90	.305	10	51	19	1
1944		117	373	95	.255	10	58	37	0
1945		115	368	113	.307	19	70	46	0
1946		88	238	69	.290	12	39	19	0
1947		48	110	31	.282	4	21	8	0
17 yrs		1853	5855	1792	.306	190	990	601	8

1938 American League — Jimmie Foxx

Year	Team	Games	AB	Hits	Avg.	HR	RBI	Runs	SB
1925	Phil AL	10	9	6	.667	0	0	2	0
1926		26	32	10	.313	0	5	8	1
1927		61	130	42	.323	3	20	23	2
1928		118	400	131	.328	13	79	85	3
1929		149	517	183	.354	33	118	123	9
1930		153	562	188	.335	37	156	127	7
1931		139	515	150	.291	30	120	93	4
1932		154	585	213	.364	58	169	151	3
1933		149	573	204	.356	48	163	125	2
1934		150	539	180	.334	44	130	120	11
1935		147	535	185	.346	36	115	118	6
1936	Bos AL	155	585	198	.338	41	143	130	13
1937		150	569	162	.285	36	127	111	10
1938		**149**	**565**	**197**	**.349**	**50**	**175**	**139**	**5**
1939		124	467	168	.360	35	105	130	4
1940		144	515	153	.297	36	119	106	4
1941		135	487	146	.300	19	105	87	2
1942	Bos AL/Chi NL	100	305	69	.226	8	33	43	1
1944	Chi NL	15	20	1	.050	0	2	0	0
1945	Phil NL	89	224	60	.268	7	38	30	0
20 yrs		2317	8134	2646	.325	534	1922	1751	87

1939 National League — Bucky Walters

Year	Team	Games	AB	Hits	Avg.	HR	RBI	Runs	SB
1931	Bos NL	9	38	8	.211	0	0	2	0
1932		22	75	14	.187	0	4	8	0
1933	Bos AL	52	195	50	.256	4	28	27	1
1934	Bos AL/ Phil NL	106	388	97	.250	8	56	46	1
4 yrs		189	696	169	.243	12	88	83	2

Year	Team	Games	W	L	ERA	IP	SO	BB	ShO
1934	Phil NL	2	0	0	1.29	7	7	2	0
1935		24	9	9	4.17	151	40	68	2
1936		40	11	21	4.26	258	66	115	4
1937		37	14	15	4.75	246.1	87	86	3
1938	Phil NL/ Cin NL	39	15	14	4.20	251	93	108	3
1939	Cin NL	39	27	11	2.29	319	137	109	2
1940		36	22	10	2.48	305	115	92	3
1941		37	19	15	2.83	302	129	88	5
1942		34	15	14	2.66	253.2	109	73	2
1943		34	15	15	3.54	246.1	80	109	5
1944		34	23	8	2.40	285	77	87	6
1945		22	10	10	2.68	168	45	51	3
1946		22	10	7	2.56	151.1	60	64	2
1947		20	8	8	5.75	122	43	49	2
1948		7	0	3	4.63	35	19	18	0
1950	Bos NL	1	0	0	4.50	4	0	2	0
16 yrs		428	198	160	3.30	3104.2	1107	1121	42

1939 American League — Joe DiMaggio

Year	Team	Games	AB	Hits	Avg.	HR	RBI	Runs	SB
1936	NY AL	138	637	206	.323	29	125	132	4
1937		151	621	215	.346	46	167	151	3
1938		145	599	194	.324	32	140	129	6
1939		120	462	176	.381	30	126	108	3
1940		132	508	179	.352	31	133	93	1
1941		139	541	193	.357	30	125	122	4
1942		154	610	186	.305	21	114	123	4
1946		132	503	146	.290	25	95	81	1
1947		141	534	168	.315	20	97	97	3
1948		153	594	190	.320	39	155	110	1
1949		76	272	94	.346	14	67	58	0
1950		139	525	158	.301	32	122	114	0
1951		116	415	109	.263	12	71	72	0
13 yrs		1736	6821	2214	.325	361	1537	1390	30

1940 National League — Frank McCormick

Year	Team	Games	AB	Hits	Avg.	HR	RBI	Runs	SB
1934	Cin NL	12	16	5	.313	0	5	1	0
1937		24	83	27	.325	0	9	5	1
1938		151	640	209	.327	5	106	89	1
1939		156	630	209	.332	18	128	99	1
1940		155	618	191	.309	19	127	93	2
1941		154	603	162	.269	17	97	77	2
1942		145	564	156	.277	13	89	58	1
1943		126	472	143	.303	8	59	56	2
1944		153	581	177	.305	20	102	85	7
1945		152	580	160	.276	10	81	68	6
1946	Phil NL	135	504	143	.284	11	66	46	2
1947	Phil NL/ Bos NL	96	252	84	.333	3	51	31	2
1948	Bos NL	75	180	45	.250	4	34	14	0
13 yrs		1534	5723	1711	.299	128	954	722	27

1940 American League — Hank Greenberg

Year	Team	Games	AB	Hits	Avg.	HR	RBI	Runs	SB
1930	Det AL	1	1	0	.000	0	0	0	0
1933		117	449	135	.301	12	87	59	6
1934		153	593	201	.339	26	139	118	9
1935		152	619	203	.328	36	170	121	4
1936		12	46	16	.348	1	16	10	1
1937		154	594	200	.337	40	183	137	8
1938		155	556	175	.315	58	146	144	7
1939		138	500	156	.312	33	112	112	8
1940		148	573	195	.340	41	150	129	6
1941		19	67	18	.269	2	12	12	1
1945		78	270	84	.311	13	60	47	3
1946		142	523	145	.277	44	127	91	5
1947	Pit NL	125	402	100	.249	25	74	71	0
13 yrs		1394	5193	1628	.313	331	1276	1051	58

1941 National League — Dolph Camilli

Year	Team	Games	AB	Hits	Avg.	HR	RBI	Runs	SB
1933	Chi NL	16	58	13	.224	2	7	8	3
1934	Chi NL/ Phil NL	134	498	133	.267	16	87	69	4
1935	Phil NL	156	602	157	.261	25	83	88	9
1936		151	530	167	.315	28	102	106	5
1937		131	475	161	.339	27	80	101	6
1938	Bkn NL	146	509	128	.251	24	100	106	6
1939		157	565	164	.290	26	104	105	1
1940		142	512	147	.287	23	96	92	9
1941		149	529	151	.285	34	120	92	3
1942		150	524	132	.252	26	109	89	10
1943		95	353	87	.246	6	43	56	2
1945	Bos AL	63	198	42	.212	2	19	24	2
12 yrs		1490	5353	1482	.277	239	950	936	60

1941 American League — Joe DiMaggio

Year	Team	Games	AB	Hits	Avg.	HR	RBI	Runs	SB
1936	NY AL	138	637	206	.323	29	125	132	4
1937		151	621	215	.346	46	167	151	3
1938		145	599	194	.324	32	140	129	6
1939		120	462	176	.381	30	126	108	3
1940		132	508	179	.352	31	133	93	1
1941		139	541	193	.357	30	125	122	4
1942		154	610	186	.305	21	114	123	4
1946		132	503	146	.290	25	95	81	1
1947		141	534	168	.315	20	97	97	3
1948		153	594	190	.320	39	155	110	1
1949		76	272	94	.346	14	67	58	0
1950		139	525	158	.301	32	122	114	0
1951		116	415	109	.263	12	71	72	0
13 yrs		1736	6821	2214	.325	361	1537	1390	30

1942 National League — Mort Cooper

Year	Team	Games	W	L	ERA	IP	SO	BB	ShO
1938	SL NL	4	2	1	3.04	23.2	11	12	0
1939		45	12	6	3.25	210.2	130	97	2
1940		38	11	12	3.63	230.2	95	86	3
1941		29	13	9	3.91	186.2	118	69	0
1942		**37**	**22**	**7**	**1.78**	**278.2**	**152**	**68**	**10**
1943		37	21	8	2.30	274	141	79	6
1944		34	22	7	2.46	252.1	97	60	7
1945	SL NL/ Bos NL	24	9	4	2.92	101.2	59	34	1
1946	Bos NL	28	13	11	3.12	199	83	39	4
1947	Bos NL/ NY NL	18	3	10	5.40	83.1	27	26	0
1949	Chi NL	1	0	0	~	0	0	1	0
11 yrs		295	128	75	2.97	1840.2	913	571	33

1942 American League — Joe Gordon

Year	Team	Games	AB	Hits	Avg.	HR	RBI	Runs	SB
1938	NY AL	127	458	117	.255	25	97	83	11
1939		151	567	161	.284	28	111	92	11
1940		155	616	173	.281	30	103	112	18
1941		156	588	162	.276	24	87	104	10
1942		**147**	**538**	**173**	**.322**	**18**	**103**	**88**	**12**
1943		152	543	135	.249	17	69	82	4
1946		112	376	79	.210	11	47	35	2
1947	Cle AL	155	562	153	.272	29	93	89	7
1948		144	550	154	.280	32	124	96	5
1949		148	541	136	.251	20	84	74	5
1950		119	368	87	.236	19	57	59	4
11 yrs		1566	5707	1530	.268	253	975	914	89

1943 National League — Stan Musial

Year	Team	Games	AB	Hits	Avg.	HR	RBI	Runs	SB
1941	SL NL	12	47	20	.426	1	7	8	1
1942		140	467	147	.315	10	72	87	6
1943		**157**	**617**	**220**	**.357**	**13**	**81**	**108**	**9**
1944		146	568	197	.347	12	94	112	7
1946		156	624	228	.365	16	103	124	7
1947		149	587	183	.312	19	95	113	4
1948		155	611	230	.376	39	131	135	7
1949		157	612	207	.338	36	123	128	3
1950		146	555	192	.346	28	109	105	5
1951		152	578	205	.355	32	108	124	4
1952		154	578	194	.336	21	91	105	7
1953		157	593	200	.337	30	113	127	3
1954		153	591	195	.330	35	126	120	1
1955		154	562	179	.319	33	108	97	5
1956		156	594	184	.310	27	109	87	2
1957		134	502	176	.351	29	102	82	1
1958		135	472	159	.337	17	62	64	0
1959		115	341	87	.255	14	44	37	0
1960		116	331	91	.275	17	63	49	1
1961		123	372	107	.288	15	70	46	0
1962		135	433	143	.330	19	82	57	3
1963		124	337	86	.255	12	58	34	2
22 yrs		3026	10972	3630	.331	475	1951	1949	78

1943 American League — Spud Chandler

Year	Team	Games	W	L	ERA	IP	SO	BB	ShO
1937	NY AL	12	7	4	2.84	82.1	31	20	2
1938		23	14	5	4.03	172	36	47	2
1939		11	3	0	2.84	19	4	9	0
1940		27	8	7	4.60	172	56	60	1
1941		28	10	4	3.19	163.2	60	60	4
1942		24	16	5	2.38	200.2	74	74	3
1943		**30**	**20**	**4**	**1.64**	**253**	**134**	**54**	**5**
1944		1	0	0	4.50	6	1	1	0
1945		4	2	1	4.65	31	12	7	1
1946		34	20	8	2.10	257.1	138	90	6
1947		17	9	5	2.46	128	68	41	2
11 yrs		211	109	43	2.84	1485	614	463	26

1944 National League — Marty Marion

Year	Team	Games	AB	Hits	Avg.	HR	RBI	Runs	SB
1940	SL NL	125	435	121	.278	3	46	44	9
1941		155	547	138	.252	3	58	50	8
1942		147	485	134	.276	0	54	66	8
1943		129	418	117	.280	1	52	38	1
1944		**144**	**506**	**135**	**.267**	**6**	**63**	**50**	**1**
1945		123	430	119	.277	1	59	63	2
1946		146	498	116	.233	3	46	51	1
1947		149	540	147	.272	4	74	57	3
1948		144	567	143	.252	4	43	70	1
1949		134	515	140	.272	5	70	61	0
1950		106	372	92	.247	4	40	36	1
1952	SL AL	67	186	46	.247	2	19	16	0
1953		3	7	0	.000	0	0	0	0
13 yrs		1572	5506	1448	.263	36	624	602	35

1944 American League — Hal Newhouser

Year	Team	Games	W	L	ERA	IP	SO	BB	ShO
1939	Det AL	1	0	1	5.40	5	4	4	0
1940		28	9	9	4.86	133.1	89	76	0
1941		33	9	11	4.79	173	106	137	1
1942		38	8	14	2.45	183.2	103	114	1
1943		37	8	17	3.04	195.2	144	111	1
1944		**47**	**29**	**9**	**2.22**	**312.1**	**187**	**102**	**6**
1945		40	25	9	1.81	313.1	212	110	8
1946		37	26	9	1.94	292.2	275	98	6
1947		40	17	17	2.87	285	176	110	3
1948		39	21	12	3.01	272.1	143	99	2
1949		38	18	11	3.36	292	144	111	3
1950		35	15	13	4.34	213.2	87	81	1
1951		15	6	6	3.92	96.1	37	19	1
1952		25	9	9	3.74	154	57	47	0
1953		7	0	1	7.06	21.2	6	8	0
1954	Cle AL	26	7	2	2.51	46.2	25	18	0
1955		2	0	0	0.00	2.1	1	4	0
17 yrs		488	207	150	3.06	2993	1796	1249	33

1945 National League — Phil Cavarretta

Year	Team	Games	AB	Hits	Avg.	HR	RBI	Runs	SB
1934	Chi NL	7	21	8	.381	1	6	5	1
1935		146	589	162	.275	8	82	85	4
1936		124	458	125	.273	9	56	55	8
1937		106	329	94	.286	5	56	43	7
1938		92	268	64	.239	1	28	29	4
1939		22	55	15	.273	0	0	4	2
1940		65	193	54	.280	2	22	34	3
1941		107	346	99	.286	6	40	46	2
1942		136	482	130	.270	3	54	59	7
1943		143	530	154	.291	8	73	93	3
1944		152	614	197	.321	5	82	106	4
1945		**132**	**498**	**177**	**.355**	**6**	**97**	**94**	**5**
1946		139	510	150	.294	8	78	89	2
1947		127	459	144	.314	2	63	56	2
1948		111	334	93	.278	3	40	41	4
1949		105	360	106	.294	8	49	46	2
1950		82	256	70	.273	10	31	49	1
1951		89	206	64	.311	6	28	24	0
1952		41	63	15	.238	1	8	7	0
1953		27	21	6	.286	0	3	3	0
1954	Chi AL	71	158	50	.316	3	24	21	4
1955		6	4	0	.000	0	0	1	0
22 yrs		2030	6754	1977	.293	95	920	990	65

1945 American League — Hal Newhouser

Year	Team	Games	W	L	ERA	IP	SO	BB	ShO
1939	Det AL	1	0	1	5.40	5	4	4	0
1940		28	9	9	4.86	133.1	89	76	0
1941		33	9	11	4.79	173	106	137	1
1942		38	8	14	2.45	183.2	103	114	1
1943		37	8	17	3.04	195.2	144	111	1
1944		47	29	9	2.22	312.1	187	102	6
1945		**40**	**25**	**9**	**1.81**	**313.1**	**212**	**110**	**8**
1946		37	26	9	1.94	292.2	275	98	6
1947		40	17	17	2.87	285	176	110	3
1948		39	21	12	3.01	272.1	143	99	2
1949		38	18	11	3.36	292	144	111	3
1950		35	15	13	4.34	213.2	87	81	1
1951		15	6	6	3.92	96.1	37	19	1
1952		25	9	9	3.74	154	57	47	0
1953		7	0	1	7.06	21.2	6	8	0
1954	Cle AL	26	7	2	2.51	46.2	25	18	0
1955		2	0	0	0.00	2.1	1	4	0
17 yrs		488	207	150	3.06	2993	1796	1249	33

1946 National League — Stan Musial

Year	Team	Games	AB	Hits	Avg.	HR	RBI	Runs	SB
1941	SL NL	12	47	20	.426	1	7	8	1
1942		140	467	147	.315	10	72	87	6
1943		157	617	220	.357	13	81	108	9
1944		146	568	197	.347	12	94	112	7
1946		**156**	**624**	**228**	**.365**	**16**	**103**	**124**	**7**
1947		149	587	183	.312	19	95	113	4
1948		155	611	230	.376	39	131	135	7
1949		157	612	207	.338	36	123	128	3
1950		146	555	192	.346	28	109	105	5
1951		152	578	205	.355	32	108	124	4
1952		154	578	194	.336	21	91	105	7
1953		157	593	200	.337	30	113	127	3
1954		153	591	195	.330	35	126	120	1

1946 National League — Stan Musial

Year	Team	Games	AB	Hits	Avg.	HR	RBI	Runs	SB
1955		154	562	179	.319	33	108	97	5
1956		156	594	184	.310	27	109	87	2
1957		134	502	176	.351	29	102	82	1
1958		135	472	159	.337	17	62	64	0
1959		115	341	87	.255	14	44	37	0
1960		116	331	91	.275	17	63	49	1
1961		123	372	107	.288	15	70	46	0
1962		135	433	143	.330	19	82	57	3
1963		124	337	86	.255	12	58	34	2
22 yrs		3026	10972	3630	.331	475	1951	1949	78

1946 American League — Ted Williams

Year	Team	Games	AB	Hits	Avg.	HR	RBI	Runs	SB
1939	Bos AL	149	565	185	.327	31	145	131	2
1940		144	561	193	.344	23	113	134	4
1941		143	456	185	.406	37	120	135	2
1942		150	522	186	.356	36	137	141	3
1946		**150**	**514**	**176**	**.342**	**38**	**123**	**142**	**0**
1947		156	528	181	.343	32	114	125	0
1948		137	509	188	.369	25	127	124	4
1949		155	566	194	.343	43	159	150	1
1950		89	334	106	.317	28	97	82	3
1951		148	531	169	.318	30	126	109	1
1952		6	10	4	.400	1	3	2	0
1953		37	91	37	.407	13	34	17	0
1954		117	386	133	.345	29	89	93	0
1955		98	320	114	.356	28	83	77	2
1956		136	400	138	.345	24	82	71	0
1957		132	420	163	.388	38	87	96	0
1958		129	411	135	.328	26	85	81	1
1959		103	272	69	.254	10	43	32	0
1960		113	310	98	.316	29	72	56	1
19 yrs		2292	7706	2654	.344	521	1839	1798	24

1947 National League — Bob Elliott

Year	Team	Games	AB	Hits	Avg.	HR	RBI	Runs	SB
1939	Pit NL	32	129	43	.333	3	19	18	0
1940		148	551	161	.292	5	64	88	13
1941		141	527	144	.273	3	76	74	6
1942		143	560	166	.296	9	89	75	2
1943		156	581	183	.315	7	101	82	4
1944		143	538	160	.297	10	108	85	9
1945		144	541	157	.290	8	108	80	5
1946		140	486	128	.263	5	68	50	6
1947	Bos NL	150	555	176	.317	22	113	93	3
1948		151	540	153	.283	23	100	99	6
1949		139	482	135	.280	17	76	77	0
1950		142	531	162	.305	24	107	94	2
1951		136	480	137	.285	15	70	73	2
1952	NY NL	98	272	62	.228	10	35	33	1
1953	SL AL/ Chi AL	115	368	94	.255	9	61	43	1
15 yrs		1978	7141	2061	.289	170	1195	1064	60

1947 American League — Joe DiMaggio

Year	Team	Games	AB	Hits	Avg.	HR	RBI	Runs	SB
1936	NY AL	138	637	206	.323	29	125	132	4
1937		151	621	215	.346	46	167	151	3
1938		145	599	194	.324	32	140	129	6
1939		120	462	176	.381	30	126	108	3
1940		132	508	179	.352	31	133	93	1
1941		139	541	193	.357	30	125	122	4
1942		154	610	186	.305	21	114	123	4
1946		132	503	146	.290	25	95	81	1
1947		**141**	**534**	**168**	**.315**	**20**	**97**	**97**	**3**
1948		153	594	190	.320	39	155	110	1
1949		76	272	94	.346	14	67	58	0
1950		139	525	158	.301	32	122	114	0
1951		116	415	109	.263	12	71	72	0
13 yrs		1736	6821	2214	.325	361	1537	1390	30

1948 National League — Stan Musial

Year	Team	Games	AB	Hits	Avg.	HR	RBI	Runs	SB
1941	SL NL	12	47	20	.426	1	7	8	1
1942		140	467	147	.315	10	72	87	6
1943		157	617	220	.357	13	81	108	9
1944		146	568	197	.347	12	94	112	7
1946		156	624	228	.365	16	103	124	7
1947		149	587	183	.312	19	95	113	4
1948		**155**	**611**	**230**	**.376**	**39**	**131**	**135**	**7**
1949		157	612	207	.338	36	123	128	3
1950		146	555	192	.346	28	109	105	5
1951		152	578	205	.355	32	108	124	4
1952		154	578	194	.336	21	91	105	7
1953		157	593	200	.337	30	113	127	3
1954		153	591	195	.330	35	126	120	1
1955		154	562	179	.319	33	108	97	5
1956		156	594	184	.310	27	109	87	2
1957		134	502	176	.351	29	102	82	1
1958		135	472	159	.337	17	62	64	0
1959		115	341	87	.255	14	44	37	0
1960		116	331	91	.275	17	63	49	1
1961		123	372	107	.288	15	70	46	0
1962		135	433	143	.330	19	82	57	3
1963		124	337	86	.255	12	58	34	2
22 yrs		3026	10972	3630	.331	475	1951	1949	78

1948 American League — Lou Boudreau

Year	Team	Games	AB	Hits	Avg.	HR	RBI	Runs	SB
1938	Cle AL	1	1	0	.000	0	0	0	0
1939		53	225	58	.258	0	19	42	2
1940		155	627	185	.295	9	101	97	6
1941		148	579	149	.257	10	56	95	9
1942		147	506	143	.283	2	58	57	7
1943		152	539	154	.286	3	67	69	4
1944		150	584	191	.327	3	67	91	11
1945		97	345	106	.307	3	48	50	0
1946		140	515	151	.293	6	62	51	6
1947		150	538	165	.307	4	67	79	1
1948		**152**	**560**	**199**	**.355**	**18**	**106**	**116**	**3**
1949		134	475	135	.284	4	60	53	0
1950		81	260	70	.269	1	29	23	1
1951	Bos AL	82	273	73	.267	5	47	37	1
1952		4	2	0	.000	0	2	1	0
15 yrs		1646	6029	1779	.295	68	789	861	51

1949 National League — Jackie Robinson

Year	Team	Games	AB	Hits	Avg.	HR	RBI	Runs	SB
1947	Bkn NL	151	590	175	.297	12	48	125	29
1948		147	574	170	.296	12	85	108	22
1949		**156**	**593**	**203**	**.342**	**16**	**124**	**122**	**37**
1950		144	518	170	.328	14	81	99	12
1951		153	548	185	.338	19	88	106	25
1952		149	510	157	.308	19	75	104	24
1953		136	484	159	.329	12	95	109	17
1954		124	386	120	.311	15	59	62	7
1955		105	317	81	.256	8	36	51	12
1956		117	357	98	.275	10	43	61	12
10 yrs		1382	4877	1518	.311	137	734	947	197

1949 American League — Ted Williams

Year	Team	Games	AB	Hits	Avg.	HR	RBI	Runs	SB
1939	Bos AL	149	565	185	.327	31	145	131	2
1940		144	561	193	.344	23	113	134	4
1941		143	456	185	.406	37	120	135	2
1942		150	522	186	.356	36	137	141	3
1946		150	514	176	.342	38	123	142	0
1947		156	528	181	.343	32	114	125	0
1948		137	509	188	.369	25	127	124	4
1949		**155**	**566**	**194**	**.343**	**43**	**159**	**150**	**1**
1950		89	334	106	.317	28	97	82	3
1951		148	531	169	.318	30	126	109	1
1952		6	10	4	.400	1	3	2	0
1953		37	91	37	.407	13	34	17	0
1954		117	386	133	.345	29	89	93	0
1955		98	320	114	.356	28	83	77	2
1956		136	400	138	.345	24	82	71	0
1957		132	420	163	.388	38	87	96	0
1958		129	411	135	.328	26	85	81	1
1959		103	272	69	.254	10	43	32	0
1960		113	310	98	.316	29	72	56	1
19 yrs		2292	7706	2654	.344	521	1839	1798	24

1950 National League — Jim Konstanty

Year	Team	Games	W	L	ERA	IP	SO	BB	Saves
1944	Cin NL	20	6	4	2.80	112.2	19	33	0
1946	Bos NL	10	0	1	5.28	15.1	9	7	0
1948	Phil NL	6	1	0	0.93	9.2	7	2	2
1949		53	9	5	3.25	97	43	29	7
1950		**74**	**16**	**7**	**2.66**	**152**	**56**	**50**	**22**
1951		58	4	11	4.05	115.2	27	31	9
1952		42	5	3	3.94	80	16	21	6
1953		48	14	10	4.43	170.2	45	42	5
1954	Phil NL/ NY AL	42	3	4	3.01	68.2	14	18	5
1955	NY AL	45	7	2	2.32	73.2	19	24	11
1956	NY AL/ SL NL	35	1	1	4.65	50.1	13	12	7
11 yrs		433	66	48	3.46	945.2	268	269	74

1950 American League — Phil Rizzuto

Year	Team	Games	AB	Hits	Avg.	HR	RBI	Runs	SB
1941	NY AL	133	515	158	.307	3	46	65	14
1942		144	553	157	.284	4	68	79	22
1946		126	471	121	.257	2	38	53	14
1947		153	549	150	.273	2	60	78	11
1948		128	464	117	.252	6	50	65	6
1949		153	614	169	.275	5	65	110	18
1950		**155**	**617**	**200**	**.324**	7	66	**125**	12
1951		144	540	148	.274	2	43	87	18
1952		152	578	147	.254	2	43	89	17
1953		134	413	112	.271	2	54	54	4
1954		127	307	60	.195	2	15	47	3
1955		81	143	37	.259	1	9	19	7
1956		31	52	12	.231	0	6	6	3
13 yrs		1661	5816	1588	.273	38	563	877	149

1951 National League — Roy Campanella

Year	Team	Games	AB	Hits	Avg.	HR	RBI	Runs	SB
1948	Bkn NL	83	279	72	.258	9	45	32	3
1949		130	436	125	.287	22	82	65	3
1950		126	437	123	.281	31	89	70	1
1951		**143**	**505**	**164**	**.325**	**33**	**108**	**90**	1
1952		128	468	126	.269	22	97	73	8
1953		144	519	162	.312	41	142	103	4
1954		111	397	82	.207	19	51	43	1
1955		123	446	142	.318	32	107	81	2
1956		124	388	85	.219	20	73	39	1
1957		103	330	80	.242	13	62	31	1
10 yrs		1215	4205	1161	.276	242	856	627	25

1951 American League — Yogi Berra

Year	Team	Games	AB	Hits	Avg.	HR	RBI	Runs	SB
1946	NY AL	7	22	8	.364	2	4	3	0
1947		83	293	82	.280	11	54	41	0
1948		125	469	143	.305	14	98	70	3
1949		116	415	115	.277	20	91	59	2
1950		151	597	192	.322	28	124	116	4
1951		**141**	**547**	**161**	**.294**	**27**	**88**	**92**	5
1952		142	534	146	.273	30	98	97	2
1953		137	503	149	.296	27	108	80	0
1954		151	584	179	.307	22	125	88	0
1955		147	541	147	.272	27	108	84	1
1956		140	521	155	.298	30	105	93	3
1957		134	482	121	.251	24	82	74	1
1958		122	433	115	.266	22	90	60	3
1959		131	472	134	.284	19	69	64	1
1960		120	359	99	.276	15	62	46	2
1961		119	395	107	.271	22	61	62	2
1962		86	232	52	.224	10	35	25	0
1963		64	147	43	.293	8	28	20	1
1965	NY NL	4	9	2	.222	0	0	1	0
19 yrs		2120	7555	2150	.285	358	1430	1175	30

1952 National League — Hank Sauer

Year	Team	Games	AB	Hits	Avg.	HR	RBI	Runs	SB
1941	Cin NL	9	33	10	.303	0	5	4	0
1942		7	20	5	.250	2	4	4	0
1945		31	116	34	.293	5	20	18	2
1948		145	530	138	.260	35	97	78	2
1949	Cin NL/ Chi NL	138	509	140	.275	31	99	81	0
1950	Chi NL	145	540	148	.274	32	103	85	1
1951		141	525	138	.263	30	89	77	2
1952		**151**	**567**	**153**	**.270**	**37**	**121**	**89**	1
1953		108	395	104	.263	19	60	61	0
1954		142	520	150	.288	41	103	98	2
1955		79	261	55	.211	12	28	29	0
1956	SL NL	75	151	45	.298	5	24	11	0
1957	NY NL	127	378	98	.259	26	76	46	1
1958	SF NL	88	236	59	.250	12	46	27	0
1959		13	15	1	.067	1	1	1	0
15 yrs		1399	4796	1278	.266	288	876	709	11

1952 American League — Bobby Shantz

Year	Team	Games	W	L	ERA	IP	SO	BB	Saves
1949	Phil AL	33	6	8	3.40	127	58	74	2
1950		36	8	14	4.61	214.2	93	85	0
1951		32	18	10	3.94	205.1	77	70	0
1952		**33**	**24**	**7**	**2.48**	**279.2**	**152**	**63**	**0**
1953		16	5	9	4.09	105.2	58	26	0
1954		2	1	0	7.88	8	3	3	0
1955	KC AL	23	5	10	4.54	125	58	66	0
1956		45	2	7	4.35	101.1	67	37	9
1957	NY AL	30	11	5	2.45	173	72	40	5
1958		33	7	6	3.36	126	80	35	0
1959		33	7	3	2.38	94.2	66	33	3
1960		42	5	4	2.79	67.2	54	24	11
1961	Pit NL	43	6	3	3.32	89.1	61	26	2
1962	Hou NL/ SL NL	31	6	4	1.95	78.1	61	25	4
1963	SL NL	55	6	4	2.61	79.1	70	17	11
1964	SL NL/ Chi NL/ Phil NL	50	2	5	3.12	60.2	42	19	1
16 yrs		537	119	99	3.38	1935.2	1072	643	48

1953 National League — Roy Campanella

Year	Team	Games	AB	Hits	Avg.	HR	RBI	Runs	SB
1948	Bkn NL	83	279	72	.258	9	45	32	3
1949		130	436	125	.287	22	82	65	3
1950		126	437	123	.281	31	89	70	1
1951		143	505	164	.325	33	108	90	1
1952		128	468	126	.269	22	97	73	8
1953		**144**	**519**	**162**	**.312**	**41**	**142**	**103**	4
1954		111	397	82	.207	19	51	43	1
1955		123	446	142	.318	32	107	81	2
1956		124	388	85	.219	20	73	39	1
1957		103	330	80	.242	13	62	31	1
10 yrs		1215	4205	1161	.276	242	856	627	25

1953 American League — Al Rosen

Year	Team	Games	AB	Hits	Avg.	HR	RBI	Runs	SB
1947	Cle AL	7	9	1	.111	0	0	1	0
1948		5	5	1	.200	0	0	0	0
1949		23	44	7	.159	0	5	3	0
1950		155	554	159	.287	37	116	100	5
1951		154	573	152	.265	24	102	82	7
1952		148	567	171	.302	28	105	101	8
1953		**155**	**599**	**201**	**.336**	**43**	**145**	**115**	**8**
1954		137	466	140	.300	24	102	76	6
1955		139	492	120	.244	21	81	61	4
1956		121	416	111	.267	15	61	64	1
10 yrs		1044	3725	1063	.285	192	717	603	39

1954 National League — Willie Mays

Year	Team	Games	AB	Hits	Avg.	HR	RBI	Runs	SB
1951	NY NL	121	464	127	.274	20	68	59	7
1952		34	127	30	.236	4	23	17	4
1954		**151**	**565**	**195**	**.345**	**41**	**110**	**119**	**8**
1955		152	580	185	.319	51	127	123	24
1956		152	578	171	.296	36	84	101	40
1957		152	585	195	.333	35	97	112	38
1958	SF NL	152	600	208	.347	29	96	121	31
1959		151	575	180	.313	34	104	125	27
1960		153	595	190	.319	29	103	107	25
1961		154	572	176	.308	40	123	129	18
1962		162	621	189	.304	49	141	130	18
1963		157	596	187	.314	38	103	115	8
1964		157	578	171	.296	47	111	121	19
1965		157	558	177	.317	52	112	118	9
1966		152	552	159	.288	37	103	99	5
1967		141	486	128	.263	22	70	83	6
1968		148	498	144	.289	23	79	84	12
1969		117	403	114	.283	13	58	64	6
1970		139	478	139	.291	28	83	94	5
1971		136	417	113	.271	18	61	82	23
1972	SF NL/ NY NL	88	244	61	.250	8	22	35	4
1973	NY NL	66	209	44	.211	6	25	24	1
22 yrs		2992	10881	3283	.302	660	1903	2062	338

1954 American League — Yogi Berra

Year	Team	Games	AB	Hits	Avg.	HR	RBI	Runs	SB
1946	NY AL	7	22	8	.364	2	4	3	0
1947		83	293	82	.280	11	54	41	0
1948		125	469	143	.305	14	98	70	3
1949		116	415	115	.277	20	91	59	2
1950		151	597	192	.322	28	124	116	4
1951		141	547	161	.294	27	88	92	5
1952		142	534	146	.273	30	98	97	2
1953		137	503	149	.296	27	108	80	0
1954		**151**	**584**	**179**	**.307**	**22**	**125**	**88**	**0**
1955		147	541	147	.272	27	108	84	1
1956		140	521	155	.298	30	105	93	3
1957		134	482	121	.251	24	82	74	1
1958		122	433	115	.266	22	90	60	3
1959		131	472	134	.284	19	69	64	1
1960		120	359	99	.276	15	62	46	2
1961		119	395	107	.271	22	61	62	2
1962		86	232	52	.224	10	35	25	0
1963		64	147	43	.293	8	28	20	1
1965	NY NL	4	9	2	.222	0	0	1	0
19 yrs		2120	7555	2150	.285	358	1430	1175	30

1955 National League — Roy Campanella

Year	Team	Games	AB	Hits	Avg.	HR	RBI	Runs	SB
1948	Bkn NL	83	279	72	.258	9	45	32	3
1949		130	436	125	.287	22	82	65	3
1950		126	437	123	.281	31	89	70	1
1951		143	505	164	.325	33	108	90	1
1952		128	468	126	.269	22	97	73	8
1953		144	519	162	.312	41	142	103	4
1954		111	397	82	.207	19	51	43	1
1955		**123**	**446**	**142**	**.318**	**32**	**107**	**81**	**2**
1956		124	388	85	.219	20	73	39	1
1957		103	330	80	.242	13	62	31	1
10 yrs		1215	4205	1161	.276	242	856	627	25

1955 American League — Yogi Berra

Year	Team	Games	AB	Hits	Avg.	HR	RBI	Runs	SB
1946	NY AL	7	22	8	.364	2	4	3	0
1947		83	293	82	.280	11	54	41	0
1948		125	469	143	.305	14	98	70	3
1949		116	415	115	.277	20	91	59	2
1950		151	597	192	.322	28	124	116	4
1951		141	547	161	.294	27	88	92	5
1952		142	534	146	.273	30	98	97	2
1953		137	503	149	.296	27	108	80	0
1954		151	584	179	.307	22	125	88	0
1955		**147**	**541**	**147**	**.272**	**27**	**108**	**84**	**1**
1956		140	521	155	.298	30	105	93	3
1957		134	482	121	.251	24	82	74	1
1958		122	433	115	.266	22	90	60	3
1959		131	472	134	.284	19	69	64	1
1960		120	359	99	.276	15	62	46	2
1961		119	395	107	.271	22	61	62	2
1962		86	232	52	.224	10	35	25	0
1963		64	147	43	.293	8	28	20	1
1965	NY NL	4	9	2	.222	0	0	1	0
19 yrs		2120	7555	2150	.285	358	1430	1175	30

1956 National League — Don Newcombe

Year	Team	Games	W	L	ERA	IP	SO	BB	ShO
1949	Bkn NL	38	17	8	3.17	244.1	149	73	5
1950		40	19	11	3.70	267.1	130	75	4
1951		40	20	9	3.28	272	164	91	3
1954		29	9	8	4.55	144.1	82	49	0
1955		34	20	5	3.20	233.2	143	38	1
1956		**38**	**27**	**7**	**3.06**	**268**	**139**	**46**	**5**
1957		28	11	12	3.49	198.2	90	33	4
1958	LA NL/ Cin NL	31	7	13	4.67	167.2	69	36	0
1959	Cin NL	30	13	8	3.16	222	100	27	2
1960	Cin NL/ Cle AL	36	6	9	4.48	136.2	63	22	0
10 yrs		344	149	90	3.56	2154.2	1129	490	24

1956 American League — Mickey Mantle

Year	Team	Games	AB	Hits	Avg.	HR	RBI	Runs	SB
1951	NY AL	96	341	91	.267	13	65	61	8
1952		142	549	171	.311	23	87	94	4
1953		127	461	136	.295	21	92	105	8
1954		146	543	163	.300	27	102	129	5
1955		147	517	158	.306	37	99	121	8
1956		**150**	**533**	**188**	**.353**	**52**	**130**	**132**	**10**
1957		144	474	173	.365	34	94	121	16
1958		150	519	158	.304	42	97	127	18
1959		144	541	154	.285	31	75	104	21
1960		153	527	145	.275	40	94	119	14
1961		153	514	163	.317	54	128	132	12
1962		123	377	121	.321	30	89	96	9
1963		65	172	54	.314	15	35	40	2
1964		143	465	141	.303	35	111	92	6
1965		122	361	92	.255	19	46	44	4
1966		108	333	96	.288	23	56	40	1
1967		144	440	108	.245	22	55	63	1
1968		144	435	103	.237	18	54	57	6
18 yrs		2401	8102	2415	.298	536	1509	1677	153

1957 National League – Hank Aaron

Year	Team	Games	AB	Hits	Avg.	HR	RBI	Runs	SB
1954	Mil NL	122	468	131	.280	13	69	58	2
1955		153	602	189	.314	27	106	105	3
1956		153	609	200	.328	26	92	106	2
1957		**151**	**615**	**198**	**.322**	**44**	**132**	**118**	**1**
1958		153	601	196	.326	30	95	109	4
1959		154	629	223	.355	39	123	116	8
1960		153	590	172	.292	40	126	102	16
1961		155	603	197	.327	34	120	115	21
1962		156	592	191	.323	45	128	127	15
1963		161	631	201	.319	44	130	121	31
1964		145	570	187	.328	24	95	103	22
1965		150	570	181	.318	32	89	109	24
1966	Atl NL	158	603	168	.279	44	127	117	21
1967		155	600	184	.307	39	109	113	17
1968		160	606	174	.287	29	86	84	28
1969		147	547	164	.300	44	97	100	9
1970		150	516	154	.298	38	118	103	9
1971		139	495	162	.327	47	118	95	1
1972		129	449	119	.265	34	77	75	4
1973		120	392	118	.301	40	96	84	1
1974		112	340	91	.268	20	69	47	1
1975	Mil AL	137	465	109	.234	12	60	45	0
1976		85	271	62	.229	10	35	22	0
23 yrs		3298	12364	3771	.305	755	2297	2174	240

1957 American League — Mickey Mantle

Year	Team	Games	AB	Hits	Avg.	HR	RBI	Runs	SB
1951	NY AL	96	341	91	.267	13	65	61	8
1952		142	549	171	.311	23	87	94	4
1953		127	461	136	.295	21	92	105	8
1954		146	543	163	.300	27	102	129	5
1955		147	517	158	.306	37	99	121	8
1956		150	533	188	.353	52	130	132	10
1957		**144**	**474**	**173**	**.365**	**34**	**94**	**121**	**16**
1958		150	519	158	.304	42	97	127	18

1957 American League—Mickey Mantle

Year	Team	Games	AB	Hits	Avg.	HR	RBI	Runs	SB
1959		144	541	154	.285	31	75	104	21
1960		153	527	145	.275	40	94	119	14
1961		153	514	163	.317	54	128	132	12
1962		123	377	121	.321	30	89	96	9
1963		65	172	54	.314	15	35	40	2
1964		143	465	141	.303	35	111	92	6
1965		122	361	92	.255	19	46	44	4
1966		108	333	96	.288	23	56	40	1
1967		144	440	108	.245	22	55	63	1
1968		144	435	103	.237	18	54	57	6
18 yrs		2401	8102	2415	.298	536	1509	1677	153

1958 National League — Ernie Banks

Year	Team	Games	AB	Hits	Avg.	HR	RBI	Runs	SB
1953	Chi NL	10	35	11	.314	2	6	3	0
1954		154	593	163	.275	19	79	70	6
1955		154	596	176	.295	44	117	98	9
1956		139	538	160	.297	28	85	82	6
1957		156	594	169	.285	43	102	113	8
1958		**154**	**617**	**193**	**.313**	**47**	**129**	**119**	**4**
1959		155	589	179	.304	45	143	97	2
1960		156	597	162	.271	41	117	94	1
1961		138	511	142	.278	29	80	75	1
1962		154	610	164	.269	37	104	87	5
1963		130	432	98	.227	18	64	41	0
1964		157	591	156	.264	23	95	67	1
1965		163	612	162	.265	28	106	79	3
1966		141	511	139	.272	15	75	52	0
1967		151	573	158	.276	23	95	68	2
1968		150	552	136	.246	32	83	71	2
1969		155	565	143	.253	23	106	60	0
1970		72	222	56	.252	12	44	25	0
1971		39	83	16	.193	3	6	4	0
19 yrs		2528	9421	2583	.274	512	1636	1305	50

1958 American League — Jackie Jensen

Year	Team	Games	AB	Hits	Avg.	HR	RBI	Runs	SB
1950	NY AL	45	70	12	.171	1	5	13	4
1951		56	168	50	.298	8	25	30	8
1952	NY AL/ Wash AL	151	589	165	.280	10	82	83	18
1953	Wash AL	147	552	147	.266	10	84	87	18
1954	Bos AL	152	580	160	.276	25	117	92	22
1955		152	574	158	.275	26	116	95	16
1956		151	578	182	.315	20	97	80	11
1957		145	544	153	.281	23	103	82	8
1958		**154**	**548**	**157**	**.286**	**35**	**122**	**83**	**9**
1959		148	535	148	.277	28	112	101	20
1961		137	498	131	.263	13	66	64	9
11 yrs		1438	5236	1463	.279	199	929	810	143

1959 National League — Ernie Banks

Year	Team	Games	AB	Hits	Avg.	HR	RBI	Runs	SB
1953	Chi NL	10	35	11	.314	2	6	3	0
1954		154	593	163	.275	19	79	70	6
1955		154	596	176	.295	44	117	98	9
1956		139	538	160	.297	28	85	82	6
1957		156	594	169	.285	43	102	113	8
1958		154	617	193	.313	47	129	119	4
1959		155	589	179	.304	45	143	97	2
1960		156	597	162	.271	41	117	94	1
1961		138	511	142	.278	29	80	75	1
1962		154	610	164	.269	37	104	87	5
1963		130	432	98	.227	18	64	41	0
1964		157	591	156	.264	23	95	67	1
1965		163	612	162	.265	28	106	79	3
1966		141	511	139	.272	15	75	52	0
1967		151	573	158	.276	23	95	68	2
1968		150	552	136	.246	32	83	71	2
1969		155	565	143	.253	23	106	60	0
1970		72	222	56	.252	12	44	25	0
1971		39	83	16	.193	3	6	4	0
19 yrs		2528	9421	2583	.274	512	1636	1305	50

1959 American League — Nellie Fox

Year	Team	Games	AB	Hits	Avg.	HR	RBI	Runs	SB
1947	Phil AL	7	3	0	.000	0	0	2	0
1948		3	13	2	.154	0	0	0	1
1949		88	247	63	.255	0	21	42	2
1950	Chi AL	130	457	113	.247	0	30	45	4
1951		147	604	189	.313	4	55	93	9
1952		152	648	192	.296	0	39	76	5
1953		154	624	178	.285	3	72	92	4
1954		155	631	201	.319	2	47	111	16
1955		154	636	198	.311	6	59	100	7
1956		154	649	192	.296	4	52	109	8
1957		155	619	196	.317	6	61	110	5
1958		155	623	187	.300	0	49	82	5
1959		156	624	191	.306	2	70	84	5
1960		150	605	175	.289	2	59	85	2
1961		159	606	152	.251	2	51	67	2
1962		157	621	166	.267	2	54	79	1
1963		137	539	140	.260	2	42	54	0
1964	Hou NL	133	442	117	.265	0	28	45	0
1965		21	41	11	.268	0	1	3	0
19 yrs		2367	9232	2663	.288	35	790	1279	76

1960 National League — Dick Groat

Year	Team	Games	AB	Hits	Avg.	HR	RBI	Runs	SB
1952	Pit NL	95	384	109	.284	1	29	38	2
1955		151	521	139	.267	4	51	45	0
1956		142	520	142	.273	0	37	40	0
1957		125	501	158	.315	7	54	58	0
1958		151	584	175	.300	3	66	67	2
1959		147	593	163	.275	5	51	74	0
1960		138	573	186	.325	2	50	85	0
1961		148	596	164	.275	6	55	71	0
1962		161	678	199	.294	2	61	76	2
1963	SL NL	158	631	201	.319	6	73	85	3
1964		161	636	186	.292	1	70	70	2
1965		153	587	149	.254	0	52	55	1
1966	Phil NL	155	584	152	.260	2	53	58	2
1967	Phil NL/ SF NL	44	96	15	.156	0	5	7	0
14 yrs		1929	7484	2138	.286	39	707	829	14

1960 American League — Roger Maris

Year	Team	Games	AB	Hits	Avg.	HR	RBI	Runs	SB
1957	Cle AL	116	358	84	.235	14	51	61	8
1958	Cle AL/ KC AL	150	583	140	.240	28	80	87	4
1959	KC AL	122	433	118	.273	16	72	69	2
1960	NY AL	136	499	141	.283	39	112	98	2
1961		161	590	159	.269	61	142	132	0
1962		157	590	151	.256	33	100	92	1
1963		90	312	84	.269	23	53	53	1
1964		141	513	144	.281	26	71	86	3
1965		46	155	37	.239	8	27	22	0
1966		119	348	81	.233	13	43	37	0
1967	SL NL	125	410	107	.261	9	55	64	0
1968		100	310	79	.255	5	45	25	0
12 yrs		1463	5101	1325	.260	275	851	826	21

1961 National League — Frank Robinson

Year	Team	Games	AB	Hits	Avg.	HR	RBI	Runs	SB
1956	Cin NL	152	572	166	.290	38	83	122	8
1957		150	611	197	.322	29	75	97	10
1958		148	554	149	.269	31	83	90	10
1959		146	540	168	.311	36	125	106	18
1960		139	464	138	.297	31	83	86	13
1961		153	545	176	.323	37	124	117	22
1962		162	609	208	.342	39	136	134	18
1963		140	482	125	.259	21	91	79	26
1964		156	568	174	.306	29	96	103	23
1965		156	582	172	.296	33	113	109	13
1966	Bal AL	155	576	182	.316	49	122	122	8
1967		129	479	149	.311	30	94	83	2
1968		130	421	113	.268	15	52	69	11
1969		148	539	166	.308	32	100	111	9
1970		132	471	144	.306	25	78	88	2
1971		133	455	128	.281	28	99	82	3
1972	LA NL	103	342	86	.251	19	59	41	2
1973	Cal AL	147	534	142	.266	30	97	85	1
1974	Cal AL/ Cle AL	144	477	117	.245	22	68	81	5
1975	Cle AL	49	118	28	.237	9	24	19	0
1976		36	67	15	.224	3	10	5	0
21 yrs		2808	10006	2943	.294	586	1812	1829	204

1961 American League — Roger Maris

Year	Team	Games	AB	Hits	Avg.	HR	RBI	Runs	SB
1957	Cle AL	116	358	84	.235	14	51	61	8
1958	Cle AL/ KC AL	150	583	140	.240	28	80	87	4
1959	KC AL	122	433	118	.273	16	72	69	2
1960	NY AL	136	499	141	.283	39	112	98	2
1961		161	590	159	.269	61	142	132	0
1962		157	590	151	.256	33	100	92	1
1963		90	312	84	.269	23	53	53	1
1964		141	513	144	.281	26	71	86	3
1965		46	155	37	.239	8	27	22	0
1966		119	348	81	.233	13	43	37	0
1967	SL NL	125	410	107	.261	9	55	64	0
1968		100	310	79	.255	5	45	25	0
12 yrs		1463	5101	1325	.260	275	851	826	21

1962 National League — Maury Wills

Year	Team	Games	AB	Hits	Avg.	HR	RBI	Runs	SB
1959	LA NL	83	242	63	.260	0	7	27	7
1960		148	516	152	.295	0	27	75	50
1961		148	613	173	.282	1	31	105	35
1962		**165**	**695**	**208**	**.299**	**6**	**48**	**130**	**104**
1963		134	527	159	.302	0	34	83	40
1964		158	630	173	.275	2	34	81	53
1965		158	650	186	.286	0	33	92	94
1966		143	594	162	.273	1	39	60	38
1967	Pit NL	149	616	186	.302	3	45	92	29
1968		153	627	174	.278	0	31	76	52
1969	Mon NL/ LA NL	151	623	171	.274	4	47	80	40
1970	LA NL	132	522	141	.270	0	34	77	28
1971		149	601	169	.281	3	44	73	15
1972		71	132	17	.129	0	4	16	1
14 yrs		1942	7588	2134	.281	20	458	1067	586

1962 American League — Mickey Mantle

Year	Team	Games	AB	Hits	Avg.	HR	RBI	Runs	SB
1951	NY AL	96	341	91	.267	13	65	61	8
1952		142	549	171	.311	23	87	94	4
1953		127	461	136	.295	21	92	105	8
1954		146	543	163	.300	27	102	129	5
1955		147	517	158	.306	37	99	121	8
1956		150	533	188	.353	52	130	132	10
1957		144	474	173	.365	34	94	121	16
1958		150	519	158	.304	42	97	127	18
1959		144	541	154	.285	31	75	104	21
1960		153	527	145	.275	40	94	119	14
1961		153	514	163	.317	54	128	132	12
1962		**123**	**377**	**121**	**.321**	**30**	**89**	**96**	**9**
1963		65	172	54	.314	15	35	40	2
1964		143	465	141	.303	35	111	92	6
1965		122	361	92	.255	19	46	44	4
1966		108	333	96	.288	23	56	40	1
1967		144	440	108	.245	22	55	63	1
1968		144	435	103	.237	18	54	57	6
18 yrs		2401	8102	2415	.298	536	1509	1677	153

1963 National League — Sandy Koufax

Year	Team	Games	W	L	ERA	IP	SO	BB	ShO
1955	Bkn NL	12	2	2	3.02	41.2	30	28	2
1956		16	2	4	4.91	58.2	30	29	0
1957		34	5	4	3.88	104.1	122	51	0
1958	LA NL	40	11	11	4.48	158.2	131	105	0
1959		35	8	6	4.05	153.1	173	92	1
1960		37	8	13	3.91	175	197	100	2
1961		42	18	13	3.52	255.2	269	96	2
1962		28	14	7	2.54	184.1	216	57	2
1963		**40**	**25**	**5**	**1.88**	**311**	**306**	**58**	**11**
1964		29	19	5	1.74	223	223	53	7
1965		43	26	8	2.04	335.2	382	71	8
1966		41	27	9	1.73	323	317	77	5
12 yrs		397	165	87	2.76	2324.1	2396	817	40

1963 American League — Elston Howard

Year	Team	Games	AB	Hits	Avg.	HR	RBI	Runs	SB
1955	NY AL	97	279	81	.290	10	43	33	0
1956		98	290	76	.262	5	34	35	0
1957		110	356	90	.253	8	44	33	2
1958		103	376	118	.314	11	66	45	1
1959		125	443	121	.273	18	73	59	0
1960		107	323	79	.245	6	39	29	3
1961		129	446	155	.348	21	77	64	0
1962		136	494	138	.279	21	91	63	1
1963		**135**	**487**	**140**	**.287**	**28**	**85**	**75**	**0**
1964		150	550	172	.313	15	84	63	1
1965		110	391	91	.233	9	45	38	0
1966		126	410	105	.256	6	35	38	0
1967	NY AL/ Bos AL	108	315	56	.178	4	28	22	0
1968	Bos AL	71	203	49	.241	5	18	22	1
14 yrs		1605	5363	1471	.274	167	762	619	9

1964 National League — Ken Boyer

Year	Team	Games	AB	Hits	Avg.	HR	RBI	Runs	SB
1955	SL NL	147	530	140	.264	18	62	78	22
1956		150	595	182	.306	26	98	91	8
1957		142	544	144	.265	19	62	79	12
1958		150	570	175	.307	23	90	101	11
1959		149	563	174	.309	28	94	86	12
1960		151	552	168	.304	32	97	95	8
1961		153	589	194	.329	24	95	109	6
1962		160	611	178	.291	24	98	92	12
1963		159	617	176	.285	24	111	86	1
1964		**162**	**628**	**185**	**.295**	**24**	**119**	**100**	**3**
1965		144	535	139	.260	13	75	71	2
1966	NY NL	136	496	132	.266	14	61	62	4
1967	NY NL/ Chi AL	113	346	86	.249	7	34	34	2
1968	Chi AL/ LA NL	93	245	63	.257	6	41	20	2
1969	LA NL	25	34	7	.206	0	4	0	0
15 yrs		2034	7455	2143	.287	282	1141	1104	105

1964 American League — Brooks Robinson

Year	Team	Games	AB	Hits	Avg.	HR	RBI	Runs	SB
1955	Bal AL	6	22	2	.091	0	1	0	0
1956		15	44	10	.227	1	1	5	0
1957		50	117	28	.239	2	14	13	1
1958		145	463	110	.238	3	32	31	1
1959		88	313	89	.284	4	24	29	2
1960		152	595	175	.294	14	88	74	2
1961		163	668	192	.287	7	61	89	1
1962		162	634	192	.303	23	86	77	3
1963		161	589	148	.251	11	67	67	2
1964		**163**	**612**	**194**	**.317**	**28**	**118**	**82**	**1**
1965		144	559	166	.297	18	80	81	3
1966		157	620	167	.269	23	100	91	2
1967		158	610	164	.269	22	77	88	1
1968		162	608	154	.253	17	75	65	1
1969		156	598	140	.234	23	84	73	2
1970		158	608	168	.276	18	94	84	1
1971		156	589	160	.272	20	92	67	0
1972		153	556	139	.250	8	64	48	1
1973		155	549	141	.257	9	72	53	2
1974		153	553	159	.288	7	59	46	2
1975		144	482	97	.201	6	53	50	0
1976		71	218	46	.211	3	11	16	0
1977		24	47	7	.149	1	4	3	0
23 yrs		2896	10654	2848	.267	268	1357	1232	28

1965 National League — Willie Mays

Year	Team	Games	AB	Hits	Avg.	HR	RBI	Runs	SB
1951	NY NL	121	464	127	.274	20	68	59	7
1952		34	127	30	.236	4	23	17	4
1954		151	565	195	.345	41	110	119	8
1955		152	580	185	.319	51	127	123	24
1956		152	578	171	.296	36	84	101	40
1957		152	585	195	.333	35	97	112	38
1958	SF NL	152	600	208	.347	29	96	121	31
1959		151	575	180	.313	34	104	125	27
1960		153	595	190	.319	29	103	107	25
1961		154	572	176	.308	40	123	129	18
1962		162	621	189	.304	49	141	130	18
1963		157	596	187	.314	38	103	115	8
1964		157	578	171	.296	47	111	121	19
1965		**157**	**558**	**177**	**.317**	**52**	**112**	**118**	**9**
1966		152	552	159	.288	37	103	99	5
1967		141	486	128	.263	22	70	83	6
1968		148	498	144	.289	23	79	84	12
1969		117	403	114	.283	13	58	64	6
1970		139	478	139	.291	28	83	94	5
1971		136	417	113	.271	18	61	82	23
1972	SF NL/ NY NL	88	244	61	.250	8	22	35	4
1973	NY NL	66	209	44	.211	6	25	24	1
22 yrs		2992	10881	3283	.302	660	1903	2062	338

1965 American League — Zoilo Versalles

Year	Team	Games	AB	Hits	Avg.	HR	RBI	Runs	SB
1959	Wash AL	29	59	9	.153	1	1	4	1
1960		15	45	6	.133	0	4	2	0
1961	Min AL	129	510	143	.280	7	53	65	16
1962		160	568	137	.241	17	67	69	5
1963		159	621	162	.261	10	54	74	7
1964		160	659	171	.259	20	64	94	14
1965		**160**	**666**	**182**	**.273**	**19**	**77**	**126**	**27**
1966		137	543	135	.249	7	36	73	10
1967		160	581	116	.200	6	50	63	5
1968	LA NL	122	403	79	.196	2	24	29	6
1969	Cle AL/ Wash AL	103	292	69	.236	1	19	30	4
1971	Atl NL	66	194	37	.191	5	22	21	2
12 yrs		1400	5141	1246	.242	95	471	650	97

1966 National League — Roberto Clemente

Year	Team	Games	AB	Hits	Avg.	HR	RBI	Runs	SB
1955	Pit NL	124	474	121	.255	5	47	48	2
1956		147	543	169	.311	7	60	66	6
1957		111	451	114	.253	4	30	42	0
1958		140	519	150	.289	6	50	69	8
1959		105	432	128	.296	4	50	60	2
1960		144	570	179	.314	16	94	89	4
1961		146	572	201	.351	23	89	100	4
1962		144	538	168	.312	10	74	95	6
1963		152	600	192	.320	17	76	77	12
1964		155	622	211	.339	12	87	95	5
1965		152	589	194	.329	10	65	91	8
1966		**154**	**638**	**202**	**.317**	**29**	**119**	**105**	**7**
1967		147	585	209	.357	23	110	103	9
1968		132	502	146	.291	18	57	74	2
1969		138	507	175	.345	19	91	87	4
1970		108	412	145	.352	14	60	65	3
1971		132	522	178	.341	13	86	82	1
1972		102	378	118	.312	10	60	68	0
18 yrs		2433	9454	3000	.317	240	1305	1416	83

1966 American League — Frank Robinson

Year	Team	Games	AB	Hits	Avg.	HR	RBI	Runs	SB
1956	Cin NL	152	572	166	.290	38	83	122	8
1957		150	611	197	.322	29	75	97	10
1958		148	554	149	.269	31	83	90	10
1959		146	540	168	.311	36	125	106	18
1960		139	464	138	.297	31	83	86	13
1961		153	545	176	.323	37	124	117	22
1962		162	609	208	.342	39	136	134	18
1963		140	482	125	.259	21	91	79	26
1964		156	568	174	.306	29	96	103	23
1965		156	582	172	.296	33	113	109	13
1966	**Bal AL**	**155**	**576**	**182**	**.316**	**49**	**122**	**122**	**8**
1967		129	479	149	.311	30	94	83	2
1968		130	421	113	.268	15	52	69	11
1969		148	539	166	.308	32	100	111	9
1970		132	471	144	.306	25	78	88	2
1971		133	455	128	.281	28	99	82	3
1972	LA NL	103	342	86	.251	19	59	41	2
1973	Cal AL	147	534	142	.266	30	97	85	1
1974	Cal AL/ Cle AL	144	477	117	.245	22	68	81	5
1975	Cle AL	49	118	28	.237	9	24	19	0
1976		36	67	15	.224	3	10	5	0
21 yrs		2808	10006	2943	.294	586	1812	1829	204

1967 National League — Orlando Cepeda

Year	Team	Games	AB	Hits	Avg.	HR	RBI	Runs	SB
1958	SF NL	148	603	188	.312	25	96	88	15
1959		151	605	192	.317	27	105	92	23
1960		151	569	169	.297	24	96	81	15
1961		152	585	182	.311	46	142	105	12
1962		162	625	191	.306	35	114	105	10
1963		156	579	183	.316	34	97	100	8
1964		142	529	161	.304	31	97	75	9
1965		33	34	6	.176	1	5	1	0
1966	SF NL/ SL NL	142	501	151	.301	20	73	70	9
1967	**SL NL**	**151**	**563**	**183**	**.325**	**25**	**111**	**91**	**11**
1968		157	600	149	.248	16	73	71	8
1969	Atl NL	154	573	147	.257	22	88	74	12
1970		148	567	173	.305	34	111	87	6
1971		71	250	69	.276	14	44	31	3
1972	Atl NL/ Oak AL	31	87	25	.287	4	9	6	0
1973	Bos AL	142	550	159	.289	20	86	51	0
1974	KC AL	33	107	23	.215	1	18	3	1
17 yrs		2124	7927	2351	.297	379	1365	1131	142

1967 American League — Carl Yastrzemski

Year	Team	Games	AB	Hits	Avg.	HR	RBI	Runs	SB
1961	Bos AL	148	583	155	.266	11	80	71	6
1962		160	646	191	.296	19	94	99	7
1963		151	570	183	.321	14	68	91	8
1964		151	567	164	.289	15	67	77	6
1965		133	494	154	.312	20	72	78	7
1966		160	594	165	.278	16	80	81	8
1967		**161**	**579**	**189**	**.326**	**44**	**121**	**112**	**10**
1968		157	539	162	.301	23	74	90	13
1969		162	603	154	.255	40	111	96	15
1970		161	566	186	.329	40	102	125	23
1971		148	508	129	.254	15	70	75	8

1967 American League—Carl Yastrzemski

Year	Team	Games	AB	Hits	Avg.	HR	RBI	Runs	SB
1972		125	455	120	.264	12	68	70	5
1973		152	540	160	.296	19	95	82	9
1974		148	515	155	.301	15	79	93	12
1975		149	543	146	.269	14	60	91	8
1976		155	546	146	.267	21	102	71	5
1977		150	558	165	.296	28	102	99	11
1978		144	523	145	.277	17	81	70	4
1979		147	518	140	.270	21	87	69	3
1980		105	364	100	.275	15	50	49	0
1981		91	338	83	.246	7	53	36	0
1982		131	459	126	.275	16	72	53	0
1983		119	380	101	.266	10	56	38	0
23 yrs		3308	11988	3419	.285	452	1844	1816	168

1968 National League — Bob Gibson

Year	Team	Games	W	L	ERA	IP	SO	BB	ShO
1959	SL NL	13	3	5	3.33	75.2	48	39	1
1960		27	3	6	5.61	86.2	69	48	0
1961		35	13	12	3.24	211.1	166	119	2
1962		32	15	13	2.85	233.2	208	95	5
1963		36	18	9	3.39	254.2	204	96	2
1964		40	19	12	3.01	287.1	245	86	2
1965		38	20	12	3.07	299	270	103	6
1966		35	21	12	2.44	280.1	225	78	5
1967		24	13	7	2.98	175.1	147	40	2
1968		**34**	**22**	**9**	**1.12**	**304.2**	**268**	**62**	**13**
1969		35	20	13	2.18	314	269	95	4
1970		34	23	7	3.12	294	274	88	3
1971		31	16	13	3.04	245.2	185	76	5
1972		34	19	11	2.46	278	208	88	4
1973		25	12	10	2.77	195	142	57	1
1974		33	11	13	3.83	240	129	104	1
1975		22	3	10	5.04	109	60	62	0
17 yrs		528	251	174	2.91	3884.1	3117	1336	56

1968 American League — Denny McLain

Year	Team	Games	W	L	ERA	IP	SO	BB	ShO
1963	Det AL	3	2	1	4.29	21	22	16	0
1964		19	4	5	4.05	100	70	37	0
1965		33	16	6	2.61	220.1	192	62	4
1966		38	20	14	3.92	264.1	192	104	4
1967		37	17	16	3.79	235	161	73	3
1968		**41**	**31**	**6**	**1.96**	**336**	**280**	**63**	**6**
1969		42	24	9	2.80	325	181	67	9
1970		14	3	5	4.63	91.1	52	28	0
1971	Wash AL	33	10	22	4.28	216.2	103	72	3
1972	Oak AL/ Atl NL	20	4	7	6.39	76.1	29	26	0
10 yrs		280	131	91	3.39	1886	1282	548	29

1969 National League – Willie McCovey

Year	Team	Games	AB	Hits	Avg.	HR	RBI	Runs	SB
1959	SF NL	52	192	68	.354	13	38	32	2
1960		101	260	62	.238	13	51	37	1
1961		106	328	89	.271	18	50	59	1
1962		91	229	67	.293	20	54	41	3
1963		152	564	158	.280	44	102	103	1
1964		130	364	80	.220	18	54	55	2
1965		160	540	149	.276	39	92	93	0
1966		150	502	148	.295	36	96	85	2

1969 National League – Willie McCovey

Year	Team	Games	AB	Hits	Avg.	HR	RBI	Runs	SB
1967		135	456	126	.276	31	91	73	3
1968		148	523	153	.293	36	105	81	4
1969		**149**	**491**	**157**	**.320**	**45**	**126**	**101**	**0**
1970		152	495	143	.289	39	126	98	0
1971		105	329	91	.277	18	70	45	0
1972		81	263	56	.213	14	35	30	0
1973		130	383	102	.266	29	75	52	1
1974	SD NL	128	344	87	.253	22	63	53	1
1975		122	413	104	.252	23	68	43	1
1976	SD NL/ Oak AL	82	226	46	.204	7	36	20	0
1977	SF NL	141	478	134	.280	28	86	54	3
1978		108	351	80	.228	12	64	32	1
1979		117	353	88	.249	15	57	34	0
1980		48	113	23	.204	1	16	8	0
22 yrs		2588	8197	2211	.270	521	1555	1229	26

1969 American League — Harmon Killebrew

Year	Team	Games	AB	Hits	Avg.	HR	RBI	Runs	SB
1954	Wash AL	9	13	4	.308	0	3	1	0
1955		38	80	16	.200	4	7	12	0
1956		44	99	22	.222	5	13	10	0
1957		9	31	9	.290	2	5	4	0
1958		13	31	6	.194	0	2	2	0
1959		153	546	132	.242	42	105	98	3
1960		124	442	122	.276	31	80	84	1
1961	Min AL	150	541	156	.288	46	122	94	1
1962		155	552	134	.243	48	126	85	1
1963		142	515	133	.258	45	96	88	0
1964		158	577	156	.270	49	111	95	0
1965		113	401	108	.269	25	75	78	0
1966		162	569	160	.281	39	110	89	0
1967		163	547	147	.269	44	113	105	1
1968		100	295	62	.210	17	40	40	0
1969		**162**	**555**	**153**	**.276**	**49**	**140**	**106**	**8**
1970		157	527	143	.271	41	113	96	0
1971		147	500	127	.254	28	119	61	3
1972		139	433	100	.231	26	74	53	0
1973		69	248	60	.242	5	32	29	0
1974		122	333	74	.222	13	54	28	0
1975	KC AL	106	312	62	.199	14	44	25	1
22 yrs		2435	8147	2086	.256	573	1584	1283	19

1970 National League — Johnny Bench

Year	Team	Games	AB	Hits	Avg.	HR	RBI	Runs	SB
1967	Cin NL	26	86	14	.163	1	6	7	0
1968		154	564	155	.275	15	82	67	1
1969		148	532	156	.293	26	90	83	6
1970		**158**	**605**	**177**	**.293**	**45**	**148**	**97**	**5**
1971		149	562	134	.238	27	61	80	2
1972		147	538	145	.270	40	125	87	6
1973		152	557	141	.253	25	104	83	4
1974		160	621	174	.280	33	129	108	5
1975		142	530	150	.283	28	110	83	11
1976		135	465	109	.234	16	74	62	13
1977		142	494	136	.275	31	109	67	2
1978		120	393	102	.260	23	73	52	4
1979		130	464	128	.276	22	80	73	4
1980		114	360	90	.250	24	68	52	4
1981		52	178	55	.309	8	25	14	0
1982		119	399	103	.258	13	38	44	1
1983		110	310	79	.255	12	54	32	0
17 yrs		2158	7658	2048	.267	389	1376	1091	68

1970 American League — Boog Powell

Year	Team	Games	AB	Hits	Avg.	HR	RBI	Runs	SB
1961	Bal AL	4	13	1	.077	0	1	0	0
1962		124	400	97	.243	15	53	44	1
1963		140	491	130	.265	25	82	67	1
1964		134	424	123	.290	39	99	74	0
1965		144	472	117	.248	17	72	54	1
1966		140	491	141	.287	34	109	78	0
1967		125	415	97	.234	13	55	53	1
1968		154	550	137	.249	22	85	60	7
1969		152	533	162	.304	37	121	83	1
1970		**154**	**526**	**156**	**.297**	**35**	**114**	**82**	**1**
1971		128	418	107	.256	22	92	59	1
1972		140	465	117	.252	21	81	53	4
1973		114	370	98	.265	11	54	52	0
1974		110	344	91	.265	12	45	37	0
1975	Cle AL	134	435	129	.297	27	86	64	1
1976		95	293	63	.215	9	33	29	1
1977	LA NL	50	41	10	.244	0	5	0	0
17 yrs		2042	6681	1776	.266	339	1187	889	20

1971 National League — Joe Torre

Year	Team	Games	AB	Hits	Avg.	HR	RBI	Runs	SB
1960	Mil NL	2	2	1	.500	0	0	0	0
1961		113	406	113	.278	10	42	40	3
1962		80	220	62	.282	5	26	23	1
1963		142	501	147	.293	14	71	57	1
1964		154	601	193	.321	20	109	87	2
1965		148	523	152	.291	27	80	68	0
1966	Atl NL	148	546	172	.315	36	101	83	0
1967		135	477	132	.277	20	68	67	2
1968		115	424	115	.271	10	55	45	1
1969	SL NL	159	602	174	.289	18	101	72	0
1970		161	624	203	.325	21	100	89	2
1971		**161**	**634**	**230**	**.363**	**24**	**137**	**97**	**4**
1972		149	544	157	.289	11	81	71	3
1973		141	519	149	.287	13	69	67	2
1974		147	529	149	.282	11	70	59	1
1975	NY NL	114	361	89	.247	6	35	33	0
1976		114	310	95	.306	5	31	36	1
1977		26	51	9	.176	1	9	2	0
18 yrs		2209	7874	2342	.297	252	1185	996	23

1971 American League — Vida Blue

Year	Team	Games	W	L	ERA	IP	SO	BB	ShO
1969	Oak AL	12	1	1	6.64	42	24	18	0
1970		6	2	0	2.09	38.2	35	12	2
1971		**39**	**24**	**8**	**1.82**	**312**	**301**	**88**	**8**
1972		25	6	10	2.80	151	111	48	4
1973		37	20	9	3.28	263.2	158	105	4
1974		40	17	15	3.25	282.1	174	98	1
1975		39	22	11	3.01	278	189	99	2
1976		37	18	13	2.35	298.1	166	63	6
1977		38	14	19	3.83	279.2	157	86	1
1978	SF NL	35	18	10	2.79	258	171	70	4
1979		34	14	14	5.01	237	138	111	0
1980		31	14	10	2.97	224	129	61	3
1981		18	8	6	2.45	124.2	63	54	0
1982	KC AL	31	13	12	3.78	181	103	80	2
1983		19	0	5	6.01	85.1	53	35	0
1985	SF NL	33	8	8	4.47	131	103	80	0
1986		28	10	10	3.27	156.2	100	77	0
17 yrs		502	209	161	3.27	3343.1	2175	1185	37

1972 National League — Johnny Bench

Year	Team	Games	AB	Hits	Avg.	HR	RBI	Runs	SB
1967	Cin NL	26	86	14	.163	1	6	7	0
1968		154	564	155	.275	15	82	67	1
1969		148	532	156	.293	26	90	83	6
1970		158	605	177	.293	45	148	97	5
1971		149	562	134	.238	27	61	80	2
1972		**147**	**538**	**145**	**.270**	**40**	**125**	**87**	**6**
1973		152	557	141	.253	25	104	83	4
1974		160	621	174	.280	33	129	108	5
1975		142	530	150	.283	28	110	83	11
1976		135	465	109	.234	16	74	62	13
1977		142	494	136	.275	31	109	67	2
1978		120	393	102	.260	23	73	52	4
1979		130	464	128	.276	22	80	73	4
1980		114	360	90	.250	24	68	52	4
1981		52	178	55	.309	8	25	14	0
1982		119	399	103	.258	13	38	44	1
1983		110	310	79	.255	12	54	32	0
17 yrs		2158	7658	2048	.267	389	1376	1091	68

1972 American League — Dick Allen

Year	Team	Games	AB	Hits	Avg.	HR	RBI	Runs	SB
1963	Phil NL	10	24	7	.292	0	2	6	0
1964		162	632	201	.318	29	91	125	3
1965		161	619	187	.302	20	85	93	15
1966		141	524	166	.317	40	110	112	10
1967		122	463	142	.307	23	77	89	20
1968		152	521	137	.263	33	90	87	7
1969		118	438	126	.288	32	89	79	9
1970	SL NL	122	459	128	.279	34	101	88	5
1971	LA NL	155	549	162	.295	23	90	82	8
1972	Chi AL	**148**	**506**	**156**	**.308**	**37**	**113**	**90**	**19**
1973		72	250	79	.316	16	41	39	7
1974		128	462	139	.301	32	88	84	7
1975	Phil NL	119	416	97	.233	12	62	54	11
1976		85	298	80	.268	15	49	52	11
1977	Oak AL	54	171	41	.240	5	31	19	1
15 yrs		1749	6332	1848	.292	351	1119	1099	133

1973 National League — Pete Rose

Year	Team	Games	AB	Hits	Avg.	HR	RBI	Runs	SB
1963	Cin NL	157	623	170	.273	6	41	101	13
1964		136	516	139	.269	4	34	64	4
1965		162	670	209	.312	11	81	117	8
1966		156	654	205	.313	16	70	97	4
1967		148	585	176	.301	12	76	86	11
1968		149	626	210	.335	10	49	94	3
1969		156	627	218	.348	16	82	120	7
1970		159	649	205	.316	15	52	120	12
1971		160	632	192	.304	13	44	86	13
1972		154	645	198	.307	6	57	107	10
1973		**160**	**680**	**230**	**.338**	**5**	**64**	**115**	**10**
1974		163	652	185	.284	3	51	110	2
1975		162	662	210	.317	7	74	112	0
1976		162	665	215	.323	10	63	130	9
1977		162	655	204	.311	9	64	95	16
1978		159	655	198	.302	7	52	103	13
1979	Phil NL	163	628	208	.331	4	59	90	20
1980		162	655	185	.282	1	64	95	12
1981		107	431	140	.325	0	33	73	4

1973 National League—Pete Rose

Year	Team	Games	AB	Hits	Avg.	HR	RBI	Runs	SB
1982		162	634	172	.271	3	54	80	8
1983		151	493	121	.245	0	45	52	7
1984	Mon NL/	121	374	107	.286	0	34	43	1
	Cin NL								
1985	Cin NL	119	405	107	.264	2	46	60	8
1986		72	237	52	.219	0	25	15	3
24 yrs		3562	14053	4256	.303	160	1314	2165	198

1973 American League — Reggie Jackson

Year	Team	Games	AB	Hits	Avg.	HR	RBI	Runs	SB
1967	KC AL	35	118	21	.178	1	6	13	1
1968	Oak AL	154	553	138	.250	29	74	82	14
1969		152	549	151	.275	47	118	123	13
1970		149	426	101	.237	23	66	57	26
1971		150	567	157	.277	32	80	87	16
1972		135	499	132	.265	25	75	72	9
1973		151	539	158	.293	32	117	99	22
1974		148	506	146	.289	29	93	90	25
1975		157	593	150	.253	36	104	91	17
1976	Bal AL	134	498	138	.277	27	91	84	28
1977	NY AL	146	525	150	.286	32	110	93	17
1978		139	511	140	.274	27	97	82	14
1979		131	465	138	.297	29	89	78	9
1980		143	514	154	.300	41	111	94	1
1981		94	334	79	.237	15	54	33	0
1982	Cal AL	153	530	146	.275	39	101	92	4
1983		116	397	77	.194	14	49	43	0
1984		143	525	117	.223	25	81	67	8
1985		143	525	116	.252	27	85	64	1
1986		132	460	101	.241	18	58	65	1
1987	Oak AL	115	419	74	.220	15	43	42	2
21 yrs		2820	9864	2584	.262	563	1702	1551	228

1974 National League — Steve Garvey

Year	Team	Games	AB	Hits	Avg.	HR	RBI	Runs	SB
1969	LA NL	3	3	1	.333	0	0	0	0
1970		34	93	25	.269	1	6	8	1
1971		81	225	51	.227	7	26	27	1
1972		96	294	79	.269	9	30	36	4
1973		114	349	106	.304	8	50	37	0
1974		156	642	200	.312	21	111	95	5
1975		160	659	210	.319	18	95	85	11
1976		162	631	200	.317	13	80	85	19
1977		162	646	192	.297	33	115	91	9
1978		162	639	202	.316	21	113	89	10
1979		162	648	204	.315	28	110	92	3
1980		163	658	200	.304	26	106	78	6
1981		110	431	122	.283	10	64	63	3
1982		162	625	176	.282	16	86	66	5
1983	SD NL	100	388	114	.294	14	59	76	4
1984		161	617	175	.284	8	86	72	1
1985		162	654	184	.281	17	81	80	0
1986		155	557	142	.255	21	81	58	1
1987		27	76	16	.211	1	9	5	0
19 yrs		2332	8835	2599	.294	272	1308	1143	83

1974 American League — Jeff Burroughs

Year	Team	Games	AB	Hits	Avg.	HR	RBI	Runs	SB
1970	Wash AL	6	12	2	.167	0	1	1	0
1971		59	181	42	.232	5	25	20	1
1972	Tex AL	22	65	12	.185	1	3	4	0
1973		151	526	147	.279	30	85	71	0
1974		152	554	167	.301	25	118	84	2
1975		152	585	132	.226	29	94	81	4
1976		158	604	143	.237	18	86	71	0
1977	Atl NL	154	579	157	.271	41	114	91	4
1978		153	488	147	.301	23	77	72	1
1979		116	397	89	.224	11	47	49	2
1980		99	278	73	.263	13	51	35	1
1981	Sea AL	89	319	81	.254	10	41	32	0
1982	Oak AL	113	285	79	.277	16	48	42	1
1983		121	401	108	.269	10	56	43	0
1984		58	71	15	.211	2	8	5	0
1985	Tor AL	86	191	49	.257	6	28	19	0
16 yrs		1689	5536	1443	.261	240	882	720	16

1975 National League — Joe Morgan

Year	Team	Games	AB	Hits	Avg.	HR	RBI	Runs	SB
1963	Hou NL	8	25	6	.240	0	3	5	1
1964		10	37	7	.189	0	0	4	0
1965		157	601	163	.271	14	40	100	20
1966		122	425	121	.285	5	42	60	11
1967		133	494	136	.275	6	42	73	29
1968		10	20	5	.250	0	0	6	3
1969		147	535	126	.236	15	43	94	49
1970		144	548	147	.268	8	52	102	42
1971		160	583	149	.256	13	56	87	40
1972	Cin NL	149	552	161	.292	16	73	122	58
1973		157	576	167	.290	26	82	116	67
1974		149	512	150	.293	22	67	107	58
1975		146	498	163	.327	17	94	107	67
1976		141	472	151	.320	27	111	113	60
1977		153	521	150	.288	22	78	113	49
1978		132	441	104	.236	13	75	68	19
1979		127	436	109	.250	9	32	70	28
1980	Hou NL	141	461	112	.243	11	49	66	24
1981	SF NL	90	308	74	.240	8	31	47	14
1982		134	463	134	.289	14	61	68	24
1983	Phil NL	123	404	93	.230	16	59	72	18
1984	Oak AL	116	365	89	.244	6	43	50	8
22 yrs		2649	9277	2517	.271	268	1133	1650	689

1975 American League — Fred Lynn

Year	Team	Games	AB	Hits	Avg.	HR	RBI	Runs	SB
1974	Bos AL	15	43	18	.419	2	10	5	0
1975		145	528	175	.331	21	105	103	10
1976		132	507	159	.314	10	65	76	14
1977		129	497	129	.260	18	76	81	2
1978		150	541	161	.298	22	82	75	3
1979		147	531	177	.333	39	122	116	2
1980		110	415	125	.301	12	61	67	12
1981	Cal AL	76	256	56	.219	5	31	28	1
1982		138	472	141	.299	21	86	89	7
1983		117	437	119	.272	22	74	56	2
1984		142	517	140	.271	23	79	84	2
1985	Bal AL	124	448	118	.263	23	68	59	7
1986		112	397	114	.287	23	67	67	2
1987		111	396	100	.253	23	60	49	3
1988	Bal AL/	114	391	96	.246	25	56	46	2
	Det AL								
1989	Det AL	117	353	85	.241	11	46	44	1
1990	SD NL	90	196	47	.240	6	23	18	2
17 yrs		1969	6925	1960	.283	306	1111	1063	72

1976 National League — Joe Morgan

Year	Team	Games	AB	Hits	Avg.	HR	RBI	Runs	SB
1963	Hou NL	8	25	6	.240	0	3	5	1
1964		10	37	7	.189	0	0	4	0
1965		157	601	163	.271	14	40	100	20
1966		122	425	121	.285	5	42	60	11
1967		133	494	136	.275	6	42	73	29
1968		10	20	5	.250	0	0	6	3
1969		147	535	126	.236	15	43	94	49
1970		144	548	147	.268	8	52	102	42
1971		160	583	149	.256	13	56	87	40
1972	Cin NL	149	552	161	.292	16	73	122	58
1973		157	576	167	.290	26	82	116	67
1974		149	512	150	.293	22	67	107	58
1975		146	498	163	.327	17	94	107	67
1976		**141**	**472**	**151**	**.320**	**27**	**111**	**113**	**60**
1977		153	521	150	.288	22	78	113	49
1978		132	441	104	.236	13	75	68	19
1979		127	436	109	.250	9	32	70	28
1980	Hou NL	141	461	112	.243	11	49	66	24
1981	SF NL	90	308	74	.240	8	31	47	14
1982		134	463	134	.289	14	61	68	24
1983	Phil NL	123	404	93	.230	16	59	72	18
1984	Oak AL	116	365	89	.244	6	43	50	8
22 yrs		2649	9277	2517	.271	268	1133	1650	689

1976 American League — Thurman Munson

Year	Team	Games	AB	Hits	Avg.	HR	RBI	Runs	SB
1969	NY AL	26	86	22	.256	1	9	6	0
1970		132	453	137	.302	6	53	59	5
1971		125	451	113	.251	10	42	71	6
1972		140	511	143	.280	7	46	54	6
1973		147	519	156	.301	20	74	80	4
1974		144	517	135	.261	13	60	64	2
1975		157	597	190	.318	12	102	83	3
1976		**152**	**616**	**186**	**.302**	**17**	**105**	**79**	**14**
1977		149	595	183	.308	18	100	85	5
1978		154	617	183	.297	6	71	73	2
1979		97	382	110	.288	3	39	42	1
11 yrs		1423	5344	1558	.292	113	701	696	48

1977 National League — George Foster

Year	Team	Games	AB	Hits	Avg.	HR	RBI	Runs	SB
1969	SF NL	9	5	2	.400	0	1	1	0
1970		9	19	6	.316	1	4	2	0
1971	SF NL/ Cin NL	140	473	114	.241	13	58	50	7
1972	Cin NL	59	145	29	.200	2	12	15	2
1973		17	39	11	.282	4	9	6	0
1974		106	276	73	.264	7	41	31	3
1975		134	463	139	.300	23	78	71	2
1976		144	562	172	.306	29	121	86	17
1977		**158**	**615**	**197**	**.320**	**52**	**149**	**124**	**6**
1978		158	604	170	.281	40	120	97	4
1979		121	440	133	.302	30	98	68	0
1980		144	528	144	.273	25	93	79	1
1981		108	414	122	.295	22	90	64	4
1982	NY NL	151	550	136	.247	13	70	64	1
1983		157	601	145	.241	28	90	74	1
1984		146	553	149	.269	24	86	67	2
1985		129	452	119	.263	21	77	57	0
1986	NY NL/ Chi AL	87	284	64	.225	14	42	30	1
18 yrs		1977	7023	1925	.274	348	1239	986	51

1977 American League — Rod Carew

Year	Team	Games	AB	Hits	Avg.	HR	RBI	Runs	SB
1967	Min AL	137	514	150	.292	8	51	66	5
1968		127	461	126	.273	1	42	46	12
1969		123	458	152	.332	8	56	79	19
1970		51	191	70	.366	4	28	27	4
1971		147	577	177	.307	2	48	88	6
1972		142	535	170	.318	0	51	61	12
1973		149	580	203	.350	6	62	98	41
1974		153	599	218	.364	3	55	86	38
1975		143	535	192	.359	14	80	89	35
1976		156	605	200	.331	9	90	97	49
1977		**155**	**616**	**239**	**.388**	**14**	**100**	**128**	**23**
1978		152	564	188	.333	5	70	85	27
1979	Cal AL	110	409	130	.318	3	44	78	18
1980		144	540	179	.331	3	59	74	23
1981		93	364	111	.305	2	21	57	16
1982		138	523	167	.319	3	44	88	10
1983		129	472	160	.339	2	44	66	6
1984		93	329	97	.295	3	31	42	4
1985		127	443	124	.280	2	39	69	5
19 yrs		2469	9315	3053	.328	92	1015	1424	353

1978 National League — Dave Parker

Year	Team	Games	AB	Hits	Avg.	HR	RBI	Runs	SB
1973	Pit NL	54	139	40	.288	4	14	17	1
1974		73	220	62	.282	4	29	27	3
1975		148	558	172	.308	25	101	75	8
1976		138	537	168	.313	13	90	82	19
1977		159	637	215	.338	21	88	107	17
1978		**148**	**581**	**194**	**.334**	**30**	**117**	**102**	**20**
1979		158	622	193	.310	25	94	109	20
1980		139	518	153	.295	17	79	71	10
1981		67	240	62	.258	9	48	29	6
1982		73	244	66	.270	6	29	41	7
1983		144	552	154	.279	12	69	68	12
1984	Cin NL	156	607	173	.285	16	94	73	11
1985		160	635	198	.312	34	125	88	5
1986		162	637	174	.273	31	116	89	1
1987		153	589	149	.253	26	97	77	7
1988	Oak AL	101	377	97	.257	12	55	43	0
1989		144	553	146	.264	22	97	56	0
1990	Mil AL	157	610	176	.289	21	92	71	4
1991	Cal AL/ Tor AL	132	502	120	.239	11	59	47	3
19 yrs		2466	9358	2712	.290	339	1493	1272	154

1978 American League — Jim Rice

Year	Team	Games	AB	Hits	Avg.	HR	RBI	Runs	SB
1974	Bos AL	24	67	18	.269	1	13	6	0
1975		144	564	174	.309	22	102	92	10
1976		153	581	164	.282	25	85	75	8
1977		160	644	206	.320	39	114	104	5
1978		**163**	**677**	**213**	**.315**	**46**	**139**	**121**	**7**
1979		158	619	201	.325	39	130	117	9
1980		124	504	148	.294	24	86	81	8
1981		108	451	128	.284	17	62	51	2
1982		145	573	177	.309	24	97	86	0
1983		155	626	191	.305	39	126	90	0
1984		159	657	184	.280	28	122	98	4
1985		140	546	159	.291	27	103	85	2
1986		157	618	200	.324	20	110	98	0
1987		108	404	112	.277	13	62	66	1
1988		135	485	128	.264	15	72	57	1
1989		56	209	49	.234	3	28	22	1
16 yrs		2089	8225	2452	.298	382	1451	1249	58

1979 National League — Willie Stargell

Year	Team	Games	AB	Hits	Avg.	HR	RBI	Runs	SB
1962	Pit NL	10	31	9	.290	0	4	1	0
1963		108	304	74	.243	11	47	34	0
1964		117	421	115	.273	21	78	53	1
1965		144	533	145	.272	27	107	68	1
1966		140	485	153	.315	33	102	84	2
1967		134	462	125	.271	20	73	54	1
1968		128	435	103	.237	24	67	57	5
1969		145	522	160	.307	29	92	89	1
1970		136	474	125	.264	31	85	70	0
1971		141	511	151	.295	48	125	104	0
1972		138	495	145	.293	33	112	75	1
1973		148	522	156	.299	44	119	106	0
1974		140	508	153	.301	25	96	90	0
1975		124	461	136	.295	22	90	71	0
1976		117	428	110	.257	20	65	54	2
1977		63	186	51	.274	13	35	29	0
1978		122	390	115	.295	28	97	60	3
1979		**126**	**424**	**119**	**.281**	**32**	**82**	**60**	**0**
1980		67	202	53	.262	11	38	28	0
1981		38	60	17	.283	0	9	2	0
1982		74	73	17	.233	3	17	6	0
21 yrs		2360	7927	2232	.282	475	1540	1195	17

1979 National League — Keith Hernandez

Year	Team	Games	AB	Hits	Avg.	HR	RBI	Runs	SB
1974	SL NL	14	34	10	.294	0	2	3	0
1975		64	188	47	.250	3	20	20	0
1976		129	374	108	.289	7	46	54	4
1977		161	560	163	.291	15	91	90	7
1978		159	542	138	.255	11	64	90	13
1979		**161**	**610**	**210**	**.344**	**11**	**105**	**116**	**11**
1980		159	595	191	.321	16	99	111	14
1981		103	376	115	.306	8	48	65	12
1982		160	579	173	.299	7	94	79	19
1983	SL NL/ NY NL	150	538	160	.297	12	63	77	9
1984	NY NL	154	550	171	.311	15	94	83	2
1985		158	593	183	.309	10	91	87	3
1986		149	551	171	.310	13	83	94	2
1987		154	587	170	.290	18	89	87	0
1988		95	348	96	.276	11	55	43	2
1989		75	215	50	.233	4	19	18	0
1990	Cle AL	43	130	26	.200	1	8	7	0
17 yrs		2088	7370	2182	.296	162	1071	1124	98

1979 American League — Don Baylor

Year	Team	Games	AB	Hits	Avg.	HR	RBI	Runs	SB
1970	Bal AL	8	17	4	.235	0	4	4	1
1971		1	2	0	.000	0	1	0	0
1972		102	320	81	.253	11	38	33	24
1973		118	405	116	.286	11	51	64	32
1974		137	489	133	.272	10	59	66	29
1975		145	524	148	.282	25	76	79	32
1976	Oak AL	157	595	147	.247	15	68	85	52
1977	Cal AL	154	561	141	.251	25	75	87	26
1978		158	591	151	.255	34	99	103	22
1979		**162**	**628**	**186**	**.296**	**36**	**139**	**120**	**22**
1980		90	340	85	.250	5	51	39	6
1981		103	377	90	.239	17	66	52	3
1982		157	608	160	.263	24	93	80	10

1979 American League — Don Baylor

Year	Team	Games	AB	Hits	Avg.	HR	RBI	Runs	SB
1983	NY AL	144	534	162	.303	21	85	82	17
1984		134	493	129	.262	27	89	84	1
1985		142	477	110	.231	23	91	70	0
1986	Bos AL	160	585	139	.238	31	94	93	3
1987	Bos AL/ Min AL	128	388	95	.245	16	63	67	5
1988	Oak AL	92	264	58	.220	7	34	28	0
19 yrs		2292	8198	2135	.260	338	1276	1236	285

1980 National League — Mike Schmidt

Year	Team	Games	AB	Hits	Avg.	HR	RBI	Runs	SB
1972	Phil NL	13	34	7	.206	1	3	2	0
1973		132	367	72	.196	18	52	43	8
1974		162	568	160	.282	36	116	108	23
1975		158	562	140	.249	38	95	93	29
1976		160	584	153	.262	38	107	112	14
1977		154	544	149	.274	38	101	114	15
1978		145	513	129	.251	21	78	93	19
1979		160	541	137	.253	45	114	109	9
1980		**150**	**548**	**157**	**.286**	**48**	**121**	**104**	**12**
1981		102	354	112	.316	31	91	78	12
1982		148	514	144	.280	35	87	108	14
1983		154	534	136	.255	40	109	104	7
1984		151	528	146	.277	36	106	93	5
1985		158	549	152	.277	33	93	89	1
1986		160	552	160	.290	37	119	97	1
1987		147	522	153	.293	35	113	88	2
1988		108	390	97	.249	12	62	52	3
1989		42	148	30	.203	6	28	19	0
18 yrs		2404	8352	2234	.267	548	1595	1506	174

1980 American League — George Brett

Year	Team	Games	AB	Hits	Avg.	HR	RBI	Runs	SB
1973	KC AL	13	40	5	.125	0	0	2	0
1974		133	457	129	.282	2	47	49	8
1975		159	634	195	.308	11	89	84	13
1976		159	645	215	.333	7	67	94	21
1977		139	564	176	.312	22	88	105	14
1978		128	510	150	.294	9	62	79	23
1979		154	645	212	.329	23	107	119	17
1980		**117**	**449**	**175**	**.390**	**24**	**118**	**87**	**15**
1981		89	347	109	.314	6	43	42	14
1982		144	552	166	.301	21	82	101	6
1983		123	464	144	.310	25	93	90	0
1984		104	377	107	.284	13	69	42	0
1985		155	550	184	.335	30	112	108	9
1986		124	441	128	.290	16	73	70	1
1987		115	427	124	.290	22	78	71	6
1988		157	589	180	.306	24	103	90	14
1989		124	457	129	.282	12	80	67	14
1990		142	544	179	.329	14	87	82	9
1991		131	505	129	.255	10	61	77	2
1992		152	592	169	.285	7	61	55	8
1993		145	560	149	.266	19	75	69	7
21 yrs		2707	10349	3154	.305	317	1595	1583	201

1981 National League — Mike Schmidt

Year	Team	Games	AB	Hits	Avg.	HR	RBI	Runs	SB
1972	Phil NL	13	34	7	.206	1	3	2	0
1973		132	367	72	.196	18	52	43	8
1974		162	568	160	.282	36	116	108	23
1975		158	562	140	.249	38	95	93	29
1976		160	584	153	.262	38	107	112	14
1977		154	544	149	.274	38	101	114	15
1978		145	513	129	.251	21	78	93	19
1979		160	541	137	.253	45	114	109	9
1980		150	548	157	.286	48	121	104	12
1981		**102**	**354**	**112**	**.316**	**31**	**91**	**78**	**12**
1982		148	514	144	.280	35	87	108	14
1983		154	534	136	.255	40	109	104	7
1984		151	528	146	.277	36	106	93	5
1985		158	549	152	.277	33	93	89	1
1986		160	552	160	.290	37	119	97	1
1987		147	522	153	.293	35	113	88	2
1988		108	390	97	.249	12	62	52	3
1989		42	148	30	.203	6	28	19	0
18 yrs		2404	8352	2234	.267	548	1595	1506	174

1981 American League — Rollie Fingers

Year	Team	Games	W	L	ERA	IP	SO	BB	Saves
1968	Oak AL	1	0	0	27.00	1.1	0	1	0
1969		60	6	7	3.71	119	61	41	12
1970		45	7	9	3.65	148	79	48	2
1971		48	4	6	2.99	129.1	98	30	17
1972		65	11	9	2.51	111.1	113	32	21
1973		62	7	8	1.92	126.2	110	39	22
1974		76	9	5	2.65	119	95	29	18
1975		75	10	6	2.98	126.2	115	33	24
1976		70	13	11	2.47	134.2	113	40	20
1977	SD NL	78	8	9	2.99	132.1	113	36	35
1978		67	6	13	2.52	107.1	72	29	37
1979		54	9	9	4.52	83.2	65	37	13
1980		66	11	9	2.80	103	69	32	23
1981	**Mil AL**	**47**	**6**	**3**	**1.04**	**78**	**61**	**13**	**28**
1982		50	5	6	2.60	79.2	71	20	29
1984		33	1	2	1.96	46	40	13	23
1985		47	1	6	5.04	55.1	24	19	17
17 yrs		944	114	118	2.90	1701.1	1299	492	341

1982 National League — Dale Murphy

Year	Team	Games	AB	Hits	Avg.	HR	RBI	Runs	SB
1976	Atl NL	19	65	17	.262	0	9	3	0
1977		18	76	24	.316	2	14	5	0
1978		151	530	120	.226	23	79	66	11
1979		104	384	106	.276	21	57	53	6
1980		156	569	160	.281	33	89	98	9
1981		104	369	91	.247	13	50	43	14
1982		**162**	**598**	**168**	**.281**	**36**	**109**	**113**	**23**
1983		162	589	178	.302	36	121	131	30
1984		162	607	176	.290	36	100	94	19
1985		162	616	185	.300	37	111	118	10
1986		160	614	163	.265	29	83	89	7
1987		159	566	167	.295	44	105	115	16
1988		156	592	134	.226	24	77	77	3
1989		154	574	131	.228	20	84	60	3
1990	Atl NL/ Phil NL	154	563	138	.245	24	83	60	9
1991	Phil NL	153	544	137	.252	18	81	66	1
1992		18	62	10	.161	2	7	5	0
1993	Col NL	26	42	6	.143	0	7	1	0
18 yrs		2180	7960	2111	.265	398	1266	1197	161

1982 American League — Robin Yount

Year	Team	Games	AB	Hits	Avg.	HR	RBI	Runs	SB
1974	Mil AL	107	344	86	.250	3	26	48	7
1975		147	558	149	.267	8	52	67	12
1976		161	638	161	.252	2	54	59	16
1977		154	605	174	.288	4	49	66	16
1978		127	502	147	.293	9	71	66	16
1979		149	577	154	.267	8	51	72	11
1980		143	611	179	.293	23	87	121	20
1981		96	377	103	.273	10	49	50	4
1982		**156**	**635**	**210**	**.331**	**29**	**114**	**129**	**14**
1983		149	578	178	.308	17	80	102	12
1984		160	624	186	.298	16	80	105	14
1985		122	466	129	.277	15	68	76	10
1986		140	522	163	.312	9	46	82	14
1987		158	635	198	.312	21	103	99	19
1988		162	621	190	.306	13	91	92	22
1989		160	614	195	.318	21	103	101	19
1990		158	587	145	.247	17	77	98	15
1991		130	503	131	.260	10	77	66	6
1992		150	557	147	.264	8	77	71	15
1993		127	454	117	.258	8	51	62	9
20 yrs		2856	11008	3142	.285	251	1406	1632	271

1983 National League — Dale Murphy

Year	Team	Games	AB	Hits	Avg.	HR	RBI	Runs	SB
1976	Atl NL	19	65	17	.262	0	9	3	0
1977		18	76	24	.316	2	14	5	0
1978		151	530	120	.226	23	79	66	11
1979		104	384	106	.276	21	57	53	6
1980		156	569	160	.281	33	89	98	9
1981		104	369	91	.247	13	50	43	14
1982		162	598	168	.281	36	109	113	23
1983		**162**	**589**	**178**	**.302**	**36**	**121**	**131**	**30**
1984		162	607	176	.290	36	100	94	19
1985		162	616	185	.300	37	111	118	10
1986		160	614	163	.265	29	83	89	7
1987		159	566	167	.295	44	105	115	16
1988		156	592	134	.226	24	77	77	3
1989		154	574	131	.228	20	84	60	3
1990	Atl NL/ Phil NL	154	563	138	.245	24	83	60	9
1991	Phil NL	153	544	137	.252	18	81	66	1
1992		18	62	10	.161	2	7	5	0
1993	Col NL	26	42	6	.143	0	7	1	0
18 yrs		2180	7960	2111	.265	398	1266	1197	161

1983 American League — Cal Ripken, Jr.

Year	Team	Games	AB	Hits	Avg.	HR	RBI	Runs	SB
1981	Bal AL	23	39	5	.128	0	0	1	0
1982		160	598	158	.264	28	93	90	3
1983		**162**	**663**	**211**	**.318**	**27**	**102**	**121**	**0**
1984		162	641	195	.304	27	86	103	2
1985		161	642	181	.282	26	110	116	2
1986		162	627	177	.282	25	81	98	4
1987		162	624	157	.252	27	98	97	3
1988		161	575	152	.264	23	81	87	2
1989		162	646	166	.257	21	93	80	3
1990		161	600	150	.250	21	84	78	3
1991		162	650	210	.323	34	114	99	6
1992		162	637	160	.251	14	72	73	4
1993		162	641	165	.257	24	90	87	1

1983 American League—Cal Ripken, Jr.

Year	Team	Games	AB	Hits	Avg.	HR	RBI	Runs	SB
1994		112	444	140	.315	13	75	71	1
1995		144	550	144	.262	17	88	71	0
1996		163	640	178	.278	26	102	94	1
1997		162	615	166	.270	17	84	79	1
1998		161	601	163	.271	14	61	65	0
1999		86	332	113	.340	18	57	51	0
2000		83	309	79	.256	15	56	43	0
2001		128	477	114	.239	14	68	43	0
21 yrs		3001	11551	3184	.276	431	1695	1647	36

1984 National League — Ryne Sandberg

Year	Team	Games	AB	Hits	Avg.	HR	RBI	Runs	SB
1981	Phil NL	13	6	1	.167	0	0	2	0
1982	Chi NL	156	635	172	.271	7	54	103	32
1983		158	633	165	.261	8	48	94	37
1984		**156**	**636**	**200**	**.314**	**19**	**84**	**114**	**32**
1985		153	609	186	.305	26	83	113	54
1986		154	627	178	.284	14	76	68	34
1987		132	523	154	.294	16	59	81	21
1988		155	618	163	.264	19	69	77	25
1989		157	606	176	.290	30	76	104	15
1990		155	615	188	.306	40	100	116	25
1991		158	585	170	.291	26	100	104	22
1992		158	612	186	.304	26	87	100	17
1993		117	456	141	.309	9	45	67	9
1994		57	223	53	.238	5	24	36	2
1996		150	554	135	.244	25	92	85	12
1997		135	447	118	.264	12	64	54	7
16 yrs		2164	8385	2386	.285	282	1061	1318	344

1984 American League — Willie Hernandez

Year	Team	Games	W	L	ERA	IP	SO	BB	Saves
1977	Chi NL	67	8	7	3.03	110	78	28	4
1978		54	8	2	3.77	59.2	38	35	3
1979		51	4	4	5.01	79	53	39	0
1980		53	1	9	4.40	108.1	75	45	0
1981		12	0	0	3.95	13.2	13	8	2
1982		75	4	6	3.00	75	54	24	10
1983	Chi NL/ Phil NL	74	9	4	3.28	115.1	93	32	8
1984	**Det AL**	**80**	**9**	**3**	**1.92**	**140.1**	**112**	**36**	**32**
1985		74	8	10	2.70	106.2	76	14	31
1986		64	8	7	3.55	88.2	77	21	24
1987		45	3	4	3.67	49	30	20	8
1988		63	6	5	3.06	67.2	59	31	10
1989		32	2	2	5.74	31.1	30	16	15
13 yrs		744	70	63	3.38	1044.2	788	349	147

1985 National League — Willie McGee

Year	Team	Games	AB	Hits	Avg.	HR	RBI	Runs	SB
1982	SL NL	123	422	125	.296	4	56	43	24
1983		147	601	172	.286	5	75	75	39
1984		145	571	166	.291	6	50	82	43
1985		**152**	**612**	**216**	**.353**	**10**	**82**	**114**	**56**
1986		124	497	127	.256	7	48	65	19
1987		153	620	177	.285	11	105	76	16
1988		137	562	164	.292	3	50	73	41

1985 National League—Willie McGee

Year	Team	Games	AB	Hits	Avg.	HR	RBI	Runs	SB
1989		58	199	47	.236	3	17	23	8
1990	SL NL/ Oak AL	154	614	199	.322	3	77	99	31
1991	SF NL	131	497	155	.312	4	43	67	17
1992		138	474	141	.297	1	36	56	13
1993		130	475	143	.301	4	46	53	10
1994		45	156	44	.282	5	23	19	3
1995	Bos AL	67	200	57	.285	2	15	32	5
1996	SL NL	123	309	95	.307	5	41	52	5
1997		122	300	90	.300	3	38	29	8
1998		120	269	68	.253	3	34	27	7
1999		132	271	68	.251	0	20	25	7
18 yrs		2201	7649	2254	.295	79	856	1010	352

1985 American League — Don Mattingly

Year	Team	Games	AB	Hits	Avg.	HR	RBI	Runs	SB
1982	NY AL	7	12	2	.167	0	1	0	0
1983		91	279	79	.283	4	32	34	0
1984		153	603	207	.343	23	110	91	1
1985		**159**	**652**	**211**	**.324**	**35**	**145**	**107**	**2**
1986		162	677	238	.352	31	113	117	0
1987		141	569	186	.327	30	115	93	1
1988		144	599	186	.311	18	88	94	1
1989		158	631	191	.303	23	113	79	3
1990		102	394	101	.256	5	42	40	1
1991		152	587	169	.288	9	68	64	2
1992		157	640	184	.287	14	86	89	3
1993		134	530	154	.291	17	86	78	0
1994		97	372	113	.304	6	51	62	0
1995		128	458	132	.288	7	49	59	0
14 yrs		1785	7003	2153	.307	222	1099	1007	14

1986 National League — Mike Schmidt

Year	Team	Games	AB	Hits	Avg.	HR	RBI	Runs	SB
1972	Phil NL	13	34	7	.206	1	3	2	0
1973		132	367	72	.196	18	52	43	8
1974		162	568	160	.282	36	116	108	23
1975		158	562	140	.249	38	95	93	29
1976		160	584	153	.262	38	107	112	14
1977		154	544	149	.274	38	101	114	15
1978		145	513	129	.251	21	78	93	19
1979		160	541	137	.253	45	114	109	9
1980		150	548	157	.286	48	121	104	12
1981		102	354	112	.316	31	91	78	12
1982		148	514	144	.280	35	87	108	14
1983		154	534	136	.255	40	109	104	7
1984		151	528	146	.277	36	106	93	5
1985		158	549	152	.277	33	93	89	1
1986		**160**	**552**	**160**	**.290**	**37**	**119**	**97**	**1**
1987		147	522	153	.293	35	113	88	2
1988		108	390	97	.249	12	62	52	3
1989		42	148	30	.203	6	28	19	0
18 yrs		2404	8352	2234	.267	548	1595	1506	174

1986 American League — Roger Clemens

Year	Team	Games	Won	Lost	ERA	IP	SO	BB	ShO
1984	Bos AL	21	9	4	4.32	133.1	126	29	1
1985		15	7	5	3.29	98.1	74	37	1
1986		**33**	**24**	**4**	**2.48**	**254**	**238**	**67**	**1**
1987		36	20	9	2.97	281.2	256	83	7
1988		35	18	12	2.93	264	291	62	8
1989		35	17	11	3.13	253.1	230	93	3
1990		31	21	6	1.93	228.1	209	54	4
1991		35	18	10	2.62	271.1	241	65	4
1992		32	18	11	2.41	246.2	208	62	5
1993		29	11	14	4.46	191.2	160	67	1
1994		24	9	7	2.85	170.2	168	71	1
1995		23	10	5	4.18	140	132	60	0
1996		34	10	13	3.63	242.2	257	106	2
1997	Tor AL	34	21	7	2.05	264	292	68	3
1998		33	20	6	2.65	234.2	271	88	3
1999	NY AL	30	14	10	4.60	187.2	163	90	1
2000		32	13	8	3.70	204.1	188	84	0
2001		33	20	3	3.51	220.1	213	72	0
18 yrs		545	280	145	3.10	3887	3717	1258	45

1987 National League — Andre Dawson

Year	Team	Games	AB	Hits	Avg.	HR	RBI	Runs	SB
1976	Mon NL	24	85	20	.235	0	7	9	1
1977		139	525	148	.282	19	65	64	21
1978		157	609	154	.253	25	72	84	28
1979		155	639	176	.275	25	92	90	35
1980		151	577	178	.308	17	87	96	34
1981		103	394	119	.302	24	64	71	26
1982		148	608	183	.301	23	83	107	39
1983		159	633	189	.299	32	113	104	25
1984		138	533	132	.248	17	86	73	13
1985		139	529	135	.255	23	91	65	13
1986		130	496	141	.284	20	78	65	18
1987	Chi NL	**153**	**621**	**178**	**.287**	**49**	**137**	**90**	**11**
1988		157	591	179	.303	24	79	78	12
1989		118	416	105	.252	21	77	62	8
1990		147	529	164	.310	27	100	72	16
1991		149	563	153	.272	31	104	69	4
1992		143	542	150	.277	22	90	60	6
1993	Bos AL	121	461	126	.273	13	67	44	2
1994		75	292	70	.240	16	48	34	2
1995	Fla NL	79	226	58	.257	8	37	30	0
1996		42	58	16	.276	2	14	6	0
21 yrs		2627	9927	2774	.279	438	1591	1373	314

1987 American League — George Bell

Year	Team	Games	AB	Hits	Avg.	HR	RBI	Runs	SB
1981	Tor AL	60	163	38	.233	5	12	19	3
1983		39	112	30	.268	2	17	5	1
1984		159	606	177	.292	26	87	85	11
1985		157	607	167	.275	28	95	87	21
1986		159	641	198	.309	31	108	101	7
1987		**156**	**610**	**188**	**.308**	**47**	**134**	**111**	**5**
1988		156	614	165	.269	24	97	78	4
1989		153	613	182	.297	18	104	88	4
1990		142	562	149	.265	21	86	67	3
1991	Chi NL	149	558	159	.285	25	86	63	2
1992	Chi AL	155	627	160	.255	25	112	74	5
1993		102	410	89	.217	13	64	36	1
12 yrs		1587	6123	1702	.278	265	1002	814	67

1988 National League — Kirk Gibson

Year	Team	Games	AB	Hits	Avg.	HR	RBI	Runs	SB
1979	Det AL	12	38	9	.237	1	4	3	3
1980		51	175	46	.263	9	16	23	4
1981		83	290	95	.328	9	40	41	17
1982		69	266	74	.278	8	35	34	9
1983		128	401	91	.227	15	51	60	14
1984		149	531	150	.282	27	91	92	29
1985		154	581	167	.287	29	97	96	30
1986		119	441	118	.268	28	86	84	34
1987		128	487	135	.277	24	79	95	26
1988	LA NL	**150**	**542**	**157**	**.290**	**25**	**76**	**106**	**31**
1989		71	253	54	.213	9	28	35	12
1990		89	315	82	.260	8	38	59	26
1991	KC AL	132	462	109	.236	16	55	81	18
1992	Pit NL	16	56	11	.196	2	5	6	3
1993	Det AL	116	403	105	.261	13	62	62	15
1994		98	330	91	.276	23	72	71	4
1995		70	227	59	.260	9	35	37	9
17 yrs		1635	5798	1553	.268	255	870	985	284

1988 American League — Jose Canseco

Year	Team	Games	AB	Hits	Avg.	HR	RBI	Runs	SB
1985	Oak AL	29	96	29	.302	5	13	16	1
1986		157	600	144	.240	33	117	85	15
1987		159	630	162	.257	31	113	81	15
1988		**158**	**610**	**187**	**.307**	**42**	**124**	**120**	**40**
1989		65	227	61	.269	17	57	40	6
1990		131	481	132	.274	37	101	83	19
1991		154	572	152	.266	44	122	115	26
1992	Oak AL/ Tex AL	119	439	107	.244	26	87	74	6
1993	Tex AL	60	231	59	.255	10	46	30	6
1994		111	429	121	.282	31	90	88	15
1995	Bos AL	102	396	121	.306	24	81	64	4
1996		96	360	104	.289	28	82	68	3
1997	Oak AL	108	388	91	.235	23	74	56	8
1998	Tor AL	151	583	138	.237	46	107	98	29
1999	TB AL	113	430	120	.279	34	95	75	3
2000	TB AL/ NY AL	98	329	83	.252	15	49	47	2
2001	Chi AL	76	256	66	.258	16	49	46	2
17 yrs		1887	7057	1877	.266	462	1407	1186	200

1989 National League — Kevin Mitchell

Year	Team	Games	AB	Hits	Avg.	HR	RBI	Runs	SB
1984	NY NL	7	14	3	.214	0	1	0	0
1986		108	328	91	.277	12	43	51	3
1987	SD NL/ SF NL	131	464	130	.280	22	70	68	9
1988	SF NL	148	505	127	.251	19	80	60	5
1989		**154**	**543**	**158**	**.291**	**47**	**125**	**100**	**3**
1990		140	524	152	.290	35	93	90	4
1991		113	371	95	.256	27	69	52	2
1992	Sea AL	99	360	103	.286	9	67	48	0
1993	Cin NL	93	323	110	.341	19	64	56	1
1994		95	310	101	.326	30	77	57	2
1996	Bos AL/ Cin NL	64	206	65	.316	8	39	27	0
1997	Cle AL	20	59	9	.153	4	11	7	1
1998	Oak AL	51	127	29	.228	2	21	14	0
13 yrs		1223	4134	1173	.284	234	760	630	30

1989 American League — Robin Yount

Year	Team	Games	AB	Hits	Avg.	HR	RBI	Runs	SB
1974	Mil AL	107	344	86	.250	3	26	48	7
1975		147	558	149	.267	8	52	67	12
1976		161	638	161	.252	2	54	59	16
1977		154	605	174	.288	4	49	66	16
1978		127	502	147	.293	9	71	66	16
1979		149	577	154	.267	8	51	72	11
1980		143	611	179	.293	23	87	121	20
1981		96	377	103	.273	10	49	50	4
1982		156	635	210	.331	29	114	129	14
1983		149	578	178	.308	17	80	102	12
1984		160	624	186	.298	16	80	105	14
1985		122	466	129	.277	15	68	76	10
1986		140	522	163	.312	9	46	82	14
1987		158	635	198	.312	21	103	99	19
1988		162	621	190	.306	13	91	92	22
1989		**160**	**614**	**195**	**.318**	**21**	**103**	**101**	**19**
1990		158	587	145	.247	17	77	98	15
1991		130	503	131	.260	10	77	66	6
1992		150	557	147	.264	8	77	71	15
1993		127	454	117	.258	8	51	62	9
20 yrs		2856	11008	3142	.285	251	1406	1632	271

1990 National League — Barry Bonds

Year	Team	Games	AB	Hits	Avg.	HR	RBI	Runs	SB
1986	Pit NL	113	413	92	.223	16	48	72	36
1987		150	551	144	.261	25	59	99	32
1988		144	538	152	.283	24	58	97	17
1989		159	580	144	.248	19	58	96	32
1990		**151**	**519**	**156**	**.301**	**33**	**114**	**104**	**52**
1991		153	510	149	.292	25	116	95	43
1992		140	473	147	.311	34	103	109	39
1993	SF NL	159	539	181	.336	46	123	129	29
1994		112	391	122	.312	37	81	89	29
1995		144	506	149	.294	33	104	109	31
1996		158	517	159	.308	42	129	122	40
1997		159	532	155	.291	40	101	123	37
1998		156	552	167	.303	37	122	120	28
1999		102	355	93	.262	34	83	91	15
2000		143	480	147	.306	49	106	129	11
2001		153	476	156	.328	73	137	129	13
16 yrs		2296	7932	2313	.292	567	1542	1713	484

1990 American League — Rickey Henderson

Year	Team	Games	AB	Hits	Avg.	HR	RBI	Runs	SB
1979	Oak AL	89	351	96	.274	1	26	49	33
1980		158	591	179	.303	9	53	111	100
1981		108	423	135	.319	6	35	89	56
1982		149	536	143	.267	10	51	119	130
1983		145	513	150	.292	9	48	105	108
1984		142	502	147	.293	16	58	113	66
1985	NY AL	143	547	172	.314	24	72	146	80
1986		153	608	160	.263	28	74	130	87
1987		95	358	104	.291	17	37	78	41
1988		140	554	169	.305	6	50	118	93
1989	NY AL/ Oak AL	150	541	148	.274	12	57	113	77
1990	Oak AL	**136**	**489**	**159**	**.325**	**28**	**61**	**119**	**65**
1991		134	470	126	.268	18	57	105	58
1992		117	396	112	.283	15	46	77	48
1993	Oak AL/ Tor AL	134	481	139	.289	21	59	114	53

1990 American League—Rickey Henderson

Year	Team	Games	AB	Hits	Avg.	HR	RBI	Runs	SB
1994	Oak AL	87	296	77	.260	6	20	66	22
1995		112	407	122	.300	9	54	67	32
1996	SD NL	148	465	112	.241	9	29	110	37
1997	SD NL/ Ana AL	120	403	100	.248	8	34	84	45
1998	Oak AL	152	542	128	.236	14	57	101	66
1999	NY NL	121	438	138	.315	12	42	89	37
2000	NY NL/ Sea AL	123	420	98	.233	4	32	75	36
2001	SD NL	123	379	86	.227	8	42	70	25
23 yrs		2979	10710	3000	.280	290	1094	2248	1395

1991 National League — Terry Pendleton

Year	Team	Games	AB	Hits	Avg.	HR	RBI	Runs	SB
1984	SL NL	67	262	85	.324	1	33	37	20
1985		149	559	134	.240	5	69	56	17
1986		159	578	138	.239	1	59	56	24
1987		159	583	167	.286	12	96	82	19
1988		110	391	99	.253	6	53	44	3
1989		162	613	162	.264	13	74	83	9
1990		121	447	103	.230	6	58	46	7
1991	Atl NL	**153**	**586**	**187**	**.319**	**22**	**86**	**94**	**10**
1992		160	640	199	.311	21	105	98	5
1993		161	633	172	.272	17	84	81	5
1994		77	309	78	.252	7	30	25	2
1995	Fla NL	133	513	149	.290	14	78	70	1
1996	Fla NL/ Atl NL	153	568	135	.238	11	75	51	2
1997	Cin NL	50	113	28	.248	1	17	11	2
1998	KC AL	79	237	61	.257	3	29	17	1
15 yrs		1893	7032	1897	.270	140	946	851	127

1991 American League — Cal Ripken, Jr.

Year	Team	Games	AB	Hits	Avg.	HR	RBI	Runs	SB
1981	Bal AL	23	39	5	.128	0	0	1	0
1982		160	598	158	.264	28	93	90	3
1983		162	663	211	.318	27	102	121	0
1984		162	641	195	.304	27	86	103	2
1985		161	642	181	.282	26	110	116	2
1986		162	627	177	.282	25	81	98	4
1987		162	624	157	.252	27	98	97	3
1988		161	575	152	.264	23	81	87	2
1989		162	646	166	.257	21	93	80	3
1990		161	600	150	.250	21	84	78	3
1991		**162**	**650**	**210**	**.323**	**34**	**114**	**99**	**6**
1992		162	637	160	.251	14	72	73	4
1993		162	641	165	.257	24	90	87	1
1994		112	444	140	.315	13	75	71	1
1995		144	550	144	.262	17	88	71	0
1996		163	640	178	.278	26	102	94	1
1997		162	615	166	.270	17	84	79	1
1998		161	601	163	.271	14	61	65	0
1999		86	332	113	.340	18	57	51	0
2000		83	309	79	.256	15	56	43	0
2001		128	477	114	.239	14	68	43	0
21 yrs		3001	11551	3184	.276	431	1695	1647	36

1992 National League — Barry Bonds

Year	Team	Games	AB	Hits	Avg.	HR	RBI	Runs	SB
1986	Pit NL	113	413	92	.223	16	48	72	36
1987		150	551	144	.261	25	59	99	32
1988		144	538	152	.283	24	58	97	17
1989		159	580	144	.248	19	58	96	32
1990		151	519	156	.301	33	114	104	52
1991		153	510	149	.292	25	116	95	43
1992		**140**	**473**	**147**	**.311**	**34**	**103**	**109**	**39**
1993	SF NL	159	539	181	.336	46	123	129	29
1994		112	391	122	.312	37	81	89	29
1995		144	506	149	.294	33	104	109	31
1996		158	517	159	.308	42	129	122	40
1997		159	532	155	.291	40	101	123	37
1998		156	552	167	.303	37	122	120	28
1999		102	355	93	.262	34	83	91	15
2000		143	480	147	.306	49	106	129	11
2001		153	476	156	.328	73	137	129	13
16 yrs		2296	7932	2313	.292	567	1542	1713	484

1992 American League — Dennis Eckersley

Year	Team	Games	W	L	ERA	IP	SO	BB	Saves
1975	Cle AL	34	13	7	2.60	186.2	152	90	2
1976		36	13	12	3.43	199.1	200	78	1
1977		33	14	13	3.53	247.1	191	54	0
1978	Bos AL	35	20	8	2.99	268.1	162	71	0
1979		33	17	10	2.99	246.2	150	59	0
1980		30	12	14	4.28	197.2	121	44	0
1981		23	9	8	4.27	154	79	35	0
1982		33	13	13	3.73	224.1	127	43	0
1983		28	9	13	5.61	176.1	77	39	0
1984	Bos AL/ Chi NL	33	14	12	3.60	225	114	49	0
1985	Chi NL	25	11	7	3.08	169.1	117	19	0
1986		33	6	11	4.57	201	137	43	0
1987	Oak AL	54	6	8	3.03	115.2	113	17	16
1988		60	4	2	2.35	72.2	70	11	45
1989		51	4	0	1.56	57.2	55	3	33
1990		63	4	2	0.61	73.1	73	4	48
1991		67	5	4	2.96	76	87	9	43
1992		**69**	**7**	**1**	**1.91**	**80**	**93**	**11**	**51**
1993		64	2	4	4.16	67	80	13	36
1994		45	5	4	4.26	44.1	47	13	19
1995		52	4	6	4.83	50.1	40	11	29
1996	SL NL	63	0	6	3.30	60	49	6	30
1997		57	1	5	3.91	53	45	8	36
1998	Bos AL	50	4	1	4.76	39.2	22	8	1
24 yrs		1071	197	171	3.50	3285.2	2401	738	390

1993 National League — Barry Bonds

Year	Team	Games	AB	Hits	Avg.	HR	RBI	Runs	SB
1986	Pit NL	113	413	92	.223	16	48	72	36
1987		150	551	144	.261	25	59	99	32
1988		144	538	152	.283	24	58	97	17
1989		159	580	144	.248	19	58	96	32
1990		151	519	156	.301	33	114	104	52
1991		153	510	149	.292	25	116	95	43
1992		140	473	147	.311	34	103	109	39
1993	SF NL	**159**	**539**	**181**	**.336**	**46**	**123**	**129**	**29**
1994		112	391	122	.312	37	81	89	29
1995		144	506	149	.294	33	104	109	31
1996		158	517	159	.308	42	129	122	40

1993 National League — Barry Bonds

Year	Team	Games	AB	Hits	Avg.	HR	RBI	Runs	SB
1997		159	532	155	.291	40	101	123	37
1998		156	552	167	.303	37	122	120	28
1999		102	355	93	.262	34	83	91	15
2000		143	480	147	.306	49	106	129	11
2001		153	476	156	.328	73	137	129	13
16 yrs		2296	7932	2313	.292	567	1542	1713	484

1993 American League — Frank Thomas

Year	Team	Games	AB	Hits	Avg.	HR	RBI	Runs	SB
1990	Chi AL	60	191	63	.330	7	31	39	0
1991		158	559	178	.318	32	109	104	1
1992		160	573	185	.323	24	115	108	6
1993		**153**	**549**	**174**	**.317**	**41**	**128**	**106**	**4**
1994		113	399	141	.353	38	101	106	2
1995		145	493	152	.308	40	111	102	3
1996		141	527	184	.349	40	134	110	1
1997		146	530	184	.347	35	125	110	1
1998		160	585	155	.265	29	109	109	7
1999		135	486	148	.305	15	77	74	3
2000		159	582	191	.328	43	143	115	1
2001		20	68	15	.221	4	10	8	0
12 yrs		1550	5542	1770	.319	348	1193	1091	29

1994 National League — Jeff Bagwell

Year	Team	Games	AB	Hits	Avg.	HR	RBI	Runs	SB
1991	Hou NL	156	554	163	.294	15	82	79	7
1992		162	586	160	.273	18	96	87	10
1993		142	535	171	.320	20	88	76	13
1994		**110**	**400**	**147**	**.368**	**39**	**116**	**104**	**15**
1995		114	448	130	.290	21	87	88	12
1996		162	568	179	.315	31	120	111	21
1997		162	566	162	.286	43	135	109	31
1998		147	540	164	.304	34	111	124	19
1999		162	562	171	.304	42	126	143	30
2000		159	590	183	.310	47	132	152	9
2001		161	600	173	.288	39	130	126	11
11 yrs		1637	5949	1803	.303	349	1223	1199	178

1994 American League — Frank Thomas

Year	Team	Games	AB	Hits	Avg.	HR	RBI	Runs	SB
1990	Chi AL	60	191	63	.330	7	31	39	0
1991		158	559	178	.318	32	109	104	1
1992		160	573	185	.323	24	115	108	6
1993		153	549	174	.317	41	128	106	4
1994		**113**	**399**	**141**	**.353**	**38**	**101**	**106**	**2**
1995		145	493	152	.308	40	111	102	3
1996		141	527	184	.349	40	134	110	1
1997		146	530	184	.347	35	125	110	1
1998		160	585	155	.265	29	109	109	7
1999		135	486	148	.305	15	77	74	3
2000		159	582	191	.328	43	143	115	1
2001		20	68	15	.221	4	10	8	0
12 yrs		1550	5542	1770	.319	348	1193	1091	29

1995 National League — Barry Larkin

Year	Team	Games	AB	Hits	Avg.	HR	RBI	Runs	SB
1986	Cin NL	41	159	45	.283	3	19	27	8
1987		125	439	107	.244	12	43	64	21
1988		151	588	174	.296	12	56	91	40
1989		97	325	111	.342	4	36	47	10
1990		158	614	185	.301	7	67	85	30
1991		123	464	140	.302	20	69	88	24
1992		140	533	162	.304	12	78	76	15
1993		100	384	121	.315	8	51	57	14
1994		110	427	119	.279	9	52	78	26
1995		**131**	**496**	**158**	**.319**	**15**	**66**	**98**	**51**
1996		152	517	154	.298	33	89	117	36
1997		73	224	71	.317	4	20	34	14
1998		145	538	166	.309	17	72	93	26
1999		161	583	171	.293	12	75	108	30
2000		102	396	124	.313	11	41	71	14
2001		45	156	40	.256	2	17	29	3
16 yrs		1854	6843	2048	.299	181	851	1163	362

1996 American League — Juan Gonzalez

Year	Team	Games	AB	Hits	Avg.	HR	RBI	Runs	SB
1989	Tex AL	24	60	9	.150	1	7	6	0
1990		25	90	26	.289	4	12	11	0
1991		142	545	144	.264	27	102	78	4
1992		155	584	152	.260	43	109	77	0
1993		140	536	166	.310	46	118	105	4
1994		107	422	116	.275	19	85	57	6
1995		90	352	104	.295	27	82	57	0
1996		**134**	**541**	**170**	**.314**	**47**	**144**	**89**	**2**
1997		133	533	158	.296	42	131	87	0
1998		154	606	193	.318	45	157	110	2
1999		144	562	183	.326	39	128	114	3
2000	Det AL	115	461	133	.289	22	67	69	1
2001	Cle AL	140	532	173	.325	35	140	97	1
13 yrs		1503	5824	1727	.297	397	1282	957	23

1995 American League — Mo Vaughn

Year	Team	Games	AB	Hits	Avg.	HR	RBI	Runs	SB
1991	Bos AL	74	219	57	.260	4	32	21	2
1992		113	355	83	.234	13	57	42	3
1993		152	539	160	.297	29	101	86	4
1994		111	394	122	.310	26	82	65	4
1995		**140**	**550**	**165**	**.300**	**39**	**126**	**98**	**11**
1996		161	635	207	.326	44	143	118	2
1997		141	527	166	.315	35	96	91	2
1998		154	609	205	.337	40	115	107	0
1999	Ana AL	139	524	147	.281	33	108	63	0
2000		161	614	167	.272	36	117	93	2
10 yrs		1346	4966	1479	.298	299	977	784	30

1997 National League — Larry Walker

Year	Team	Games	AB	Hits	Avg.	HR	RBI	Runs	SB
1989	Mon NL	20	47	8	.170	0	4	4	1
1990		133	419	101	.241	19	51	59	21
1991		137	487	141	.290	16	64	59	14
1992		143	528	159	.301	23	93	85	18
1993		138	490	130	.265	22	86	85	29
1994		103	395	127	.322	19	86	76	15
1995	Col NL	131	494	151	.306	36	101	96	16
1996		83	272	75	.276	18	58	58	18
1997		**153**	**568**	**208**	**.366**	**49**	**130**	**143**	**33**
1998		130	454	165	.363	23	67	113	14
1999		127	438	166	.379	37	115	108	11
2000		87	314	97	.309	9	51	64	5
2001		142	497	174	.350	38	123	107	14
13 yrs		1527	5403	1702	.315	309	1029	1057	209

1996 National League — Ken Caminiti

Year	Team	Games	AB	Hits	Avg.	HR	RBI	Runs	SB
1987	Hou NL	63	203	50	.246	3	23	10	0
1988		30	83	15	.181	1	7	5	0
1989		161	585	149	.255	10	72	71	4
1990		153	541	131	.242	4	51	52	9
1991		152	574	145	.253	13	80	65	4
1992		135	506	149	.294	13	62	68	10
1993		143	543	142	.262	13	75	75	8
1994		111	406	115	.283	18	75	63	4
1995	SD NL	143	526	159	.302	26	94	74	12
1996		**146**	**546**	**178**	**.326**	**40**	**130**	**109**	**11**
1997		137	486	141	.290	26	90	92	11
1998		131	452	114	.252	29	82	87	6
1999	Hou NL	78	273	78	.286	13	56	45	6
2000		59	208	63	.303	15	45	42	3
2001	Tex AL/ Atl NL	118	356	81	.228	15	41	36	0
15 yrs		1760	6288	1710	.272	239	983	894	88

1997 American League — Ken Griffey, Jr.

Year	Team	Games	AB	Hits	Avg.	HR	RBI	Runs	SB
1989	Sea AL	127	455	120	.264	16	61	61	16
1990		155	597	179	.300	22	80	91	16
1991		154	548	179	.327	22	100	76	18
1992		142	565	174	.308	27	103	83	10
1993		156	582	180	.309	45	109	113	17
1994		111	433	140	.323	40	90	94	11
1995		72	260	67	.258	17	42	52	4
1996		140	545	165	.303	49	140	125	16
1997		**157**	**608**	**185**	**.304**	**56**	**147**	**125**	**15**
1998		161	633	180	.284	56	146	120	20
1999		160	606	173	.285	48	134	123	24
2000	Cin NL	145	520	141	.271	40	118	100	6
2001		111	364	104	.286	22	65	57	2
13 yrs		1791	6716	1987	.296	460	1335	1220	175

1998 National League — Sammy Sosa

Year	Team	Games	AB	Hits	Avg.	HR	RBI	Runs	SB
1989	Tex AL/ Chi AL	58	183	47	.257	4	13	27	7
1990	Chi AL	153	532	124	.233	15	70	72	32
1991		116	316	64	.203	10	33	39	13
1992	Chi NL	67	262	68	.260	8	25	41	15
1993		159	598	156	.261	33	93	92	36
1994		105	426	128	.300	25	70	59	22
1995		144	564	151	.268	36	119	89	34
1996		124	498	136	.273	40	100	84	18
1997		162	642	161	.251	36	119	90	22
1998		**159**	**643**	**198**	**.308**	**66**	**158**	**134**	**18**
1999		162	625	180	.288	63	141	114	7
2000		156	604	193	.320	50	138	106	7
2001		160	577	189	.328	64	160	146	0
13 yrs		1725	6470	1795	.277	450	1239	1093	231

1998 American League — Juan Gonzalez

Year	Team	Games	AB	Hits	Avg.	HR	RBI	Runs	SB
1989	Tex AL	24	60	9	.150	1	7	6	0
1990		25	90	26	.289	4	12	11	0
1991		142	545	144	.264	27	102	78	4
1992		155	584	152	.260	43	109	77	0
1993		140	536	166	.310	46	118	105	4
1994		107	422	116	.275	19	85	57	6
1995		90	352	104	.295	27	82	57	0
1996		134	541	170	.314	47	144	89	2
1997		133	533	158	.296	42	131	87	0
1998		**154**	**606**	**193**	**.318**	**45**	**157**	**110**	**2**
1999		144	562	183	.326	39	128	114	3
2000	Det AL	115	461	133	.289	22	67	69	1
2001	Cle AL	140	532	173	.325	35	140	97	1
13 yrs		1503	5824	1727	.297	397	1282	957	23

1999 National League — Chipper Jones

Year	Team	Games	AB	Hits	Avg.	HR	RBI	Runs	SB
1993	Atl NL	8	3	2	.667	0	0	2	0
1995		140	524	139	.265	23	86	87	8
1996		157	598	185	.309	30	110	114	14
1997		157	597	176	.295	21	111	100	20
1998		160	601	188	.313	34	107	123	16
1999		**157**	**567**	**181**	**.319**	**45**	**110**	**116**	**25**
2000		156	579	180	.311	36	111	118	14
2001		159	572	189	.330	38	102	113	9
8 yrs		1094	4041	1240	.307	227	737	773	106

1999 American League — Ivan Rodriguez

Year	Team	Games	AB	Hits	Avg.	HR	RBI	Runs	SB
1991	Tex AL	88	280	74	.264	3	27	24	0
1992		123	420	109	.260	8	37	39	0
1993		137	473	129	.273	10	66	56	8
1994		99	363	108	.298	16	57	56	6
1995		130	492	149	.303	12	67	56	0
1996		153	639	192	.300	19	86	116	5
1997		150	597	187	.313	20	77	98	7
1998		145	579	186	.321	21	91	88	9
1999		**144**	**600**	**199**	**.332**	**35**	**113**	**116**	**25**
2000		91	363	126	.347	27	83	66	5
2001		111	442	136	.308	25	65	70	10
11 yrs		1371	5248	1595	.304	196	769	785	75

2000 National League — Jeff Kent

Year	Team	Games	AB	Hits	Avg.	HR	RBI	Runs	SB
1992	Tor AL/ NY NL	102	305	73	.239	11	50	52	2
1993	NY NL	140	496	134	.270	21	80	65	4
1994		107	415	121	.292	14	68	53	1
1995		125	472	131	.278	20	65	65	3
1996	NY NL/ Cle AL	128	437	124	.284	12	55	61	6
1997	SF NL	155	580	145	.250	29	121	90	11
1998		137	526	156	.297	31	128	94	9
1999		138	511	148	.290	23	101	86	13
2000		**159**	**587**	**196**	**.334**	**33**	**125**	**114**	**12**
2001		159	607	181	.298	22	106	84	7
10 yrs		1350	4936	1409	.285	216	899	764	68

2000 American League — Jason Giambi

Year	Team	Games	AB	Hits	Avg.	HR	RBI	Runs	SB
1995	Oak AL	54	176	45	.256	6	25	27	2
1996		140	536	156	.291	20	79	84	0
1997		142	519	152	.293	20	81	66	0
1998		153	562	166	.295	27	110	92	2
1999		158	575	181	.315	33	123	115	1
2000		**152**	**510**	**170**	**.333**	**43**	**137**	**108**	**2**
2001		154	520	178	.342	38	120	109	2
7 yrs		953	3398	1048	.308	187	675	601	9

2001 National League — Barry Bonds

Year	Team	Games	AB	Hits	Avg.	HR	RBI	Runs	SB
1986	Pit NL	113	413	92	.223	16	48	72	36
1987		150	551	144	.261	25	59	99	32
1988		144	538	152	.283	24	58	97	17
1989		159	580	144	.248	19	58	96	32
1990		151	519	156	.301	33	114	104	52
1991		153	510	149	.292	25	116	95	43
1992		140	473	147	.311	34	103	109	39
1993	SF NL	159	539	181	.336	46	123	129	29
1994		112	391	122	.312	37	81	89	29
1995		144	506	149	.294	33	104	109	31
1996		158	517	159	.308	42	129	122	40
1997		159	532	155	.291	40	101	123	37
1998		156	552	167	.303	37	122	120	28
1999		102	355	93	.262	34	83	91	15
2000		143	480	147	.306	49	106	129	11
2001		**153**	**476**	**156**	**.328**	**73**	**137**	**129**	**13**
16 yrs		2296	7932	2313	.292	567	1542	1713	484

2001 American League — Ichiro Suzuki

Year	Team	Games	AB	Hits	Avg.	HR	RBI	Runs	SB
2001	Sea AL	**157**	**692**	**242**	**.350**	**8**	**69**	**127**	**56**
1 yr		157	692	242	.350	8	69	127	56

Index